DETAINED IN CHINA AND TIBET

A Directory of Political and Religious Prisoners

Asia Watch

Human Rights Watch
New York • Washington • Los Angeles • London

Library of Congress Catalog Card Number: 93-78900
ISBN 1-56432-105-3

HUMAN RIGHTS WATCH

Human Rights Watch conducts regular, systematic investigations of human rights abuses in some seventy countries around the world. It addresses the human rights practices of governments of all political stripes, of all geopolitical alignments, and of all ethnic and religious persuasions. In internal wars it documents violations by both governments and rebel groups. Human Rights Watch defends freedom of thought and expression, due process and equal protection of the law; it documents and denounces murders, disappearances, torture, arbitrary imprisonment, exile, censorship and other abuses of internationally recognized human rights.

Human Rights Watch began in 1978 with the founding of its Helsinki division. Today, it includes five divisions covering Africa, the Americas, Asia, the Middle East, as well as the signatories of the Helsinki accords. It also includes four collaborative projects on Arms, Free Expression, Prisoners' Rights, and Women's Rights. It now maintains offices in New York, Washington, Los Angeles, London, Moscow, Belgrade, Zagreb and Hong Kong. Human Rights Watch is an independent, nongovernmental organization, supported by contributions from private individuals and foundations. It accepts no government funds, directly or indirectly.

The board includes Robert L. Bernstein, chair; Adrian W. DeWind, vice chair; Roland Algrant, Lisa Anderson, Peter D. Bell, Alice L. Brown, William Carmichael, Dorothy Cullman, Irene Diamond, Jonathan Fanton, Alan Finberg, Jack Greenberg, Alice H. Henkin, Stephen L. Kass, Marina Pinto Kaufman, Alexander MacGregor, Peter Osnos, Kathleen Peratis, Bruce Rabb, Orville Schell, Gary G. Sick, and Malcolm Smith.

The staff includes Kenneth Roth, executive director; Holly J. Burkhalter, Washington director; Gara LaMarche, associate director; Susan Osnos, press director; Ellen Lutz, California director; Jemera Rone, counsel; Richard Dicker, associate counsel; Michal Longfelder, development director; Rachel Weintraub, special events director; Allyson Collins, research associate; and Ham Fish, senior advisor.

The regional directors of Human Rights Watch are Abdullahi An-Na'im, Africa; Juan E. Méndez, Americas; Sidney Jones, Asia; Jeri Laber, Helsinki; and Andrew Whitley, Middle East. The project directors are Kenneth Anderson, Arms Project; Gara LaMarche, Free Expression Project; Joanna Weschler, Prison Project; and Dorothy Q. Thomas, Women's Rights Project.

Addresses for Human Rights Watch

485 Fifth Avenue
New York, NY 10017-6104
Tel: (212) 972-8400
Fax: (212) 972-0905
email: hrwatchnyc@igc.apc.org

1522 K Street, N.W., #910
Washington, DC 20005
Tel: (202) 371-6592
Fax: (202) 371-0124
email: hrwatchdc@igc.apc.org

10951 West Pico Blvd., #203
Los Angeles, CA 90064
Tel: (310) 475-3070
Fax: (310) 475-5613
email: hrwatchla@igc.apc.org

90 Borough High Street
London, UK SE1 1LL
Tel: (071) 378-8008
Fax: (071) 378-8029
email: hrwatchuk@gn.apc.org

TABLE OF CONTENTS

ACKNOWLEDGEMENTS

This report is primarily the work of two people: Robin Munro, Hong Kong director of Asia Watch and China specialist, and Mickey Spiegel, an Asia Watch researcher on China based in New York.

Mickey Spiegel assembled and drafted much of the primary data that constitutes the core of this report. That material was then entered into a database on Chinese and Tibetan prisoners with the help of Renee Chiang and Shanti Hixon.

Robin Munro then took the database material and edited, updated and substantially expanded it. He also organized the report and wrote the introduction.

Many people gave unstintingly of their time and knowledge to make the publication of this report possible. To those inside China and Tibet, who often took great personal risks in order to transmit information on imprisoned dissidents to the outside world, we are especially grateful.

We are also indebted to numerous colleagues at Human Rights Watch and in the human rights field more broadly for their assistance. Special thanks are due to Robbie Barnett and friends of the Tibet Information Network in London, who checked and re-checked lists of Tibetan prisoners; Liu Qing, Xiao Qiang, and Sophia Woodman of Human Rights in China, who supplied extensive case details and were always ready to help in a crisis; John Kamm, Sue Whitfield, Jim Seymour, Philip Baker, Lau Bing-sum, Richard Dicker, Mike Jendrzejczyk and Jeannine Guthrie for information, advice, practical assistance, computer know-how and moral support.

INTRODUCTION

Overview

Nineteen ninety-three was without doubt the worst year for political arrests and trials in China since mid-1990 and the aftermath of the June 4, 1989 crackdown on the pro-democracy movement. Asia Watch documented almost 250 such cases in 1993, including thirty-two dissident trials resulting in average sentences of four years' imprisonment, and 216 new arrests. Almost eighty percent of these cases occurred in Tibet, where a continuing Chinese government campaign of repression against peaceful pro-independence activities by Buddhist monks and nuns sharply intensified during the year. In addition, Asia Watch received information on some 140 arrests or trials of persons whose names are as yet unknown. Set against this invidious record were reports of a mere thirty-seven dissidents having been released from jail during the period from January 1993 to January 1994, although at the time this report went to press, rumors were circulating of the pending release of several well-known political prisoners, including Wang Juntao and Bao Tong. Among those freed were a number of prominent dissidents, notably Wei Jingsheng, whose releases appeared to be carefully timed by the Chinese authorities to influence important international events. Having served the greater part of fourteen and a half years of his fifteen-year sentence in solitary confinement, Wei was released just days prior to the International Olympics Committee's decision on the host-city for the 2000 Summer Olympics, for which Beijing was a leading contender.

This report provides the most complete available accounting of the nature and extent of political and religious imprisonment in China today. It contains information on a total of some 1,700 persons known or believed to be presently imprisoned in connection with their political, ethnic or religious views. Reaching back well before the June 1989 crackdown in Tiananmen Square, it records the cases of dissidents arrested in the late 1970s and early 1980s and extends through arrests that took place as late as January 1994. Around 1,230 of those listed are persons detained or convicted solely on account of their non-violent beliefs or activities; more than 760 are confirmed or "status known" cases, while the remaining 470 are "status unclear" cases on which no firm or reliable information has been received for several years. Asia Watch calls upon the Chinese government immediately and unconditionally to release all prisoners in the former category, and to provide a full accounting of all those in the latter category and to free those still jailed. The true number of people detained in China on account of their peacefully held views remains impossible to determine. Asia Watch's best estimate is that the figure is many times higher than the 760 known cases listed here.

The report also contains information on some 460 persons detained or convicted in China for allegedly violent or other criminal acts committed during various pro-democracy, ethnic-separatist or religious movements; of these cases, 190 are "status known" and 270 are "status unclear." In view of the low standards of criminal justice prevailing in China and the general absence of safeguards for defendants' rights, which greatly increase the likelihood of wrongful or unsafe convictions, Asia Watch calls upon the Chinese government to make publicly available the evidence upon which these convictions were based and, where appropriate, to reopen the cases and conduct a judicial review.

In addition, the report contains two key lists of specific classes of prisoners. The first is a list of almost one hundred non-violent political, ethnic or religious prisoners in China known to be currently serving sentences of between ten years' and life imprisonment. This forms, in effect, Asia Watch's priority list, a targeted index of those jailed dissidents who are in most urgent need of international and domestic pressure to secure their release at the earliest possible date. Some of these dissidents have been behind bars for more than a decade. For all such long-term prisoners, the difference between early release and serving out a sentence in full may be the difference between the capacity eventually to resume a normal life and permanent physical or psychological damage. Most of those on the list were sentenced within the last five years and thus still have the major part of their terms left to serve. More numerous by far than their known counterparts of the early 1980s, they represent what might aptly be called a "new generation of Wei Jingshengs." A clear symbol of the retrograde direction taken by the Chinese leadership over human rights issues in recent years, these long-term political prisoners of the 1990s should be the yardstick against which any evaluation of "overall significant progress" by the regime is made.

The other key list (included as Appendix I) is a compilation of all prisoners currently known or believed to be under arrest or serving sentences in China on charges of "counterrevolution." Although the authorities continue to maintain that there are "no political prisoners in

China," this complex category of detainees comprises probably the closest and most inclusive equivalent of those falling within the internationally-accepted "political prisoner" definition. The overwhelming majority of so-called counterrevolutionaries (currently almost eighty percent, according to the authorities)[1] are peaceful dissidents, while a significant number are persons convicted of violence, espionage or other recognized criminal offenses. Many peaceful dissidents, however, are sentenced, either with or without trial, on charges other than "counterrevolution," and this number is likely to increase in coming years as China's judicial authorities move toward replacing such charges with less obviously political ones.

As the first systematic attempt by any independent organization to assemble such data, Asia Watch's list of "counterrevolutionaries" is inevitably incomplete. In September 1993, Chinese officials for the first time gave a total figure for this category -- 3,317 -- of whom 144 were women. Asia Watch cannot confirm the accuracy of this statistic, and thus far, no actual list of names has been forthcoming from the authorities. The list presented here includes the names of more than 1,200 prisoners (900 of whom were arrested or convicted for purely peaceful activities), or just over one third of the officially cited total. We publish the list in the hope that it may contribute to the process of eliciting from the Chinese government a complete accounting and eventually release of all non-violent, sentenced "counterrevolutionaries."

Also listed in the report are details of more than 1,000 prisoners who are either confirmed, reported or presumed to have been released from prison since June 1989, mostly after months or years of detention without trial or after completing their sentences in full. This documentation provides a background history of much of China's dissident movement. In many cases, those listed have faced continuing persecution after their release and remain at high risk of being rearrested for continuing their dissident activities.

---

[1] "On the Determination of the Crime of Counterrevolutionary Propaganda and Incitement," *Xiandai Faxue (Modern Jurisprudence)*, No.1, 1990, p.44. This represents a significant recent change in the composition of those sentenced on such charges. According to a 1992 analysis by the Supreme People's Procuracy, "Over the past decade, those sentenced on charges of counterrevolutionary propaganda and incitement accounted for around 20 percent of all sentenced counterrevolutionaries." (In CCS, p.238)

The Detainees

One of the most daunting aspects of the problem of political and religious imprisonment in China concerns the sheer number of the detainees involved. While every effort has been made to organize the report data in a useful and accessible format, the vast quantity of unfamiliar names and case details can still have an almost mind-numbing effect to all but the most dedicated of readers. For every Wang Juntao or Chen Ziming - the "black hand" Tiananmen Square intellectuals whose cases are by now familiar to most observers of China's political scene, there are dozens of other imprisoned dissidents, often similarly inspiring figures, of whom the outside world has little or no knowledge at all. Availing itself of this situation, the Chinese government has in recent years begun to practice a new diplomatic tactic - a kind of "hostage *politik*," whereby certain political or religious prisoners whose cases have received special attention from Western governments or human rights groups are effectively turned into bargaining chips, to be released at key moments for maximum publicity effect. In the process, those eager to sideline human rights considerations and resume business as usual in the burgeoning China market all too often welcome these isolated releases as representing "significant progress" or even "major concessions," while the largely anonymous majority of such prisoners are quietly forgotten.

The following cases, almost none of which have previously received public attention, afford a brief glimpse into this forgotten archive of human persecution and suffering, serving to remind us that each of the cases recorded in this report concerns a real person, rather than just one more statistic on a list.

* **Jampa Ngodrup**, a 45-year-old Tibetan doctor, sentenced to thirteen years' imprisonment in 1990 on charges of "counterrevolution" for copying and distributing name-lists of those arrested or injured during two 1988 pro-independence demonstrations in Lhasa. According to the court, a heavy sentence was called for "in order to strengthen the unity of the Motherland...and to stabilize the democratic rights of the people." The lists were regarded by the authorities as being "state secrets" and Jampa was thus convicted of "espionage." Held in Lhasa's Drapchi Prison, as of May 1993 he was reported to have fallen gravely ill as a result of ill-treatment by prison officials; suffering severe fluid retention such that his entire body had become bloated, he appeared to have developed tuberculosis and was unable to walk without the aid of crutches.

* **Huang Junjie**, 72, a retired railroad worker from Hengyang

City in Hunan Province, sentenced to ten years' imprisonment on charges of "counterrevolution." According to an internal report by the Supreme People's Court, "On June 5, 1989, Huang made two speeches to students...in which he spread rumors, inflamed people's emotions and spread counterrevolutionary propaganda and incitement." He reportedly said, "There has been bloodshed at Tiananmen, the People's Liberation Army has gunned down with automatic weapons or crushed to death with tanks between one and two thousand people; among the dead were old ladies and even children." He also allegedly "incited" police officers by saying, "The Public Security Bureau must not suppress the students and the masses, you should stand on the side of the people." Place of imprisonment unknown.

* **Yang Lianzi**, 48, described by the authorities as a "private performance artist" and a figure familiar to many first-hand observers of the May 1989 Tiananmen protest movement, sentenced to fifteen years' imprisonment in October 1990 on charges of "counterrevolution." According to China's judicial authorities, "After the announcement of martial law, Yang roamed around Tiananmen Square and the Xinhuamen Gate area [residence of the senior Communist Party leadership] wearing a headband bearing the words 'Wild Man of Huaxia'. By means of singing songs, playing stringed instruments and giving speeches, Yang engaged in counterrevolutionary propaganda and incitement, attacking the Chinese Communist Party and the socialist system and cursing and ridiculing Party and state leaders." Place of imprisonment unknown.

* **Gyaltsen Lhaksam**, 23, a Tibetan Buddhist nun from Garu Nunnery, arrested in August 1990 for staging a peaceful demonstration, and later sentenced to seven years' imprisonment. Other nuns are also serving prison terms in connection with the incident, which occurred at the Norbulingka, the Dalai Lama's former summer palace near Lhasa, during the week-long Shoton (Yoghurt) Festival. After shouting slogans in support of the Dalai Lama and calling upon Chinese settlers to leave Tibet, the demonstrators were seized by police and taken to Gutsa Detention Center for interrogation; after trial, they were transferred to Drapchi Prison, where Gyaltsen Lhaksam and several others still remain. Although her sentence was later reduced by two years, news received in mid-April 1991 said that she had subsequently been placed under "special discipline" - probably in solitary confinement - for unknown prison-rule infractions. Present condition unknown.

* **Zheng Yunsu** and some thirty-six leaders of the Jesus Family

in Douyigou, Shandong Province, including Zheng's four soons, were sentenced to long prison terms. Zheng, the local leader, received a twelve-year term which he was serving in a labor camp called the Shengjian Motor Factory, not far from Jinan, the provincial capital. His oldest son, **Zheng Jiping**, and his third son, **Zheng Jikuo**, each received a nine-year term. Charges against them included holding illegal religious gatherings, leading a "collective life," disturbing the social order, resisting arrest and beating up public security personnel. The latter charge probably referred to an attempt on May 21, 1992 by a crowd of believers to prevent their church from being razed.

* **Wan Yansheng** and **Zong Rongkun**, religious sectarian leaders who, if still alive, would now be in their seventies or early eighties, arrested in central China in 1988 on charges of leading a branch of the *Da Cheng Men (Mahayana Gate)* sect and later sentenced to unknown terms of imprisonment for "counterrevolution." According to the authorities, "The order to ban and eradicate the *Da Cheng Men* was given in the 1950s. In 1983, Wan and Zong...under the banner of 'freedom of religious belief' and on pretexts such as 'adopting the prohibitions of vegetarianism' and 'cultivating the future life rather than one's present existence', secretly recruited into the sect over one hundred new members. All this exerted an extremely bad influence among the masses." No further news of the two elderly sectarians' fate since late 1988.

* **Liu Baiqiang**, 26, a prisoner serving a ten-year sentence for robbery in Guangdong Province in June 1989, sentenced to an additional eight-year term for writing leaflets in his prison cell expressing support for the crushed pro-democracy movement. According to an internal report by the Supreme People's Court, on June 6 that year, Liu secretly wrote out three leaflets bearing the words, "Long Live Freedom," "Deng Xiaoping should step down" and "Tyranny." After showing these to his cellmates, "He attached them to the legs of locusts and released the insects out of the prison cell [in the aim of] inciting people to overthrow the political power of the people's democratic dictatorship." At his trial, the court pronounced Liu guilty of "counterrevolutionary propaganda and incitement" and declared that "his crimes are heinous and he must be severely punished."

* **Jampel Changchup** and **Ngawang Phulchung**, Tibetan Buddhist monks in their mid-thirties, arrested in early 1989 for staging a peaceful protest and later sentenced to nineteen years' imprisonment for "espionage" and "forming a counterrevolutionary group." The two monks were accused of "collecting information and passing it on to the enemy,"

charges which appear to have referred primarily to their contacts with the Dalai Lama's government-in-exile and to unofficial publishing activities. Significantly, their first major publication was a Tibetan translation of the *Universal Declaration of Human Rights*. Together with eight other monks sentenced in connection with the same case, they are currently serving their sentences at Drapchi Prison. They are among twenty inmates who in April 1991 were beaten unconscious by prison guards for protesting the punishment of two other prisoners who had attempted to hand then U.S. Ambassador to China, James Lilley, a letter exposing conditions at Drapchi.

   * **Zheng Qiuwu**, arrested in Hainan Island in 1986, tried on charges of "organizing and leading a counterrevolutionary group" and sentenced to 14 years' imprisonment. Zheng is currently being held in a special unit for political prisoners at Huaiji Prison, Guangdong Province, where he has been in solitary confinement for most of the past seven years. Among the "ideological heterodoxies" of which he was accused was his outspoken advocacy of establishing stock markets in China - a notion that was officially condemned at the time but which now forms a central part of the government's economic reform policy. According to a former political inmate of Huaiji Prison, Zheng had by 1991 become mentally disturbed as a result of his solitary ordeal.

Fair Trial Concerns

   Anyone who has examined trial documents in the cases of political prisoners in China can hardly fail to be struck by one oddly consistent fact, namely that court verdicts follow, virtually verbatim, the text of the original prosecution indictment. This textual correspondence is unerringly repeated, moreover, when the time for the appeal hearing duly arrives. Far from demonstrating, as Chinese judicial authorities might suppose, the estimable rigor and diligence of the court system, this state of affairs means one thing only: that guilt has been predetermined and the verdicts decided upon in advance.

   A brief outline of China's criminal justice system suffices to confirm this impression. First, court authorities explicitly reject the principle of "presumption of innocence," a cornerstone of internationally recognized due process and a principle enshrined in the *Universal Declaration of Human Rights*. (To adopt such a rule, argue the Chinese authorities, would be tantamount to saying that China's policemen could never arrest anyone.) Instead, the first thing detainees encounter when

xvii

they enter police cells is a large sign on the wall proclaiming "Lenience to Those Who Confess, Severity to Those Who Resist." Confession is an integral and required part of the system, and is the only viable route for detainees wishing to avoid the full weight of the law.

Second, detainees in China are by official regulation denied all access to defense lawyers until after the prosecution has wrapped up its case and is ready to go to trial, by which time the accused will commonly have been held for a period of between several months and over a year. This usually leaves no more than a few days for counsel to prepare a defense, and even then lawyers are often informed that the court will only accept guilty pleas. Visits by family members may only commence once the verdict has been handed down and the prisoner transferred to the facility where he or she is to serve sentence.

Third, the inevitable outcome of such prolonged incommunicado detention is widespread police torture and ill-treatment aimed at forcing the requisite confessions. An official newspaper revealed in October 1993 that no less than 1,687 cases of police and justice officials extracting confessions by torture had occurred nationwide since 1988.[2] Despite China's ratification that year of the U.N Convention Against Torture, "The trend of torture has not declined. On the contrary, more and more bloody incidents have occurred....[And] methods of torture have become more cruel." In Henan Province alone, "Forty-one criminals and innocent suspects were killed by torture from 1990 to 1992. Seventeen, or more than forty percent of the victims, died last year, during which sixty-two cases of torture were uncovered, twenty-four percent more than in 1991." And perhaps most disturbing of all, "Officers that rely on torture to break a case are not criticized but are cited for meritorious service and rewarded."

Fourth, there is no meaningful independence of the judiciary in China, especially where political cases are concerned. According to information supplied by the Chinese government in 1993 to the U.N. Committee Against Torture, "The Communist Party [does] not intervene at all in decisions of the courts."[3] The reality, however, is very different. Courts at all levels are subject to close scrutiny and control by parallel

---

[2] *Henan Legal News*, October 7, 1993, in *Agence France Presse*, October 15.

[3] Official Records of the 48th Session of the General Assembly, Supplement No.44 (A/48/44), p.65.

and superior organs of the Communist Party known as "politics and law committees" *(zheng-fa weiyuanhui.)* In addition, "adjudication committees" *(shenpan weiyuanhui)* within each court, composed of the court president and other senior judicial cadres, are required by the Party not only to screen all so-called major, important or thorny cases *(da-yao yinan anjian)*, but also to render a verdict in advance of the actual trial. This procedure, a novel one by international standards, is openly referred to in China's legal press as "verdict first, trial second *(xianpan houshen.)* A concise explanation of the practice, which remains the norm for all political cases, was given in July 1988 by an unusually outspoken advocate of judicial reform, writing in the Shanghai journal *Democracy and Law:*

> Our current trial practice in all cases, regardless of whether they are major or minor, criminal, civil, economic or administrative ones, is that the adjudication committee must first give its opinion on what the appropriate ruling should be, and this is then implemented [in court] by the panel of judges....Even if they [i.e. the committee] reach an erroneous verdict, the panel of judges must submit to it completely and unconditionally; there is no room allowed for debate or disagreement.[4]

With such perverse rules of legal process in operation, a high incidence of wrongful conviction becomes a virtual certainty. But what is most surprising is that so few real lessons appear to have been learned by China's senior judicial officials in the aftermath of the Cultural Revolution. According to a confidential report prepared over a decade ago by the Fujian provincial justice authorities, 93 out of a total of 750 "counterrevolutionaries" sentenced by the province's courts during the two-year period 1977-78 received the death penalty and were executed. Subsequently, the government conducted a review of altogether ninety-eight of the sentences of "counterrevolution" passed during the period in question by intermediate courts in the province's two main cities, Fuzhou and Xiamen, and by six other municipal and county courts in the province. The findings were shocking:

---

[4] *Minzhu Yu Fazhi*, July 1988.

We discovered serious problems with regard to 93 of the cases, amounting to 94.3 percent of the total. Among these, 67 of the convicted persons, or 68.36 percent of all the cases reviewed, were in fact completely innocent. Two persons, or 2.05 percent of the total, should have been exempted from criminal punishment. In 21 cases, or 21.4 percent of the total, either the wrong charges had been applied or the sentences imposed were too heavy. And in a further three cases, or or 3.06 percent of the total, either the facts were unclear or the evidence was insufficient.[5]

Among twenty-one of the "counterrevolutionaries" sentenced by the Fuzhou Intermediate Court, "Seventeen, or seventy-seven percent of the total, were found to have been completely innocent....The original verdict was upheld in only one case." And of nine such verdicts rendered by the Xiamen Intermediate Court, "All were found to have problems." The government report carefully avoided specifying how many wrongfully convicted persons had been among the list of those actually executed, confining itself to the comment, "A small number of persons who should not have received the death penalty were sentenced to death." But the figures spoke clearly enough for themselves: virtually all of the cases had been miscarriages of justice.

All but two of the twelve main counts of "counterrevolutionary crime" with which political defendants may be charged in China are currently punishable by the death penalty. The present report contains summaries of sixty-seven such cases of execution that occurred during the 1980s, including seven cases of persons who were accused solely of non-violent activities; also listed are the names (without case details) of a further thirty-eight executed "counterrevolutionaries." But this is just the tip of the iceberg. Most of those executed each year in China are so-called common criminals, rather than political prisoners. Although the authorities have consistently refused to make public the nationwide statistics for executions, independent monitoring groups estimate the

---

[5] "Many 'Unjust, False and Erroneous' Verdicts Also Found Among Cases Tried Between 1977 and 1978," *Renmin Sifa Xuanbian* ("A Compilation of Articles from *People's Justice* Magazine"), Law Publishing House, February 1983, pp.116-8. The volume is marked "For internal distribution only."

average annual figure to be at least several thousand.[6] Wrongful execution is, to be sure, only the most heinous among an extensive range of human rights violations that occur all too often as a result of the currently deplorable state of criminal justice in China. But when lives can be so casually dispensed with, few judicial safeguards for prisoners' rights - short of a fundamental reform of the entire court system - are likely to be forthcoming in the case of non-capital offenders, especially those political and religious activists whom the Communist Party still views as being among its most dangerous enemies.

Accountability

In assessing what steps the international community might usefully take in order to promote an improvement in China's human rights situation, three separate but interrelated issues need to be considered. The first is prisoner accountability. Thus far, efforts by foreign governments and rights groups to secure even the most basic accounting from the Chinese authorities of its political and religious prisoner population have not produced encouraging results. In fact the process has been much like pulling teeth. A series of political and religious prisoner lists, often running to several hundred names in length, have been presented to Beijing by the U.S. and other Western governments since 1991, but these have brought forth partial and extremely limited responses from the authorities. This still represents progress, as compared to those times when the lists have simply been ignored. While seizing upon every available inaccuracy or inconsistency on the lists in order to downplay the reliability of the information as a

---

[6] International pressure on the issue is steadily mounting. In its annual report of 1993 to the United Nations General Assembly, the U.N. Committee Against Torture noted that it had formally requested from the Chinese government "precise statistical data concerning the number of persons...sentenced to capital punishment and executed." (Official Records of the 48th Session of the General Assembly, Supplement No.44 [A/48/44], p.67.) *Amnesty International*, which monitors use of the death penalty worldwide, recorded a total of 1,249 confirmed executions in China between January and November 1993, while noting that "These figures are believed to be far below the actual number." In the month of September alone, "570 people were sentenced to death...of whom at least 373 were executed." (*ASA 17/02/94*, January 1994.)

whole, Chinese officials have expended little equivalent effort either to correct them or to supply the missing details. Meanwhile, all the information needed to promote the process of accountability, were the authorities so minded, no doubt sits readily accessible in the archives of the central and provincial justice departments.

The absolute minimum that the international community should expect to achieve in what has by now become something of a cat-and-mouse game with Beijing, is an adequate accounting of the present status and circumstances of those prisoners appearing on the lists presented. If certain names genuinely cannot be identified, the authorities should request further information where available and make good-faith efforts to cooperate in the search. Beyond this, however, they should also be asked to supply copies of the court verdicts or police sentencing documents in all confirmed or "status known" cases. Access to such documents by human rights groups and others would probably be the single most effective means of evaluating the charges laid against imprisoned dissidents and of establishing whether or not internationally accepted standards had been violated by the courts.   The government maintains that all trials in China, including those of "counter-revolutionaries" (and excluding only those of minors or ones where "state secrets" are involved), are conducted openly and publicly. If this were indeed true, then the trial proceedings would surely be a matter of public record, freely available to any Chinese citizen or other concerned party. The claim, however, is false, and there appear to be no such public archives anywhere in China. Sometimes even the families of the accused are denied a copy of the sentencing document. As regards the prisoners listed in this report, it should be stressed that probably the majority of cases summaries were obtained from officially published Chinese sources. On all such cases, there can be no excuse for the government to plead ignorance or lack of information. All that is clearly lacking is the inclination on its part to play ball.

Access

Even assuming that the major hurdle of prisoner accountability is somehow eventually cleared, there still remains the problem of access. At present, all prisoners in China serve out their sentences in a harshly punitive penal environment over which there is no outside scrutiny or independent monitoring worth mentioning. The recently established "prisons bureau" (*jian-suo jiancha bumen*) of the Chinese procuracy, which is meant to perform this role, remains a weak and ineffective body with no powers other than those bestowed and withdrawn at the whim of Party officialdom. As noted above, serious abuses by prison officials, including forcing inmates to work 14-hour days in order to boost the prison enterprise's earnings or torturing them with electric batons as punishment for minor infractions of the rules, thrive in such an environment. A most pressing and immediate need is therefore to secure agreement from the Chinese authorities for regular access to prisoners by independent humanitarian or rights monitoring groups.

The International Committee of the Red Cross (ICRC), which in early 1994 was negotiating with the Chinese government for such access, is certainly more than qualified to perform this role. However, even if access is finally agreed upon, it will only be to one particular sector of the Chinese prisoner population, most probably either sentenced "counter-revolutionaries" or imprisoned Tibetan pro-independence activists. (Actually, almost all Tibetan political prisoners appear to have been convicted of "counterrevolution," and so in effect form a subset of the former group.) So-called common criminals, who constitute the great majority of Chinese prisoners but fall outside these two categories, also have human rights, and they are often subjected to just as severe treatment as the political inmates. The Chinese government will also almost certainly limit visits to the relatively small number of penal facilities in which the chosen target group is for the most part confined. (In accordance with the principle of "separate management and separate custody" *[fenguan fenya]*, most "counterrevolutionaries" are nowadays concentrated in two or three high-security prisons located in each major province.)

China's prison and labor-camp system is the most extensive in the world. According to the Chinese government's 1993 reply to the U.N. Committee Against Torture, it currently comprises "684 reform-through labor centers, 155 prisons, 492 rehabilitation centers [including both administrative "labor re-education" camps and "women's re-education" centers] and thirty-seven social reintegration centers for juvenile offenders. And that only includes the facilities for sentenced criminals administered by the Ministry of Justice. Pre-trial detention centers of all types, including jails *(kanshousuo)*, "shelter for investigation centers" *(shourong shencha suo)* and police lockups at county, district and neighborhood levels number several thousand in all. In addition, the People's Liberation Army (PLA) administers, under the aegis of its "Production and Construction Corps" *(shengchan jianshe bingtuan)* a separate network of several dozen large prison camps for sentenced criminals in the far northwestern region of Xinjiang. The inmates of these camps are not included in any prisoner statistics issued by the Ministry of Justice, and it is unlikely that any agreement eventually concluded by the ICRC will confer access to them.

The disproportionately large number of Tibetan political prisoner cases listed in this report lends particular importance to one further complication in the overall administrative anatomy of the Chinese prison system. Although almost entirely unknown, the fact is that the greater part of the prison system in Tibet, unlike that elsewhere in China, falls under the jurisdiction of the Ministry of Public Security - the police - rather than that of the Ministry of Justice. Unless carefully investigated and negotiated, this and other administrative hurdles could potentially result in the ICRC being denied access to a sizable and key portion of China's political prisoner population. According to an article published some years ago in a confidential magazine for prison officials,

> By rights, China's organs of labor-reform administration [i.e. prisons and labor camps] should form a single, highly-concentrated and unified system. But in reality, the various units fall under the separate administrative purview of the departments of justice, public security and agricultural reclamation. Qincheng Prison, for example, and also the labor-reform units in Tibet, fall under the administration of the public security authorities; and in Xinjiang, several dozen labor-reform units are run by the Production and Construction Corps.[7]

The Ministry of Public Security's retention of jurisdiction over major prisons and labor camps in Tibet, despite a nationwide reform of 1983 which ended such control elsewhere in China, means that police

---

[7] "Thoughts on Reforming the Labor-Reform System's Administrative Structure," *Laogai Laojiao Lilun Yanjiu (Theoretical Studies in Labor Reform and Labor Re-education)*, No.2, 1990, p.43. The mention of prisons run by the "agricultural reclamation department" *(nongken bumen)*, is probably a reference to the labor camp system in China's most northeasterly province, Heilongjiang. It was previously believed that all these camps had been handed over to the Ministry of Justice by the early 1980s at the latest.

investigative power and prison administrative authority remain in the hands of a single government agency - a situation condemned under international standards as being likely to lead to the occurrence of torture and other human rights violations.[8]

A final group of prisons which are also not administered by the Ministry of Justice, but to which particular attention should probably be paid by the ICRC, are ones mentioned fleetingly in a internal directive issued jointly in June 1983 by the Justice and Public Security authorities. The directive set forth detailed arrangements for the administrative transference of all labor-reform and labor re-education facilities from the Ministry of Public Security to the Ministry of Justice, an important penal reform which duly took place later that year. The passage in question reads,

> In view of the ongoing requirements of our struggle against the enemy, the public security departments will need to continue to maintain a number of prisons across the country for the incarceration of spies, espionage agents and other major criminals, and also for criminals with knowledge of state secrets. Detailed plans for this are to be drawn up by the Ministry of Public Security and submitted to the CPC Central Committee for approval and authorization.[9]

The only such prison in China that is known to the outside world is Qincheng, which lies about 40 miles north of Beijing. Formerly a top-

---

[8] An example of a slightly different nature arising from the proliferation of penal jurisdictions in China can be seen in the case of the PLA-run labor camps in Xinjiang, where, according to the article cited above, the percentage of prisoners sentenced to death with a two-year reprieve who were actually executed after the probationary period is almost twice as high as that in any other part of the country.

[9] "Various Regulations by the Ministry of Public Security and the Ministry of Justice Concerning the Detailed Implementation of the Central Committee's Transferral of Administrative Authority Over the Work of Labor-Reform and Labor Re-education," June 6, 1983, in *Zhonghua Renmin Gongheguo Falü Guifanxing Jieshi Jicheng - Zengbuben* (A Collection of Standard Interpretations of the Laws of the PRC - Supplementary Volume), Jilin People's Press, December 1991, p.813.

secret facility for senior political prisoners, it still holds a number of prominent detainees, notably Bao Tong, the former chief aide to deposed Party leader Zhao Ziyang. Officially, however, the prison does not exist, and the passage cited above contained the first indication that there may actually be several more like it.

Prominent attention should also be paid to one of the most striking features of the prisoner data contained in this report. Why is it that in Tibet, a country whose population accounts for only around 0.2 percent of the total population of China, there are currently more known political and religious prisoners reported to be in jail than in the rest of the country combined? And why are so many of these prisoners, the great majority of whom are peaceable Buddhist monks and nuns, so often arrested and sentenced on charges of "counterrevolution" rather than less serious counts? The answer to these questions is far from clear, but the following statistics may provide an answer of sorts. In October 1993, Minister of Justice Xiao Yang publicly announced that in China as a whole, sentenced "counterrevolutionaries" accounted for only 0.3 percent of the total convicted prisoner population. According to an article published in October 1991 in a confidential journal for prison officials, the corresponding figure for Tibet stood at an astonishing 6.5 percent.[10] In other words, the proportion of "counterrevolutionaries" to common criminals in Tibetan jails today is almost twenty-one times higher than in China proper.

Releases

Securing an accounting from the Chinese government of its political and religious detainees would certainly be a welcome first step in the direction of longer-term human rights improvements. And gaining ICRC access to prisoners would greatly consolidate the process, placing it on a broader and more flexible footing. But neither of these measures really address the crux of the problem, which is the continued arbitrary detention of thousands of peaceful dissidents all over China. Unless substantial numbers of those on Asia Watch's priority list and other urgently required releases are carried out by the authorities, then

---

[10] "A Discussion of the Special Characteristics of Ethnic Prisoners in the Tibetan Region and of Measures to Deal With Them," *Fanzui Yu Gaizao Yanjiu (Research in Crime and Reform)*, No.5, 1991, p.42.

progress on the other two issues might even have the unintended consequence of appearing to confer international respectability or legitimacy upon the repressive status quo.

Economic reforms may indeed, as those who oppose sanctions against China maintain, result eventually in a freer and more democratic type of society. But that change will not come easily, and it will be strenuously resisted by the country's present rulers, for whom a compliant court system and the ever-available charges of "counterrevolution" remain the weapon of choice against citizens actively seeking to promote a more pluralist outcome. A clear case in point is that of the *Democratic Youth Party*, a dissident group that was based in Kai County, Sichuan Province. In May 1992, according to an internal government report, no fewer than 179 members of the group were "netted" by the police for having "opposed the Three Gorges Dam." (Most of Kai County is destined to disappear forever under the floodwaters of the massive dam project.) There were no public reports on the case and it is not known what became of any of the detainees. As good a test as any of the government's readiness to show progress on the human rights front would be to request that it first provide a list of names of the 179 detainees and then grant Asia Watch or some other monitoring group access to those still being held. China's record for 1993 speaks for itself: accountability was minimal, access was nil and a handful of releases were accompanied by a wave of new arrests. In retrospect, it looks more like regress than progress.

As the years go by since the June 1989 Tiananmen Square events and as China's developing economy exerts an ever-growing influence on the West's policy toward Beijing, a certain hesitancy seems to be emerging on the part of many who were formerly convinced of the need for continued pressure over the human rights issue. An interim assessment of how effective the pressure has been to date is no doubt in order, and results have indeed been patchy. But one thing is clear: international pressure over the past few years has been virtually the only factor serving to keep in check, the more flagrantly repressive impulses of the Chinese authorities. Any move now by the international community to abandon that pressure would send an entirely inappropriate signal to Beijing, one that would probably be interpreted as a green light to commence open season on the dissidents for the foreseeable future.

-- January 31, 1994

A NOTE ON THE TEXT

Certain conventions and phrases are used in the text of this report as follows:

CCS refers to an important source used in documenting some cases of counterrevolutionary prisoners. Entitled *Criminal Case-Studies Series (Vol.1: Crimes of Counterrevolution)*, it was compiled by the Supreme People's Procuratorate and published in Beijing in 1992.

TC refers to an analysis of ten trials arising out of the June 4, 1989 demonstrations, published in a restricted-circulation (*neibu*) document called *Handbook of Criminal Adjudication and Supervision, Volume 2, Parts 1 and 2 (Second Criminal Court Book of the Supreme People's Court Adjudication)*. It was published by the People's Court Publishing House in Beijing in 1991.

Superscripts appearing after names are used to distinguish several prisoners with the same name, as in Zhang Jie[1] and Zhang Jie[2].

The Chinese government uses terms such as "never accused of any offense" and "not pursued for legal responsibility" to refer to people known to have been arrested after whom government and individuals have inquired. Such terms often mean that the detainees in question were given administrative, rather than judicial sentences of up to three years in labor re-education camps.

Many Tibetan prisoners are listed as being detained in prisons known by their location in and around Lhasa: Drapchi, Gutsa, Sangyip and so on. Drapchi is officially Prison No.1 of the Tibetan Autonomous Region (TAR) and holds only sentenced prisoners, men and women. There appears to be a second prison called Trisam. There are also two labor reform camps run by the TAR's Bureau of Labor Reform, No.1 in Sangyip and No.2 in Nyingtri, but each of these appears to have several branches. The TAR Public Security Bureau runs an interrogation and detention center called New Seitru, which is in the Sangyip area. Gutsa is the municipal detention center of Lhasa.

I. CRACKDOWN OF 1993

1. Died in Prison/Under Surveillance

Catholics and Protestants

Hebei

■ Bishop Paul **LIU Shuhe**, the second bishop of Yixian, Hebei Province, died at the age of 74 on May 2, 1993 and was buried on May 10 in his village, Chunmuyu, Xuhui County. Extremely ill with kidney disease, he had been in hiding after escaping from an "old-age home" (see **Chen Jianzhang**, p.392) in April 1992, and was unable to get medical attention without risking arrest or having severe restrictions placed on his movements. An earlier report (said to have originated with the Chinese authorities claimed that he had been transferred from a "re-education through labor" facility to government care in an "old-age home," thus implying that he was free. At that time, however, neither his friends nor family were able to contact him.

In October 1988, Bishop Liu was accused of possessing two scripts for "illegal" sermons and a typewriter, and for this was sentenced administratively to three years' "labor re-education." Other charges reportedly stemmed from his meeting with a visiting cleric from the Philippines. A year later, in June 1989, ill with severe cirrhosis of the liver, Bishop Liu was permitted to return home for medical treatment but was kept under strict house arrest. In mid-December 1990, his term of "re-education" still incomplete, he was again incarcerated, probably in a labor re-education facility. The police officers who came to the bishop's home said they were "taking him to Baoding for a discussion"; they promised to bring him home once matters were settled, but he never returned. In mid-December 1991, after Bishop Liu's original sentence of "re-education" had expired, family members repeatedly asked the Public Security Bureau for his release. They were finally told, "He is kept and provided for by the state. Don't ask any more where he is now." Family requests to visit the bishop were denied.

First jailed as a "counter-revolutionary" from 1958 until 1980, Bishop Liu spent, during his life, a total of more than 25 years in prison. Ordained in 1944 and consecrated on May 18, 1982, he was elected Secretary-General of the clandestine Bishop's Conference held in Shaanxi Province in November 1989, although he did not directly take part.

. . . . [DEAD]

1

Shaanxi

■   In late March 1993, five
Protestants, all from Shaanxi, were
detained and severely tortured in
Shaanxi Province's Taoyuan Village (in
Lijia Township, Xunyang County). One
of the five, 22-year-old **LAI Manping**,
died as a result of his wounds.
According to a firsthand account by
one of the victims, which was made
available to Asia Watch by a Protestant
church source, the police attacked a
group of worshippers at a religious
meeting in Taoyuan on March 27.
Eight or nine Public Security Bureau
officers broke into the gathering and
"without a word of explanation began
to beat us with rods and put handcuffs
on the five who came from Ankang,"
three men and two women. (The five
were reportedly singled out because the
authorities suspected them of
connections with foreigners.)
According to the account,

*The officers stripped three brethren
naked from the waist and forced the
women to stand with them. Not only did
they then beat them, moreover they
forced each of the 26 other local people
to beat each one 100 times with
bamboo rods. If they refused [said the
police], they would in turn be beaten.
The three men were beaten until they
were totally covered with blood and
had gaping wounds and injuries all
over their bodies. As if such violent
beating wasn't enough, the officers then
hung them up and began to hit them
with the rods on their backs. They did
this until the three men were
unconscious and barely breathing. We*

*could only hear the sound of the
beating and the cursing of the officers.*
        The two women from Ankang
were also violently beaten and
eventually passed out. On regaining
consciousness, they found, "Two of us
sisters had been placed on the stove and
a large millstone of over 100 catties
[130 pounds] placed on our backs while
they continued to beat us with rods.
They also...ripped open our
pants...using the most cruel methods to
beat our private parts."
        The following morning, the
five victims were taken first to the
Taoyuan police station and then to the
Public Security Bureau in Lijia. But the
officers at Lijia refused to accept them,
so they were sent back to Taoyuan and
remained there for eight days "under
the most primitive conditions." When
the officers realized the full extent of
Lai Manping's injuries, a doctor was
summoned to give minimal medical
treatment. However, "Realizing Lai
was about to die, the guards ordered
him to leave. He struggled along,
walking some and crawling some for
ten kilometers....And then he
collapsed. The local people found him
and carried him to a small house, but
after one day and night he died."
        According to the Chinese
government's subsequent account of the
incident, Lai Manping had travelled
from Ankang to Taoyuan on March 27
with "two accomplices." The three men
had "seriously disturbed the public
order by organizing an illegal
meeting," which was later "stopped" by
the police. "Local people, enraged by
Lai's unlawful activities," said the
authorities, "beat him up with bamboo

sticks" and left him "slightly injured" on the back. Lai's death on April 6, concluded the official version, was "the result of a heart attack brought on by a lung ailment."

The author of the firsthand acount cited above, a 21-year-old woman from Ankang County named **XU Fang**, went on to report that by early May 1993, police had rounded up some 90 Christians in the area, both men and women, in an attempt to suppress all news of the incident. By the end of June, all but two of the detainees had been released after paying the police stiff fines of 500-700 *yuan* ($90-$130) each; in many cases, the detainees were reportedly severely beaten to force them into paying. In September, police in Ankang County again rounded up 25 local Christians in an attempt to discover who had leaked the news of Lai Manping's death to the outside world, according to the Hong Kong-based *Chinese Church Resource Centre*. By mid-October, six persons still remained in police custody. Ms. Xu Fang was one of those detained, moreover, and as of late January 1994 she was reportedly still being held and believed likely to face eventual trial for revealing the truth of Lai's killing.

. . . . [DEAD]

Shanghai

■   Jesuit Father Vincent **ZHU Hongsheng**, born July 17, 1916, died on July 6, 1993 of a heart ailment. Five months earlier, on February 17, *Xinhua*, the official Chinese news agency, had announced with much fanfare Father Zhu's "early release"

from a 15-year prison term. What the official reports neglected to mention, however, was that Father Zhu, who was arrested on November 18, 1981 and sentenced on March 22, 1983, had actually been released on medical parole on February 6, 1988 and for the past few years had been living with relatives in Shanghai. (His original sentence, to be followed by five years' subsequent deprivation of political rights, had previously been reduced to twelve years in prison and subsequent loss of political rights. Another priest sentenced at the March 1983 trial, Father **Chen Yunshang**, received an 11-year prison term.) In reality, the Shanghai Intermediate People's Court had merely canceled the remaining months of Father Zhu's suspended sentence and restored his civil rights. In other words he was officially no longer under police surveillance and was technically free to vote, to travel around China and to apply for a passport.

The announcement also neglected to mention that Father Zhu had suffered a serious heart attack on Christmas Eve 1992, followed by another in January 1993, that is, just weeks before the *Xinhua* announcement of his "release," and that there was good reason to doubt even then that he would survive. He returned home in February, but as of late March 1993 was back in hospital. Father Zhu had been hospitalized once before, in 1987, suffering from heart problems and high blood pressure, and his release from prison to house arrest at that time apparently was a response by the authorities to his deteriorating health.

Father Zhu's trial in March 1983 was attended by some 100 officially invited guests; no family members were allowed to attend. According to unofficial sources, he was probably sentenced under Articles 91 and 102 of the Chinese Criminal Code for various "counterrevolutionary" activities, including "colluding with foreign countries," "endangering the sovereignty and security of the motherland," "collecting intelligence reports," and "fabricating rumors and carrying out incitement or subversive activities." The charges referred to Father Zhu's contacts with the Vatican, his independent religious activity including the circulation of unofficial religious literature, and his contacts with unapproved foreign visitors during the time between his release from prison in 1979 and his re-arrest on November 19, 1981. On that day, 20 police officers searched his home from 9 A.M. until midnight.

Father Zhu had already spent 24 years in prison, prior to his last (post-1981) term. He was first arrested in 1953 and held for a year, then on September 8, 1955, he was again arrested and held for five years before being sentenced on March 17, 1960 to 15 years' hard labor. He was not released until 1978, when the Cultural Revolution received official condemnation. Father Zhu was held for those 24 years in a variety of labor camps in Anhui Province and in northern China. In 1970 he began work in a prison-run pesticide factory and taught cadres' children English and French. He also translated western books into Chinese.

Born into a wealthy Shanghai family that had practiced Catholicism for over 300 years, in his youth Father Zhu was sent to study in France, Belgium, Ireland and the U.S. He became a priest in 1944 and returned to China in 1947 to head a Jesuit school, the St. Ignatius High School in Shanghai. His uncle, Bishop **Zhu Kaimin**, was one of the first six Chinese bishops ordained in Rome. Bishop Zhu died in 1960 while under house arrest by the government.

. . . . [DEAD]

2. Sentenced

Students and Intellectuals

Beijing

■   **BAI Weiji**, 36, was sentenced on May 20, 1993 to ten years in prison for the alleged crime of "illegally providing national secrets to a foreigner." The foreigner in question was Lena Sun, Beijing bureau chief of the *Washington Post*. Bai's appeal was rejected on July 5. Moreover, his wife, **ZHAO Lei** (Lily), received a six-year term for the same offense. Bai was arrested at home after midnight on May 5, 1992, and Zhao almost a year later, on April 21, 1993. The couple were tried in secret, Bai reportedly on March 13, 1993.

Prior to his arrest, Bai had maintained friendly contacts with several foreign journalists, among them Lena Sun. On May 17, 1992, Ms.

Lena Sun. On May 17, 1992, Ms. Sun's office was raided by five plainclothes security agents, who opened her safe, searched through her notes and documents and confiscated a large quantity of material. *Xinhua*, the official Chinese news agency, subsequently claimed that ten secret government documents had been found in the safe.

Two friends of Bai and his wife were also tried and sentenced in connection with the case. One, named **TANG Yi**, 36, assistant to Commerce Minister Hu Ping (*New York Times*, July 30, 1993), received a four-year sentence. Tang is said to have admitted that he showed documents to Bai Weiji but was unaware that they would be turned over to a foreigner. The other, **WANG Jun**[1], a journalist for the *People's Daily Overseas Edition* who reportedly was arrested around May 25, 1992, was sentenced to two years in prison. After June 1989, Wang was reportedly disciplined for his participation in the pro-democracy movement (*Committee to Protect Journalists*, July 29, 1992) and banned from continuing to work as a journalist. After Tang's arrest, his wife was passed over for a routine promotion at the hospital where she works, presumably on account of her husband.

Bai Weiji graduated from Beijing University in 1981 with a degree in political science and was assigned to work at the General Office of the Communist Party where he helped resolve complaints from the general public. Before going to work in the Foreign Ministry, where he monitored foreign news and wrote news summaries for ministry employees, he acquired a master's degree. During the 1989 pro-democracy movement, Bai reportedly organized a march of some younger ministry employees, for which he lost his job and was expelled from the Party.

Zhao Lei graduated from the Beijing Foreign Affairs College and also worked for a time at the Foreign Ministry. She later did part-time translation work for Lena Sun, among other foreign residents of Beijing. Bai and Zhao have a one-and-a-half-year-old daughter, who is currently being cared for by a woman hired by their families.

. . . . [10, 6 YRS]

■   **LIAO Jia'an**, 24, a graduate student in philosophy at People's University was sentenced by the Beijing Intermediate People's Court in August 1993 to a three-year prison term for, among other things, planning activities to mark the second anniversary of the June 1989 crackdown in Beijing. Arrested on June 8, 1992, he was tried on June 19, 1993. The trial notice did not go up until the day before the proceedings, preventing Liao's relatives from getting to Beijing on time. **WANG Shengli**, an alleged accomplice detained at the same time as Liao, was released in April 1993 after charges against him were withdrawn. According to an unconfirmed report, the men's families were unable to find lawyers willing to defend them, after judicial authorities warned law firms in Beijing not to serve as counsel (*Hua Qiao Ribao*, January 10, 1993, in FBIS,

January 11).

On the morning of May 28, 1991, Liao and Wang, who was also a graduate student in philosophy, allegedly distributed on the Beijing University campus some 4,000 leaflets urging students to wear white shirts and black armbands commemorating the Tiananmen anniversary and to petition the government for political reform. In addition, the two men allegedly hung a large banner, "We have not forgotten June 4," from the upper story of Student Dormitory No.46.

The arrests in June 1992 were also related to Liao and Wang's role in distributing *Tides of History*, a book of essays by members of the reformist faction of the Communist Party which backed the drive for economic reform but also called for political change. The book, which was legally published in April 1992 by People's University Press, was later criticized by Chinese authorities and withdrawn from circulation. In addition to staging a reading of *Tides of History*, Liao and Wang had earlier organized a student group called the *Study Club (Dushu She)* at People's University. Although the organization, which rapidly became the largest student association in all of Beijing, was founded in accordance with university regulations, it soon came under official scrutiny because of a series of public lectures that it sponsored on controversial topics and because of the reformist political commentary which appeared in the group's journal, *Dajia (Everyone)*. Liao and Wang edited the journal, which was banned after four issues. In September 1992, the *Study Club* was

also forced to disband.

Liao, an aesthetics major in the philosophy department, who worked part-time at Beijing's *San Wei Shushi (Three Flavors Study)*, a privately-run bookstore, was called out from his dormitory room by university authorities at 9 P.M. on June 8, 1992 and arrested. Wang, also a philosophy major, was seized at 3 P.M. by the Beijing police while visiting his wife, who worked for the army in Tuan County, Hebei Province. Both men's dormitory rooms were searched and a printing machine and books and papers were reportedly confiscated. On June 9, the Beijing Public Security Bureau officially took Wang and Liao in for "shelter and investigation," an extra-judicial form of detention. On June 12, People's University officials announced to the assembled students and faculty that the two had been involved in distributing "counter-revolutionary leaflets" and would consequently be prosecuted on charges of "counterrevolutionary propaganda and incitement." Liao and Wang were initially held in Banbuqiao Detention Center in Beijing, where Liao contracted hepatitis for which he has reportedly received no treatment. While at Banbuqiao, Wang is said to have suffered severe physical ill-treatment from the common criminals with whom he shared a cell.

Prior to June 4, 1989, Liao was an undergraduate at Beijing Normal University; Wang, a Communist Party member, worked in a provincial justice department. At the time of their arrests, they had already successfully defended their master's theses and passed their doctoral examinations.

. . . . [3 YRS]

■ **WU Shisen** (Shishen), an editor in the domestic news department of *Xinhua* and a graduate of Fudan University's journalism department, was sentenced to life imprisonment in April 1993 by the Beijing People's Intermediate People's Court on charges of "leaking state secrets overseas." The charges referred to Wu's provision to a Hong Kong reporter, **Leung Wai-man** (see p.426), of an advance copy of Party leader Jiang Zemin's speech to the 14th Party Congress (*Washington Post*, August 31, 1993). **MA Tao**, an editor at the magazine *China Health Education News*, received a six-year sentence as an accomplice. According to a *Xinhua* report, on October 4, 1992, Wu secretly copied the "most confidential document" and gave it to Ma, who then gave it to the reporter in exchange for $867. *Xinhua* further reported that Leung had confessed and that Wu and Ma had both pleaded guilty. But the account claimed that Wu "was the engineer of the crime and the principal culprit" and that he "should be punished severely for the vile nature of the crime and for the odious way it was committed and its serious consequences." The text of Jiang Zemin's speech was made public by the Chinese government only days after this allegedly serious offense took place. . . . . [LIFE]

Hebei

■ **WAN Jianguo**, from Shijiazhuang in Hebei Province, was sentenced to a four-year prison term for re-printing some 60,000 copies of *Golden Lotus*, a 400-year-old Chinese erotic classic (*South China Morning Post*, March 19, 1993). The book is banned from public sale in China but is available to the Communist Party leadership and other members of China's elite in "restricted circulation" editions.

. . . . [4 YRS]

Hubei

■ **QIN Yongmin**, 44, a Wuhan Democracy Wall participant who spent several years in prison during the 1980s, was administratively sentenced in Wuhan during the third week in January 1994 to a two-year term of "labor re-education." His wife was notified of the decision on January 24 and reportedly informed that he had seriously "disturbed the social order." Qin had been taken into custody for questioning along with another activist, **Yang Zhou** (see p.478) on November 14, 1993 after taking part in a dissident meeting in Beijing to discuss a "Peace Charter" (*Heping Xianzhang*) promoting non-violent political reform in China. (See also **Zhou Guoqiang**, above.) Initially held at Beijing's Paoju Lane Detention Center, the two men were later transferred to police custody in their hometowns. Yang was subsequently released, but as of January 1994, Qin remained in detention at an unknown location in Wuhan. In a written statement issued to the foreign press, Qin's wife, Li Jinfang, said: "I strongly urge the

Chinese government to immediately cease acting in violation of human rights. If my weak call isn't enough to win my husband's release, if his concern for the fate of the Chinese people can't be protected by law, then I say again, 'People, be silent no more!'." In early December, two other signatories of the "Peace Charter," former pro-democracy movement student leaders **MA Shaohua** (see below), both of whom spent time in jail after the June 4, 1989 crackdown, were also detained and transferred to police custody in their hometowns. As of January 1994, the two men were still being held.

Qin had been in and out of jail for most of that summer on account of his dissident activities. On August 11, after publicly protesting for the third time against Beijing's bid to host the 2000 Olympics he was detained by police and held incommunicado for the next six weeks. Unfurling a banner, "Oppose the Beijing Olympics," outside a meeting of the China Olympic Committee that day, he had said to the crowd of foreign and Chinese journalists following him that the country was too poor to host the games. He also demanded the release of three Shanghai dissidents and protested the punishment he had received for previous acts of opposition. Surprised committee members quickly arranged a meeting between Qin and the committee's vice-chairman, Wu Zhongyuan, who later accused him of "discriminating against the right of developing countries to host the Olympics." He was detained by police upon his return to Wuhan and

held in a detention center until September 24, the day after the International Olympics Committee announced its decision on the host city for the 2000 Olympics.

Qin was arrested on April 23, 1993 in Beijing for similar activities. Escorted back to Wuhan, Hubei Province, and held for two weeks for "shelter and investigation," he was released after signing a paper accusing him of committing the crime of "incitement" (*South China Morning Post*, May 13, 1993). Earlier, on March 26, after Qin returned from another trip to Beijing, he was held for 40 hours and then released "under supervision." His home was searched and personal papers, including a draft of his autobiography and some of his poems, were confiscated. According to Qin, after his second release, the police came to his home "many times" to intimidate him; his phone was tapped and his mail stopped. Qin, who operates a street stall, was warned not to talk about his opposition to the games with foreign journalists, not to form any anti-Olympic bid organization and not to distribute anti-Olympic bid literature.

Originally arrested in November 1979 for selling unofficial pro-democracy magazines, Qin was released some time later, then re-arrested in April 1981 when the government carried out its final crackdown on those involved in Democracy Wall activities, and subsequently sentenced to undergo several years' "labor re-education." A former worker in the Wuhan Steel Mill, Qin edited and wrote articles during the Democracy Wall movement for the unofficial journal *Sound of the Bell (Zhong Sheng)* and was a chief organizer of the dissident *April Fifth Study Society (Si-Wu Xueshe)*.

. . . . [2 YRS]

■ **WANG Shuxiang**, 29, from Hubei Province, was sentenced to death with a two-year reprieve by the Beijing Intermediate People's Court for allegedly selling pornography and illegally trading in publishing quotas (*Reuters*, April 14, 1993). Some of the "low taste" titles he allegedly published included *A Dark Massage House*, *Sex Desire*, and *An Elementary Course on Marriage*. According to the official newspaper *Beijing Wanbao* (April 13, 1993), Wang's assets, amounting to some $603,500, would be confiscated by the state. In addition, **LI Dasheng**, a 40-year-old resident of Beijing, was charged with illegal publishing and distribution of more than 600,000 copies of similar works, including such titles as *Sex Swindling Cases* and *A Flesh Deal*, and received a 12-year prison sentence.

[DEATH W/REPRIEVE, 12 YRS]

■ **YU Zhuo**, a 24-year-old former computer science student at Hubei University (1985-89), was sentenced on October 12, 1993, by the Wuhan Intermediate People's Court to two years' imprisonment on charges of "counterrevolutionary propaganda and incitement." According to an appeal letter issued by Yu's father, Yu had pasted up in Wuhan around June 4, 1992 more than thirty wall-posters commemorating the repression of June

4, 1989, demanding that the "murderers" responsible be brought to trial, that an amnesty for political prisoners be declared, that pro-democracy exiles be permitted to return to China and that the families of June 4 massacre victims be given support. Two of the slogans read: "Blood debts must be paid for in blood" and "Put the chief murderers on trial."

Detained on September 3, 1992, Yu was held incommunicado for administrative "shelter and investigation" until May 27, 1993, when formal charges and arrest were made. He was indicted on July 5 and the trial began on August 16, but it was temporarily suspended when the public prosecutor failed to show up. His family was denied all access to him throughout the pre-trial period, during which he was held in Wuhan No.1 Detention Center, Hubei Province. Attempts by his father, **Yu Mingchu**, to gain information about Yu's whereabouts and condition were met with official stonewalling. The Wuhan Public Security Bureau chief insisted he had no responsibility for the case, although Yu was clearly his responsibility at the time. When Yu Mingchu tried to file an administrative lawsuit challenging his son's detention, Wuhan court officials referred him to a local government complaints office, despite the fact that the court had a clear obligation under the Administrative Litigation Law of 1990 to read the submission and decide whether the case should be tried.

Yu Zhuo had previously been detained for more than a year in connection with his involvement in the

1989 pro-democracy movement. After his release in 1990, Yu, under the pseudonym **YANG Yujun**, entered Wuhan Polytechnic's department of economic management as a graduate student.

. . . . [2 YRS]

Shanghai

■   **FU Shenqi,** 40, a prominent veteran of the 1978-81 Democracy Wall movement, was sentenced without trial on July 4, 1993 to three years' "re-education through labor" for allegedly "inciting trouble" among Shanghai's dissident community and speaking to foreign reporters (*New York Times*, July 12, 1993). According to the authorities, Fu had instigated a letter-writing campaign on behalf of a detained workers' rights activist, Wang Miaogen (see p.27), and had incited a hunger strike outside police headquarters in early June following the arrest of fellow dissident Zhang Xianliang (*AP* July 11, 1993) (see p.13). The four activists involved in the hunger strike (see Yang Qinheng p.50) subsequently released a signed statement denying Fu Shenqi's involvement, and Fu's wife has likewise denied that he took part in the campaign on Wang Miaogen's behalf.

Imprisoned twice before for dissident activities, Fu was seized by the Shanghai police on June 26, 1993 in order to prevent him from speaking to foreign reporters during the visit of Australian Prime Minister Paul Keating. (A journalist from the Australian Broadcasting Corporation, Ali Moore, was detained for several

hours in connection with the incident.) According to Fu's wife, **Li Liping**, it was not until mid-September that Chinese authorities informed her of the labor camp where he was being held, the Dafeng County Labor Re-education Farm in the coastal district of Yancheng in northern Jiangsu Province. She was then allowed to visit him, but only once every three months. On her first visit, Li found that Fu did not have enough to eat, that other prisoners were barred from talking to him and that some had been ordered to spy on him; on a later visit, he complained of severe stomach pain.

Fu asked for an administrative review by the Labor Re-education Administrative Committee (LRAC) of Shanghai, but the committee upheld the original sentence. Li Liping then called upon the authorities to permit her husband an open hearing in court. (According to current Chinese law, those sentenced administratively to "labor re-education" can appeal direct to the courts after an unsuccessful administrative review of the sentence by the LRAC.) In addition, Li expressed concern that her husband's Shanghai residency might be canceled and transferred to the administration of the labor camp. The court hearing was held in mid-November, but according to Li, the magistrate repeatedly interrupted and ignored evidence presented by Fu's lawyers. This second appeal, also in the form of a civil suit, was turned down by the Huangpu District Court in Shanghai on December 28, 1993. The hearing was closed, and Fu did not appear in court.

Fu Shenqi had previously been detained between May 24, 1991 and February 26, 1993, at which time he was released after being sentenced to two years' deprivation of political rights. Together with his codefendant, **ZHANG Rujun**, 38, also held since May 1991, Fu had been tried in secret by the Shanghai Intermediate People's Court in late March 1992. (Zhang received a sentence of one year's deprivation of political rights; nothing further is known about him.) During his two years in Shanghai No.1 Detention Center, Fu Shenqi was never let out of his cell. Visits from his wife were prohibited, and letters from family members often "got lost." According to an Asia Watch source, the charges of "counterrevolutionary propaganda and incitement" that were brought against Fu at his trial referred to his publication of four issues of *Fuxing (Renaissance),* an underground pro-democracy journal, and a bulletin entitled *Private Voice.* (See also *Ming Bao,* February 27, 1993, in FBIS, March 1; and *South China Morning Post,* June 4, 1991.) The magazine appealed to the people of Shanghai to show concern for the condition of imprisoned dissidents and published the proceedings of the February 1991 trials of Wang Juntao and Chen Ziming (see p.63), together with a copy of Wang's letter to his lawyer. Speaking after his release, Fu argued that he had never committed "counterrevolutionary activities" or sought to overthrow the government. His magazine, he said, was not publicly circulated and only went out to about 100 intellectuals.

Originally a worker in a Shanghai generator factory and a member of the Communist Youth League, Fu Shenqi, who is from Nanchang city in Jiangxi Province, was first arrested in April 1981 in connection with two unofficial journals that he edited during the Democracy Wall movement. *Minzhu Zhi Sheng (Voice of Democracy)* was founded in 1979; and *Zeren (Responsibility),* the journal of the *National Association of Unofficial Magazines,* began publication shortly after the organization's founding in October 1980. Fu was charged with "counter-revolutionary" offenses, both in connection with the case of Xu Wenli (see p.510) and for his Democracy Wall-related activities in Shanghai. He was sentenced in 1981 to a seven-year prison term, much of it spent in solitary confinement in a Shanghai prison. After his release (two years before his term expired), Fu continued his pro-democracy activities, taking part in the 1986-87 student protests. Prior to his most recent arrest, he made a modest living running a private bookstall in Shanghai and was a frequent participant in an unofficial "Sunday salon" which met regularly in a Shanghai park.

. . . . [3 YRS]

■   **YAO Kaiwen**, a 53-year-old former high school teacher, arrested on May 1, 1993, and **GAO Xiaoliang**, a 22-year-old former member of the banned Shanghai Workers Autonomous Federation (SWAF), also arrested in early May, were tried by the Shanghai Intermediate People's Court on

September 24, 1993 (one day after the International Olympics Committee awarded the 2000 Summer Olympics to Sydney instead of Beijing), on charges of "organizing and leading a counter-revolutionary group" known as the *Mainland Headquarters of the Democratic China Front*. Both men had been charged on June 5. The sentences were not announced until December 23: Yao received a ten-year prison term, with three years' subsequent deprivation of political rights, and Gao a nine-year term with two years' deprivation of rights. Members of China's dissident comunity "expressed shock at the severity of the sentences" (*South China Morning Post*, January 4, 1993).

Two other members of the alleged "counterrevolutionary" group, **YAO Tiansheng**, a factory worker, and **HAN Lifa**, a motorcycle mechanic and former SWAF member, both of whom had been arrested on May 26, were released on September 5, apparently for lack of evidence. As of late October 1993, neither of the two had been formally cleared of their "crimes," and both demanded that the Chinese authorities publicly declare their innocence. The four arrests were apparently prompted by the group's plan to hold commemorative activities on the fourth anniversary of the 1989 Tiananmen Square crackdown.

Gao was accused of demanding the abolition of "rule by the communist spies," and Yao Kaiwen of issuing "counterrevolutionary" slogans calling for the overturning of the official verdict on the 1989 pro-democracy movement, the holding of a

plebiscite, greater freedom of speech and a purge of the Communist Party. Yao allegedly also called for people to take over the state-run radio station and to stage demonstrations objecting to Communist rule. Both had earlier served time in prison for pro-democracy activities, Gao a two-year term for taking part in the 1989 workers' protests, and Yao an 18-month sentence of "labor re-education" following his repatriation from Hong Kong, where he had unsuccessfully sought political asylum in June 1989. All four men were initially held at the Shanghai No.1 Detention Center.

According to the court verdict, in September 1992, Yao drafted a 10-point manifesto whose aim was "ending the dictatorial rule of the Communist regime." The document also allegedly stated that the dissident group was ready to take "peaceful and bloody, legal and illegal, domestic and foreign-aided actions" to promote its pro-democracy goals. The authorities further alleged that Gao and the two Yaos had met in a Shanghai park to discuss a plan of action which (according to *SCMP*) included "street demonstrations, forming brigades of workers, occupying radio and television stations and detaining Party and government leaders." (These damaging allegations have not been independently confirmed, and as a Shanghai sources familiar with the case later commented, "That adherents of the Front do not seem to have ruled out acts of violence in their theoretical discussions does not mean they will actually commit them.") The two activists' current place of detention is not known.

. . . . [10, 9 YRS]

■ **ZHANG Xianliang**, a 47-year-old veteran pro-democracy campaigner and former clothing store manager, was sentenced without trial in July or August 1993 to three years' "labor re-education" for allegedly "inciting incidents." Family members, who had been barred from obtaining legal counsel, received formal notice of the verdict on August 21, but were not granted permission to visit him until late October. They are concerned that his Shanghai residency permit may be canceled and transferred to the administration of the Qindong Labor Re-education Farm, Qingpu County, where he is now being held. Arrested for the second time in five days on June 5, 1993, after he had given numerous interviews to foreign reporters calling, as he has since the late 1970s, for political reform, freedom of the press, freedom of speech and greater human rights, Zhang was then placed by the police under "domestic surveillance" at an undisclosed location prior to his trial. (On June 3, he had been detained for 24 hours to prevent him meeting with other dissidents at a teahouse in Shanghai People's Park, where Zhang had arranged a private commemoration of the fourth anniversary of the 1989 crackdown on the pro-democracy movement. At that time, he was freed "on bail to await trial.")

This was Zhang Xianliang's second sentence for dissident activities. In 1978, he founded a *samizdat*-style pro-democracy journal entitled *Science and Democracy*, and ever since then has used the pen-name "Shen Mo." In 1983, he was jailed in Anhui Province for five years on charges of "counter-revolutionary propaganda and incitement." Upon his release, moreover, the Shanghai authorities began to harass and persecute his daughter, Zhang Bing. Denied a job allocation by the government for several years, despite holding excellent graduation certificates, she was finally granted a passport in the late summer of 1993 and in November was preparing to travel to the U.S. to begin college.

. . . . [3 YRS]

Workers

Beijing

■ **XIAO Delong**, whose name, address and photograph appeared on a secret "most wanted" list issued by the Chinese government on August 19, 1989, has reportedly been sentenced to a three-year prison term in connection with his participation in the Beijing Workers Autonomous Federation (BWAF). A 45-year-old Beijing worker who lived on the Qinghua University campus, Xiao was arrested in September 1992 and was reportedly tried in early 1993. According to one account, he mutilated his face while on the run in an attempt to disguise his identity. No further details are currently available.

. . . . [3 YRS]

Hubei

■ **ZHANG Minpeng**, a 37-year-old worker arrested on July 16, 1992 in Wuhan, Hubei Province for his alleged leadership of an underground dissident organization, was sentenced on August 5, 1993 (under Articles 51, 52 and 98 of the Criminal Law) to a five-year prison term and two year's subsequent deprivation of political rights. Twelve other members of the dissident group were arrested at the same time and were due to be tried separately. Formally arrested on April 30, Zhang, a veteran pro-democracy activist, was tried on June 21 by the Wuhan Intermediate People's Court. According to the official court verdict (which, however, contained no allegations of violent activity by the dissident group), there was "solid" evidence that from April 1991 until his arrest Zhang had formed and led an underground organization called the Republican Party *(Gong He Dang)*. According to the verdict, Zhang had arranged meetings, printed material and drafted the Party's bylaws and also a manifesto calling for the "eradication of autocracy and re-establishment of the republic." In addition, he gave various speeches including one entitled "The Fate of Chinese Intellectuals" in which he "blasphemed against the Chinese Communist Party." Moreover, he had allegedly "failed to reform himself" while serving a previous administrative sentence of three years' "re-education through labor," imposed in April 1981 for publishing so-called "illegal" materials. (This almost certainly means that Zhang was an editor-activist during the Democracy Wall period.)

According to the August 5, 1993 verdict against Zhang, the twelve other members of his "counter-revolutionary clique" were **WANG Yangli**, **ZHANG Hanjiang**, **LIU Bangming**, **HU Gang**, **DING Hancong**, **LIU Gui**, **WU Yingling**, **LU Zhonghua**, **LIU Chongyun**, **WANG Yuqing**, **ZENG Dazhao** and **ZHANG Weidong**. The outcome of the court proceedings against these twelve are not known, although according to one report **Liu Gui** received a two-and-a-half-year sentence.

    . . . [5 YRS] [12 X ? YRS]

Shanghai

■ **GAO Xiaoliang** - see p.11
  . . . . [9 YRS]

Tianjin

■ **HUANG Shixu**, a member in May-June 1989 of the *Tianjin Democratic Revival Association (TDRA)*, was arrested sometime after meeting with the U.S.-based dissident student Shen Tong, who returned to China in August 1992. The two met in Tianjin that same month. In the summer of 1993, he was sentenced without trial to a three-year term of "labor re-education" for "counter-revolutionary" offenses. First detained after June 1989 on account of his involvement in the *TDRA,* Huang spent several months in Tianjin No.1 Prison before being released.

  . . . . [3 YRS]

■ **LU Gang**, 30, was administratively sentenced in summer

1993 to a second three-year term, this one a "labor re-education" sentence for alleged "counterrevolutionary offenses." He was arrested on or about September 13, 1992 on account of his involvement with Shen Tong (see above entry.) At the time, Lu was working in the home appliance section of the Tianjin Far Eastern Department Store, having been out of prison less than two months. He was first arrested in June 1989 and sentenced to three years' imprisonment on charges of "counter-revolution" for his activities as a Standing Committee member of the Tianjin Workers Autonomous Federation, a dissident labor group formed during the May 1989 protests. Prior to that arrest, Lu had worked at the Tianjin No.2 Woolen Thread Factory.

. . . . [3 YRS]

Tibetans

Monks and Nuns

Ganden Monastery

- **NORBU**[2] - see p.35

- **PENPA**[2] - see p.35

Garu Nunnery

- **GYALTSEN TSULTRIM** (lay name MIGMAR TSAMCHOE or MIGMAR CHOEKYI) and **NGAWANG YANGKYI** (also known as NGAWANG YANGDROL; lay name KUNSANG[1]), 22-year-old Garu nuns from Ngangra Township or

Nyara, have been sentenced and transferred to Drapchi Prison. They were arrested around noon on June 4, 1993 on the Barkhor in Lhasa, while attempting to lead a small demonstration, then taken to Gutsa Detention Center. It is not known what happened to four men (names unknown) who were taken away with them.

. . . . [2 X ? YRS]

- Of a large group of nuns from Garu Nunnery who were arrested on June 14, 1993 and taken to Gutsa Detention Center, eleven have since been sentenced and transferred to Drapchi Prison (*South China Morning Post* (July 22, 1993). According to the report, the nuns, who may not have been demonstrating at the time, were seized as part of a crackdown, including a "re-education campaign," at Garu, whose members have been active leaders and participants in the Tibetan pro-independence movement. Prison terms have been reported for **GYALTSEN KELSANG**[1] (lay name KELSANG DROLMA), 23, from Ngangdren or Nyara, two years; **NGAWANG KELDRON** (lay name GOEKYI or GORKYI), in her early twenties, from Medro Gongkar Gyama, five years; **NGAWANG DEDROL**[1] (lay name RINCHEN CHOEDRON), 25, from Medro Gongkar, seven years; **NGAWANG CHENDROL** (or NGAWANG PELDROL; lay name PHURBU DROLKAR), 19, from Phenpo Lhundrup, three years; **GYALTSEN SANGMO** (lay name ACHOK ZOMPA), 24, from Kongpo Gyada Krugla district, three years;

RINCHEN DROLMA[1], 23, from Phenpo Lungshoe, two years; and **PHUNTSOG CHOEKYI** (lay name DEKYI[1]), 22, from Phenpo Lhundrup, seven years.

[2, 5, 7, 3, 3, 2, 7 YRS]

Others who were moved to Drapchi but whose sentences have not been reported include: **GYALTSEN KUNGA** (lay name YANGKYI), 23, from Nyemo Thonchue; **NGAWANG CHIME** (lay name PHURDROL), 19, from Drigung; **NGAWANG CHOEKYI[1]** (lay name CHELMO or CHOENGA), 22, from Phenpo Lungshoe; and **NGAWANG PEMO[1]** (lay name TSERING[3]), 22, also from Phenpo Lungshoe.

. . . . [4 X ? YRS]

According to an unconfirmed report, **GYALTSEN PELSANG** (lay name NYIMA[3] or MIGMAR[4]), 14 or 15 years old, from Medro Gongkar Gyama, has also been moved to Drapchi Prison despite being too young for legal admittance to a prison. And there is no further word on **PHUNTSOG CHENGA** (lay name SONAM ZOMPA or CHENGA), 22, from Lhundrup Phodo.

. . . . [2 X ? YRS]

Pomda Monastery

■   **JAMPA[1]** (referred to by the Chinese as GYAGA), a monk or cook at Pomda Monastery, about thirty years old, was found guilty of "counterrevolutionary propaganda and incitement" by the Intermediate People's Court of Chamdo Prefecture and sentenced to a four-year prison term and three years' subsequent deprivation of political rights (*Tibet People's Broadcasting Service*, November 21, 1993). On July 6, he allegedly wrote "reactionary slogans" and posted them on the "house number plate of the [Pomda] township's family planning service station," for which he was arrested on or about August 1. Pomda (called Bangda by the Chinese), is a rural area in Kham, close to the Tibet Autonomous Region's border with Sichuan Province. The report of Jampa's sentencing, which noted that he had "confessed," that his action had "created a very bad impact on society" and that "the trial of this specific case served as an example in educating the masses and played a positive role in promoting stability in the Chamdo area," was the first report by the official media of a political arrest or trial in Tibet since March 3, 1991.

. . . . [4 YRS]

Lay persons

■   **SONAM TSERING[1]**, 27, and **BAGDRO[1]**, 25, arrested on May 6 or 7, 1993 for writing pro-independence slogans on the walls of government buildings, reportedly have been sentenced to unknown terms and transferred to Drapchi Prison. It is unclear if the men, from Gyama Trikhang Village, Medro Gongkar County, 40 kilometers east of Lhasa, are monks or farmers. Sonam Tsering is the son of Tsering Dhondrup (father) and Rigzin Choedron (mother); Bagdro's father is named Kunchok.

. . . . [2 X ? YRS]

■ **LODROE**[1], a 24-year-old nomad and former farmer, and two farmers, **TENPA SONAM**, a 26-year-old Communist Party member from Medro Gyama Trikhang, and **DORJE**[2] (also known as KHANGSAR DORJE), 25, from Medro Gyama Dashar, were among fourteen persons arrested on May 4, 5 or 7, 1993 in Medro Gyama. They have reportedly been sentenced and transferred to Drapchi Prison. Along with eleven others, the three allegedly participated in a February 22 demonstration (the first day of the Tibetan New Year), shouting pro-independence slogans and calling for the return of the Dalai Lama. The protests were said to have sparked off a series of local incidents, the nature of which is unclear, but may have included a demonstration in a neighboring town. In that incident, a crowd which had surrounded the house of a known police informer was dispersed by police fire.

. . . . [3 X ? YRS]

Protestants

■ **DAI GUILIANG**, 45, **GE XINLIANG**, 27, and **DAI LANMEI**, a 27-year old woman, three of eight preachers and laymen from northern Anhui Province who were arrested in late summer 1993, were sentenced on September 10, 1993 to terms of "labor re-education" by the Fuyang Prefectural Labor Re-education Administrative Committee. The three prisoners, farmers from Mengcheng County, Yuefang Township, were detained on August 25. Dai Guiliang, from Simen Village, Daiqui Hamlet, received a three-year sentence; Ge Xinliang, from Gejing Village in Jing Hamlet, and Dai Lanmei from Jintou Village in Qiu Hamlet, both received two-year sentences.

According to the sentencing documents, the three preachers "conspired together using their belief in the 'Spiritual Truth' sect to proclaim that tribulation was coming, thus causing believers to stop participating in production. They also organized sessions for listening to Hong Kong gospel radio broadcasts and they received overseas versions of the Bible. From December 31, 1992 to January 5, 1993, the three also organized a 'Preachers' Training Class' in Dai Guiliang's home, in which about 60 people participated. On the evening of March 6, Ge Xinliang and Dai Lanmei held a 'Gospel University' session in Dai Lanmei's home and trained 36 people. On the evening of August 24, 1993, [the three] held a 'Fellowship Prayer Meeting' in Simen Village, Qin Hamlet, attended by more than one hundred people. They seriously interfered with production and social order." According to informed sources, the various meetings were all held in the evenings and the charge that they interfered with production in the villages is untrue.

A fourth house church activist, **GUO MENGSHAN**, was sentenced on October 11, 1993 to a three-year "labor re-education" term for engaging in "itinerant preaching" activities. Together with **LIU WENJIE** and **ZHENG LANYUN**, both of whom were arrested with him on July 20 (case dispositions currently unknown), Guo was officially charged with "conducting 'New Believers Edification' training classes." Another church member, **ZHANG JIUZHONG**, from Jiwangchang Township in Lixin County, received a two-year "labor re-education" sentence. **LI HAOCHEN**, from Mengcheng County, Sanyi Township, was originally reported to have received a one-year term of re-education, but according to a later account (*South China Morning Post*, December 15, 1993), the sentence was actually three years. The same source also reported that a 45-year-old woman (name unknown) had been arrested in Mengcheng County in early November after she refused to close her house church; on November 17, she was sentenced to a two-year "labor re-education" term. Moreover, Hong Kong church sources reported that as of December 1993, police in Anhui were still searching for another preacher (name unknown) who had gone into hiding following the arrest of his church colleagues.

[2 X 3 YRS] [4 X 2 YRS] [1 YR] [2 X ? YRS]

3. Trial Imminent

Between May and July 1992, several dozen students, intellectuals and workers were seized by the authorities in Beijing and elsewhere on charges of alleged involvement in several peaceful underground pro-democracy groups that had been formed the previous year. The government crackdown of mid-

1992 apparently succeeded in virtually eliminating these groups, which included the **China Progressive Alliance** (CPA), the **Free Labor Union of China** (FLUC) and the **Liberal Democratic Party of China** (LDPC), all based in Beijing; and also the Lanzhou-based **Social Democratic Party of China** (SDPC) and the Hunan-based **All-China People's Autonomous Federation** (ACPAF). The groups, most of which were formed in 1991, called for greater democracy and human rights and advocated peaceful, non-violent opposition toward the Communist one-party system. In addition, a secret government report revealed that no less than 179 members of a group known as the **Democratic Youth Party** (DYP), a pro-democracy group based in Wanxian District, Sichuan Province (the heart of the government's massive "Three Gorges Dam" project)" had been "netted" by the authorities in May 1992. While it is possible that many of the Wanxian detainees were either eventually released or subjected to relatively minor penalties, the authorities' crackdown on the DYP, the details of which remain almost entirely unknown, constitutes the largest single reported case of government repression against peaceful dissent in China since the summer of 1989. (For further details of the case, see p.145.)

By September 1993, some 16 of at least 20 detainees in the Beijing area, together with three activists in Henan Province, had been formally indicted and were awaiting trial. The charges ranged from "engaging in counterrevolutionary propaganda and incitement" to "organizing and leading a counterrevolutionary clique." Other activists were picked up in mid-1992 in Gansu, Hunan and Anhui provinces and in Tianjin and Shenzhen. (The Hunan detainees were reportedly released in late 1992, while those in Anhui are thought to have been released on medical parole in early September 1993.) In mid-November, the long-anticipated trials were abruptly postponed by the authorities, in order, according to numerous reports, to avoid adverse publicity for the Chinese government on the eve of President Jiang Zemin's meeting with U.S. President Clinton at the APEC summit conference in Seattle. In December, rumors surfaced that the original prosecution indictments had been withdrawn following objections by court officials that insufficient evidence had been presented to support the intended convictions. It is possible that the final bill of indictment will list somewhat different charges against the various defendants than those described below.

State-run law firms were reportedly instructed not to defend the Beijing prisoners (most of whom, as of January 1994, were being held in Beijing's Banbuqiao Detention Center), and some of the families were subsequently unable either to find or afford private defense lawyers. Some of the families, none of whom were allowed to see their detained relatives prior to trial, were informed that the trials would be held in secret and that they would be barred from attending the proceedings (Reuters, September 17, 1993). In addition, several families

were made to pay up to 500 yuan to prison authorities to cover their detained relatives' daily necessities. Trials of the underground Party activists detained in other Chinese provinces in mid-1992, including at least ten in Lanzhou, Gansu Province, were either still pending as of January 1994 or had already been conducted in secret. (For additional information on some forty of the activists detained during the mid-1992 crackdown on underground pro-democracy groups, see **Economic Reform, Political Repression**, Asia Watch, Vol.5, No.4, March 2, 1993.)

Students, Intellectuals and Officials

Beijing

■   **CHEN Wei**[1], a 24 or 25-year-old native of Suiming County in Sichuan Province and a former student of applied science at the Beijing University of Science and Engineering *(Li-Gong Daxue)*, was secretly arrested in late May 1992 in Beijing. In September 1993, Chen, one of 16 co-defendants from the Beijing area formally indicted by the Beijing Municipal Procuracy, was arraigned on charges of carrying out "counter-revolutionary propaganda and incitement."

Chen Wei's latest detention is his fourth since June 1989, when he was imprisoned for more than 18 months in Qincheng Prison for having led the student movement at his college in May-June of that year. At Qincheng, he shared a cell with Xiong Yan, one of the 21 "most wanted" student leaders of the 1989 movement who was eventually released, tried to organize an underground network, and escaped from China in mid-1992. Chen, who is single, was expelled from college after his release from Qincheng in early 1991 and was then sent back to his hometown in Sichuan Province. He soon returned to Beijing, however, and continued living there as an unauthorized resident. Chen was detained for the second time in early June 1991, apparently as a preventive measure in advance of the June 4 anniversary; no specific reason was ever given. His third arrest was in connection with the funeral of student activist Wen Jie in December of that year (see Wang Guoqi, p.26). The reason for Chen's latest incarceration may have been related to his links to Xiong Yan, although it is not known if he was active in Xiong's network.

By March 1993, Chen's family had reportedly received no information from the police about his conditions of detention or even where he was held. Only when the prosecution indictment was issued did they learn that he was being held in Beijing's Banbuqiao Detention Center. Chen Wei is a short, thin young man, extremely bright and said to be an excellent ping-pong player. As of January 1994, the trials of Chen and the 15 others, together with those of three others in Beijing (see **An Ning** p.24), were reported to be imminent.

■   **HU Shenglun**, a 38-year-old lecturer at the Beijing Languages Institute, Chinese-Western Comparative Literature Department, was arrested at the home of a friend on May 27, 1992, together with **GAO Yuxiang**, a street-stall owner at the Hongqiao Agricultural Products Market in Beijing's Xuanwu District. The police reportedly found a large quantity of pro-democracy literature in the two men's possession, and on June 6, 1992, officers from the No.7 Department of the Beijing Public Security Bureau searched their homes without warrants and confiscated notebooks, name cards, photographs and a shortwave radio.

Nothing further was heard of either Hu Shenglun (also known as **Hu Shigen**) or Gao Yuxiang until September 1993, when their names appeared on the joint bill of indictment issued by the Beijing Municipal Procuracy. Hu, singled out in the indictment as being one of the groups' "leaders," was arraigned on dual charges of "organizing and leading a counterrevolutionary group" and "counterrevolutionary propaganda and incitement." Wang was charged solely on the former count. Both defendants are being held in Beijing's Banbuqiao Detention Center, and as of January 1994, the trial was reported to be imminent.

■   **KANG Yuchun**, 28, a medical researcher in the Department of Psychiatry at Beijing's Anding Hospital and a 1991 master's graduate of the Beijing College (or Institute) of Chinese Medicine, was secretly arrested in Beijing on May 6, 1992. home and reportedly confiscated a quantity of pro-democracy leaflets. Officials of the Anding Hospital told

Kang's relatives that the State Security Ministry was involved in his arrest and it would therefore be best if they made no further inquiries. In September 1993, Kang was formally indicted on charges of "counterrevolution" for alleged involvement in underground pro-democracy organizations. As of early November, 1993, when Kang's trial was reported to be imminent, the authorities had failed to inform his parents (a peasant couple living in the outskirts of Beijing) of either the reason for his arrest or his place of detention. (The location is probably Beijing's Banbuqiao Detention Center.) In June 1993, Asia Watch formally reported Kang Yuchun's case to the U.N. Working Group on Enforced or Involuntary Disappearances. In the joint prosecution indictment, Kang, identified as being a "chief conspirator" in the case, was formally arraigned on dual charges of "organizing and leading a counterrevolutionary group" and carrying out "counterrevolutionary propaganda and incitement." As of January 1994, the trial was reported to be imminent.

■   **L U   Z h i g a n g** , a n undergraduate law student at Beijing University, arrested some time in mid-1992, was indicted by the Beijing Municipal Procuracy in September 1993 on dual charges of "organizing and leading a counterrevolutionary group" and carrying out "counterrevolutionary propaganda and incitement." As of March 1993, Lu, said by the authorities to be a "chief conspirator" in the case, was being held in Pinggu County jail, but by

September 1993 he had been transferred to Beijing's Banbuqiao Detention Center in readiness for his forthcoming trial.

■   **WANG Peizhong**, a graduate student at either the Oil Prospecting and Exploration Research Institute or at Beijing University who was arrested in mid-1992 in connection with the authorities' crackdown on alleged underground dissident group members, was formally indicted in September 1993 on charges of "actively participating in a counterrevolutionary group" and carrying out "counter-revolutionary propaganda and incitement." As of January 1994, Wang's trial was reportedly imminent.

■   **WANG Tiancheng**, 29, a law lecturer at Beijing University and editor of the college journal *Zhong-Wai Faxue (Chinese and Foreign Jurisprudence)*, was secretly arrested on November 2, 1991 in Beijing, just prior to leaving for Germany to take up a visiting scholarship. He was formally indicted in September 1993 on charges of "actively participating in a counter-revolutionary group" and carrying out "counterrevolutionary propaganda and incitement." He was still awaiting trial as of January 1994.

Wang is reported to have been the chief secretary of two underground political groups, the *Young Marxism Party* and the *Democratic Freedom Party*. According to an Asia Watch source, the Public Security Bureau was aware of both groups as early as October 1991, but for reasons unknown waited until after the visit to China of the Japanese emperor to make the arrests. There have been several unconfirmed reports that a number of other students at the law faculty, possibly as many as seven, were detained around the same time as Wang, but officials at Beijing University have denied all knowledge of the cases (*South China Morning Post*, November 18, 1992).

Wang Tiancheng's major academic interest is administrative law, and at a 1988 conference on the Chinese constitution (another interest of his) he described the current state of administrative law in China as "feudal" (a comment which reportedly brought down Party censure upon Wang's mentor, **Luo Haocai**, a vice-president of Beijing University.) Wang is said to have written an article, "Constitution and Human Rights," for the Beijing University law journal based on the theories of the 18th century philosopher Montesquieu, whom he much admires.

NB: The following persons are also reported to have been detained in the Beijing area during the mid-1992 government crackdown on underground pro-democracy groups:

■   **GUO Shaoyan**, a Beijing University graduate student; **LI Ji** (possibly a pseudonym); **WANG Qishan**, an employee at the Institute of Geology in Beijing; and **WANG Xiaodong**, a former student at the Beijing Institute of Technology, were all reportedly arrested in connection with the 1992 roundup of alleged underground dissident group members. There has been no subsequent news of

them, but it is believed they may also be scheduled to face trial.

■   **LI Yan**, a graduate student in the geology department at Beijing University, was reportedly arrested in June 1992. Other than that as of August 1993 he was still imprisoned for allegedly trying to form an "illegal" organization, no further information on Li's status is currently available.

■   **LU Mingxia,** a former student at People's University who served as head of finance in the 1989 *Beijing Students Autonomous Federation*, was arrested sometime between mid-1992 and mid-1993 in connection with the government's crackdown on peaceful underground pro-democracy groups. In the Beijing Municipal Procuracy's joint indictment of September 1993, Lu was named as being one of the "co-conspirators" in the case, but he was listed as "to be tried separately." As of January 1994, there had been no further news of his trial.

■   **REN Jun**, a lawyer and former student at Beijing University, has disappeared, according to an Asia Watch source. No additional information is available, but Ren may be one of several students from the Beijing University law department known to have been detained since early 1992 in connection with the case of Wang Tiancheng (see p.21; see also Lu Zhigang, above).

■   **ZHAO Xin**, a former student at the Beijing University of Science and

Engineering who was imprisoned for 15 months following the June 1989 government crackdown, was detained again in early June 1992, together with three others (names unknown) at the Beijing University of Agriculture and Trade. Although he was later released and sent back to his hometown in Yunnan Province, there are unconfirmed reports that Zhao was subsequently detained again in connection with the government crackdown on underground pro-democracy groups. His present circumstances are unknown.

Gansu

■   During April and May 1992, around twenty members of the dissident *Socialist Democratic Party of China* (SDPC), a peaceful underground organization based in the northwestern province of Gansu, were reportedly arrested in and around the provincial capital Lanzhou. According to Asia Watch sources, as of September 1993 at least ten of the detainees had been formally indicted and were awaiting trial on charges of "counterrevolution." They included six activists associated with Lanzhou University, namely **LIU Wensheng**, 24, a former history major from Ningxia Hui Autonomous Region, and **LIU Baiyu**, a 25-year-old former philosophy major; **GAO Changyun**, a 28-year-old management studies teacher; **LU Yanghua**, 25, a graduate student in physics and a participant in the 1989 pro-democracy movement; and **XING Shimin** (Ximan), 22, and **DING Mao**, 25, both philosophy students.

Ding, Liu Baiyu and Liu Wensheng were all active during the 1989 pro-democracy movement and were arrested following the June 4 crackdown. Ding and Liu Baiyu - who was listed as "already arrested" on a September 1989 Ministry of Public Security "most wanted" notice - were jailed for nine and 19 months respectively, and after his release, Liu was expelled from Lanzhou university. Prior to his arrest in mid-1992, Liu Wensheng, whose name also appeared on the September 1989 secret "most wanted" list, had eluded capture for almost three years.

Also detained in April and May 1992 were **ZHANG Jian**, 25, a worker at the Gansu Provincial Library; **XU Zhendong**, 25, a cadre in the Tianshan Boiler Factory in Urumqi, capital of the Xinjiang Uygur Autonomous Region; **LU Yalin**, a 24-year-old teacher at the Yancheng Institute of Light Industries in Jiangsu Province; and **CAO Jianyu**, a staffer at the Gansu Public Relations Association. All ten were reportedly secretly arrested, and subsequent requests from family members about their whereabouts went unanswered (*South China Morning Post*, August 15, 1992). As of January 1994, it was likely that the ten activists had already been secretly tried and convicted.

According to an Asia Watch source, the SDPC was headquartered in Lanzhou but also had cells in other parts of China. According to its manifesto, the organization was founded in 1991 and its membership comprised students, entrepreneurs, workers and cadres "opposed to the one-party dictatorship." In April 1992, when the SDPC first surfaced, it called upon China's National People's Congress to implement democratic reform and to release all political prisoners.

Henan

■   **AN Ning**, a former graduate student in Beijing University's archaeology department, was seized by police at the Beijing Railway Station in early September 1992 on suspicion of involvement in underground pro-democracy organizations. Subsequently, a pile of political leaflets was found in his home in Zhengzhou, capital of Henan Province. An Ning was formally indicted one year later, in September 1993, on charges of "counter-revolution" together with numerous other alleged underground Beijing activists (see **Hu Shenglun** *et al,* p.20), and as of early November his trial was reportedly imminent. According to his friends, the immediate cause of An's arrest was his contacts with Shen Tong, a U.S.-based student dissident who returned briefly to China in August 1992 (see p.452). This was An's second arrest. He spent time in prison for his role in the 1989 pro-democracy movement, and after his release the only job he could find was as an office boy in Zhengzhou. According to the September 1993 joint indictment issued by the Beijing Procuracy, An Ning's case was to be "tried separately."

■   **MENG Zhongwei**, formerly a chemistry student at Zhengzhou University and a friend of An Ning

(see above), was detained in Guangzhou by the State Security Bureau sometime in September, also reportedly on account of his contacts with Shen Tong. Meng, who was also involved in the 1989 pro-democracy protests, was subsequently transferred by the police to Zhengzhou, Henan Province, for questioning. There has been no further news about him since then.

■   The name of **WANG Jianping** also appears on the Beijing Procuracy's joint indictment of September 1993 concerning those to be tried on charges of "counterrevolution" for organizing underground pro-democracy groups. However, Wang's case is listed as "to be tried separately." There has been no further information on Wang's case since then.

Tianjin

■   **CHEN Qinglin**, 25, a government cadre from Tianjin working at the Han Gu Salt Farm weather forecasting station in Changlu, near Tianjin, and a 1987 graduate of the Beijing Meteorological Institute, was arrested on June 7, 1992 in connection with the government's roundup of alleged underground dissident group members. Held since his initial arrest at Banbuqiao Detention Center (Dept. No.7 of the Beijing Public Security Bureau), Chen was formally indicted for trial on charges of "actively participating in a counter-revolutionary group" in September 1993 along with 15 activists from

Beijing (see **Hu Shenglun** *et al,* p.20). During the 1989 pro-democracy movement, Chen served in a minor liaison capacity for the now-banned Beijing Students Autonomous Federation. Born and raised in Inner Mongolia, Chen, who is in his early twenties, is an ethnic Han. As of January 1994, Chen's trial was reported to be imminent. According to an Asia Watch source, Chen's father, **CHEN Mingxin**, was arrested together with his son.

Workers and Business Persons

Beijing

■   **GAO Yuxiang** - see p.20

■   **LIU Jingsheng**, 38, a veteran pro-democracy activist and a worker at the Tongyi Chemicals Accelerator Fluid Plant, Tongxian County, Beijing, was arrested on or around June 1, 1992 at his home in connection with the government's crackdown on "counter-revolutionary groups." So-called reactionary leaflets found at his home were later confiscated by the police. Together with many other suspected underground pro-democracy group members (see **Hu Shenglun** *et al,* p.20), Liu, who was singled out as a "chief conspirator," was formally indicted in September 1993. The specific charges against him were "organizing and leading a counter-revolutionary group" and carrying out "counterrevolutionary propaganda and incitement." As of January 1994, his trial was reported to be imminent. During the 1978-81 Democracy Wall

movement, Liu was co-editor with Wei Jingsheng (see p.507) of *Explorations (Tansuo),* a well-known dissident journal of that period. Arrested along with Wei in March 1979, Liu was called upon to give evidence at Wei's trial that October. After his release later that year, Liu resumed his job as a bus driver and nothing further was heard of him outside China until his arrest in mid-1992. His wife has not been allowed to see him since his latest arrest, although he is known to be held at Beijing's Banbuqiao Detention Center.

■   **RUI Chaohuai**, a worker at the Beijing Construction Materials and Machinery Plant; **ZHANG Guojun**[1], a private businessman (name also reported as **LI Guojun** - may be the same person as Zhang Guojun[2], see p.384); **XU Dongling**, a worker at the Beijing Paper Mill; and **ZHANG Chunzhu**, unemployed, were all named as defendants in the Beijing Procuracy's September 1993 joint indictment against underground pro-democracy group members in the Beijing area. The four were charged with carrying out "counterrevolutionary propaganda and incitement," and as of January 1994 their trials were believed to be imminent. Another activist, **LI Quanli**, a worker at the Beijing Automobile Plant's electrical appliances section, was also listed on the indictment, but under the more serious charge of "actively participating in a counterrevolutionary group." In fall 1993, reportedly following the death of his wife, Li Quanli was released "on bail awaiting trial." It is not known whether he too will eventually face trial.

- **WANG Guoqi**, 31, formerly a worker at the printing plant of the Beijing Languages Institute, was detained for the fifth time on June 22, 1992 for planning activities to commemorate the third anniversary of the crackdown in Tiananmen Square, and also for his alleged membership in underground pro-democracy organizations. Wang was seized at his ex-wife's home in Beijing by uniformed police who (rather unusually) produced a formal warrant; but he was not formally indicted until September 1993, when his name appeared along with those of 15 other codefendants on the Beijing Procuracy's joint bill of indictment (see **Hu Shenglun** *et al,* p.20). The specific charge against Wang was "actively participating in a counterrevolutionary group." As of January 1994, his trial was reported to be imminent.

Wang served two years in prison after June 1989 for printing leaflets protesting the Tiananmen crackdown. After his release, he was briefly detained again for questioning along with five former students (all of whom had spent time in Qincheng Prison for involvement in the 1989 democracy movement) on suspicion of having co-organized the funeral of **WEN Jie**, a former teacher at Beijing University who was imprisoned for 18 months after June 1989 and who died of cancer on December 20, 1991. The others briefly held included **ZHANG Qianjin**, **ZHAO Xin**, 24, **LI Xiang** and **CHEN Wei**, who was also

formally indicted in September 1993 for alleged involvement in underground pro-democracy groups and was awaiting trial as of early November (see p.19). Another activist, **WANG Tao**, and former Beijing student leader **LU Mingxia** (also indicted in September 1993 and awaiting trial as of November - see p.22) are also thought to have been detained after the funeral, together with the deceased's sister **WEN Ning**. The security authorities are said to have been particularly concerned about a white wreath with six black and four red paper roses, symbolizing June 4, 1989, which appeared at the funeral.

Wang Guoqi was detained for a third time on February 29, 1992, while hosting a birthday party for fellow dissident Zhang Qianjin, a former student leader from Hunan who had studied at the Beijing Languages Institute. Zhang was released on January 5, 1991 after completing a two-year prison term on charges of assembling crowds, undermining public order and impeding the advance of martial law troops in Beijing in early June 1989. At least eight others, including Zhao Xin (see p.22) and **LIU Di**, a veteran democracy activist in his late thirties, were also detained in connection with the birthday party. Plainclothes police followed them to Wang's apartment at Beijing's China Geological University, and when the dissidents asked why they were being followed, the police promptly laid into them and bloodied their noses (*South China Morning Post*, March 2, 1992). In addition to these various earlier detentions, Chen, Zhao and Wang

Guoqi were briefly detained in early June 1991, apparently as a government precaution against June 4 anniversary celebrations.

Place Unknown

■ **XING Hongwei**, formerly a cadre at the Chengdu City Jianjiang Coal Mine's attached flour mill, was arrested in Beijing shortly before June 4, 1992 in connection with alleged pro-democracy activities. In September 1993, Xing was formally indicted along with 15 other codefendants in the Beijing area for involvement in underground pro-democracy groups. The specific charge against Xing was carrying out "counterrevolutionary propaganda andincitement." (See Hu Shenglun *et al*, p.20.) (In other reports, Wang is described as being a private businessman from Weinan, Shaanxi Province, and as having worked at a fertilizer factory.) As of January 1994, his trial was reported to be imminent.

4. Psychiatric Confinement

Shanghai

■ **WANG Miaogen**, chairman of the Shanghai Workers Autonomous Federation (SWAF) during the 1989 pro-democracy movement, was forcibly committed on April 27, 1993 to a psychiatric hospital run by the police in Shanghai to ensure that he would not disrupt that city's East Asian Games. The 10-day event in May 1993 was to help showcase Beijing's ability to host the 2000 Olympics (*AP*, May 19, 1993). Before his commitment, Wang, 41, reportedly was beaten up by the police, kicked in the head, tied up and gagged with a sock on several occasions (*Agence France Presse*, June 4, 1993). He is not permitted visitors. (Another dissident, **Wang Wanxing**, p.114, has been forcibly incarcerated in the Beijing PSB Ankang Psychiatric Hospital since June 1992, when he was seized after unfurling a protest banner in Tiananmen Square.)

Wang Miaogen had his 1989 sentence remitted or he was "released after re-education through labor," according to the Chinese government's response to inquiries by the International Labor Organization (November 1990). He was one among a group of nine (see Li Zhibo p.162) arrested on June 9, 1989 for holding secret meetings, "spreading rumors," distributing leaflets, advocating strikes, chanting reactionary slogans, advocating the overthrow of the government, setting up roadblocks, and disrupting traffic (*Beijing Radio* in FBIS, June 12, 1989). Allegedly, "they also vilified the Shanghai Council of Trade Unions as being totally paralyzed."

. . . .   [INDEFINITE]

■ **XING Jiandong**, a 28-year-old man from Shanghai who unsuccessfully sought political asylum while studying in Australia in 1991 and was then deported back to China in August 1992, was arrested on September 7, 1993 outside the Australian Consulate in Shanghai. Xing had been staging a series of peaceful sit-ins outside the consulate in protest at what he claimed to be his violent mistreatment at the hands of the Australian authorities during his detention in that country. Initially served with a seven-day administrative detention order, Xing was forcibly committed on September 13 to Shanghai's Ankang Psychiatric Hospital, a Public Security Bureau-run detention facility for the criminally insane.

According to Amnesty International (ASA 17/WU 16/93), Xing's family were pressured by the Shanghai police to give their consent to his confinement in the psychiatric prison and were told that he would otherwise be sent to a labor camp for one to three years. Following his committal to Ankang Hospital, Xing is alleged to have been tied to a bed continuously for three days and nights. The Australian Embassy in Beijing was later reported as saying that it would approach the Chinese Foreign Ministry for information on Xing's case and that its Shanghai consulate had already sought clarification from the local authorities (*South China Morning Post,* October 21, 1993). (See also Wang Wanxing p.114.)

.... [INDEFINITE]

5. Arrested

Students, Intellectuals and Officials

Beijing

■   **GAO Yu**, 49, a former deputy chief editor of *Jingjixue Zhoubao (Economics Weekly,* the banned newspaper formerly run by leading dissidents Wang Juntao and Chen Ziming - see p.63) was arrested by police in Beijing on October 2, 1993, two days before she was due to arrive in Hong Kong on her way to New York to take up a one-year fellowship at the Columbia School of Journalism. Gao was formally charged eleven days later with "illegally providing state secrets to people outside the borders" *(wei jingwai renyuan feifa tigong guojia mimi).* As of November 1993, she was being held incommunicado at the Beijing Municipal State Security Detention Center *(Beijing Anquanju Kanshousuo).* According to her family, Gao suffers from heart trouble developed during a previous period in detention between June 1989 until August 1990, but she has reportedly been denied proper treatment or medication. Chinese government officials have declined to comment on her case, beyond confirming that she has been detained.

Although Gao was never formally arrested or charged during her first period of imprisonment, her interviews with reformist intellectuals Wen Yuankai and Yan Jiaqi, published in Hong Kong's *Mirror* magazine, were characterized by Beijing Mayor Chen Xitong in his June 1989 "report on the turmoil" as having been part of "laying the foundations in public opinion" for the so-called counterrevolutionary rebellion of May-June that year. Prior to her latest arrest, Gao had continued to suffer harassment by being denied a new job assignment (her former newspaper was closed down after June 1989), having her phone tapped and being periodically threatened by the authorities for writing for the Hong Kong media. Gao's earnings from her part-time journalism were her only source of income.

Before joining *Jingjixue Zhoubao* in 1988, Gao worked for *China News Service*, a semi-official Chinese news service. Prior to that, she was a student in the language and literature department at People's University, and during the Cultural Revolution she was sent to Datong, Shanxi Province. Upon her return to Beijing she worked for the Beijing Municipal Department of Culture.

■ **XI Yang**, a reporter for the Hong Kong newspaper *Ming Pao*, was detained by the Beijing Municipal State Security Bureau on September 27, 1993. According to an official report in *Xinhua* (September 27, 1993), Xi had "stolen and spied on financial secrets of the state in violation of the State Security Law." On September 28 (according to Xi's editor at *Ming Pao*), Beijing Public Security Bureau officials searched his hotel room in Beijing and confiscated all his materials and those of his roommate, and took a fax machine used by Xi from the room of another *Ming Pao* reporter. Formal arrest followed on October 7. According to the government, Xi, who had been based in Hong Kong for several years, later pleaded guilty to the charges against him. The Chinese authorities' definition of "state secrets" is highly elastic and over-inclusive, and

in March 1993 the National People's Congress revised the Criminal Law to make the crime of "leaking state secrets" punishable, in serious cases, by the death penalty. Xi has been held incommunicado ever since his initial detention and there remain firm grounds for skepticism as to the validity of the charges against him.

A clerk at the People's Bank, **TIAN Ye**, was also detained in connection with the case. He was later accused of being the "main culprit" for having allegedly provided Xi Yang with confidential documents concerning the government's plans for interest rate changes and its policy on international gold transactions. Tian reportedly has also pleaded guilty.

■ On July 8, 1993 in Tiananmen Square, police seized a man (name unknown) who had thrown ink at the massive portrait of Mao Zedong which hangs in the square. A foreign witness was also detained, and film of the incident taken by a Chinese news photographer was reportedly destroyed by the authorities. No further information on the case is currently available.

Hainan

■ **LIU Taiheng**[1], a publisher at the Hainan Publishing House, was arrested in mid-October 1993 and as of December was still being held by the provincial police in connection with a best-selling book that he had published that August entitled *Citizens Sue the China-Invading Japanese Army*. The book reflected the views of a growing grassroots movement called the Preparatory Committee on Japan War Reparations (led by Tong Zeng, a Beijing academic), which is pressuring the Beijing authorities into demanding reparations from the Japanese government for that country's invasion and occupation of China between 1932 and 1945. According to officials of the Shanghai Press and Publications Bureau, "The book violates the spirit of a Central Communist Party document...and could provoke another 1989-type political disturbance." At last information, **Wang Zhonglun**, compiler of the book, was reportedly under continuing investigation in his hometown of Chongqing, Sichuan Province; and **Liu Yu**, its editor, was in danger of being fired.

Hubei

■ **FANG Junjie,** a pro-democracy activist in Wuhan, was arrested sometime during the third week of September, 1993, according to Qin Yongmin (see below), a fellow dissident from the same city who was detained on several occasions this year on account of his opposition to Beijing's bid to host the 2000 Summer Olympics. It is not known if Fang was also opposed to the Beijing bid, and there has been no further news on his situation since the time of his arrest. (*South China Morning Post,* September 25, 1993).

Shaanxi

■ **MA Shaohua** and **ZHENG Xuguang**, two former pro-democracy

movement student leaders who had spent time in jail after the June 4, 1989 crackdown and both of whom were signatories of the "Peace Charter" launched in Beijing in November 1993 (see **Qin Yongmin** p.7), were detained in the Chinese capital in early December and later transferred to police custody in their hometowns. As of January 1994, the two men were reportedly still being held. In November, Ma, a resident of Xi'an, the provincial capital of Shaanxi, had organized a public protest and staged a hunger strike to demand the release of a local worker, **GAO Ping'an**, arrested some weeks earlier for resisting eviction from his home as part of an "urban renovation" scheme planned by the municipal authorities. (As of January 1994, Gao was believed to be still held.) On October 29, Ma Shaohua, the author of a recently published 369-page book on the fall of Communism in Eastern Europe that was swiftly banned as "subversive" by the authorities, had been detained and questioned by police in Xi'an for more than 30 hours. He then went to Beijing and, together with Zheng Xuguang, joined the just-launched "Peace Charter" initiative led by former free-trade union activist **Zhou Guoqiang** (see p.51).

A native of Sichuan Province and formerly a student at Chinese People's University, Ma was first arrested on June 16, 1989 in Zhigong Village, Baitian Township, Hebei Province, then transferred back to Beijing on June 19. A Standing Committee member of the Beijing Students Autonomous Federation, Ma allegedly was in possession of "reactionary propaganda" at the time of his arrest (*Hunan Provincial Radio*, June 19, 1989, in FBIS, June 20).

Zheng Xuguang, a 23-year-old former engineering student at the Beijing Aeronautics Academy, sentenced to a two-year term on January 5, 1991 by the Beijing Intermediate People's Court, was released in July 1991. He was No.9 on the list of "21 Most Wanted Students" issued by the Chinese authorities shortly after the June 1989 crackdown and was among the first "most wanted" student leaders to be tried. Held in Qincheng Prison, Zhang shared a cell with two other pro-democracy students. Fan Shumi, a spokesperson for the Beijing Intermediate People's Court, said Zheng was tried in open court (*AP*, December 4, 1990) and more than 60 Beijing residents, as well as relatives of the defendant, were present when the sentences were announced. Foreign journalists and international observers were barred from the trial.

Zheng reportedly went on trial November 27, 1990. According to the official notice of his indictment, posted on November 27 (*Reuters*, November 29, 1990), Zheng, a member of the Standing Committee of the Beijing Students Autonomous Federation, was charged with "counter-revolutionary propaganda and incitement" and trying to escape from China. He was further accused of "inciting subversion against the people's government and the [attempt at] overthrowing the socialist system during the 1989 turmoil and rebellion." Zheng, a native of the Mi District in

Hunan Province, was arrested, probably in late July 1989 in Guangzhou, while attempting to escape (*Ming Bao*, June 20, 1990, in FBIS, June 20).

Shandong

■ On October 12, 1992, **two youths** from Shandong Province threw eggs at Mao's portrait overlooking Tiananmen Square. Plainclothes public security personnel immediately hustled them away. An official press report (*Jingji Ribao*, October 13, 1992, in FBIS, same date), claimed that the youths were angry about business losses they had incurred and that they were not politically motivated.

Shanxi

■ **QIAO Anyou**, 43, a cadre in the Fenxi Water Conservation Bureau of Linfen Prefecture, Shanxi Province; **ZHANG Weijia**, 40, a deputy section chief in the Linfen Party Committee's policy research office; and **ZHANG Jinlan**, 60, a retired former deputy bureau chief in the prefecture's Xiangfen County transportation bureau, were all secretly detained on May 12, 1993 and then formally arrested ten days later. Although they are sure to face trial, there has been no further news on their situation since then. Qiao, a long-time active campaigner against official corruption, had participated in the street demonstrations in Shanxi in May 1989 and been expelled from his post during the crackdown of the following month. Zhang Weijia had witnessed the May-

June pro-democracy movement in Beijing, while on a work assignment there.

The three men's arrests followed an incident in late 1992 in which they went to Beijing and knelt before the Tiananmen Gate in an attempt to draw the central government's attention to a case of official corruption that had occurred in Shanxi's Xiangfen County. In February 1992, officials of the county Public Security Bureau had allegedly confiscated and then privately resold for profit more than sixty different household-registration, employment, marriage, birth-control and electoral identity cards, thereby arousing much public anger. Qiao and the two Zhangs petitioned the local authorities to investigate the case, but to no avail. After then unsuccessfully staging the public petition activity in Tiananmen Square, the three men applied to the Beijing PSB for permission to hold a public protest demonstration. Not only was this refused, but they were forcibly escorted back to Linfen by police authorities. They continued their fight for justice and were eventually arrested as described above. The Party Secretary of Shanxi Province, Wang Maolin, reportedly said of their case, "These men are [June 1989-style] turmoil elements, and they're still trying to create turmoil."

Workers and Peasants

Guangdong

■ **LI Guohen, LIANG Weimin** and **WU Songfa** were arrested on April 6, 1993 at Baiyun Airport in Guangzhou for allegedly planning to distribute handbills calling for the gradual introduction of democracy and political freedom to accompany economic reform (*AP*, May 25, 1993). The three were part of a loosely organized group whose other members, all workers or traders, reportedly fled Shunde, their home county, after the arrests. Li, Liang and Wu had planned to fly from Guangdong where they lived, to Shanghai, and were carrying several hundred copies of a flyer entitled "Letter to the Citizens of Shanghai." After the arrests, Li Guohen's home was searched and a letter, notebook and papers were confiscated. According to family members, the men were being held in a detention center in Shunde, Guangdong Province. Li is reportedly in poor health and has been badly beaten. In a letter to his wife, he wrote, "If I die you must not be sad," and asked for painkillers and medication to treat broken bones (*South China Morning Post*, June 23, 1993, and July 7). The 31-year-old sales manager and former teacher also reportedly participated in the 1989 democracy movement.

Sichuan

■ **XIANG Wenqing**, a Sichuan farmer, and his "followers" were arrested for allegedly "inciting riots" after a combination of high local taxes and severe drought led to widespread unrest in Renshou County, Sichuan Province in June 1993. Their arrests then provoked large-scale anti-government protests. Residents claimed that Xiang was no troublemaker. Rather, they said, he was arrested for showing others government documents which revealed how local officials had abused their authority by levying unreasonable taxes (*South China Morning Post*, July 10, 1993). Xiang's whereabouts are currently unknown and there is no information as to how many others were arrested with him.

Tibetans

Monks and Nuns

Chubsang Nunnery

■ **NGAWANG KARTSO**, a Chubsang nun, from Nyangtrel Xiang, was arrested on June 14, 1993.

Donphu Choekhor Monastery

■ Eighteen monks from Donphu Choekhor Monastery were arrested on or about May 30, 1993. They include: **SONAM CHOEPHEL**[1], 12; **JAMPEL DORJE**, 15, who joined in 1988; **PHURBU TASHI**, 15, who joined in 1988; **LOBSANG**[1], 22; **TASHI CHUNGCHUNG**, 17; **TSERING DONDEN**, 26; **CHIME**, 25; **MIGMAR TSERING**[1], 20; **LHAKPA TSERING**[1], 20; **MIGMAR**[1], 17; **DRADUL**[1], 23; **PASANG**[1] 24; **PENPA**[1], 19; **CHOEPHEL**, 20; **DORJE**[1], 15, (there is a **PEMA DORJE**, from the same monastery, also 15, who may possibly be the same person); **NORZANG**, 15; **THAPKE**, 17; and **MIGMAR**[2], 27, The men's

offenses are unknown, but the arrests took place at about the same time pro-independence protests erupted in nearby Kyimshi, a group of villages in the Upper Chideshol valley, Gongkar County, Lhokha Prefecture, 45 kilometers south of Lhasa, and at Sungrabling Monastery, also in the upper valley. Donphu Choekhor is in the lower reaches of the Chideshol valley. As a result of the unrest, hundreds of Chinese troops took over the villages, dug gun emplacements into the mountains overlooking the site, set up guards at each house, and conducted house-to-house searches. By July 5, 35 people from the three sites had been arrested, and some tortured. Sonam Choephel, Lhakpa Tsering, Jampel Dorje, Phurbu Tashi had also been arrested in September or October 1992 (see Gelong Tsering, p.204).

The initial demonstrations reportedly were started by Sungrabling monks on May 29 at the time of local elections. Their call for a boycott on the grounds that the election was pointless, in that it would only return a Chinese appointee to office, rapidly turned into calls for Tibetan independence. Local police were unable to handle the incident and on June 1, one day after they were denied access to Sungrabling Monastery, 200 police in twelve trucks reportedly showed up to make arrests. Villagers set up a road block and denied the police access to the monastery. On June 2, a "work team" was dispatched to Sungrabling Monastery to conduct political re-education. Four weeks later, on June 28, 1,700 soldiers in 57 trucks reportedly surrounded the village and began the arrests.

A number of arrests apparently preceded the June 28 raid. **DILA**, a farmer, reportedly was arrested on May 30. Two nuns, **PALDEN**[1], 23, and **LOBSANG PALDEN**[1], 22, associated with Lhodrak Monastery in Chideshol, were arrested June 6. Among those arrested on June 28 in the upper Chideshol valley were three monks from Sungrabling: **YESHE JINPA** (lay name PEMA SAMDRUP), 20, who alternately has been reported as being a farmer; **TSULTRIM TOPGYAL** (lay name PENPA[3]), 20; and **NGAWANG LAMCHEN** (lay name SHILOK[1]), 23; **TSERING**[1], a 28-year-old monk from Lhodrak Monastery; and **NGAWANG CHOEDRON**[1] (lay name CHIME CHOEDRON), 17; and **TENZIN CHOEKYI**[1] (lay name WANGDEN CHOEKYI), 17, both nuns at Choebup Nunnery, originally from Drongshur Village.

Farmers arrested from Upper Chideshol included **PHURBU NAMDROL** (also known as PHURBU GYEN) (another report lists him as being a monk with the monastic name of PHURGEN); **SONAM**[1]; **GYALTSEN NORBU**[1]; **NORBU**[1]; **NYIMA**[1]; and **TSERING**[2]. Those arrested on July 5 included three monks from Sungrabling, **TSULTRIM GYALTSEN** (lay name BUCHUNG DAWA), 23; **TSULTRIM ZOEPA** (lay name PENPA[4]), 23; and **TSULTRIM SHERAB** (lay name PENPA[5] or PENDOR), 19. **DAWA TSERING**[1] (also known as TENNUP), a farmer was reported to have been

arrested July 5. Another account lists **DAWA TSERING**[5], a monk from Lhodrak, arrested June 6. The two may or may not be one person. **NGAWANG DONYO**, a monk and former elected leader at Sungrabling was arrested sometime after July 5. His room was searched and a camera found in his pillow. Concern has since been expressed about his health and welfare in custody. Later in July, the villagers, still subject to intense security measures, issued an appeal for help to the international community and to the United Nations declaring, "We Tibetans have no human rights and are at risk of being exterminated."

Drak Yerpa Hermitage

■   **LOBSANG DONYO**[1] (lay name PASANG[3]), 19, and **LOBSANG CHOEDRAG**[1], 22, (lay name JAMPA SONAM[1]), two monks from the hermitage at Drak Yerpa, a cave-temple 30 kilometers northeast of Lhasa, have been arrested. According to a report from the *Tibet Information Network* (December 4, 1993), their detentions came after the local Party Secretary visited the main temple on August 27, 1993 at Drak Yerpa and discovered a banned Tibetan flag. At noon the next day, two members of the Public Security Bureau checked Lobsang Donyo's room and arrested him, although a ninety-minute search had reportedly yielded no incriminating evidence. He was taken to the local jail in Taktse. Two weeks later, at 7:30 A.M. on September 15, Lobsang Choedrag was arrested. According to local residents, he was badly beaten in a police ride to the village of Yerpa, a distance of four kilometers.

Drepung Monastery

■   **LOBSANG DONYO**[2] (lay name JAMPA TASHI), 19, and **NGAWANG SONAM** (lay name JAMPA SONAM[2]), 22, monks from Drepung Monastery, picked up on "suspicion and doubt," were detained on March 4, 1993 and sent to Gutsa Detention Center.

■   **NGAWANG TSONDRU**[1] (lay name TSONDRU[1]),23, from Phenpo Lhundrup, and **PASANG**[2], both from Drepung Monastery, were detained in June 1993. No further information is available.

Ga Lakhang Monastery

■   There are unconfirmed reports that six monks from Ga Lakhang Monastery were arrested in early June 1993 after demonstrating in the town of Tsethang, the capital of Lhokha, 40 kilometers south of Lhasa (*Tibet Information Network*, July 31, 1993). No further information is available.

Ganden Monastery

■   **NGAWANG LOBSANG**, a 23-year-old Ganden monk, from Medro Gyama, was arrested on June 14, 1993. No further information is available.

■   **NGAWANG LOSEL** (lay name TENZIN[1]), 23, from Medro Gyama Trikhang; and **NGAWANG**

TOPCHU (lay name PALJOR), 22, from Medro Gyama, both Ganden monks, were among six arrested on June 4, 1993, a few minutes after they appeared in Barkhor Square carrying Tibetan flags.

■   **NGAWANG SANGYE** (lay name TSUNPA JOWA; also known as JOPHO), 20, from Thankgya Xiang; **TENZIN DRADUL** (lay name TENZIN CHOEPHEL[1]) 18; **LOBSANG SAMTEN** (lay name TOPJOR[1]), 18, from Medro Jara; **JAMPA GYATSO** (lay name THUPTEN SHERAB), 20, from Medro Gyama; **JAMPA GELEK** (lay name KELSANG YONTEN), 18; **YESHE GYALPO** (lay name DONDRUP YUGYAL), 23, from Gyama in Medro County; **NORBU**[2], 20, from Taktse Dargye; and **PENPA**[2], 20, from Medro Dushi, were arrested on the morning of March 9, 1993 at a pro-independence demonstration in Lhasa while trying to reach the Barkhor. All eight, unofficial monks at Ganden Monastery, were taken to Gutsa Detention Center; one, who was carrying a Tibetan flag, reportedly was beaten by the police at his arrest. Of the eight, two, Norbu and Penpa, are known to have been sentenced to four and three years' imprisonment respectively and transferred to Drapchi Prison.

■   **PHUNTSOG WANGDU**, 24, from Taktse Dushi, expelled from Ganden in 1990 along with seventeen others for his alleged involvement in a pro-independence demonstration, was arrested on June 18, 1993 four months after he returned from India to visit his aged grandmother. He had escaped there in October 1990. According to unofficial reports, he returned with **TSENYI**, a 22-year-old woman from Lhasa Kyirey Lane 4, also arrested on June 18, 1993. The sister of Pema Tsamchoe, (see p.42) from whose home she was seized, Tsenyi had spent two years studying in India. Despite an unconfirmed report that she had been released, as of August 1993, Tsenyi was still in Seitru Prison. (A listing for **TSEKYI**, 23, a female student from Tsenor, arrested on June 17, 1993, may actually refer to Tsenyi.) Phuntsog Wangdu is the nephew of Yulo Dawa Tsering (see p.179).

■   **TOPJOR**[2], a Ganden monk from Medro Jharado, was arrested on May 28, 1993. No additional information is available.

Garu Nunnery

■   **GYALTSEN PELSANG** - see p.15

■   **NGAWANG THUPTEN**[1], 18, a Garu nun from Phenpo, was arrested on May 29, 1993. No further information is available.

■   **PHUNTSOG CHENGA** - see p.15

Kirti Monastery

■   **KUNCHOK TENPA**, 28, a monk from Kirti Monastery, originally from Zhagdom, was arrested sometime in 1993. Located in Ngaba County in Kham (Aba Xiang in Chinese), Kirti is the largest extant monastery in Tibet.

Kyemolung Monastery

■   **NGAWANG SHERAB**[1] and **SHENYAN LOBSANG**, monks from Kyemolung Monastery, were arrested on June 16, 1993. No further information is available.

Michungri Nunnery

■   Three Michungri nuns, **PHUNTSOG DROLMA**, 16, from Lhokha Danang; **TENZIN CHOEKYI**[2], 19; and **TSERING**[4], both from Medro Gongkar, were arrested on March 11, 1993. No further information is available.

■   **TENZIN DEKYONG**, a 17-year-old novice from Michungri Nunnery and a native of Medro Gongkar Gyalayok; **NGAWANG DROLMA**[1], an 18-year-old from Toelung Dechen Norluk; and **JAMPA DEDROL**, 15, from Medro Gongkar Thompogang, were arrested by plainclothes police during a demonstration on the Barkhor in Lhasa on March 13, 1993 at 3 P.M. Taken to the South Barkhor Police Station, they were severely beaten, then transferred to Gutsa Detention Center.

Nagar Nunnery

■   Four nuns, **DAKAR**, 20; **JAMPA DROLKAR**[1], 21; **PEMA OEZER**, 16; and **TSAMCHOE**[1], 19, from Nagar Nunnery in Chegar Township, Phenpo Lhundrup County,

45 kilometers north of Lhasa, were seized by plainclothes police on the Barkhor at 6 P.M. on August 17, 1993. Their protest, encircling the Jokhang Temple shouting pro-independence slogans, lasted only a few minutes before they were arrested.

Nyemo Gyaltse Monastery

■ **LOBSANG GYALTSEN**[1], a monk and chantmaster *(umze)* from Nyemo Gyaltse Monastery, was detained in June 1993. No further information is available.

■ **NGAWANG CHOEDRAG**, a monk and chantmaster at Nyemo Gyaltse Monastery, from Nyemo County, was arrested sometime between April and June 1993 for alleged involvement in political activities. No other information is available.

■ **NGAWANG KELSANG** and **PEMA YESHE**, two nuns affiliated with the Nyemo Gyaltse Monastery in Nyemo County, were arrested in early June 1993 following a "very active" demonstration. No further information is available.

Phenpo Monastery

■ Five monks from Phenpo Monastery reportedly were arrested in 1993. **TENGYE**, 27, arrested March 5, and **NGAWANG TSULTRIM**[1], 23, arrested in May, are both originally from Phenpo. **LOBSANG TENPA**[1], 32, arrested May 24, was born in Toelung. **DHONNOR**, 29, from

Nyemo; and **THUPTEN TSERING**[1], 24, from Phudo Lungshe, were both arrested May 20.

Sangrikor Monastery

■ A monk (name unknown) from Sangrikor Monastery in Nyemo County, previously a student at the Nechung Buddhist Institute in Lhasa, reportedly was arrested in May 1993 for distributing Tibetan nationalist literature *(Tibet Information Network, July 31, 1993)*.

Sera Monastery

■ **TENPA DARGYE** and **THUPTEN TSERING**[2], monks from Sera Monastery, were reportedly both arrested in June 1993.

Shelkar Choede Monastery

■ Seven monks from Shelkar Choede Monastery, in Shelkar Xiang, Dingri County, were arrested on April 28, 1993. **LOBSANG PALDEN**[2], 22, from Marshag or Lazag; **LOBSANG GYALTSEN**[2], 22, from Drag or Gyagur Jhagnag; and **TENZIN RABTEN**, 21, from Rikor, were still being held as of August 1993. **SANGYE TENZIN**, 19, from Dushi; **KHYENRAB TENDAR**, 21, from Po; **KHYENRAB DRAGYE**, 21,, from Kyishong; and **KHYENRAB CHOEPEL**, 22, from Danag, reportedly have managed to escape to India.

Shungsep Nunnery

Buddhist nuns from Tibet demonstrated in Lhasa for six days beginning on December 4, 1993, in protest against a three-month campaign to re-educate Tibetan nuns. Of at least twenty-two women arrested, the names of seventeen are known. All reportedly belong to Shungsep Nunnery. Eight were detained for shouting "Tibet is independent" on December 9 at 10 A.M. on the Barkhor. Plainclothes policemen immediately took **RIGZIN TSONDRU, NORZIN, JAMPA CHOEKYI, NAMGYAL CHOEDRON, CHOENYI DROLMA, SHERAB DROLMA, NORBU YANGCHEN** and **LODROE PEMA** to the police station in Barkhor Square. On December 11, a similar protest resulted in the arrests of six more nuns: **PENDROL**[2], **YANGDRON, YESHE KUNSANG, YESHE CHOEZANG, CHIME WANGDU** and **TSERING CHOEDRON**[3]. Three more nuns, **YESHE TSONDRU, TSULTRIM THARCHIN** and **TSERING CHOEKYI** were arrested the following day.

The re-education campaign was carried out by "work teams" who spent up to three months regularly visiting the five main nunneries in the Lhasa area, Chubsang, Garu, Michungri, Shungsep and Ani Tsangkhung. The teams, consisting of nine or ten Party cadres, imposed new regulations including denial of admission to nunneries in the case of any woman detained for political activities (see Phuntsog Tseyang, p.534), expelling nuns suspected of pro-independence sympathies, and banning nuns from traveling to Lhasa without permission. As a result the population at Michungri was reduced from ninety nuns in 1989 to thirty-seven or thirty-eight. In April 1993, work teams decreed that no more than 130 nuns could live at Shungsep, resulting in loss of residence for some seventy nuns (*Tibet Information Network*, January 12, 1994).

Tashilhunpo Monastery

▪   **NYIMA PHUNTSOG** and **SONAM GYALPO**[1], monks from Tashilhunpo, were arrested in July 1993 and are reportedly being held in a prison in Shigatse. Another monk from the same monastery, **PHURBU TSERING**[1], detained on June 15, is also being held in Shigatse.

Tsamkhung Nunnery

▪   **TSERING YUDON**, 27, a Tsamkhung nun, from Lhasa, was arrested on June 14, 1993.

Tsepak Lhakhang Monastery

▪   Six monks from Tsepak Lhakhang Monastery, located in Ramchoe, were arrested on June 3, 1993, a date coinciding with Sagadawa, one of the most sacred Buddhist holy days. **PASANG**[4], 15; **LANGDOR**, 19; **GYAGPA**, 16; **KELSANG**[1], 16; **PHURBU**[1], 16; and **CHANGLOCHEN**, 17, all originally from Phenpo, reportedly are held in Gutsa Detention Center.

Nunnery Unknown

- **TSAM-LA**[1], 27, a nun from Lhasa Barnag, was arrested in May 1993.

Lay Persons

- **TSETHAR**, from Medro; **PHUNTSOG THOSAM**, 24, from Phenpo; **TENPA PHULCHUNG**[1]; and **TENPA WANGDRAG**[1], were all arrested on May 28, 1993. It is not known, however, if their arrests were connected.

- **DODRONG NGAWANG DORJE**, 41, a mason from Lhasa, was arrested in June 1993 at the headquarters of the Lhasa City People's Political Consultative Congress, where he was staying with his mother. She had been given an official title and a stipend.

- **DROLMA**, a 53-year-old woman, **JAMPEL**, 25, and **KUNCHOK TENZIN**, 27, were three of eight peasants and nomads arrested for participating in a series of small pro-independence demonstrations in rural central Tibet between late February and April 1993. As of mid-May they were being held in the county prison in Medro Gongkar. The three were jailed between April 21 and April 28 in Rinchenling, a group of villages in the Draklok district of Medro Gongkar County, after round-the-clock interrogation in the nearby village of Tashigang. They allegedly led an April demonstration during which they shouted slogans and interrupted an official meeting.

- **INCHUNG** (not his real name but the one by which he is commonly known), about 36, from Phenpo Ramchoe, reportedly was arrested on June 11 or 12, 1993. He is identified as being a former carpenter, now a trader. (He may possibly be the same person as **IKCHUNG**, a staff member of the Economic Affairs Office, now a resident of Lhasa Drongsar, originally from Phenpo, who was reportedly arrested on May 28, 1993.)

- **KARTSE**, 43, a trader from Ngaba (Aba in Chinese), was arrested in August 1993, approximately one month after his return from a visit to India. He reportedly was taken to Barkham Prison the day after his arrest.

- **KELSANG DAWA**[1], 29, from Lhasa Tsomolung, was arrested in September 1993.

- **LHAKPA**[1], a school teacher at a school established by the villagers in Nemo, Tsondoe Township, Lhundrup County, was arrested on June 21, 1993 for alleged involvement in political activities, probably in connection with a demonstration the day before. Reportedly taken to Lhundrup County Jail, he was so severely beaten that, as of a July 31 report (*Tibet Information Network*), he was in "critical condition."

On June 26, farmers from the same village overturned a police car and freed two monks from Nemo Monastery who were being driven to the Lhundrup County Jail. The monks had been arrested earlier that day after a police search of the monastery in connection with Lhakpa's arrest had turned up pro-independence literature. On June 27, 200 soldiers surrounded the village and arrested four other Tibetans, including two farmers, **NGAWANG TSERING** and **TSEWANG**[1] (also listed as TSERING[5] and TSEWANG TASHI). According to unconfirmed reports, all four were later tortured. Three others, all monks, managed to run away before they could be detained; a "wanted" order for their arrest is reportedly now in force.

■   **LHAKPA**[2], a layman from Lhasa Kyire was arrested on May 24, 1993.

■   **LHAKPA**[3], a 28-year-old mason from Lhasa Sector 1, originally from Toelung Kyawo, and **YANGCHEN**[1], a woman from Lhasa Shardo, were detained on June 20, 1993. At the time of his 7 P.M. arrest, Lhakpa was at his wife's ancestral home in a remote area near Drepung Monastery.

■   **LHASANG**, about 40, from Lhasa, probably a resident of Karma Shargyu, was arrested in May 1993.

■   As many as sixty people, some from as far away as Xining, the provincial capital, were arrested in Tsolho (Hainan Prefecture) in Qinghai Province, probably in early July, in an effort by the authorities to "prevent incidents" during a visit later that month by President Jiang Zemin to the prefectural capital Gonghe (Chabcha in

Tibetan). All had reportedly been suspected of preparing pro-independence leaflets. The eight whose names have been confirmed include Tibetan intellectuals, students, and officials. **LHATRIGYA** (LHATRUGYAL) (lha-'phrug rgyal), from Tsolho, reportedly was severely tortured and injured after confinement in a Xining prison. **MENLHA KYAB** (MENLHA CHA) (smen-lha-skyaba), a 35-year old native of Gonghe, is a comedian and writer widely known for radio broadcasts featuring "cross-talk" *(xiang sheng),* the art of comic dialogue, and for his articles in the magazine *Qinghai People's Art.* A member of the Tsolho Theater Company, he also worked in the Xining Film Company dubbing films into Tibetan.

SHAWO DORJE (sha-bo rdo-rje) and **HUACHEN KYAB** (dpal-chen skyabs), 27, are both officials at the Nationality Languages Committee in Tsolho, a government-sponsored body dedicated to promotion of the use of Tibetan (see also Tenpa Kelsang p.43). **SAMDRUP TSERING** (bsam-grub tshe-ring), a 26-year-old 1988 graduate of the Qinghai Nationalities Institute in Xining and a native of Rongbo village, Tongren County, worked as a translator in his home county until 1991. He then returned to the institute to do post-graduate research. **DUNGKAR TSO** (dung-dkar 'tsho) was studying at the Xining Teachers Training College at the time of her arrest. She is from Tsolho. **PALJOR TSERING** (dpa'-'byor tshe-ring) is a minor official in Gonghe. At the time of his arrest, after his return from a visit to India, he was taking a two-year refresher course at Qinghai Nationalities Institute in Xining. **LHASHAMHUA** (**LHACHO LHAWA**) (lha-byams dpal), 43, is a senior member of the Chinese People's Political Consultative Conference in Tsolho. The reported arrest of **TSERING THAR** (tshe-ring thar), a student from Tsolho, has not yet been confirmed.

Fourteen more Tibetans, all working for the Chinese government and all suspected of involvement in political activities, reportedly were among the sixty arrested between July 10 and August 1 in Qinghai. Details are sparse: those listed include **WANGDU**[1], from Gonghe; **DUGBUNTHAR**; **JAMYANG**[1]; **YIDAN TSERING**; **WANGDEN**; **NAM LOYAK**; **GYALPO**[1]; **PEMA GYAL**; **RINCHEN NORBU**; **SONAM TSERING**[2]; **TSEGOEN GYAL**, secretary of the Kagyur Xiang Administration; **GYATSO**[1]; **KHARMO**; and **DORJE**[3]. An unnamed man, reportedly the principal of a school in Kagyur Xiang, also is listed as arrested. (Another listing, for **SHAWO**, a teacher, may actually refer to Shawo Dorje.)

■ **LOBSANG CHOEDRAG**[2], a 43-year-old worker at the Tromsigang meat market when he was detained for the second time on June 17, 1993, is currently being held in Seitru Prison. He had returned a few days earlier from Sikkim, where he had attended the Kalachakra Initiation at which the Dalai Lama officiated. Arrested late at night from his home in Lhasa Kyedrong Khansgar, perhaps together with his younger sister (thought to be named **Lhakdron** - see p.163), Lobsang Choedrag is a member of a politically active family (see Choezed Tenpa Choephel p.163). He previously served a four-year prison term (1980-84), the last year of which was spent in the notorious labor camp in Powo Nyingri, where his jaw was broken as a result of beatings. According to some sources, he was shot and injured during a demonstration in December 1988. Lobsang Choedrag is married and has three children.

■ **LOBSANG DAWA**[1], a Lhasa businessman who "disappeared" on September 1, 1993, reportedly is in police custody. It took three weeks for family members to find out that the 35 or 36-year-old motorcycle mechanic had been arrested. Police later informed them that he was under suspicion for involvement in the Tibet independence movement, but refused to revel where he was being held. He may be in Seitru Prison, along with some ten others arrested by the State Security Bureau since May 1993. Before 1991, when he started selling and repairing motorcycles, Lobsang Dawa worked as a receptionist at a hotel in Lhasa. (A brother of his, name unknown, imprisoned in 1989 for involvement in a pro-independence demonstration in 1989, has since been released from prison.)

■ **LOBSANG GYALTSEN**[3], a 33-year-old farmer from Nyemo Sangri, was arrested on May 20, 1993 on suspicion of belonging to a pro-independence organization. He is the uncle of Damchoe Pemo (see p.516). No additional information is available.

■ **LODROE PHUNTSOG**, 53, a Communist Party member who worked as a security guard at the Public Hospital in Lhasa, was arrested May 23, 1993.

■ **LOTEN**[1] - see p.518

■ **NGAWANG RIKHAR**, 41, was arrested on April 8, 1993. No further information is available.

■ **NYIMA**[2] - see p.518

■ **PALDEN CHOEDRAG**, a 42-year-old carpenter from Lhasa Garu Shar; **RABGYAL**, a 45-year-old mason from Lhasa Kyire; and **TENPA**, 35, a construction worker from Lhasa, who had worked previously in a government shop, were arrested on June 6, 1993. Palden Choedrag, arrested from his home during the night, was in Seitru Prison as of August 1993. Tenpa had earlier spent three years in prison for trying to escape to India in 1978 or 1979.

■ **PASANG**[5], 24, a driver for hire, originally from Lhokha, reportedly was arrested in early June from the home of a relative with whom he was staying at Shakabpa House in Lhasa.

■ **PELKYI**, a Garu Nun, reportedly is in Trisam Prison as of November 1993. No additional information is available.

■ **PEMA NGODRUP**, a native of Kham, was arrested from his residence in Dokhang Lhasa on May 28, 1993.

■ **PEMA TSAMCHOE**, a 31-year-old housewife from Lhasa Kyire, was arrested in early July 1993 for her alleged involvement in the massive May 24, 1993 demonstration in Lhasa. One report stated that she stood up on a bicycle and lectured to the crowd of demonstrators. Pema Tsamchoe is the sister of Tsenyi (see p.36).

■ **PE-NGOE**, a 45-year-old carpenter from Lhasa Kashali, was arrested from his house between 10 and 11 P.M. on May 25, 1993.

■ **SONAM GYALPO**[2], formerly a trader from Lhokha Gongkar, was arrested on July 22, 1993. There is a small possibility that he has since been released.

■ **SONAM TASHI**, a 40-year-old draftsman from Lhasa Phunkhang, was arrested from his house at 9 P.M. on May 27, 1993.

■ **SONAM TSERING**[3], a 39-year-old English interpreter, originally from Nyemo, was arrested on May 6, 1993.

■ **SONAM TSETEN**, from Lhasa, Phunkhang House, was arrested either on May 20 or 30, 1993.

■ **TASHI TOPGYAL** - see

p.516

■   **TENPA KELSANG**, a 30-year-old Tibetan academic, was arrested at the University of Tibet in Lhasa on August 6, 1993. A 1985 graduate of the university, he worked for the Lhasa branch of the Tibetan Language Committee and his arrest may have been in connection with the crackdown in Tsolho Prefecture (see Lhatrigya p.40).

■   **THUBGO**, 27, a layman from Ngaba, reportedly was arrested on June 13, 1993.

■   **TOPGYAL[1]**, a tailor from Lhasa Jamangkyil, was arrested on July 5, 1993.

■   **TSETEN DORJE** who worked at the Religious Affairs Bureau in Lhasa, was arrested from his home at 2 A.M. on May 9, 1993. His arrest may have been in connection with those of Gendun Rinchen (see p.519) and Damchoe Pemo (see p.516). A report that **SISHIYI (SEGSHINGPA) TSETEN DORJE**, 50, a trader from Lhasa Jamyang Tara, was arrested in June, may in fact refer to the same person.

■   **TSETEN YARPHEL**, 35, a worker at Hydro-electric Brigade No.2., was arrested on July 8, 1993.

■   There is scant information about a further thirteen people reportedly arrested in 1993. **ZOEPA CHOWANG**, 20, and **TOPGYAL[3]**, 20, are from Medro Gongkar;

NGAGCHUNG, 21, is from Toelung; **DAWA DOL**, 21, and **DEKYI[2]** 22, are both from Taktse; **NGAWANG CHOEDRON[3]**, 22, is from Lungshoe; and **RINCHEN DAWA[1]**, 20, is from Phenpo. **ASHANG LA**, from Lhasa Gyalka Lam, is known to be a layman; **PENDROL[1]** is known to be a lay woman from Lhasa Metog Changseb; **LHAKPA[4]** and **BAGDRO[2]**, are known to be farmers from Nyemo County; there is no information about **TENDAR[1]** and **JAMYANG[2]**.

■   On August 18, 1993, two or three Tibetans in lay clothes staged a brief protest at the Norbulingka, former summer palace of the Dalai Lama. At least two of the three were arrested (*Tibet Information Network*, September 12, 1993).

■   According to an unconfirmed report, three students, one female and two male, all students at a Lhasa secondary school, were detained after they led a two-day protest in April 1991 against the imposition of school fees (*Tibet Information Network*, July 31, 1993).

Inner Mongolians

■   **DELGER**, 32, and his brother-in-law, **HE Quan**, 30, were formally arrested and charged with "counterrevolutionary propaganda" in January 1993. At the end of April or the beginning of May 1992, Delger, a teacher in the Mongolian literature department at Inner Mongolia University wrote a letter addressed to his department chairman saying that the suppression of Mongolian culture and people was wrong. The letter went on to say, that the department head, because of his position, bore some responsibility for the lack of progress in educating Mongolians about their own culture. Delger further suggested that the chairman was, thus, serving the authorities. Having written the letter in the evening, Delger posted it on the department head's office door, where it was seen by the Party Secretary of the department. He immediately called the chairman; the police were called; and Delger was detained. He Quan, a policeman, was not seized until shortly before his formal arrest.

■   According to an Asia Watch source, three or four men from Inner Mongolia were seized on the border between China and Mongolia at the end of April or beginning of May 1993. It is still not clear if they were seized in Mongolia and forcibly repatriated or if they had not yet crossed the border. The only identifying information available is that one of the men graduated from Northwest Minorities College.

Catholics and Protestants

■   **Father CHU Tai and Father ZHANG Li** and one other priest were arrested in Zhangjikaou, Hebei Province in early November 1993. According to an unconfirmed report, Father Chu was sentenced administratively to one year of labor re-education and Father Zhang to three

years. Both reportedly were sent to a labor camp in Zhangjiakou.

■   Bishop **HAN Dingxiang**, 57, clandestine Vicar-General of Handan (Yongnian) diocese, Hebei Province, was arrested again on November 18, 1993. Since his last release from detention in 1991, he had been under severe restrictions. Father Han (he had not yet been made a bishop) had been arrested on December 26, 1990 after saying Mass, and served a summons by public security officers to attend a study seminar. The "study camp," organized in Handan County, Hebei Province, for Catholic religious personnel from Daming and Handan dioceses, was part of an "Anti-Pornography, Evil-ridding, Anti-Convert Activities Campaign" to which certain Catholics were "invited." As of January 1991, more than 20 people, including Father Han, were in camp. All were eventually permitted to leave but some were placed under restrictions, including Father Han, whose freedom of movement was tightly controlled. An official Chinese response to requests for information by the U.S. government (November 1991), listed Father Han as "under investigation," but supplied no further information.

Father Han was imprisoned in Beijing for 19 years, 1960-1979, while still a layman. He was finally ordained after his release. In 1989, Father Han was re-arrested and held for several months.

■   Bishop Julius **JIA Zhiguo**,

the 58-year-old clandestine bishop of Zhengding diocese, Hebei Province, was taken away by the Public Security Bureau on January 7, 1994 and as of January 19 had no returned home. He had been last detained on April 5, 1993 to prevent him from saying an anniversary Mass for Bishop Fan Xueyan, who had died in April 1992 (see p.228). He was later released, as were eight other priests detained with him at the same time. The 58-year-old Bishop Jia was first arrested on April 7, 1989 in Beijing, then released back to his village, Wuqiu, on September 11 the same year, reportedly without having been charged but with an order restricting his movements for the next three years. (In November 1991, in response to requests for information by the U.S. government, Chinese authorities said Bishop Jia had "never been accused of any offense," a phrase which does not preclude detention without trial or other restrictions on movement.)

On December 11, 1991, Bishop Jia was again detained, although news of this did not surface until April 1992. According to an Asia Watch source, the bishop had been taken on a "compulsory tour" by the authorities as a way of keeping him under surveillance. He was arrested yet again in November or December 1992 at his home, released just before Christmas, and then picked up again shortly after the holiday and held for a further month before being released under restrictions.

A native of Luan Xian in Hebei, Bishop Jia was secretly consecrated in February 1981. After the death of Bishop Liu Shuhe in May 1992 (see p.1), Bishop Jia became Secretary-General of the clandestine Bishops' Conference, first organized in November 1989.

■   **LIN Zilong,** an 80-year-old district leader of the Shouters, a Protestant sect, was arrested on December 23, 1993 in Fuqing County, Fujian Province and as of January 19, 1994 was in the Fuqing Public Security Bureau lockup. He has been arrested three times since the 1970's for religious activities outside the official church. Lin's family were permitted to see him and bring him food daily.

■   **MA Shuishen,** one of between 120 and 160 Chinese and three foreigners arrested on September 8, 1992 during a raid on a church meeting in Guofa Village, Wuyang District, Henan Province, was reportedly re-arrested at the beginning of January 1993. All those rounded up and accused of taking part in illegal religious activities, were attending a training seminar held at Ma's house. Some escaped, while others, primarily the older participants, were released by the authorities after several weeks. The last eight were released in January 1993. Some who were released, however, were told they would be subject to re-arrest in their home provinces. The meeting place itself was unregistered, technically a breach of the government regulations restricting religious practice.

Some 40 Public Security Bureau officers armed with walkie-talkies conducted the raid. All those present were ordered to "get down on the floor" while the village was searched for some house church members who were not present and while a long harangue was delivered by one of the PSB cadres. According to numerous reports, some participants were handled very roughly. They were tied with rope and electrical wire and hit in the face and head. At the Wuyang PSB office, those detained were ordered to empty their pockets of money. Some were interrogated every day. Others, including one woman whose legs were all black and blue, were beaten severely. Some were removed to other detention centers in Shipo District, Xiping District, Fangcheng, and to detention centers in Anhui, Shandong, Hubei and other parts of Henan. Many of those released were made to pay steep fines, ostensibly for room and board.

While they were in detention, some of the worshippers' homes were searched, family members beaten and everything of value confiscated. The family which hosted the meeting had its home stripped bare. Furniture, clothes, blankets and cooking materials were taken. Handmade prayer mats and stools were burned. Bibles and other religious literature was destroyed. Even farm equipment and animals were removed.

■   **Father MAO Lehua and Father GUO Xijian** were arrested together with four nuns and three "brothers" on December 16, 1993 in Fuan, Fujian Province by the Public Security Bureau during a Mass in a private house. According to an Asia Watch source, the police are actively searching for another four priests connected to those already in custody.

■   **Father PEI Ronggui** was picked up on January 7, 1994 and by mid-month had not returned home. A 60-year-old Trappist priest from Youtong village, Luancheng County, Hebei Province, had only been released from prison on March 31, 1993 after serving more than three years in prison. He had been arrested on September 3, 1989 by the Shijiazhuang Public Security Bureau while administering last rites, and was charged on December 15 of the same year with three counts of "disturbing the social order." He was accused of instigating a group that used force to try and take over a primary school in Youtong in March 1989. According to Chinese officials, there were mass gatherings at the school as a result and classes had to be suspended for 60 days. Pei also allegedly ministered to demonstrators in Beijing during the 1989 pro-democracy demonstrations and he allegedly officiated at unapproved religious activities, presumably in Youtong. On January 7, 1991, he was sentenced to five years in prison by the Luancheng County Court; he was held in Prison No.4 in Shijiazhuang.

Father Pei's name first appeared on a government wanted list in April 1989; he had refused to join the Catholic Patriotic Association. On April 18, 1989, in an early morning confrontation with police who came to destroy his church, a tent located in a schoolyard on property which had originally belonged to the church, over 300 people reportedly were injured, and two died. Thirty-two people were arrested. The tent had been erected on March 17 to facilitate the Easter celebration, and to protest a government decision to deny compensation for church property confiscated or destroyed during the Cultural Revolution. The raid reportedly was carried out by at least 3,000 police armed with electric batons, sticks, bricks and water guns, and 270 military vehicles. Youtong village, with a population of some 3,500 people, is about 50 percent Catholic.

■   Several Catholic and Buddhist clerics were arrested in Shanghai during October 1993, according to one of the city's leading dissidents, **Yang Zhou** (see p.478). In addition, reported Yang, a number of junior army officers who had tried to form a protest group in the city were detained in a separate case around the same time. (*South China Morning Post*, October 20, 1993). Neither the detainees' names nor the reason for the various arrests is known, although they may have been part of a general tightening up on dissent by the Shanghai authorities following Beijing's failed bid to host the 2000 Summer Olympics.

6. Briefly Detained

Students and Intellectuals

Beijing

■   **GUO Baosheng**, 21, a third-year philosophy student at People's University; **LIN Jianhua**, 25, a worker in an advertising company; **HUANG Jingang**, a Beijing University student and a rock-and-roll singer active in the 1989 pro-democracy movement; and possibly other students from Beijing University and People's University were arrested around June 4, 1993 for allegedly trying to organize a petition advocating the overthrow of Premier Li Peng (*Ming Bao*, June 21, 1993, in FBIS, June 22). Some of those arrested, including Guo, Lin and Hua, also were accused of printing and wearing T-shirts featuring three footprints linked by a chain. By June 22, all those involved were thought to have been released, although uncertainty remained as to the status of Guo Baosheng.

■   **LI Minqi**, 24, an economics major in his junior year at Beijing University at the time of his first arrest on June 4, 1990, was detained again on June 2, 1993 at his home in Beijing and held three days for printing an underground magazine entitled *Bi An (Other Side of the River)*. One hundred copies of the magazine's second issue were confiscated by the authorities (*Kyodo*, July 17, 1993, in FBIS, July 19). Li had been released on June 14, 1992 after completing a two-year sentence for "counterrevolutionary propaganda and incitement." His political rights remained suspended for another year and he was not allowed to resume his studies.

A member in May-June 1989 of the *Beijing Students Autonomous Federation,* Li was detained one year after the June 4th crackdown in Beijing in connection with a commemorative speech he had made at an unauthorized midnight rally on the campus of Beijing University. In addition to calling China's rulers "wild and savage autocrats," Li called for direct elections to the National People's Congress, for improved treatment of intellectuals and for land and factories to be turned over to peasants and workers (*Boston Globe*, December 7, 1991). The rally followed a protest during which about 1,000 students sang songs, shouted slogans and threw small bottles (a symbolic reference, in China's political culture, to leader Deng Xiaoping) from dormitory windows. Labeled by university authorities as the "chief instigator of an anti-party conspiracy," Li was eventually sent to Qincheng Prison, charged with "counter-revolutionary propaganda and incitement" on September 25, formally indicted in April 1991, tried in December that year and sentenced to two years' imprisonment on February 25, 1992. According to friends, Li made the unplanned speech on campus because "he knew it would be the last major demonstration in Beijing in the near future."

■ **YAN Zhengxue,** a delegate to the People's Congress (local legislature) in the Zhejiang provincial city of Shujiang, was illegally detained in mid-July 1993 in the Haidian district of Beijing and tortured by public security officials for three hours. On July 19, Yan filed an administrative lawsuit against the police officers concerned; as of December 1993, the outcome of the case remained unknown. From November onward, however, he received numerous threatening phone calls from persons who identified themselves only as being from the Public Security Bureau; Yan was warned that he and his family, and in particular, his son and daughter, would suffer if he continued with his lawsuit against the police. The following month, Yan's son was run over and killed in Beijing by an unmarked but apparently "official-looking" vehicle. In letters to senior Beijing security officials after the incident, Yan reportedly stated that while there was no proof that his son had been murdered, the striking and sinister coincidence of the "accident" having occurred soon after the threatening calls clearly presented the authorities, in his view, with a *prima facie* case to answer.

Yan's July 1993 detention was illegal, as Chinese law forbids the arrest or detention of any People's Congress delegate without special authorization from the senior authorities. It occurred after he got into an argument with a surly bus conductor in Beijing. According to Yan, he was seized by police at the scene of the argument, taken to a local police station and then beaten up. "Without asking about the facts," reported Yan, "the officers forced me into the back of the station with electric batons, illegally handcuffed me and then tortured me for three hours." He reportedly suffered contusions over his entire body, a punctured eardrum and serious damage to one eye. Photographs showed broad patches of discolored skin and also marks on his wrists apparently left by handcuffs. (*Reuters,* July 24, 1993).

Shanghai

■ **LIN Muchen**, an art designer and member of a Shanghai dissident group (see **Zhang Xianliang**, p.13) that had been meeting each week at a local coffee shop, was detained and interrogated for two hours on December 4 after police broke up a meeting attended by around 30 dissidents. He was warned not to organize any such activities in future.

■ **SUN Lin**, 36, formerly a cameraman for *Shanghai Television*, and **FU Jiqing**, a 47-year-old engineer, were detained in Shanghai on or around March 1, 1993 and reportedly taken into criminal custody (*South China Morning Post*, March 9, 1993). The incident followed attempts by Sun and Fu to communicate with senior Chinese dissident Wang Ruowang (see p.463), who had been allowed to leave for the U.S. some months earlier.

On the day of her arrest, Fu Jiqing, formerly Wang Ruowang's translator, went out to mail some letters from him to his friends in China but failed to return home. Later that evening, Public Security Bureau officers searched her house, confiscating newspaper clippings and magazine articles about Wang and

taking away copies of his writings. The police initially informed Fu's son that she had been detained on a gambling charge. According to the son, however, his mother did not gamble. Later, the charge was altered to one of "colluding with hostile overseas groups." After more than a month, Fu was finally released, but her work unit, the Shanghai Reform Electrical Machinery Factory, demoted her from cadre to ordinary worker for having allegedly committed "a grave political error." Fu had suffered harassment from the authorities ever since the 1989 pro-democracy movement. Her telephone line was cut several times and her house searched on three occasions. In 1989, her plans to study in Australia were ended when the police confiscated her passport and visa.

Sun Lin was formally arrested at the end of May 1993 but later "exempted from prosecution" by the authorities and released in late July. ("Exempt from prosecution" *[mian yu qisu]*, a legal category under which the detainee does not go to trial but is still considered guilty, acquires a criminal record and subsequently encounters all the attendant problems such as dismissal from previous employment and loss of housing, is technically distinct under Chinese law from a decision "not to prosecute" *(bu qisu)*, which leaves the person concerned more or less free from legal taint.) Sun, who disappeared at the same time as Fu, had received a fax from Wang Ruowang on the day before his arrest. After his detention, his home was searched and notebooks and newspapers were confiscated. Sun had been arrested once before, after June 4, 1989, for taking home videotapes about the student pro-democracy movement. He subsequently lost his job and had his passport and visa confiscated.

■   **YANG Qinheng, WANG Yonggang** and **GONG Xingnan**, four Shanghai dissidents active since the 1978-81 Democracy Wall period, and **BAO Ge**, a teacher and researcher at the Shanghai Medical School, went on a hunger strike in June 1993 outside the Petitions Office of the Shanghai Public Security Bureau to call for the unconditional release of Zhang Xianliang (see p.13). They were taken into police custody on June 7 and released some hours later. Bao reported that the police went to his school on June 4 and threatened to send him to a mental institution if he did not cooperate (*South China Morning Post*, June 11, 1993). After the protest, his phone line was cut. On October 19, 1993, Bao Ge was informed by his superiors at the Shanghai Medical School that he was being suspended from duties for a three-month period, ostensibly because of a lack of teaching work at the school.

Yang Qinheng, a private entrepreneur, was co-editor of the unofficial journal *Responsibility* during the Democracy Wall period and was imprisoned from 1883-85. Gong Xingnan, also a private businessman, was jailed for at least four years starting in March 1979. Wang Yonggang, who works at a wool factory, was co-editor of the unofficial journal *Voice of Democracy*.

In an attempt to prevent any activities marking the fourth anniversary of the June 4 crackdown, some 50 Shanghai dissident intellectuals reportedly had to appear at the police station. They were held for 24 hours under the guise of "improving communications with the city's intellectuals" and released. Among those who had to report were **WANG Fuchen**, the 38-year-old secretary-general of the *Zhongguo Renquan Wenti Yanjiuhui* (*China Study Group on Human Rights* - see also Wang Ruowang, p.463); ten of the group's members; and most of those who had received a letter from Zhang suggesting the commemorative meeting. Wang, a businessman, was picked up again on June 9 and held for several hours to prevent a protest against the detention of the hunger-strikers.

On the same day, a colleague of Wang Fuchen's, **YANG Zhou** (see p.478), who was also detained on June 4, was forbidden to leave his apartment. The association has written to the Standing Committee of the National People's Congress protesting interference in its members' civil rights. Yang Zhou and Wang Fuchen were detained again on June 26, during the visit of Australian Prime Minister, Paul Keating (see Fu Shenqi p.10). The three and Bao Ge had planned to meet with a journalist traveling with the Prime Minister. Bao escaped detention, fleeing when he saw plainclothesmen outside his house. The journalist was detained for three hours. In addition to the detentions, Yang's telephone line was cut and plainclothesmen surrounded his house around the clock.

■   **LI Gaotao,** president of the unofficial, Shanghai-based *China Study Group on Human Rights,* was detained for 24 hours on October 13, 1993 by the Shanghai police and badly beaten, according to fellow member Yang Zhou (see p.478). A former teacher at the Institute of Mechanical Engineering in Shanghai, Li had already served a two-year jail sentence for his role in the 1989 pro-democracy protests in the city.

Workers

Beijing

■   **ZHOU Guoqiang**[1], a leading member of a dissident labor group in Beijing, was detained and interrogated for four hours on April 10, 1993 after he and other group members had sought to provide legal services to taxi drivers who wanted to stage a demonstration in the Chinese capital to protest their working conditions. Police succeeded in intimidating most of the drivers and breaking up the demonstration. While being interrogated, Zhou reportedly argued that he had an obligation to provide legal services to the workers and also that they had a constitutional right to obtain them.

A few weeks later, on May 1, 1993, Zhou was placed under house arrest for 16 hours after organizing, together with **Han Dongfang** (see p.55 and p.419) an outing on May 2 by members of the dissident labor group to celebrate May 1, International Labor

Day. The Chaoyang branch of the Public Security Bureau first took him to the police station, warned him that the gathering would be an "illegal activity" and told him to cancel it. When he protested that the event had been organized by word of mouth and would therefore be difficult to cancel, he was made to call foreign journalists to tell them he was calling it off. Several other labor activists, including Song Jie, Zhang Qianjin and Qian Yumin, who had been imprisoned during the June 1989 crackdown, were also briefly detained again at this time.

In August 1993, Han Dongfang, former leader of the Beijing Workers Autonomous Federation (BWAF), an independent trade union banned after June 4, 1989, was forcibly ejected from China back to Hong Kong a day after he had returned there from the U.S. A week later, his PRC passport was canceled by the Chinese government. When Han then brought an administrative lawsuit against the Ministry of Public Security for violating his rights in this way, Zhou Guoqiang acted as his legal representative. In early November, however, the case was rejected by the Beijing Intermediate People's Court without a hearing.

Originally arrested in July 1989 and charged with "counter-revolutionary propaganda" and instigating workers to go on strike, Zhou had earlier, in fact, led the only successful strike in his factory's history and was instrumental in forming the BWAF. Released without charge on January 10, 1990, he was eventually allowed to resume his old job at the

Beijing Broadcasting Facilities and Equipment Company, an acoustical equipment factory, although the Public Security Bureau pressured his former employer not to give him any work. Zhou, who served as an army recruit in Tibet during the late seventies, is also an accomplished poet. In 1987, under his pen name, **AQUQIANGBA**, he edited and helped publish a poetry collection entitled *Sixteen Young Beijing Poets*. The Lijiang Publishing House in Guilin, Guangxi Province, which published the volume, in 1989 also published a collection of Zhou's own work. (See also p.419.)

Catholics and Protestants

■   Bishop **SONG Weili**, the 76-year-old underground bishop of Langfang diocese, Hebei Province, was detained twice between December 1992 and the beginning of March 1993, each time for several weeks. During his detention, he was reportedly forced to study government religious policy and the role of the official "patriotic associations," engage in self-criticism, examine his attitude toward the Vatican and "learn how to be patriotic." As of April 21, 1993, Bishop Song, despite continued restrictions on his movements, was reportedly back in charge of the reformed Langfang diocese. It is unclear, however, if the official Chinese Catholic Patriotic Association has sanctioned his recent activities.

Bishop Song was earlier detained in late December 1990 or early January 1991. An official Chinese response to requests for information on

that detention by the U.S. government (November 1991) listed him as having "never been accused of any offense." According to an Asia Watch source, Bishop Song, who was ordained by Bishop Fan Xueyan (see p.228) in 1981, had been sent for "re-education in a study camp" and then later released.

■   Reports mounted throughout 1993 of a widespread pattern of detentions, beatings and finings by local police of house church Christians, mainly poor farmers, in the three north-central provinces of Henan, Anhui and Shaanxi. (See case of **Lai Manping**, p.2, for a detailed account of one such incident.) In July, unofficial church sources reported that the total number of those so detained in the three provinces since late 1992 was at least several hundred and possibly as many as one thousand. The detainees were said mostly to have been freed after paying fines (for which no receipts were given) ranging from 50 yuan to as high as 500 yuan. (The latter sum is equivalent to at least a year's earnings for many rural dwellers.) Subsequent investigations by outside church and human rights groups confirmed the general substance of these reports. Police repression was reportedly most severe in the Sheqi and Zhoukou regions of Henan Province and in Ankang and Xunyang counties, Shaanxi Province. In one such incident, Henan police were reported to have poured boiling water over the head of a Christian from Taihe township, Sheqi County, after he refused to hand over money; unable to withstand the torture, the man eventually paid up. In the case of house church detainees who refused to pay even after being beaten, police would frequently resort to confiscating their oxen or other household belongings in lieu of payment.

■   On September 19, 1993, more than 80 armed Public Security Bureau officers surrounded an unregistered church in the eastern Guangzhou City suburb of Hak Shan (Black Mountain), Baiyun District, at around 2.00 P.M., shortly before a service was to begin (*News Network International*, October 1993). According to NNI, "Authorities searched all 30 members of the congregation, and confiscated their Bibles, hymnals, and one member's address book." No search warrant was produced during the raid. Four members of the church were then detained and interrogated for five hours at the PSB headquarters. The report continued, "Among the four was church leader **LU Zhoushen**, a close associate of renowned Guangzhou house church pastor, Lin Xianggao (Samuel Lamb or Lam). During the interrogation, PSB officials charged the house church was 'illegal' because it violated a 1988 Guangdong provincial law which requires all religious groups to register with the [government-run] Religious Affairs Bureau. Prior to their release, the members were warned not to attend Lin's prominent Damazhan house church." The Hak Shan church is a satellite congregation of the Damazhan church. The 69-year-old Pastor Lin has continually refused to register his church with the official

Protestant "Three-Self Patriotic Movement" authorities.

In a related incident, another unregistered church, also in Guangzhou's Baiyun District and linked to Pastor Lin's congregation, was raided and ordered closed by the PSB on September 13. Authorities temporarily detained the church's leader, interrogated her for at least three hours and warned her not to resume services or associate with Lin or his house church.

7. Exit Denied

Beijing

■   Three leading intellectuals, **TONG Dalin**, head of the official Research Society for Reform of the Economic Structure; **WU Mingyu**, former deputy head of the State Council's Economic Development Center; and **ZHENG Zhongbing**, a liberal author and former editor of the now-defunct journal *New Observer (Xin Guanchajia)*, were all refused visas in October 1993 to attend an academic conference held in Princeton, N.J., on the topic of relations between China and Hong Kong. The conference, which was convened by the *Future China Society*, run by a group of respected Chinese scholars in the U.S., was also attended by several independent pro-democracy representatives from the Hong Kong legislature, including Szeto Wah, Emily Lau and Christine Loh. A major theme of the meeting was "the problem of 1997," when Hong Kong will revert to mainland Chinese control, and the visa refusals are thought to have followed Beijing's perception of the event as being too "politically sensitive."

■   **YU Haocheng,** former chief editor of Masses Publishing House (an organ of the Ministry of Public Security), was barred by the authorities from leaving China in mid-October 1993, the eighth occasion in two years that he has been denied permission to travel abroad. A leading expert on constitutional law, Yu was imprisoned without trial for more than one year after the June 1989 crackdown on the pro-democracy movement. Since his release in 1990, he has continued to speak out on the need for fundamental legal reforms and to publish dissident-style views in the foreign media. His latest denial of permission to travel was in connection with an invitation to attend a seminar at the Chinese University of Hong Kong entitled "Symposium on the Concept of Human Rights in Asia and Europe." Yu was to have spoken at the conference on the topic "Human Rights and their Guarantee by Law." The Beijing public security authorities, however, failed to provide him with any reason for their refusal to allow him to attend the meeting. Previous such denials to travel have been in connection with other conferences and research fellowships in Europe and the U.S. (See also p.483.)

Hunan

■   Dr. Philip H. **CHENG Wai-wo,** an American-Chinese businessman, was detained in Changsha, Hunan

Province on August 26, 1993 and held incommunicado for four days by the local public security authorities. For three of those days, Dr. Cheng, a diabetic, was interrogated constantly and not permitted to sleep. He was then conditionally released, but his passport was confiscated and he was forbidden to leave Changsha. In early October he was allowed to travel to the Zhuhai Special Economic Zone in southern China, where he owns a manufacturing company, Zhuhai Golex Ltd., but as of early November he was still barred from leaving the country, pending resolution of a lawsuit currently being waged against him by the Hunan Arts and Crafts Import-Export Company. Dr. Cheng's detention and ill-treatment by the Hunan police followed a claim by Hunan Arts and Crafts that he had reneged on a joint venture contract with their company. In fact, the Hunan company officials had suddenly demanded that Cheng return to them the sum of U.S. $165,000 which they had earlier, under contract, invested in his Zhuhai-based manufacturing facility. The demand came after orders were issued nationwide by the central government in Beijing in July to recall all unauthorized bank loans and clamp down on further investment projects. Dr. Cheng's arrest and detention appear to have been a blatant attempt by local police to extort the money from him in disregard of the terms of his contract with Hunan Arts and Crafts.

Shanghai

■   **XU Keren,** a senior editor at

Shanghai's *Xinmin Evening News*, was prevented from leaving China on October 1, 1993. When Xu checked in for his flight to Tokyo to visit his wife and daughter, his passport and other documents were confiscated. According to the *South China Morning Post* (October 3, 1993), Xu had been under scrutiny ever since publishing a story about alleged ties between public security officials and nightclub owners in Shanghai. As of October 5, Xu's whereabouts were unknown.

Other Cases

■ As of December 1993, the Chinese government was continuing to block the issuance of passports and exit permits to family relatives of the exiled Chinese dissidents **Cai Chongguo, Chai Ling, Chen Yizi, Lü Jinghua, Wan Runnan** and **Zhang Gang**, all of whom were placed on "most wanted" lists by the Public Security Bureau after June 4, 1989, but who later escaped from China and now reside in the U.S.

8. Entry Denied

■ On November 11 and 13, 1993, **HAN Dongfang**, a prominent exiled labor leader, was stopped from returning to China, first by air and then by land from Hong Kong. It was the third time he had tried to return. On August 13, 1993, Han, the 29-year-old founder and leader of the *Beijing Workers Autonomous Federation,* China's first post-1949 independent labor union, returned to China on a valid Chinese passport after undergoing

almost a year's intensive medical treatment in the U.S. for tuberculosis he had contracted during his two years' imprisonment after the June 1989 crackdown. The following day, he was seized in Guangzhou by the Public Security Bureau, roughed up and forced back across the border to Hong Kong. $1600 of Han's money was confiscated and, since he had a still valid visa for Switzerland, an air ticket for travel there was purchased for him by police officials. In Hong Kong on an emergency seven-day transit visit, Han insisted he wished only to return to his country, that he had no intention of trying to overthrow its government but wanted to establish a free trade union to help the average worker bargain for his rights in China's new economic climate. He refused to apply for a visa to any other country.

On August 21, before Han's visa expired and before the Hong Kong government unilaterally extended it for another 30 days, Chinese officials announced that his passport had been cancelled on orders from "relevant government departments." At no time during several subsequent visits by Han to the Hong Kong branch of China's *Xinhua* news agency, however, did any Chinese official ask him to surrender his passport or even to produce it so that it could be marked as cancelled. The authorities' intent in applying the "cancellation" was clearly to prevent Han from returning to China, while at the same time hoping that he would use the passport to return to the U.S. Despite this legally anomolous outcome and Han's subsequent refusal to leave Hong Kong or seek asylum elsewhere,

Beijing's action effectively rendered him stateless. What had appeared as a humanitarian gesture to permit Han to travel abroad for one year, starting in September 1993, to seek medical treatment for drug-resistant tuberculosis, became instead enforced exile. In so doing, Chinese officials flouted Article 13 of the Universal Declaration of Human Rights under which everyone has "the right of return to his or her country," a document which every member-state of the United Nations is pledged to uphold by virtue of its membership in the body.

According to a Chinese government spokesperson, Han was aware of the conditions under which he was permitted to travel abroad, among which (the spokesperson falsely claimed) was "a promise not to engage in activities harmful to the Chinese state." Instead, Han allegedly "opposed and attacked China, betraying it and his Chinese citizenship, undermining the interests of the country and harming its international prestige," all of which violated Article 51 of the Chinese constitution which states that citizens "may not infringe upon the interests of the state, of society or of the collective..." The Ministry of Public Security also said Han was in violation of Article 4 of a new state security law, issued some four months after he left China. Should Han ever be convicted under its provisions, which include "conspiring to subvert the government and dismember the state and overthrow the socialist system" and "undertaking tasks for foreign espionage organizations," he could receive a life sentence. And in an attempt to rebut

the charges of violating international law, *Wen Wei Po* (August 19, 1991), a Hong Kong newspaper which mirrors the Chinese government position, cited the 1961 U.N. *Convention on the Reduction of Statelessness*. The article not only ignored the fact that China never ratified the Convention but chose selectively from its provisions to bolster the Chinese position.

Among the "subversive" activities cited in support of the government's decision to bar Han from returning to China were his acceptance of the National Endowment for Democracy Award; a speech he made in which he said he asked President Clinton to support a free trade union in China; his attendance in June 1993 at the U.N. World Conference on Human Rights in Vienna; and a speech to the International Labor Organization on June 21, 1993 in which he called on governments to recognize the right of workers to organize and join independent unions. He also was said to have "fanned activities against the Chinese government and besmirched China's international prestige, colluded with and controlled from a distance illegal domestic organizations which he provided with financial backing, incited people to go on strike and made preparations to set up illegal organizations."

In reply, Han stated he had no desire to embarrass or insult the Chinese government nor to promote chaos. Rather, he wished to educate workers about their lawful rights and duties so they could benefit from economic growth. In October, Han's legal agent, Zhou Guoqiang (see p.51) filed an administrative lawsuit on his behalf via the Beijing Intermediate People's Court, challenging the Ministry of Public Security's decision to deny him entry to China and accusing the ministry of violating his civil rights. The suit was dismissed by the court without even a hearing. (See also p.419.) As of January 1994, Han still remained in Hong Kong seeking re-entry to China.

This was at least the third such incident in just over a year. On May 28, 1992, **GONG Xiaoxia**, a Harvard doctoral candidate, was sent back to Hong Kong by the Chinese authorities when she attempted to enter Guangzhou, her home city, to visit family and friends (*South China Morning Post*, June 7, 1992). From there she returned to Boston. A student in the U.S. during the 1989 crackdown in Beijing, Gong went on radio and television at the time to publicly protest the Chinese government's repressive actions.

■   **LÜ Jinghua**, a U.S.-based dissident and formerly a small private entrepreneur active in 1989 with the Beijing Workers Autonomous Federation in Tiananmen Square, was prevented from returning to China to visit her mother and small daughter. According to Lü's own account, on June 13, 1993 in the airport in Beijing, 18 Chinese officials including police and border patrol officers, many in plainclothes, handcuffed and interrogated her for over an hour, then forcibly put her on a Hong Kong-bound plane. She was traveling at the time on a U.S. government-issued travel document stamped with a valid Chinese tourist visa. Lü, 32, who now works in New York for the International Ladies Garment Workers Union, was placed on a secret "most wanted" list by the Chinese government after June 4, 1989 and escaped from the country shortly thereafter.

■   Following the Han Dongfang incident in August (see above), **Richard TSOI Yiu-Cheong**, a Hong Kong trade union activist who had accompanied Han on his abortive trip back to China, was formally notified by the Hong Kong branch of the *New China News Agency (Xinhua)* that his "PRC Document of Return" *(Hui Xiang Zheng)*, a travel document used by most Hong Kong Chinese when travelling to China, had been cancelled for a three-year period as punishment for his involvement in the Han affair.

■   **YAO Yongzhan** (Cantonese name YIU Yung-Chin), a mainland student activist who was detained for one year in Shanghai following the May-June 1989 pro-democracy protests and then released and allowed to return to Hong Kong, where he had previously resettled, was informed by the Chinese authorities in late October that his application for a "PRC Document of Return" had been rejected. No reason was given, but it is believed that the refusal of permission to return to China stemmed from Yao's continued pro-democracy activities in Hong Kong.

9. List of 1993 Releases

The following 37 persons were either confirmed or reported as having been released from prison in China between January 1993 and January 1994:

- **Baatar** - see p.514

- **Chen Jianyong** - see p.495

- **Chen Jianzhang** - see p.392

- **Damchoe Pemo** - see p.516

- **Dorje Dradul** - see p.518

- **Gao Shan** - see p.415

- **Gendun Rinchen** - see p.519

- **Guo Haifeng** - see p.418

- **Hu Hai** - see p.499

- **Huang Jinwan** - see p.444

- **Huchuntegus** - see p.216

- **Jiang Bing** - see p.499

- **Li Guiren** - see p.427

- **Liu Jihua** - see p.437

- **Liu Peigang** - see p.501

- **Lobsang Yonten²** - see p.519

- **Ma Lianggang** - see p.444

- **Ngodrup Wangmo** - see p.531

- Bishop **Shi Enxiang** - see p.395

- **Tian Yang** - see p.444

- **Tseten Norgye** - see p.540

- **Wang Bo** - see p.505

- **Wang Dan** - see p.459

- **Wang Shengli** - see p.5

- **Wang Xizhe** - see p.506

- **Wei Jingsheng** - see p.507

- **Wu Xuecan** - see p.471

- **Xie Changzhong** - see p.495

- **Xu Wenli** - see p.510

- **Xu Yiruo** - see p.475

- **Shen Liangqing** - see p.444

- **Zhai Weimin** - see p.486

- **Zhang Dapeng** - see p.397

- **Zhang Weiming** - see p.398

- **Zhang Youshen** - see p.399

- **Zhou Zhirong** - see p.494

- **Zhu Guoqiang** - see p.495

II. DEMOCRACY MOVEMENT PRISONERS

II. DEMOCRACY MOVEMENT PRISONERS

1. Current Status Known

Sentenced

Students, Intellectuals, Journalists and Officials

Anhui

- **QI Dafeng**, a former graduate student in the management department at Nankai University in Tianjin, was sentenced administratively by the Beijing Labor Re-education Administration Committee to two years' "re-education through labor" and on December 25, 1992 was transferred to the Xuancheng Labor Re-education Camp in Anhui Province. The committee's verdict accused him of "anti-government activities," a reference to his cooperation with **SHEN Tong**, 24, a U.S-based student dissident (see below and p.452). Qi immediately appealed the verdict, then went on a protest hunger strike when the authorities denied his right to appeal. He was force-fed after four days and, as of August 1993,

reportedly was in poor health from the experience. The camp at Xuancheng is a graphite mine, but it is unknown what particular work tasks Qi has been assigned.

Qi Dafeng was arrested on September 1, 1992 along with **QIAN Liyun**, the 26-year-old wife of escaped student leader Xiong Yan (see p.474), and Shen Tong, who planned to hold a news conference in Beijing that day to announce the opening of a Beijing branch of his Boston-based Democracy for China Fund. Shen, who had quietly entered China in August, was released and deported back to the U.S. on October 24. Qian Liyun was held in the Red Flag Hotel in an eastern suburb of Beijing until September 26, then moved to a prison, before being released without charge on October 30. Some months later, she was granted a passport and has since rejoined her husband in the U.S.

Qi was originally arrested in June 1989 for his role as a leader of the Tianjin Students Autonomous Federation (see Lu Gang p.14) and spent twenty months in the detention center at Tianjin No.1 Prison before being tried, declared innocent and released. Known externally as the Tianjin Hinge Factory, the prison is a forced labor facility which manufactures door hinges, electrical batteries, water pumps, transformers and steel tubing.

. . . . [2 YRS]

Beijing

■ **BAI Weiji** - see p.4

. . . . [10 YRS]

■ **BAO Tong**, a leading political reformer and former aide to ousted Party leader Zhao Ziyang, was sentenced to seven years' imprisonment on July 21, 1992, by a three-judge panel of the Beijing Intermediate People's Court. Bao Tong had been taken into custody on May 28, 1989 and held without charge, incommunicado for much of the time, until January 15, 1992. Bao's trial, the most important political proceedings in China for twelve years, reportedly took less than six hours to complete. Bao is currently being held in solitary confinement in Qincheng Prison, China's main detention facility for top political prisoners.

Bao Tong was sentenced to four years' imprisonment for "leaking an important state secret" and an additional five-year sentence, with two years' subsequent deprivation of political rights, for engaging in "counterrevolutionary propaganda and incitement" during what the judges called the "serious disturbances" in Beijing in May 1989. In accordance with Article 64 of China's Criminal Law, the total sentence was reduced to seven years' imprisonment minus time already spent in detention, so that Bao will be due for release in 1996. His appeal was routinely turned down by a "collegiate bench" of judges of the Beijing Municipal High People's Court on August 6, 1992.

Despite a report by *Xinhua* (the official Chinese news agency) implying that Bao's wife, daughter, brother and sister had attended the trial along with some 230 others, family members were in fact allowed into the courtroom only to hear the ten-minute verdict. Court employees who had been ordered to attend made up the bulk of the audience, and they too were only admitted to the courtroom when Bao's sentence was announced. Other spectators arrived and departed in government cars. It was not a public trial in any meaningful sense of the word. Bao's family were denied visits with him for a period of eight months prior to his trial, and subsequently, the authorities violated PRC prison regulations by only permitting bimonthly visits. Finally, in March 1993, the prison authorities agreed to allow one visit per month.

Bao Tong's health has seriously deteriorated during his time in prison. He has undergone five operations for polyps on his colon, most recently in April 1993. His white blood count is well below the normal minimum, and his carcinoembryonic antigen (CEA) level has been increasing steadily and is now well above normal. An elevated CEA can indicate the presence of cancer. A request by members of Bao's family to allow him to see his own doctor was denied. Two petitions for his "release on bail to seek medical treatment" have been denied, once in March 1993 and again in May. "If we must wait until the end of Bao's life for the authorities to allow him out on bail for medical treatment," read one of the petitions, "his release will be meaningless." The prison authorities apparently denied the requests for bail on the grounds that Bao is able to care for himself. An earlier petition for review of Bao's case was dropped by the family after prison authorities ruled in October 1992 that should the appeal go ahead, it would be considered a lawsuit and family members would thus again have to be denied visitation privileges.

Prior to his detention, Bao Tong, now 60, was political secretary to the Politburo's Standing Committee and a member of the Party's Central Committee. An adviser to ousted Party leader Zhao Ziyang for ten years, first as chief of staff and later as senior aide, Bao is widely credited with being the chief architect of Zhao's economic and political reforms. Until 1987, he directed the State Commission on Economic Reform and, from 1987 to 1989, he was Director of the Central Research Institute for the Reform of the Political Structure. In Bao's view, political reform required strengthening respect for the rule of law and separating the government from the Party, but did not mean the adoption of Western-style democracy. In the *Working Report of the Central Committee to the Thirteenth Party Congress* (1987), which Bao authored,

he had called for the phasing out of centralized economic planning in favor of a free market economy and emphasized the need for accompanying political reform. As recently as January 1992, Deng Xiaoping again referred to this report as being the blueprint for China's future reforms.

Bao Tong has a long and distinguished history of service to China. His Party career extends back to the 1940s when, as a high school student, he first joined the Communist underground. During the 1950s, he served as secretary to the chief of the Central Committee's Organization Bureau and later headed its policy division. Bao was purged during the Cultural Revolution as a "capitalist roader" and spent several years as a laborer on a tobacco farm in a Henan prison camp. He resumed his Party work soon after Deng Xiaoping's return to power in 1978. On March 26, 1992, Bao Tong was formally expelled from the Chinese Communist Party.

. . . . [7 YRS]

■ **CHEN Yanbin**, 23, a student at Beifang Communications University, and **ZHANG Yafei**, 24, a graduate of Qinghua University, were tried by the Beijing Intermediate People's Court March 5, 1991 on charges of "organizing a counterrevolutionary group" and sentenced to 15 years and 11 years' imprisonment respectively. In addition, after release Chen will be stripped of political rights for four years and Zhang for two years. The "principal ringleaders" of a peaceful opposition group called the *Chinese Revolutionary Democratic Front* and editors of a dissident publication entitled *Tielu (Iron Currents)*, Zhang had been arrested in September 1990 and Chen later that same year. According to the court verdict, Zhang and Chen, in denouncing the Tiananmen Square crackdown, had slandered the leadership of the Chinese Communist Party by calling it "an authoritarian tyranny." "Their crimes," the document stressed "were serious, their nature sinister and the offense grave." Subsequent U.S. government enquiries about the men's whereabouts and condition elicited no response from the Chinese government in a November 1991 reply by the latter on other political prisoner cases. In October 1993, Asia Watch learned that Chen Yanbin is currently being held at Beijing No.1 Prison and Zhang Yafei is being held at the Shengjian Vehicle Repair Plant, a prison-labor factory in Jinan, capital of Shandong Province. Zhang, who was divorced by his wife last year, is said to be seriously ill in prison.

A man named **ZHANG Donghui** and four others (names unknown) were also, according to the verdict on Chen and Zhang Yafei, tried and sentenced for joining the "counterrevolutionary" *Chinese Revolutionary Democratic Front,* which was founded in 1990, and for distributing "on buses, campuses and in residential areas" over 400 copies of the one published issue of the group's "reactionary" journal *Iron Current.* No sentencing or other details for these five are known.

. . . . . [11, 15 YRS] [5 X ? YRS]

■ **CHEN Ziming**, 41, a veteran

dissident, publisher and social scientist whom the authorities labeled a "black hand" of the 1989 pro-democracy movement, was tried on February 11, 1991 by the Beijing Intermediate People's Court on charges of "conspiracy to subvert the government" and "counterrevolutionary propaganda and incitement." (See also **Wang Juntao**, p.70.) The following day, he was sentenced to 13 years' imprisonment and four years' subsequent deprivation of political rights. Although detained since October 1989, Chen was not formally charged until February 5, 1991, leaving the lawyer hired by his family less than a week before the trial to prepare his defense. On February 7, Chen went on a hunger strike in an effort to secure more time, but to no avail. Chen's trial was closed to the public, and police officers stood outside the courtroom to bar foreigners from even reading the posted trial notice (*AP,* February 11, 1991). The thirty or so people seated in the public gallery were all, with the exception of two of Chen's relatives, either police officers or court officials. Chen's mother and sister were admitted to the courtroom, but his wife, father, younger brother and uncle were all barred. The authorities had threatened that none of the family could attend if Chen continued his hunger strike. Chen's subsequent appeal to the Beijing High People's Court was routinely rejected (*South China Morning Post,* March 28, 1991).

On April 2, 1991, Chen was transferred from Qincheng Prison to Beijing No.2 Prison. Initially placed in a "strict regime" solitary confinement cell measuring only four square meters, Chen was transferred in September 1991 to a 12-square meter cell housing four prisoners, where he currently remains. Since his imprisonment, Chen has acquired a serious skin ailment and suffers also from heart trouble and high blood pressure. When he asked to see a doctor, however, he was told, "The doctor is too busy to see you" (*AP*, May 30, 1991) His cellmates, "common criminals," are required to report on his activities, thoughts and moods.

Prison food at Beijing No.2 is meager and sanitation is rudimentary, and Chen is confined to his cell all day long. Family visits are limited to thirty minutes once a month and prison conditions are a taboo topic at the meetings. Requests for him to be housed with other political prisoners, for a larger desk with enough light to read by, for more regular family visits, to be granted exercise time and be allowed to read English-language books (instead of only materials produced by state-run publishing houses) have all been ignored by the Bureau of Labor Reform and the Ministry of Justice. In addition, his application to People's University to pursue an external doctorate in Chinese modern history has been turned down, as has his petition to the National People's Congress asking for release on bail for medical treatment (*South China Morning Post*, March 13, 1993).

A series of libel suits lodged by Chen against *Xinhua*, *People's Daily*, *The Earth* publishing house, the Public Security Bureau and the State Education Commission in connection with their allegations that he urged violent protest action during the 1989 democracy movement, have all been arbitrarily blocked by the courts. Nor has there been any response to an April 1992 petition from Chen's wife **WANG Zhihong** to the National People's Congress complaining that her husband's trial did not even meet the PRC's own standards of legal fairness and adequacy. In particular, she noted that Chen's lawyer was refused permission to examine the tapes of two key witness's statements and had been barred by the court from freely entering counter-evidence (FBIS April 29, 1992).

Chinese leaders had reportedly branded Chen and his colleague Wang Juntao as being "the black hands behind the black hands," accusing them of manipulating the Tiananmen Square protestors in an attempt to overthrow the government. According to *Xinhua news agency:* "They gathered together some illegal organizations in Beijing" and helped organize "attacks against the armed forces" (in *AP*, February 12, 1991). Moreover, alleged *Xinhua,* in a reference to Chen, Wang and their two colleagues and codefendants Liu Gang (see p.65) and Chen Xiaoping (see p.410), "Some of the four defendants gathered together and used illegal organizations to resist and sabotage the implementation of state laws and decrees and carried out a series of conspiratorial activities to subvert the government.... Others resorted to a variety of means to wantonly and blatantly incite the masses to subvert the people's political power and the socialist system." Commenting on the sentences (Chen Ziming and Wang Juntao 13 years each, Liu Gang six years, Chen Xiaoping released), the agency claimed that the verdicts had combined "punishment with leniency...according to the circumstances and degree of harmfulness of the crimes and the defendants' attitudes toward their crimes and punishments."

Chen, former head of the Beijing Social and Economic Sciences Research Institute (SERI), and his wife Wang Zhihong were arrested sometime in October 1989 in the southern coastal city of Zhanjiang while pursuing a secret escape route (*Reuters*, November 9, 1989). A Shanghai native and formerly the Deputy Director of the Beijing Human Resources Testing and Evaluation Center (a division of SERI), Wang Zhihong was released sometime in mid-November 1990 after spending over a year in prison without charge. For further information on Chen Ziming, Wang Juntao and Liu Gang, see "Rough Justice in Beijing" (*News From Asia Watch*, January 27, 1991) and "Defense Statement of Chen Ziming" (*News From Asia Watch*, June 10, 1992).

.... [13 YRS]

■ **LI Jijun**, former commander of the Beijing-based 38th Army, was court-martialled in the summer of 1989 and sentenced to five years in prison for disobeying orders during the June 4 crackdown in Beijing. He allegedly failed to execute the Central Military Commission order to "arm the troops and send them to Beijing city" (FBIS, September 18, 1990). Li filed an appeal against conviction on the grounds of "improper administrative procedures," arguing that his orders were not issued in accord with regulations. While Li was originally placed under house arrest, it is unclear whether he subsequently served his sentence in or out of prison.

.... [5 YRS]

■ **LI Nong, HU Ruoyang** and **XIAO Feng**[1] were sentenced on January 26, 1991 to five years, four years and three years' imprisonment respectively for helping "most wanted" student leader Wuerkaixi escape from China (*Shijie Ribao*, January 29, 1991). In a November 1991 response to U.S. government inquiries, Chinese officials confirmed that Hu Ruoyang had been sentenced, gave no information about Li Nong and claimed that Xiao Feng had already been freed. According to an account reportedly later confirmed by Wuerkaixi, Xiao, a 21-year-old student at Beijing Normal University, and Li, a 29-year-old from the music department at Central Minorities Institute in Beijing, had escorted the fugitive student leader on the Henan Province-Guangzhou leg of his escape route from China. Hu, 37, a staff member at a trading company in Guangdong, and three others who later managed to escape, then completed the assignment. Li, Xiao and Hu were arrested shortly afterwards.

.... [5 YRS]

■ **LIAO Jia'an** - See p.5

.... [3 YRS]

■ **LIU Gang**[1], 32, a graduate physics

student and Tiananmen Square activist who ranked third on the Chinese government's list of 21 "most wanted" students, was tried by the Beijing Intermediate People's Court on February 6, 1991 on charges of "conspiracy to subvert the government" and sentenced on February 12 to six years' imprisonment and two years' subsequent deprivation of political rights. A native of Liaoyan, Jilin Province, Liu was arrested in Baoding, Hebei Province, on June 19, 1989 while trying to buy a railway ticket. Local residents reportedly turned him in to the police after noticing that, although dressed in worker's clothing, he did not have calloused hands. His trial lasted for three and a half hours, and Liu, who had been allowed to hire his own lawyer, spoke for one hour in his own defense. He denied the charges of sedition and demanded that all earlier statements made by him to police interrogators be discounted, as they had been extracted under threat of death. According to *Xinhua*, however, Liu had "acknowledged his crimes and showed willingness to repent" and so received a "mitigated sentence" (*Reuters*, February 12, 1991).

In April 1991, Liu, a close colleague of imprisoned dissidents Chen Ziming and Wang Juntao, was transferred from Beijing's Qincheng Prison to the infamous Lingyuan Labor-Reform Camp in Liaoning Province, a vast penal-industrial complex where prisoners are forced to produce a wide range of goods for export. According to several first-hand accounts smuggled out of the prison, from the time of his arrival at the

prison's No.2 Detachment until at least April 1993, Liu was subjected to a wide range of severe physical and psychological torture, including beatings and long periods of solitary confinement in a small, "strict regime" cell where he was required to sit on a bench facing the wall for 14 hours a day. Denied the right to exercise or to maintain personal hygiene, he has since developed arthritis, and suffers from a prolapsed anus, hemorrhoids and psoriasis (a disease of the scalp). According to the first-hand accounts, he suffers from unspecified heart and stomach problems for which he has not been permitted appropriate medical treatment; in addition, his face often appears swollen and his hair has started to turn white and fall out.

Members of Liu's family are allowed to visit him only on condition that they "refuse to believe" his allegations about prison conditions, and Liu himself was reportedly forced under torture on at least one occasion to "confess" that he was not being ill-treated. In November and December 1993, his father, Liu Guichun, a retired Public Security Bureau official, and his younger sister, Liu Ming, and her husband made separate atempts to visit Liu Gang at the Lingyuan penal colony. They were turned away by prison officials and informed that all future visits would be cancelled since Liu had been "telling lies" about his ill-treatment in prison. When Liu Ming continued to insist on seeing her brother, a prison official flung her bodily out of the main gate, injuring her head in the process.

Since first arriving at Lingyuan

labor camp, Liu had staged a series of solo hunger strikes and led other political prisoners in doing the same in a sustained and persistent effort to draw attention to the flagrant human rights abuses being committed there. One strike took place in November 1991 on the occasion of then U.S. Secretary of State James Baker's visit to China. (For further details, see Asia Watch, "Chinese Political Prisoners Abused in Liaoning Prison," *News From Asia Watch*, vol.4, no.23). In May 1990, Liu had been moved to solitary confinement in Qincheng Prison as punishment for trying to organize a prisoners' hunger strike to commemorate the June 4 massacre. For two months he lay shackled in leg irons, his arms also lashed tightly together for a week. Also at Qincheng, he was denied a last meeting with his mother prior to her death from cancer.

In response to rising international concern over Liu's plight, the Chinese government in 1991-92 mounted an intensive propaganda campaign aimed at portraying Liu as being a chronic liar who had spread reports of his mistreatment for "ulterior motives and personal purposes" (*Beijing Weekly*, August 22, 1993 and *Xinhua*, August 12, 1993). According to the official accounts, Liu has gained weight in prison, is in good general health, has never been beaten and is excused from physical labor because he is an intellectual. One magazine article, which carried pictures of a healthy-looking Liu happily at work at a computer, even quoted him as saying that he spends an hour each day "sunbathing" in the prison grounds.

Liu Gang's role in the spring of 1989 included organizing key student networks among the major Beijing colleges, and he was prominently associated with SERI, the influential private think-tank headed by Chen Ziming (see p.63) and Wang Juntao (p.70). But Liu's pro-democracy activities began earlier. After graduating from the Chinese Institute of Science and Technology in Hefei, he had eschewed study abroad or work in Beijing, instead accepting a position in a technology development center in Ningbo, Zhejiang Province, where he hoped that his education and ideas would be better utilized. Those hopes were not realized. Upon returning to Beijing, he began to speak out in favor of freedom of the press, the need for multiparty elections and greater respect for human rights. Liu was active in the various student protests of the mid-1980s. After graduating from Beijing University in 1987 with a master's degree in physics, he went on to play a central role the following year in the setting up of campus "democracy salons," which in turn became the springboard for the 1989 pro-democracy movement.

After Liu's arrest, the government cited these and similar activities as showing conclusive proof of a long-standing attempt "to overthrow the leadership of the Chinese Communist Party and the socialist system." Moreover, Liu was accused of being one of the "key agents" of dissident astrophysicist Fang Lizhi and his wife Li Shuxian. (Professor Fang was one of Liu's teachers during his undergraduate study at the Chinese Institute of Science and Technology, and in 1988 Liu campaigned to have Li Shuxian's candidature for election to the National People's Congress restored after her name was arbitrarily removed from the ballot just prior to the election.) At his trial, Liu was also accused of having co-drafted and distributed a "Letter to the People" in Beijing on May 19, 1989 warning of the imminent imposition of martial law and calling upon citizens to block the army's advance, so preparing the ground for the June 4 "counterrevolutionary rebellion."

. . . . [6 YRS]

■ **MA Tao** - see p.7

. . . . [6 YRS]

■ **REN Wanding** (Ren An), 46, a veteran human rights and pro-democracy activist and formerly an accountant in Beijing, was tried by the Beijing Intermediate People's Court on charges of "counterrevolutionary propaganda and incitement" and sentenced on January 26, 1991 to seven years' imprisonment with three years' subsequent deprivation of political rights. According to *Xinhua*, the official Chinese news agency, he "was found guilty of grave crimes and showed no repentance." Ren's wife and young daughter were not even informed of the trial. Following rejection of his appeal by the higher court, Ren was transferred from Banbuqiao Detention Center to Beijing No. 2 Prison, where he is still being held.

Since entering prison, Ren Wanding's health has markedly deteriorated. He is in danger of losing

his eyesight from retinal and cataract problems, but is being denied the medical attention he desperately needs. A thorough examination of both eyes with proper modern equipment is essential. Ren's condition is not new. In November 1989, when he had been in custody for five months at Qincheng Prison, his left eye suddenly became hot and painful. He experienced shadows and decreased visual acuity including the inability to read newsprint. No one examined him until January or February 1990, when doctors at the Public Security Hospital diagnosed his condition as "degenerative macular hemorrhage," for which herbal medicine was prescribed. No further examination was conducted until more than a year later. In July 1991, Ren was examined at the Bin He Hospital, a medical center attached to the Beijing No.1 Prison. The original diagnosis of macular degeneration of the left eye was reportedly confirmed, and he was found also to have cloudiness in the vitreous matter of both eyes, together with bilateral cataracts and severe bilateral myopia (near-sightedness). Oral medication was prescribed and an injection administered. The shadows became less noticeable and Ren's sight improved temporarily. In April 1992, the shadow in Ren's left eye reportedly became larger and more dense. In June, his visual acuity was reportedly down to 0.3; it is unclear when or how this low reading was obtained.

In June 1993, Ren requested an official investigation into why three-quarters of his prison medical records have apparently gone missing, a situation which seriously reduces his chances of securing medical parole. To call attention to his demands, Ren threatened to go on a hunger strike. On June 15, however, during his wife's monthly visit, Ren was reportedly manhandled by guards when he got into an argument with a prison official about his medical condition. Ren's other medical disabilities have been exacerbated by prison conditions. A January 1992 operation for a prolapsed rectum brought some relief, but painful internal and external hemorrhoids persist. He cannot sit for any length of time. Sciatica and chronic lower back pain also prevent prolonged sitting. Chronic gastritis and stomach pain require medication; the dampness of his cell has aggravated both severe chronic nasal sinusitis and pharyngitis and also an upper respiratory tract infection. His request for a vegetarian diet to alleviate his alimentary condition, has reportedly been granted; but he is allergic to pork fat, which the authorities continue to include in his rations. Another request, to be free of handcuffs when he goes for medical checks, has been ignored.

Ren Wanding is one of the few leading activists from the Democracy Wall period of 1978-81 who also played a leading role in the 1989 pro-democracy protests. When the first crackdown on Democracy Wall came in 1979, Ren, as founder of the *China Human Rights League* - the first-ever such organization in China - was denounced by the authorities as a non-Marxist. Arrested in April 1979 after publicly protesting the government's seizure of Wei Jingsheng (see p.507) a few weeks earlier, Ren

spent the next four years in prison, his initial sentence having been extended when, rather than making an acceptable self-criticism, he wrote two volumes attacking the government. In 1988, on the tenth anniversary of the founding of the Democracy Wall, Ren published an article in the *New York Times* in which he called upon Chinese students and intellectuals to speak out for the release of all political prisoners in China and called upon the international business community to make its investments in China conditional upon an end to the suppression of dissidents.

During the spring of 1989, Ren, the acknowledged "father of the China human rights movement," made numerous public speeches in Tiananmen Square and other parts of Beijing calling for the release of political prisoners and for a society based on respect for human rights. He also wrote and distributed articles calling for freedom of expression, the rule of law as guaranteed by the Chinese constitution and promotion of a "pluralistic society and culture" to accompany the economic reforms. For this, he was singled out for special criticism in Beijing Mayor Chen Xitong's June 30, 1989 speech summarizing the main antecedents and course of the June 4 "counter-revolutionary rebellion." After the June 4 massacre, Ren reportedly sought sanctuary at the U.S. Embassy in Beijing but was turned away by American officials. He was arrested on June 9 at about 8 P.M. and initially held in Qincheng prison, although his detention was never acknowledged by the government until November 1990, when he was formally charged with "counterrevolution." His wife, **Zhang Fengying**, who before June 1989 had worked as an accountant at SERI (Chen Ziming's now-banned private think-tank), was denied permission to see him from the time of his arrest until after his January 1991 trial.

Since then, Zhang and her 13-year-old daughter, who suffers from a nervous complaint, have met with repeated harassment and persecution from the authorities. Several days prior to Ren's sentencing, they were evicted from the family's company-allocated apartment, although Zhang managed to salvage temporary use of a 15-square meter space. In April 1992, however, Ren's former employer, a refrigeration supply firm, shuttered up the apartment with most of the family's possessions still inside. The police then pressured Zhang to move back to Tianjin, her original place of residence, but she has insisted on staying in Beijing so that she can visit her husband. After moving around between friends' houses and unable to find steady employment, in November she demonstrated outside a Beijing police station to demand proper housing. In early July, 1993, she and her daughter were detained for ten days at a guest house outside Beijing, in an attempt by the authorities to prevent Zhang from demonstrating again or holding a news conference in support of her husband's request for medical parole.

. . . . [7 YRS]

■ **WANG Juntao**, 35, labeled by the government as one of the "black hands" behind the 1989 pro-democracy

movement, was tried and sentenced on February 12, 1991 by the Beijing Intermediate People's Court to 13 years' imprisonment and four years' deprivation of political rights on charges of "conspiracy to subvert the government" and "counterrevolutionary propaganda and incitement." Wang's trial was closed to the public, and police officers stood outside the courtroom to bar foreigners from reading even the officially posted trial notice. The 30 or so people seated in the public gallery were, with the exception of a few of Wang's relatives, either police officers or court officials. The Beijing High Court subsequently rejected Wang's appeal, after blocking his defense lawyers from continuing with the case. The court gave no serious consideration to the points raised in the appeal submission (which was prepared by Wang's wife, Hou Xiaotian - see p.422) and failed to supply any evidence in refutation. As of early November 1993, Wang, by now seriously ill, was being held at the People's Liberation Army (PLA) No.302 Military Hospital in Beijing under armed guard and in strict, prison-style isolation.

Chinese leaders had accused Wang and his colleague Chen Ziming of manipulating the Tiananmen Square protestors in an attempt to overthrow the government. According to *Xinhua*, "They gathered together some illegal organizations in Beijing" and helped organize "attacks against the armed forces" Moreover, alleged the official news agency, in a reference to Wang, Chen, and their two colleagues and codefendants Liu Gang (see p.65) and

Chen Xiaoping (see p.410), "Some of the four defendants gathered together and used illegal organizations to resist and sabotage the implementation of state laws and decrees and carried out a series of conspiratorial activities to subvert the government.... Others resorted to a variety of means to wantonly and blatantly incite the masses to subvert the people's political power and the socialist system."

Already suffering from Hepatitis-B at the time of his one-day trial, Wang was denied appropriate medical treatment both before and after his transfer on April 1, 1991 from Qincheng Prison to solitary confinement in Beijing No.2 Prison. From then on, his health steadily deteriorated as a result of prison conditions that Wang called "squalid, inhumane and illegal" (UPI, July 27, 1991). At the time of his transfer to Beijing No.2 Prison, the Qincheng authorities failed to inform officials at the new prison about his medical condition, and the latter subsequently claimed he was not ill. Repeated requests for medical treatment were ignored, but after Wang staged a hunger strike in August 1991, he was moved the next month to Yanqing Prison, a hospital detention facility located about 50 miles north of Beijing. Apparently as a result of international pressure, Wang was given a spacious cell with his own television set, though remaining in strict isolation from other inmates. Sixty to seventy percent of the prisoners patients hospitalized at Yanqing suffer from mental illness, however, and medical facilities were inadequate to deal with his condition.

The extent of Wang's physical deterioration surfaced in April 1993 when it was learned that his liver function had worsened and he had symptoms consistent with serious heart disease. On March 1, an electrocardiogram taken at the No.302 Military Hospital in Beijing showed an inverted T-wave. Even then, petitions for release on medical parole were denied. Wang was transported between the hospital and central Beijing for evaluation and treatment during March and April, then at the end of May a noted heart specialist from Beijing's Fuwei hospital was asked by the Ministry of Justice to treat Wang in prison. Finally, during the week of June 7, 1992 he was transferred to the custody of No.302 Military Hospital, where family members were promptly asked to contribute as much as 5,000 yuan per month towards medical care expenses. The high cost was attributed by hospital officials to the fact that Wang was housed in a four-person room, although prison guards occupied two of the beds and the fourth was empty. In the event, the demand for payment was apparently not enforced, although prison authorities had reportedly paid the hospital 10,000 yuan. Asking families to contribute toward prisoners' medical care is a contravention of the United Nation's *Body of Principles for all Persons Under Any Form of Detention or Imprisonment,* and the Chinese government subsequently denied that any such request had ever been made (*Xinhua,* July 243, 1993 in FBIS, July 26).

In addition to his health problems,

Wang has been barred from pursuing due legal remedies while in prison. Attempts to sue Qincheng Prison and police authorities for deliberate delays and inadequacies in his medical treatment have met with no success; similar attempts to sue *Xinhua* news agency for libel over its false reporting of his role in the 1989 democracy movement have all been blocked; and he has been unable to recover property and cash confiscated in fall 1989 at the time of his arrest in Changsha, Hunan Province. (The court held that the money was for purposes of assisting Wang's escape from China and so could not be returned.) Prison visits by his wife were suspended as punishment for her public appeals on his behalf through the foreign media. Then on August 12, 1992, after prison authorities prevented Wang from passing petition materials and evidence to Hou, his legal representative, Wang started a hunger strike in prison despite his deteriorating medical condition. He continued the strike in modified form, allowing himself to be intermittently force-fed liquid nutrients by the authorities, for the next two months, but to no avail. When Hou Xiaotian threatened to stage a public protest on August 20 in his support, the police detained her for four days at the Yanshan Sanatorium in Changping County, some 40 kilometers from Beijing, for "discussions" on her husband's case. Prison visits by both his parents and Hou were suspended throughout August and September on account of Wang's alleged "bad attitude."

A co-founder with Chen Ziming of the Beijing Social and Economic Sciences Research Institute (SERI), China's first private research institute, Wang has been active as a dissident since 1976, when at the age of sixteen he was imprisoned for 224 days for participating in the April 5 protests in Tiananmen Square against the "Gang of Four." During the 1978-81 Democracy Wall movement, he helped Chen edit the unofficial journal *Beijing Spring*, although both avoided arrest at that time. Wang graduated from the physics department of Beijing University in 1981 and, after a brief spell working at a nuclear physics institute outside Beijing, spent the next few years travelling around China teaching and conducting social and economic research. After joining SERI, he served as deputy editor of *Economics Weekly,* the institute's newspaper, until the time of the June 1989 crackdown. (For further information on Wang and Chen, see *Rough Justice in Beijing,* Asia Watch, January 27, 1991; and *The Case of Wang Juntao,* Asia Watch, March 11, 1991.

. . . . [13 YRS]

■ **WU Shisen** - see p.7

. . . . [LIFE]

■ **YANG Jianwen**, 37, was reportedly sentenced to a 10-year prison term for taking part in May 1989 in the protest activities of the Writer's Class (a prestigious annual group of young professional writers from around the country) at Beijing University. After the crackdown, Yang went to Nanchang, capital of Jiangxi Province, to help organize demonstrations there. Aware that a government "wanted notice" for him had been issued, Yang went on the run but was finally arrested. No further information on his case is currently available.

. . . . [10 YRS]

■ **YANG Lianzi**, 48, a man described by the authorities as a "private performance artist" from Wuchuan County, Gansu Province, was tried in late 1990 by the Beijing Intermediate People's Court on charges of "counterrevolutionary propaganda and incitement" and sentenced to 15 years' imprisonment and three years' subsequent deprivation of political rights. Yang's appeal was rejected by the Beijing High People's Court on October 29, 1990. He is probably currently being held in either Beijing No.1 or No.2 Prison.

Yang was a well-known figure to the numerous foreign journalists and others who followed at first hand the events in Tiananmen Square during May-June 1989. According to the *1991 Beijing Yearbook,* Yang arrived in Beijing from Gansu on May 18 that year. "After the announcement of martial law, Yang roamed around Tiananmen Square and the Xinhuamen Gate area [the residence of many senior Communist Party leaders] wearing a headband bearing the words 'Wild Man of Huaxia'*(Huaxia Kuangren)."* (*Huaxia* is a poetic term meaning the Chinese nation.) "By means of singing songs, playing stringed instruments and giving speeches," continued the official account, "Yang engaged in counter-revolutionary propaganda and

incitement in which he attacked the Chinese Communist Party and the socialist system and cursed and ridiculed Party and state leaders."

. . . . [15 YRS]

■ **ZHANG Yafei** - see p.62
. . . . [11 YRS]

■ **ZHAO Lei** - see p.4
. . . . [6 YRS]

Fujian

■ **SUN Xiongying**, 25, a cadre at the Fuzhou Sparetime University, was sentenced on December 21, 1989 by the Fuzhou Intermediate People's Court to 18 years' imprisonment and five years' subsequent deprivation of political rights. (In November 1991, Chinese authorities confirmed to the U.S. government that Sun was sentenced and still being held, but the prison term was not mentioned.) According to a government radio broadcast (FBIS, November 2, 1989), Sun was arrested in fall 1989 in Fuzhou's Gulou Precinct after local residents informed the authorities about his protest activities. These allegedly included "the counterrevolutionary activities of writing reactionary slogans and defacing and damaging the statues of state leaders." In addition, Sun was implicated in five different cases of "counterrevolution," all of which had been under investigation by the Fuzhou and Xiamen authorities since June 4, 1989.

"After listening to reactionary radio broadcasts for a long time," said the official report, "Sun cherished the ideals of bourgeois liberalization and became greatly dissatisfied with the Party, government and socialist system." He then "successively wrote reactionary slogans and defaced and damaged Chairman Mao's statue, the government name plaques at Wuyi Plaza, the Workers Cultural Palace and the entrance to the city government building in Fuzhou. On September 18, 1989, he posted reactionary slogans at Xiamen University." Sun's current place or conditions of imprisonment are not known.

. . . . [18 YRS]

Guangdong

■ **CHEN Zhixiang**, 29 years old, formerly a teacher at the Guangzhou Maritime Transport Academy, was tried by the Guangzhou Intermediate People's Court on January 11, 1990 on charges of "counterrevolutionary propaganda and incitement" and sentenced to ten years' imprisonment and three years' subsequent deprivation of political rights. An official Chinese response in November 1991 to inquiries by the U.S. government confirmed the conviction.

According to the court verdict, Chen, a native of Nantong in Jiangsu Province, organized student demonstrations in Guangzhou City during the May 1989 protests and wrote "reactionary articles" which had an "extremely bad influence in institutions of higher education." On June 7, 1989, he allegedly painted 20-meter long slogans on the walls along Yanjiangzhong Road and Huanshizhong Road in Guangzhou, in which "he attacked state, military and Party leaders" and called "for the overthrow of the People's Democratic Dictatorship." Chen, who is said to have had a previous "reactionary historical background," was arrested shortly thereafter and eventually convicted, as described, under Articles 102 and 52 of the PRC Criminal Law. In fall 1992, Chinese officials stated that Chen was being held at the Shaoguan Labor Reform Detachment, which is in the northern part of Guangdong Province.

. . . . [10 YRS]

■ **LIN Songlin**, 46, formerly a physician at the ship-building section of the No.3 Engineering Company, Fourth Maritime Bureau of the PRC Ministry of Transportation, was sentenced after June 1989 by the Zhanjiang City Intermediate People's Court, Guangdong Province, to eight years' imprisonment on charges of "counter-revolutionary propaganda and incitement." According to an internal report by the Supreme People's Court (see TC p.380), "Defendant Lin Songlin frequently listened to rumor-mongering broadcasts put out by *Voice of America* and the British BBC, and made tape-recordings of them. On May 17 and 18, 1989, he took a tape of these broadcasts to his work-unit's medical clinic and incited his colleagues by playing it to them. On the morning of May 19, Lin Songlin was caught in the act by his work-unit leadership and subjected to severe criticism, but he remained unrepentant."

On May 21, "Lin sneaked into Leizhou Special Teachers Training

College, Zhanjiang City, and spread rumors, liaised with others and incited the students to make trouble. He told several leaders of the Student Association, 'The Beijing people have all now arisen. Hand in hand, they formed a human wall and blocked the street intersections by means of gasoline bottles. In clashes between the army and the students, soldiers beat and injured more than 60 students. The government's dispatching of the army into Beijing to impose martial law is a barbarous suppression of the patriotic student movement.'" The official report added that Lin had denounced Party and state leaders as being "autocratic rulers," called for the "implementation of consensual multi-party government" and "incited students to solicit donations from the public, take to the streets and demonstrate, thereby creating political turmoil." After his arrest, the police found at his home "one counterrevolutionary banner and one reactionary article written by Lin." His current place of imprisonment is not known.

. . . . [8 YRS]

Hebei

■ **WAN Jianguo** - see p.7

. . . . [4 YRS]

Hubei

■ **GAO Yuan**, formerly a student at a teachers' training college in Huang District, Hubei Province; **JIANG Pinchao**, a former student in Jingzhou, Hubei, at a vocational college *(shifan zhuanke)* for the training of elementary

school teachers; **PAN Huijia**, a middle school teacher in Yangxing, Hubei; and **YE Youwen**, formerly a student at the Jingzhou Agricultural School in Hubei, were tried and sentenced after June 1989 for alleged involvement in the 1989 pro-democracy movement. After sentencing, all four were sent to the Hubei No.1 Labor Reform Detachment (New Life Plastics Factory). The specific charges, dates of trial and prison terms are not known.

. . . . [? YRS]

■ **YU Zhuo** - see p.9

. . . . [2 YRS]

Hunan

■ **AH Fang** (nickname), 23, and **ZHANG Jie**[1], 25, two scientific researchers from Changsha, Hunan Province who left the Changsha Nonferrous Metal Design Academy in September 1989 to found a private company, were arrested at the end of 1989 along with their company's entire staff. The authorities closed down the company, branding it a "counter-revolutionary organization" and a front for pro-democracy activities. In mid-1990, the two founders were convicted by the Changsha Intermediate People's Court on charges of being "members of a counterrevolutionary clique" and each sentenced to five-year prison terms. Initially held in Changsha No.1 and No.2 Detention Centers, Ah Fang was transferred after trial to Yuanjiang Prison (Provincial No.1), where Zhang is also being held. It is not known what became of the other staff members, all of whom had worked at various research institutes before joining Ah Fang and Zhang.

Ah Fang was originally a student at Changsha University; Zhang was a graduate of Hefei University. During the 1989 pro-democracy movement, Ah Fang took part in the Students Autonomous Federation, but withdrew from its activities early on and so was not investigated by the authorities immediately after the June 4 crackdown.

. . . . [2 X 5 YRS]

■ **DUAN Ping**, a 32-year-old from Yongzhou City, Hunan Province, formerly a teacher in Qiyang No.1 Middle School, was sent to Xinkaipu Labor Re-education Center for three years. He was arrested after the August 1991 attempted coup in the Soviet Union, apparently for making statements welcoming the coup's failure. Duan previously served a two-year "re-education through labor" sentence for allegedly "making secret link-ups and stirring up disturbances" during the 1989 pro-democracy movement. After his release from his first sentence, Duan opened an electronic games parlor.

. . . . [3 YRS]

■ **HUANG Zhenghua**, a 54-year-old cadre from a government department in Nan County, Yiyang Prefecture, Hunan Province who had been assigned to work in Changsha, was sentenced to six years' imprisonment by a district court in Changsha in October 1990 on a charge of "economic criminal activity." Arrested in early 1990, Huang had made numerous public speeches in May 1989 in support of the demonstrating students, and was accused by the authorities of "inciting hostile feelings among the masses toward the government" and of "conspiring to form an underground organization."

. . . . [6 YRS]

■ **JIANG Zhiqiang**, 37, from Shaoyang City, Hunan Province, was tried by the Shaoyang Intermediate People's Court in early 1990 on charges of "counterrevolutionary propaganda and incitement" and sentenced to 13 years' imprisonment. Arrested in August 1989 and initially detained in Shaoyang Jail, he was held in Longxi Prison (Provincial No.6) after his trial, then transferred to another prison. During the 1989 pro-democracy movement, Jiang allegedly engaged in extensive "incitement" of the local populace by advocating the parliamentary political system and promoting theories against dictatorship. He reportedly also posted up a large number of "counter-revolutionary articles," and was involved in secret liaison activities in preparation for the founding of a "counterrevolutionary organization."

. . . . [13 YRS]

■ **LIU Jian'an** - see p.378

. . . . [10 YRS]

■ **LIU Xin**, a 15-year-old, ninth-grade *(chu san)* middle school student in Shaoyang City, Hunan Province, was tried and sentenced in September 1989 by the Shaoyang City Intermediate People's Court to 15 years' imprisonment on a charge of "arson." On May 19, 1989, Liu, who was with his older sister's husband on the streets watching people burn an imported car, allegedly supplied some matches. Arrested in June, he is serving his sentence in Longxi Prison (Provincial No.6) where he has been treated as an adult and made to work cutting marble slabs. Liu, who is illiterate and of frail health, denies having supplied any matches during the incident, and insists he was merely a spectator. His sister's husband, whose name is not known, was sentenced to life imprisonment.

. . . . [15 YRS]

■ **LÜ Riying**, 30, a special representative in Shenzhen of the Light Industrial Department of Shaoyang City, Hunan Province, was charged in March 1990 with the alleged crime of "hooliganism" and sentenced to 13 years' imprisonment. Currently held in Longxi Prison (Hunan Provincial No.6), he has submitted numerous petitions to the higher authorities, all of which have been rejected.

During the 1989 pro-democracy movement, Lu returned to Shaoyang several times, allegedly to "spread rumors from Hong Kong and Taiwan." On the night of May 19, 1989, he participated in a large demonstration march protesting Li Peng's imposition of martial law in Beijing. During a violent clash between police and demonstrators, "a police vehicle was burned and several officers were injured." Lu was arrested in early August, after again returning to Shaoyang from Shenzhen, and initially detained in Shaoyang Jail. According to sources familiar with the case, Lu was not involved in any violence.

. . . . [13 YRS]

■ **MAO Genhong**, a 25-year-old graduate of the Hunan College of Finance, and his 22-year-old brother MAO Genwei, and six other people, names unknown, were arrested in late 1990 and tried in mid-1991 by the Changsha Intermediate People's Court on charges of "forming a counter-revolutionary clique." The highest prison sentence imposed was reportedly five years, but the name of the person who received this sentence is not known. Mao Genhong was sentenced to three years' imprisonment, and has presumably now been released; Mao Genwei was exempted from criminal punishment and released after the trial. According to an internal government source, "After graduation, Mao Genhong, together with his younger brother Mao Genwei and others, in mid-1990 set up an underground organization which was broken up by the authorities at the end of 1990." The two brothers were held in Changsha No.1 Prison before their trial. Mao Genhong was then sent to Lingling Prison (Provincial No.3) and later transferred to Yuanjiang Prison (Provincial No.1).

. . . . [NAME? 5 YRS]

■ **Teacher LIU** (given name unknown), 37, a teacher in the politics department of Yiyang Teachers College, Hunan Province, was sentenced in early 1990 by the Yiyang City Intermediate People's Court to seven years' imprisonment. During the 1989 pro-democracy movement, Liu allegedly made speeches in Yiyang, Changsha, and other places and published "reactionary articles." He was arrested after June 4 that year and is serving his sentence at the Jianxin Labor Reform camp near Yueyang, Hunan. He reportedly also was involved in an earlier protest movement in the province in 1980.

. . . . [7 YRS]

■   **Teacher X** (name unknown), in his thirties, a teacher in the linguistics department at Changde Normal University, Hunan Province, and a graduate of the Chinese department of Hunan Normal University, was reportedly sentenced at the end of 1989 by the Changde City Intermediate People's Court to 12 years' imprisonment on charges of "counter-revolutionary propaganda and incitement" and for "being in secret contact with foreign countries" *(litong waiguo)*. He is currently being held in Hengyang Prison (Provincial No.2).

The teacher was reportedly involved in pro-democracy activities for a long time and joined the 1989 movement in its early stages. He organized student demonstrations, wrote "reactionary articles" and made speeches demanding the restoration of basic rights. After June 4, 1989, at a commemorative meeting held in front of the municipal government offices to mourn those killed in Beijing, he allegedly called upon the people to rise up to resist the regime. He was arrested shortly thereafter.

. . . . [NAME? 12 YRS]

■   **WANG Changhong**[1], a resident of Changsha City, Hunan Province and a participant in the 1989 pro-democracy movement, was tried by the Changsha Intermediate People's Court in late 1990 on a charge of "forming a counterrevolutionary group." He was sentenced to five years' imprisonment. In early 1990, Wang established an underground pro-democracy group. He was arrested shortly thereafter and accused of "leaking state secrets." Several other people were arrested and tried in connection with the same case, but no details about them are known. Wang is currently held in Lingling Prison (Hunan Provincial No.3).

. . . . [5 YRS]

*[NB: As of summer 1993, a large number of political prisoners from the 1989 pro-democracy movement in Hunan had reportedly been transferred from other prisons and concentrated in the Changde Labor Reform Detachment (also known as the Hunan Diesel Engine Factory). The names of those transferred are not known, but for details of more than 200 persons detained after June 4, 1989 in Hunan, see **Anthems of Defeat: Crackdown in Hunan Province, 1989-1992**, Asia Watch, June 1992.]*

Jiangsu

■   **Li Lifu**, formerly a graduate student at the Nanjing China Medical College, Jiangsu Province, was detained in October 1990 in connection with the 1989 pro-democracy movement. He was later tried and sentenced to an eight-year prison term. No further details are available.

. . . . [8 YRS]

■ **PENG Wanquan**, formerly a graduate student at China Medical College, possibly in Jiangsu Province, was detained in October 1989 in connection with the 1989 pro-democracy movement and later tried and sentenced to an eight-year term. No further information is available.

. . . . [8 YRS]

■ **YANG Tongyan**, a Christian detained in Nanjing, Jiangsu Province, on June 1, 1990, was tried and sentenced to ten years' imprisonment in November 1991 for allegedly "organizing a counterrevolutionary group," the *China Social Democratic Party* (also referred to as the "China Domestic Rally.") Yang was arrested in Nanjing, secretly and without a warrant, on June 1, 1990, but his wife was not officially informed of his arrest and sentencing until December 28 the same year. Yang is now reportedly being held in the Jiangsu No.17 Labor Reform Detachment, at Nongtan, near his home city of Nanjing. (Another report describes his place of detention as the "Ninth Branch [Gold] Factory No.2"). His wife, Zhang Xiaoli, is permitted to visit him there once a month. After graduating in 1981 from the history department of Beijing Normal University, Yang later worked as a researcher in Chinese and western history at the Jiangsu Social Research

Institute in Nanjing. After resigning from his job in early 1990 he went to Hong Kong. While there, Yang was baptized, then decided to return to China as a missionary. His wife, a graduate of the Nanjing Art Institute, has reportedly been under surveillance since her husband's arrest.

According to a rough English translation recently received by Asia Watch, the court verdict states: "Yang's thoughts were counter-revolutionary. He worked together with armies, developed a counter-revolutionary organization, and wanted to destroy proletarian rule....He is the vice-chairman of the counter-revolutionary organization, *China Domestic Rally*. What he has done is to found, organize, and lead a counter-revolutionary organization. According to the Criminal Law of the People's Republic of China, Articles 98, 60, and 52, Yang is [hereby] sentenced for a term of 10 years, beginning on June 1, 1990 and ending on May 31, 2000." The court alleged that Yang had helped organized and lead the "counter-revolutionary party" and drafted its "Principles and Plan of Activities," and that during his time in Hong Kong he had provided "counterrevolutionary information" about the party to the newspaper *Ming Bao* (which it reportedly published on February 7 or 9, 1990).

Also arrested for involvement in Yang's "counterrevolutionary" party were **CHEN (Sun) Zhongming,** a poet, who was sentenced to six years' imprisonment; and **ZENG Yanzhuo** (also reported as **FENG Yanzhao**), described as a "specialized soldier," who received a four-year term. Both men are reportedly being held at the Suyang Zhuanghu Prison Farm, which is believed to be in Jiangsu Province. Other party members known to have been arrested, but of whom there has been no further news, include **ZHANG Yaowei**, who was accused of helping Yang distribute "counterrevolutionary materials," and **ZHANG Yi**[1], who was allegedly the chairman of the new party.

. . . . [4, 6, 10 YRS]

Another detained member, **ZHANG Yuxiang**, a former PLA district-level political propaganda cadre, was sentenced to two or three years in prison and has reportedly now been released. According to the court verdict, on May 23-25, 1990, Yang Tongyan, Zhang Yi, Chen Zhongming and **ZHANG Heping** (a vice-chairman of the party) made plans to hold a rally or demonstration by the new party, and during this time Yang allegedly received $1,900 in U.S. currency and 750 *yuan*. (Zhang Heping is subsequently believed to have escaped from China.) Three others detained at the time are also thought to have been involved in the Yang Tongyan case, although they were not named in the court verdict: **WANG Zhan**, who received a two-year sentence, which he has presumably now completed; and **ZHAN Weiou** and **XIAO Yong**, who were later released.

Jilin

■ **AN Fuxing**, a college graduate and cadre at the Jilin Chemical Industry Corporation, and **LI Jinge**, a college graduate and formerly an instructor at the plant, were tried (probably in 1990) and sentenced for their participation in demonstrations which occurred at the chemical company in May-June 1989. An, 40, who helped organize the demonstrations, was convicted of "organizing and leading a counter-revolutionary group" and received a five-year term of imprisonment with two years' subsequent deprivation of political rights. Li, 25, received a three-year term and two years' subsequent deprivation of political rights for "actively taking part in the activities of a counterrevolutionary group." (Li, who was arrested in December 1989, has presumably been released upon completion of his term.)

The two men were sent to serve their sentences in Lingyuan Prison in Liaoning Province, where An Fuxing, along with numerous other political prisoners (see Tang Yuanjuan p.105, and Liu Gang p.65, has since been repeatedly subjected to torture, solitary confinement and other brutalities. In attempts to alleviate their conditions and focus international attention on their plight, political prisoners at Lingyuan have staged collective hunger strikes at least twice.

. . . . [5 YRS]

Liaoning

■ **TIAN Xiaoming**, a 28-year-old college graduate and native of Dandong Municipality, Liaoning Province, was sentenced to a seven-year prison term on charges of "counterrevolutionary propaganda and incitement." Tian is held under appalling conditions in Lingyuan Prison in Liaoning, where he, along with other political prisoners, has been subjected to torture, solitary confinement and other brutalities. In attempts to alleviate their conditions and focus international attention on their plights, political prisoners at Lingyuan have staged collective hunger strikes at least twice. (For details, see Tang Yuanjuan p.105.)

. . . . [7 YRS]

Qinghai

■ **YU Zhenbin**, a 28-year-old cadre from the Qinghai Provincial Archives Bureau, was sentenced to 12 years in prison for organizing a "counter-revolutionary clique" in Qinghai in June 1989 (*Reuters*, January 16, 1991). That he was sentenced was confirmed by Chinese officials in response to requests for information by the U.S. government (November 1991). No date was given. According to *Renmin Ribao* (June 30, 1989), Yu who was arrested on June 27, 1989 near Xining City, organized the illegal *Chinese People's Democratic Opposition Party Alliance* in order to overthrow the Communist party and "seize power." He also allegedly wrote and distributed leaflets calling for a revision of the Chinese constitution, the establishment of a new central government and an end to one-party rule.

. . . . [12 YRS]

Shaanxi

■ **ZHANG Ming[1], HE Hua, SUN Zhenggang** and **XU Jianxiong**, all students from Northwest University *(Xibei Daxue)* in Xi'an, capital of Shaanxi Province, were sentenced to terms of five to ten years' imprisonment for allegedly organizing an informal current-affairs discussion group known as a "democracy salon" and for sending a telegram in May 1989 to Mikhail Gorbachev calling for free elections in the Soviet Union. It is believed that other students were also arrested in connection with the case. The group also put up "big character" posters, travelled to Beijing sometime in May 1989 and called for the resignation of Premier Li Peng. Arrested later that month, they were held together in Xi'an's "Fifth Branch" (possibly the PSB Dept. No.5) Detention Center, where they were separated from common criminals but forced to work in the jail's factory making matches. Convicted in March 1990 for "counterrevolutionary organizing," they were transferred in June to the Shaanxi Provincial No.2 Prison (a convict-labor boiler factory) in Weinan to serve their sentences.

Zhang Ming, a former history major, and Xu Jianxiong (both around 26 or 27 years old), argued at their trial that they had done nothing wrong and would be exonerated by history. Convicted of "counterrevolutionary propaganda and incitement," they were each sentenced to ten years' imprisonment. Sun Zhenggang and He Hua received five and four-year sentences respectively on the same charges. (The latter has presumably now been released upon completion of his term.) University officials initially denied that any of their students had been imprisoned; later, judicial and "foreign affairs" officials in Xi'an and in Shaanxi Province said they were either "not clear" or denied all knowledge of the cases (UPI, December 26, 1991). (Zhang Ming is not be confused with the "most wanted" student leader of the same name who was convicted in January 1991; see p.445.)

. . . . [5, 5, 10, 10 YRS]

■ **ZHANG Zongai**, a former professor of either Tong Ji University in Xi'an, Shaanxi Province, or the Xi'an Institute of Statistics, was still in Shaanxi No.2 Prison in Weinan as of June 1993, according to an Asia Watch source. Zhang was tried in March 1991 on charges of "counterrevolutionary propaganda and incitement" and sentenced to a five-year prison term for his participation in the demonstrations in Xi'an in April 1989.

. . . . [5 YRS]

Shandong

■ **CHEN Lantao**, a marine biologist born in October 1963, was sentenced on August 23, 1989 to a term of 18 years' imprisonment with five years' subsequent deprivation of political rights and confiscation of items of personal property. His sentence is nearly the maximum allowed by law as "combined punishment for more than one crime" (Articles 64, 158, 159, 102 of the 1979 Criminal Law). Charges included "counterrevolutionary propaganda and incitement" and "disturbing the social order and traffic." The Qingdao Intermediate

People's Court where Chen was tried labeled him a "ringleader." Chen did not appeal his sentence and a 1991 appeal to the Qingdao Higher People's Court on his behalf was rejected. Eight others, whose names are unknown, reportedly received terms ranging from 18 to seven years' imprisonment. Before trial, all nine were held at the Laixi County Prison in Qingdao municipality.

According to an Asia Watch source, Chen's major "offense" was a public speech he gave on June 8, 1989, in which he attacked the government for the military crackdown in Beijing, demanded greater democracy and called upon the Communist Party to step down. Before June 4, Chen had taken part in the peaceful pro-democracy demonstrations in Qingdao and made contact with the leaders of the Qingdao College Students Autonomous Federation (*Qing-Gao-Lian*). Another accusation made against him by the government was that he had listened to *Voice of America* broadcasts since 1981. After Chen's arrest, his personal diary and black head-bands that he and his wife, **SUN Lijuan**, had worn to commemorate the victims of the June 4 massacre were seized by the authorities as evidence.

A 1988 master's graduate of the Oceanography University of Qingdao, where he was chairman of the graduate student union, and later an associate engineer at the Beihai branch of the State Commission of Oceanography in Qingdao, Chen was arrested, together with his pregnant wife, on a Qingdao street on June 12, 1989. The security officers who carried out the arrest carried warrants issued by the Qingdao Intermediate People's Court. Chen's wife was released after 53 days, but Chen was formally arrested on July 21. Initially held in the Dashan Detention Center, he was later moved to Changzhou Lu Detention Center. After his trial, Chen was sent to Laixi County Prison and from there to the Shandong Provincial No.3 Prison in Weifang to serve his sentence and perform hard labor. Chen's protest activities extend back to the 1986 nationwide student demonstrations, and he was first criticized by the authorities for his pro-democracy stance in 1987 during the official "campaign against bourgeois liberalization."

.. [18 YRS] [8 OTHERS: 7+ YRS]

■ **ZHANG Xiaoxu**, 32, formerly an assistant engineer at the No.2 Telephone Substation of the Qingdao Bureau of Post and Telecommunications, Shandong Province, was tried on charges of "counterrevolutionary propaganda and incitement" sometime before the end of 1989 and sentenced to 15 years' imprisonment and five years' subsequent deprivation of political rights. According to the official *1990 Qingdao Yearbook,* "On June 5 and 6, 1989, Zhang went on two separate occasions to the front gate of the Qingdao Municipal People's Government offices and delivered counterrevolutionary speeches before a crowd of several thousand people; he openly advocated the overthrow of the proletarian dictatorship and the socialist system, thereby committing the crime of counterrevolutionary propaganda and

incitement." (By the end of 1989, moreover, "a total of nine people were convicted of counterrevolutionary crimes in Qingdao" in connection with the May-June pro-democracy movement there.)

Zhang Xiaoxu is a veteran dissident. In 1980, according to the official source, he took part in an "illegal organization" known as the *Friends of Democracy Study Society.* After the banning of this group, which was presumably one of the many such organizations that emerged during the nationwide 1978-81 Democracy Wall movement, Zhang was "criticized and educated" by the authorities. His current place of imprisonment is not known.

. . . . [15 YRS]

Shanghai

■ **FU Shenqi** - see p.10
. . . . [3 YRS]

■ **PAN Weiming**, 42, was sentenced to four years in prison on January 24, 1992 for alleged "hooligan offenses" (*New York Times,* February 13, 1992) including a liaison with a prostitute on March 4, 1991 in a hotel in Chengdu, the capital of Sichuan Province. According to an Asia Watch source, not only was the police raid on his hotel room an entrapment, but his December 26, 1991 secret trial had less to do with the "womanizing" with which he was charged and which he did not deny, than with his support for the pro-democracy movement. In particular, Pan is said to have been involved as an adviser to pro-democracy activists in Shanghai who had tried, in early 1991, to launch more organized activities. Instead of the 15-day period of detention and administrative fine which is normally imposed for patronizing a prostitute, Pan was brought back to Shanghai by the authorities on March 21, held under a warrant of "shelter and investigation" in the city's No.1 Detention Center, repeatedly quizzed about his pro-democracy contacts and formally arrested on June 19, 1991. His apartment was thoroughly searched and notebooks, letters, address books and manuscripts were confiscated.

During the mid-1980s, Pan served as head of the Shanghai Propaganda Department, and during his time in office he loosened Party control over the city's writers and artists. He lost that post in 1987 after the removal from office of his patron, the late Party chief Hu Yaobang. Demoted to the post of Party secretary for the Shanghai News and Publication Bureau, Pan was then suspended from that position also soon after the June 1989 crackdown in Beijing and reportedly expected to be expelled from the Party. Unemployed, Pan eventually found work as a free-lance film-maker and photographer, and he was engaged in a film project at the time of his arrest.

. . . . [4 YRS]

■ **ZHANG Xianliang** - see p.13

. . . . [3 YRS]

■ **ZHOU Yuan**, **LIU Kai** and **TANG Weihua** were convicted on July 8, 1992 by the Shanghai Municipal People's Court on charges of forming a "counterrevolutionary organization," the *Zhonghua Tongmeng Hui (Chinese Alliance Association)*. The group, which was smashed by the police in April 1992, had been established with a total of eight members two years earlier. Zhou received a five-year term and is now being held at the Shanghai Municipal Prison, his appeal to the Shanghai Supreme People's Court having been rejected in October. In prison, he has reportedly been put to work making expensive gloves for export, and monthly visits by his family are canceled if he fails to meet his production quotas. Both Liu Kai, 22, formerly a waiter at the Westin Hotel in Shanghai, and Tang Weihua received two-year sentences.

. . . . [2, 2, 5 YRS]

Shanxi

■ **DING Junze**, a 52-year old former lecturer in the department of philosophy at Shanxi University, was sentenced on June 25, 1990, to 12 years' imprisonment and three years' subsequent deprivation of political rights on charges of "counter-revolutionary propaganda and incitement." By 1992, Ding had developed a series of severe medical ailments in prison, and by July 1993, his condition had worsened to the point that he had to be transferred to the Shanxi No.109 Labor-Reform Hospital, located at Dongtaipu. In August that year, Ding's wife **Zhang Ye**, a teacher at Taiyuan No.22 Middle School, revealed that Ding had been close to death, suffering from high blood pressure, heart disease and arteriosclerosis as well as bone spurs on his cervical vertebra *South China Morning Post* (August 25, 1993).

Zhang went on to recount that when moved to the hospital in early July, Ding was in a semiconscious state and experiencing severe chest pains. A week later, when she saw him on her monthly visit, he was on an intravenous drip, too weak to read a newspaper's headlines. He recovered somewhat, but in addition to his cardiovascular problems, Ding was said to be suffering from malnutrition. Moreover, his toe, which had been broken in prison, reportedly had not healed properly; although it had been re-set three times, Ding reportedly was using crutches and moving with great difficulty. There is concern that he may even be crippled for life. Prison doctors reportedly confirmed to Zhang that Ding was suffering from various heart problems including arrhythmia, high blood pressure, hardening of the arteries and severe heart pain (possibly angina). In addition, he suffers from Meunier's Disease, an affliction of the middle ear that causes painful dizziness. Despite her husband's rapidly deteriorating condition, Zhang's frequent applications to the judicial authorities for his release on bail to secure proper medical treatment have all been ignored.

For refusing to sign his arrest warrant in June 1989, Ding was attacked by a police officer with an electric baton and badly beaten. After sentencing, along with eleven other Shanxi intellectuals, all also convicted of "counterrevolutionary propaganda and incitement," he was sent to the Shanxi Provincial No.1 Prison in Qi County. On August 12, 1992, when Ding's terminally ill mother was hospitalized, managers of the Xinhua Chemical Factory submitted medical certificates to the prison authorities and requested that Ding be released on medical bail. Permission was denied, and Ding was not even allowed to attend his mother's funeral. Since his arrest, the family has undergone severe financial hardship.

Ding, who is originally from Tianjin, was first detained on June 27, 1989 and formally arrested on July 3. Following his conviction in June 1990, Ding appealed, but the Shanxi Provincial High People's Court upheld the original verdict. The court declared that during May and June 1989, Ding had "conspired to form the Shanxi University Students Autonomous Federation" and helped set up a broadcasting station, *Wind of Democracy*. He allegedly "criticized the government" and "directed others to take to the streets and factories to conduct counterrevolutionary propaganda and incitement." In addition, "Ding interfered in the activities of the [banned] Provincial Workers Autonomous Federation and influenced Li Fufa (see p.112), a worker at Yuantai Steel Factory to lead workers in the factory to participate in illegal activities by students. After Li was taken into custody, Ding organized students to demonstrate outside the factory, disrupting the normal production schedule." After June 4, 1989, moreover, he "organized a memorial service for those who died in Beijing." The Chinese authorities have never publicly reported Ding's arrest and sentencing, and requests for information by the U.S. government in November 1991 elicited no response from Chinese officials. In mid-summer 1993, a report surfaced that Ding had been released, but this appears to have been a misconstrual of the news of his transfer to the prison hospital.

. . . . [12 YRS]

■ **GE Hu**, 33, a lecturer at the Shanxi College of Coal Industry Management and one of a group of twelve intellectuals from Shanxi Province (see Ding Junze, above), was tried on charges of "counter-revolutionary propaganda and incitement" in November 1989 by the Shanxi Taiyuan Intermediate People's Court and sentenced to seven years' imprisonment and three years' subsequent deprivation of political rights. Like most of the political prisoners at Shanxi No.1, Ge's health has seriously deteriorated since his arrival there. On September 8, 1993, he suddenly lost sight in his right eye, and four days later was admitted to the No.109 Labor-Reform Hospital (located in Taiyuan City's Dongtaipu district), where doctors made a confirmed diagnosis that he had suffered a cerebral thrombosis. Despite the gravity of his condition and the prison hospital's inability to provide adequate treatment, Ge has been refused "release on bail for medical treatment" *(baowai jiuyi)*.

First detained on June 13, 1989, Ge was formally arrested on July 27 and is serving his sentence at Shanxi Provincial No.1 Prison in Qi County.

According to the court verdict, on June 5, 1989 Ge made a speech in May 1 Square on behalf of the faculty and staff of Taiyuan colleges at a memorial meeting commemorating the victims of the June 4 Beijing massacre. In it, he graphically described how tanks had crushed young demonstrators, a statement the verdict condemned as "provocative." After organizing a large scale "illegal" demonstration, Ge, on the afternoon of June 6 "called a meeting to reorganize the *Shanxi University Planning Committee* in order to broadcast the truth about June 3 and 4" (see also Zhao Jinwu p.491). At the meeting, he "received people from Beijing University and other higher educational institutions who claimed to be eyewitnesses [to the events in Tiananmen Square]." Ge then again went to May 1 Square and made further "counterrevolutionary speeches."

Since her husband's trial, Ge Hu's wife, a teacher in the foreign language department of Shanxi University, has experienced extreme hardship in caring for herself, Ge and their small child. Prison guards demand payment for various "services" when she visits her husband, and she has effectively to pay for his upkeep in prison. Numerous petitions for a reduction of Ge's sentence have gone unanswered.

. . . . [7 YRS]

■ **HU Jian**[1], 43, formerly a lecturer in the Department of Business Administration at Taiyuan Industrial College, was tried on June 20, 1990 by the Shanxi Taiyuan Intermediate People's Court on charges of "counterrevolutionary propaganda and incitement" and sentenced to ten years' imprisonment for his role in the 1989 pro-democracy movement in Taiyuan, Shanxi Province (see Ge Hu, above). (NB: It is possible that this is the same person as Hu Jian[2], see p.147.) Hu, currently held at the Shanxi Provincial No.1 Prison in Qi County, was reported in summer 1993 to have become mentally disturbed as a result of abusive prison conditions.

. . . . [10 YRS]

■ **WANG Xinlong**, 50, a deputy director and assistant professor in the Department of Political Studies at Shanxi University was tried on March 23, 1990 on charges of "counter-revolutionary rioting" and later sentenced to eight years' imprisonment and three years' subsequent deprivation of political rights. Held at Shanxi Provincial No.1 Prison in Qi County, Wang has reportedly suffered a steady decline in his health over the past three years, to the point where he is now said to be "extremely frail."

According to the court verdict, on the morning of May 17, 1989 Wang delivered a pro-democracy speech to students and teachers in front of the main building at the university. That afternoon, "He strongly supported a student going on hunger strike in front of the provincial government building." In an allegedly "inflammatory" speech in the city's May 1 Square on May 20, moreover, Wang further declared, "What Li Peng says cannot represent the central government. A government which sustains itself by knives cannot last long." He characterized Premier Li

as "the butcher who suppressed the student movement" and "a political hooligan," and led the crowd in shouting such slogans as "down with Li Peng." On May 24, according to the verdict, Wang "incited students and teachers at Shanxi university, saying: 'Today's demonstration is to attack Li Peng.'" That afternoon, Wang and another man "decided to demonstrate in the name of Shanxi intellectuals," ordering a third man to make banners for the occasion. On June 4, he again "spread rumors" in May 1 Square and denounced the government's suppression of the student movement.

Wang, a native of Lingchuan County, was taken into custody on June 16, 1989 and formally arrested on January 2, 1990. In October 1991, his wife, **Zhao Hongyue**, who had been diagnosed as having a uterine tumor and required a total hysterectomy and three-month recuperative period, wrote to the provincial Party Secretary and to prison authorities requesting Wang's temporary release. In her letters she explained she had a 95-year-old mother and a teenage daughter at home, both of whom required care. All the letters went unanswered, as have repeated requests for a reduction of her husband's sentence. Zhao teaches at the No.27 Middle School in Taiyuan.

. . . . [8 YRS]

■ **YAO Huxian**, 37, president of his class (the 1985 entering class) in the pediatrics department of Shanxi Medical College, was tried by the Shanxi Taiyuan Intermediate People's Court on charges of "counter-revolutionary propaganda and incitement" and sentenced on February 12, 1990 to six years' imprisonment and three years' subsequent deprivation of political rights. A native of Licheng County, Yao was taken into custody on October 17, 1989 and formally arrested on November 17. According to the verdict, on June 6, 1989 Yao drafted an open letter and urgent appeal to the people, for which the court accused him of openly spreading rumors and plotting to overthrow the government. The letter reportedly said: "Li Peng and a small group of anti-communists committed bloodshed in Tiananmen Square and brutally suppressed the patriotic students. This action clearly demonstrates that they are the true public enemy of the people of China." In addition, Yao allegedly "instigated students to write big character posters and post them up on doors of the medical school, in May 1 Square and at the provincial government building."

At the end of July 1991, equipped with a medical notice from the People's Hospital of Licheng County, his relatives requested Yao's temporary release from prison to visit his dying father. Permission was denied, as was permission to attend the subsequent funeral. Yao's wife, a teacher at Shanxi Normal University, reportedly has great financial difficulties in providing for herself, Yao and their small child.

. . . . [6 YRS]

Sichuan

■ **LIAO Yiwu**, 34, a poet from Chongqing who worked at the Fuling City Cultural Center, was arrested in March 1990 in Chengdu, Sichuan Province together with five other poets for making a secret videotape, *The Massacre*, commemorating the June 4, 1989 crackdown. Liao was later tried and sentenced to four years' imprisonment for "counterrevolutionary propaganda and incitement." Initially detained in Sichuan Province No.2 Prison in Chongqing, he is currently being held in the Dazu County Prison, Sichuan Province. Liao, who authored the video script, had also earlier recorded an audiotape, *The Requiem*, criticizing the Chinese leadership for ordering the army to fire on protesters in June 1989. Both the audio and video tapes were distributed by the group in an effort to break the government's news blockade and convey the truth about the "counterrevolutionary rebellion." The others, who were released without charge at the end of February 1992, included **WAN Xia**, a 31-year-old with a heart condition who held no formal job prior to his arrest; **LI Yawei**, a 30-year-old middle school teacher; **LIU Taiheng**[2], 37; **WANG Qing** (pen name **BA Tie**), a 37-year-old office worker; and **XUN Mingjun**, 29, also an office worker. According to the authorities, the five, who were held with Liao Yiwu in the Chongqing Detention Center, had "made mistakes, but were not guilty of crimes." (See also p.459).

. . . . [4 YRS]

■ **LIU XX** (given name unknown), 51, a teacher from Chongqing, was arrested sometime after 1989 and sentenced to four years' imprisonment for writing a letter to senior Communist Party leaders expressing his views on China's domestic political situation. He is currently being held at the Sichuan Province No.2 Prison in Chongqing (also known as the Sichuan New Life *Laodong* Factory).

. . . . [4 YRS]

■ **ZHENG Hengkang,** former general manager and vice-chairman of the Xinguang Industrial Import and Export Corporation in Sichuan Province, received a ten-year sentence from the Chengdu Intermediate People's Court for allegedly passing state secrets to a foreign reporter and "viciously attacking the policies of the Chinese Communist Party and socialist system" (*Zhongguo Qingnian Bao*, August 14, 1992, in *Reuters*, same day). Ousted from his job on August 1, 1989 after incurring "serious losses to the state" in a joint venture undertaken with a Hong Kong firm in 1986, Zheng fled on September 11. By June 29, 1990, he had escaped to Kunming. While there, Zheng allegedly obtained more than ten secret documents, including one described as containing "important state secrets," and then passed them via his son to a foreign journalist (identity unknown). The subsequent publication of the document "had a severe political effect at home," according to *Zhongguo Qingnian Bao*.

. . . . [10 YRS]

Tianjin

■ **CHEN Jie,** a 33-year-old man, was arrested during the June 1989 crackdown and later sentenced to eight years' imprisonment for alleged "counterrevolutionary propaganda and incitement." Other than that he is currently being held at the Tianjin No.1 Prison, no further information on Chen's case is available.

. . . . [8 YRS]

■ **LIAO Zheng,** a 30-year-old former teacher at the Tianjin Textile Industry College, was arrested on June 15, 1989 and later tried for "counter-revolutionary activities" and sentenced to seven years' imprisonment. After witnessing the crackdown in Beijing on June 3-4, 1989, Liao returned to Tianjin, made speeches at his school about what he had seen and called for the removal of Premier Li Peng. Liao's imprisonment has destroyed his marriage. After his trial, his wife was forced to give up their housing, her application for a passport to study abroad was rejected, and the couple eventually agreed to divorce. Liao is serving his sentence at Tianjin No.1 Prison.

. . . . [7 YRS]

■ **LI Zhongjie,** around 40, an instructor at the Tianjin Textile Industry College, was arrested shortly after June 4, 1989 and later tried on charges of "counterrevolutionary propaganda and incitement." According to Asia Watch's information, Li received a six-year sentence; in October 1993, however, Chinese officials said he had been sentenced to five years. He is serving his sentence at Tianjin No.1 Prison.

. . . . [5-6 YRS]

■ **ZHU Wenhua,** a cadre at the Tianjin No.2 Wristwatch Factory, and

WANG Ning, about 35, a trade union official at Tianjin Hongqiao District College of Planning and Design, were tried after June 1989 on charges of "organizing a counterrevolutionary group" and "counterrevolutionary propaganda and incitement" and sentenced to, respectively, six years and eight years' imprisonment. The charges referred to Zhu's role as a standing committee member of the Tianjin Workers Autonomous Federation (TWAF), a dissident labor group founded during the May 1989 protests, and to Wang's role as chairman of the group.

Initially held in Tianjin No.1 Prison, Zhu was subjected to severe physical abuse, including beatings, shocks with electric batons and being made to wear tight handcuffs which painfully restrict blood circulation. In addition, Zhu, a 33-year-old graduate of the Tianjin Staff and Employees University, was repeatedly held in prolonged solitary confinement, once for a period of six months without break. He was later transferred from Tianjin No.1, and his current place of detention is not known.

Wang Ning, about 35, was knocked from his bicycle shortly after June 4, 1989 by the security officials who arrested him, and suffered untreated injuries which reportedly left him crippled in one leg. Currently held in Tianjin No.1 Prison, Wang has reportedly been beaten and tortured by prison guards. In October 1993, Chinese officials confirmed that Wang's jail term was eight years.

. . . . [6, 8 YRS]

Zhejiang

■ **CHEN Gang**[1], a student from Ningbo, Zhejiang Province, was tried and sentenced for his part in the 1989 pro-democracy movement, according to a November 1991 official Chinese response to inquiries from the U.S. government. Chen's sentence has been variously reported as being either three years or five years' imprisonment.

. . . . [3-5 YRS]

■ **CUI Jiancheng**, 28, and **ZHANG Weiping**, 27, both formerly students of traditional Chinese painting at the Zhejiang Academy of Fine Arts, were both sentenced soon after June 4, 1989 in connection with an unauthorized flag-lowering to commemorate the victims of the Beijing massacre. Zhang, the first student known to have been tried after June 4, 1989, was tried by the Hangzhou Intermediate People's Court on August 26, 1989 on charges of "counterrevolutionary propaganda and incitement," and sentenced to nine years' imprisonment and three years' subsequent deprivation of political rights after reportedly "confessing" to all charges. In fall 1993, a report surfaced that Zhang may have been released, but the news was never confirmed and probably was incorrect.

According to a restricted-circulation *(neibu)* official account, "On the morning of June 5, Zhang witnessed fellow-student Cui [Jiancheng] lowering by one section the national flag of China that flew above the provincial government offices. At 3:00 P.M. the following day, Zhang made an international telephone call to

Voice of America [VOA]...and informed it of the incident." That same evening, VOA broadcast the news, which Zhang then taped and gave to his campus radio center for re-broadcasting. The official source added, "During the turmoil, Zhang drew numerous cartoons insulting and slandering State leaders, and spread political rumors that he heard on VOA and BBC." (In CCS pp.252-3: see note on p.276, below; see also *New York Times,* June 21, 1989.)

The authorities have never revealed what sentence Cui Jiancheng, who presumably was viewed as the "chief culprit" of the case, received. Both he and Zhang were confirmed as sentenced, however, in a November 1991 official Chinese response to U.S. government inquiries.

.... [9, ? YRS]

Place Unknown

■ **LI * dong**, 33, a medical worker; **CHEN * feng**, 25, unemployed; **PAN * hui**, 27, a primary school teacher; **RUAN * xue**, 24, and **YU * you**, 33, both peasants; **CHEN * juan** (female), 25, a middle school teacher; **LIN * shou**, 27, a primary school teacher; **LI * jin**, 27, a peasant; and **CHEN * chun**, 26, and **XIE * ying** (female), 20, both middle school teachers, were all sentenced to unknown terms for "counterrevolutionary activities" sometime after June 1989. According to the authorities, in February 1987 they organized a "counterrevolutionary group" called the *China People's Democratic Party (Zhongguo Renmin Minzhu Dang),* which allegedly called

for "the overthrow of the Communist Party and the present autocratic state power." By May 1987, "ringleaders Li [* dong], Chen [* feng] and Pan had recruited a total of 35 counter-revolutionary members across six different districts and counties," and the group proceeded to hold a series of secret "counterrevolutionary meetings" at which the dissident party's charter and rules of organization were formulated.

Between October 1987 and February 1988,

*Li, Chen and Pan actively operated a dried mushroom factory, making it the office for their 'temporary provincial committee of the * region' and using the profits to fund their counter-revolutionary activities...they established a 'youth corps' (shaonian tuan) and a 'spiritual combat center' (jing-wu guan) [possibly some kind of martial arts salon], and other such counterrevolutionary front organizations...They also hatched a counterrevolutionary plot to infiltrate the army, public security organs and Chinese Communist Party."*

In March 1989, "Li * dong, Chen * feng and Pan * hui hatched a conspiracy to travel to Guangdong, Hebei, Yunnan and other provinces to set up counterrevolutionary bases. Li * dong even went to a foreign country [name censored] to seek support from enemy forces." In December 1987, the group had "bought an ink-mimeograph machine and printed more than 200 counterrevolutionary leaflets, which they distributed at the * Provincial

Hospital, * Park, * Provincial Museum and at the provincial government building." Then in June 1989, "they printed a further 100 or more counterrevolutionary leaflets, which they distributed at the * Supply and Marketing Cooperative, the bus station and other places."

At their trial, which probably occurred later in 1989 or sometime in 1990, Li * dong, Chen * feng and Pan * hui were convicted on charges of "organizing and leading a counter-revolutionary group" and "counter-revolutionary propaganda and incitement." The other seven defendants were all convicted on charges of "actively participating in a counterrevolutionary group" and "counterrevolutionary propaganda and incitement." Although the sentences are unknown, it is likely that all the defendants received long prison terms and were therefore still behind bars in early 1994. The official account of the case (in CCS pp.135-38: see note on p.276, below) censored both the prisoners' middle names (denoted above by asterisks) and also the location of the alleged activities.

. . . . [10 X ? YRS]

Workers and peasants

Beijing
■ **CHEN Yong** - see p.355
. . . . [LIFE]

■ **WANG Yongming**, 32, from the Beijing Data Processing Research Institute, and **DOU Linhuai,** a cadre in charge of a street in the Haidian District of Beijing, were arrested after driving the corpse of a nine-year-old boy around the city on June 4-5, 1989. Their purpose reportedly was to show citizens that martial law troops had even slain children. Wang was sentenced to five years' imprisonment and is currently being held in Beijing No.2 Prison. Charged with violating the traffic law and creating a disturbance, Dou was sentenced to a four-year prison term and presumably has now been released.

. . . . [5 YRS]

■ **GUO Jinghua**, a fruit tree expert from the Haidian District of Beijing, was sentenced to five years' imprisonment on charges of "counter-revolutionary propaganda and incitement" in connection with the May 1989 protests. Other than that Gao was arrested in July 1989, no additional information on the case is available.

. . . . [5 YRS]

■ **LI Hongjiang**, 23, was sentenced in May 1990 to life in prison for alleged corruption and for spreading rumors, according to an Asia Watch source. Li, who was arrested in early January 1990, reportedly made a donation of funds to the pro-democracy movement from the joint venture company where he was employed as assistant to the manager. According to the source, Li had the authority to approve the donation. There is speculation that the harshness of Li's sentence was attributable to his close relationship with **Ke Feng**, a leading democracy figure who escaped from China.

. . . . [LIFE]

■ **LI Nan,** the 35-year-old owner of The Unique House, a restaurant in Beijing, and the youngest chef ever to reach China's "Special First Level," was sentenced to a seven-year prison term for "counterrevolutionary propaganda and incitement." According to an account in the *San Francisco Examiner* (November 19, 1991), even after the declaration of martial law in Beijing, Li provided large quantities of food and financial support to the students in Tiananmen Square. In addition, he recorded nine hours of videotape of events during the crackdown in Beijing on June 3-4.

Li was arrested by officers of the People's Liberation Army on June 14, 1989 and sent to the Xuanwumen Detention Center. After six months of intensive interrogation, he reportedly signed a confession. After another eight months, he was transferred to Beijing No.1 Prison, before finally being transferred to the Shandong Province Beishu Labor Reform Detachment (also known as the Beishu Shengjian Graphite Mine). In its sales brochures, the Beishu Graphite Mine boasts that its products "are sold in 31 countries and regions in five continents." Li Nan, however, has reportedly been put to work in the prison kitchen.
. . . . [7 YRS]

■ **SUN Chuanheng,** a 22-year-old unemployed worker arrested on June 7, 1989 and charged that September, was sentenced to life imprisonment on a charge of arson. On the night of June 3, 1989, he allegedly "directed others" to burn a People's Liberation Army vehicle. Held in Beijing Prison No.2,

Sun suffers from a serious stomach ailment and a deteriorating eye condition. He reportedly has severe back pain resulting from torture. According to an Asia Watch source personally acquainted with Sun, the government's allegations of violence are entirely spurious.
. . . . [LIFE]

■ **TIAN Bomin,** a 24-year-old studio worker and member of the Beijing Workers Autonomous Federation who allegedly drafted and distributed the leaflet, "Declaration of the Dragon" (see Guo Yaxiong p.563) in Tiananmen Square, was sentenced to five years' imprisonment for larceny and fraud, according to a Chinese response to International Labor Organization inquiries (November 1991). He was arrested on June 26, 1989 in Yunnan Province, where he had allegedly fled in order "to spread unrest" through audio and video tapes of speeches and demonstrations by students and workers in Beijing. (According to an August 4, 1989 *Agence France Presse* dispatch, 36 others who were trying to flee the country were also arrested in Yunnan. They allegedly took part in "counter-revolutionary rebellion" in Beijing or provoked "turmoil" in Shanghai or Chengdu. Border police seized some 200 reactionary books, poems and video cassettes.)
. . . . [5 YRS]

■ **WANG Guoqing, LI Baoqin, DONG Huaimin, WANG Zhongxian** and **WEI Ren** were sentenced for "counterrevolutionary propaganda and incitement," according to notices posted outside the Beijing Intermediate People's Court on February 25, 1992. Wang Guoqing and Li Baoqin received five-year terms; Dong Huaimin was jailed for four years; and Wang Zhongxian and Wei Ren received three-year terms (*Da Gong Bao*, February 28, 1992, in FBIS, same date). Two others, **WANG Lidong**, who apparently was arrested in 1990, and **BAI Chunxiang**, were also convicted. Wang received a two-year sentence, while Bai, for reasons unknown, was "exempt from criminal punishment."

Li Baoqin, a construction worker about 30 years old, was reportedly a picket team leader in the Beijing Workers Autonomous Federation (BWAF) and participated in the May 28, 1989 negotiations with the Public Security Bureau for the release of BWAF members. Arrested after the June 4 crackdown, he was held successively in Paoju and Banbuqiao Detention Centers and at Qincheng Prison. Li's whereabouts as of December 1993 were unclear, but he and Wang Guoqing, about whom nothing else is known, are probably being held at either Beijing No.1 or No.2 Prisons.
. . . . [2 X 5 YRS]

■ **WANG Jiansheng**[1], a worker at the Beijing Glass Factory, was sentenced to six years in prison after his trial and conviction on January 5, 1991 (*Reuters*, April 9, 1991). No additional details are available.
. . . . [6 YRS]

■ **WANG Lianxi** - see p.354
. . . . [LIFE]

■ **WANG Yasheng**, a Beijing city bus driver, charged with using his bus to block the entrance of martial law troops into the city, was sentenced to five years in prison for "undermining transportation" (Human Rights in China).
. . . . [5 YRS]

■ **XIAO Delong** - see p.13
. . . . [3 YRS]

■ **ZHAO Pinju**, who ran a small printing shop, was arrested in July 1989 and is serving a 13-year sentence in Beijing No.2 Prison for allegedly stealing guns, carrying arms and engaging in violence. According to a reliable Asia Watch source, however, Zhao had found a gun during the June 4, 1989 crackdown in Beijing, but quickly discarded it. In prison, Zhao is suffering from hepatitis and a stomach ailment, frequently vomits blood and is severely emaciated. According to his elder brother, **ZHAO Pinlu**, Zhao Pinju was tortured in prison in part because he refused to reveal Zhao Pinlu's whereabouts.

Zhao Pinlu, whose name, address and photograph appeared on the Chinese government's August 19, 1989 secret compilation of "most wanted lists," and whom the government declared dead and missing in 1991, escaped China after almost three years on the run. A 36-year-old Beijing native, formerly employed at the housing management section of the Ministry of Railways but suspended from his duties prior to June 4, 1989, Zhao was active in the Beijing Workers Autonomous Federation. He now lives in the U.S.

. . . . [13 YRS]

Guizhou

■ **LI Xinfu (Xingfu)** and **CHEN Jiahu**, arrested in late August 1989 while allegedly in possession of "counterrevolutionary" programs, letters and membership registration forms, were charged with "organizing a counterrevolutionary group" known as the *China Savior Party* in 1988 in the Wuchuan Gelao-Miao Autonomous County of Guizhou Province. Both were later reportedly sentenced to "long prison terms" (*Renmin Gong'an Bao [People's Public Security News]*, in FBIS, November 3, 1989; *Fazhi Ribao*, in FBIS, November 7). Chinese officials confirmed the sentencing to the U.S. government in November 1991.

In addition, ten other leaders and core activists of the underground party were reportedly denounced by informers in late November 1989, then arrested and put on trial. The twelve were described as "mainly counter-revolutionaries and criminal offenders who continued to oppose the people after their [previous] release from prison." The accused were charged with "forging central documents and cheating people out of more than 7,000 *yuan* in cash by means of purchasing counterrevolutionary money and shares." However, the main charges apparently related to the defendants activities during the 1989 pro-democracy movement. "In May of this year, while turmoil occurred in the whole nation, Li Xinfu went to

Chongqing to watch the situation and to collect and copy leaflets, and he encouraged core members to 'put objectives and aspirations into practice'" in order to overthrow the Chinese Communist Party. Li and Chen had allegedly served previous prison terms for organizing a "counter-revolutionary party."

The *China Savior Party*, dedicated to upholding Sun Yatsen's Three People's Principles, reportedly comprised a total of 118 members from four counties and 28 towns. The Public Security Bureau of Wuchuan was said to have cracked the case under the leadership of higher public security organizations and with the cooperation of police bureaus from Meiyun, Zhengan and Fenggang counties.

. . . . [12 X ? YRS]

Guangdong

■ **HUANG Junjie**, 72, a retired railroad worker from Hengyang City in Hunan Province, was sentenced after June 1989 by the Guangzhou City Intermediate Railways Court, Guangdong Province, to 10 years' imprisonment and three years' subsequent deprivation of political rights on charges of "counter-revolutionary propaganda and incitement." According to an internal report by the Supreme People's Court (see TC p.379), "Between noon and 3:00 P.M. on June 5, 1989, Huang made two speeches to students who were blocking trains at the Hengyang Railway Station and to the surrounding crowd...in which he spread rumors, inflamed people's emotions and spread counterrevolutionary propaganda and incitement."

Huang allegedly declared, "There has been bloodshed at Tiananmen, the People's Liberation Army has gunned down with automatic weapons or crushed to death with tanks between one and two thousand people; among the dead were old ladies and even children"; "The students have been bloodily suppressed at Tiananmen Square, and blood debts must be repaid in kind"; "Deng Xiaoping, Li Peng and Yang Shangkun must step down"; and "China is now being run by a gang of profiteers." Huang was also accused of encouraging the students to "emulate the spirit of the 1927 Beijing-Hankou Railroad Strike" and of inciting police officers by saying, "The Public Security Bureau must not suppress the students and the masses, you should stand on the side of the people." In view of Huang's considerable age, there is cause for serious concern as to his likely state of health in prison. His current place of incarceration is not known.

. . . . [10 YRS]

▪ **Liu Baiqiang**, 26, a prisoner originally serving a 10-year sentence for robbery in Guangdong Province at the time of his second "offense," was sentenced to an additional eight years' imprisonment after June 1989 for writing leaflets in his prison cell expressing support for the pro-democracy movement. According to an internal report by the Supreme People's Court (see TC p.377), on June 6, 1989, upon hearing of the "counter-revolutionary rebellion" in Beijing, Liu

secretly wrote out three leaflets bearing the words, "Down with Deng Xiaoping and Li Peng," "Long Live Freedom," "Deng Xiaoping should step down" and "Tyranny." After showing these to his cellmates, he "attached them to the legs of locusts, and then released the insects out of the prison cell [with the aim of] inciting people to overthrow the political power of the people's democratic dictatorship." At his subsequent trial, the Jiangmen City Intermediate People's Court of Guangdong Province pronounced Liu Baiqiang guilty of "counter-revolutionary propaganda and incitement" and declared that "his crimes are heinous and he must be severely punished." The court sentenced him to serve a total of 17 years' imprisonment, including the remaining nine years of his original sentence, and five years' subsequent deprivation of political rights.

. . . . [8 YRS]

Hubei

▪ **LIANG Xiaozhong** and **SU Jingping**, both workers in the Wuhan (Hubei Province) Steel Factory and members of the Wuhan Workers Autonomous Federation, were sentenced for involvement in the 1989 pro-democracy movement. According to an Asia Watch source, Su Jingping was sentenced to a five-year term for "disturbing the social order" and as of June 1993 was being held, reportedly in extremely poor health, at the Shayang Labor Reform Detachment, a vast prison-labor camp in Hubei Province. Liang Xiaozhong also received a five-year sentence, but nothing further is known about his case.

. . . . [2 X 5 YRS]

■ **SUN Sanbao**, a worker at a shipbuilding facility in Hubei Province, was sentenced to eight years' imprisonment for allegedly organizing a strike during the 1989 pro-democracy movement. According to an Asia Watch source, he was one of 19 people in Hubei heavily sentenced for "counterrevolutionary" activities. Two others from the shipyard in Wuchang, **LIN Ziyong** and **SUN Wufu**, were also sentenced. The latter, a leading member of the Workers Autonomous Federation, was being held in Hubei No.1 Prison as of May 1993.

. . . . [8 YRS] [2 X ? YRS]

Hubei

■ **ZHANG** Minpeng - see p.14

. . . . [5 YRS]

Hunan

■ **CHEN GANG**[2], a factory worker in Xiangtan, Hunan Province, was arrested in June 1989 and sentenced to death (later reduced to death with a two-year reprieve) for calling for justice for his younger brother, **CHEN Ding**. A student in the 1987 entering class at Changsha Railroad College in Hunan Province, Chen Ding was sentenced in July 1989 to one year's imprisonment on charges of "counter-revolutionary propaganda and incitement." He was released in mid-1990 and permitted to resume his studies. Shortly after the June 4 crackdown, Chen Ding returned to Xiangtan and, along with a group of fellow students, urged the workers at a local factory, the Xiangtan Electrical Machinery Plant (a large factory in Hunan with several tens of thousands of employees), to stage a strike in opposition to the government repression. When the young Chen's arm was broken by a group of factory security men led by the factory's security section chief, more than 1,000 workers spontaneously broke into the security chief's home and carried off or burned expensive furnishings and electrical goods. Six or seven workers, including **PENG Shi**, **LIU Zhihua** and **LIU Jian**[1], Chen, and his elder brother **CHEN Gang** - who did not, however, take part in the break-in - were then arrested. Seven days later, Chen Ding was indicted by the Xiangtan City Intermediate People's Procuracy; his trial was held the next day.

Shortly afterwards, Chen Gang was also arrested. At first, his crime was said to be "counterrevolutionary propaganda and incitement," but when charges were laid seven days after his arrest, the crime had been changed to one of "assembling a mob for beating, smashing, and looting." And when the public trial was held the next day, the charges had been raised once again to "hooliganism." Chen Gang received a death sentence, commuted in May 1990 to death with a two-year suspension of execution. For ten months, from the time of his initial detention until the final review of death sentence, Chen Gang was kept shackled hand and foot.

Peng, 21 or 22, Liu Zhihua, 21,

and Liu Jian, 26, were sentenced to life imprisonment by the Xiangtan City Intermediate People's Court on charges of "hooliganism," Peng for having led the attack and Liu Zhihua for "incitement through anti-government speeches." All four men are currently being held in Longxi Prison (Hunan Provincial No.6).

[DEATH W/REPRIEVE] [3 X LIFE]

■ **DING Longhua**, a factory worker in his thirties and a member of the Standing Committee of the Hengyang Workers Autonomous Federation in Hunan Province, was tried in February 1990 by the Hengyang City Intermediate People's Court on a charge of "counterrevolutionary propaganda and incitement" and sentenced to six years' imprisonment. During the 1989 pro-democracy movement, Ding made public speeches and organized strikes among workers. After June 4, he organized a city-wide general strike in coordination with the Hengyang Students Autonomous Federation, and was arrested shortly thereafter.

. . . . [6 YRS]

■ **DONG Qi, HE Jianming, LIANG Chao** and **DAI Dingxiang**, all workers or residents in Changsha, Hunan Province, were sentenced respectively to five, four, three and three years by the Changsha Eastern District Court in October 1989 on charges of "assembling a crowd to create a disturbance." He, Liang and Dai have presumably now been released upon completion of their terms. During the 1989 pro-democracy movement, the four men helped organize citizens groups in support of the students. On the evening of May 20, hearing a rumor that the army had entered the city and was heading for Dongfanghong Square, they went to the Changsha Railway Station to discuss countermeasures with student leaders, but were intercepted by police officers who discovered that the four were all carrying small pen-knives (a common and by no means necessarily sinister act). Arrested on charges of "carrying weapons," they were held prior to trial at the Changsha No.1 Jail. Dong Qi's current place of imprisonment is not known.

. . . . [5 YRS]

■ **GONG Songlin**, a resident of Xiangtan City, Hunan Province, in his twenties, was tried as a "common criminal" shortly after June 4, 1989 by the Yuhu District Court, Xiangtan, and sentenced to five years' imprisonment. During the 1989 pro-democracy movement, he took part in numerous demonstrations and other protest activities, and was subsequently arrested for his alleged participation in the "Pingzheng Road Police Station Incident" (see p.561).

. . . . [5 YRS]

■ **HU Min, GUO Yunqiao, MAO Yuejin, WANG Zhaobo, HUANG Lixin, HUANG Fan, WAN Yuewang, PAN Qiubao**, and **YUAN Shuzhu**, workers or residents of Yueyang City, Hunan Province, between 20 and 35 years old, were sentenced in September 1989 by the Yueyang City Intermediate People's Court on charges of "hooliganism." Guo received a death sentence, suspended for two years; Hu and Mao were given 15-year prison terms; Wang, Huang Lixin, Huang Fan, Wan, Pan and Yuan received sentences ranging from 7 to 15 years. Arrested on June 9, and detained first in Yueyang Prison, all nine were being held in Hengyang Prison (Provincial No.2) as of May 1992.

During the 1989 pro-democracy movement, the men organized the Yueyang Workers Autonomous Federation and on several occasions led demonstrations and strikes. After the events of June 4, they lay down on the railroad tracks on Yueyang's Baling Railway Bridge to protest the violent acts of the government. Then, along with over 10,000 others, they marched carrying wreaths and setting off firecrackers, to the offices of the municipal government and the seat of the municipal [Party] committee. There, they allegedly took down the sign saying "City Government" and trampled it underfoot, resulting in an "extremely odious influence."

. . . . [DEATH W/REPRIEVE]
[2 X 15 YRS] [6 X 7-15 YRS]

■ **HU Nianyou** - see p.355

. . . . [LIFE]

■ **LI Wangyang**, a 36-year-old worker at a Shaoyang (Hunan Province) factory, was tried in early 1990 by the Shaoyang City Intermediate People's Court on charges of "counterrevolutionary propaganda and incitement" and sentenced to 13 years' imprisonment. Initially held at Longxi Prison (Hunan Provincial No.6), he was later transferred to do hard labor at Yuanjiang Prison (Provincial No.1). (More recently, he may have been moved to a labor-reform farm near Yueyang.) During the 1989 democracy movement, Li helped organize the Shaoyang Workers Autonomous Federation and served as its chairman. Arrested on June 9 in Shaoyang City, he and his colleagues were charged with having "posted up banners, issued leaflets, carried out liaison trips, spread rumors, uttered reactionary slogans, incited workers to go on strike and proclaimed the founding of a completely independent and autonomous [workers] organization" (Hunan Ribao). There have been persistent reports that Wang has been severely ill-treated in prison over the past two years.

. . . . [13 YRS]

■ **LI Xiaodong**, a 25-year-old worker formerly employed at the Zhongnan Pharmaceutical Plant in Shaoyang City, Hunan Province, was tried in October 1989 by the Shaoyang Intermediate People's Court on charges of "counter-revolutionary propaganda and incitement" and sentenced to 13 years' imprisonment. He is now being held at Yuanjiang Prison (Provincial No.1). Li was a member of the Shaoyang Workers Autonomous Federation during the 1989 pro-democracy movement. On the evening of May 19, he led a group of workers to People's Square, the local government offices and to other sites around the city to demonstrate against the imposition of martial law in Beijing. As they marched, the workers shouted slogans which allegedly "incited the masses to

break into the government
headquarters." A clash with the police
followed. Li was arrested the following
day and taken to the Shaoyang jail.
.... [13 YRS]

■ LI Xiaoping, 28, a worker at a
factory in Shaoyang, Hunan Province,
was tried in early 1990 by the
Shaoyang Intermediate People's Court
on charges of "hooliganism" and
sentenced to six years' imprisonment
which he is serving in Longxi Prison
(Provincial No.6). He had served as
deputy-chief of the picket squad for the
Shaoyang Workers Autonomous
Federation during the 1989
pro-democracy movement and
participated in student demonstrations
and petition groups. On May 20, Li
allegedly led a crowd of citizens who
pushed their way into the municipal
Party Committee and government
offices. He was arrested the following
month.
.... [6 YRS]

■ LIANG Jianguo, a 26-year-old
employee of a guesthouse run by the
Hunan Provincial People's Political
Consultative Conference, was tried in
mid-1990 by the East District Court of
Changsha on "common criminal"
charges and sentenced to six years'
imprisonment. He allegedly was
involved both in the 1989 democracy
movement and in underground
pro-democracy work early in 1990.
Arrested in June 1990 and tried shortly
thereafter, Liang is held in Lingling
Prison (Provincial No.3).
.... [6 YRS]

■ WU Jianwei, in his twenties, a
worker at the Xiangtan Electrical
Machinery Plant, Hunan Province, was
tried at the end of 1989 by the Yuetang
District Court, Xiangtan Municipality,
on unknown charges and sentenced to
14 years' imprisonment. During the
1989 pro-democracy movement, he
allegedly "took part in creating
disturbances" and "shouted reactionary
slogans." These actions were said by
the authorities to have "led to serious
consequences." Wu was arrested soon
after June 4.
.... [14 YRS]

■ WU Tongfan, 40, a resident of
Fuzhong Alley, Nanyang Street,
Changsha, Hunan Province, was
sentenced in mid-1990 by the Changsha
Intermediate People's Court on a
charge of "counterrevolutionary
propaganda and incitement." The length
of his term is unknown. During the
1989 pro-democracy movement, Wu
allegedly had contacts with He Zhaohui
(see p.565), a leader of the Changsha
Workers Autonomous Federation, and
others in the pro-democracy movement.
Accused of "directing events from
behind the scenes," Wu is currently
imprisoned in Yuanjiang Prison (Hunan
Provincial No.1).
.... [? YRS]

■ XIONG Xiaohua, a 25-year-old
technician at the Xiangtan Power
Machinery Factory, Hunan Province
and a graduate of the Xiangtan
Mechanization Special School, was
sentenced in November 1989 by the
Xiangtan City Intermediate People's
Court to 13 years' imprisonment on a

charge of "hooliganism." He allegedly organized a group of former classmates to print and distribute propaganda materials during the 1989 pro-democracy movement and he shouted slogans during the Xiangtan May 29 Incident. Arrested in July 1989, Xiong is serving his sentence in Longxi Prison (Provincial No.6). His family lives near the Xiangtan Municipal People's Congress Building.

. . . . [13 YRS]

■ **YAN Bingliang**, a peasant from Dake in the Loudi District of Hunan, was sentenced to seven years' imprisonment for allegedly "disrupting traffic" during the May 1989 protests. According to sources familiar with the case, however, his real offense was to have conducted numerous "liaison trips" around Hunan Province during the protest movement. Held at first in Loudi Jail, Yan was transferred after trial to a nearby labor-reform farm to serve his sentence.

. . . . [7 YRS]

■ **YAN Xuewu**, a 26-year-old worker at the Xiangtan Municipal Motor Vehicle Parts Factory, Hunan Province, was tried soon after June 4, 1989 by the Yuhu District Court on a charge of "disturbing public order" and sentenced to five years' imprisonment. He was arrested for allegedly participating in an incident on May 22, 1989, during which a group of people were said to have "burst into" the Pingzheng Road Police Station in Yuhu (see p.561).

. . . . [5 YRS]

■ **YAO Guisheng** (alleged robbery, but principal activity was rescuing Workers Federation members) - see p.355

. . . . [15 YRS]

■ **YU Zhijian**, a 27-year-old teacher in the Tantou Wan Primary School in Dahu Town, Liuyang County, Hunan; **YU Dongyue**, fine arts editor of the *Liuyang News*; and **LU Decheng**, a 28-year-old worker in the Liuyang (Hunan Province) Public Motorbus Company, were tried on August 11, 1989 by the Beijing City Intermediate People's Court on charges of "counter-revolutionary sabotage and incitement." They were sentenced to, respectively, life, 20 years and 16 years' imprisonment.

During the 1989 pro-democracy movement, Yu Zhijian gave speeches in Liuyang, Changsha and other places. On May 19, together with Yu Dongyue and Lu, he went to Beijing. On May 23, the three defaced the large portrait of Mao Zedong overlooking Tiananmen Square by throwing ink and paint-filled eggs at it. They were arrested on the spot by student pickets and handed over to the authorities.

All three were sent back to Hunan to serve their sentences in Lingling Prison (Provincial No.3). Beijing officials reportedly instructed Hunan prison authorities to hold them in a "strict regime" unit. Although regulations permit a maximum of 15 days' solitary confinement, Lu was kept in this condition for six months, and Yu Zhijian and Yu Dongyue were held in solitary for at least two years.

Yu Zhijian's health deteriorated drastically, and he became severely emaciated. Yu Dongyue became severely psychologically disturbed and lost control of his excretory functions. The manifold forms of physical torture and ill treatment to which both men were subjected was ostensibly because they had uttered "reactionary statements" about certain government officials and failed to reform. Yu Dongyue and Lu were transferred in early 1992; as of April 1992, however, Yu Zhijian was still being held in solitary at Lingling Prison.

.... [16, 20 YRS] [LIFE]

■ **ZHANG Jingsheng[1]**, a veteran pro-democracy activist arrested just after June 4, 1989, was tried on December 7, 1989 by the Changsha Intermediate People's Court on charges of "counterrevolutionary propaganda and incitement" and sentenced to 13 years' imprisonment (*Hunan Ribao,* December 9, 1989, FBIS, December 14, 1989). A worker at the Hunan Shaoguan Electrical Engineering Plant, Zhang, 37, made speeches during the May 1989 protest movement at Hunan University and at the Changsha Martyrs' Mausoleum calling for the release of Wei Jingsheng (see p.507), the leading Democracy Wall prisoner. On May 21, Zhang became an informal adviser to the Changsha *Workers Autonomous Federation* (WAF) (see **Zhou Min** p.103), and allegedly urged workers to go on strike and students to boycott classes. After the June 4 crackdown in Beijing, Zhang wrote a letter of appeal, distributed by the WAF, urging that resistance to the

government continue.

During the Democracy Wall period, Zhang Jingsheng was chief editor of two unofficial pro-democracy journals, *The Republican (Gonghe Bao)* and *The Wanderer.* Arrested for the first time in April 1981, Zhang spent the next four years in prison for spreading "counterrevolutionary propaganda." While serving this sentence, Zhang composed numerous prison songs, many of which have since become popular throughout China, particularly among political prisoners. At least one cassette version of the songs was unofficially released in China in 1988.

Also tried and sentenced with Zhang on December 7, 1989 was former WAF member **WANG Changhuai**. Wang, who had turned himself in on June 15, 1989 (see Zhou Min p.103), was given a three-year prison sentence with one year's subsequent deprivation of political rights. A worker at the Changsha Automobile Engine Factory, Wang, 30, was both head of the Changsha Workers Autonomous Federation (WAF) and its propaganda section chief. He was presumably released upon completion of his term.

.... [13 YRS]

■ **ZHANG Xiong**, 24, a worker at the Changsha Woolen Mill and a resident of Liu Zheng Street in Changsha, Hunan Province, was sentenced in November 1989 by the Changsha Eastern District Court to five years' imprisonment on a charge of "robbery." Apparently the only grounds for the charge, however, was that

Zhang's former girlfriend had reported to the authorities that a small tape player in his possession might have been obtained from "beating, smashing, and looting." In June 1990, Zhang was sent to Changsha's Pingtang Labor Reform Camp.

During the 1989 pro-democracy movement, Zhang reportedly organized demonstrations and strikes by the mill workers, and he participated in the Changsha Workers Autonomous Federation's special picket squad. He was arrested along with his younger brother in June 1989 on a charge of harboring **ZHOU Yong** (see p.564), former head of the Changsha WAF. Zhou was later acquitted; Zhang's younger brother was released.

. . . . [5 YRS]

■ **ZHOU Min**, 26, founder and standing committee member in May 1989 of the Changsha *Workers Autonomous Federation* (WAF) and formerly a worker at the Changsha Nonferrous Metallurgy Design Academy, was rearrested (probably in 1990) and sentenced to six years' imprisonment for allegedly "leading a counterrevolutionary group." On June 8, 1989, the Changsha WAF had helped organize a mass mourning meeting *(zhuidao hui)* at the Changsha Railway Station. According to the official *Hunan Daily*, at the rally Zhou Min "viciously attacked Party and state leaders, incited the workers and shopkeepers to go on strike, and workers to boycott classes." Arrested after June 4, 1989, Zhou was held for several months at the Changsha No.1 Jail, where he was frequently subjected

to corporal punishment and other ill-treatment. After his release, however, he allegedly secretly continued his WAF organizational activities and was eventually rearrested. Sentenced to six years in jail by the Changsha Intermediate People's Court, Zhou was then transferred to Yuanjiang Prison (Hunan Provincial No.1) to serve his sentence. He has reportedly now become mentally disturbed and his speech is incoherent. (See also p.564).

. . . . [6 YRS]

■ **ZHU Fangming**, a 28-year-old worker at the Hengyang City (Hunan Province) Flour Factory, was sentenced in December 1989 by the Hengyang City Intermediate People's Court to life imprisonment on a charge of "hooliganism." As vice-chairman of the Hengyang City Workers Autonomous Federation, Zhu organized demonstrations and took part in a sit-in in front of the municipal government offices. After the events of June 4, he allegedly led workers to the municipal Public Security Bureau to demand justice; a clash with police followed, although it is not known if Zhu was actually involved. Arrested shortly thereafter along with Ding Longhua, Zhu is currently being held in Hengyang Prison (Hunan Provincial No.2).

. . . . [LIFE]

Jiangsu

■ **WU Jianmin**, an employee at a passenger vehicle plant in Nanjing, Jiangsu Province, was arrested in October 1990 for pro-democracy activities and subsequently sentenced to ten years' imprisonment. No further details are currently available.

. . . . [10 YRS]

■ **ZHU Xiangzhong**, 26, an unemployed resident of Nanjing, was detained sometime after the June 4, 1989 crackdown and formally arrested on September 26 that year. On December 27, he was tried by the Nanjing Intermediate People's Court on charges of "counterrevolutionary propaganda and incitement" and sentenced to seven years' imprisonment and two years' subsequent deprivation of political rights. According to the official *1990 Nanjing Yearbook*, Zhu, an unemployed university graduate who was then living in the dormitory of the Nanjing Special Light Bulb Factory, felt "extremely dissatisfied with the socialist system" after the June 4 crackdown. "Between June 6 and 9," continued the account, "Zhu painted more than ten counterrevolutionary slogans in red ink at various sites, including on the concrete pillars at the east side of the city's Daqiao Hotel and on the walls around the PLA College of Politics and the Nanjing College of Construction Engineering."

. . . . [7 YRS]

Jilin

■ **CHI Shouzhu** (also reported as CHI Mengzhu), arrested in June 1989, was sentenced to ten years' imprisonment on charges of "counter-revolutionary propaganda and incitement." The 32-year-old senior high school graduate, who lived in the Chuanying District in Jilin City, allegedly "took part in demonstrations and made speeches." Chi is currently held under appalling conditions in Lingyuan Prison in Liaoning Province, where, along with numerous other political prisoners, he has been subjected to torture, solitary confinement and other brutalities. In attempts to alleviate their conditions and focus international attention on their plights, political prisoners at Lingyuan have staged collective hunger strikes at least twice. (For further details see Tang Yuanjuan p.105.)

. . . . [10 YRS]

■ **LI Jie**[1] and **SI Wei** were both sentenced on charges of "counter-revolutionary propaganda and incitement" for allegedly printing and distributing leaflets disclosing the truth about the June 4 crackdown in Beijing and protesting the government's brutality. Li, a 27-year-old intermediate technical school graduate and former cadre at the Bank of Shuangliao County in Jilin Province, received a five-year prison term with two years' subsequent deprivation of political rights. He had been arrested in May 1990. Si Wei, a 32-year-old high school graduate from Tonghua Municipality, Jilin Province, was sentenced to four years' imprisonment with one year's subsequent deprivation of political rights.

Both men are being held under appalling conditions in Lingyuan Prison in Liaoning Province, where along with numerous other political prisoners, they have been subjected to torture, solitary confinement and other brutalities. In attempts to alleviate their conditions and focus international attention on their plights, political prisoners at Lingyuan have gone on hunger strike at least twice.

. . . . [4, 5 YRS]

■ **TANG Yuanjuan**, **LI Wei**, and **LENG Wanbao**, three workers accused of leading an alleged "counter-revolutionary group" in Jilin Province before June 1989, were detained on June 10, 1989 and tried in late November 1990 by the Changchun City Intermediate People's Court. The sentences handed down ranged from eight to 20 years' imprisonment. The three men are currently being held in the massive Lingyuan Prison complex in Liaoning Province, where all reportedly have been subjected to repeated torture, solitary confinement and other brutalities.

Tang, a former assistant engineer at the assembly branch of the Changchun No.1 Motor Works and the alleged leader of the group, was sentenced to 20 years' imprisonment and five years' subsequent deprivation of political rights on charges of "organizing and leading a counterrevolutionary group" and "carrying out counterrevolutionary propaganda and incitement." Appeals for clemency to Party Secretary Jiang Zemin and the Supreme People's Court by Tang's father have all failed. Born on March 27, 1957 in Yangzhou, Jiangsu Province, Tang was sent to the countryside to work after he completed high school. When permitted to return to his hometown, Changchun, he found work at the No.1 Motor Works and

later graduated from its college for employees. Tang's political ideas included "eradicating feudalism, instituting democracy, reforming the Communist Party and establishing a commonwealth." Chinese authorities, in an official response to U.S. government inquiries, confirmed he had been sentenced (November 1991).

Li Wei, a worker in the factory's crankshaft workshop, was sentenced to a 13-year prison term and four years' deprivation of political rights for "actively taking part in a counter-revolutionary group" and for "counter-revolutionary propaganda and incitement." In November 1991, the Chinese authorities confirmed to the U.S. government that he had been sentenced. Li was born in 1976 in Ninghe County, Hebei Province and graduated from high school in 1985. He then became a worker at the Changchun No.1 Motor Works, where he earned a college equivalency diploma after taking an examination for the "self-taught."

Leng Wanbao, a worker in the tooling section of the Motor Works' engine-building branch, received an eight-year sentence and three years' deprivation of political rights on the same charges. Born in 1960 in Huaide County, Jilin Province, he graduated from high school in 1979. In 1987, like Li Wei, Leng earned a college equivalency diploma.

The men were tried at the end of November 1990, together with **Li Zhongmin** and **Liang Liwei** (both now presumed released - see p.567), by the Changchun City Intermediate People's

Court. The sentences were upheld on appeal on April 6, 1990 by the Jilin Province High People's Court. Tang was at home at the time of his arrest, and ten members of the Public Security Bureau searched his house, confiscating letters and filming the entire process.

According to the authorities, over a two-year period, the five men (and one other unnamed defendant) recruited 11 other workers into their group, "instigating [them] to go on strike and to organize illegal demonstrations" (*Jilin Provincial Radio*, in FBIS, July 10, 1989), Moreover, the group was said to have planned a city-wide strike designed to "topple the socialist system" (UPI, July 19, 1989). In fact, the alleged "counterrevolutionary clique," which was organized in 1987 as a discussion salon, met only a few times during its first year and soon disbanded when its members could not agree on which issues to discuss. Tang reportedly initiated other meetings in 1988, and later that year and early the next he requested permission from the local Communist Party to hold a meeting under its auspices at the factory. Permission was never granted. On May 19, 1989, during the pro-democracy movement, Tang and others led a peaceful demonstration of several thousand workers in support of the Beijing student hunger-strikers. On June 6, after learning of the Beijing massacre, the group organized a protest march by workers, which joined up with a rally of some 10,000 demonstrators in the city's Geological Palace Square, where several car factory workers called for a general strike at their plant.

Lingyuan Prison, in which the men are held, is a forced-labor camp known to the outside world as the Lingyuan Automobile Assembly Factory. Cells of less than 60 square meters often hold more than 40 prisoners. Common criminals are appointed to act as guards, a day's labor is fourteen hours long, and if work quotas are not met or if prisoners fail to "reform" their political views, the guards beat them with fists, belts and electric batons. Medical care and nutrition at the prison are highly deficient, and political prisoners, of which there are reportedly at least 30, are permitted neither books nor newspapers. Chinese officials insist, however, that there are only four prisoners to a cell and that they only have to work for three to five hours a day, are not beaten and have full access to newspapers, TV and books. (See also Liu Gang, p.65.)

Perhaps the most significant protest action carried out by the Lingyuan political prisoners was a collective hunger strike in November 1991 to protest their continued persecution, torture and beatings. The strike coincided with then U.S. Secretary of State James Baker's visit to China, but according to the government, foreign news reports of the impending strike were a "sheer fabrication with ulterior motives" (*Xinhua*, November 12, 1991, in FBIS, same date). From mid-November onwards, the prisoners' families lost their visitation rights on the grounds that their relatives had "violated prison regulations." Correspondence privileges were rescinded, and permission to receive food parcels and other supplies was also denied. Families were told that their relatives were "in excellent physical condition and still in one piece...their treatment accords with the prison regulations on strict regimen [i.e. solitary-confinement]punishment." Supporters of the prisoners have since called publicly for an international inquiry to be held into their conditions of detention. (For details, see *News From Asia Watch*, "China: Political Prisoners Abused in Liaoning Province as Official Whitewash of Labor Reform System Continues," September 1, 1992.)

. . . . [8, 13, 20 YRS]

Liaoning

■ **WEI Shouzhong**, a 23-year-old Shenyang (Liaoning Province) native, arrested in June 1989, was later sentenced to 15 years' imprisonment on charges of "counterrevolutionary propaganda and incitement." He is currently being held at the Lingyuan Labor Reform Detachment. So far as is known, Wei was not involved in any of the hunger strikes at the prison. (See Tang Yuanjuan, above.)

. . . . [15 YRS]

■ **XIAO Bin**[1], 44, a former salesman at the Dalian Xinghai Aluminum Window Factory, was sentenced on July 13, 1989 to ten years' imprisonment and three years' subsequent deprivation of political rights by the Dalian Intermediate People's Court. His term was later reduced by six months, allegedly because he admitted guilt, accepted efforts to reform him and followed prison regulations *(Liaoning Fazhi Bao [Liaoning Legal Journal])*, *Reuters*, August 17, 1992). Xiao was convicted of "propagating counterrevolutionary lies" for stating many times in public that 20,000 people had been killed on June 4, 1989 and that some had been crushed by tanks. He also was found guilty of "vilifying the righteous acts of the martial law troops." Requests by the U.S. government for information about Xiao's whereabouts elicited no response from Chinese officials (November 1991).

Xiao, who was arrested on June 10, 1989 in Dalian shortly after *Beijing Television* appealed to viewers to turn him in for "rumor-mongering," had been interviewed about the Tiananmen Square massacre by the U.S.'s ABC News. The broadcast showed him imitating machine guns mowing down demonstrators in Beijing. The official *People's Daily* claimed that Xiao had engaged in "counterrevolutionary incitement" out of resentment and personal frustration at the loss of his job. The article quoted from Xiao's "confession" (which was almost certainly forced) to the effect that he had told students in Tiananmen Square how corrupt the government was and that officers and soldiers responsible for martial law must be killed. Xiao "confessed" that he had spread untrue rumors in order "to make the masses doubt the Communist Party and the government." According to *People's Daily*, the ten-year sentence Xiao received was "reasonable, justifiable and lawful, as well as appropriate." (The fullest account available of Xiao's case can be found in TC pp.376-377.)

. . . . [9.5 YRS]

■ **XU Boquan**, a 28-year-old high school graduate and Liaoning Province peasant, arrested in June 1989, was sentenced after June 1989 to eight years' imprisonment on charges of "counterrevolutionary propaganda and incitement" and is currently being held in Lingyuan Prison. So far as is known, Xu was not involved in any of the hunger strikes at the prison. (See Tang Yuanjuan p.105.)

. . . . [8 YRS]

■ **ZHAO Junlu**, a 23-year-old native of Danding Municipality, Liaoning Province, was sentenced to ten years' imprisonment on charges of "counter-revolutionary propaganda and incitement." A "vagrant," arrested in June 1989 by police in Tieling City, Liaoning, Zhao was alleged to have joined student protests in Beijing on May 31, 1989, giving lectures to students and collecting donations for them. He also was accused of inciting more than 600 Fuxin City students to storm police headquarters there (Amnesty International, July 6, 1989). Zhao is currently being held in Lingyuan Prison. So far as is known, he was not involved in any of the hunger strikes at the prison. (See Tang Yuanjuan p.105.)

. . . . [10 YRS]

Shaanxi

■ **ZHOU Feng**, a 24 or 25-year-old peasant and correspondence student from Shaanxi Province, was sentenced to eight years in prison on charges of "counterrevolutionary propaganda and incitement." He is held in Shaanxi No.1 Prison in Fuping County. According to an Asia Watch source, Zhou wrote letters to several Shaanxi newspapers supporting the student movement. Arrest and sentencing dates are unknown.

. . . . [8 YRS]

Shandong

■ **HAO Fuyuan**, 40, a peasant from Haojia village in Tianzhen Town, Gaoqing County, Shandong Province, was sentenced sometime after June 1989 to 10 years' imprisonment on charges of "counterrevolutionary propaganda and incitement," according to an internal report by the Supreme People's Court (see TC p.374). The report stated that on May 18, 1989, Hao "sneaked into a crowd of students and forced his way on to a train bound for Beijing, where he became involved in the Tiananmen Square activities." On May 22, he returned to Jinan City, Shandong, and made a "reactionary tape-recording" containing such statements as, "Deng Xiaoping has seven billion dollars' savings in the United States and his entire family have become U.S. citizens"; "On May 15, the foreign ministries of all the foreign nations declared that the Li Peng government is an illegal government"; "[The authorities] have cut off the water supply in Tiananmen Square and want to force the students to their deaths"; and "Li Peng's speeches are designed to deceive the masses and we should on no account believe them."

He also allegedly called on school students to boycott classes and workers to stage strikes across the country, and urged people to ignore government radio broadcasts and listen to *Voice of America* instead.

. . . . [10 YRS]

■ **Farmer X**, an unidentified peasant from Tianzhen was sentenced to ten years' imprisonment for engaging in "counterrevolutionary provocation," according to *Fazhi Ribao* (in FBIS, November 3, 1989). In May 1989, the man travelled to Beijing with a group of students to participate in pro-democracy demonstrations; upon his return to Shandong, he joined demonstrating students in Jinan and gave allegedly "reactionary" lectures in his home village.

. . . . [10 YRS]

■ **JIANG Fuzhen**, a 36-year-old worker in a Qingdao (Shandong Province) factory, was arrested in August 1989 for helping to disseminate "counterrevolutionary propaganda," was later sentenced to an eight-year prison term. He had been arrested once before, in 1980, for publishing a magazine entitled *Hai Min Hua*.

. . . . [8 YRS]

■ **JIAO Zhijin** (Zhixin), a 58-year-old salesman from Shandong Province was sentenced to 15 years in prison on charges of "organizing a counter-revolutionary group," the *China Democratic Political Party*, according to an Asia Watch source. He is currently serving his sentence at the Lingyuan No.2 Labor Reform

Detachment in Liaoning Province. In an official response to International Labor Organization inquiries (November 1991), however, the Chinese government said that he was "never brought to court." Jiao, a high school graduate, was arrested on June 13, 1989 in Dalian, Liaoning Province, where he gone on March 30, 1989 (see also Zheng Quanli p.110).

Allegedly a "chieftain" of a "counterrevolutionary party," Jiao was accused of "inciting and participating in riots and conspiring to overthrow the government" (*Zhongguo Qingnian Bao*, June 14, 1989) and of helping to send fourteen "counterrevolutionary declarations, guiding principles and letters of application" to other Chinese cities and "formulating regulations on establishing counterrevolutionary armed forces."

. . . . [15 YRS]

■ **SUN Weibang** (SUN Feng), a veteran Democracy Wall activist who spent several years in prison in the early 1980s, was re-arrested after June 1989 in connection with the pro-democracy movement and later sentenced to 12 years' imprisonment. A worker who joined the student demonstrations on May 14, 1989 and was in charge of the Beijing Students Autonomous Federation's broadcasting station, Sun was arrested on June 2, 1989 and charged with spreading rumors, blocking traffic and disturbing the social order (*Beijing Ribao*, June 4, 1989). According to an official Chinese response to U.S. government inquiries, however, Sun was "not found legally responsible" by the courts after June

1989. Since there is no doubt that Sun was sentenced to 12 years, the authorities may have either confused his name with someone else's or been trying to conceal the fact of his long sentence.

Sun, 43, a worker who in 1979 was employed in the Qingdao, (Shandong Province) Handicrafts Factory, first went to Beijing in March 1979 to display posters at the Democracy Wall. He became a close friend and colleague of Xu Wenli (see p.510) another leading dissident worker. In August 1979 in Qingdao, Sun founded the unofficial journal *Hailanghua (Foam of the Wave)*. First arrested in April 1981, he was held for three years without trial or sentence and then released in 1984.

. . . . [12 YRS]

■ **ZHANG Jie**[2], 26, an unemployed worker from Jinan, Shandong Province, was sentenced to either 15 or 18 years' imprisonment on charges of "counter-revolutionary propaganda and incitement" in October 1989. According to *Jinan Masses Daily* (October 15, 1989), the sentence was 18 years, but an internal report by the Supreme People's Court (see TC p.373) said that Zhang had been sentenced to 15 years. According to the latter account, between June 5 and 7, 1989, Zhang led several thousand people in holding a "funeral meeting" *(zhuidaohui)* outside the Qingdao municipal government offices to commemorate the victims of the Beijing crackdown.

He also allegedly made a series of "subversive and inflammatory statements" at the crossroads of Taidong No.1 Road and Weihai Road. These included: "a major massacre occurred in Beijing on June 4 in which 3,000 people were killed and more than 10,000 were injured"; "the army has committed towering crimes against the people"; "a pile of 48 corpses lay piled outside the Great Hall of the People in Beijing"; the tanks ran over whoever they encountered on the streets, an old lady was beaten to death, and four female students who knelt on the ground and pleaded for mercy were also shot dead." Zhang also allegedly called for the overthrow of the government and shouted the slogans, "Throttle Deng Xiaoping and Li Peng," "Overthrow fascism" and "Put Deng Xiaoping and Li Peng on public trial." In a November 1991 response to inquiries from the U.S. government, Chinese officials confirmed that Zhang was sentenced but gave no indication of the prison term.

. . . . [15 OR 18 YRS]

■ A man named **ZHENG Quanli** (Chuanli, Jinli), 38, who travelled from Shandong Province to Dalian, Liaoning Province on March 30, 1989, was arrested in Dalian on June 13 the same year and later sentenced to 12 years' imprisonment on charges of "organizing a counterrevolutionary group" (see Jiao Zhijin p.109), according to an Asia Watch source. In a Chinese government response to the International Labor Organization (November 1991), however, Zheng was listed as being "never brought to court." (In a further complication, another ILO report [March 1992] listed an unemployed worker from Dalian, **SONG Tianli**, as having received a 15-year prison term. There is reason to believe that the two names refer to the same person, although the discrepancy in sentencing cannot be resolved.) Allegedly the "chieftain" of a "counter-revolutionary party," Zheng was accused of "inciting and participating in riots and conspiring to overthrow the government" (*Zhongguo Qingnian Bao*, June 14, 1989). He was also accused of helping to send fourteen "counter-revolutionary declarations, guiding principles and letters of application" to other Chinese cities and of "formulating regulations on establishing counterrevolutionary armed forces."

. . . . [12 YRS]

Shanghai

■ **DAI Zhenping** was sentenced to an eight-year prison term for the "serious crime of disturbing the traffic and social order by participating in the riots" in Shanghai, according to a Chinese response to requests for information by the International Labor Organization (March 3, 1992). His name also appeared on an official list of those sentenced which Chinese officials gave to the U.S. government (November 1991). His real offense, however, was listed as "spreading rumors" on June 9, 1989 at the Shanghai railway station about the deaths of demonstrators. Dai was arrested sometime before August 23 (*Jiefang Ribao*, August 23, 1989).

. . . . [8 YRS]

■ **GAO Xiaoliang** - see p.11

. . . . [9 YRS]

■ **HUANG Jianhu(a)**, an assembly worker at the Shanghai Water Company's water meter plant, was sentenced in Shanghai to a four-and-a-half-year term of imprisonment for disturbing the public peace, according to the report made by Chinese authorities to the International Labor Organization (November 1990). In response to requests for information by the U.S. government, Chinese authorities confirmed that he had been sentenced (November 1991). Huang was arrested on June 8, 1989 for allegedly directing a "flying vehicle squad" to set up road barricades. According to *Shanghai Radio* (June 10, 1989), squad members, some 200 in all, shouted "reactionary slogans" and incited workers to strike.

. . . . [4.5 YRS]

■ **QI Hongjun** and **ZHOU Hongbin** were sentenced on September 12, 1989 for allegedly stealing a fire hose that was being used to put out a fire on a train which hit demonstrators at a Shanghai rail junction on June 6. Qi, unemployed, received a 12-year sentence; Zhou, a fruit seller, received a ten-year sentence (*Shijie Ribao*, September 16, 1989). An official Chinese response to U.S. government requests for information confirmed that Zhou was sentenced but gave no information about Qi (November 1991).

. . . . [10, 12 YRS]

■ **TANG Guoliang**, a 29-year-old unemployed worker, was sentenced to a term of imprisonment, according to an official Chinese response to U.S. government inquiries (November 1991). Other sources reported he received a ten-year term on July 6, 1989. According to *Jiefang Ribao* (July 13, 1989), one month earlier, on June 6, Tang pretended he was a Shanghai Railroad Institute student and incited people to block trains.

.... [10 YRS]

■ **YAN Tinggui**, one of ten members of the Shanghai Patriotic Workers Organization in Support of the Beijing People, was sentenced to an eight-year prison term for the "serious crime of disturbing the traffic and social order by participating in the riots" in Shanghai, according to a Chinese response to requests for information by the International Labor Organization (March 3, 1992). His name also appeared on an official Chinese list of those sentenced which was handed to the U.S. government (November 1991). Arrested for allegedly forcing the director of his factory to call a strike in support of the people of Beijing following the crackdown there, Yan was seized before August 23, 1989. According to a report on that date in *Jiefang Ribao*, the Shanghai government newspaper labeled him a "bad element" because he had once been convicted of gambling.

.... [8 YRS]

■ **YAO Kaiwen** - see p.11

.... [10 YRS]

Shanxi

■ **LI Fufa**, a worker at the Yuantai Steel Factory in Taiyuan, Shanxi Province, was sentenced to seven years' imprisonment after June 1989 for allegedly leading workers at the factory to participate in "illegal" student demonstrations. Li's role in the protests was outlined in a court document rejecting the appeal of another Shanxi dissident, **Ding Junze** (see p.84), who was said to have "influenced" Li. Two other members of Li's group, **LI Suping**, a railway worker, and **QIN Huaiqing**, a farmer, were each sentenced to four-year prison terms. Assuming both were arrested shortly after the events of June 1989, they should already have been released after completing their terms.

.... [7 YRS]

Sichuan

■ **LAI Bihu** and **LIN Qiangguo** were sentenced to ten years' imprisonment for their participation in the pro-democracy movement in Chengdu, Sichuan Province. Three others, unnamed, were sentenced at the same time (*Shijie Ribao*, August 10, 1989). Requests to Chinese authorities by the U.S. government (November 1991) for information about the men elicited no response.

.... [2 X 10 YRS]

■ **PU Yong**, 22, a medical worker and minor administrator in Nanjiang County, Sichuan Province, has been sentenced, according to an official response by Chinese authorities to U.S.

government inquiries (November 1991). The length of his term and the place of imprisonment were not reported. An earlier account said he was arrested in connection with "a major counterrevolutionary propaganda and incitement case" (*Sichuan Ribao*, in FBIS, November 1, 1989.) Pu, who was elected deputy director of Liangshui Township in May 1988 and was a worker at the Nanjiang County Hospital of Traditional Chinese Medicine, allegedly had "listened to the *Voice of America*, read reactionary publications and worshipped the capitalist social system practiced in Western countries." During the "counterrevolutionary rebellion," the high-school educated Pu had "posted big-character slogans in Nanjiang County and, on the night of October 29-30, he secretly wrote more than 400 counterrevolutionary leaflets which he distributed in 13 places in Nanjiang's downtown area, including bus stations, movie houses and the people's assembly hall." He also allegedly "took down and threw away the signboard of a government and Party organ" and viciously attacked the Chinese Communist Party and China's socialist system and slandered its leaders."

. . . . [? YRS]

■ **MA Xiaoyu**, 28, a special (vocational) middle school graduate, was arrested sometime after June 4, 1989 and is currently serving a seven-year sentence at the Sichuan Province No.1 Prison (also known as the Sichuan New Life *Laodong* Factory). Ma received a three-year term for "counterrevolution" and a four-year

term, to be served consecutively, for alleged economic crimes. According to an Asia Watch source, Sichuan No.2 Prison is subdivided into 11 "brigades" *(dadui)*, each of which at present holds two to three "counterrevolutionaries" and "spies." The source reported that there are currently between 20 and 30 sentenced "counterrevolutionaries" being held at the prison.

. . . . [7 YRS]

Tianjin

■ **HUANG Shixu** - see p.14

. . . . [3 YRS]

■ **LI Yongsheng**, an unemployed worker about 30 years old, arrested in Tianjin on or around June 11, 1989, organized the "Tianjin Residents' Petitioning Team" and engaged in "rumor-mongering" and "instigation" at Nanyuan Airport in Beijing, according to *Tianjin Ribao*. Requests for information by the U.S. government about his whereabouts elicited no response from Chinese officials (November 1991), but according to an Asia Watch source, Li is serving a 12-year sentence at Tianjin No.1 Prison for "counterrevolutionary propaganda and incitement." Eventually, in October 1993, Chinese officials confirmed both the location and the length of sentence.

. . . . [12 YRS]

■ **LI Zhenqi**, a worker who participated in a group called the Tianjin Democratic Revival Association *(Tianjin Minzhu Zhenxing Hui)* during the May 1989 protests, was arrested and later tried on charges of belonging

to a "counterrevolutionary organization" and sentenced to five year's imprisonment. Li is currently serving his sentence at the Tianjin No.1 Prison. (See also LIU Peigang, p.501.)
.... [5 YRS]

■ **LU Gang** - see p.14
.... [3 YRS]

Zhejiang

■ According to an Asia Watch source, **CHEN Bo**, a worker from Ningbo, Zhejiang Province. received a six-year sentence in connection with the 1989 pro-democracy movement. No other information is available.
.... [6 YRS]

■ **LIU Heping**[1], a 32-year-old pharmacist from the Red Cross Hospital in Hangzhou, Zhejiang Province, reportedly was sentenced to a 12-year prison term for allegedly putting up a wall poster critical of the Chinese government. According to an Asia Watch source, he was accused of three crimes, corruption, damaging government property and "counter-revolutionary propaganda and incitement." Liu is serving his sentence in Zhejiang Provincial Prison No.1, also known as Wuyi (May 1st) Machinery Plant or Zhejiang Light Duty Lifting Machinery Plant, where he makes chains and lever hoists reportedly for export to the U.S. and other countries (*Laogai Report*, July 1993). The dates of arrest and sentencing are not known.
.... [12 YRS]

2. Psychiatric Confinement

Beijing

■ **WANG Wanxing**, 43, unemployed, was transferred from Beijing's Chao Yang Detention Center on June 30, 1992 and forcibly admitted to the Ankang Psychiatric Hospital in southwestern Beijing, an institution for the criminally insane run by the Beijing Public Security Bureau, having been diagnosed by police doctors as suffering from "paranoid psychosis." Wang, a veteran dissident, had been arrested in Tiananmen Square on June 3, 1992 by some 30 plainclothes officers after unfurling a banner at the Monument to the People's Heroes demanding redress for his previous periods of imprisonment as a political dissident. The banner also condemned Deng Xiaoping and other Chinese leaders for the 1989 Beijing massacre and castigated Deng for his appointment of senior leaders without "fair competition" (*South China Morning Post*, June 7, 1992). According to Wang's wife, a doctor at the hospital diagnosed Wang's condition as "political paranoia." Upon being told that Wang would not be sentenced and would be released earlier if she signed a document confirming that he had psychiatric problems, she succumbed to the pressure and signed. (See also Wang Miaogen p.27, and Xing Jiandong p.27.)

In a subsequent letter addressed to U.N. Secretary-General Boutros Boutros-Ghali and to U.S. President Bush, which Wang had smuggled out from the Ankang Hospital (*Reuters*, July 28, 1992), he said, "I am not a psychiatric patient but they are giving me medication every day. They are forcibly administering drugs to me...and trying all the time to destroy my body and spirit." In July 1992, Asia Watch received specimen samples of the drugs Wang is being forced to take. According to a pharmacological analysis of the pills subsequently carried out by the U.S.-based Physicians for Human Rights, they comprise drugs of the opiate and benzodiazepine class. Opiates are usually reserved for those in pain and create a "high" effect which also sedates. In U.S. psychiatric institutions, opiates are used only in cases of addictive drug "withdrawal." Benzodiazepines are a type of tranquilizer normally used to sedate patients who are anxious and easily excitable. Effects in both cases vary from the mild to the extreme, depending upon the dosage given. According to Wang, the drugs make him feel numb, dizzy, nauseous and fatigued.

Wang has been jailed twice before, in 1966 and 1976, both times for expressing his support for Deng Xiaoping, who was then out of favor with the ruling clique. He was formally rehabilitated by the Party in the early 1980s and his case declared an injustice. At the time of his 1992 protest, Wang was pressing the government for monetary compensation for his previous imprisonments. In August 1993, an interview with Wang that had been secretly filmed at the Ankang Hospital several months earlier was shown on British television as part of a Yorkshire Television documentary program, "Laogai: Inside the Chinese Gulag."

. . . . [INDEFINITE]

Shanghai

- **WANG Miaogen** - see p.27
  . . . . [INDEFINITE]

- **XING Jiandong** - see p.27
  . . . . [INDEFINITE]

3. Arrested/Awaiting Trial (1992-93)

Students, Intellectuals, Workers and Peasants

Beijing

- **BAO Liangqing** - see p.146

- **CHEN Mingxin** - see p.24

- **CHEN Wei**[1] - see p.19

- **GAO Yu** - see p.28

- **GAO Yuxiang** - see p.20

- **GUO Baosheng** - see p.47

- **GUO Shaoyan** - see p.22

- **HU Shenglun** - see p.20

- **KANG Yuchun** - see p.20

- **LI Ji** - see p.22

- **LI Quanli** - see p.25
- **LI Yan** - see p.22
- **LIU Jingsheng** - see p.25
- **LU Mingxia** - see p.22
- **LU Zhigang** - see p.21
- **REN Jun** - see p.22
- **RUI Chaohuai** - see p.25
- **TIAN Ye** - see p.29
- **WANG Guoqi** - see p.26
- **WANG Peizhong** - see p.21
- **WANG Tiancheng** - see p.21
- **WANG Qishan** - see p.22
- **WANG Xiaodong** - see p.22
- **XI Yang** - see p.29
- **XU Dongling** - see p.25
- **ZHANG Chunz(h)u** - see p.25
- **ZHANG Guojun[1]** - see p.25
- **ZHAO Xin** - see p.22

  Gansu

- **CAO Jianyu** - see p.23
- **DING Mao** - see p.23
- **GAO Changyun** - see p.23

- **LIU Baiyu** - see p.23
- **LIU Wensheng** - see p.23
- **LU Yalin** - see p.23
- **LU Yanghua** - see p.23
- **XING Shimin** - see p.23
- **XU Zhendong** - see p.23
- **ZHANG Jian** - see p.23

  Guangzhou

- **LI Guohen** - see p.32
- **LIANG Weimin** - see p.32
- **WU Songfa** - see p.32
- **LIU Taiheng[1]** - see p.29

  Henan

- **AN Ning** - see p.24
- **MENG Zhongwei** - see p.24
- **WANG Jianping** - see p.24

  Hubei

- **FANG Junjie** - see p.30
- **HE Quan** - see p.43
- **QIN Yongmin** - see p.7

  Jiangxi

- **LUO Guilong, 26, and ZHANG**

Shidong, 35, peasants from Jiangxi Province, were arrested sometime prior to February 1992 for allegedly campaigning against Communist Party rule. According to the February 11, edition of *Jiangxi Legal News* (*Agence France Presse*, February 19, 1992, in *fbis*, same date), the two men, who were later denounced by their fellow villagers, had posed as special envoys of the Party's Central Committee and attempted to "infiltrate the villages," telling local residents that Beijing had sent them "to do secret work." Until October 1991, the account continued, the two men, who reportedly had failed to benefit from China's agricultural reforms, "hysterically attacked the socialist system, attacked the Party's policy of reform and opening and attacked Party and state leaders." In addition, they had "tried to contact domestic and foreign reactionary forces."

■ **ZHANG Shidong** - see p.116

Shaanxi

■ **XING Hongwei** - see p.27

Shanxi

■ **QIAO Anyou**, **ZHANG Weijia** and **ZHANG Jinlan** - see p.31

Sichuan

■ **XIANG Wenqing** - see p.32

Tianjin

■ **CHEN Qinglin** - see p.24

4. Died in Prison/Under Surveillance

Beijing

■ **WEN Jie,** deputy head of the propaganda section of the Command Center to Protect Tiananmen Square, died from colon cancer on December 20, 1991 at the age of 27. He had become ill while detained without charge in Qincheng Prison, but timely and appropriate treatment was reportedly denied by the prison authorities at that time. Formerly a graduate student in ancient Chinese literature at Beijing University and a teacher at the Beijing Fashion Institute, Wen was arrested in June 1989 and either paroled in December 1990 for medical reasons or was one among a group of student leaders released without charge on January 27, 1991. After his funeral on December 24, 1991, at least six former students (see Wang Guoqi p.26), were detained for questioning.
. . . . [DEAD]

Hunan

■ **LI Maoqiu,** formerly a senior engineer at the Changsha (Hunan Province) Non-Ferrous Metals Design Academy, died in November 1990 while in Changsha No.1 Prison, Cell 12, reportedly from rupturing of the blood vessels of the heart. Li, who had reportedly acquired almost 10 million yuan in assets by early 1989 from running his own breeding business, was in his mid-fifties when he died. Arrested shortly after June 4, 1989, Li was accused in mid-1990 of "economic crimes," officials claiming that eight million *yuan* had been obtained by fraud. All his assets, including home electronic equipment, were confiscated. His wife, **Yu Ziyu**, later reportedly tried unsuccessfully to commit suicide.

Li's businesses included a chicken farm, a dog farm, a salted goods shop and a roasted snack shop. His only known involvement with the 1989 pro-democracy movement was his contribution of 10,000 *yuan* to the demonstrating students. He had inherited "historical problems," however: both his mother's father and his father-in-law had been students at the Whampoa Military Academy, and during the War of Liberation (the 1945-49 civil war), they were high-ranking KMT (Chinese Nationalist) generals.
. . . . [DEAD]

[NB: For details of Catholics and Protestants who died in prison or under restriction, see p.228 and p.244.]

2. Current Status Unclear

Sentence Unknown

Students, Intellectuals, Journalists and Officials

Anhui

■ **ZHANG Lin**, head of the Students Autonomous Union in Bengbu City, was arrested in Bengbu on June 8, 1989 (*Anhui Radio*, June 14, 1989) and later tried and sentenced. The length of sentence is not known, but Zhang was listed as being still jailed in a November 1991 official Chinese response to enquiries from the U.S. government. A student at Qinghua University in 1985, Zhang was later that year assigned to work at the Bengbu Knitwear Mill. He resigned from the mill sometime afterwards and remained unemployed until his arrest. Zhang allegedly established the Autonomous Union on May 19, 1989 at Bengbu Medical College and made an "extremely reactionary" speech on May 21. He helped stage sit-ins and began a hunger strike on May 25, saying he wanted to turn Bengbu Medical College into a "center of democratic politics and to set up a human rights office at the college." According to Amnesty International (*ASA 17/54/90*), Zhang also allegedly led a "Dare-to-Die Corps" against the offices of the city Party committee and the city government during the period June 5-7, 1989. From March 1989, Zhang had traveled repeatedly between Beijing and Bengbu, and in a letter (apparently confiscated by the authorities) he wrote of his intention to make contact with dissident astrophysicist Fang Lizhi.

. . . . [? YRS]

Beijing

■ The whereabouts of **WANG Haidong**, who went on trial on January 15, 1991, are uncertain. Requests for information on his case by the U.S. government to Chinese officials went unanswered (November 1991). According to a notice posted at the Beijing Intermediate People's Court, Wang, who was associated with the Chinese Academy of Social Sciences, was charged with "counterrevolutionary propaganda and incitement" (UPI, January 15, 1991).

. . . . [? YRS]

■ **ZHANG Donghui** - see p.62

. . . . [? YRS]

Guizhou

■ **ZHANG Shen(g)ming** (Xingming), an engineer at a farm machinery plant in Guiyang City, was arrested on June 24, 1989 for sending anonymous "reactionary letters" to government officials and Party leaders. He reportedly wrote the notes over a two-year period starting in July 1987, and in them allegedly attacked Party and government officials. He was charged with the crimes of, variously, "counterrevolutionary propaganda" and "insulting individuals" (*Agence France Presse*, June 25, 1989, in FBIS, June 26.) In November 1991, the Chinese authorities confirmed to the U.S. government that Zhang had been sentenced and was still in prison. The length of sentence was not disclosed.

. . . . [? YRS]

Henan

■ **ZHAO Shujian**, 33, was arrested on November 7, 1989 for alleged counterrevolutionary crimes committed on May 20 that year in the city of Kaifeng, central Henan Province. An official Chinese response in November 1991 to U.S. government inquiries confirmed that Zhao was sentenced and still detained, but the prison term was not disclosed. According to an official press report, Zhao, a cadre in the Kaifeng Housing Construction Company, posted more than 30 "reactionary slogans" on streets, schools and factories at the height of the May 1989 protests; organized illegal demonstrations; gave "counter-revolutionary speeches" at Henan University; and spread news reports broadcast by *Voice of America* at his workplace. For this, he was branded a "criminal" by the police and accused of trying to "overthrow the Communist Party" and of "viciously attacking and vilifying state and Party leaders."

Previous alleged offenses by Zhao included writing posters on April 25, 1989 and January 18, 1987. According to the authorities, Zhao Shujian later "confessed to all his crimes."

. . . . [? YRS]

Hubei

■ **WANG Yangli, ZHANG Hanjiang, LIU Bangming, HU Gang, DING Hancong, LIU Gui, WU Yingling, LU Zhonghua, LIU Chongyun, WANG Yuqing, ZENG Dazhao** and **ZHANG Weidong** - see p.14

. . . . [12 X ? YRS]

Hunan

■ **QIN Hubao,** formerly a senior cadre in the Office of Discussion and Criticism (ODC) in Yueyang City, Hunan Province, was reportedly sentenced in December 1989 by the Yueyang City Intermediate People's Court to ten years' imprisonment on a charge of "counterrevolutionary propaganda and incitement." The report of Qin's trial and sentencing, however, has never been confirmed. The ODC, established by the reformist vice-mayor of Yueyang, Yin Zhenggao, for the purpose of criticizing cadres, was closed down by the senior authorities in late 1988. Qin was tried on some of the same charges as other officials from Yin's administration (see Xie Yang p.552). However, Qin was accused of additional "counterrevolutionary acts." During the 1989 pro-democracy movement, he allegedly went to Beijing and from there smuggled to Hunan the banned No.5, 1989 issue of *Reportage Literature* [*Baogao Wenxue*], which included an investigative article about Yin Zhenggao's removal from power. Qin distributed copies widely in Changsha, Yueyang and other cities. He was arrested in July 1989.

.... [10 YRS?]

■ **WANG Xinlin**, 24, a former officer of the People's Liberation Army, was tried and sentenced, according to an official Chinese response to requests for information by the U.S. government (November 1991), but no further information was given. Wang was officially arrested on June 21, 1989 by the Jinggangshan City Public Security Bureau on the charge of carrying out "counterrevolutionary propaganda and incitement." He was accused of putting up "reactionary" posters on June 5, 1989 at the former residence of Chairman Mao in Jinggangshan, on wire poles along highways and in long-distance buses. In addition, he allegedly "viciously attacked" Party and state leaders, vilified martial law troops and shouted "reactionary" slogans. Wang, born in Jinggangshan and a 1987 graduate of the PLA Engineering Institute in Changsha, was described as one with a "history of grievances." He was a platoon leader until his dismissal from that position in November 1988. As a soldier, Wang was presumably tried by a military court (*Jiangxi Provincial Radio*, June 22, 1989, in FBIS, June 23).

.... [? YRS]

Liaoning

■ **LI Xiuping** (or **LIU Shuping**, also known as **Er Mei**), a woman, and **YANG Zhiwei** (Dehui), two key members of the Autonomous Federation of Students from Outside Beijing, were detained in Baoding, Hubei Province in mid-June 1989 and then handed over to the Beijing Public Security Bureau for "further hearing" (*Chinese Central Television*, June 18, 1989). According to a November 1991 official Chinese response to inquiries by the U.S. government, Li was later tried and sentenced. Yang's current circumstances are unknown. According to the *Hong Kong Standard* (June 19, 1989), Li and Yang took part in the May 1989 "dialogue" talks between the State Council and the independent student movement, and had meetings with the Chinese Red Cross Society. Yang was a journalism student at Hebei University. Li, a student at China Medical University in Shenyang, Liaoning Province, allegedly confessed to taking part in "major activities" during the 1989 protests.

.... [2 X ? YRS]

Shandong

■ **SHAN Zhenheng**, formerly a history student at Beijing Normal College, was sentenced for his participation in the 1989 pro-democracy movement, according to a former fellow prisoner, **XU Yiruo** (see p.475). The two met sometime after late 1991 when they were both mining flint clay at the Shandong No.1 Re-education through Labor Camp (also known as the Shandong Province Shengjian August 3rd Factory). Shan was detained for over a year after June 1989, during which time he tried to commit suicide by slashing his wrists. After his release, he continued pro-democracy activities and was then rearrested and sentenced without trial to a several-year term of "labor re-education."

. . . . [? YRS]

Shanxi

■ **ZHAO Hongyue**, a student at the Taiyuan No.27 Middle School, reportedly received an unknown term of imprisonment; and an unnamed student at the Institute of Medicine was sentenced to six years' in prison. A third student, **WANG X** (given name not known) who gave speeches in Taiyuan's May Day Square on May 20 and June 4, 1989 (his June 4 speech was entitled "Li Peng is a Political Bandit") was also sentenced to an unspecified term and is believed to be incarcerated in Qi County Prison. According to the source, none of the accused was charged with committing any acts of violence. In an official Chinese response to U.S. government requests for information (November 1991), Zhao was listed as having "never been accused of any offense."

. . . . [6 YRS] [2 X ? YRS]

Sichuan

■ **LEE BUN** (Li Ben) and her husband, **LI Qingming**, both university graduates who claimed to have been active during the 1989 pro-democracy

movement, were reportedly executed in Sichuan early 1990, within a month of their deportation back to China from Hong Kong following a failed asylum bid in the colony. The report has never been officially confirmed, but authoritative sources in the Hong Kong administration are said to have privately expressed belief that the report was accurate. The couple fled to Hong Kong on September 2, 1989 after allegedly learning that they were wanted by the Chinese police. On December 6, they were arrested by Hong Kong police during a raid on a passport-forging syndicate in Mongkok. After a series of court hearings in connection with their asylum claim, the couple was deported to China in February 1990.

. . . . [2 X EXECUTED?]

Tianjin

■ **XU Liguang**, a graduate student in the management department at Nankai University in Tianjin, was arrested in June 1989 for his role as a leader in the Students Autonomous Federation. He was reportedly tried and sentenced, but no further details are available (Amnesty International, *ASA 17/24/90*). Requests for information from the U.S. government about Xu's whereabouts elicited no response from Chinese authorities (November 1991).

. . . . [? YRS]

Yunnan

■ **SHI Qing, SHANG Jingzhong, YU Anmin** and **JI Kunxing** and three others (names unknown) were all tried in Kunming on September 16, 1989 on charges of fomenting a "counter-revolutionary plot" *(Yunnan Ribao, September 28, 1989)*. **Shi**, 27, named as the leader, allegedly went to the town of Zhuzhou in Hunan Province on June 9, 1989, and at the train station there he publicly denounced the military crackdown in Beijing. He later went to Kunming "to take part in agitation" and decided, together with Shang, Yu and Ji, to found a "counter-revolutionary party." The group then allegedly established an underground magazine called *Pioneers*, circulated anti-government leaflets and put up "counterrevolutionary posters" (FBIS, October 5, 1989). They also allegedly "sought contacts abroad" and attempted "to spirit their leaders out of the country." U.S. government inquiries to the Chinese authorities about the cases of Shi, Shang, and Ji elicited no response, although a government reply of November 1991 confirmed that Yu Kunxing had been sentenced. The sentences of the four men have never been made public; and there has been no further word on the fate of the three unnamed defendants who were also tried.

. . . . [7 X ? YRS]

■ **WANG Cun** and **YANG Hong** were arrested on June 13, 1989 in Kunming, Yunnan Province (see also Wu Haizen p.551). According to an official Chinese response to U.S. government inquiries (November 1991), both men were later sentenced to imprisonment (terms unknown). Wang, 27, an accounting supervisor at the Kunming Jinglong Hotel, was accused of being head of propaganda for the Yunnan Students Autonomous Federation. According to an official radio report, he "took advantage of his position to spread rumors" and "did a lot of evil through his contacts with Hong Kong and other regions." Yang, 36, a reporter at the Kunming paper *Zhongguo Qingnian Bao (China Youth News)*, was charged with circulating "rumor-mongering leaflets" and protesting against corruption (*Kunming Radio*, in FBIS, June 16, 1989). He reportedly "participated in writing slogan banners attacking leading central comrades" and "spread reactionary news to an illegal organization, the Yunnan Patriotic Students Democracy Movement Committee." In addition, he was accused of being a "corrupt element" for allegedly cohabiting with a married woman and owning two pornographic video tapes.

. . . . [2 X YRS]

Zhejiang

■ **LI Nannan**, formerly a student of veterinary medicine at Zhejiang Agricultural University, was arrested and sentenced sometime after June 1989, according to an official Chinese response to inquiries from the U.S. government (November 1991). He was arrested for allegedly organizing demonstrations, making speeches and putting up protest posters in Zhangzhou, Zhejiang Province (Amnesty International, *ASA 17/24/90*).

. . . . [? YRS]

■ **ZHANG Cheng** (Zhen), a former

student at Zhejiang Medical College, was arrested on June 15, 1989 by the Hangzhou City Public Security Bureau. According to an official Chinese response to inquiries from the U.S. government. Zhang was later sentenced and had not been released as of November 1991. According to a report on *Hangzhou Radio* (June 23, 1989, in FBIS, July 3), Zhang was expelled from his college on theft charges but stayed on campus and became head of the Students Autonomous Federation. He allegedly went first to Beijing, then returned to Hangzhou with "reactionary propaganda material" and then made speeches, "orchestrated attacks" on railway stations and blocked trains. Zhang was among 151 persons from 18 "illegal organizations" said by the authorities to have been arrested in Hangzhou, Ningbo, Wenzhou and Jinhua soon after June 4, 1989.

. . . . [? YRS]

Workers and Peasants

Beijing

■ **CAO Yingyun**, 36, a worker at the Second Machine Tool Factory in Beijing, was sentenced after the June 1989 crackdown, according to an official Chinese response to U.S. government inquiries (November 1991). He was arrested in the Fengtai district on May 24, 1989 for desecrating slogans that supported Li Peng and for spreading material that "attacked the leader of the Party and the government" (*Beijing Wanbao*, June

3, 1989).

. . . . [? YRS]

■ **HAN Binglin** was reportedly tried by the Beijing Intermediate People's Court on March 8, 1991 on charges of "counterrevolution" (*Shijie Ribao*, from Hong Kong, March 9, 1991). U.S. government requests for further information on Han's case elicited no response from the Chinese authorities (November 1991).

. . . . [? YRS]

■ **JIA Guanghua**, a 22-year-old construction worker, was sentenced after the June 1989 crackdown, according to the November 1991 official response to U.S. government inquiries. He was arrested sometime prior to September 13, 1989 after a fellow-worker allegedly reported to the police that on June 4, 1989, Jia had stolen a submachine gun from a soldier at the Muxidi interchange in Beijing and thrown it in a trash can (Amnesty International, *ASA 17/24/90*).

. . . . [? YRS]

■ **WANG Liqiang** and **LIN Qiang** were tried in July 1989 by a Beijing district court for allegedly inciting workers at the Capital Iron and Steel Company to join the democracy protests on May 20, 1989 (*Beijing Wanbao*, July 16, 1989). The outcomes of the trials were not reported, and later inquiries by the U.S. government on the men's cases elicited no response from the Chinese authorities (November 1991). (See also **Yi Jingyao** and **Tan Minglu**, below.)

. . . . [2 X ? YRS]

■ **WANG Zhaoming** and **WANG Jiaxiang** were sentenced by a Beijing court on December 7, 1989 for spreading "counterrevolutionary propaganda" and "inciting rebellion." Neither the dates of their arrests nor the terms of their sentences have been announced (*South China Morning Post*, December 15, 1989); however, an official Chinese response to U.S. government inquiries confirmed that Wang Zhaoming was sentenced and listed Wang Jiaxiang as "under investigation" (November 1991).

. . . . [2 X ? YRS]

Hebei

■ **CUI Guoxin**, who reportedly surrendered to the Public Security Bureau in Huanghua, Hebei Province (*Hebei Ribao*, July 11, 1989), was later sentenced, according to an official Chinese response to inquiries by the U.S. government (November 1991). He was allegedly involved in "illegal organizations" in either Hebei or Beijing.

. . . . [? YRS]

■ **LIU Tong**, a worker from Hubei Province, was sentenced in connection with 1989 pro-democracy activities and sent to the Hubei No.1 Labor Reform Detachment (New Life Plastics Factory). The date and length of sentencing are unknown.

. . . . [? YRS]

Shandong

■ **LI Weiguo**, 23, a peasant from Shili Village, Mazhai Township, Juancheng County in Shandong Province, was arrested on June 8, 1989 for allegedly taking part in the Beijing "Dare-to-Die Corps" and distributing leaflets entitled "The Truth of June 3" in front of the Heze City Specialized Teachers School. He was confirmed as sentenced on a list presented to the U.S. government by Chinese officials in November 1991. According to *Shandong Radio*, Li went to Beijing on May 15, 1989 to support the student hunger strikers. Once there, he made contact with students from Heze and through them entered the "Dare-to-Die Corps." On June 5, Li allegedly left Beijing to go to the Shandong cities of Qingdao and Yantai to make contact with unidentified persons; he returned to Heze on June 8 and was promptly arrested.

. . . . [? YRS]

Shanghai

■ **LIU Jian**[2], a worker at the Shanghai No.1 Aluminum Alloy Plant, was arrested between June 6 and 9, 1989 on charges of setting up roadblocks in Shanghai, instigating others to do the same and attempting to "stop and overturn police cars" (see Cheng Qiyang p.497 and Zhu Genhao p.582). Altogether 130 "lawless elements" were reported arrested in Shanghai for "disrupting traffic and obstructing official business" between June 6 and 9. In an official Chinese response to inquiries by the U.S. government (November 1991), once person named Liu Jian was listed as released and another of the same name was listed as sentenced, but the lack of additional identifying information made it impossible to know which of the two was still in prison.

. . . . [? YRS]

■ **SHEN Zhigao**, a worker at the Shanghai Toy Company warehouse and allegedly head of a "rebellious faction" during the Cultural Revolution, was tried and sentenced after the June 1989 crackdown, according to an official Chinese response to requests for information by the U.S. government (November 1991). Requests by the International Labor Organization for further information about his whereabouts have elicited no response (March 1992). Arrested on June 11, 1989 for spreading "counter-revolutionary propaganda" at People's Square and at the Finance and Economics University, Shen was also accused of carrying out unspecified "instigation" at the gate of Tongji University in Shanghai.

. . . . [? YRS]

■ **ZHAO Guozheng**, arrested and accused of blocking traffic and deflating tires on June 8, 1989 in connection with the Shanghai demonstrations in support of Beijing's pro-democracy movement (*Jiefang Ribao*, August 23), was later sentenced to a term of imprisonment, according to an official Chinese response to requests for information by the U.S. government (November 1991). No further details are known.

. . . . [? YRS]

Yunnan

■ **Li Hongbing** and two other leaders of the Kunming City (Yunnan Province) Residents Group for Supporting Patriotism and Democracy allegedly surrendered to the police and confessed their crimes after June 4, 1989. (According to a Kunming police spokesperson, an additional 15 "criminal elements," some of whom were accused of "beating, smashing, looting and burning," infiltrated the organization and were arrested on June 11, 1989.) (Amnesty International, *ASA 17/24/90*.) An official Chinese response to inquiries from the U.S. government confirmed Li as sentenced (November 1991).

. . . . [3 X ? YRS]

Zhejiang

■ **WANG Lin**, 25, was the target of a special October 24, 1989 "wanted notice" issued by the Hangzhou Municipal Public Security Bureau. She is from Heilongjiang Province and was a mining department student at China Mining Industry Institute. According to the notice, Wang was the leader of an "illegal" organization, the branch office of the *Students Alliance of the China Mining Industry Institute*d, in Xuzhou, Jiangsu Province. She allegedly "actively organized and plotted the turmoil, and is moreover suspected of having participated in the counter-revolutionary rebellion in Beijing. She has committed serious criminal acts..." There has been no news about Wang since June 1989, and the strong likelihood is that she was eventually caught and sentenced. (In response to inquiries by the U.S. government (November 1991), Chinese officials listed **"WANG Min"** as released, but that name did not appear on the U.S. inquiry list. While this may have been a mistaken reference to Wang Lin, the chances of such an error seem highly remote, given that Wang Lin was the subject of a "most wanted" notice and her case was thus clearly well known to the authorities.)

. . . . [? YRS]

Place Unknown

■ **TANG Kai** was arrested and sentenced after June 4, 1989, according to an official Chinese response (November 1991) to government inquiries about some 800 prisoners. His name was not on the list submitted by the U.S. side, however, and no additional information about him is available.

. . . . [? YRS]

■ **ZHAO Xiangzhang**, a retired worker, was reportedly sentenced at the end of April 1990 for setting up an illegal committee and preparing to dismiss village cadres (Amnesty International, *ASA 17/34/91*). No further details are known.

. . . . [? YRS]

Occupation Unknown

Beijing

■ A man named **ZHANG Hua** was tried by a Beijing court on charges of "counterrevolutionary propaganda and incitement" on August 2, 1992, according to a court proclamation. Zhang is believed to have received a five-year prison term, although this has not been confirmed. No further details of the case are known.

. . . . [5 YRS?]

Hunan

■ **BAI Xiaomao**, 29, a resident of Chenzhou Municipality and an employee of the Zixing Municipal Mining Bureau's Tangdong Coal Mine, was sentenced after June 1989 on charges of belonging to a "counter-revolutionary clique," according to an Asia Watch source. It is not known what sentence Bai received.

. . . . [? YRS]

■ **GAO Longfa**, 20, a resident of Tuyan Village (No.2 Group) in Rongjiang Township, Jishou Municipality, was sentenced after June 1989 on charges of "counter-revolutionary propaganda and incitement," according to an Asia Watch source. It is not known what sentence Gao received.

. . . . [? YRS]

■ **JIANG Fuxing**, 29, a resident of Chenzhou Municipality and an employee of the Zixing Municipal Mining Bureau's Baoyuan Coal Mine, was sentenced after June 1989 on charges of belonging to a "counter-revolutionary clique," according to an Asia Watch source. It is not known what sentence Jiang received.

. . . . [? YRS]

■ **JIANG Qianguo** - see p.257

. . . . [? YRS]

■ **LI Defeng** - see p.258

. . . . [? YRS]

■ **OUYANG Xinming**, 23, a resident of Xiangxi Municipality, was sentenced after June 1989 on charges of "counterrevolutionary propaganda and incitement," according to an Asia Watch source. It is not known what sentence Ouyang received.

. . . . [? YRS]

■ **TANG Ping**, a resident of Fenghuang County in the Xiangxi Tujia-Miao Autonomous Prefecture, was sentenced after June 1989 on charges of "counterrevolutionary propaganda and incitement," according to an Asia Watch source. It is not known what sentence Tang received.

. . . . [? YRS]

■ **WEN Xinyuan** - see p.264

. . . . [? YRS]

■ **XIA Lihuai** - see p.265

. . . . [? YRS]

■ **ZENG Chuqiao** - see p.267

. . . . [? YRS]

■ **ZHANG Shanguang**, a resident of Xupu County in Huaihua District, was sentenced after June 1989 on charges of "counterrevolutionary propaganda and incitement," according to an Asia Watch source. It is not known what sentence Zhang received.

. . . . [? YRS]

■ **ZHU Yiqun**, 30, a resident of Hengyang, was sentenced after June 1989 on charges of "counterrevolutionary propaganda and incitement," according to an Asia Watch source. It is not known what sentence Zhu received.

. . . . [? YRS]

■ **ZHUANG Lixin**, 27, a resident of Taoyuan County in Changde Municipality, was sentenced after June 1989 on charges of "counterrevolutionary propaganda and incitement," according to an Asia Watch source. It is not known what sentence Zhuang received.

. . . . [? YRS]

2. Arrested/Outcome Unknown

Students, Intellectuals and Journalists

Anhui

■ **XU Chong**, the general secretary of an independent students' union in Anhui Province, was "under investigation," according to an official Chinese response to an inquiry by the U.S. government (November 1991). He was arrested in a hotel in Nanjing, the provincial capital of Jiangsu (*Xinhua*, July 22, 1989), one among a total of 3,182 people arrested there in the three-day period July 13-15, 1989. Public security officials who made the arrest reportedly uncovered $1000 which allegedly had been hidden by a woman, **ZHENG Mingxia**, Chief of Finance for the Beijing student movement. (NB: This may actually be a reference to **Lu Mingxia**, see p.22.)

■ **YANG Fang** (Feng), a mechanics department engineering student at Anhui Engineering Institute, was arrested sometime in early July 1989 for alleged "counterrevolutionary propaganda and incitement" *(Hefei Radio,* in FBIS, July 10, 1989). The report identified Yang, a Hefei native, as chairman of the Institute's Students Autonomous Federation and a member of the provincial Students Autonomous Federation in Hefei. Yang allegedly organized a boycott of classes at local universities, took part in underground meetings and set up road barricades to block traffic. According to a UPI report, *Hefei Radio* also accused Yang of setting up a radio station called *Voice of the People* which, following the June 4, 1989 crackdown in Beijing, broadcast over loudspeakers set up outside the city government building in Hefei. Transmissions by the station included *Voice of America* programs and various other speeches which Yang personally recorded at Tiananmen Square. Yang was further accused of distributing pictures of the "alleged military crackdown." Inquiries to Chinese officials from the U.S. government as to Yang's whereabouts elicited no response (November 1991).

Beijing

■ **CHANG Jin(g)**, treasurer and Standing Committee member of Beijing University's Students Autonomous Federation, reportedly was arrested some time after June 4, 1989. Chang was a geography student at Beijing University from 1986 until his detention.

■ **CHEN Zhubai**, an engineering student at the Beijing University of Science and Technology, was arrested, possibly in July 1989, for organizing demonstrations at the Northwestern Agricultural University in Yangling, Shaanxi Province, where he stayed in May and June 1989 (Amnesty International, *ASA 17/24/90*). Requests by the U.S. government for information about Chen elicited no response from Chinese authorities.

■ **FAN Jianping**, an editor at *Beijing Ribao*, was arrested sometime after the June 4 crackdown, according to an Asia Watch source. Requests by the U.S. government for information about him have elicited no response from Chinese officials (November 1991).

■ **FAN Weijun**, a professor at the Law Research Institute of the Chinese University of Politics and Law and leader of the Beijing Citizens Autonomous Federation, was arrested in August 1989. As of November 1993, no further information was available.

■ **GONG Hui**, **LIU Jianqiang** and **GUO Yonggang**, natives of Beijing Municipality and "major participants" in the pro-democracy movement, were arrested on June 15, 1989 at the Dezhou railway station, Jinan County, during a spate of arrests in that province (*Shandong Radio*, June 22, 1989, in FBIS, June 23). All were characterized as "ringleaders of illegal student organizations" and were handed over to the Beijing Public Security Bureau. According to an official Chinese response to U.S. government inquiries (November 1991), Liu Jianqiang was released, but no information about either Gong Hui or Guo Yonggang was given.

■ **JI Funian**, in charge of logistics for the Beijing Students Autonomous Federation; and **WANG Zhigang**, a key member of the same organization; and three others, were arrested on June 15, 1989 by the Xushui County (Hebei Province) Public Security Department for "taking part in the counter-revolutionary rebellion in Beijing" (*Beijing Domestic Service*, June 20, 1989, in FBIS, June 27, 1989). In response to inquiries from the U.S. government, in November 1991 Chinese officials listed **WANG Shigang**, presumably the same person, as having "never been accused of any offense."

■ **JIA Aimin**, a student leader from Beijing, was reportedly arrested shortly after June 4, 1989. There has been no further news of his situation since then.

■ A person named **JIAN Jiliang** was reportedly arrested after June 4, 1989 and possibly held in Qincheng Prison, Beijing. There has been no further information on the case.

■ **JIN Naiyi**, 30, a journalist at *Beijing Ribao*, was arrested sometime after the June 4 crackdown, according to an Asia Watch source. No further information is available.

■ **LI Hongyu**, a psychology student at Beijing Normal University, was taken into custody in Chengdu, Sichuan on July 30, 1989 and transferred to Beijing on August 6. A Reuters report said that police officers uncovered 216,000 *yuan* or $58,000 that had been donated to the Beijing Students Autonomous Federation at the home of Li's boy friend, **LI Ming**[1], a researcher in the philosophy department at the Chinese Academy of Social Sciences. He reportedly was arrested at the end of 1989 and dismissed from his job. Requests for information by the U.S. government to Chinese authorities concerning the whereabouts of both dissidents elicited no response (November 1991). The cash allegedly was given to Li Hongyu by one of the students on China's "21 most wanted students" list, 21-year-old **Liang Qingtun**, another psychology student. Liang escaped from China in the summer of 1990. Li Ming, an associate of Li Shengping, joined Wang Juntao (see p.70), Chen Ziming (p.63) and Min Qi, as a participant in the "Beijing Spring" movement of the late 1970s.

■ **LI Jian**[1], a journalist at *Wenyi Bao*, a Beijing literature and arts journal, was arrested sometime after June 4, 1989, according to an Asia Watch source. His current status is unclear. The list of prisoners submitted in 1991 to Beijing by the U.S. government includes three different persons named Li Jian, and when the Chinese authorities responded in November 1991, they listed one Li Jian as being released, a second as being sentenced (i.e. still imprisoned), and no information was given on the third. Since no additional details (apart from the identical names) were revealed, however, it was not possible to identify which of the three had reportedly been released. (See also p.564 and p.564.)

■ **LI Shuguang**, an associate at the Chinese Legal History Institute, was arrested in June 1989. There is no further information on the case.

■ **LI Xiaohua**, an amateur writer, was arrested in mid-June 1989, according to an Asia Watch source. Li, who is about 35, was an editor at the People's Liberation Army Literature Publication House in Beijing. A 1988 national poetry award winner, he reportedly was arrested in Guangzhou on June 12, 1989 after fleeing there from Beijing. Requests by the U.S. government for information about Li's whereabouts elicited no response from Chinese officials (November 1991).

■ **LIU Bingjiang**, an artist and lecturer at the National Minorities University, reportedly was arrested in August 1989 for taking part in pro-democracy protests (Amnesty International, *ASA 17/24/90*). Requests by the U.S. government for information about him elicited no response from Chinese officials (November 1991). Liu is in his forties.

■ **LIU Huo**, a medical student, possibly from Beijing University, who was described on national television as "an important member of the student movement," was arrested shortly after June 4, 1989. He was accused of misappropriating donations worth $4,000 and of staying in an expensive hotel and eating and drinking lavishly. It was not clear, however, whether the funds referred to had in fact been collected in support of the students (Amnesty International, *ASA 17/24/90*). Requests by the U.S. government to Chinese authorities for information about Liu elicited no response (November 1991).

■ **LIU Xianbin**, a student in the personnel management department of People's University, was arrested sometime in April 1991 for publishing an unauthorized journal, Democracy Forum, which advocated reform of the Communist system (*South China Morning Post*, May 6, 1991; see also *Hong Kong Standard,* December 18, 1991). Liu was reportedly to face trial after mid-December 1991, but there has been no further information on his case.

■ **LU Feng**, a student at Beijing University of the Medical Sciences, reportedly was arrested on June 24, 1989. Requests by the U.S. government for information about his whereabouts elicited no response from Chinese officials (November 1991).

■ **MA Chengyi,** PLA Publishing House editor of *White Snow, Red Blood*, a controversial work of military history (see Zhang Zhenglong p.490), was detained in 1990 (*Christian Science Monitor*, September 27, 1990). There is no further information available.

- **OUYANG Ping**, a lecturer at the Institute of Sociology at Beijing University, was taken into custody in late June 1989. Requests by the U.S. government for information about him elicited no response from Chinese officials (November 1991).

- **PENG Kehong**, deputy director of the Marxist-Leninist Institute, was arrested on February 28, 1990. According to an Asia Watch source, he was sent to Qincheng Prison, but because of his heart condition was not admitted by the authorities there. Instead he was placed under house arrest. Peng's only activities in connection with the pro-democracy movement were to send a wreath to Tiananmen Square commemorating Hu Yaobang - he was the first one to do so - and to attend several meetings of "unauthorized" organizations at the Institute.

- A person named **QU Zijiao** was reportedly arrested at Beijing airport (date unknown) as he was preparing to leave for France to take part in a festival. According to a second report, a person named **YANG Xinghua** was arrested at Beijing airport before leaving to attend a ballet festival in France. There has been no further information on either case.

- **SUN Lu** and **XIA Kai** were arrested for involvement in the 1989 Beijing student movement, according to

People's Daily Overseas Edition (June 27, 1989). However, requests by the U.S. government to Chinese officials for information about the men's whereabouts elicited no response (November 1991). Sun is a graduate of Qinghua University and formerly a former secretary at Wanke Inc., in Shenzhen. Xia was a student at Shenzhen University.

- **TAO Yongyi**, director of the propaganda department for the Beijing Students Autonomous Federation, was arrested in the Mengcun Hui Nationality Autonomous County of Hebei Province sometime prior to July 6, 1989 (*Hebei Ribao*). Requests by the U.S. government for information about him elicited no response from Chinese officials (November 1991).

- A man named **WANG Jun**[3] was reportedly arrested in Shanghai for pro-democracy activities sometime in January 1990. There has been no further word on his situation since then.

- **WANG Xuezhi**[1], from the Beijing College of Chinese Traditional Medicine, was arrested in Beijing in June 1989 while trying to assist a wounded student (Amnesty International, *ASA 17/73/90*). Requests by the U.S. government for information about him elicited no response from Chinese officials (November 1991).

- The whereabouts of **WANG Yumin**, a junior at Beijing University when he was arrested in connection with the 1989 pro-democracy movement, are currently unknown. He may still be imprisoned.

■ **WU Bin** (Bing), a student in charge of the Beijing Students Autonomous Federation's reception center in Tiananmen Square, may have been arrested. According to an August 1989 official report, Wu appeared on an official video which recounted events of the night of June 3-4, 1989. Other people shown on the video are known to have been arrested (Amnesty International, *ASA 17/24/90*). Requests by the U.S. government for information about Wu have elicited no response from Chinese officials (November 1991).

■ **WU Xiaoming**, formerly a Beijing Normal College student, was held for at least a year-and-a-half for his participation in the 1989 pro-democracy movement. There is an unconfirmed report he was then sentenced to a four-year prison term and moved to another facility.

■ **WU Yun**, 24, a student in a Beijing institute of higher education and a core member of the Beijing Students Autonomous Federation, reportedly was transferred to an unknown location in Beijing from Changsha No.1 Prison in Hunan Province sometime after his arrest on June 13, 1989. According to the authorities, "From June 3 to June 4, he blocked military vehicles in Beijing, beat PLA soldiers with pop bottles, and stole an army helmet." On June 4, he fled to Guangzhou through Changsha, returning to Changsha on

June 8 to join a mourning ceremony organized by the Hunan Students Autonomous Federation. When Wu was arrested in a hotel, he had on him "a large quantity of reactionary handbills and propaganda materials" (*Hunan Ribao*, June 17, 1989).

■ **XIAO Wei**, a young man who came to Beijing to take his graduate school entrance examinations and had been staying at an unoccupied house in Shen Yuan Qiao owned by **YANG Liwen**, a professor of history at Beijing University, was arrested in early August 1991 for reasons unknown. According to an Asia Watch source, the police then placed Professor Yang's house under surveillance, questioning all those who came looking for Xiao. A self-paying student of economics at Beijing University, **LIU Mingtao**, who did not even know Xiao but whom Professor Yang had offered a bed for the night, was later taken into custody. On November 10, 1991, a schoolmate of Liu's received a letter from him asking that bedding and a toothbrush be sent to the Xuan Wu District Jail. The letter arrived after a deadline to deliver the package had passed, and when the friend tried to deliver it he was turned away by prison officials. As of January 1992, Professor Yang was still under investigation by the Beijing Public Security Bureau and his house had been confiscated. There has been no further news about either Xiao Wei or Liu Mingtao.

■ **XIONG Dayong**, a Chinese literature department student in his senior year at Beijing University, was arrested for organizing a July 23, 1989 demonstration on campus to protest the government's method of job assignment. The more than 300 students who attended the peaceful demonstration also commemorated those killed as a result of the June 4 crackdown. University officials alleged that Xiong was arrested for breaking martial law, but they also claimed he had previously been caught stealing bicycles and had been "warned for assault." Requests by the U.S. government for information about Xiong's whereabouts elicited no response from Chinese officials (November 1991).

■ **YANG Yiping**, a member of the *Stars (Xing Xing)* group of artists, reportedly was arrested in late July or early August 1989; his arrest is unconfirmed. A *Stars* group, probably the one to which Yang belonged, was active during the Democracy Wall movement.

■ **YUE Wenfu**, a student at the Lu Xun Academy of Literature and a leading activist in the Tiananmen Square occupation, was arrested and badly beaten while in prison, according to an Asia Watch source. Yue is thought to have helped erect barricades in Beijing in order to block the PLA's entry into the capital. Requests by the U.S. government for information about Yue elicited no response from Chinese officials (November 1991).

■ **ZHANG Jia**, head of a picket team of the Beijing Students Autonomous Federation, reportedly was arrested on June 16, 1989 by the Shahe City (Hebei Province) Public Security Department for "taking part in the counterrevolutionary rebellion in Beijing" (*Beijing Domestic Service*, June 20, 1989, in FBIS, June 27, 1989). There is no additional information available.

■ **ZHANG Nuanxiu**, a film director and signer of the February 1989 petition calling for amnesty for political prisoners, reportedly was arrested on June 11, 1989 (China Concern Group, Hong Kong University). Requests by the U.S. government for information about Zhang elicited no response from Chinese officials (November 1991).

■ **ZHANG Zhiqing**, on the June 13, 1989 "21 most wanted students" list, was arrested almost two years after he went on the run. No further details about the date or circumstances of his arrest or his place of imprisonment are known.

■ **ZHAO Jun**[1], an officer with the PLA's General Political Department, Division of Cultural Affairs, was secretly arrested at the end of summer 1990, according to an Asia Watch source. The report suggested that a contributory factor in Zhao's arrest was the fact that he was not in uniform on June 4, 1989. No additional information is available.

■ **ZHAO Yiqiang**, a radiation research office technician at Beijing Medical University's basic science department; his wife; and a graduate student at the university were among a number of people, including student leaders, reportedly detained in Zhangjiakou over the weekend of June 17-18, 1989. Their arrests followed the detention of **LIU Fuan**, now released, who reportedly "confessed" that the various parties had fled Beijing together. Zhao and his wife allegedly assisted students involved in the hunger strike (*Kyodo*, June 23, 1989, in FBIS, June 26, 1989). However, according to an official report, neither one was ever detained or arrested. Others arrested around the same time included **LIU Jiayu**, a student; **LIU Weidong**, a student leader and Liu Fuan's wife; **CHEN Weidong** and **LIU Jiaming** (Jianing). A report by *Beijing Central Television* (June 18, 1989, in *Kuai Bao*, June 19) that **LU Jieming** and four other student leaders were arrested in Zhangjiakou, Hebei Province, probably referred to the same case, i.e. "Liu Jiaming" and "Lu Jieming" may be the same person. All were accused of holding secret meetings, advocating strikes and chanting reactionary slogans. Requests by the U.S. government to Chinese authorities for information about Liu Weidong, Liu Jiayu, Chen and Zhao elicited no response, but Liu Jiaming was reported as released (November 1991).

■ A person named **ZHENG Chengli** was reportedly arrested at Beijing Railway Station on or shortly before June 13, 1989 while trying to leave the capital. There has been no further information on the case.

Gansu

■ Eight Lanzhou University student activists reportedly were arrested in January 1990 for their part in the pro-democracy movement (*Hong Kong Sing Tao Wan Bao* and *Agence France Presse*, in FBIS, January 8, 1990). Three of the arrested were on an official list of "most wanted" student leaders. While Asia Watch cannot confirm the report, it is known that Lanzhou University sent a delegation, reportedly of as many as 800 students, to Beijing during the pro-democracy protest. On January 11, 1990, an official at the university said she knew nothing about the report and denied there was a new wanted list; no new lists, she said, had been published in local newspapers since June 1989. Unofficial Chinese sources report, however, that regional governments issued their own lists apart from those from Beijing; such lists were not made public and circulated only in security units (FBIS, January 11, 1990).

Hainan

■ **GUO Xiaohong** and **GUO Yong**, cadres of the Communist Youth League at Hainan Normal University, were reportedly arrested in July 1989. Guo Yong, vice-secretary of the university's Youth League Committee, allegedly was one of the organizers of several demonstrations in Haikou, Hainan Province in May 1989 (Hong Kong *Kaifang*, April 1990). Inquiries by the U.S. government concerning the men's whereabouts elicited no information from Chinese authorities (November 1991).

Hebei

▪ **CHENG Zhedong**, a student, reportedly was arrested in Zhangjiakou, Hebei Province, on June 19, 1989 (China Concern Group, Hong Kong University). No further details are available.

Heilongjiang

▪ **CAI Sheng**, a grade two student at Wuchang Senior Middle School, was handed over to the police by Harbin Engineering University on June 7, 1989. He was accused of lying that his sister was a student in the Politics and Law Department at Beijing University and that she had been killed on campus by a shot to the chest. Cai also was accused of stealing a mini-cassette and other articles while housed overnight by sympathetic students at a Harbin university. Requests by the U.S. government for information about his whereabouts elicited no response from Chinese officials (November 1991).

According to a report in the June 8, 1989 *Heilongjiang Ribao* (in FBIS, August 4), Cai asked for leave on June 3, 1989 and took a train to Harbin. He later confessed that he went there to develop some film and do some shopping, but after seeing some leaflets he decided to "take advantage of the opportunity to cheat." On June 6, he allegedly made a speech in front of Harbin Construction Engineering College, saying he was a senior middle school student from Jilin and was an

eyewitness to the events of June 4 in Beijing. He said he witnessed many students killed in Tiananmen Square by vehicles running over them. He also reported he lost his watch and 300 *yuan* at the Square.

Henan

▪ **LU Yichun**, 32, was re-arrested on March 7, 1991 after having been forcibly repatriated to China, according to a January 1993 report from a source close to the case. In January 1991, Lu left China for Hong Kong. Once there, he denounced the Communist Party in a local newspaper. Originally arrested on June 25, 1989 for his part in pro-democracy activities, Lu remained in detention until July 10, at which point the Luoyang (Henan Province) Procuratorate decided not to prosecute him for his part in the "turmoil." He was said to have "made a serious political mistake," "inciting rumors of military rebellion" in Beijing and asking students in Luoyang to support the rebellion, but he later allegedly admitted his guilt and was freed. According to the State Education Commission, Lu was then disciplined by his institute. A 1984 graduate of the Wuhan College of Iron and Steel Technology, at the time of his second arrest Lu was a graduate student at the Luoyang Institute of Fire Resistant Materials. His present whereabouts are unknown.

▪ **WANG Qi**, formerly a student at the PLA's Foreign Languages School in Luoyang City, disappeared on approximately June 24, 1990, after being summoned back to China from Warsaw, where he had been studying Polish since 1986. In the spring of 1990, Wang was informed that he would have to return to China during the summer vacation since the Chinese Embassy had not received his scholarship funds, but that he could collect the money in China and resume his studies later. Upon returning to Luoyang on or around June 23, 1990, he reported to his college the following day, and has reportedly not been seen or heard of since. Friends who knew him in Poland have received no word from him, although he left all his property in that country and had only two more examinations to take before graduating from Warsaw University. It is believed that the Chinese authorities may have suspected Wang of participating in protest activities in Poland following the June 1989 government crackdown.

Hubei

■ **CHEN Zhiyang**, a staff member at the Wuhan Research Center for the Application of Higher Technology, reportedly was arrested in December 1989 for helping conceal Wang Juntao (see p.70) and sentenced in January 1991 to 13 years in prison as a "black hand" dissident (Amnesty International, *ASA 17/24/90*). However, requests for information to Chinese authorities by the U.S. government about Chen's case elicited no response. In the indictment statement of others involved in the case, Wu Litang *et al* (see p.436), there is mention of a **SHEN Qiaxiang**, prosecuted separately, who may be

Chen Zhiyang. For additional information, see also Xiao Yuan p.472. It is possible that Chen has now been released.

■ **GUO Yue** - see p.421

■ **XIAO Guangjian**, about 25 years old, a third or fourth-year student in the department of industrial technology at Wuhan (Hubei Province) University, was arrested on June 3, 1989 in Wuchang, according to an Asia Watch source. Xiao, who reportedly was one of the 20 or so top student organizers at Wuhan University, was at the front of a June 3 protest parade going from Wuchang Railway Station to the City Hall, when the demonstrators encountered a police blockade. He was arrested on the spot and there has been no further reports on his situation. Requests by the U.S. government to Chinese authorities for information about Xiao's case elicited no response (November 1991).

■ **ZH(O)U Xiaotong** (pen name **ZHOU Jiajun** and possibly the same person as **ZOU Xiaotong**), a young writer and student at the University of Wuhan (Hubei Province), was reportedly arrested in Wuhan sometime before June 17, 1989. Zh(o)u, who was affiliated with the 164th infantry battalion of the 55th army, allegedly burned his military uniform on the street to protest the massacre in Beijing. At last information, he was to face a military court if formally charged. (Requests by the U.S. government to Chinese authorities in November 1991 for information about

Zh(o)u elicited no response, but a person named "Zou Xiaotong" was listed by the authorities as released.)

Hunan

■ **CHEN Bing**, a student in the 1986 entering class at the Hunan Academy of Finance and Economics, was arrested at the end of 1989 after having been on the run for several months. Originally held in Cell 22 at Changsha No.1 Prison, his circumstances as of July 1993 were unknown. One report said he was accused of acts of violence. Chen reportedly was a "radical activist" during the 1989 pro-democracy movement, advocating no compromise with the government and opposing all dialogue and links. He was an important member of the Changsha Workers Autonomous Federation.

■ **HOU Liang'an**, 35-year-old head of the Changsha (Hunan Province) Soccer Fans' Association and a member of the Changsha branch of the Chinese People's Political Consultative Conference (CPPCC), was re-arrested at the end of 1990 and accused of establishing an underground organization. He had submitted a petition to the central and provincial governments after his release from a six-month prison term for alleged "extortion." Hou's circumstances as of July 1993 were unknown.

During the 1989 pro-democracy movement, Hou contributed over 2,000 *yuan* to the students in the name of the Soccer Fans' Association; and he organized deliveries of food to students engaged in sit-ins. While Hou was in detention in Changsha No.1 Prison, his father died. Several tens of thousands of people reportedly held a commemorative ceremony, both to mourn the dead man and to express support for Hou.

■ **HUANG Haizhou**, a 28-year-old employee of the Hunan People's Publishing House, was arrested and held in Changsha No.1 Prison for denouncing the Li Peng regime. During the 1989 pro-democracy movement, Huang organized a "Publishing Industry League in Support of the Students," allegedly wrote "reactionary articles" and planned demonstrations by League members. His circumstances as of July 1993 were unknown.

■ **WEN Quanfu**, 38, formerly general manager of the Hunan Province Overseas Chinese Enterprise Company, was arrested in September 1989 after a reportedly thorough investigation and held in Changsha No.1 Prison, Cell 10, before being transferred to Changsha County Detention Center. His circumstances as of July 1993 were not known. Wen's support of the students during the 1989 pro-democracy movement was characterized by the authorities as "having encouraged reactionary ideas" within the company and "creating an extremely bad influence among the masses." His case allegedly included "complex political aspects."

■ **XIONG Gang**, 23, a student from Hanshou County, Hunan Province, studying in the Chinese department of Yuncheng Teachers College in Shanxi

Province, was held for several days in Changsha's No.1 Prison before being transferred to Beijing. His circumstances as of July 1993 were unknown. In June 1989, *Hunan Ribao* reported Xiong's arrest by the Public Security Bureau in his home town. He had fled there after June 4. Xiong had gone to Beijing during the 1989 pro-democracy movement where he became general director of the Federation of Students in Higher Education from Outside Beijing. While in Beijing, he allegedly made "reactionary speeches."

■ **YAN Jiazhi** - see p.385

■ **YI Yuxin**, a 36-year-old cadre at the printing factory of Central-South Industrial University, Hunan Province, was arrested at the end of 1989 and held in Changsha No.1 Prison. His circumstances as of July 1993 were unknown. After the suppression of the 1989 pro-democracy movement, Yi allegedly continued to print and distribute propaganda materials.

■ **ZHENG Yuhua**, a 37-year-old teacher who operated his own private school, was arrested in July 1989 and held in Changsha No.1 Prison, Hunan Province, then transferred to an unknown location in December. Zheng reportedly had a good understanding of political theory, and, during the 1989 pro-democracy movement, acted as an advisor to the Standing Committee of the Hunan Students Autonomous Federation. He also organized a think tank.

■ **ZHOU Peiqi**, a 29-year-old technician with the Central-South No.5 Construction Company in Hunan Province, and a graduate of Central-South Industrial University, was arrested at the end of July 1989. His current situation is unknown. Before the 1989 pro-democracy movement, Zhou was already publicizing democratic thinking and reportedly was involved in a "secret organization." He actively participated in the movement in 1989, and after May 4, was in charge of the cash raised by the "Provincial Provisional Committee of Schools of Higher Education." Towards the end of May, Zhou, together with **LIU Zhongtao** (also known as **CHEN Le**), since released, and others, planned to set up a "Democracy Movement Lecture Center." Their plans never bore fruit.

Inner Mongolia

■ **WANG Shufeng**, 21, a student at Beijing University, and **QIAN Shitun** (Jitun/Chitong), described as core members of the Autonomous Federation of Students from Outside Beijing, were arrested on June 20, 1989. **YUAN Chihe** (Shihe/Cihe), 23, alleged chief director of the same organization, reportedly surrendered himself to the Baotou City (Inner Mongolia) Public Security Department that same day. On June 21, Yuan and Wang reportedly were turned over to the Beijing Municipal Public Security Department for further investigation. Requests for information by the U.S. government to Chinese authorities about the whereabouts of the three elicited no response (November 1991).

Yuan, a student at the Baotou Teachers Training School, was accused of "inciting, organizing and directing students who came to Beijing from other provinces to engage in demonstrations, sit-ins and strikes." He reportedly was interviewed several times by foreign reporters at Tiananmen Square; and after returning to Baotou he allegedly "continued to spread rumors and to incite students to go on strike and engage in demonstrations and other illegal activities." Yuan apparently also goes by the name **TASU**.

Wang was accused of having served as chief director of a group of demonstrators from Beijing University. He allegedly was responsible for organizing and directing "illegal" student demonstrations, sit-ins and hunger strikes and was a chairman of the Tiananmen Square student finance department. No biographical information or details about the charges against Qian were reported (*Inner Mongolia Radio*, June 23, 1989, in FBIS, June 27).

Jiangsu

■ **WANG Bin**, a member of the Beijing Students Autonomous Federation, reportedly was detained by the Nanjing (Jiangsu Province) Public Security Bureau for interrogation. He was discovered carrying "reactionary leaflets" and trying "to establish illicit ties in Nanjing's Hehai University" (*Beijing Radio*, June 16, 1989 in FBIS, June 21).

■ **WANG Yang**[1], Standing Committee member of the Students Autonomous Federation and a student at the Nanjing (Jiangsu Province) Institute of Mechanical and Electrical Engineering, was arrested on June 14, 1989. He allegedly tried to steal a bag of aluminum ingots. Wang not only did not register and confess his crimes as urged by the Public Security Bureau on June 13, but allegedly continued his illegal activities (*Beijing Radio*, June 16, 1989, in FBIS, June 21).

■ **WU Jianlin**, deputy head in May 1989 of the "solidarity group in the north" and a student at the Jiangsu Provincial Institute of Business-Management Cadres (*Beijing Radio*, June 16, 1989, in FBIS, June 21); **JI Tengheng**, a Nanjing University post-graduate student; and **HUANG Yongxiang**, a standing committee member of the Nanjing Students Autonomous Federation and a postgraduate student at Nanjing University, together with 16 members of outlawed student and worker organizations in Nanjing, reportedly turned themselves in to the authorities as requested as of June 15, 1989. Huang reportedly sent a cable to the Nanjing Public Security Bureau from his home in Fuzhou County, Fujian Province, asking that he be registered as a member of the illegal student union. According to an official Chinese response to U.S. government inquiries (November 1991) about the three men, Huang Yongxiang had been released and Wu Jianlin was still "under investigation." No information was given concerning Ji Tengheng.

■ **ZHOU Chengyu**, a 35-year-old graduate student in the history department of East China Normal University and a former education official in the Nanjing military region, was arrested in Jiangsu Province for giving shelter to Bao Zunxin (see p.405), according to an confirmed report. A request to Chinese officials by the U.S. government for information about Zhou elicited no response (November 1991).

Jiangxi

■ **XIONG Jiang**, formerly a student in the philosophy department at Beijing University, was detained in the summer of 1991 for pro-democracy activities. Other than that he is from a village in Jiangxi Province, no further information is available.

Jilin

■ **ZHOU Chifeng**, liaison officer of the Sit-in Command at Tiananmen Square who was interviewed frequently by a *New York Times* reporter, was arrested by the Changchun City Public Security Bureau, Jilin Province, on June 12, 1989. He had been in hiding in Changchun and was turned in to the authorities by members of Changchun Architecture College. Zhou, a former student at Wuhan University and probably originally from Hubei Province, reportedly made an initial confession. It is likely he was sent back to Beijing for investigation (*Beijing Radio*, June 21, 1989, in FBIS, same day). Requests by the U.S. government to Chinese authorities for information

about Zhou's whereabouts have elicited no response (November 1991).

■ According to a *Beijing Radio* dispatch (June 21, 1989, in FBIS, same day), an unnamed Jilin Industry University student who formerly headed the Organization Department of the Autonomous Federation of Students from Outside Beijing turned himself in to the public security organs and "confessed" to his pro-democracy activities in Beijing. Nothing is known of what became of him.

Liaoning

■ **CHEN Yang**, a 23-year-old student in the law department at the University of Politics and Law in Beijing who was allegedly director of the Beijing Citizens Autonomous Federation, was arrested on June 15, 1989 in Shenyang, Liaoning Province. A radio broadcast in Shenyang on June 17, 1989 said Chen had helped organize a "Dare-to-Die Corps," distributed "reactionary leaflets" and participated in "counterrevolutionary rebellion activities." He fled to Shenyang on June 9, 1989 and was arrested at his home by the Heping District Public Security Sub-bureau (FBIS, June 19, 1989). Chen was probably brought back to Beijing to face charges. Requests by the U.S. government for information about his whereabouts elicited no response from Chinese officials (November 1991).

■ **HUI Cheng**, a student at Northwest Engineering College and allegedly a member of a Beijing

"Dare-to-Die Corps," was arrested prior to June 20, 1989, possibly in Liaoning Province. Requests by the U.S. government for information about his whereabouts elicited no response from Chinese officials (November 1991).

■ **LI Shaopin**, a medical student at Shenyang University and a representative of the Autonomous Federation of Students from Outside Beijing, was arrested on June 18, 1989 in Baoding (*China Central Television*, June 18, 1989). Requests by the U.S. government for information about his whereabouts have elicited no response from Chinese officials (November 1991).

■ **YU Lin,** a student at Northwest Engineering College in Shenyang, Liaoning Province, and allegedly one of the key members of the Shenyang Students Autonomous Federation, was arrested sometime during June 14-20, 1989. Requests by the U.S. government for information about his whereabouts elicited no response from Chinese officials (November 1991).

■ **ZHOU Guijin** and **ZHI Chengyi** reportedly registered themselves with the Public Security Bureau of Shenyang City, Liaoning Province, on June 22 and June 21, 1989 respectively. Zhou, 24, a student at the Shenyang Teachers Training College, was described as a member of the Shenyang Students Autonomous Federation and general director of the "illegally-organized" Patriotic Society of Shenyang Teachers Training College. He allegedly directed a group of people to block traffic and roads on June 4, 1989 in order to prevent workers from getting to their jobs. On June 7, he organized a group of people to go to the Shenyang airplane manufacturing company and the Shenyang instrument-making company to block the workers' route to work. Zhou reportedly had shown a willingness to "confess his crimes."

Zhi, a student at Shenyang City's Medical College, was described as having been the Shenyang Students Autonomous Federation liaison and vice-chairman of a China Medical College "illegal" organization. He reportedly "accurately confessed to his illegal activities" (*Liaoning Provincial Radio*, June 23, 1989, in FBIS, June 27). Requests by the U.S. government for information about Zhi's whereabouts elicited no response from Chinese officials (November 1991).

Shaanxi

■ **HU Changsheng**, an assistant to the president of Baoji Teachers College in Shaanxi Province, was placed under investigation for his role in the 1989 democracy protests and may later have been taken into custody (Amnesty International, *ASA 17/24/90*). According to the authorities, "During the turmoil [Hu] gave some students written permission to go to Beijing to establish ties with Beijing students." On August 5, 1989 at an enlarged meeting of his college's Communist Party Committee, Hu allegedly "spread reactionary views" and "asserted that he could not associate with murderers."

The meeting had been called to discuss a Communist Party Central Committee document on "stopping the turmoil and putting down the counterrevolutionary rebellion." Hu was expelled from the Communist Party the following day. The U.S. government included his name on a list of prisoners submitted to Beijing in early 1991, but in its November 1991 response the Chinese government failed to give any accounting of Hu's current status.

■ The name and photograph of **QU Biao** appeared on a secret "most wanted" list issued by the government on August 19, 1989 as part of its crackdown on the pro-democracy movement. Qu, 29 years old, from Hengshan County in Shaanxi Province, was said to be a lecturer in the Weihai Annex of Shandong University. No details of his pro-democracy activities were given and his current status and whereabouts are unknown. He is one of the few of those who appeared on government wanted notices after June 1989 to have not yet been accounted for, and there is a high likelihood that he was eventually caught and sentenced.

■ The status and whereabouts of **ZI Yue**, formerly an editor of *Changan Review*, a literary magazine in Shaanxi Province, are unknown. He disappeared along with **DAO Zi**, his co-editor, in April 1989 after the two men had tried to publish a collection of essays and poems dedicated to the memory of Hu Yaobang (*South China Morning Post*, May 3, 1991). Dao later surfaced in Beijing, but there has been no further

information on Zi Yue.

Shandong

■ **PENG Jiang**, a student leader, was arrested on June 22, 1989 in Jinan (*Agence France Presse*, June 24, 1989). Requests to Chinese authorities by the U.S. government for information about him elicited no response (November 1991).

Shanghai

■ **SUN Mingzhang**, the 27-year-old deputy secretary general of the European Research Institute of the Shanghai Academy of Social Sciences, was reportedly arrested in Shanghai in the summer or autumn of 1989 and held in a secret detention center at No.5 Yin Gao Road in Shanghai (Amnesty International, *ASA 17/24/90*). However, requests by the U.S. government for information on Sun elicited no response from Chinese officials (November 1991). He was accused of having liaised with the foreign ministries of several governments.

■ A person named **XIE Zhilu** was reportedly arrested in Shanghai on June 5-6, 1989. There has been no further information on the case.

■ **YU Zhongmin** and **SHI Binhai**, both reporters for the Shanghai *Fazhi Yuekan (Law Monthly,* published by the East China Institute of Government and Law), were arrested during the summer or autumn of 1989 for their involvement in the democracy movement *(Shijie Ribao,* October 10, 1989). Both were cited in a long article, "The Facts about the Shanghai Riot" *(Wen Wei Bao,* June 28, 1989), which described them as "agitators" who "controlled and exploited the students during the turmoil in Shanghai." The article was later reprinted in several other major Chinese newspapers. According to an official Chinese response to U.S. government requests for information, Shi was released (November 1991); however, no information about Yu Zhongmin was forthcoming.

■ **ZHAO Wenli,** a female student from the class of 1988 at Northwestern College of Politics and Law, was identified in an article entitled "Facts about the Shanghai Riot" as the former head of the "Student Propaganda Delegation to the South." The article alleged that she had gone to various universities in Shanghai on May 24, 1989 to "stir up problems." Her arrest although likely, was never reported; and inquiries by the U.S. government about her status elicited no response from Chinese officials (November 1991).

Shanxi

■ **TIAN Junjie,** described only as "a student," was seized by the police at 9:30 P.M. on June 8, 1989 outside the Datong Station ticket office in Datong, Shanxi Province as he was "distributing mimeographed reactionary leaflets and spreading counterrevolutionary rumors" *(1990 Datong Yearbook,* p.51). Also arrested at the same time was a worker

activist from Beijing named **Zhao Changlin** (see p.150). The current circumstances of Tian and Zhao are unknown.

Sichuan

■ **CHEN Dali,** an instructor in the history department at Chengdu University and a leader of the student demonstrations in Chengdu, Sichuan Province, was arrested after the June 5-6, 1989 riots in that city, according to an Asia Watch source. Inquiries by the U.S. government about Chen elicited no response from Chinese officials (November 1991).

■ **JIANG Jiliang,** 27, a teacher at the Chengdu Geological Institute and one of a group of five or six academics detained in Chengdu after June 4, 1989, on charges of "counter-revolutionary propaganda" is still unaccounted for. In April 1990, *Jiushi Niandai* reported that **LI Xiaofeng,** a young philosophy researcher at the Sichuan Academy of Social Sciences, had been temporarily released on bail and that **LI Jing,** a young assistant researcher at the academy's Institute of History, had been freed due to ill-health. And responding to inquiries by the U.S. government, Chinese officials said in November 1991 that **TU Qiusheng,** 35, and **WANG Chengzong,** also philosophy researchers at the Sichuan Academy of Social Sciences, were released and that **WANG Zhilin,** a 32-year-old researcher at the academy and an editor in its intelligence section, had "never been accused of any offense" (a common euphemism for an administrative sentence of "labor re-education.") U.S. government requests for information about **JIANG Jiliang**, however, elicited no response.

- The arrest of **XUN Jianshen(g)**, 34, an instructor in Marxist philosophy at the Sichuan Provincial Youth League College, was announced at a mass rally in Chongqing, Sichuan Province on September 13, 1989 *(Chongqing Evening News*, September 14). On June 8, 1989, Xun spoke out in his classroom against the government repression in Beijing, and for this was later accused of attacking the Party's leaders and the People's Liberation Army and charged with "counter-revolutionary propaganda and incitement." (According to *Ming Bao* (October 10, 1989), one of Xu's pupils denounced him for saying that "several hundreds or even thousands of people" had been killed in Beijing.) Expelled from the Party and dismissed from his post after his arrest, as of September 1991 he was still being held at a detention center in Chongqing and his family had not been informed of his whereabouts. Inquiries to the Chinese authorities about Xun by the U.S. government elicited no response (November 1991).

- An unusually large dissident pro-democracy group, the *Democratic Youth Party (Minzhu Qingnian Dang)*, was uncovered and smashed by the authorities in Kai County, Wanxian District of Sichuan Province in May 1992. According to a confidential report by the Wanxian District Public

Security Section, no less than 179 members of the group, which was specifically described as having "opposed the Three Gorges Dam Project" (one of the largest civil engineering projects ever undertaken) were "netted" in the crackdown. (Report published in a restricted-circulation *[neibu]* journal entitled *Research in Crime and Reform,* No.2, 1993.) Most of Wanxian District, a relatively prosperous region of fruit tree and orchard cultivation, is scheduled to disappear forever under the flood area of the Three Gorges Dam, should the project eventually be completed as planned. There have been no public reports of the *Democratic Youth Party* case and it is not known either how many of the 179 reported detainees have by now been brought to trial and sentenced, or how many may already have been released or are still awaiting trial.

Tianjin

- **CHEN Xuezhao** and **LI Shi**, students at Nankai University in Tianjin, were reportedly arrested during the crackdown on the 1989 democracy movement and there had been no news of them since. Chen, a graduate student in sociology, was detained in August 1989 for allegedly writing a "Letter to All Chinese" and posting it up at Beijing University. Li, a graduate student in biology, was detained in June 1989 for allegedly writing a poster attacking Prime Minister Li Peng (Amnesty International, *ASA 17/24/90*). Inquiries by the U.S. government on the status of Chen and Li elicited no response from Chinese officials (November 1991).

Xinjiang Uygur Autonomous Region

- **WANG Xuecheng**, 26, a trainee associate at the Xinjiang Academy of Science's Institute of Biological, Soil and Desert Research, was arrested on June 13, 1989 in Urumqi, capital of the Xinjiang Uygur Autonomous Region after allegedly listening to *Voice of America* broadcasts and then putting up posters that "spread rumors" about the June 4 crackdown in Beijing (Amnesty International, *ASA 17/24/90*). Requests by the U.S. government for information on Wang's status elicited no response from Chinese authorities (November 1991).

Zhejiang

- **LI Yunshou**, a Zhejiang Agricultural University graduate student, was seized in Yunnan sometime after June 4, 1989, according to an Asia Watch source. Inquiries to Chinese officials by the U.S. government on Li's status elicited no response (November 1991).

- **LIU Xiaoqu**, 27, and **LU Zhuru**, 29, two women accused of involvement in the "counterrevolutionary rebellion," were reportedly arrested at Beijing Airport sometime during June 1989 while preparing to board a plane for Paris. According to *South China Morning Post* (June 23, 1989), their passports had been mailed to them from

outside China and a customs official spotted forged entry stamps. Liu and Lu, teachers in Wenzhou, Zhejiang Province, were reportedly travelling under the assumed names of **GU Fengjuan** and **HUANG Hongyu**. Inquiries to Chinese officials by the U.S. government on the women's status elicited no response (November 1991).

- **WANG Hong**[1], a second-year English student at the Zhejiang Normal University in Jinhua, was reportedly arrested on campus when he returned from summer recess, probably in early September 1989, and then held incommunicado and denied family visits. Wang, in his early twenties, was charged with writing slogans in his own blood and burning posters bearing quotations from Chairman Mao. Requests for information on Wang's status by the U.S. government elicited no response from the Chinese authorities (November 1991).

- A person named **ZHANG Zhen** was reportedly arrested in Hangzhou, Zhejiang Province, on June 15, 1989 after he was found with "counter-revolutionary" printed material that he had brought back from Beijing. There has been no further information on the case.

Place unknown

- **BAO Liangqing**, the first Chinese procuratorial official reported to have been detained in connection with pro-democracy activities, is believed to have been arrested in April 1992. (The duties of the procuracy include conducting state prosecutions and monitoring law-enforcement by the police and courts.) On August 19, 1991, eight months prior to his arrest, Bao is said to have participated in a celebration of the failure of the Soviet coup to oust Mikhail Gorbachev. No further details of the case are known.

■ Nothing is known about the current status of **LIU Ruilin, HU Jian²**, **MA Xiaojun** and **SHADIKEJIANG**, all of whom were listed as "already arrested" in a secret compilation of "most wanted" notices issued by the Ministry of Public Security in September 1989. The confidential document gave no details about the four other than their names, and subsequent inquiries by the U.S. government on the cases elicited no response from Chinese officials (November 1991). Some of them may be workers rather than students or intellectuals. The name "Shadikejiang" is certainly not that of a Han Chinese - the person concerned is probably of ethnic-group origin, most likely a Uygur. As for Hu Jian, a person of that name from Shanxi Province was arrested during the 1989 crackdown and later sentenced to ten years' imprisonment (see p.86), but that may be a different person.

According to another report, a government cadre named **YU Liangqing** was arrested in Anhui Province sometime around June 1992 on suspicion of involvement in pro-democracy activities; it is possible that both names refer to the same person. (More likely, however, is that the latter

name refers to **Shen Liangqing** [see p.444], a cadre who was released in September 1993.)

Workers, Peasants and Business Persons

Anhui

■ **CHEN** Ting and **LIANG Jianshe**, deputy heads of the Worker Volunteer Brigade in Hefei, Anhui Province, were reportedly arrested sometime after June 4, 1989 in the coastal city of Wenzhou, Zhejiang Province. Both men were allegedly active in demonstrations that rocked Hefei between June 4 and June 9. Subsequent inquiries by the U.S. government about the two elicited no response from Chinese officials (November 1991).

■ **GAO Jingshan**, one of seven alleged leaders of "illegal organizations" in Anhui Province, was arrested sometime before June 19, 1989 in Hefei. Requests from the U.S. government for further information on Gao's case elicited no response from Chinese officials (November 1991).

■ **YIN Guohua**, allegedly a key member of a Hefei "illegal organization," was detained sometime before June 18, 1989. No additional details are available (Amnesty International, *ASA 17/24/90*). Subsequent inquiries by the U.S. government on Yin's case elicited no response from Chinese officials (November 1991).

■ **ZHANG Guorong**, a young

worker and leader of the Hefei City Workers Spontaneous Group, Anhui Province, reportedly turned himself in to the Public Security Bureau on June 10, 1989. He was accused of "taking advantage of the social unrest" to stage demonstrations, shout slogans, incite strikes and vilify Party and state leaders. Zhang allegedly was detained twice before, and on one occasion served time in a "re-education through labor" center (*Beijing Radio*, June 13, 1989, in FBIS, June 22). Requests from the U.S. government for further information elicited no response from Chinese authorities (November 1991).

Beijing

- **BAI Fengying** - see p.365

- **BAI Xinyu** - see p.359

- **CHENG Yufei**, 26, was arrested at the end of 1989 while at work at the Changcheng Hotel in Beijing. He was reportedly a member of the Beijing Workers Autonomous Federation and participated in "counterrevolutionary activities." At last report, in mid-1991, family members and workers at the hotel had received no news of his whereabouts. No further information is currently available.

- **GAO Feng²**, who was alleged to have gone from Beijing to Xi'an on May 19, 1989, to stir up people and urge them to initiate a hunger strike in Xincheng Square, was arrested on June 5 or 6, 1989. According to a report in *Zhongguo Qingnian Bao (China Youth*

Daily) on July 1, 1989, Gao, an unemployed worker, "spread rumors" on May 20 and 22 at Northwestern University and pretended to be a *Zhongguo Qingnian Bao* reporter. Requests for information about two people named Gao Feng (see p.160) were submitted to Chinese authorities by the U.S. government. In the official Chinese response (November 1991), one was listed as having "never been accused of any offense"; the other was not mentioned. Since additional details were provided it was unclear to whom the comment referred.

- **LI Mou**, an employee of the Merchant and Industry Station in Huilongguan, Changping County and a Beijing Workers "Dare-to-Die Corps" member, was arrested on June 13, 1989 in Huoying, Changping County near Beijing for allegedly joining the June 3-4 turmoil (*Beijing Ribao*, June 15, 1989). Subsequent inquiries by the U.S. government on Li's case elicited no response from Chinese officials (November 1991).

- **LI Zixin**, 21, from Dongzhao Village, Fashang Brigade, Daxing County near Beijing, was arrested for allegedly joining a group that attempted to block the progress of military vehicles on May 22, 1989 (*Beijing Wanbao*, June 3, 1989). Requests by the U.S. government for information about Li's whereabouts elicited no response from Chinese officials (November 1991).

- **LIANG Zhenyun**, a self-employed auto mechanic, was arrested for allegedly taking a machine gun and a pistol from a soldier on June 4, 1989 (*Beijing Wanbao*, in UPI July 14, 1989). No further information is available.

■ **LIU Beihong**, arrested in June 1989 by the Beijing Public Security Bureau for his membership in the Beijing Workers Autonomous Federation, was held incommunicado after his arrest. No further information is available.

■ **LIU Weipu**, **WU Zhijun** and **ZHANG Shaoying** were shown on *China Central Television* on June 16, 1989 being paraded at a public trial. Placards announced the charges as being "counterrevolutionary propaganda." According to the *New York Times* (June 16, 1989), Zhang was later sent to a labor camp for "spreading rumors." According to a November 1991 official response to U.S. government inquiries, Wu and Zhang were later released. The current status of Liu Weipu is unknown.

■ **MIAO Deshun** - see p.359

■ **SHI Guoquan** - see p.359

■ **SUN Peng**, the executive housekeeper at the Beijing International Hotel, was reportedly arrested for his involvement in the May 1989 demonstrations in Beijing. He was later, however, charged with beating his wife and mother-in-law and taking money from a guest at the hotel (Amnesty International, *ASA 17/24/90*). Subsequent requests by the U.S. government to Chinese authorities for information on Sun's case elicited no response (November 1991).

■ **TAN Pinggan**, a Beijing painter, was reportedly arrested in late July or early August 1989 (Amnesty International, *ASA 17/24/90*). Subsequent inquiries by the U.S. government on Tan's case elicited no response from Chinese officials (November 1991).

■ **WANG Guoqiang** - see p.359

■ **WANG Shuwei**, in his early twenties and a bell-boy at the Beijing International Hotel, was reportedly arrested for "counterrevolutionary" offenses (Amnesty International, *ASA 17/24/90*). Requests by the U.S. government for information about his whereabouts elicited no response from the Chinese authorities (November 1991).

■ The fate of **WANG Weilin**, the young man who stood in front of a column of tanks near Tiananmen Square just after June 4, 1989 as millions worldwide watched on television, is still unknown. The London *Daily Express* (June 18, 1989) reported that Wang, then 19, the son of a factory worker, was later arrested by the secret police and charged with "political hooliganism" and "attempting to subvert members of the People's Liberation Army." According to the newspaper, friends of the young man recognized him after seeing a line-up of pro-democracy detainees with shaven heads appear on state television.

Another account, from the Hong Kong press, reported that Wang had been executed.

In a reply to inquiries from the International Labor Organization (November 1990), Chinese officials claimed that Wang had never been arrested or brought before the judicial authorities. This could mean, however, that he was sentenced without trial to "re-education though labor." The U.S. Department of State's *Country Reports on Human Rights Practices for 1990* (February 1, 1991) concluded that none of the various accounts, including the official Chinese disclaimer of Wang's arrest, could be confirmed. And subsequent requests for information by U.S. government for information about Wang (November 1991) elicited no response from Chinese officials. It is even quite possible that the man who stood in front of the tanks in Beijing was not, in fact, named Wang Weilin after all.

■   **YANG Ensen**, a worker at the Sixth Construction Company, was arrested in Beijing (*Xinhua*, June 16, 1989; *Renmin Ribao*, June 19). At 8 A.M. on June 4, 1989, Yang reportedly saw several military vehicles stopped in the middle of a road and shouted at them. For this he was later charged with committing the crime of "counter-revolutionary incitement."

■   **YANG Jing**, 44, a former steel worker, served in full an eight-year sentence for peaceful dissident activities before being released in April 1989, subject to one year's further deprivation of political rights. An

editor of *April Fifth Forum* during the Democracy Wall movement, he was arrested for advocating improvement in the human rights situation in China and for pressing for the release of other Democracy Wall activists. Yang served eleven months in solitary confinement, much of it in handcuffs and leg irons, for attempts to contact friends among fellow inmates. He was advised upon his release to avoid his former colleagues. However, Yang made speeches in Tiananmen Square during the 1989 pro-democracy movement and is thought to have been re-arrested sometime after June 4. Requests by the U.S. government for information about him elicited no response from Chinese officials (November 1991).

■   **ZHAI Yicun** - see p.359

■   **ZHAO Changlin**, described in the *1990 Datong Yearbook* as being a "diehard member of the Beijing Workers Autonomous Federation," was arrested at 9:30 P.M. on June 8, 1989 outside the Datong Station ticket office in Datong, Shanxi Province, together with a student named **Tian Junjie** (see p.144) and nine other "criminal elements." The current circumstances of Zhao and Tian are unknown.

Gansu

■   **YANG Zhengyi, PENG Shangzhi** and **XIAO Bin**[2] were all arrested in Lanzhou, Gansu Province on June 8, 1989 for allegedly spreading rumors and organizing an illegal demonstration there. According to a Chinese response to U.S. government inquiries (November 1991), Peng was later released; it is not known whether he served a sentence or was released without charge. The authorities gave no response to inquiries about either Xiao Bin (not to be confused with another person of that name who received a ten-year sentence - see p.107) or Yang Zhengyi. Described by the authorities as a "criminal on the run," Xiao Bin is from Yinchuan in Ningxia Hui Autonomous Region.

■ Trials of sixteen pro-democracy activists reportedly took place in Lanzhou, Gansu Province, on July 15-20, 1989. According to an Asia Watch source, all those tried were charged with either "counter-revolutionary propaganda and incitement" or "obstructing public order." One of those convicted was an elderly woman who, after June 4, allegedly spread a story that Deng Xiaoping had died, and then lit firecrackers in celebration. This prompted similar celebrations all over Lanzhou which continued until a police crackdown at 3:00 A.M. the next morning; the woman's arrest is said to have aroused much public indignation. Neither the names of the sixteen defendants nor the lengths of their prison sentences are known.

Guangdong

■ LU Zhanbiao, FENG Zechao and ZHOU Yiming were arrested in Guangzhou, Guangdong Province, sometime prior to July 20, 1989. Feng and Zhou were suspected of engaging in "counterrevolutionary propaganda," and Lu, a 30-year-old private

businessman, was charged with creating "counterrevolutionary disturbances" (Amnesty International, *ASA 17/66/90*). Subsequent requests by the U.S. government for information about the three men elicited no response from Chinese officials (November 1991).

■ XIAO Shifu, owner of a photo-processing shop; LI Lixin (Lixian), his wife; and LIN Weiming were arrested on July 15, 1989 in Guangzhou, Guangdong Province. Xiao and Li were accused of trying to use fake Singapore passports to flee the country. Lin, a Hong Kong resident, was accused of providing the passports in exchange for the sum of HK$300,000. Reports gave no indication of why the couple were trying to flee the country, but their attempt coincided with a large series of escapes from China by pro-democracy activists wanted by the security authorities, and it is possible that Xiao and Li were also fleeing repression. Requests by the U.S. government for further information on their cases elicited no response from Chinese officials (November 1991).

■ YANG Guixi, deputy manager of the Wanzai Tour Company in Zhuhai, was arrested on November 28, 1989 in his native Guangdong Province for allegedly selling a ferry ticket for Macao to a person on the run who then escaped from China (Amnesty International, *ASA 17/24/90*). Requests to Chinese authorities by the U.S. government for further information on Yang's case elicited no response (November 1991).

Hebei

■ **DING Peilin** and **DING Jie**, father and son, were arrested sometime before July 6, 1989 for allegedly beating martial law enforcement troops during the crackdown in Beijing. Both were arrested in Xingtai City, Hebei Province (*Hebei Ribao*, July 12, 1989). There has been no further information on the case.

■ **LIU Jianli**, a "ruffian," was arrested on June 15, 1989 by the Xianghe County Public Security Bureau during a reported roundup of 44 people in Hebei Province. Requests by the U.S. government for information about his whereabouts elicited no response from Chinese officials (November 1991).

■ **SUN Baochen**, **BAI Zenglu** and **MA Jianxin**, all from Dingxian County, Hebei Province, were arrested on June 6, 1989 in Zhuozhou City for allegedly joining the "counter-revolutionary protests" in Beijing (*Zhongguo Qingnian Bao*, June 14, 1989). Requests by the U.S. government for information about Sun and Bai's whereabouts elicited no response from Chinese officials (November 1991).

Henan

■ **ZHANG Wei**[1] - see p.435

Hunan

■ As of May 1992, **LIU Fuyuan**, a 35-year-old private businessman in Changsha City, Hunan Province, was still being detained. His fate since then is unknown. While in prison, Liu reportedly went on hunger strikes to protest his treatment; his weight dropped from over 80 to under 40 kg. In addition, he developed kidney stones which caused him excruciating pain. Doctors recommended that he be released for medical treatment, but the authorities refused permission.

During the 1989 pro-democracy movement, Liu reportedly organized local residents to donate money to the students, and he participated in a hunger strike and a sit-down protest outside provincial government offices. After June 4, he allegedly "spread rumors" that "several thousand people were killed by the troops in Beijing." Liu then fled China for Thailand. After returning in mid-1990, he was arrested in Changsha and imprisoned in the Changsha No.1 Jail (Cell 13). As a youth, Liu was involved in dissident activities with the Cultural Revolution pro-democracy activist Chen Guangdi, who later died in prison.

■ **LIU Yi**, a 24-year-old worker at the Changsha Power Machinery Factory, Hunan Province, was re-arrested in August 1990 on a charge of posting "counterrevolutionary slogans." He was first arrested in June 1989 and held in Changsha No.1 Jail (Cell 11), then released in December. During the 1989 pro-democracy movement, Liu served as treasurer of the Changsha Workers Autonomous Federation. There has been no further news on his fate.

■ **LUO Ziren**, a 25-year-old Guizhou Province native, and a temporary [contract] worker at the Changsha (Hunan Province) Cigarette Factory, was re-arrested in November 1991 for posting "reactionary handbills." He had been released in 1990 from his first arrest which took place shortly after June 4, 1989 in his home town in Guizhou. During the 1989 pro-democracy movement, Luo was a member of the Picket Squad of the Hunan Students Autonomous Federation (HSAF) and was responsible for the safety of HSAF leaders and for some of the organization's documents. There has been no further news on his fate.

■ **TANG Zhijian**, 31, formerly a worker at the Hengyang Railway Maintenance Department, Hunan Province, was re-arrested in May 1991 and taken to Baishazhou Detention Center. The ostensible charge against Tang was that he had "stolen a tape-recorder on a train." He was first arrested in March that year by the Hengyang Jiangdong Railway Police for assisting the brothers Li Lin and Li Zhi (see p.500) and others to flee China on a direct Hengyang-Hong Kong train in July 1989 and for taking part in the 1989 demonstrations in Hengyang. He reportedly confessed, and after one week was freed upon payment of a fine of 1,000 *yuan*. Tang's wife was assured by the Public Security Bureau that if he signed a confession he would not be prosecuted. In May 1991, he did so, stating that he was unaware that the people he helped were involved in the pro-democracy movement. He was then rearrested. Tang told Li Zhi that he was being pressured to say he had received money for helping the Li brothers escape in 1989. In mid-1991, Li Zhi was being held two cells away, having been arrested along with his brother after returning to China from Hong Kong. As of January 1992, Tang was still in prison. Following international pressure, the Lis were freed and now live in the U.S.

■ **XU Yue**, a 25-year-old employee in the maintenance workshop of the Tianjin Nail Factory, was arrested on June 13, 1989 in a hotel in Changsha, Hunan Province, and held in Changsha No.1 Jail before being transferred to an unknown location. Reportedly a core member of the Beijing Students Autonomous Federation, Xu was also responsible for logistics for the support group from Hong Kong stationed in Tiananmen Square. After the June 4 massacre, he fled to Guangzhou via Changsha, and on June 8 returned to Changsha to take part in a mass public mourning ceremony organized by the Hunan Students Autonomous Federation. According to the authorities, Xu also took photographs "with the intention of carrying out additional reactionary propaganda all over the place" (*Hunan Ribao*, June 17, 1989). His current circumstances are unknown.

Jiangsu

■ **FANG Jingdong**, 28, an employee of the China Trust Company's energy division, was arrested in January 1990 at the Nanjing railway station (Jiangsu Province), allegedly carrying the original copy of a late May 1989 petition calling upon the National People's Congress to convene an emergency session to discuss, among other things, freedom of the press. Fang allegedly organized the drive and obtained about 200 signatures from the company's employees; the authorities apparently only knew the identities of about 50 participants. After June 4, 1989, Fang was made to write a self-criticism and was placed under surveillance. It was during a permitted trip to visit his family in Nanjing that he was seized. Requests by the U.S. government for further information on Fang's case elicited no response from Chinese officials (November 1991).

Jilin

■ **LI Xiexian, LIU Yusheng** and 23 others were arrested and "punished" publicly in Changchun, capital of Jilin Province, on June 10, 1989, according to Chinese television. Li allegedly took advantage of student disturbances to commit murder and theft. The charges against Liu, one of six people sentenced to "re-education through labor," are not known (Amnesty International, *ASA 17/24/90*.) However, Chinese officials told the International Labor Organization in March 1992 that, of the 26 "ruffians" reportedly tried on June 10 in Changchun, the seven sentenced to labor re-education camps had been released "a year ago," approximately June 1991. Liu was presumably among them.

Liaoning

■ **WANG Di**, 42, was arrested on June 11, 1989 in Dalian, Liaoning Province for speaking with a foreign television crew in Beijing about the June 4 massacre in Beijing (Amnesty International, *ASA 17/24/90*). Excerpts of the interview were broadcast on Chinese television on June 10, 1989; on June 11, Chinese television broadcast Wang's arrest and described him as a "dangerous counter-revolutionary instigator." Requests by the U.S. government for information about his whereabouts elicited no response from Chinese officials (November 1991).

■ **XIAO Han** was arrested in Dalian for stirring up "counterrevolutionary" activities first in Beijing and then in Dalian, according to *Shenyang Radio* (Hong Kong Alliance, June 16, 1989). No further information is available.

■ **XU Guocai**, a peasant from Songjiaguo village, Huanhe township, Tieling County, Shenyang, Liaoning Province, was arrested for sending 13 "counterrevolutionary letters" between April 20 and May 26, 1989, according to a provincial radio broadcast. In the name of a group called the "Special Administrative Team of the Northeast China Joint Forces for Saving the Country," the letters allegedly called on military districts in the region to overthrow the government, stage mutinies and support student unrest. Requests by the U.S. government for further information on Xu's case elicited no response from Chinese officials (November 1991).

■   **YANG Dongju**, a worker at the repair unit of the engineering section of the Shenyang (Liaoning Province) Railway Bureau, and **QUAN Baogui**, a worker at the Dandong No.4 Vehicle Parts Factory, were arrested sometime between June 15 and June 20, 1989 by the Dandong City Public Security Bureau for allegedly making "inciting speeches and spreading rumors in the streets" and "attacking Party leaders and the PLA." During the week prior to their arrests, the Dandong television station broadcast a videotape of Yang and Quan speaking. Yang reportedly was punished by being given a warning and a "demerit" for his alleged participation in gambling and for damaging public property, but may also have been charged with "counter-revolutionary propaganda and incitement" under Article 102 of the Chinese Criminal Code. Quan reportedly was punished by receiving a "demerit in line with administrative action" and was dismissed from the Party *(Liaoning Provincial Radio*, June 22, 1989, in FBIS, June 23). Requests by the U.S. government for information about the men's whereabouts elicited no response from Chinese officials (November 1991).

■   **ZHU Yunfeng**, a worker in the service committee of the Fushun Carbon Plant, was arrested in Fushun City, Liaoning Province on June 15, 1989 together with five other members of a "people's corps." All were accused of blocking traffic and shouting slogans such as "Down with official

speculation!" Requests by the U.S. government for further information on Zhu's case elicited no response from Chinese officials (November 1991).

Shandong

■   **LI Fenglin's** name, address, photograph and I.D. number appeared on a secret "most wanted" list issued by the Chinese government on August 19, 1989. A 31-year-old, he was a vegetable farmer from Zhudian Village, Honglou Town, Jinan, Shandong Province. No details of his pro-democracy activities were given and his whereabouts are unknown. He is one of the few persons named on known top "wanted" lists after June 4, 1989 who still remain unaccounted for, and the strong likelihood is that he was eventually caught and sentenced.

■   **LI Wenting**, a peasant from Feicheng County, Shandong Province, was arrested on June 24, 1990 in Tai'an. He allegedly had links to the Beijing Students Autonomous Federation. Requests for information by the U.S. government about his whereabouts elicited no response from Chinese officials (November 1991).

■   **NIU Shengchang**, 39, a peasant from Niulin Village, Yunshang Township, Dongping County, Shandong Province, was arrested on June 16, 1989 in Tengzhou and accused of going to Beijing on May 18 to join the Peasants Autonomous Union. After allegedly resisting martial law troops, Niu returned to his home on June 4, but reportedly then traveled to other provincial localities where he posted "reactionary" posters and distributed "counterrevolutionary leaflets" (*Shandong Provincial Radio*, June 17, 1989, in FBIS, June 20). Niu allegedly had "a record of dissatisfaction." Between 1984 and 1986 he went to Beijing eight times, said the report, to present unspecified appeals to higher authorities. Requests to Chinese authorities by the U.S. government (November 1991) for information about Niu elicited no response.

■   **ZHAO Gang**[1], a cotton mill worker in Zouping County, Shandong Province, was arrested after June 4, 1989 in connection with the pro-democracy movement, according to an Asia Watch source. Nothing further is known about his case.

Shanghai

■   **CHEN Dao** (also known as **CHEN Yuan**); **JIANG Zhi'an**, a worker for the Shanghai Construction Company's No.301 Team; **DAI Yue**; and **YANG Xiuping** were arrested for setting up an "illegal organization," the broadcasting station *Voice of Democracy and Freedom*, in Shanghai's People's Square. The station allegedly began "counterrevolutionary propaganda broadcasts" on May 23, 1989 (*Jiefang Ribao*, August 23, 1989). Jiang, Dai and Yang were later released, according to a Chinese response to requests for information by the U.S. government (November 1991). but requests for information about Chen Dao elicited no response.

■   **GENG Xiuchong**, 30, a Shanghai resident, was accused of "faking a bloody cloth on June 5, 1989 as evidence of the Beijing massacre" (*Beijing Ribao*, June 29, 1989). Requests by the U.S. government for further information on Geng's case elicited no response from Chinese officials (November 1991).

■   **LI Rongfu** was arrested on June 7, 1989 and accused of instigating students to obstruct transportation. According to *Shanghai Radio*, the 39-year-old Shanghai taxi driver approached a group of students gathered at the intersection of Siping and Xingang Roads and urged them to adopt new "struggle tactics," including setting up roadblocks. Requests by the U.S. government for further information on Li's case elicited no response from Chinese officials (November 1991).

■   **WU Qihao** and **LU Guodong**, two Shanghai workers, were arrested for their alleged attempt, on June 8, 1989, to lower the flag on the Huangpu District Government building out of respect for the victims of the Beijing massacre (*Jiefang Ribao*, August 23, 1989). Arrest dates are unknown, and requests for further information by the U.S. government elicited no response from Chinese officials (November 1991).

Sichuan

- **YAO Yuan**'s name, address and photograph appeared on a secret "most wanted" list issued by the Chinese government on August 19, 1989. He is a 28-year old from Ziyang County, Sichuan Province. No details of his pro-democracy activities were given. Yao is one of the few people named on known top "wanted" lists after June 4, 1989 who still remain unaccounted for, and it is most likely that he was eventually caught and sentenced.

Tianjin

- **WANG Jin(g)ji**, 30, was arrested in Tianjin on June 10, 1989 and accused of collecting funds for student demonstrators (Amnesty International, *ASA 17/24/90*). It is not known what then happened to him. Requests by the U.S. government for further information on Wang's case elicited no response from Chinese officials (November 1991).

- **YE Fuzhan** and **FENG Guowei**, both allegedly former labor-camp inmates, were re-arrested in Tianjin sometime in mid-June 1989, according to a report in *Tianjin Ribao* (June 12, 1989). They were accused of taking part in a "Residents Support Group" which helped student demonstrators, and of gathering in front of colleges and universities to shout "reactionary slogans." Feng, together with a third person arrested at the same time, Jia Changling, from Siping City, were later released, according to an official Chinese response to requests for

information by the U.S. government (November 1991). Inquiries about Ye Fuzhan's case, however, elicited no response.

- **ZHOU Liwei**, an unemployed worker, was arrested in Tianjin on June 11, 1989. He allegedly acted as a bodyguard to members of the Beijing Students Autonomous Federation and was "among rioters and criminal elements who incited and created turmoil" (*Tianjin Ribao*, June 13, 1989). Requests for information by the U.S. government about Zhou's whereabouts elicited no response from Chinese officials (November 1991).

Yunnan

- **WANG Gang**, 27, manager of the Jinlong Hotel in Kunming, Yunnan Province, was arrested and charged with engaging in "counterrevolutionary propaganda" and with contacting people from Hong Kong (see Wu Haizen see p.551). The date of Wang's arrest is unknown, and requests by the U.S. government for further information elicited no response from Chinese officials (November 1991).

- **ZHANG Jun**[1], a self-employed worker, was reportedly arrested on June 14, 1989 in Chuxiong, Yunnan Province. Using the pen-name **TANG Shijie**, Zhang wrote for *Qinghai Literature (Qinghai Wenxue Bao)* and was editor-in-chief of *Xiaoxi Bao* and *Xinfeng Zaobao*, newspapers which apparently circulated during the pro-democracy demonstrations in Kunming. He was accused of doing "a great deal of evil" during the May-June

1989 "turmoil" as a reporter for the Yunnan Students Federation. Requests by the U.S. government for further information on Zhang's case elicited no response from Chinese officials (November 1991).

Zhejiang

■ **HE Jian**, in his thirties, who worked in a state-owned company in Hangzhou, Zhejiang Province, was arrested shortly after June 4, 1989 in Changsha, Hunan Province, and detained there for several months before being transferred to a detention center in his native province. During the 1989 pro-democracy movement, He allegedly travelled to several major cities and "incited local people to create disturbances." There has been no further news about him since his arrest.

Occupation Unknown

Hebei

■ **LIU Jingliang,** a man allegedly involved in "illegal organizations" either in Hebei or Beijing, reportedly surrendered to the Public Security Bureau in Nanpi, Hebei Province in June or early July 1989 (*Hebei Ribao*, July 11, 1989). There has been no further news about Liu, and requests by the U.S. government for further information his case elicited no response from Chinese officials (November 1991).

■ **WANG Shuangqing**, who was allegedly involved in "illegal organizations" either in Hebei or Beijing, reportedly surrendered to the Public Security Bureau in Hengshui, Hebei Province in June or early July 1989 (*Hebei Ribao*, July 11, 1989). There has been no further news about him since then.

Henan

■ **XIONG Mingqiang,** a 26-year-old from Luoyang, Henan Province, was arrested in connection with the 1989 pro-democracy movement, according to an Asia Watch source. There has been no further news about him since then, and requests by the U.S. government for further information on his case elicited no response from Chinese officials (November 1991).

3. Inadequate Official Accounting

NB: The following cases concern persons who were reportedly arrested after June 4, 1989 but whom the Chinese government, in replies to separate inquiries from the International Labor Organization and the U.S. Government, variously reported had been "never brought to court," "not pursued for their legal responsibility" or "never accused of any offense." Such references often mean that detainees were sentenced without trial by the police to terms of up to three years of "labor re-education" - a punishment which in practice differs little from penal custody. That "no legal responsibility" was reportedly pursued (meiyou zhuijiu falü zerenzhe) by no means precludes such extrajudicial sentencing, "labor re-education" being defined by the authorities as a so-called administrative rather than a "legal" sanction.

In addition, the phrase "never accused of any offense" (cong wei bei tichu renhe zhikongzhe) is a misleading, non-legal term which can encompass either administrative sentences of "labor re-education" or lengthy periods (sometimes extending to several years) spent in so-called "shelter for investigation" - an extrajudicial and almost entirely unregulated form of police custody. Some of the 46 persons listed by the authorities in November 1991 as "never accused of any offense" actually appeared on the Chinese government's "most wanted" lists after June 1989. Despite official denials, therefore, the status of these cases remains unclear.

Students, Intellectuals and Journalists

Beijing

- **WANG Zhigang** - see p.130

Heilongjiang

- **ZHONG Zhanguo, ZHANG Jianhua** and fourteen other leaders (names unknown) of the Harbin City Students Autonomous Federation reportedly surrendered to the Harbin public security authorities on or before June 23, 1989. According to the authorities, they handed over the seals of their "unlawful" organizations and "presented the facts of [their] unlawful activities committed since May 15, 1989 with regard to organizing students in higher educational institutions in Harbin City to strike and conduct street demonstrations, conduct petitions and set up road blocks in order to prevent workers from attending their production sites" (*Heilongjiang Provincial Radio*, June 23, 1989, in FBIS, June 27). According to the authorities' November 1991 accounting, Zhang Jianhua was already released and Zhong Zhanguo had "never been accused of any offense" (a common euphemism for an administrative sentence of "labor re-education.") The current status of the other fourteen student leaders is unknown.

Hubei

- **LIAO Baobin**, a 22-year-old student from the Chinese department at Central China Normal University, class of 1985, was reportedly arrested in the latter half of 1989 after his name appeared on a September 1989 secret "most wanted" list. In November 1991, however, Liao was declared by the authorities to have "never been accused of any offense." The striking contradiction between this statement and the known inclusion of his name on a still-valid "wanted" list was left unexplained.

- The whereabouts of **MIN Yue** (MIN Dongxiao), arrested for making counterrevolutionary speeches in the streets of Wuhan, are unknown.

Requests for information to Chinese authorities by the U.S. government elicited no response (November 1991). Min was involved with Li Haitao, whose arrest and sentencing for helping plan a memorial meeting in Wuhan on June 4, 1989, commemorating those who died that day in Beijing, was previously reported. **GUO Yue**, **HE Libin** and **ZHANG Jianchao**, all probably students, were arrested in connection with the same event. Li and Zhang were released, according to the Chinese government reply cited above; no information about Guo was provided. (See p.421.)

Jiangsu

■ **HAN Xiaodong**, a third-year physics major at Nanjing University who led the Nanjing Students Autonomous Federation, an organization banned on June 14, 1989, was reported as arrested by *China Central Television* on June 16, 1989. According to the broadcast, Han had organized citizens on June 7 for the purpose of "sabotaging" a train. In November 1991, however, the authorities listed him as "never accused of any offense."

Jiangxi

■ **HONG Yibin** (pen name for **HONG Liang**), a poet and editor of the arts journal *Bai Hua Zhou (Hundred Flowers Continent)* at the Jiangxi People's Publishing House, was arrested sometime after June 4, 1989 by the Nanchang Public Security Bureau. According to an Asia Watch source, he was arrested because of his position as editor during the time when *Utopia*, a work by Su Xiaokang, a leading intellectual once on the "most wanted" list and now in the U.S., was published in the journal. There was no news of his subsequent release, but in November 1991 the authorities reported that he had "never been accused of any offense."

Shandong

■ **FANG Wensheng**, **JIANG Tao** and **GAO Feng**[1], heads of the Students Autonomous Federation at the Qingdao Architectural and Engineering Institute and the Marine College, reportedly turned themselves in to the authorities sometime before June 13, 1989. In November 1991, the authorities told the U.S. government that the three had "never been accused of any offense." The status of Gao Feng remained particularly unclear, however, since the U.S. side had asked about two persons of that name but a reply was received on only one. The non-provision of any additional details made it impossible to know to which case the authorities were referring.

■ **PAN Qiang**, a leader of the Autonomous Federation of Students from Outside Beijing whom the authorities accused of participating in and plotting the "counterrevolutionary riot," was arrested at Shandong University on the evening of June 20, 1989 *(Shandong Provincial Radio*, June 22, 1989, in FBIS, June 23). A graduate of Shandong University's foreign literature department, Pan reportedly led the university's support group to Beijing on May 18, 1989 and served as a member of the liaison command of the Shandong provincial colleges. After his arrest, the authorities announced that he was wanted by the Beijing police and would be returned there for "further investigation and trial." In November 1991, the government claimed that Pan had "never been accused of any offense."

Sichuan

■ **WANG Zhilin** - see p.144, 145

Zhejiang

■ The current status of **CHEN Xuanliang**, who was identified on a secret government "most wanted" list of August 17, 1989 as being "a diehard element of the illegal organization, the Association of Beijing Intellectuals...[who] actively participated in inciting and organizing the turmoil and counterrevolutionary rebellion, committing serious criminal acts," is not known. Chen, 43, is from Dongyang County in Zhejiang Province. Prior to June 1989, he lived and taught at the China Youth Politics College. Despite Chen's earlier inclusion on the wanted list, the Chinese authorities stated in November 1991 that he had "never been accused of any offense." It is probable that he was in fact eventually caught and sentenced.

Workers and Peasants: Occupation Unknown

Guangxi

■ **PAN Haihong,** from Guangxi Hui Autonomous Region, was never arrested or brought before judicial authorities, according to the Chinese government's November 1990 reply to an International Labor Organization inquiry. He may have been administratively sentenced instead to "re-education through labor." There is no additional information available about Pan or the circumstances of his arrest.

Inner Mongolia

■ **BAO Huilin, ZHANG Lishan, WEN Lihua, CAI Shi** and **YANG Xudong,** five members of a group of 15 leaders of the Hohhot Workers Autonomous Federation, Inner Mongolia, who were detained prior to June 14, 1989 for allegedly joining a student march and establishing ties with a university's "Dare-to-Die" team, were never arrested or brought before the judicial authorities, according to a Chinese government report to the International Labor Organization (November 1990). The men may instead have been administratively sentenced to "re-education through labor." Inquiries by the U.S. government on their cases elicited no response from the Chinese authorities (November 1991).

Shaanxi

■ **TANG Zibin,** from Shaanxi Province, reportedly detained after June 4, 1989, was never arrested or brought before the judicial authorities, according to a Chinese government report to the International Labor Organization (November 1990). This may mean that he was instead administratively sentenced to a term of "re-education through labor." A request by the U.S. government for clarification of Tang's status elicited no response from Chinese officials (November 1991). Nothing further is known about his case.

Shanghai

■ **FAN Jin(g)chun**, a Shanghai worker, was arrested and accused of spreading rumors such as "the police are beating people" and "Deng Xiaoping has been killed" (*Jiefang Ribao*, August 23, 1989). According to an official Chinese response to requests for information by the U.S. government (November 1991), in Fan's case, "no legal responsibility was pursued" - often a euphemism for an administrative sentence of "re-education through labor."

■ **LI Zhibo** (Zhibao, on the ILO list), a leader of the Shanghai Workers Autonomous Federation and one of nine activists detained in Shanghai on June 9, 1989, was never arrested or subsequently brought before the judicial authorities, according to a Chinese government response to repeated inquiries from the International Labor Organization (November 1990). This may mean that he was instead sentenced administratively to "re-education through labor." According to *Beijing Radio* (in FBIS,

June 12, 1989), the nine (see also Wang Wang p.506) were seized by security authorities for "holding secret meetings, spreading rumors, distributing leaflets, advocating strikes, chanting reactionary slogans, advocating the overthrow of the government, setting up roadblocks and disrupting traffic." Allegedly, they also "vilified the Shanghai Council of Trade Unions as being totally paralyzed." Requests by the U.S. government for clarification of Li's status elicited no response from the Chinese authorities (November 1991).

Place unknown

■ A man named **JI Changpeng** was described by the Chinese government, in its November 1991 response to a list of Chinese prisoners compiled by the U.S. government, as having "never been accused of any offense." This was surprising, since Ji's name was not among the 800 or more included on the U.S. list. There is no information available on who Ji Changpeng is, or why the authorities should have wished it to be known that he was "never accused."

[NB: See also Catholics: Father An Shi'an (p.235), Father Pei Zhenping (p.233), Father Shi Wande (p.239) and Father Wei Jingyi (p.544).]

III. ETHNIC NATIONAL PRISONERS

1. Tibetans

Died in Prison/Under Surveillance

■ **CHOEZED TENPA CHOEPHEL**, a 66-year-old Lhasa native, arrested on December 15, 1987, reportedly for possessing a copy of the Dalai Lama's autobiography, died on August 25, 1989 in Lhasa People's Hospital. He had been transferred there the day before from Drapchi Prison where he had been held for twenty months. According to witnesses, his body was severely bruised on transfer. Choezed Tenpa Choephel had been a groundskeeper at the Norbulingka, and he and his wife operated a small shop in Lhasa. His entire family had been politically active. His wife, **TSERING LHAMO**, was imprisoned for a year starting in October 1979 for shouting pro-democracy slogans during the 1979 visit of a Tibetan exile delegation. She was detained again in 1980 for protesting the arrest of her son. One of their daughters, perhaps the one named **Lhakdron**, was arrested in March 1989 for demonstrating and served two years in Gutsa. Their son, **Lobsang Choedrag**[2] (see p.41), formerly a worker in a truck repair shop, spent four years in prison, from 1980 to 1984, for putting up pro-independence posters, and as a result of his involvement with Geshe Lobsang Wangchuk (see below), now deceased, who had been Tibet's best known dissident. (For further probable detail on Choezed Tenpa Choephel's case, see **"Qunze ****," p.170).

. . . . [DEAD]

■ **GESHE LOBSANG WANGCHUK**, the most well known political dissident in Tibet and an important religious leader in Nagchu, was two days past his 73rd birthday when he died in prison on November 4, 1987. After authorities initially denied reports of Lobsang Wangchuk's death, it was finally acknowledged, with the official cause listed as lung cancer. A lama, originally from Amdo, Lobsang Wangchuk spent a total of sixteen years in prison between 1962 and his death. During those years, much of it in Drapchi Prison, he sustained torture and mistreatment during "struggle sessions." As a result, he lost his eyesight and the use of his hands.

Originally arrested in 1962, Lobsang Wangchuk was sentenced to ten years in prison. In 1970, when his term was coming to an end, he was attached to a work team and sent to break rocks. After the completion of his sentence, he was made to work in the Nyethang brick factory and in farming and herding, work and working conditions that hardly differed from his prison experiences. After Deng Xiaoping came to power, Lobsang Wangchuk, while editing medical texts for publication by the Tibetan Medical Center, secretly wrote and pasted up posters rebutting what the official Chinese press was saying about Tibet. On December 3, 1981, he was re-arrested and subsequently sentenced to a three-and-a-half-year term for writing a book or booklet, *A History of Tibetan Independence*, and preparing it for secret distribution. His sentence was later extended to eighteen years because of his refusal to confess the error of his views during interrogations and criticism meetings. On February 24, 1987, after previous severe beatings for allegedly not being able to perform hard labor, Lobsang Wangchuk had his hands "twisted beyond normal limits" and was "excused" from work. Once he could no longer work, his contact with others was cut off except for minimal interaction with those who brought him food and other necessities.

It was reliably reported in October 1983, that Lobsang Wangchuk was scheduled for execution as part of a group of Tibetan prisoners caught up in a mass anti-crime campaign then raging throughout China. He was spared, reportedly because of pressure exerted by international groups. There were reports that he was kept shackled hand and foot from September 1983 until February 1984.

. . . . [DEAD]

■   **JAMPA TENZIN**[1], 49, was found dead in the Jokhang Temple on February 22, 1992. According to the police he committed suicide; according to Tibetan sources, foul play was involved. Public Security Bureau officials in Lhasa reportedly examined the body on the spot and insisted officials at the temple accept the suicide ruling. There was no known investigation. Jampa Tenzin became a symbol of Tibetan independence on October 1, 1987 after he ran through flames to rescue prisoners trapped inside a burning police station. Hidden and treated by western doctors, he was imprisoned on October 13 after he turned himself over to the police in response to an offer of partial amnesty and a need for hospitalization. After a month in the hospital, under guard and under interrogation, he was sent to Seitru Prison. There he faced both threats and offers of release in an attempt to coerce him into divulging the names of others involved in the demonstration (*Tibet Information Network*, March 8, 1992). Released in an amnesty arranged by the Panchen Lama in January 1988, Jampa Tenzin was badly beaten and kept under surveillance after a demonstration later in 1988.

. . . . [DEAD]

■   **LHAKPA DONDRUP**, from Lhasa Chakshi, died in custody in November 1991 in People's Hospital in

Lhasa after repeated severe beatings in Gutsa Detention Center. He was in his early twenties at the time. Among his injuries was a ruptured spleen; he may also have been suffering from hepatitis and leukemia. Arrested in 1989 for "beating, looting, setting fires [and] smashing public property" (*People's Daily*, August 7, 1989), he was sentenced on July 29, 1989 to a prison term of two-and-a-half years.

. . . . [DEAD]

■ Of six Lhasa Middle School students arrested on November 4, 1989, one died in prison, two have been released, one received an administrative sentence of "labor re-education," and the other two are unaccounted for (see Migmar Tsering[4] p.527). Five arrests were confirmed by the government on December 8, 1989 (*Radio Lhasa*, December 8, 1989; *Reuters*, December 9, 1989; and FBIS, December 19, 1989). Group members were accused of "ganging up together to illegally establish a counterrevolutionary organization, the *Gangchen Youth Association* [also known as the *Young Lions*], in March 1988, with the aim of carrying out counterrevolutionary activities. The youths allegedly wrote and printed a large number of reactionary propaganda materials and produced banners marked with lions of the snowy mountains, the symbol of Tibetan independence, which they then posted in many streets, temples and in the school. They vilified the Chinese Communist Party and the socialist system, plotting to undermine the unity of the motherland and national solidarity. They also preached

Tibetan independence."

According to the authorities, "This counterrevolutionary organization was cracked down upon by our public security organ on November 4, 1989 and its members arrested on December 8, 1989. To consolidate our proletarian dictatorship and severely punish counterrevolutionary elements who are guilty of the crime of splitting the motherland, the Lhasa City Public Security Bureau, with the approval of the Lhasa City People's Procuratorate, arrested the five..." (*Reuters*, December 19, 1989, in FBIS, December 19, 1989).

LHAKPA TSERING[3], 20, died in Drapchi Prison on December 15, 1990, probably as a result of a beating by prison personnel in retaliation for refusing to accept restrictions imposed prior to an expected visit from foreigners. He was serving a three-year sentence. After his relatives received Lhakpa Tsering's body on December 16, they asked for an inquest. At the post-mortem, held at the burial site and attended by a Tibetan doctor and an official from the local People's Procuratorate, it reportedly was evident that Lhakpa Tsering's body "bore many bruise marks." Unofficial statements made by the doctors and officials who conducted the autopsy implied that the prisoner had died as a result of internal infection due to failure to treat intestinal lacerations caused by beatings. There has never been a detailed official report, nor has a full scale inquiry ever been conducted.

Another detailed but unconfirmed account, that Lhakpa Tsering's family was offered help with funeral expenses, food, butter and a payment of 30 *yuan*, equivalent to two month's salary, has fueled suspicion of prison complicity in his death. *Xinhua* (April 6, 1991) quoted a speech by Gyaltsen Norbu, the chairman of the Tibet Autonomous Region, to then U.S. Ambassador James Lilley, in which he stated that Lhakpa Tsering had become ill in November 1991 and had died of appendicitis and peritonitis. Chinese authorities have not, however, explained why Lhakpa Tsering was never hospitalized. Unofficial sources report that doctors at the prison hospital refused him treatment. A silent protest over Lhakpa Tsering's death, by ninety-three prisoners in the male section of Drapchi, resulted in several unprecedented moves by authorities. People's Liberation Army troops were brought into the prison on December 16. They remained until the next morning. Visitors on December 20 were offered tea and food in order to dissuade them from reporting that almost all the prisoners had swollen faces and many had bruises on their heads.

. . . . [DEAD]

■ **NGAWANG TSONDRU**[3] - see p.183

. . . . [DEAD]

■ **RIGZIN CHOEDRON** (lay name KUNSANG CHOEKYI), a Shungsep nun from Lhokha Gongkar, died on October 10, 1992 at the age of 26, one month after her release from Trisam Prison. She had served a three-year sentence. Death probably resulted from kidney damage due to prison beatings and torture. One report said that Rigzin Choedron had been subject to a form of crucifixion, forced to remain for days with her hands and feet tied to opposite ends of planks of wood (*Tibet Information Network*, December 21, 1992). At the time of her release, she had "abscesses and wounds" on her back. For information about Rigzin Choedron's alleged activities, see Choenyi Lhamo (p.515).

. . . . [DEAD]

■ **YESHE**, a 25-year-old painter, died 59 days after his release from prison on August 22, 1989. He had been arrested at midnight on March 7. At the time of his release he could not urinate nor could he walk on his own. According to official reports, his death was attributed to poisoning. Unofficial reports said his injuries and death could be attributed to the severe beatings, particularly to his genitals, which he sustained during the five months he was in prison.

. . . . [DEAD]

Sentenced

Monks and Nuns

Chamdo Monastery

■ **NGAGCHOE**, a 28-year-old Chamdo monk, arrested in December 1989, was sentenced by the Chamdo Court on February 2, 1991, to a five-year prison term which he is serving in

Chamdo Prison.

. . . . [5 YRS]

Chubsang Nunnery

■ Five Chubsang nuns, arrested in connection with a demonstration on March 21, 1992, included **GYALTSEN KELSANG**[2], a 22-year-old from Lhasa Nyangden; **YANGZOM**[1], 23; **PHUNTSOG LOCHOE**, 24; **NGAWANG CHOEZOM**[1], 22; and **PHUNTSOG TSAMCHOE**, 22. The latter two, from Toelung and Taktse respectively, are serving five-year sentences in Drapchi Prison. Phuntsog Lochoe, from Taktse, received a seven-year sentence. At last report, Gyaltsen Kelsang and Yangzom were still in Gutsa Detention Center.

. . . . [5, 5, 7 YRS]

■ **GYALTSEN SHERAB**, a 25-year-old Chubsang nun, from Phenpo, arrested May 10, 1992, was sentenced to a five-year prison term. Other than that as of August 1993, she was in Drapchi Prison, no additional information is available.

. . . . [5 YRS]

■ Five of six nuns from Chubsang Nunnery, arrested on August 18, 1991 for allegedly leading a pro-independence demonstration around the Barkhor in Lhasa in either June or August, have been sentenced to three years in prison. **GYATSO NGODRUP**, (lay name DADRON[1], a contraction of DAWA DROLMA[1]), 21 or 24, from Lhasa Phunkhang, who allegedly carried a banned Tibetan flag during the demonstration; **NGAWANG**

TSETEN, (lay name PHURBU[3]), from Nyethang; **NGAWANG YUDRON**[1], (lay name TASHI DROLMA[1]), 23, from Toelung; **GYATSO DAMCHOE**, (usually known as GYALTSEN DAMCHOE, lay name TRINLEY LHAMO), from either Phenpo Lhundrup or Phenpo Phomdo; and **TSULTRIM SANGMO**, (lay name DROLKAR), 22, from the village of Gyama, were all held in Gutsa Detention Center, then transferred to Trisam. It is not known what happened to **PHETHO**, the lay name for a 21-year-old native of Nyethang Ratoe, who was in Gutsa and is known to have been expelled from the nunnery.

. . . . [5 X 3 YRS]

■ **NAMDROL LHAMO**, a 28-year-old Chubsang nun, from Rinpung, is serving a six-year prison term in Drapchi Prison. Other than that she was arrested on May 12, 1992, no additional information is available.

. . . . [6 YRS]

■ Some nine people were arrested in connection with a demonstration on July 6, 1992 at the site of birthday celebrations for the Dalai Lama. **NGAWANG NYIDROL**, a 23-year-old nun from Chubsang Nunnery, received a three-year prison term for her participation. Held first at Gutsa Detention Center, she was transferred to Drapchi Prison upon sentencing. **LOBSANG THUPTEN**[1], 32, a Sera monk from Phenpo, arrested the same day, reportedly is still in Gutsa.

. . . . [3 YRS]

Dingkha Monastery

■ Five Dingkha monks, arrested for shouting pro-independence slogans and trying to unfurl the Tibetan flag in front of the Jokhang Temple on March 17, 1991, were transferred from Gutsa to Drapchi after sentencing. **KELSANG GYALTSEN**, 27, from Yangpachen, received a six-year term; **NGAWANG ZOEPA**[2], 28, from Toelung, a chantmaster, was sentenced to five years' imprisonment; **NGAWANG TSONDRU**[2], 28, and **NGAWANG LEGSHE**, 24, both from Toelung, received four-year sentences; and **NGAWANG NAMGYAL**[1], 24, from Damshung, was sentenced to a three-year term. **NGAWANG OEZER**[1], 28, another Dingkha monk, from Toelung, arrested in March 1991 and sentenced to five years' imprisonment may also have been involved with the March 17 demonstration.

. . . . . . [6, 5, 5, 4, 4, 3 YRS]

■ **NGAWANG LHUNDRUP**[2] (lay name PENPA[8]), a 22-year-old Dingkha monk from Toelung Dechen County, was sentenced to a six-year term for putting up pro-independence posters in the monastery. His arrest came in the last week of April 1991. Initially held in a local prison in Dechen County, Ngawang Lhundrup is serving his sentence in Drapchi Prison. According to another monk's report, there "were (posters) on the walls in Toelung. They charged him and said the handwriting was similar. So they...put him in prison."

. . . . [6 YRS]

Donphu Choekhor Monastery

■ **JAMYANG KUNGA** - see p.204
. . . . [4 YRS]

■ **NGAWANG PALDEN**[1], 28, and **THUPTEN MONLAM**, 20, monks from Donphu Choekhor Monastery, from Gongkar County, originally received four-and-a-half-year terms which they are serving in Drapchi Prison. However, an unconfirmed report claims the two had their sentences increased to ten years. **THUPTEN NAMLHA**, 21, another monk, received a two-year term. He is also in Drapchi. Other than that the three were arrested on August 28, 1992, no further information is available.

. . [2 X 4½ OR 10 YRS] [2 YRS]

■ **TENZIN TRINLEY** - see p.204
. . . . [3 YRS]

■ **THUPTEN KUNKYHEN** - see p.204
. . . . [3 YRS]

■ **THUPTEN TSONDRU**, 23, a monk from Donphu Choekhor Monastery, originally from Lhokha, arrested April 6, 1992, is serving a four-year term in Drapchi Prison.
. . . . [4 YRS]

Dralhaluphug Monastery

■ **DAWA TSERING**[2], 22, a monk from Dralhaluphug Monastery, born in Lhundrup County; and **TENZIN CHOEPHEL**[2], 21, a Ganden monk born in Tsang Penam County, were paraded along with at least four others before a mass public meeting in Lhasa on November 3, 1989, during which their sentences were announced, eight years for Dawa Tsering and three years for Tenzin Choephel (*Tibet Daily*, November 6, 1989, in *Reuters*, November 16 and FBIS, November 20), who presumably has been released. The two monks were among at least six who allegedly demonstrated "illegally" around the Jokhang Temple in Lhasa on September 30, 1989, during which Tenzin Choephel reportedly brandished a banned Tibetan flag which Dawa Tsering had made. Dawa Tsering was arrested on the spot, accused of organizing separatist activities, as well as taking part in "rioting" on March 5, 1989. Tenzin Choephel was not arrested until October 25, 1989. Initially held in Sangyip Prison, Dawa Tsering was transferred to Drapchi and Tenzin Choephel finished his sentence in Trisam.

. . . . [8, 3 YRS]

■ Of four monks from Dralhaluphug Monastery, arrested on October 25, 1989 and administratively sentenced to three-year "labor re-education" terms on November 3 after being paraded before a mass public rally, (*Tibet Daily*, November 6, 1989 in *Reuters*, November 16 and in FBIS, November 20), one has been released. He is **LEGTSOG**, 23, from Ledro Gongkar Thankgya, who allegedly shouted "independent Tibet" and other reactionary slogans while marching around the Jokhang Temple in Lhasa. Originally held in Sangyip, he was

released from Trisam. **LOBSANG TRINLEY**[2], 20, from Yamdrog Nangkar Tse, who also demonstrated, was originally sentenced to a three-year term but had his sentence extended to four-and-a-half years. Originally held in Sangyip, he was later moved to Trisam. **LHAKPA**[6], (sometimes spelled LAWA), 26, from Lhokha Tongra Chu, who joined the demonstration, had his term extended to eight years for his involvement in a Sangyip prison protest on May 20, 1991. He was transferred to Drapchi Prison on September 28. **PHURBU**[6], in his twenties, reportedly had his sentence extended by one-and-a-half years for a total term of four-and-a-half-years. It is unclear if he was then moved to either Drapchi or Trisam Prison or remained at Sangyip. For more information about the protest, see p.186.

. . . . [4½, 4½, 8, YRS]

■ **THUPTEN NAMDROL** (also known as NAMDROL), a 63-year-old Dralhaluphug monk probably from Lhokha Lhodrak, arrested on December 14, 1987, was sentenced to a nine-year term. He is in the Fifth Division, Sixth Section at Drapchi Prison and reportedly is suffering from severe swollen joints due to hard labor (*Tibet Information Network*, October 19, 1993); the charges against him are not known. Thupten Namdrol, along with twenty others, were harshly disciplined for protesting the April 27, 1991 transfer of five Drapchi prisoners, two of whom had handed then U.S. Ambassador James Lilley a letter about torture and ill-treatment in the prison (see Tenpa Wangdrag[2] p.177). Thupten

Namdrol has also been referred to as a caretaker monk at the Jokhang. This confusion over his affiliation is due to the fact that Dralhaluphug monks are under the administrative jurisdiction of the Jokhang Temple in Lhasa.

An official Chinese compilation of "counterrevolutionary" cases (CCS p.246: see note on p.276, below) described the case of one "TUDENG **" (a partially-censored Chinese transliteration), who is believed actually to be Thupten Namdrol. According to the account, "Tudeng **" served a 20-year prison term after 1959 for participating in the Tibetan rebellion that year against rule by Beijing. In 1986, he allegedly collaborated with another Tibetan, "DANBA **" - who was described only as "tried separately" (sentence unknown) - in writing a "counterrevolutionary letter," which Tudeng then passed on to foreign tourists in Tibet. In February and March 1987, "Danba wrote three documents entitled 'The Tibetan Nation on the Brink of Extinction', 'The Danger of the [Tibet Autonomous] Region Becoming a Rebel Zone' and 'How the Enemy Has Deceived Us After Its [December 1978] 3rd Plenum,' which he variously signed in the name of the 'Truth and Struggle Society of the Three Tibetan Regions' and the 'Peasants and Herders of Northern Tibet.'" Tudeng is said to have distributed these documents also to foreign tourists in Tibet, which they then carried overseas, and to have "circulated numerous other counter-revolutionary leaflets and posters which incited ethnic discord and national dismemberment." On September 27 and October 1, 1987, Tudeng allegedly had another Tibetan, QUNZE ** , also described as "tried separately" (sentence unknown), "prepare ten copies of a counterrevolutionary article entitled 'History and Law Fully Prove that Tibet is an Independent Country.'"

The person named as "Danba **" is probably in fact **Tenpa Phulchung**[2] (see p.200), who was arrested in December 1987 and sentenced to seven years' imprisonment for allegedly possessing posters advocating Tibetan independence. Similarly, "Qunze **" is probably a reference to **Choezed Tenpa Choephel** (see p.163) a 66-year-old political activist who died in police custody at Lhasa People's Hospital on August 25, 1989.

. . . . [9 YRS]

Drepung Monastery

■ **JAMPEL PHUNTSOG**, 27, from Tsal Gungthang; and **NGAWANG RAPJOR**, 23, from Damphag, both Drepung monks, arrested on September 27, 1991, were sentenced to six-year prison terms. **NGAWANG SUNGRAB**, 20, from Damphag, received a ten-year term. First held in Gutsa Detention Center, they were transferred after sentencing to Drapchi Prison.

. . . . [10, 6, 6 YRS]

■ **LOBSANG TSONDRU** (also known as LOBSANG TSULTRIM, HOR GYESHI and HOR LAGEN), an 84-year-old native of Sok County in Nagchu and resident monk at Drepung Monastery, reportedly was sentenced to six or seven years' imprisonment for "failure to reform." He was formally arrested on April 14 or 15, 1990 and held until October 13, 1990 in Outridu, a section of the Sangyip Prison Complex, then transferred to Drapchi Prison, Fifth Division and later to Section Four. His arrest apparently was part of a campaign to expel several hundred monks and nuns from their religious institutions in the few weeks before martial law was to be lifted in Lhasa. At a meeting in Drepung's main prayer hall, Chinese officials read out the names of 37 Drepung monks, including Lobsang Tsondru, who were to be expelled. They then singled him out, read a warrant for his arrest and a list of charges, and led him away in handcuffs. According to the charges, "despite opportunities given to Lobsang Tsondru to reform himself through re-education, he nevertheless became a reactionary with the hope of splitting the great motherland and [he] carried out unlawful activities which are forbidden by the constitution of the country" (*Tibet Information Network*, June 17, 1990).

On April 27, 1991, prisoners in Drapchi protested following the transfer of five prisoners, two of whom, Tenpa Wangdrag[2] (see p.177) and Lobsang Tenzin[2] (see p.351), had handed then U.S. Ambassador to China, James Lilley, a letter about torture and ill-treatment in the prison. Lobsang Tsondru was among about twenty who were harshly disciplined for the protest. He was placed in solitary confinement and reportedly was beaten by PLA soldiers until he was bleeding from the mouth and ears. Along with some of the others punished, he was handcuffed

and manacled until May 2 (*Tibet Information Network*). Reports have expressed grave alarm over the state of his health. He reportedly has heart disease. Lobsang Tsondru was arrested once before, in 1988.

. . . . [6-7 YRS]

■   **NGAWANG BUMCHOG**, 22; **NGAWANG KHEDRUP**, 24; and **NGAWANG PELGON**, 33, all Drepung monks originally from Toelung, arrested on June 15, 1992, were sentenced respectively to five, six, and five-year prison terms. They are in Drapchi Prison.

. . . . [6, 5, 5 YRS]

■   Five Drepung monks, arrested September 14, 1991, are serving prison terms in Drapchi after transfer from Gutsa Detention Center. **NGAWANG CHOEJOR**, 18, and **NGAWANG TENSANG**, 24, both from Toelung, have been sentenced to three and ten years respectively. **PHUNTSOG GONPO**, 24, from Phenpo and **PHUNTSOG THUTOP**, 22, from Lhokha, received five-year terms. **PHUNTSOG CHANGSEM**, 21, from Lhokha, is serving an eight-year term.

. . . . . . [10, 8, 5, 5, 3 YRS]

■   A group of 14 Drepung monks were arrested probably on May 13, 1992 (despite reports which give the date as May 12), for "demonstrating"; they were later sentenced to terms of up eight years' imprisonment. **PHUNTSOG DRIME**, 22, originally from the Lhasa Cement Factory, and **PHUNTSOG SEGYI** (lay name TOPGYAL[2]), 22, from Phenpo

Phondo, both received eight-year sentences. **PHUNTSOG LEGSANG**, 21, from Nyendrong, **PHUNTSOG SAMTEN**[1], from Damshang, and **PHUNTSOG NAMGYAL**, 23, from Phenpo, all received six-year sentences.

.... [2 X 8 YRS] [3 X 6 YRS]

NGAWANG LHAKSAM, 24, from Phenpo, **NGAWANG LUNGTOK**, 20, from Phenpo, and **NGAWANG SOTHAR**, 24, from Toelung, all received five-year sentences. **NGAWANG DIPSEL**, 28, from Phenpo, and **PHUNTSOG DRADAG**, 20, from Toelung, were sentenced to four years each. And **TRINLEY CHOEDRON**, 28, from Phenpo, **NGAWANG CHOSHE**, 24, from Drigung Lungshoe, and **TRINLEY TENZIN**, 31, from Toelung, all received three-year sentences. After sentencing, the thirteen monks were transferred from Gutsa Detention Center to Drapchi Prison. Another monk, **TENZIN NYIMA**, 22, received a one-year sentence and presumably was released upon its completion. (See also Jampa Tenzin[2] p.176, and Ngawang Choekyi[2] p.191.)

[3 X 5 YRS] [2 X 4 YRS] [3 X 3 YRS]

■ **NGAWANG DAWA**, a Drepung monk, from Lhasa, arrested on September 10, 1991, is serving a six-year term in Drapchi Prison.

. . . . [6 YRS]

■ **NGAWANG DECHOE**, a 21-year-old Drepung monk from Phenpo Lhundrup County Dongpo Village, arrested from his dormitory room in Drepung Monastery probably on the evening of March 21, 1991, has received a three-year sentence. Initially held in Gutsa Detention Center, he was moved later to Trisam.

. . . . [3 YRS]

■ **NGAWANG JANGCHEN**, a 20-year-old Drepung monk from Tsethang, arrested September 1991, received a five-year prison sentence. First held in Gutsa Detention Center, he was later transferred to Drapchi Prison.

. . . . [5 YRS]

■ Several Drepung monks, including **NGAWANG JIGME**, 19, from Toelung; **NGAWANG THUPTEN**[2], 21, from Lhasa; **PHUNTSOG JORCHU**, 27, from Toelung; **LOBSANG PHUNTSOG**, 22, from Toelung, are serving respectively six, four, five, and four-year terms in Drapchi Prison. Their respective dates of arrest were September 20, 1991, September 10, August 2, and sometime in August.

. . . . [6, 5, 4, 4 YRS]

■ **NGAWANG PEKAR**, a 29-year-old Drepung monk from Toelung Dechen, arrested on July 12, 1989, was sentenced to eight years in prison for allegedly putting up pro-independence posters and participating in demonstrations. He is in Drapchi Prison. At the time of his arrest, Ngawang Pekar reportedly was arranging to escape to India. For details of a previous arrest, see Ngawang Topchen (p.528).

. . . . [8 YRS]

■ Eleven Tibetans, charged with "counterrevolutionary" advocacy of Tibetan independence, were tried at a mass public meeting in Lhasa on November 30, 1989 and given harsh prison sentences ranging from five to nineteen years (*Xinhua*, in *Reuters*, December 12, 1989). All are held in Drapchi Prison. Ten of the eleven are monks from Drepung Monastery. For information about the eleventh, see Dondrup Dorje (p.193).

NGAWANG PHULCHUNG, 34, from Toelung Dechen, allegedly the leader of the monks' protest, was arrested on April 16, 1989, and sentenced to nineteen years in prison with five years' subsequent deprivation of political rights. He was charged with founding a "counterrevolutionary clique" in January 1988, with "spreading counterrevolutionary propaganda and inflammatory agitation," and with "collecting information and passing it on to the enemy, seriously undermining national security" (*Xinhua*, in *Reuters*, December 12, 1989). **NGAWANG OEZER**[2] (lay name JAMYANG[5]), 22, from Lhokha Dranang, was also arrested on April 16 and sentenced to seventeen years in prison with five years' subsequent deprivation of political rights for his alleged activities as a "main culprit" in organizing a "counterrevolutionary clique" and spreading propaganda.

. . . . [19, 17 YRS]

JAMPEL CHANGCHUP, (lay name YUGYAL), 33, from Toelung Dechen Dhinga, arrested on March 16,

1989, in addition to being charged as "a main culprit" (*Radio Lhasa*, November 30, 1989), was accused of espionage. He received a nineteen-year sentence and five years deprivation of political rights. **JAMPEL KHEDRUP**, (lay name KELSANG THUTOP), 47, from Toelung Dechen County, Gewu Chu, arrested on April 16, received an eighteen-year sentence and five years' subsequent deprivation of political rights. In addition to the charges detailed above, he allegedly crossed the national border illegally.

. . . . [19, 18 YRS]

NGAWANG RIGZIN, 32, from Phenpo Lhundrup County, arrested in March 1989 and charged as an "accessory offender" for "collecting intelligence according to foreign demand and printing and distributing reactionary leaflets," thus "viciously slandering the people's democratic dictatorship," was given a nine-year sentence and three years' deprivation of political rights. The leaflets which he and the others were accused of printing were consistently non-violent in content and were primarily confined to reports on Tibetan dissident activity. The group's first major publication was a Tibetan translation of the *Universal Declaration of Human Rights* (*Tibet Information Network*, December 8, 1990).

. . . . [9 YRS]

NGAWANG GYALTSEN[1] (lay name NGOEGYAN), 36, from Toelung Dechen, arrested on April 16, was sentenced to a seventeen-year term and five years' subsequent deprivation of political rights. As an "accessory offender," he was charged with "actively participating in criminal activities, engaging in espionage, and illegally crossing the national boarder." Ngawang Gyaltsen was arrested together with Tenzin Phuntsog[2] (see p.353) while they were trying to flee the country, and he is almost certainly the same Ngawang Gyaltsen as the one implicated for sending information about the violence in Lhasa out of the country. **JAMPEL MONLAM** (lay name DRADUL[2]), 28, from Lhasa Trengkan Chu (the Tibetan quarter around the Jokhang), arrested in March, was sentenced to five years' imprisonment and two years' subsequent deprivation of political rights as an "accessory."

. . . . [17, 5 YRS]

Two others charged as "accessories," **NGAWANG KUNGA**, (lay name DORJE TRINLEY), 29, from Medro Gongkar County Drigung; and **JAMPEL TSERING**, 25, from Medro Gongkar, were arrested on July 18. They both received five-year prison terms with two years' deprivation of political rights. According to a former prisoner, in Ngawang Kunga was forced to run with a stone on his back in 1990 or 1991, and has liver problems as a result of heavy labor. **JAMPEL LOBSANG**, (also known as JAMPEL LOSEL), 27, from Taktse County, another "accessory offender," arrested in March 1989, was sentenced to ten years in prison and three years' subsequent deprivation of political rights.

. . . . [10, 5, 5 YRS]

All except Jampel Lobsang and Jampel Khedrup were among the group of 21 monks who, arrested on September 27, 1987 for taking part in a pro-independence demonstration, began the current wave of Tibetan unrest. All were released in January 1988 after the intervention of the Panchen Lama and after signing confessions admitting to "political crimes" and acknowledging Chinese sovereignty over Tibet. In addition, three of the monks, Ngawang Phulchung, Jampel Changchup, and Jampel Tsering, were among the twenty prisoners harshly disciplined for protesting the April 27, 1991 transfer of five Drapchi prisoners (see Tenpa Wangdrag[2] p.177).

■   **NGAWANG SAMTEN[2]**, a 25-year-old Drepung monk from Phenpo Lundrup Gyepo, arrested March 9, 1991 for putting up pro-independence posters on the walls of Drepung Monastery, which he had joined the year before, received a four-year sentence. Initially held in Gutsa Detention Center, Ngawang Samten was transferred to Drapchi Prison Block 5, Section 7. As a result of hard labor in prison, he reportedly suffers from severely swollen joints.

. . . . [4 YRS]

■   **NGAWANG TENRAB[1]**, a 36-year-old monk from Drepung Monastery, originally from Taktse County, was sentenced to a seven-year prison term for participating in demonstrations and putting up posters in the monastery in March 1989. In mid-October 1992, he was moved from

Drapchi Prison to Kuwang Yiyong Hospital, then later returned to the prison. Despite the hospital claim that he "fell down while doing work," it is suspected that he had some ribs broken during a beating. Ngawang Tenrab was detained once before, on September 27, 1987 and released after a few days.

. . . . [7 YRS]

■ **PHUNTSOG DONDRUP**, a 20-year old Drepung monk, from Phenpo Lundrup, arrested on October 10, 1991, has received a four-year prison sentence which he is serving in Drapchi.

. . . . [4 YRS]

Drongtse Monastery

■ **LOBSANG TENPA**[2], a 27-year-old Drongtse monk, from Gyaltse County, was arrested in September 1990 and originally sentenced to a two-and-a-half-year term and sent to Drapchi Prison. At some point his sentence was extended to eight years.

. . . . [8 YRS]

Ganden Monastery

■ Two Ganden monks, **DORJE**[4], 25, from Medro, and **JAMPA RANGDROL**, 21, from Taktse, are in Drapchi Prison. Dorje is serving either a six or eight-year term, and Jampa Rangdrol a sentence of six years. Other than that they were arrested on April 11, 1992, no further information is available.

. . . . [6-8, 6 YRS]

■ A group of monks from Ganden

monastery and two from Drepung were arrested during a demonstration around the Jokhang Temple on March 20, 1992 and taken to Gutsa Detention Center. Those known to have later been sentenced and transferred to Drapchi Prison include, from Ganden, **JAMPEL GENDUN**, a 31-year-old native of Medro, who received a nine-year sentence; **LOBSANG JAMPA**[1], sentenced to eight years' imprisonment; **LOBSANG LUNGTOG**, 23, from Lhasa, seven years; **TENZIN PHUNTSOG**[1], 24, from Medro, six years; and **LOBSANG YESHE**[1], 21, from Medro, and **LOBSANG LEGSHE**, 24, from Medro, each five years. **TSULTRIM DONDEN**, 23, a Drepung monk, originally from Toelung, was sentenced to four years' imprisonment and is also in Drapchi.

[9, 8, 7, 6 AND 4 YRS] [2 X 5 YRS]

Others from Ganden arrested, but so far as is known still detained in Gutsa, include **JAMYANG**[3], 28, from Medro Thagya, who served in the People's Liberation Army before joining the monastery in 1984; **LOBSANG TENZIN**[1], 21, from Lhasa Nyangden; **DAWA**[1], 21, from Medro Jaramdo; **DAWA**[2], 27, from Medro Thankgya Drok Township; **TSERING PHUNTSOG**[1], 26, from Lhasa Kyire; and **SONAM BAGDRO**, 24. **THUPTEN KUNPHEL**, also still in Gutsa, is from Drepung Monastery.

In the course of the demonstration, in which some 250 peaceful protestors carried a Tibetan flag and shouted pro-independence, anti-Chinese slogans, plainclothes and uniformed police beat and arrested the monks. Jamyang[3], who was lying motionless on the ground, was repeatedly kicked.

■ During May 1992, monks from Ganden Monastery demonstrated on five occasions, May 7, 8, 11, 13, and 14. The May 7 protests took place around the Barkhor and involved a home-made Tibetan flag and pro-independence posters. **JAMPA TSETEN**, 22, from Medro; **LOBSANG GELEK**[1], 23, from Medro; and **YESHE KHEDRUP**, 20, from Medro, all arrested on May 7, although some reports read May 6, are now in Drapchi Prison serving seven, five and six-year sentences respectively. They initially were detained in Gutsa. Of those arrested on May 13, **JAMPA TENZIN**[2], 22, from Phenpo, received a two-year sentence. Two other monks, also arrested on May 13, **GYALTSEN CHOEZIN**, from Nechung Monastery (part of Drepung), and **JORDEN**, a 23-year-old Drepung monk, who reportedly lost an eye as a result of torture, so far as is known are still in Gutsa. For other Ganden monks arrested in May 1992, see Dawa Sonam (p.206).

. . . .   [7, 6, 5, 2 YRS]

■ Nine monks from Ganden Monastery, arrested on March 7, 1988 for their involvement in the March 5, 1988 demonstration in Lhasa, received long prison sentences and were initially sent to Drapchi Prison. One of the monks, **LHUNDRUP GADEN**, (lay name TASHI[1] or TASHI GYATSO[1]; also known as GANDEN TASHI), 22, from Medro Gongkar Gyama, is now at home, paralyzed from the neck down from prison-sustained injuries.

Although it is unclear when he was injured sufficiently to paralyze him, it is known that he was beaten unconscious at the time of his initial arrest and suffered serious head injuries. The terms and conditions of his release are not known.

Lhundrup Gaden originally was sentenced on January 18, 1989 to a three-year term and deprivation of political rights for one-year for his involvement in the demonstration, for making posters, for speaking for Tibetan independence, and for demanding the release of Yulo Dawa Tsering (see p.179). The official charge was "instigating counterrevolutionary propaganda." On May 14, 1990, the Lhasa Intermediate People's Court, the same court that had initially sentenced him, increased his sentence by nine-and-a-half years and three years' deprivation of political rights for shouting slogans while in prison, for planning escape schemes and "organizing a jailbreak," and for forming a pro-independence group within Drapchi Prison. That indictment had come in November 1989. On December 17, 1991, Lhundrup Gaden was transferred to the Public Security Bureau Hospital in Lhasa.

. . [12½ YRS/MEDICAL PAROLE]

Four of the monks, along with one other person, were discovered with a leaflet or letter from a "foreigner," possibly a Tibetan exile, which read "The Chinese should leave Tibet." **LOBSANG CHOEJOR**[1], (lay name KUNSANG TSERING), 35, from Medro Gongkar Gyama, considered by Chinese authorities to be a leader or instigator, was sentenced to nine years in prison on charges of openly supporting Tibetan independence and corresponding with foreign reactionaries. **TENZIN TSULTRIM**, (lay name TSERING SONAM), 26, from Taktse County Cha, one of the five allegedly caught with the letter, received a five-year sentence; he was presumably released after its completion. **PHUNTSOG GYALTSEN**, (lay name LOBSANG YESHE[2]), 26, from Medro Gongkar Drigung Jo, received a sentence of twelve years. Not only was he charged with possession of the letter and participation in the March demonstration, but it was alleged he made the Tibetan national flag which the monks used, and acted as a leader or instigator. Phuntsog Gyaltsen was arrested once before. After a demonstration in October 1987, he was held in a "labor re-education" camp.

. . . . [12, 9 YRS]

LOBSANG TASHI[1], (lay name CHUNGDAG[1]), 33, from Taktse County, originally a peasant farmer, received a seven-year sentence with two years' subsequent deprivation of political rights for his part in the demonstration and for possession of the letter. He also allegedly instigated lamas to parade in the streets during the 1987 Lhasa riot (*Xinhua*, September 21, 1989) and openly supported Tibetan independence at an assembly meeting in the monastery. Lobsang Tashi, who joined the monastery when he was 21, was deputy director of its Democratic Management Committee and a council member of the Tibet Branch of the Buddhist Association of China. He was expelled from the latter body in September 1989.

. . . . [7 YRS]

TENPA WANGDRAG[2], (lay name SONAM[2]), 49, from Yartoe Yarzam in Lhokha Nedong County, received a fourteen or possibly a fifteen-year prison term for openly supporting the independent status of Tibet. On March 31, 1991, along with Lobsang Tenzin[2] (see p.351), he attempted to hand then U.S. Ambassador to China, James Lilley, a letter protesting prison conditions. The letter was snatched from Lilley's hands by the official interpreter. The two prisoners were severely beaten and moved to unlit isolation cells. On April 27, after protests by other prisoners against their continued isolation, the two, along with three others who were present at the time of the initial incident, (see Lobsang Palden[4], below; Tenpa Phulchung[2] p.200; and Penpa[10] p.532), were chained hand and foot and taken to Sangyip Prison. The following day, in handcuffs only, they were moved to what may be the Tibet Autonomous Region Prison Center No.2 or may be a labor camp *(laogai)* in Powo Tramo County in Nyingtri (called Kongpo by the Tibetans). The five probably were held in Damchu, a unit within the prison complex. A report that they were in an isolated work camp, may simply describe Damchu; reports that they were under a regime of hard labor and reduced rations could not be confirmed. The April 27 protest against moving the prisoners was violently suppressed.

About twenty prisoners asked a guard about the missing men; the guard phoned for assistance and a large contingent of armed soldiers moved in. Each protestor was tied with rope. Four or five guards then beat each one unconscious, some several times. Prison staff were not permitted to intervene. Most of the protesting men were put in isolation cells, some in manacles. Until June 1, Tenpa Wangdrag was in isolation, much of the time in the dark.

. . . . [14-15 YRS]

LOBSANG PALDEN[4], (lay name GYALTHAR, probably short for GYALTSEN THARCHIN), 32, from Chamdo Pakshoe County, was sentenced to ten years in prison for demonstrating and on charges of "reactionary behavior" for demanding the release of Yulo Dawa Tsering (see p.179), a senior Ganden monk and longtime political prisoner. As described above, Lobsang Palden was one of the prisoners punished in connection with the James Lilley affair.

. . . . [10 YRS]

DRAKPA TSULTRIM, (lay name TSONDRU[2]), 41, a storekeeper monk from Kyipo Gakyi, Medro Gongkar County, was sentenced to eight years' imprisonment for helping make the flag used in the March 1988 demonstration and for supporting independence. He was one of some twenty Drapchi prisoners harshly disciplined for involvement in the James Lilley incident (see above). **DRAKPA TENGYE**, (lay name

TSERING[8]), 26, from Medro Gongkar, was sentenced to four years in prison on similar charges and was also disciplined for involvement in the Lilley affair. He presumably has been released.

. . . . [8, 4 YRS]

■ **LOBSANG DADAK**, a 23-year-old Ganden monk, from Taktse County, arrested in September 1989, was sentenced to a nine-year prison term which he is serving in Drapchi. No additional information is available.

. . . . [9 YRS]

■ Four Ganden monks, **LOBSANG DRADUL** (lay name LOBSANG GYATSO[1]), 18; **LOBSANG YARPHEL**[1] (lay name PENPA[6]) 20; **TENZIN DRAKPA** (lay name TSERING BAGDRO), 26; and **TENZIN WANGDU** (lay name possibly DONDRUP[1]), 19, all from Medro Gongkar, arrested on June 10 or 13, 1992, were sentenced on August 30 in connection with a June 10 demonstration on the Barkhor during which they shouted "reactionary slogans." As part of the indictment, the four were accused of meeting together on June 9 in Tenzin Dragpa's room to make a copy of the banned Tibetan national flag. Charged with "counterrevolutionary propaganda and incitement," they received respectively five, seven, eight, and six-year sentences. The four were transferred from Gutsa Detention Center to Drapchi Prison after sentencing.

. . . . [8, 7, 6, 5 YRS]

■ **LOBSANG KHEDRUP**, 16, a

Ganden monk from Medro, arrested on June 17, 1992, was sentenced to a five-year prison term which he is serving in Drapchi.

. . . . [5 YRS]

■ **NGAWANG THONGLAM** (lay name LOBSANG CHOEJOR[2]), a 23-year-old Ganden monk, from Medro Gongkar Dro, Thankgya Chu, where his family farms, was initially sentenced on October 10, 1989 to a three-year prison term. He was arrested immediately after being spotted carrying a Tibetan flag toward the Barkhor in mid-September 1989. After his alleged involvement in a prison protest on May 20, 1991 in Sangyip (see p.186), Ngawang Thonglam was held in isolation for three weeks and his sentence was extended by one and a half years. Later, he was transferred to Trisam Prison. At some point, he was expelled from his monastery. Ngawang Thonglam's sister, Ngawang Tsepak (see p.529), is a Chubsang nun who completed a two-year prison sentence on September 2, 1991 and fled to India. Once there, she gave a detailed account of torture in prison.

. . . . [4½ YRS]

■ **PHURBU**[5], a 23-year-old Ganden monk from Taktse County, was arrested on October 10, 1989 and initially sentenced to a three-year prison term. After his sentence was extended by four years due to his alleged involvement in a protest within Sangyip Prison on May 20, 1991, he was moved to Drapchi Prison (see p.186).

. . . . [7 YRS]

■ **TENZIN LOBSANG** (lay name SONAM DORJE[2]), a 26-year-old Ganden monk, from Medro Gongkar Gyama, arrested on October 1, 1989 and originally sentenced to a three-year term, had his sentence extended by one-and-a-half-years for participating in a demonstration in Sangyip Prison on May 20, 1991 (see p.186). He subsequently was moved to Trisam Prison.

. . . . [4½ YRS]

■ **YULO DAWA TSERING**, a 67-year-old senior monk from Ganden Monastery, born in Dushi Taktse County, and a member of the Political Consultative Conference, was arrested on December 26, 1987, but not sentenced until January 19, 1989 when the Lhasa Intermediate People's Court handed down a ten-year term. There is an unconfirmed report that his sentence has been reduced by two years for good behavior. The charges against Yulo Dawa Tsering stemmed from remarks allegedly made to two visitors from Italy, one an exiled Tibetan monk and the other an Italian tourist, Dr. Stefano Dallari, who videotaped the conversation. Yulo Dawa Tsering reportedly suggested that foreign journalists should be permitted to enter Tibet and the Dalai Lama should not return until "everything had been changed." **THUPTEN TSERING**[3], a 67-year-old treasurer or storekeeper at Sera Monastery, born in Damshung County or Nagchu, was videotaped along with Yulo Dawa Tsering and faced the same charges. Arrested December 16, he received a six-year sentence and presumably was released upon its completion. Both monks were in the Fifth Division of Drapchi.

According to a March 1988 *Radio Lhasa* broadcast, "...on the afternoon of July 26, 1987, (the two monks) spread reactionary views, such as Tibetan independence, to foreign reactionary elements who came to Tibet as tourists and viciously vilified the policies adopted by the Chinese Communist Party and the people's government." Both monks were charged under Article 102(2) of China's Criminal Law for spreading "counterrevolutionary propaganda." According to *Xinhua* (September 21, 1989), Yulo Dawa Tsering had been sentenced to life imprisonment in 1959 but was released under an amnesty twenty years later.

On three occasions, Chinese authorities "permitted" visitors to "meet" with Yulo Dawa Tsering in Drapchi Prison. In October 1993, U.S. Assistant Secretary of State for Human Rights and Humanitarian Affairs John Shattuck met with him under "severely controlled circumstances with the prison authorities in attendance" and, said Shattuck, "[W]e were unable to have any conversation with him more than to obtain...a statement about his view of the circumstances that led to his arrest." In 1991, then U.S. Ambassador to China, James Lilley, met with Yulo Dawa Tsering but he, too, indicated that no genuine conversation was possible. During a November 1990 visit to Tibet, diplomats from four Scandinavian countries met Yulo Dawa Tsering. According to their report, he appeared in good health and was able to walk across the prison courtyard to meet them.

. . . . [8 OR 10 YRS]

Garu Nunnery

■ **GYALTSEN KELSANG**[1] - see p.15

. . . . [2 YRS]

■ **GYALTSEN KUNGA** - see p.16

. . . . [? YRS]

■ A group of at least 16 pro-independence demonstrators, including seven nuns from Garu Nunnery, eight from Michungri Nunnery, and one monk from Sera Monastery, were detained on August 21, 1990 at the Norbulingka, the Dalai Lama's former summer palace about a mile outside of Lhasa. According to *Tibet Information Network*, the sixteen demonstrators allegedly disrupted a state-run festival during the first day of the week-long Shoton (Yoghurt) Festival. They shouted slogans in support of the Dalai Lama and called on Chinese settlers to leave Tibet. All of those apprehended were first taken to Gutsa Detention Center for interrogation and later were transferred to Drapchi Prison. Among those formally arrested on September 11, 1990 and sentenced on December 2 under Articles 102, 22-24, 14 and 52 of the Criminal Law, were four Garu nuns.

GYALTSEN LHAKSAM[1] (lay name KELSANG CHOEDRON), 23, born either in Gyaltse or Gyama, received a seven-year sentence with two years off for good behavior.

However, a mid-April 1991 account (*Tibet Information Network*, August 31, 1991) reported that Gyaltsen Lhaksam[1] had been under special discipline, probably in solitary confinement, for unknown prison rule infractions. **GYALTSEN DROLKAR** (lay name **DAWA**[6]), 19, born in Medro Gongkar, and **GYALTSEN MONLAM** (lay name YANGCHEN[2]), 18, from Phenpo Lhundrup, were each sentenced to four years' imprisonment with one year off for good behavior. The latter reportedly has been released. There is a report that Gyaltsen Drolkar had her sentence increased by three or four years for singing pro-independence songs during May or June 1993. **GYALTSEN CHOEZOM** (lay name PENPA CHOEZOM), 21, from Taktse, was sentenced to five years in prison, less one year off for good behavior.

.... [7+YRS?] [4 YRS]

Among the Michungri Nuns sentenced were **GYALTSEN CHOEDRON**[1] (lay name PEMA DROLKAR[1]), 15, from Medro. She received a five-year term with one year off for good behavior. **TENZIN THUPTEN** (lay name DAWA YANGCHEN), 20, and **LOBSANG CHOEDRON**[4] (alternately known as SONAM CHOEDRON[1], 26, both from Medro; and **GYALTSEN LUNGRING** (lay name TRAZANG), 19, from Lhokha Dranang also were sentenced to five years' imprisonment reduced to four. However, there is a report that Tenzin Thupten had her sentence increased by nine years. **LOBSANG CHOEDRON**[2] (lay name SANGMO[1]), 23, from Medro was sentenced to seven years' imprisonment, reduced to five. **KARMA TRINLEY** (lay name PEMA), 23, from Toelung Dechen; **TENZIN NGAWANG** (lay name PEDRON), 21, from Medro; and **LHUNDRUP SANGMO** (lay name SANGMO[2]), 23, from Lhundrup, received four-year sentences with one-year reductions. With the exception of Lhundrup Sangmo who may have had her sentence increased by three years, they presumably have been released.

.... [5, 4, 4, 4 YRS]

■ Two outlawed flags were carried around the Potala about 9 A.M. either on June 15 or June 22, 1992 during a demonstration by sixteen nuns from Garu Nunnery. Thirteen reportedly were arrested and initially taken to Gutsa Detention Center. Among those known to have been sentenced on April 23, 1993 in connection with the protest were **GYALTSEN KUNSANG**[1], a 24-year-old Phenpo Lhundrup Ding native; **GYALTSEN NYINYI**, 23, from Taktse Pennyak; **NGAWANG KYENMA**, 22, from Phenpo Lhundrup Kolmo; **DAMCHOE GYALTSEN**, 24, from Toelung; **RINCHEN SANGMO**, 22, from Phenpo Lungshoe Phongdo; **NYIMA TSAMCHOE**, 24, from Toelung Sunrawa; and **NGAWANG NYIMA**[1], 23, from Nagchu Yabchishak, all serving four-year terms. **LOBSANG CHOEKYI**, 20, from Lhasa Dode, and **NGAWANG RIGDROL**, a 20-year-old from Medro Gongkar Yiche, received six-year sentences; **LOBSANG DROLMA**[1], 18, from Toelung Wangkar, received a five-year sentence.

[2 X 6 YRS] [5 YRS] [7 X 4 YRS]

NGAWANG PELKYI, 23, from Phenpo, is serving a three-year term; **NGAWANG TENKYI**, 18, from Taktse Tsangdok, has a two-year sentence. All those sentenced were sent to Drapchi Prison with the exception of Ngawang Pelkyi who went to Trisam. Nothing further is known about another Garu nun, **NGAWANG DADROL**, 17, from Medro Gongkar Chakgalgang, arrested the same day and still in Gutsa. Gyaltsen Nyinyi was arrested once before, for demonstrating with some Chubsang nuns on March 21 or May 14, 1992 (see Gyaltsen Kelsang[2], p.167). Ngawang Rigdrol also was arrested on March 21. It is possible that other Garu nuns, among them **NGAWANG JAMPA, NGAWANG SAMTEN[1], RINCHEN DROLMA[2]** and **TSAMCHOE[2]** were arrested in connection with the June demonstration.

. . . . [3, 2 YRS]

■ **GYALTSEN LODROE[1]** - see p.585

. . . . [3 YRS]

■ **GYALTSEN PELSANG** - see p.16

. . . . [? YRS]

■ **GYALTSEN SANGMO** - see p.15

. . . . [3 YRS]

■ **GYALTSEN TSULTRIM** - see p.15

. . . . [? YRS]

■ **KUNCHOK TSOMO**, a 17-year-old nun from Garu Nunnery, was arrested on June 17, 1992 and subsequently sentenced to a three-year prison term which she is serving in Drapchi Prison. Other than that she is from Medro, no further information is available. In a similar case, **NGAWANG SANGDROL** a 18-year-old Lhasa native, also from Garu Nunnery, was arrested on the same date for participating in a demonstration that took place on the Barkhor at 11.30 A.M. Held first at Gutsa Detention Center, she was transferred to Drapchi Prison after receiving a three-year term. Ngawang Sangdrol was imprisoned for four months in 1990 for her alleged participation in a demonstration on August 21 in Norbulingka Park (see Gyaltsen Lhaksam[1], p.16, 180).

. . . . [2 X 3 YRS]

■ **NGAWANG CHENDROL** - see p.15

. . . . [3 YRS]

■ **NGAWANG CHIME** - see p.16

. . . . [? YRS]

■ **NGAWANG CHOEKYI[1]** - see p.16

. . . . [? YRS]

■ **NGAWANG DEDROL[1]** - see p.15

. . . . [7 YRS]

■ **NGAWANG KELDRON** - see p.15

. . . . [5 YRS]

■ **NGAWANG KUNSANG** (lay name TSETEN[1]), a 24-year-old Garu nun from Phenpo, arrested on January 27, 1990, was sentenced to a six-year prison term and transferred from Gutsa Detention Center to Drapchi Prison. She has been expelled from her nunnery. A report giving the date of her arrest as January or February 1991, may actually refer to the date of her transfer to Drapchi.

. . . . [6 YRS]

■ **NGAWANG PEMO**[1] - see p.16

. . . . [? YRS]

■ **NGAWANG YANGKYI** - see p.15

. . . . [? YRS]

■ **PELKYI** - see p.42

. . . . [? YRS]

■ **PHUNTSOG CHENGA** - see p.16

. . . . [? YRS]

■ **PHUNTSOG CHOEKYI** - see p.15

. . . . [7 YRS]

■ **RINCHEN DROLMA**[1] - see p.15

. . . . [2 YRS]

Kyemolung Monastery

■ Four monks from Kyemolung Monastery, **NGAWANG TENZIN**[3] (lay name NYIMA[4]), 25; **NGAWANG SHENYEN** (lay name PHUNTSOG DORJE[1]), 27; **NGAWANG TSULTRIM**[2] (lay name PENPA[9]), 27; and **NGAWANG RABSANG** (lay name NORBU[3]), 18; all natives of Toelung Dechen, arrested on March

18, 1989, were sentenced to eight, six, six and three-year prison terms respectively. All were held in Drapchi Prison; Ngawang Rabsang presumably was released upon completion of his term. The four monks, along with two others, were first arrested in June 1988 for shouting slogans from the front of the Jokhang Temple in Lhasa on June 1. Although they were only held forty days, all were beaten during their detentions. One month later, in August 1988, a Work Inspection Team which came to the monastery interrogated the monks. Seven months later, on March 12, 1989, the four put up independence posters in the monastery; six days later they were arrested for the second time. Interrogation did not start until November. A fifth monk, **NGAWANG TSONDRU**[3], 22, who reportedly was implicated in the first case and spent 18 months in prison, from March 1988 until September 1989, committed suicide by hanging on December 25, 1989 as a result of at least two weeks of intensive and continuous interrogation by the Toelung Dechen Work Team. A sixth monk, **PHUNTSOG JAMPA**, was also interrogated, but his whereabouts are unknown.

. . . . [8, 6, 6 YRS]

Lhokha Ngari Dratsang Monastery

■ **NGAWANG DAMCHOE** (lay name SONAM DAMCHOE), a 21-year-old monk from Lhokha County Kyipa Xiang, arrested July 11, 1989, was sentenced to a four-and-a-half-year prison term. He reportedly was transferred to Trisam Prison after his initial detention in Sangyip.

. . . . [4½ YRS]

Lo Monastery

- **THUPTEN KELSANG**[1], a 19-year-old monk from Lo Monastery, originally from Taktse, was sentenced to a six-year prison term. Arrested on May 4, 1992, he is serving his sentence in Drapchi Prison.

. . . . [6 YRS]

Michungri Nunnery

- **PENPA WANGMO**[1], a 20-year-old Michungri nun, from Taktse, arrested on February 13, 1992, is serving a five-year sentence in Drapchi Prison.

. . . . [5 YRS]

- **PHUNTSOG NYIDRON** (lay name TSETEN[2]), from Phenpo Lhundrup County, and **PHUNTSOG PEMA**, from Toelung, both 23-year-old Michungri nuns, reportedly received nine and eight-year prison terms respectively for demonstrating and/or putting up posters. Both allegedly were "ringleaders." Originally sent to Gutsa Detention Center, they were later transferred to Drapchi Prison. There is some inconsistency in the reports of their activities and treatment. The two nuns were arrested on October 14, 1989 (see Phuntsog Sangye, p.533) and then disappeared from view. A later account reports their "arrests on December 14, 1990," probably a Tibetan calendar date. Since they were accused as "ringleaders" in the first demonstration and the others

involved received three-year terms, it is unlikely Phuntsog Nyidron and Phuntsog Pema were freed, then rearrested as the second report implied. More likely, both accounts refer to the 1989 event.

. . . . [9, 8 YRS]

Nyemo Gyache Monastery

- **LOBSANG CHOEDRAG**[3] (lay name THUPTEN NORBU), an 18-year-old monk from Nyemo Gyache Monastery or Sera Monastery, arrested for demonstrating along the Barkhor with five Michungri nuns on February 3, 1992, was formally arrested on April 23. Sentenced to a five-year prison term and two years' deprivation of political rights on August 3, he was transferred from Gutsa Detention Center to Drapchi Prison. Three of the nuns received prison terms on charges of "spreading counterrevolutionary propaganda." **LOBSANG DROLMA**[2] (lay name DAWA TSEDRON), 22, from Toelung, identified as the "principal culprit" because she had "ganged up" with two other nuns and suggested they go to Lhasa to demonstrate, received a seven-year prison term and three years' subsequent deprivation of political rights. **PHUNTSOG YANGKYI** (lay name MIGZANG), 19, from Medro Chubla, and **TRINLEY CHOEZOM** (lay name GORGYAL), an 18-year-old from Medro, treated as "minor offenders," were sentenced to five-year terms and two years' deprivation of political rights. All three were sent to Drapchi from Gutsa. The sentences and whereabouts of two other nuns,

LOBSANG CHOEDRON[1], a 17-year-old Lhokha Dranang Gyaling native, and **SHERAB NGAWANG**, 15, from Medro Gongkar Thankgya, found guilty of taking part in the protest, are unknown. They originally were held in Gutsa.

The protest erupted the day before the Chinese New Year while the governor of the region, the vice-mayor of Lhasa and fifteen other officials were paying a visit to the Barkhor Police Station.

. . [7, 5, 5, 5 YRS] [2 X ? YRS]

Nyethang Tashi Monastery

■ **PHUNTSOG SAMTEN**[2], a 24-year-old Nyethang Tashi monk and chantmaster, and **PHUNTSOG TSERING**, 25, a monk, were arrested for their participation in a demonstration on September 4, 1991 and sentenced respectively to ten and five-year terms. First detained in Gutsa, they were moved to Drapchi Prison after sentencing. **PHUNTSOG WANGDEN**, also a Nyethang Tashi monk, from Chushul, received a five-year sentence and is also in Drapchi. His date of detention is listed as September 1991 but it is unclear if he was part of the September 4 demonstration.

. . . . [10, 5, 5 YRS]

Palkhor Choede Monastery

■ Two accounts about **LHUNDRUP MONLAM**, a 26-year-old Palkhor Choede monk, born in Gyaltse County, differ as to date of arrest and length of sentence. The first reported he was arrested on March 15, 1990 and was sentenced to a four-and-a-half-year term; the second that he was arrested a year earlier and received a four-year sentence, in which case he would have completed his term and presumably been released. Both agree he was in Drapchi Prison, Fifth Division.

. . . . [4 OR 4½ YRS]

■ **LHUNDRUP TOGDEN**, a 25-year-old monk from Palkhor Choede Monastery, from Gyantse, arrested in December 1989, has been sentenced to a prison term of fourteen years. There is no additional information available.

. . . . [14 YRS]

■ **TSERING PHUNTSOG**[2], a 26-year-old monk from Palkhor Choede Monastery, detained in August 1990, has received a thirteen-year prison term. Other than that he is detained in Drapchi Prison, no additional information is available.

. . . . [13 YRS]

Pomda Monastery

■ **JAMPA**[1] - see p.16

. . . . [4 YRS]

Potala

■ **NGAWANG CHAMTSUL**, (lay name LOYAK[2]), 34, arrested on March 10, 1989, was sentenced to fifteen years' imprisonment and five years' deprivation of political rights by the Lhasa Intermediate People's Court at a mass public rally on December 6, 1989. Charged with "counterrevolutionary propaganda, inflammatory delusion and espionage" under Articles 102, 97 and 52 of the Chinese Criminal Law, he is serving his sentence in Drapchi Prison. According to *Tibet Radio* (December 7, 1989, in FBIS, December 20), Ngawang Chamtsul "actively collected intelligence for the enemy abroad, instigated the masses to hinder the enforcement of state laws and regulations, and jeopardized national unity." Before his arrest, Ngawang Chamtsul was a caretaker monk at the Potala Palace. He is 34 years old and is a native of Phenpo Lhundrup County.

. . . . [15 YRS]

■ **TENDAR PHUNTSOG**, a 62-year-old caretaker monk from the Potala Palace, from Phenpo, arrested March 8, 1989 for reasons unknown, reportedly had his sentence extended to ten years for leading a protest within Sangyip Prison on May 20, 1991. On that date, three days before the fortieth anniversary of the 17-point agreement between China and Tibet, political prisoners delivered a petition to prison authorities describing the agreement as having been imposed by force on an independent Tibet. As a result, eleven prisoners were beaten and spent at least three weeks in solitary confinement; some ten were given new sentences, some for as long as five years; and some were moved to Drapchi Prison. Those involved included Wangdu[2] p.191, Lhakpa[6] p.169, Phurbu[6] p.169, Sodor p.190, Phurbu Tsering[2] p.198, Ngawang Thonglam p.179, Jigme Wangchen p.523, Phurbu[5] p.179, Tenzin Lobsang p.179, and Jamyang[6]

p.195.

. . . . [10 YRS]

Phurchok Hermitage

■ **LOBSANG DORJE** (lay name KELSANG WANGDU), from Lhundrup Songban; **LOBSANG LHUNDRUP**[3] (lay name PALDEN[2]), from Phenpo Sege Nang; and **LOBSANG SHERAB**[1] (lay name KELSANG LHUNDRUP), from Lhundrup Songban, all 20 years old; and **THUPTEN KELSANG**[2] (lay name PENPA[7]), 18, from Taktse Kangba, monks from Phurchok Hermitage, were sentenced respectively to nine, seven, eight and six-year prison terms for demonstrating with a flag and shouting "Tibetan independence" outside the Jokhang Temple on May 16, 1992. In addition to their sentences, the men's political rights were suspended for four, two, three, and two or three years. Formally arrested on August 21, the monks were sentenced on September 16 by the Lhasa Intermediate People's Court on official charges of "counterrevolutionary propaganda and incitement" as defined in Articles 102, 11, 23, 24 and 52 of the Criminal Code. According to the court, the sentences were imposed to "protect the dictatorship of the proletariat, preserve the unification of the motherland, and severely crack down on the criminal activities of the counterrevolutionaries in their attempts to separate the motherland." No lawyers represented the defendants in court.

. . . . [9, 8, 7, 6 YRS]

RINCHEN DAWA[2] (also known as REZENG), a 25-year-old farm woman from Lhundrup, and **NGAWANG TENZIN**[1] (lay name RINZEN WANGMO; also known as NAMDROL KUNCHOK), a 23-year-old Chubsang nun originally from Jorenang, described as minor offenders because they arrived late and only followed the other four, received five-year sentences and two years' subsequent deprivation of political rights. All six are in Drapchi Prison. This was Ngawang Tenzin's second arrest; she had been expelled from her nunnery in 1989 for a "similar political offense," but nothing further is known about the circumstances of that first arrest.

. . . . [2 X 5 YRS]

According to eye witnesses (*Tibet Information Network*, September 16, 1992), once inside the Barkhor police station, the detainees were severely beaten. By the time they left for Gutsa Detention Center, some had bandages on their heads and blood coming from their mouths and faces. Others reportedly left the station unconscious. According to a second *Tibet Information Network* report (November 8, 1992), in late October a Chinese cellmate (a "common" criminal) in Gutsa beat Ngawang Tenzin over the head with a thermos and a rod. Guards, responding to Ngawang Tenzin's cries, continued to beat her, then denied her medical care because she had no money. Even after local people raised the necessary funds, treatment was refused. When they were finally permitted to take her to hospitals in Lhasa, People's Hospital refused to accept her, saying she had no need of treatment. Only after "sympathizers" put up a *renminbi* 500 deposit, was she finally accepted in the inpatient unit of the Hospital of Traditional Tibetan Medicine (*Mentse Khang*).

Rame Monastery

- **THUPTEN PHUNTSOG**[1] (lay name JAMPA[2]), 26, arrested June 22, 1992, received a five-year prison term for putting up posters. He is a monk from Rame Monastery, originally from Gongkar County. Initially held in Tsethang Jail, Thupten Phunstog was moved to Drapchi after sentencing.
. . . . [5 YRS]

Rong Jamchen Monastery

- **NGAWANG SHERAB**[2] and **NGAWANG ZOEPA**[1], both 24-year-old monks from Jamchen Monastery, arrested on March 11, 1992, were originally sentenced to four-and-a-half-year prison terms which they are serving in Drapchi Prison. However, an unconfirmed report claims that both monks had their sentences increased to ten years. Other than that the two are from Rinpung, no additional information is available.
. . . . [2 X 4½ OR 10 YRS]

Samye Monastery

- **LHAGYAL**[1], a 35-year monk from Samye Monastery, originally from Rinpung, detained in September 1991, has received a four-year sentence and is in Drapchi Prison.

. . . . [4 YRS]

■ **TENZIN SAMPHEL**, a 35-year-old native of Kongpo Lushar, was arrested in Lhokha sometime in 1991 for putting up posters and shouting slogans calling for Tibetan independence. Tried by the Lhasa Intermediate People's Court on charges of carrying out "separatist activity," he was sentenced to three years "reform through labor" and sent to the Toelung Reform Through Labor Camp near Lhasa. There has been a report that due to ill-treatment and poor prison conditions, Tenzin Samphel's health is precarious.

Tenzin Samphel was born in Tibet but spent his childhood in the Mysore Tibetan Settlement in South India where he received a formal education. In 1984 he returned to Tibet, taught English, and later became a monk at Samye Monastery. His is the first known case of a Tibetan who, having been educated and raised in India, returned to live in Tibet and was later tried and sentenced for involvement in non-violent pro-independence activities. Tenzin Samphel's father, Pema Tenzin, 53, lives in Switzerland.

. . . . [3 YRS]

■ **UGYEN CHOEKYI** (lay name DORJE TENZIN), a 31-year-old Samye Chimpuk monk, originally from Kongpo Miling, was arrested on November 1, 1991 and subsequently sentenced to a three-year prison term which he is serving in Trisam.

. . . . [3 YRS]

Sangyak Khargon Monastery

■ **LOBSANG DARGYE**, a 23-year-old monk from Sangyak Khargon Monastery in Dechen County, originally from Taktse, was sentenced to a seven-year prison term for demonstrating. Arrested on either May 15 or 16, 1992, he was detained first in Gutsa, then transferred to Drapchi Prison. Another monk, name unknown, from the same monastery was also arrested (see also Sonam Drolkar[1], p.204).

. . . . [7 YRS]

Sera Monastery

■ **LOBSANG GELEK[2]**, a 22-year-old Sera monk from Toe Lhatse or Nyemo, arrested November 17, 1989, was sentenced at the latest in October 1990 to twelve years in prison for allegedly taking part in demonstrations and distributing leaflets. He is in Drapchi Prison, having been transferred there from Sangyip.

. . . . [12 YRS]

■ **LOBSANG GYATSO[2]** (lay name NGODRUP[1]), a 24-year-old Sera monk from Phenpo Lhundrup, was arrested on June 2, 1991 and sentenced to a three-year prison term. First detained in Gutsa, he was moved later to Trisam.

. . . . [3 YRS]

■ **LOBSANG LHUNDRUP[1]** (lay name KELSANG TENZIN[1]), a 22-year-old from Sera Monastery, originally from Lhokha Chonggye, is in Trisam Prison. He was sentenced to a three-year term for demonstrating on May 26, 1991 on a road in Lhasa unofficially called Rangzem Lam. He may have been stabbed by police at the time he was apprehended. At least one, and maybe two other monks from Sera Monastery, were detained at the same time. **LOBSANG TOPCHU**, (lay name KUNKHYAB), 18, reportedly from Medro Lapdong, was stabbed several times and hospitalized after his arrest. Initially interned in Gutsa Detention Center, he may now be released. The whereabouts of **PHUNTSOG TSUNGME**, (lay name THUPTEN[1]), 21, a non-registered Sera monk, from Toelung, who reportedly received harsh treatment in Gutsa because of a previous arrest in 1986 or 1987, are uncertain. As of August 20, 1991, he was still in Gutsa.

. . . . [3 YRS]

■   **LOBSANG NYIMA[1]**, a 21-year-old Sera monk, from Medro Gyama, was sentenced to a three-year prison term for demonstrating for Tibetan independence. Arrested on May 26, 1991, he was detained first in Gutsa and then transferred to Trisam.

. . . . [3 YRS]

■   **LOBSANG TENPA[3]**, (lay name KELSANG TENZIN[2]), a 20-year-old Sera monk from Toelung Dechen County, reportedly a printer at the monastery, was sentenced to three years' imprisonment and transferred from Gutsa Detention Center to Trisam. He had been arrested on August 4, 1991 for an unknown offense. Lobsang Tenpa was imprisoned for two months in October

1987 for his alleged involvement in the October 1, 1987 demonstration. Later, during the December 10, 1988 demonstration, he was shot. After a one-month hospital stay, he was returned to his monastery and subjected to five months of investigation, then expelled. The expulsion, effective March 17, 1989, was announced on April 14 at which time Lobsang Tenpa was escorted to his home village and placed under restrictions.

. . . . [3 YRS]

Serkhang Monastery

■   **NGAWANG YESHE**, 22, and **YESHE JAMYANG**, 19, monks from Serkhang Monastery in Phenpo, were arrested on February 11, 1992 for putting up pro-independence, anti-Chinese posters. Held first in Gutsa Detention Center, they were transferred to Drapchi Prison after receiving prison terms of three and four years respectively.

. . . . [4, 3 YRS]

Shungsep Nunnery

■   Six Shungsep nuns, detained together for "shouting independence slogans and demonstrating" on October 1, 1990, have been sentenced and were in Drapchi Prison as of January 1994. They included **CHIME DROLKAR** (also known as CHIME DEKYI), 18; **JIGME YANGCHEN**, 23; **YANGZOM[3]** (lay name RIGZIN CHOEKYI[2]), 24; **OEZER CHOEKYI**, 23, all from Lhokha; and **PALDEN CHOEDRON** (lay name PALDEN YANGKYI), 19, from Nyemo. All were sentenced to seven-year terms, but according to a January 1994 report, Chime Drolkar may have been released early and Palden Choedron may have had her sentence extended by three or four years. **PEMA DROLKAR[2]**, 19, from Lhokha, received a three-year term and presumably was released.

... [4 X 7 YRS] [7 + 3-4 YRS]

■ **RINCHEN CHOENYI** - see p.515

. . . . [7 YRS]

■ **TAPSANG[1]**, a 22-year-old Shungsep nun from Lhasa, has been sentenced to five years in prison and expelled from her nunnery. The date of her arrest and her alleged offense are not known, but as of late 1991 she was held in Gutsa Detention Center.

. . . . [5 YRS]

Sungrabling Monastery

■ Six monks from Sungrabling monastery in Lhokha, Gongkar County, all natives of the area, were charged with involvement in the March 1989 demonstrations and sentenced to prison terms of two to six years. **TSULTRIM JAMPA**, 25, and **CHIME TSERING**, 20, who served three and two-year prison terms respectively, have been released from Drapchi Prison. **YESHE TSERING**, 26, who received a four-year term, probably has been released. **YESHE DRADUL**, 27; **YESHE NGAWANG**, 26; and **YESHE PALJOR**, 23, serving six, six, and five-year terms respectively, are still in Drapchi. The three were arrested on March 13. According to an August 10,

1993 report from *Tibet Information Network*, another Sungrabling monk, **SOTOP** (also known as SONAM TOPGYAL[1] and SONAM TOPJOR), 23, from Lhokha Gongkar, who was also arrested in 1989, was sentenced to a seven-year term and is in Drapchi.

. . . . [7, 6, 6, 5 YRS]

Sungthang Monastery

■ **SODOR** (lay name SONAM DORJE[3]; also known as SOETOP), a 25-year-old monk from Sungthang Monastery, originally from Lhokha Gongkar Namgyal Shol, arrested on August 16, 1989, originally received a two-year prison term. As part of a protest in Drapchi Prison on May 20, 1991 (see p.186), he was moved to Sangyip Prison and had his sentence extended, probably by five years.

. . . . [7 YRS?]

Thankgya Monastery

■ **NGAWANG PALDEN[2]** (lay name SONAM NORBU), a monk from Thankgya Monastery, was arrested on July 12, 1992 and subsequently sentenced to three years' imprisonment. He is in Trisam Prison in the Lhasa area. No further information is available.

. . . . [3 YRS]

Toelung Nyengon Nunnery

■ Six nuns, arrested on May 14, 1992 for taking part in a demonstration the day before (see Jampa Tenzin[2], p.176, and Ngawang Choshe, p.172) have all been sentenced. **NGAWANG**

CHOEKYI[2], 23; NGAWANG LOCHOE, 19; and NGAWANG TSAMDROL, 21, were each sentenced to five years' imprisonment. NGAWANG NAMDROL[1], 23, and NGAWANG PHUNTSOG, 22, received seven-year terms. NGAWANG TENDROL, 18, was sentenced to three years' imprisonment. Detained first at Gutsa, the five were transferred to Drapchi after sentencing. Ngawang Choekyi and Ngawang Tsamdrol are from Toelung Nyengon Nunnery; the others are from Samdrup Drolma Lhakhang Nunnery. Ngawang Choekyi came originally from Medro or Toelung; the others from Toelung. Four other names, NGAWANG NGONDRON, NGAWANG GYATSO[1], NGAWANG NORDRON and NGAWANG PHURDRON[1] have been cited in connection with the demonstration; however, it is unclear if they are alternate names for those already listed or represent other arrests.

[2 X 7 YRS] [3 X 5 YRS] [3 YRS]

Toelung Tsongmed Monastery

■ KELSANG DAWA[2], a 22-year-old monk from Toelung Tsongmed Monastery, is serving a three-year term in Drapchi Prison. Other than that his date of arrest was May 15, 1992, no additional information is available.
. . . . [3 YRS]

Tsuglhakhang

■ LHUNDRUP JINPA, (also known as DAWA WANGDU, lay name DAWA[8]), a 25-year-old Phenpo

Lhundrup County native, and a monk at the Jokhang (Tsuglhakhang) Temple in Lhasa, arrested on June 11, 1989, received a five-year prison term for his alleged participation in demonstrations and for putting up pro-independence posters. He is in the Fifth Division of Drapchi Prison.
. . . . [5 YRS]

■ NGAWANG SONGSTEN, a 24-year-old Tsuglhakhang (Jokhang) monk, from Taktse, arrested in March 1989, is serving a seven-year prison sentence in Drapchi Prison. The length reflects either a four-year extension of an original three-year term or vice versa.
. . . . [7 YRS]

■ WANGDU[2], a 27-year-old caretaker monk at the Jokhang (Tsuglhakhang), originally from Taktse, arrested on March 8, 1989, probably received a three-year prison sentence. After he took part in a prison protest in Sangyip on May 20, 1991 (see p.186), he had his term extended five years and was moved to Drapchi Prison.
. . . . [8 YRS]

Zitho Monastery

■ LOBSANG TASHI[2], a 41-year-old monk from Zitho Monastery, born in Lho County, arrested on March 4, 1990, was sentenced on January 5, 1991 by the Chamdo court (*Tibet Information Network*) to a five-year prison term which he is serving in Powo Zungma Prison. There is a report, however, of a 1988 arrest of a

25-year-old with the same name who was sentenced to life in prison and held in Powo Zungma Prison. Despite the discrepancies, it appears as if the reports refer to the same person.

. . . . [5 YRS OR LIFE]

Lay Persons

■ **BAGDRO**[1] - see p.16
. . . . [? YRS]

■ **BUCHUNG**, 20, a trader from Dromo County, was arrested on December 2, 1991 and sentenced to a five-year prison term which he is serving in Drapchi Prison. No additional information is available.
. . . . [5 YRS]

■ **CHOEDAK**, 38, and **HA RANGGON**, 40, two Tibetan businessmen, were tried and sentenced on March 22, 1990 in Ngaba for allegedly writing and putting up posters advocating Tibetan independence. Choedak, also accused of distributing political pamphlets brought in from Lhasa, received a seven-year term. There have been no reports on his condition since 1992, when he reportedly was in ill-health. Ha Ranggon, reportedly a "regular guest at local government meetings" received a two-and-a-half-year term and presumably has been released. No information about **TSENDAK** has been available since he was arrested along with the others. The 25-year-old teacher from the Ngaba Minority High School allegedly participated in pro-

independence activities.
. . . . [7 YRS]

■ **CHUNGDAG**[2] (or PUMO CHUNGDAG), a 36-year-old businesswoman from Lhasa, arrested March 14, 1989, is serving a seven-year sentence in Drapchi Prison.
. . . . [7 YRS]

■ **DAWA**[9], a 27-year-old nomad from Chushul County, arrested on March 26, 1989 in Chushul, was sentenced to a five-year prison term. Other than that he is in Drapchi Prison, no additional information is available.
. . . . [5 YRS]

■ **DAWA DROLMA**[2], a 26-year-old Nyemo native, formerly a temporary teacher at the Lhasa Cement Plant School, was in Drapchi Prison as of March 6, 1992. On that day, she was beaten and placed in solitary confinement after she and some 25 other female prisoners, 22 of whom were nuns, in an attempt to honor the Tibetan tradition of wearing new clothes on the New Year, donned their own clothes or pieces of clean prison clothing. When told to wear their usual clothing, they responded by making nationalist statements. According to one source, there was a disagreement among the prison staff as to whether the clothing change was acceptable. After one Section Head denounced the women, they became angry and some shouted that Tibet was independent and they were not afraid to die for it. The thirty to forty armed policemen who were summoned, beat the women so severely that they all needed medical attention the next day. Two of the nuns reportedly were unable to walk without assistance. Three women were placed in solitary confinement following the incident. **RIGZIN CHOEKYI**[1] (probably an alternative name for **RINCHEN CHOENYI**, currently serving a seven-year sentence: see p.515), a Shungsep nun pegged as the leader of the protest, was reportedly still in isolation as of March 30.

Charged with "counter-revolutionary instigation" for writing a "reactionary song" on her classroom blackboard on September 14, 1989, and then teaching it to her students, and for providing shelter for "rioters" and "encouraging" them, Dawa Drolma was granted bail on December 8, 1989, by the Lhasa People's Procuratorate pending further investigation. According to a *Radio Lhasa* report (December 8, 1989), the action had been taken so that she could continue to feed her one-year old son. Dawa Drolma finally received a five-year sentence but it is unclear from what date it commenced, September 14, 1989 or November 17, 1990 when she was either re-arrested or was returned to prison.

. . . . [7 YRS] [5 YRS]

■ **DONDRUP DORJE**, a 45-year-old driver for the Lhasa Shoe and Hat Factory, arrested on May 26, 1989, was sentenced at a mass public meeting in Lhasa on November 30, 1989 (see Ngawang Phulchung, p.173) to five years in prison on charges of "counterrevolutionary agitation" and mimeographing "reactionary leaflets to slander the socialist system." He was

deprived of his political rights for an additional two years. Detained first at Gutsa, Dhondrup Dorje was transferred to Drapchi after sentencing. During his first imprisonment, which started on October 15, 1987 and lasted nine months, and was for demonstrating on October 1, Dhondrup Dorje was regularly and severely beaten, leaving him partially deaf. He also was chained hand and foot for three months in a cell he shared with twenty others.

. . . . [5 YRS]

■ **DORJE**[2] - see p.17

. . . . [? YRS]

■ **DRADUL**[3], a 23-year-old ex-soldier from Lhasa Town-2, arrested March 12, 1989, was sentenced to sixteen years in prison. Other than that he is in the Fifth Division of Drapchi Prison, no additional information is available.

. . . . [16 YRS]

■ **DROLMA SANGMO** (also listed as **TASHI SANGMO**), 24, from Chamdo, and her husband **JIGME DORJE**, 22, were sentenced to three-year prison terms for allegedly carrying flags and political leaflets when they crossed from Nepal to Tibet in April or May 1991. The couple was arrested in Lhatse and sent to Sangyip Prison. Drolma Sangpo, who reportedly was in isolation because she "chants scriptures," has been transferred to Trisam, as has Jigme Dorje.

. . . . [2 X 3 YRS]

■ **GELEK YONTEN**, a 38-year-old tailor from Phenpo, was sentenced on

February 28, 1991 to a seven-year prison term which he is serving in Drapchi Prison. According to *Tibet Information Network* (February 28, 1991), Gelek Yonten, married with two children ages nine and seven, was detained by police in Lhasa on August 9, 1990. An unconfirmed account reported that he was accused of involvement with a foreign journalist who was trying to learn about conditions in Tibet. According to a close associate, he was tortured during preliminary interrogation and forced to name as his accomplice Sonam Drolkar[2] (see p.590), a 25-year-old nun who was tortured, hospitalized, but then was able to escape from Tibet and give her testimony.

. . . . [7 YRS]

■   **JAMPA NGODRUP**, a 45-year-old doctor from Lhasa, employed at the Barkhor Nangrong East Clinic (*Chengguan Qu* Barkhor Clinic), was sentenced to thirteen years in prison as an "agent," for copying, at two different times, lists of names of those arrested or injured during two 1988 pro-independence demonstrations in Lhasa. Initially detained on October 10, 1989, Jampa Ngodrup was held without charge for ten months, until August 13, 1990 when he was officially charged. Tried in Lhasa Municipal People's Court on December 24, he was sentenced the following day. The decision characterized the verdict as necessary "in order to strengthen the unity of the Motherland...and to stabilize the democratic rights of the people." Jampa Ngodrup, who allegedly "confessed," was described as

"harboring counterrevolutionary aims." According to Chinese authorities, he committed two crimes. He gave Lhamo Yangchen, a Tibetan woman, the names of some of those arrested from the March 5, 1988 demonstration. And in December 1988, Lhamo Yangchen gave another list, this one from the December 10, 1988 demonstration, to Jampa Ngodrup and "made" him copy it. Since she is considered a "foreign resident" by the Chinese and the lists were considered "state secrets," Jampa Ngodrup was charged under Article 97(1) of the Chinese Criminal Code. The article generally deals with acts of espionage; Section 1 deals with "stealing or secretly gathering or providing intelligence for the enemy."

A Ratoe monk named Choejor, who was employed at the clinic and reportedly had just been released from prison, also was implicated. He allegedly supplied some of the names for the first list, and it is not clear whether he has been re-arrested. Choejor and Lobsang Choejor[3] (see p.540), who was arrested in 1988 for demonstrating at Ratoe Monastery, may be the same person. (See also Tseten Yangkyi, p.589.)

Jampa Ngodrup is held in the Fifth Division of Drapchi Prison. A May 1993 report characterized him as severely ill from prison maltreatment. He is suffering extreme fluid retention such that his entire body is bloated; he is unable to walk without the aid of crutches and he may have tuberculosis (*Tibet Information Network*, October 19, 1993). Jampa Ngodrup was detained once before, on October 27,

1987.
. . . . [13 YRS]

■   It is unclear if **JAMYANG**[6], a 20-year-old layman, either from Tsawa Pomda in Chamdo or from Dakyab County, arrested in 1989 and sentenced to a three-year term, has been released from Drapchi Prison. His sentence had been extended, length unknown, after his involvement in a May 20, 1991 protest within Sangyip (see p.186).
. . . . [3 + ?YRS]

■   **JAMYANG SAMTEN**, a 35-year-old road worker in Chamdo, arrested on September 8, 1989, was sentenced to a five-year prison term and three years' deprivation of political rights for "opposing progress" (*Radio Lhasa*, February 8, 1991), a Chinese government euphemism for opposing the Communist Party or government. The public rally at which he was sentenced took place on February 8, 1991. His trial before the Chamdo Court may have occurred a day or two earlier; he is held at Powo Tramo Prison. A *Tibet Information Network* source (June 1991) reported that, "...these political prisoners were charged for writing slogans and putting them up in the streets; in particular I am definite about Jamyang Samten."
. . . . [5 YRS]

■   **JIGME GYATSO**[1] was reportedly arrested sometime in 1987 and tried "about a year" later, then transferred from Gutsa Detention Center to Drapchi Prison. As of early 1992, he was still there. A *Xinhua* report of March 11, 1988, confirmed that he had

been arrested and charged. According to unconfirmed reports, Jigme Gayatso's trial was attended by relatives who reported that he received a life sentence. In November 1991, he reportedly became severely ill, "trembling and unable to stand up." Although he was refused medical treatment in prison, relatives were permitted to take him to a clinic for a one-time visit, and by February 1992, his condition had reportedly improved. There are unconfirmed allegations that Jigme Gyatso was repeatedly beaten in prison. Formerly a monk at Labrang Tashi Khyil Monastery, he left the monastic life in order to marry. At the time of his arrest, he was selling incense from a stall on the South Barkhor.
. . . . [LIFE?]

■   **KHAMSANG GYALTSEN**, 27, a farmer from Zozang County, arrested on June 7, 1989, was tried in Chamdo Court on July 5, 1990 and sentenced to a five-year term which he is serving in Powo Tramo Prison.
. . . . [5 YRS]

■   A political re-education meeting in the village of Medro Gyama Trikhang, Medro Gongkar, on June 30, 1992, was disrupted when **KUNCHOK LODROE**, 23; **SONAM DORJE**[1], 23; **LHUNDRUP DORJE** (also known as LHUNDRUP), 23; and **SONAM RINCHEN**, 23, four farmers from Dashar, a village in the district, rushed the stage, seized the microphone, tangled with officials, shouted pro-independence and anti-Chinese statements, and unfurled a Tibetan flag.

After the four original demonstrators were dragged away and beaten by the People's Armed Police, some 100 villagers joined the shouting. Fourteen arrests followed immediately; three came later. Some of the participants were sent to Gutsa Detention Center in Lhasa, 60 kilometers west of the village; some were held at the local Medro Gyama Jail.

On October 20 the Lhasa Intermediate People's Court handed down judgements. Kunchok Lodroe, the leader, and Sonam Dorje and Sonam Rinchen were each sentenced to thirteen years in prison and four years' subsequent deprivation of political rights; Lhundrup Dorje, who was severely injured with a rifle butt during the protest, received a fifteen-year term and five years' deprivation of rights. All four, charged with "spreading p r o p a g a n d a   r e g a r d i n g counterrevolution" and "launching wanton attacks on the socialist system to divide the Motherland," are in Drapchi Prison.

. . . . . . [15 YRS] [3 X 13 YRS]

A 41-year-old farmer, **THUPTEN YESHE**[1], was detained on July 6 after security officers and legal cadres from Lhasa arrived in the village to search the houses of those initially arrested. Although he reportedly did not take part in the protest, he received a fifteen-year sentence and five years' deprivation of political rights on a charge of "cooperating with the demonstrators." According to court documents, Thupten Yeshe, formally arrested on August 14, made three pro-independence posters "attacking the

socialist system, opposing the socialist ideological education, and encouraging peasants to rebel, and hung them on a tree on April 24. In June, he and Lhundrup Dorje discussed plans to fly a Tibetan flag from the local government offices, offenses which constituted "spreading propaganda regarding incitement to revolution." He, too, is in Drapchi. Another member of Thupten Yeshe's family also was detained, but no details are available. **SAMTEN GYATSO**, 27, who reportedly helped make the flag, was released on August 22, 1992. **LHAKSAM**, 27, who shouted slogans, was released on August 16. **LHAKYET**, also detained, has probably been released. (For further details about resistance to mining and deforestation in Medro Gyama Trikhang, see Gyatso[2] p.212.)

. . . . [15 YRS]

■   **LEGDRUP**, 27, who is either a farmer or tailor in Gyaltse County, was arrested on January 7, 1991 and subsequently sentenced to a three-year prison term. He is in Drapchi Prison.

. . . . [3 YRS]

■   **LOBSANG LHUNDRUP**[2], in his fifties; **TSONDRU TENPHEL**, 29; **PEMA   KELSANG**, 34; and **LODROE**[2], 39, all farmers from Lhokha Kyiru Township, arrested October 11, 1991, were sentenced for putting up anti-Chinese posters. Lobsang Lhundrup received a seven-year sentence and two years "under watch at home"; the others are serving respectively three, four, and two-year terms. All are in Drapchi Prison, except Lodroe who presumably was released upon completion of his term. Lodroe was arrested in August; the others on October 11, 1991.

.... [7, 4, 3 YRS]

■ **LODROE**[1] - see p.17

.... [? YRS]

■ **MIGMAR**[3], a 32-year-old projectionist at the Chideshol Cinema, is serving a five-year sentence for distributing and putting up posters in Chideshol (see Shilok[2], p.205). Held in Tsethang Jail after his arrest on April 5, 1992, he was later transferred to Drapchi Prison.

.... [5 YRS]

■ **NAMGYAL TASHI**[1], 62, from Lhasa, was sentenced to an eight-year prison term for alleged "splittist" activities, including involvement in demonstrations, links with westerners involved in anti-Chinese activity, and distribution of posters. Arrested on June 3, 1991, he is in Drapchi Prison.

.... [8 YRS]

■ **NGODRUP**[2] (also known as NGODRUP PHUNTSOG and NGO-PHUN), 37, formerly a member of the Chinese People's Political Consultative Conference (CPPCC) from Lhasa, arrested in March 1989, was sentenced to eleven years in prison and deprived of his political rights for four years. There is speculation that the reason for Ngodrup's arrest had to do with his supplying food and tea from his restaurant in Lhasa to participants in the 1988 demonstrations. The restaurant, which he had opened with

his three sisters, was a meeting place for people wanting to discuss politics. It is possible this was Ngodrup's second arrest, the first coming in 1987 immediately after he returned from India where he had gone in late 1985. Prior to his work at the CPPCC, Ngodrup was employed in the Municipal Housing Construction Company, first as a construction worker and later in so-called managerial positions. Prior to 1959, Ngodrup's father was a member of the Tibetan army with some 100 people under his command; his mother was a small stall-keeper in Lhasa. One sister was active in a volunteer attempt to rebuild Ganden Monastery after the Cultural Revolution; another was imprisoned during the Cultural Revolution.

.... [11 YRS]

■ **NYIMA**[5], a 31-year-old married man with two young children, was transferred from prison to People's Hospital No.2 (also known as Workers' Hospital No.1) on or just before February 1, 1992. Suffering from acute kidney failure as a result of kicks received while incarcerated, he reportedly lapsed into a coma shortly after admission (*Tibet Information Network*, March 10, 1992). Nyima reportedly recovered, but has since disappeared from view. He had been in prison since at least June 1990, when he was arrested during a pro-independence demonstration.

.... [? YRS]

■ **PENPA DRUGYAL**, a 23-year-old painter from Gyantse County,

arrested on October 28, 1991, was sentenced to three years' imprisonment and sent to Drapchi Prison. He had been arrested for putting up posters reading 'Independence for Tibet,' 'Chinese leave Tibet,' and 'Tibet for Tibetans.' According to a *Tibet Information Network* report (January 8, 1992), at the beginning of November 1991, he was chained, denounced and punched by police during a public rally in Gyantse, 250 kilometers southwest of Lhasa. An official announced that Penpa Drugyal was "a separatist and a black social element [and] "a spy and enemy." He was dragged back and forth in front of the crowd while two Public Security officers kept punching his head to keep it lowered.
. . . . [3 YRS]

■   **PENPA TSERING**[2], 26, from Lhasa, arrested October 9, 1991, is serving a four-year prison term in Drapchi.
. . . . [4 YRS]

■   **PHUNTSOG DORJE**[2], a 36-year-old native of Lhasa, arrested on November 7, 1990 at his workplace, the Snowlands Restaurant, has been sentenced to a ten-year term which he is serving in Drapchi Prison, Block 5, Section 2, after transfer from Sangyip. He reportedly is ill with kidney problems attributed to extraordinarily heavy labor (*Tibet Information Network*, October 19, 1993). According to unofficial reports from Lhasa, the Chinese authorities suspected him of links with a pro-independence organization. Phuntsog Dorje had been arrested once before, on December 20,

1989, and held for eight months.
. . . . [10 YRS]

■   **PHURBU TSERING**[2] (also known by the Chinese name SHAO MI), a 27-year-old "family" man from Lhasa Tsemonling, arrested on March 7, 1989 and initially sentenced to a three-year prison term had his sentence extended to seven years and was moved to Drapchi Prison after he took part in a protest in Sangyip Prison on May 20, 1991 (see p.186).
. . . . [7 YRS]

■   **SONAM TOPGYAL**[2], a 24-year-old painter and tailor from Lhasa Dharpa Ling, arrested March 10, 1989, was sentenced to a five or possibly a six-year prison term. Held in Drapchi Prison, he was one among some twenty prisoners harshly disciplined in connection with the James Lilley letter affair (see Tenpa Wangdrag[2] p.177).
. . . . [5/6 YRS]

■   **SONAM TSERING**[1] - see p.16
. . . . [? YRS]

■   **TANAK JIGME SANGPO** (also known as JIGSANG), a 64-year-old former teacher at Lhasa Primary School No. 1, born in Gyantse, is currently serving a cumulative sentence of 28 years in Drapchi Prison, Block 1, a unit reserved for "bad social elements." A famous dissident, well known for his continued defiance within prison, he has been held continuously since September 1983, initially because he shouted slogans and/or put up posters criticizing Deng Xiaoping, and later for political acts within prison. Jigme Sangpo's 1983 original 15-year sentence was increased, either in 1987 or 1989, to 19 years after he shouted pro-independence slogans.

The Lhasa Intermediate People's Court increased Jigme Sangpo's sentence again in 1991, this time to 28 years for shouting pro-independence slogans on December 6 during the prison visit of a Swiss delegation. As the delegates, including Switzerland's ambassador to China, approached Jigme Sangpo's cell, he and three other prisoners began to shout. The delegates were quickly led away by their Chinese hosts who said the prisoners were mad. Minutes later, the four prisoners were dragged from their cells, beaten, and placed in isolation. Jigme Sangpo reportedly was beaten so harshly that his body turned numb. Fellow prisoners in Drapchi, knowing he would face an additional sentence, smuggled out a letter for the delegation informing them that the man who had shouted during their visit was not mad but a political prisoner, and urging them to attend his trial.

Continuing reports of beatings, torture and isolation have led to grave concern over Jigme Sangpo's well-being. The most recent report detailed a new method, "cold cell torture," in which the prisoner is surrounded by cold metal sheets. It was first used on Jigme Sangpo in 1991 after the second extension of his 1983 sentence. He was placed in an isolation cell lined with the sheets which were designed to lower cell temperature, but permission to put on extra clothing was denied. The average winter temperature in Lhasa is 3.5° C below zero and can drop to as low as 10° C below. After at least six weeks of such treatment, Jigme Sangpo was removed from the cold cell. An October 19, 1993 account of his torture (*Tibet Information Network*) reports he is ill with high blood pressure.

As of 1993, Jigme Sangpo had already spent at least 25 years in prison. He was first arrested in 1959 and sentenced to three years' "labor re-education" for "corrupting the minds of children with counterrevolutionary ideas." A student had written a criticism of Mao on a bathroom wall. Jigme Sangpo chastised the student and made him erase the slogan but had not reported the incident to the authorities. Arrested again in 1964 for having made a negative comment about the "political struggle sessions" of the Panchen Lama, which all Lhasa primary school teachers were required to attend, he received another three-year "labor re-education" term. In 1969, Jigme Sangpo was either re-arrested or has his sentence extended after his niece, a member of a pro-independence organization, was arrested while trying to escape from Tibet. She was carrying Jigme Sangpo's photograph. Accused of sending her to report to the Dalai Lama, he was required to spend another ten or fifteen years' in prison (reports vary), much of it at the Nyethang Lime Works. Following his "release," he was required to remain at work as a "forcibly retained laborer."
. . . . [28 YRS]

■   **TASHI TSERING**, a 55-year-old prominent public figure and former member of the Chinese People's

Political Consultative Conference (CPPCC), from Area No.3 in Shigatse, was sentenced to a seven-year prison term for "counterrevolutionary propaganda and incitement" (FBIS, December 1, 1989). Following his arrest on November 28, 1989, his case was described in detail in a *Radio Lhasa* report (November 29, 1989). "For a long time [Tashi Tsering] has been slack in remolding his ideology, showing great discontent against the Party and about the reality. He wrote a total of 73 slogans and leaflets supporting independence for Tibet this year and put them into complaint letter boxes at the central airport of the prefecture...the general office of the CPPCC Prefectural Committee and the head office of the Shigatse City Party Committee. These slogans and leaflets, venomously slandering the Chinese Communist Party and the socialist system, reflected his very reactionary thinking. They have had extremely bad influence among the public and have seriously undermined political stability and unity..." An unofficial report lists Tashi Tsering, in the Fifth Division in Drapchi Prison, as ill with heart problems. He reportedly was briefly admitted to the prison clinic in April 1991.

. . . . [7 YRS]

■   **TENPA PHULCHUNG**[2], 47, an accountant in a city shoe factory co-operative in Lhasa, was arrested on December 15, 1987 and sentenced to seven years in prison for allegedly possessing posters advocating Tibetan independence. (For important further information on Tenpa Phulchung, see

case of "**Danba ***," p.170.) Held after sentencing in the Fifth Division, Drapchi Prison, he was moved after a prison protest (see Tenpa Wangdrag[2] p.177) to Powo Tramo County in Nyingtri (called Kongpo by the Tibetans), to what may be the Tibet Autonomous Region Prison No.2 or else a labor camp *(lao gai)*. He and possibly other protestors were reportedly held at Damchu, a unit within the prison complex removed from the main body of the prison. Another report, that they were in an "isolated work camp," may simply refer to Damchu. Initial reports that Tenpa Phulchung was being held under a regime of hard labor and reduced rations which greatly weakened him have not yet been confirmed.

. . . . [7 YRS]

■   **TENPA SONAM** - see p.17

. . . . [? YRS]

■   **TENZIN**[2], a 23-year-old from Lhasa, arrested March 9, 1989, was sentenced to a five-year prison term. He is in Drapchi Prison.

. . . . [5 YRS]

■   **TSETEN DONDRUP**, 26, a student from Shigatse, was sentenced sometime between March and October 1990 to a seven-year term for carving "Tibet is independent" on a woodblock. The last report of his whereabouts was as of September 1991, when he was being held in Outhridu, a section of Sangyip Prison Complex. During an earlier imprisonment, for four months in the winter of 1988, Tseten Dondrup was reportedly tortured.

. . . . [7 YRS]

■ **TSERING**[9] (also known as TSERING KYOKPA), a 48-year-old carpenter from Kham Minyak, tried and sentenced on October 5, 1989 by the Lhasa Intermediate People's Court, is serving a seven-year sentence in Drapchi Prison. As a Sera monk, Tsering took part in two demonstrations, one on December 10, 1988, during which he was shot in the abdomen and one on March 5, 1988 during which he carried a flag and shouted "reactionary slogans." Tsering was one of twenty-some prisoners disciplined for their participation in the James Lilley incident (see Tenpa Wangdrag[2] p.177). According to an unofficial report, Tsering has gone deaf as a result of severe beatings (*Tibet Information Network*, 10/19/93).

. . . . [7 YRS]

■ **TSERING**[10], a 30-year-old, born in Lhasa Town-2 Ramoche, arrested on December 10, 1988 and sentenced to six years' imprisonment, is serving his sentence in the Fifth Division of Drapchi Prison. No other information is available.

. . . . [6 YRS]

■ **TSERING NGODRUP**, a 59-year-old from Lhokha Lhuntse, employed at the Lhasa Gernyer Restaurant, arrested on April 7, 1989 and sentenced on September 12, 1989 by the Lhasa Municipal People's Court, is serving a twelve-year term in the Fifth Division of Drapchi Prison. He also has been deprived of his political

rights for four years. *Radio Lhasa* (September 13, 1989) reported that during the March 1989 demonstration in Lhasa, Tsering Ngodrup incited young people to sing "reactionary" Tibetan independence songs, "delivered speeches stirring up separatist emotion, wantonly robbed, destroyed and set on fire public and private properties, and beat up public security officers. In doing so, [he] ran utterly rampant, seriously disrupting social order and upsetting stability and unity in Lhasa." He was further accused of contacting Tibetan exile authorities. Upon his return from abroad, Tsering Ngodrup allegedly engaged in "espionage activities," including gathering lists of those detained by the Chinese for interrogation and of those wounded during the March 5 and July 10, 1988 demonstrations in Lhasa and then attempting to send the information abroad. He reportedly visited relatives in India in 1987 and wrote a coded letter in October 1988 to the "security department of the Dalai Lama clique" (*Amnesty International*, ASA 17/10/90). For all of this, he was accused of spying for the Dalai Lama, and charged with engaging in "counterrevolutionary propaganda and incitement." (See also Tenzin Phuntsog[2], p.353).

According to another official account, in which Tsering Nogodrup's name appeared as "CIWANG **" (a partially-censored Chinese transliteration), he allegedly told a student named **PENPA TSERING**[3] (given as "BIANBA **" - see p.527), "If disturbances break out in Tibet, you young people should all take part. We older people want to do so, but we're too frail." The account continued, "In February 1989, Ciwang ** instigated Bianba ** to tape-record a series of reactionary songs about [Tibetan] independence. Ciwang ** also secreted away a large quantity of other reactionary propaganda materials on the subject of [Tibetan] independence, and distributed copies of these to Bianba and others." On the morning of March 5, 1989, Ciwang allegedly said to young people in the canteen, "The disturbances have now begun - the sun has risen. All you young people should stiffen your resolve and go out and demonstrate." (CCS p.253: see note on p.276, below.) Penpa Tsering's current status is unknown.

. . . . [12 YRS]

■   **WANG LANGJIE**, (possibly WANGCHUK NAMGYAL), was tried and sentenced to an unspecified period of imprisonment on January 23, 1990, on the charge that he "wandered about the environs of Beijing East Road, Lhasa, on January 5, 1990, yelling 'Tibetan independence' and other reactionary slogans." Such behavior was characterized by the authorities as "sufficient to constitute the crime of counterrevolutionary propaganda and incitement" (*Tibet Daily*, January 24, 1990, in *Reuters*, February 2). Twenty-one other Tibetans, also accused of "counterrevolutionary offenses," were paraded before the public at a mass sentencing rally that same day. Ten were sentenced to penal terms of "reform through labor," one youth was sentenced to "juvenile correction

procedures," and the fates of the other ten are unknown.

. . . . [11 X ? YRS]

■   **ZHILING**, a 20-year-old from Lhasa Town-3, arrested in 1989 and sentenced to five years in prison, reportedly was in Drapchi Prison as of late 1991. There is no confirmation of the initial report, which may mean either that he has been released or that the name, Zhiling, is incorrect.

. . . . [5 YRS?]

■   On February 10, 1991, the Shigatse Intermediate People's Court sentenced two Tibetans for "counterrevolutionary propaganda and incitement." The *Tibet Daily* (February 25, 1991) failed to report either the names of those imprisoned or the length of their sentences (*Agence France Press*, March 7, 1991, in FBIS, March 8.)

. . . . [2 X? YRS]

Arrested/Sentence Unknown

Monks and Nuns

Amdo Rabkung Monastery

■   **DONDRUP**[2], a monk from Amdo Rabkung Monastery and a medical student at the *Mentse Khang* (Hospital of Tibetan Medicine) in Lhasa, was arrested from his dormitory room on September 30, 1990. Police searched his room and reportedly found illegal posters and a Tibetan flag (*Tibet Information Network*, 1990.)

Chubsang Nunnery

■ Between thirteen and seventeen monks, nuns and lay people demonstrated about 10 A.M. on August 12, 1992 on the Barkhor. Among those known to have been arrested were two nuns from Chubsang Nunnery, **DORJE TSOMO**, 18, and **YESHE DROLMA**, 25. Dorje Tsomo is from Kongpo Gyama Gachung and Yeshe Drolma is from Medro Gongkar Drongkogeng. **NGAWANG DORJE** (lay name TSERING DORJE[1]), 21; **NGAWANG LHUNDRUP**[1] (lay name TSERING[6]), 19, both monks from Shedrupling Monastery, and originally from Lhokha Gongkar Shol and Medro Gongkar Shol respectively, were arrested the same day. All were taken to Gutsa Detention Center. **TSERING YANGZOM**[1], an 18-year-old nun (nunnery unknown) from Dromo County, may also have been detained at the same time.

■ **GYALTSEN KELSANG**[2] - see p.167

■ Six nuns from Chubsang Nunnery, arrested on May 14, 1992 for demonstrating on the Barkhor, were taken to Gutsa Detention Center. They included: **NGAWANG DEDROL**[2], a 23-year-old from Chuda; **NGAWANG NYIMA**[2], 22, from Jangpa; **NGAWANG TSEDROL**, 22, from Lhokha; **NGAWANG WANGMO**[1]; **NYIDROL**; and **TSERING CHOEDRON**[1].

■ **NGAWANG KARTSO** - see p.33

■ **PHETHO** - see p.167

■ **YANGZOM**[1] - see p.167

Dakpo Monastery

■ Five monks from Dakpo Monastery, **KELSANG TSERING**; **LI-ZE**; **LOBSANG TRINLEY**[1]; **PASANG**[6]; and **SONAM TENZIN**, were arrested in January 1992 after putting up posters in and around the monastery over a period of several days. They were initially detained in the Medro Jail.

■ **KUNSANG JAMPA**, 20, from Medro Samling; **LOBSANG CHOEDRAG**[4] (lay name KUNSANG[2]), 18, from Medro Dakpa; and **LOBSANG NGAWANG**[1], 22, from Medro Balok, monks from Dakpo Monastery, were arrested on March 11, 1992 and sent to Gutsa Detention Center. Other than that some "printed matter" was involved, no other information about their alleged offenses was available. Despite the case discrepancies, Lobsang Ngawang may be the same person as another monk listed as **LOBSANG NGAWANG**[2], 21, a Lhasa native, from Nechung Monastery (a part of Drepung), arrested on May 13, 1992. A report that Lobsang Ngawang[2] received a one-year sentence and was transferred to Drapchi Prison seems doubtful, since prisoners with short sentences are not usually held in Drapchi. If the information is correct, then he should have been released upon completion of his term.

Dechen Khul Nunnery

■ **SONAM DROLKAR**[1], a nun from

Dechen Khul Nunnery, was arrested for "demonstrating" probably on May 16, 1992 in Lhasa. Other than that she was initially held at Gutsa Detention Center, no further information is available (see also Lobsang Dargye, p.188.)

Donphu Choekhor Monastery

■ **CHIME** - see p.33

■ **CHOEPHEL** - see p.33

■ **DAWA TSERING[1]** - see p.34

■ **DAWA TSERING[5]** - see p.34

■ **DILA** - see p.34

■ **DORJE[1]** - see p.33

■ **DRADUL[1]** - see p.33

■ Between September and November 1992, eleven monks from Donphu Choekhor Monastery were seized there and taken in chains to the Tsethang Jail after refusing to confess to chanting anti-Chinese slogans, putting up posters, and spreading leaflets around the village of Chideshol in August and September. Once at the jail, under threats and torture, they allegedly confessed. Those held included **GELONG TSERING** (Gelong is a title conferred on a fully ordained monk), 26, arrest date September 10; **DAWA[3]**, 20, who reportedly joined the monastery in 1987; **SHILOK[3]**, 18, who joined in 1988; **MIGMAR GYALTSEN**; **MIGMAR TSERING[2]**, 17, from Tsong, who joined in 1986;

and **TSERING[7]**, 20. **MIGMAR[5]**, 21, from Nyamgyal Shol, who joined the monastery in 1986 and was also arrested with the others, is probably the same Migmar arrested in March or April 1992 (see above.) For information about the four others arrested, Sonam Choephel[1], Lhakpa Tsering, Jampel Dorje and Phurbu Tashi, see (p.33).

Three of those arrested, reportedly on November 7, 1992, have been sentenced under their monastic names and moved to Drapchi Prison. They are listed as **THUPTEN KUNKYHEN**, 17, a three-year term; **TENZIN TRINLEY**, 23, a three-year term; and **JAMYANG KUNGA**, 22, a four-year term. As of August 1993, it could not be determined to whom the monastic names referred.

■ **GYALTSEN NORBU[1]** - see p.34

■ **JAMPEL DORJE** - see p.33

■ **LHAKPA TSERING[1]** - see p.33

■ **LOBSANG PALDEN[1]** - see p.34

■ **LOBSANG[1]** - see p.33

■ **MIGMAR TSERING[1]** - see p.33

■ **MIGMAR[1]** - see p.33

■ **MIGMAR[2]** - see p.33

■ **NGAWANG CHOEDRON[1]** - see p.34

■ **NGAWANG DONYO** - see p.34

- **NGAWANG LAMCHEN** - see p.34

- **NORBU**[1] - see p.34

- **NORZANG** - see p.33

- **NYIMA**[1] - see p.34

- **PALDEN**[1] - see p.34

- **PASANG**[1] - see p.33

- **PEMA DORJE** - see p.33

- **PENPA**[1] - see p.33

- **PHURBU NAMDROL** - see p.34

- **PHURBU TASHI** - see p.33

- **SHILOK**[2], 33, a monk from Donphu Choekhor Monastery; and **NAMGYAL CHOEWANG**, a 38-year-old farmer from Lhokha Chideshol, Phuphuk Village, were arrested at the end of March or beginning of April 1992 and held in Tsethang Jail. Migmar[5], another monk arrested at the same time, was probably released, then re-arrested in September or October 1992 (see Gelong Tsering above.) The three had distributed and put up posters in Chideshol calling on Tibetans to unite and to assert they were being denied their human rights. The arrests came only days before the start of an official four-month Socialist Education Campaign. All Chideshol residents between 16 and 60 were obliged to attend minimally 80 percent of the sessions.

- **SONAM CHOEPHEL**[1] - see p.33

- **SONAM**[1] - see p.34

- **TASHI CHUNGCHUNG** - see p.33

- **TENZIN CHOEKYI**[1] - see p.34

- **THAPKE** - see p.33

- **TSERING DONDEN** - see p.33

- **TSERING**[1] - see p.34

- **TSERING**[2] - see p.34

- **TSULTRIM GYALTSEN** - see p.34

- **TSULTRIM SHERAB** - see p.34

- **TSULTRIM TOPGYAL** - see p.34

- **TSULTRIM ZOEPA** - see p.34

- **YESHE JINPA** - see p.34

  Drak Yerpa

- **LOBSANG CHOEDRAG**[1] - see p.34

- **LOBSANG DONYO**[1] - see p.34

  Drepung Monastery

- **GYALTSEN CHOEZIN** - see p.176

- **JORDEN** - see p.176

- **LOBSANG DONYO**[2] - see p.35

■ **LOBSANG JAMPEL** (also known as LOBSANG JAMPA[2]) a 44-year-old Drepung monk from Nyemo, was arrested on the street on July 6, 1991, the Dalai Lama's birthday. A police search of his room that night uncovered independence posters and leaflets and two books produced by the Tibetan Administration in Exile. As of April 1992, he was in Seitru. Lobsang Jampa had been imprisoned once before, from 1959 until 1977.

■ **NGAWANG LHUNDRUP[3]**, a 33-year-old Drepung monk from Toelung, reportedly was arrested in his dormitory room in Drepung Monastery on May 16, 1991. There has been no further word since late 1991, when he reportedly was being held in Gutsa Detention Center.

■ **NGAWANG SONAM** - see p.35

■ **NGAWANG TENZIN[4]**, a 21-year-old Drepung monk from Toelung, was held in Gutsa Detention Center as of late 1991. The date of his arrest, his prison sentence, his alleged offense and his current whereabouts are not known.

■ Since late 1991, there has been no word of **NGAWANG THUTOP**, an 18-year-old Drepung monk from Phenpo, who at that time was being held in Gutsa Detention Center.

■ **NGAWANG TSONDRU[1]** - see p.35

■ **PASANG[2]** - see p.35

■ **THUPTEN KUNPHEL** - see p.175

Ganden Monastery

■ **DAWA[1]** - see p.175

■ **DAWA[2]** - see p.175

■ A group of Ganden monks, arrested in May 1992 and initially taken to Gutsa, but whose dates of arrest are uncertain, include **DAWA SONAM**, a 16-year old from Medro; **DELO**, 23, from Medro; **KAGYE**; **KELSANG[2]**; **NGAWANG TENGYE**; **PEPAR**, 21, from Medro; **TASHI DAWA**; **TSETEN NYIMA**; **TSETEN SAMDRUP**, 27, from Phenpo Lhundup Shen; and **TSULTRIM NYIMA**, from Taktse. Some of those listed are feared to have been severely wounded during the course of their arrests.

■ **JAMPA GELEK** - see p.35

■ **JAMPA GYATSO** - see p.35

■ **JAMYANG[3]** - see p.175

■ **LOBSANG SAMTEN** - see p.35

■ **LOBSANG TENZIN[1]** - see p.175

■ **NGAWANG LOBSANG** - see p.35

■ **NGAWANG LOSEL** - see p.35

■ **NGAWANG SANGYE** - see p.35

■ **NGAWANG TOPCHU** - see p.35

■ **NORBU[2]** - see p.35

■ **PENPA[2]** - see p.35

- **PHUNTSOG WANGDU** - see p.35

- **SONAM BAGDRO** - see p.175

- **TENZIN DRADUL** - see p.35

- **TOPJOR[2]** - see p.36

- **TSENYI** - see p.35

- **TSERING PHUNTSOG** - see p.175

- **YESHE GYALPO** - see p.35

Garu Nunnery

- **GYALTSEN CHOEZANG** - see p.585

- **GYALTSEN LHAZOM** - see p.585

- **NGAWANG DADROL** - see p.181

- **NGAWANG JAMPA** - see p.181

- **NGAWANG SAMTEN** - see p.181

- **NGAWANG THUPTEN[1]** - see p.36

- **RINCHEN DROLMA[2]**- see p.181

- **TSAMCHOE[2]** - see p.181

Gyumed Monastery

- **TSERING DORJE[2]**, a 26-year-old monk from Phuntsok Ling in Phenpo, was arrested after flying a Tibetan flag from the roof of Gyumed Monastery in Lhasa about 5 A.M. on October 1, 1990, China's National Day. The police reportedly first saw the flag about 7 A.M., then searched all the monks' rooms. When they found it in Tsering Dorje's room, he allegedly confessed. Tibetan sources said he was initially held in "Kuwang Ting," probably a local police station in Lhasa, but there has been no further word on his whereabouts. A young girl, Dawa Kyizom (see p.517), was later arrested for giving the flag to Tsering Dorje.

Kirti Monastery

- **KUNCHOK TENPA** - see p.36

Kyemolung Monastery

- **NGAWANG LAMCHUNG** (lay name DAWA[4]), 22, and **NGAWANG TENZIN[2]** (lay name PHURBU[2]), 18, both originally from Toelung Dechen Kyemolung, and both monks at Kyemolung Monastery, were arrested on December 19, 1992 for participating in a demonstration. They were sent to Gutsa Detention Center.

- **NGAWANG SHERAB[1]** - see p.36

- **SHENYAN LOBSANG** - see p.36

Michungri Nunnery

- **JAMPA DEDROL** - see p.36

- **NGAWANG DROLMA[1]** - see p.36

- **PEMA DROLKAR[3]**, an 18-year-old Michungri nun from Medro Gongkar, date of arrest unknown, as of

February 1992 was being held at Gutsa Detention Center. No other information is available.

- **PHUNTSOG DROLMA** - see p.36

- **TENZIN CHOEKYI**[2] - see p.36

- **TENZIN DEKYONG** - see p.36

- **TSERING**[4] - see p.36

Nagar Nunnery

- **DAKAR** - see p.36

- **JAMPA DROLKAR**[1] - see p.36

- **PEMA OEZER** - see p.36

- **TSAMCHOE**[1] - see p.36

Nyemo Gyaltse Monastery

- **LOBSANG GYALTSEN**[1] - see p.37

- **NGAWANG CHOEDRAG** - see p.37

- **NGAWANG KELSANG** - see p.37

- **PEMA YESHE** - see p.37

Palkhor Choede Monastery

- **CHIGCHEN**, 21, and **DAWA NORBU**, 19, monks at Palkhor Choede Monastery who were attempting to flee to India, were apprehended in Khamar Shan and returned to the Gyangtse Public Security Bureau on July 3, 1992. A search of their rooms yielded

cassettes of Buddhist teachings by the Dalai Lama and a map of India. On the basis of this "evidence," they were detained in Gyangtse Jail on suspicion of being separatists.

Phenpo Monastery

- **DHONNOR** - see p.37

- **LOBSANG TENPA**[1] - see p.37

- **NGAWANG TSULTRIM**[1] - see p.37

- **TENGYE** - see p.37

- **THUPTEN TSERING**[1] - see p.37

Phurchok Hermitage

- **LOBSANG THUPTEN**[2] (lay name MIGMAR[6]), a 16-year-old monk from Phurchok Hermitage, arrested May 8, 1992 for participating in a demonstration, was sent to Gutsa Detention Center. There has been no further news.

Rong Jamchen Monastery

- **THUPTEN KUNGA**, in his seventies, a monk and chantmaster (umze) at Rong Jamchen Monastery, was seized from his home at midnight on April 9 or 10, 1992 on suspicion of being involved in demonstrations at the monastery. A search of his quarters turned up nothing incriminating, but as of August 1992, his whereabouts remained unknown. Thupten Kunga's arrest came in the aftermath of a major demonstration at the monastery on

March 10 in commemoration of the 1959 Tibetan uprising on that date. During the protests, monks put up posters calling for Tibetan independence. The following day, police arrested six monks, two to five of whom were under age 15. Soon afterwards - the exact date is unclear - they returned to arrest the dean of the monastery and an additional seventeen to thirty-eight monks, leaving only six at the monastery. All those arrested were taken to Rinpung County Jail. Their names and current whereabouts are unknown.

Rakya Monastery

■ **LOBSANG PALDEN**[3], who led a demonstration of Rakya monks in the Tsonyon Golok Autonomous Region on November 16, 1992 during the enthronement of the Shingsa Pandita Lama, was arrested that same day and detained in Tsonyon Golok Jail. As of February 23, 1993, no additional information about him was available nor, with one exception, was anything known about the up to 80 monks who may have taken part in the same demonstration, shouting slogans, distributing leaflets and putting up posters. Another detainee, **TSERING DONDRUP**[3], from Rekong County in Qinghai Province, reportedly organized the printing of the pro-independence leaflets in October 1992, from woodblocks produced by the monks. Slogans included "Free Tibet" and "Chinese go away." After his release, Tsering Dondrup attempted to reach India, but died on the way.

Sera Monastery

■ **KELSANG PHUNTSOG**, a 21-year-old monk and woodblock printer from Sera Monastery, was reportedly arrested while distributing leaflets on the Barkhor on August 4, 1991. Since his transfer to Gutsa Detention Center from an overnight stay in the Barkhor Police Station, nothing further has been heard of him (Amnesty International *ASA 14/19/92*). The distributed leaflets called for Tibetan independence and human rights for the Tibetan people.

■ **LOBSANG DELEK** (lay name SONAM CHOEPHEL[2]), a 22-year-old Sera monk, was arrested on May 13, 1991 (Amnesty International, *AI 17/19/92*.) At last report, in October 1991, no additional information was available.

■ **LOBSANG NAMDROL**, 26, a Sera monk from the village of Lhalung Dongtso in Medro Gongkar, was arrested with a friend in a restaurant in Lhasa sometime in 1992, and has disappeared. He had been arrested once before, on July 3, 1988 and held briefly at Outridu. After his release, Lobsang Namdrol who had become a monk in 1985, was in charge of the printing house at Sera. Before 1985, he taught elementary school in his home village.

■ **LOBSANG TENZIN**[3] (lay name SAMDRUP[1]), an 18-year-old Sera monk from Lhokha Dranang, arrested August 14, 1991, was initially sent to Gutsa Detention Center. No other information is available.

■ **LOBSANG THUPTEN**[1] - see p.167

■ **LOBSANG YONTEN**[2] (lay name YONTEN PHUNTSOG), 28, a private teacher and monk from Sera Monastery, arrested on August 16, 1991 in connection with "printed matter," was initially held in Gutsa Detention Center. Other than that he is from Phenpo Lhundrup Lungshoe, no further information is available.

■ **NGAWANG DEBAM**, a 24-year-old Sera monk from Toelung, arrested August 8, 1991, was initially held in Gutsa Detention Center. No other information is available.

■ **NGAWANG GYALTSEN**[2], a 21-year-old Sera monk from Phenpo, was arrested without warrant on May 3, 1991. As of late 1991 he was being held in Gutsa Detention Center.

■ **PHUNTSOG TSUNGME** - see p.188

■ **TENPA DARGYE** - see p.37

■ **THUPTEN TSERING**[2] - see p.37

Shelkar Choede Monastery

■ **KHYENRAB CHOEPEL** - see p.37

■ **KHYENRAB DRAGYE** - see p.37

■ **KHYENRAB TENDAR** - see p.37

■ **LOBSANG GYALTSEN**[2] - see p.37

■ **LOBSANG PALDEN**[2] - see p.37

■ **SANGYE TENZIN** - see p.37

■ **TENZIN RABTEN** - see p.37

Tashilhunpo Monastery

■ **NYIMA PHUNTSOG** - see p.38

■ **SONAM GYALPO**[1] - see p.38

■ **PHURBU TSERING**[1] - see p.38

Thangkyap Monastery

■ **NGAWANG CHOKLANG** (lay name LHAKPA TSERING[2]), a 16-year-old monk from Thangkyap Monastery, was arrested on July 14, 1992 for "involvement with printed materials." Originally from Medro Gyama, he was detained in Gutsa.

Tsamkhung Nunnery

■ **TSERING YUDON** - see p.38

Tsepak Lhakhang Monastery

■ **CHANGLOCHEN** - see p.38

■ **GYAGPA** - see p.38

■ **KELSANG**[1] - see p.38

■ **LANGDOR** - see p.38

■ **PASANG**[4] - see p.38

■ **PHURBU**[1] - see p.38

Upper Tantric College

■ **LOBSANG NAMGYAL**, a monk and teacher at Upper Tantric College, was taken into custody on March 3, 1992 for reasons unknown. As of August 1993, he was being held in Seitru Prison.

Monastery unknown

■ There is no information as to the whereabouts or date of arrest of **TSONDRU**[3], a 26-year-old monk from a monastery in Ngaba, who received a three-year sentence for distributing pamphlets (Amnesty International, *ASA 17/34/91*). He was originally held in Mengxian Prison.

Nunnery Unknown

■ **TSAM-LA**[1] - see p.38

Lay Persons

■ **ASHANG LA** - see p.43

■ **BAGDRO**[2] - see p.43

■ **DAWA DOL** - see p.43

■ **DEKYI**[2] - see p.43

■ **DEKYI**[3], a 30 or 40-year-old businesswoman in the Barkhor area in Lhasa, was arrested in her home at midnight in December 1991 just prior to her departure for Nepal. Her travel documents were all in order at the time. Dekyi may be held in Drapchi Prison.

■ **DODRONG NGAWANG DORJE**

- see p.39

■ **DONDUL**, a Lhasa Weather Office employee, was arrested on September 27, 1992 and sent to Sangyip. No additional information is available.

■ **DORJE**[3] - see p.41

■ There has been no additional information since the reported arrests in Ngaba on or about July 27, 1990 of two Tibetans, **DORJE**[6] and an unnamed male companion. According to an Asia Watch source, they were accused of printing and distributing pro-independence literature in Lhasa. Dorje, in her mid-forties, and her alleged accomplice, approximately ten years her junior, reportedly were held in the local Ngaba jail and subjected to beatings and other ill-treatment. In order to avoid arrest, the two Lhasa residents left the city after martial law was declared. They returned to their native Ngaba and went underground. In response to minor pro-independence disturbances in Ngaba in February and March 1990, Chinese authorities began a heightened political campaign, including "struggle sessions," aimed at ferreting out dissidents. It is possible that the presence in Ngaba of Dorje and her companion was discovered in the course of that campaign.

■ **DROLMA** - see p.39

■ **DUGBUNTHAR** - see p.41

■ **DUNGKAR TSO** - see p.40

■ **GARCHU**, 32, from Ngaba in

Amdo (a part of Sichuan Province), was arrested at the end of June 1990 from the house of a relative in Thail Pung Gang, Lhasa. He reportedly had fled there after he made strong nationalist statements, overheard by informants, during an argument in a bar in Ngaba. Search parties were looking for him by the time he reached Lhasa (*Tibet Information Network*, August 11, 1990). Garchu's present whereabouts are unknown.

■ **GYALPO¹** - see p.41

■ **GYATSO¹** - see p.41

■ **GYATSO²**, 22, a carpenter; **KARMA¹** (also known as JAMYANG⁴), a 42-year-old farmer; and **MONLAM GYATSO** (previously named as **PALDEN³**), 21, a farmer, all from Medro Gyama Trikhang (see Kunchok Lodroe, p.195), were arrested on March 5, 1992 during the Tibetan New Year for putting up posters calling for independence and opposing local mining projects. Karma, arrested at his home and accused of being a "counterrevolutionary," was taken away in handcuffs. As of July 1992, the three reportedly were detained "in the custody of the district security forces [in a jail in Medro], undergoing unspeakable tortures and beatings" (quoted in a *Tibet Information Network* report, January 21, 1993.) In November 1992, Chinese officials told the UN that they had no records of the three being held in prison, a wording which could mean the men were still in detention centers or in "labor re-education" camps. Karma had been

detained for interrogation once before, in 1990.

According to a second report, three people with the same names as the above three were arrested on June 30, 1992 and held in Gutsa Detention Center. There are several possible explanations: that the three were released and then re-arrested; that they were transferred from Medro to Gutsa; that in fact they are three different people.

■ **HUACHEN KYAB** - see p.40

■ **INCHUNG** - see p.39

■ **JAMPEL** - see p.39

■ **JAMYANG¹** - see p.41

■ **JAMYANG²** - see p.43

■ **KARTSE** - see p.39

■ **KELSANG DAWA¹** - see p.39

■ **KHARMO** - see p.41

■ **KUNCHOK TENZIN** - see p.39

■ **LHAGYAL²** - see p.527

■ **LHAKPA¹** - see p.39

■ **LHAKPA²** - see p.40

■ **LHAKPA³** - see p.40

■ **LHAKPA⁴** - see p.43

■ **LHASANG** - see p.40

- **LHASHAMHUA** - see p.40

- **LHATRIGYA** - see p.40

- **LOBSANG CHOEDRAG[2]** - see p.41

- **LOBSANG DAWA** - see p.41

- **LOBSANG GYALTSEN[3]** - see p.42

- **LODROE PHUNTSOG** - see p.42

- **LOTEN[1]** - see p.518

- **MENLHA KYAB** - see p.40

- The present status of **MIGMAR[7]**, a 20-year-old from Lhasa, arrested on April 20, 1991 as part of a series of preventive arrests in connection with the May 23 commemoration of the "liberation" of Tibet, is unknown. Originally arrested in 1989 and sentenced to a year in prison which he served in Sangyip, Migmar continued to be harassed after his March 6, 1990 release. He was not permitted to return to school and could not find work. Other than that Migmar's mother, Phurdron, works in a restaurant, no other information is available.

- **NAM LOYAK** - see p.41

- **NGAGCHUNG** - see p.43

- **NGAWANG CHOEDRON[3]** - see p.43

- **NGAWANG RIKHAR** - see p.42

- **NGAWANG TSERING** - see p.40

- **NYIMA[2]** - see p.518

- **PALDEN CHOEDRAG** - see p.42

- **PALJOR TSERING** - see p.40

- **PASANG[5]** - see p.42

- **PENPA TSERING[3]** - see p.527

- **PE-NGOE** - see p.42

- **PEMA GYAL** - see p.41

- **PEMA NGODRUP** - see p.42

- **PEMA TSAMCHOE** - see p.42

- **PENDROL** - see p.43

- **PHUNTSOG THOSAM** - see p.39

- **PHUNTSOG[1]**, a driver for the Association of Foreign Commerce, Industry and Trade, who fled Lhasa for India before the 1990 Tibetan New Year, has disappeared. After a change of heart, Phuntsog went to the Chinese Embassy in Katmandu, Nepal and wrote a letter of self-criticism. In return, he reportedly received a letter guaranteeing his safe return. There have been reports that he was arrested in June 1991 and has undergone harsh treatment, including repeated beatings, in an unknown prison.

- **RABGYAL** - see p.42

- **RINCHEN DAWA[1]** - see p.43

■ **RINCHEN NORBU** - see p.41

■ **SAMDRUP TSERING** - see p.40

■ **SHAWO DORJE** - see p.40

■ **SHERAB** - see p.527

■ **SICHOE DORJE**, (probably same person as SONAM DORJE[4]), a small businessman in his forties from the Tromsigang district of Lhasa, was arrested at home on March 1, 1990 and subsequently underwent intensive interrogation in Sangyip Prison. Eight officers of the Public Security Bureau participated in the arrest; his home was searched and his wife was questioned about family ties with exiled Tibetans. Sources in Lhasa claimed that Sichoe Dorje had not taken part in any pro-independence demonstrations, and there has been speculation that the authorities were trying to establish links between Sichoe's family and the exiled Tibetan community (Amnesty International, *UA 231/90.*)

■ **SISHIYI (SEGSHINGPA) TSETEN DORJE** - see p.43

■ **SONAM GYALPO[2]** - see p.42

■ **SONAM TASHI** - see p.42

■ **SONAM TSERING[2]** - see p.41

■ **SONAM TSERING[3]** - see p.42

■ **SONAM TSETEN** - see p.42

■ **SONAM WANGDU[2]**, a 23-year-old resident of Lhasa, was still in Gutsa Detention Center as of March 1992. He was arrested on February 5, 1991 for "carrying a large amount of reactionary material, flags of so-called independent Tibet, and money for operations." A report on *Lhasa Television* (March 2, 1991), claimed that he had been sent to "collaborate with reactionary organizations in disseminating reactionary leaflets and video tapes to hoodwink and mislead the masses." A *Radio Lhasa* report (March 3, 1991) described a **SONAM WANGDEN** from Shigatse, presumably the same person, as a "spy sent by the security ministry and espionage agency of the so-called Government in Exile." It is noteworthy that during all of 1991, Sonam Wangdu's arrest was the only one that Chinese authorities in Tibet announced. A man and a woman, both unidentified, reportedly were arrested on March 3, 1991 in the Chushul area in connection with the same case. They, too, allegedly had large quantities of "illegal" leaflets for distribution (*Tibet Information Network*, August 31, 1991).

■ **TASHI TOPGYAL** - see p.516

■ **TASHI WANGDU** - see p.527

■ **TENDAR[1]** - see p.43

■ **TENPA KELSANG** - see p.43

■ **TENPA PHULCHUNG[1]** - see p.39

■ **TENPA** - see p.42

■ **TENPA WANGDRAG[1]** - see p.39

■ **TENZIN CHOEDRAG**, a worker at the Zhangmu Restaurant in Lhasa, was arrested in July 1991, reportedly because of alleged contacts with other Tibetans while he was in Nepal. There have been reports that he received frequent beatings while in detention in Seitru Prison.

■ **THUBGO** - see p.43

■ **TOPGYAL**[1] - see p.43

■ **TOPGYAL**[3] - see p.43

■ **TSEGOEN GYAL** - see p.41

■ **TSENDAK** - see p.192

■ **TSERING CHOEDRON**[2], a 30-year-old female from Lhasa, was summoned to the local Public Security Bureau on the evening of March 3, 1992, and has not been seen since. So far as is known, she was interrogated and sent to Gutsa Detention Center. **TSERING DEKYI**, 30, from Lhasa, also was summoned that same evening to "sort something out," then sent to Gutsa. In late 1991, Tsering Dekyi sent her two sons to India without documentation. She later joined them, but returned to Lhasa in early 1992.

■ **TSERING GYALTSEN**, 30, from Lhasa, was arrested at home at midnight on March 22, 1992 and his house thoroughly searched because, it was alleged, he was "involved" in undesirable activities.

■ **TSERING THAR** - see p.40

■ **TSETEN DORJE** - see p.43

■ **TSETEN YARPHEL** - see p.43

■ **TSETHAR** - see p.39

■ **TSEWANG**[1] - see p.40

■ **TSEWANG PALDEN**, a 59-year-old carpenter and the father of Sonam Drolkar[2] (see p.590), was arrested somewhere between Lhatse and Dhingri in central Tibet in either December 1991 or January 1992. He had been visiting relatives. At last report, April 6, 1992, he was in Gutsa Detention Center. During the night of February 2 or 3, his house in Rabsel Tsanghang, Lhasa, was raided by the police. At the same time, **TATRU**, a relative of Tsewang Palden's deceased wife, was detained at Sangyip Prison. According to an unconfirmed report, she was interrogated there under torture during a seven-day period. Nothing further is known of her current situation.

■ **WANGDEN** - see p.41

■ **WANGDU**[1] - see p.41

■ **YANGCHEN**[1] - see p.40

■ **YANGZOM**[2], a 32-year-old woman from Nyemo Phusum Township, was arrested in July 1992 for distributing and putting up posters. No further information is available.

■ **YIDAN TSERING** - see p.41

■ **ZOEPA CHOWANG** - see p.43

2. *Inner Mongolians*

Sentenced

■ **AMUGULANG**, the leader of the *Bayannur League National Modernization Society* in Inner Mongolia, was sentenced to a three-year prison term which he is serving at a labor reform camp in Linhe. He was reportedly arrested by plainclothes police at the end of July 1991. According to a report on April 9, 1992 *(Far Eastern Economic Review)*, three other teachers and a student from a local high school were arrested along with Amugulang. The *Modernization Society* had been formed by Mongolian intellectuals and Party cadres interested in regenerating the region's ethnic and cultural identity. It was crushed by Chinese authorities in 1991 for allegedly "opposing the leadership of the Communist Party and the socialist system, and inciting a national split and undermining the unification of the motherland" *(Inner Mongolian League for the Defense of Human Rights*, May 21, 1991).

. . . . [3 YRS]

■ **BAYANTOGTOKH**, a secondary school teacher and a leader of the *Bayannur League National Modernization Society of Inner Mongolia* who was seized by security authorities in July 1991 along with seven other key members of the society, was formally arrested in April 1992. After a secret trial at which he reportedly was sentenced to a term of one-and-a-half years, Bayantogtokh was sent to a prison in Hohhot administered by Section 5 of Inner Mongolia's Public Security Bureau. As of July 1993, two years after his detention, Bayantogtokh for reasons unknown remained in prison. (It is possible either that his sentence was extended or that he was forcibly "retained for in-camp employment" in the prison enterprise following completion of his term.) The seven others detained with Bayantogtokh in July 1991 were reportedly taken into police custody in Linhe, the League's capital, and there has been no further information about them since then.

The *National Modernization Society*, a study group formed by Mongolian intellectuals and Party cadres in an attempt to regenerate the region's ethnic and cultural identity, was crushed by Chinese authorities for allegedly "opposing the leadership of the Communist Party and the socialist system, and inciting a national split and undermining the unification of the motherland" *(Inner Mongolian League for the Defense of Human Rights*, June 30, 1991).

. . . . [2-? YRS]

■ **WANG Manglai**, 30, a leader of the *Ih Ju League National Culture Society*, Inner Mongolia, arrested on May 15, 1991, was sentenced on June 6, 1992, to a two-year prison term. Another of the ethnic dissident group's leaders, **HUCHUNTEGUS**, 36, arrested and sentenced at the same time as Wang to three years' imprisonment, was granted early release in August 1993; as of January 1994, however, he remained under a form of house arrest. Wang Manglai, who should have been released on completion of his term, was reportedly still being held in an unknown prison as of early 1994.

According to secret "Document No.13" of the Inner Mongolian Office of the Chinese Communist Party, security authorities arrested the two intellectuals in their homes in Dongsheng, the local capital, for "attempting to overthrow Communist Party leadership" and for "creating ethnic divisions" (*Shijie Ribao,* June 10, 1991). According to a June 30, 1991 report from the *Inner Mongolian League for the Defense of Human Rights,* Wang and Huchuntegus were first held incommunicado for "shelter and investigation" in a secret prison in Hohhot, the regional capital. (The prison reportedly is administered by Section 5 of Inner Mongolia's Public Security Bureau.) Huchuntegus' trial reportedly was postponed several times until the court agreed, as he requested, to hear the case in the Mongolian language. After the trial, he was held in two separate labor camps in the Ih Ju League, one in Wushen Banner and the other in the municipality of Dongsheng. His wife, **Dagushlata**, was reportedly subjected to frequent harassment and surveillance following her husband's arrest.

Also in May 1991, twenty-six members of the Ih Ju League National Culture Society's provisional council were placed under house arrest or close surveillance by the authorities; others were reportedly "black-listed." The group, composed primarily of ethnic Mongol intellectuals, college students and cadres, was formally banned as an "illegal organization" in May 1991. Another scholarly organization, the *Bayannur League National Modernization Society* (see **Bayantogtokh,** p.216), was also proscribed at the same time. According to Asia Watch sources, however, both groups were in fact academic discussion groups that had attempted to legally register with the proper authorities and which were dedicated to researching and promoting traditional Mongolian culture and identity.

According to Document No.13, Wang Manglai and Huchuntegus "organized home gatherings and conferences and made speeches" on twelve occasions. The report continued, "They selected, printed and distributed various illegal propaganda items and expanded their influence by making connections outside the region. Under the guise of ethnic modernization, they opposed the Communist Party, attempted to demolish Marxism in the region and tried to change the nature of socialism in order to overthrow the leadership of the Communist Party."

The document also charged that the two "illegal organizations" had pursued a three-stage strategy, namely: within a two to four-year period, to publicize and study the strategy of "ethnic florescence" and to determine the policies and goals of ethnic unity; to establish a fully-fledged organization within three to five years; and, within a fifteen-year period, to achieve a solid foundation for ethnic development and florescence. According to the authorities, the groups' main aim was to unite the Mongolians under the communists' own slogan: "one country, two systems." The groups' leaders were purported to have said, "No matter what, we should not let this chance go. It is a matter of life and death for the whole race." The document made clear that the authorities' main concern was to deter attempts to develop ethnic cohesion among the separate Mongol communities of Inner Mongolia, the Mongolian People's Republic and the Buryat region of the Soviet Union.

Wang Manglai graduated from the department of Mongolian language and literature at Inner Mongolia Normal University. Huchuntegus studied at the Inner Mongolia College for Professional Training in the department of Mongolian language, and in the political education department of Inner Mongolia Normal College. Prior to their arrest, both men worked with the Ih Ju League Department of Education. Huchuntegus was previously imprisoned between 1982 and 1984 for opposing China's attempts to "destroy grasslands, dig mines, and set up factories in Inner Mongolia." (See also **Baatar** and **Bao Hongguang**, p.514.)
. . . . [2 YRS]

■ **MONKHBAT**, a young ethnic Mongol, was sentenced in 1992 in Inner Mongolia to three years' imprisonment for involvement in an underground network dedicated to the peaceful promotion of Mongolian cultural identity, according to an Asia Watch source. He is currently serving his sentence at a labor reform farm in the region.

A resident of Inner Mongolia's Ih

Ju League, in 1989 Monkhbat passed the entry exams for the Xilin Gol League Nationalities Finance Academy, graduating in 1991. While at the college, he was an active participant in the ethnic Mongolian movement and reportedly printed a large number of pro-ethnic Mongolian leaflets. For this he was intensively investigated by the Public Security Bureau and ordered to stop attending classes until the investigation was concluded. At some point (date unknown) Monkhbat had studied under Huchuntegus, the now-imprisoned leader of the outlawed *Ih Ju League National Culture Society*. Denied a job placement after graduation, Monkhbat continued to be active in the ethnic Mongolian movement, editing and producing an underground journal entitled *Mongolian Free Forum (Menggu Ziyou Luntan)*.

In March 1992, Monkhbat was detained by the authorities, placed under arrest, then tried and sentenced. He is reportedly being held in the Dongtucheng Labor Reform Farm in Wuyuan County, Bayannur League. The main charge against him was apparently that he had written a letter to the Party Committee of Ih Ju League demanding the release of Huchuntegus. The authorities later characterized this as being an "attempt to intimidate" them.
. . . . [3 YRS]

■ **ULAN Shovo**, a 37-year-old history professor at the University of Inner Mongolia who was arrested on around July 11, 1991, was secretly tried and sentenced to between five and eight years' imprisonment, either in late 1991 or early 1992, according to Asia Watch sources. The charges are believed to have referred to his alleged provision to a foreigner of confidential government information about the May 1991 crackdown against Mongol dissident groups. (See Huchuntegus *et al*, p.216.) According to one Asia Watch source, Ulan Shovo was arrested outside a friend's house where he had gone to play Chinese chess. The arrest was witnessed by a friend. Prior to his arrest, Ulan Shovo had reportedly been tape-recorded and photographed passing confidential documents to a foreigner. As a result, the State Security Bureau took charge of the case investigation.

On June 12, 1991, Andrew Higgins, Beijing correspondent for the British *Independent* newspaper, was detained at Yantai airport and found to be in possession of confidential government documents on the crackdown against Mongol dissent. He was later expelled from China. Ulan Shovo's detention is believed to have been in connection with this incident, although it is known that Ulan did not pass the documents to Higgins. After his detention, Ulan Shovo reportedly was sent to Inner Mongolia No.1 Prison; his whereabouts as of November 1993, however, were unknown. Following reports of his trial, an unnamed government official from a "relevant department" denied that Ulan Shovo had ever been tried and sentenced (*Xinhua*, in *AP*, April 2, 1992). In February 1993, however, an official report stated that "the persons who gave secret information to Higgins and [Lena] Sun [see case of **Bai Weiji**, p.4] have all been suitably punished"

(*Liaowang [Outlook] Weekly,* February 22, 1993, p.11).

. . . .   [5-8 YRS]

Arrested/Sentence Unknown

■ **DELGER** - see p.43

Under surveillance

■ **ALTAN**, 29, formerly a student in Inner Mongolia University's language department, who worked at the Ih Ju League's Party School, as of July 1993 was being kept under police surveillance. Altan was initially placed under house arrest, along with 25 other ethnic Mongol intellectuals (see below for details), on or about May 15, 1991, for his participation as a Provisional Council member in the *Ih Ju League's National Culture Society*. Some of those under house arrest were repeatedly questioned and harassed by secret police from the Public Security and State Security Bureaus, and at times were subjected to intimidation, insults and corporal punishment. The society, a study group for Mongolian intellectuals and Party cadres interested in regenerating the region's ethnic and cultural identity, was crushed by Chinese authorities for "opposing the leadership of the Communist Party and the socialist system, and inciting a national split and undermining the unification of the motherland" (*Inner Mongolian League for the Defense of Human Rights*, June 30, 1991.) (See also **Huchuntegus**, p.216.)

- **AMURHESHIG**, 40, who worked at the Marin Caidam Unit in the cooperative of Tonegchi, Toli Commune. His name is on a "black list" reported to be collectively maintained by local Public Security Bureaus in Inner Mongolia. The 1,000 or so on the list are considered to be politically "unstable elements" and kept under observation. Amurheshig was formerly a student at Uyushin Banner's 1st High School.

- **HASACHINGEL**, 31, who worked at the Ih Ju League's Mongolian High School, was placed under house arrest, as were 25 others, on or about May 15, 1991, for his participation as a Provisional Council Member in the Ih Ju League's *National Culture Society*. As of November 1993, his situation was not known. Hasachingel was formerly a student in the history department at Inner Mongolia Normal University.

- **HASCHULUU**, 24, who worked at the Ih Ju League's Ordos News Bureau, and formerly was a student at the Inner Mongolia Special School for Mongolian Language.

- **HASHUYAG**, who worked at the Ih Ju League's Propaganda Bureau, and formerly was a student at Inner Mongolia University.

- **HUCHUNTEGUS** - see p.216

- **NASUN**, 40, who worked at the Ih Ju League's News Bureau, and formerly was a student majoring in translation at the Inner Mongolia

Special School for Mongolian Language. He is kept under very heavy surveillance and supervision; his home has been repeatedly searched.

- **SECHENBAATAR**[1], 32, who worked at Ih Ju League's Mongolian High School, and formerly was a student in the history department at Inner Mongolia Normal University.

- **SECHNEBAYAR**, 30, who worked at the Ih Ju League's Chinggis Khan Research Center, and formerly was a student at Inner Mongolia Normal University.

- **WANG Buu Shan**, 58, the assistant manager of the Ih Ju League's Political Council's Committee on Religion. He is kept under heavy surveillance and required to attend political study class and write repeated self-criticisms.

Status unclear

- **B. JORIGTU**, 26, was placed under house arrest, as were 25 others, on or about May 15, 1991, for his participation as a recording secretary of the Provisional Council of the Ih Ju League's *National Culture Society* (see **Altan**, p.219). As of July 1993, his situation was not known. He formerly was a student in the history department at Inner Mongolia Normal University. Others whose situation is unclear include:

- **BATUCHINGGEL**, 28, who worked in the philosophy section of the

Ih Ju League's Party School, and formerly was a student in Inner Mongolia University's philosophy department. Although his situation is not known with certainty, he reportedly has had his work "adjusted" and can no longer teach.

■ **BAYAN**, 30, who worked at the Ih Ju League's Records Office, and formerly was a student at Inner Mongolia University.

■ **HASBAYAR**, 26, who worked at the Ih Ju League's People's District Court, and formerly was a student in Xinjiang University's law department.

■ **HASERDENI**, 29, who worked at the Ih Ju League's Mongolian School, and formerly was a student at the Ih Ju League's Special Teachers School.

■ **JIANG Peng**, 28, who worked at the Ih Ju League's College of Education, and formerly was a student at Inner Mongolia Normal University.

■ **MANDULA**, 24, who worked at the Dongsheng City Branch of the Ih Ju League's Bank for Commerce and Industry, and formerly was a student at Xinjiang College of Commerce and Economy.

■ **OULA**, 28, who worked at the Mongolian Kindergarten, and formerly was a student at the Ih Ju League's Mongolian Teachers School.

■ **OYUNBAATAR**, 25, who worked at the Ih Ju League's Second Light Industry Factory, and formerly was a

student at the Inner Mongolia Special Mongolian Language School.

■ **SARANGUA**, a 26-year-old female, who worked at the Ih Ju League's Party School, and formerly was a student in Inner Mongolia University's Mongolian language department.

■ **SECHENBAATAR**[2], 24, who worked at the Dongsheng City Office for Commerce and Industry, and formerly was a student at the Inner Mongolia School for Industry and Marketing.

■ **SECHENNORBU**, 31, who worked at the Ih Ju League's Office of Investigation, and formerly was a student in the Economic management department of the Central Committee's Party School.

■ **SECHENTU**, 28, who worked at the Ih Ju League's Office of Education, and formerly was a student at Inner Mongolia Normal University.

■ **UDHAOCHIR**, 33, who worked in the scientific socialism section of the Ih Ju League's Party School, and formerly was a student in Inner Mongolia University's language department.

■ **ULJEI**, 29, who worked on the Ih Ju League's Political Advisory Committee, and formerly was a student at Inner Mongolia University.

■ **WANG Hasbayar**, 35, who worked at the Ih Ju League's 3rd

Woolen Textile Factory, and formerly was a student at Ih Ju League's Health Welfare school.

3. Moslems

Sentenced

■ **ABDUL MALIK, ABDU KADIR AYUP**, 45; **ABDURAHMAN ABLIZ**, 47; **ALIMJAN KARIHAJIM**, 60; and **OMER KHAN MAHSUN**, 70, were detained in July and August 1990 for circulating a pamphlet protesting curbs on religious activities including mosque closures in Yecheng, southwest Xinjiang. Abdul Malik, detained on August 10, was sentenced in October to a five-year prison term. There has been no further news of the other four, all detained in July 1990 and believed still held.

. . . . [5 YRS] [4 X ?YRS]

■ **ABDUREHIM TURDY, JAMAL MAMAT, AHAD TILIWALDY, TURGUN ISAAK, SIDIKHAJY ISAAK** and **ABLA KASIM** were tried in 1990 or 1991 on charges of having organized the April 1990 Baren protests in Xinjiang. (For information about the Baren incident, see Kerim Kari p.225.) Some of the men may have received the death penalty and may already have been executed (Amnesty International *ASA 17/50/92*).

. . . . . [POSSIBLE EXECUTIONS]

■ **KAJIKHUMAR SHABDAN**, 69, an ethnic Kazakh writer and poet, was reportedly detained in December 1988 in the Tacheng District of northern Xinjiang (an area directly adjacent to the border with the former Soviet Republic of Kazakhstan, now an independent state.) He was later charged with "espionage" and sentenced to either twelve or fifteen years' imprisonment. Altogether ten other persons are reported to have been detained at the same time in connection with "disturbances" that occurred in Tacheng in the summer of 1988, following a series of protest demonstrations during June-August that year in several cities in Xinjiang (*Amnesty International, ASA 17/50/92.*) Born in 1924 in Kazakhstan, Kajikhumar Shabdan ("Hajihumaer" in Chinese transliteration) emigrated to Xinjiang in 1931 and trained as a teacher, but was imprisoned there in the 1930s and 1940s on suspicion of having "nationalist" sympathies. In 1958, he was sentenced by the PRC authorities to 18 years' imprisonment for "opposing socialism." He served his sentence in full, and was released only in 1976. Between 1982 and 1988, the first three volumes of his novel *Crime*, a history of central Asia from the 1920s onward and a critique of the policies of successive Chinese governments toward the Turkic minorities living there, were published in China. Parts of this epic work are believed to have been written during his long period of imprisonment. The publication of Volume IV was banned by the authorities.

. . . . [12 OR 15 YRS]

A restricted-circulation *(neibu)*

compilation of "counterrevolutionary cases," published by the Chinese government in November 1992 (CCS pp.95-6: see note on p.276, below), revealed, for the first time, details of the court's charges and allegations against Kajikhumar Shabdan and seven other codefendants. The account began by listing the four principal defendants, all of whom were duly convicted of the "counterrevolutionary" crime of "espionage." (Date of trial and length of sentences were not specified, and ages listed for the accused were presumably those as at the time of trial; asterisks in the following denote where middle or last names were censored from the official account by the authorities.)

"Defendant **HAJI** *** [i.e. **Kajikhumar Shabdan**], male, 62, ethnically Kazakh, higher-middle school education, a full-time author employed in the Xinjiang Autonomous Region's Writers Federation.

"Defendant **MUER** ***, male, 67, ethnically Kazakh, lower-middle school education, a retired cadre from the X District Court.

"Defendant **WUHE** ***, male, 56, ethnically Kazakh, primary school education, a retired worker from the X Cigarette Factory of X Municipality.

"Defendant **MAIHAN** **, male, 48, ethnically Kazakh, higher vocational college education, a cadre in the People's Government of X Municipality."

"In 1979, the espionage agency of Country X secretly dispatched a person named **AH** * **ti** (case tried separately), who had fled to that country in 1978, back to City X in China. Ah * ti [NB: full Chinese transliteration of this Kazakh name is probably "Ahfanti"] went first to the home of **WUHE** ***, his father, and exploited his family relationship to persuaded Wuhe *** into also joining the espionage ring. Moreover, he turned Wuhe's place of residence into a liaison point and intelligence gathering center for Country X's espionage operations in China.

"Between October 1979 and the fall of 1980, Ah * ti, who had made many covert trips back into China, arranged for Wuhe *** and his wife, **AI** * **sha** (case tried separately), to meet on two occasions at his father's home with **SU** * **tang** (died of illness in December 1980), an undercover espionage agent. In October 1980, Ah * ti delivered a walkie-talkie set and other communications equipment to Wuhe ***, which the latter then used to relay information and intelligence acquired by Su * tang back to Country X's espionage agency. In October 1982, Ah * ti made another covert trip to China, during which defendant Wuhe *** arranged for defendant **HAJI** *** to meet secretly with him. From then on, Haji ***, following instructions from Country X's espionage agency, became actively engaged in spying activities. Between October 1982 and March 1986, he supplied a large quantity of political and economic information [about

China] to the foreign spy center.

"In 1983, Haji *** and defendant **MUER** *** conspired together to induce **HAXI** *** (case tried separately) into joining the spy ring as a liaison person. Between September 1983 and September 1986, Haxi *** on six occasions left China by stealth and brought back to Haji *** secret letters, operating funds, walkie-talkies and other items given to him by Country X's espionage agency. In October 1985, Haxi *** used the walkie-talkie on numerous occasions to communicate with the foreign spy center, relaying to it materials and information that had been gathered by Haji ***.

"In 1985, Haji *** and Muer ***conspired together to induce **MAIHAN** **, a cadre of the municipal government, into also joining their activities. Defendant Maihan ** took advantage of his official position to steal secret and top-secret documents and other relevant information, and in December of that year he passed these on to Haji ***; they were then delivered to Country X's espionage agency by Haxi ***. In June 1986, Maihan *** [NB: three asterisks rather than two appear this time] again gathered a large quantity of information on China's political and national defense situation; he supplied these to Haji ***, who then used the communications equipment to relay the information to the foreign spy center. Also in 1985, after Wuhe *** had emigrated to Country X, Haji *** used the operating funds to purchase Wuhe ***'s home, which he then handed over to Haxi *** for continued use as their liaison center for espionage activities."

Despite the government's allegations of spying, Asia Watch is concerned that, in view of Kajikhumar Shabdan's long record of ethnic dissidence and his repeated lengthy imprisonment by successive governments, it is probable that he and at least some of his colleagues are in fact being held by the authorities principally on account of their dissident or peacefully pro-separatist views.

. . . . [7 X ? YRS]

■ Three men were sentenced, probably in April 1991, in connection with demonstrations in Moyu and Yutian, southwestern Xinjiang, in April 1990. **NAMAT ABDUMAT** (Namadi Abudoumadi) from Moyu, received a 15-year prison sentence and five years' subsequent deprivation of political rights on two charges, one of "counter-revolutionary propaganda and incitement"; the other of "counter-revolutionary arson." **UBUL EMIL** and **BALAT NIYAZ MOHAMMAT TOHTI**, both under 18, probably accused of complicity, were each sentenced to three years in prison and one year's deprivation of political rights (*Xinjiang Daily*, April 13, 1991). The three allegedly put up posters in four places in Moyu, including the post office, middle school and government offices, criticizing the Communist Party and its family planning policies. In addition, Namat Abdumat allegedly set fire to a family planning office. It is presumed that the two who received three-year sentences have by now been released.

. . . . [15 YRS]

■ **ZHANG Jianxin** and four other taxi drivers were administratively sentenced to three years' re-education through labor for taking part in an illegal demonstration on October 1, 1991. According to *Xinjiang Daily* (October 31, 1991), the five, on the pretext that the municipal government was taxing them too heavily, drove "their cars through some main thoroughfares...finally seriously blocked traffic on the People's Square, jeopardizing social order and the order of the people's daily life."

. . . . [3 X 3 YRS]

Arrested/Sentence Unknown

■ **ABDU KADIR AYUP** - see p.222

■ **ABDUKERIM KARI**, 65; **ABDUKERIM YAKUP**, 58; and **OMAR TURDI**, 26, three "intellectuals and religious personalities," (Amnesty International *ASA 17/50/92*) reportedly were arrested in Yecheng, Xinjiang, as religious dissidents. Omar Turdi was detained on March 13, 1992; the others on March 17.

■ **ABDURAHMAN ABLIZ** - see p.222

■ **ABDUWELI, NURMUHAMMED ABDURAHMAN, AHMET JAN** and **MUHTAR CHONG KADIR**, four ethnic Uygurs from the Xinjiang Uygur Autonomous Region (XAR), were arrested between June and September 1992 (Amnesty International, *ASA 17/07/93*). Ahmet Jan, a 26-year-old

graduate of Xinjiang Technology Institute employed in the XAR's Personnel Department, was detained in Urumqi, the capital, in September 1992. He reportedly was accused of establishing a "reactionary organization." Nurmuhammed Abdurahman, 28, a graduate in architecture from the same institute, who worked in a housing planning office in Urumqi, also was detained in September. Abduweli, 27, and Muhtar Chong Kadir, 26, two university students, reportedly were detained for "counterrevolutionary activities," the former in Urumqi and the latter in Kashgar on June 23. The current whereabouts of the four detainees are not known, but it appears they are being held incommunicado.

■ **ALIMJAN KARIHAJIM** - see p.222

■ **KERIM KARI** *et al.* In April 1990, large-scale protests described by Chinese officials as pro-independence and "counterrevolutionary" took place in Baren in Xinjiang. According to published reports, the incident was in response to the closing of a local mosque just before a religious festival, and a ban on building new mosques and religious schools. On April 5, after large groups of Uygurs refused to abandon their peaceful protest, army troops and units of the People's Armed Police used force to stop the demonstrations. Local authorities reported that some 200 people were detained following the incident; unofficial reports put the figures in the thousands for all of Xinjiang; the number of deaths is still not known. It was reported that those held were subjected to torture and beatings (Amnesty International *ASA 17/50/90*). Others, including **Abdurehim Turdy** (see p.222), may have been sentenced to death and executed for their role in the Baren protests.

Among all those detained, the following seven names are known: **KERIM KARI**, a 29-year-old Kuche native, arrested in Urumqi in July 1990; **ABAYDULLA MAROP DAMOLLAN**, 52, from Shaya, arrested there in April 1990; **YASIN TURDI**, 48, also from Shaya, arrested in Kuche probably in June 1990; **ISMAIL HAJI**, 25, and **MUHAMMAD AMIN YAPQAN**, 26, both Yingjisha natives and both arrested there in July; **ABDULKADIR**, from Kashgar, arrested there in October; and **MUKARRAM HADJI NENIM**, a 22-year-old female from Kuche where she was arrested sometime in 1990.

- **MA Zhongping**, accused as a leader of the 1989 pro-democracy movement in Urumqi, capital of Xinjiang region, reportedly was detained on October 9, 1992 in Yunnan Province (*Xinjiang Daily*). A Gansu Province resident, he was cited as the "main criminal" in the May 19 incident" in Urumqi, which the report characterized as "violent." Ma allegedly "distributed leaflets and incited the population to rebel; he went into Party and government premises where he hit officials and vandalized and set fire to the offices before

fleeing."

- **MANTIMYN (Maimaitiming)**, the administrator of No.5 Middle School in Urumqi, was detained in southern Xinjiang in April or May 1990. He reportedly was suspected of writing a 1988 appeal to the United Nations detailing Chinese human rights violations in Xinjiang. Mantimyn, about 50 years old, from Wusu District, Yili Kazakh Autonomous Prefecture in northern Xinjiang, was detained incommunicado for at least a year; his present status and whereabouts are unknown (Amnesty International *ASA 17/50/92*).

- **OMER KHAN MAHSUN** - see p.222

- **YASIN KARI**, 28; **ABDUREZZAK**, a 35-year-old food processing worker; and **KAWOL KURBAN**, 39, have been arrested for political activities in Xinjiang. Yasin Kari and Kawol Kurban were detained in their home district of Jiashi in March and February 1992 respectively; Abdurezzak, from Guma, was detained in January (Amnesty International *ASA 17/50/92*).

Restricted

- **TURGUN ALMAS (Tuergong Alemasi)**, a 68-year-old Uygur historian and formerly a researcher at the Xinjiang Academy of Social Sciences, reportedly is under house arrest in Urumqi, having been barred from publishing and dismissed from his job; his home has been repeatedly searched and his relatives harassed. Turgun Almas is the author of several books on history and music. One, *The Uygurs*, was criticized in 1990 and 1991 in four lengthy articles in the official *Xinjiang Daily* for presenting a "nationalistic" view of Uygur history and supporting "independence and separatism." Intellectuals have reportedly been urged to criticize his works at political study meetings (Amnesty International *ASA 17/50/92*).

IV. RELIGIOUS PRISONERS

1. Catholics

Died in Prison/Under Surveillance

■ Bishop **FAN Xueyan**, perhaps the most influential of China's underground Catholic bishops, died in police custody on April 13, 1992, the day before his ten-year sentence would have expired. Ordained by Pope Pius XII on June 24, 1951, Bishop Fan in turn ordained many of the Chinese bishops loyal to the Vatican. The Chinese government attempted to weaken his authority throughout his career, and this effort continued at his wake and funeral in his home village of Wangting in Dingxing County, Hebei Province.

Bishop Fan was 85 years old at the time of his death and had retired in 1990 from his duties as (clandestine) bishop of Baoding diocese. His body was released to his family on April 16, 1992. Color photographs taken on April 16 or 17 showed large marks on his forehead and on one cheek. Both legs appeared to be dislocated below the knee. No definitive analysis as to the cause of death could be made from the photos, but the marks were consistent with violence suffered shortly before death. Government cadres keeping watch at the funeral, when asked, attributed Bishop Fan's bruises to his own carelessness, suggesting, among other stories, that he was weak from diarrhea and had tripped over a threshold or fallen out of

bed. There were also unconfirmed reports that Bishop Fan died from a pneumonia which went untreated. He was buried on April 24, 1992.

An eyewitness account of the events surrounding Bishop Fan's wake and burial gave details of Public Security Bureau surveillance of, and interference in, the religious rites and mourning rituals. Local PSB bureaus first imposed martial law on all the villages in four Catholic dioceses in Hebei Province, Yixian, Anguo, Zhengding, as well as Baoding. Police officers then prevented Catholics from leaving their home villages and ordered the local bus company not to sell tickets on part of the Baoding-Anxin route, forcing anyone who could manage the journey to walk the last four miles to the funeral site. A few taxis still got through. Soldiers, stationed at every important crossroads, examined travelers; every Catholic village in Dingxing was surrounded by PLA troops; and all civil defense forces in the vicinity of Baoding were placed on alert. Outside Wangting itself, there was a sentry or guardpost every few feet and all those entering or leaving the village were interrogated. Plainclothesmen with walkie-talkies or video cameras were stationed on all rooftops overlooking the funeral tent. By the evening before the funeral, some 10,000 Catholics had already official vehicles ringed the village and mounted loudspeakers announced that if Catholics in the village had overnight visitors, they would be fined.

Many Catholics who persisted in their attempts to reach the funeral site on tractors, tricycles or motorcycles had their vehicles confiscated and were forced to pay fines as high as *Renminbi* 1,600 ($280). Harassment of Catholics in attendance was continuous. The day before the funeral, for example, local authorities dragged a Catholic youth from Biyangcheng village into the government compound and beat him. Some of those who attempted to assist the youth were also beaten. In addition, several persons were arrested in connection with their attendance at the funeral (see Ji Xiaoshang p.234).

In an obvious attempt to hasten Bishop Fan's burial and thus avoid what was rapidly becoming a rallying point for the Catholics of Hebei Province, for some four days prior to the funeral, authorities prevented food supplies and the ice needed to preserve the body from entering the village. During the two days immediately preceding the services, children were enlisted to help smuggle in food. No attention was paid to the Catholic request that Bishop **Chen Jianzhang** (see p.392) be permitted to conduct the rites. One year later, Chinese officials again attempted to interfere with religious rites, this time at a requiem Mass for Bishop Fan. Despite their efforts, 7,000 Catholics participated in the event, at which Bishop Liu Guandong (see p.394) presided.

Fan Xueyan was born on February 11, 1907 in Xiaowangting Village,

Qingyuan County, Hebei. He studied for the priesthood in Beijing and Rome. On December 22, 1934, he was ordained as a priest and went to serve in Wanxian diocese in Sichuan Province. During the war against Japan, Father Fan, by then living in Baoding, contributed medical and material services to the Communist Party's Eighth Route Army in Hebei.

First arrested in 1958, Bishop Fan was sentenced to 15 years' hard labor for his opposition to the Chinese Church's "anti-imperialist, self-governing policy" and for "stubbornly refusing to accept" the official Catholic Patriotic Association. He served his sentence in labor camps in Laishui, Huanghua and Anxin counties. Released at the end of 1969, Bishop Fan returned to his home village but remained subject to supervision. He was arrested again on April 15, 1978 and held without charge in a local county jail until January 14, 1980. During the early 1980s, Bishop Fan continued his underground church activities, secretly ordaining three bishops and several priests. On April 13, 1982, he was arrested again, charged with "colluding with foreign forces to jeopardize the sovereignty and security of the motherland" and sentenced to a ten-year term and jailed at Hebei's No.2 Prison in Shijiazhuang, the provincial capital. Following an intervention by Cardinal Jaime Sin of Manila, Bishop Fan was released on parole in November 1987, but he remained under virtual house arrest in a church compound in Baoding. On feast days, to prevent him from meeting with his followers, Bishop Fan was taken on tours outside his area of influence. When the clandestine Chinese bishops formed their own Episcopal Conference on November 21, 1989, he was elected, in absentia, as honorary president.

Since November 3, 1990, when Bishop Fan again disappeared from Baoding, until his death almost a year and a half later, his whereabouts were often unknown as he was moved from place to place by Chinese authorities. During the early part of his confinement, relatives reportedly could visit him in the presence of security police. In 1991, a statement put out by the government said Bishop Fan would henceforth "be staying at a pleasant location" and did "not wish to be disturbed by anyone."

The authorities have consistently denied persecuting Bishop Fan Xueyan. According to Liu Bainian, lay member of the Standing Committee of the Catholic Patriotic Association, Bishop Fan's arrest after 1979 was purely "for political, not religious" reasons. According to Liu, no one has been jailed in China for religious reasons since the Cultural Revolution.

. . . . [DEAD]

■ Father **HUO Bingzhang** - see p.394

. . . . [DEAD]

■ Bishop **LI Zhenrong**, who eluded arrest for two years following his involvement as vice-president in the November 1989 clandestine Bishops' Conference, died from cancer on April 19, 1992, having four months earlier (on December 11, 1991) been forcibly

removed from Tianjin No.2 Hospital by the authorities. The government later insisted that Bishop Li was not arrested but had left the hospital of his own free will and against doctor's orders. And in an official (November 1991) response to requests for information by the U.S. government, Chinese authorities falsely listed Bishop Li as having "never been accused of any offense" *(cong wei bei tichu renhe zhikongzhe)*. (This term does not appear in the Chinese Criminal Procedure Law and has no legal significance; it does not preclude detention without trial or other restrictions on movement.)

On November 28, 1991, Bishop Li, ill with stomach cancer and using the name **LI Mu**, had two-thirds of his stomach surgically removed. Authorities discovered his presence at the Tianjin No.2 Hospital on December 8, and three days later he was transferred to an undisclosed location by plainclothes Public security officers from Cangzhou County, Hebei Province. Several people who had helped care for the bishop were briefly detained. Some time afterwards, however, Bishop Li was permitted to hold a public Mass.

Born on September 29, 1919, Bishop Li was ordained a priest on May 3, 1951. He had entered the Xianxian Minor Seminary in September 1935, the Jiangxian Major Seminary in 1940 and later studied at the Shanghai Jesuit School of Theology. First arrested in 1955, Bishop Li was sentenced to a seven-year prison term and three years' subsequent deprivation of political rights for refusing to join the Catholic Patriotic Association. He was not released, however, until December 1968. In April 1977, Bishop Li was again tried and sentenced, this time to twelve years in prison and five years' deprivation of rights. He was released on parole in 1980. Three years later, he was secretly ordained as a bishop and thereafter served clandestinely in the Xianxian diocese.

. . . . [DEAD]

■ Bishop **LIU Difen**, a Catholic bishop from Anguo Diocese, Hebei Province disappeared in December 1990. At the time, he was 78 years old. There was no further news of Bishop Liu until November 15, 1992, when his corpse was suddenly handed over to his family. They were told he had died on November 14, 1992 at 1:10 P.M. from high blood pressure and a brain embolism. Although rumors of the Bishop's death had been circulating for some time, it took almost five months for the reports to be confirmed.

Bishop Liu had a long history of difference with the official Chinese Catholic Church. He was first arrested during the 1950s for refusing to take part in the government-sponsored Three Self Movement. After his release, he worked in the hospital of the 85th Commune of Anguo until the start of the Cultural Revolution, when he again became the target of official persecution. In 1980, he resumed working at the hospital until his retirement in 1984, after which he turned his full attention to church matters.

The circumstances of Bishop Liu's death, as described in a first-hand account dated November 1992 and delivered to Asia Watch on April 6, 1993, show striking similarities to those surrounding the deaths of Bishop Fan Xueyan (see p.228) and Bishop Shi Chunjie (see p.232). Taken together, the reports suggest that the Religious Affairs Bureau, in conjunction with the official Catholic Patriotic Association, maintain places of extra-judicial detention euphemistically called "old-age homes," to which elderly clergy are sometimes forcibly removed. Friends and relatives are denied access to these "old-age homes," and it appears that medical care is at best rudimentary.

On November 2, less than two weeks before Bishop Liu's death, a delegation of officials including the head of the Religious Affairs Bureau visited the bishop's relatives in Biandukou Village, Renqiu District, Hebei. They told his nephew, "Your uncle is sick, he cannot walk, he has high blood pressure, and his mind is not very clear. He would like to come home to rest. Will you receive him?" Bishop Liu's relatives readily agreed and offered to immediately send a car to fetch him. The official replied, "There is no need to go fetch him. 'They' will bring him back here." He did not, however, specify any time or indicate who, precisely, "they" were.

There was no further news until November 11, when the official returned to tell the bishop's relatives that he would be brought home that same day at 5:00 P.M. But that afternoon, they were told, "The bishop is very sick. Some of his relatives can go to see him at the hospital in Kuancheng District" [a mountainous area, 500 kilometers distant, in the extreme northern part of Hebei Province]. Three of the bishop's nephews "hurried" to the hospital, traveling through the night. When they arrived, Bishop Liu was already unconscious and unable to breath without supplementary oxygen. But his nephews could not take him home as they did not have the money to pay the exceptionally high price the hospital was demanding for the oxygen. A request from the bishop's doctor to the Secretary of the hospital to lower the price was unsuccessful. According to the first-hand account, the high charge for oxygen was dictated by the authorities in a deliberate attempt to prevent Bishop Liu's relatives from removing him. A nephew "rushed the 500 kilometers home," rented a car and returned to the hospital with a doctor and an oxygen tank, but by then the bishop had already died. His relatives were forbidden to remove the corpse without permission from the Religious Affairs Bureau.

The nephews later asked what crime Bishop Liu had committed. They were informed, "He has committed no violation, no crime. He was brought up here to rest." When Bishop Liu's body was dressed, however, relatives found what they considered to be evidence of numerous injuries. Among other marks, they found two unhealed wounds in the middle of his back; his left shoulder bore scars; and there were two holes under his left armpit. Family members concluded that he had died "from serious ill treatment." As confirmation, they quoted the head of the Kuancheng Religious Affairs Bureau, who told

them, "When the Bishop arrived at Kuancheng, he had no shoes. So I sent him a pair but he refused to take them, saying, 'You have reduced me to this state and now you give me a pair of shoes. I won't wear them!...' I replied that the ill-treatment against him was all 'their' problem. For my part, I was only offering him this out of humanitarian compassion." In an attempt to keep control over Bishop Liu's funeral, government officials proposed to exclude all participation by underground bishops, priests and laypersons and limit attendance to "affiliated" priests from Xianxian (Hebei Province). The bishop's relatives resisted this ban and succeeded in rallying the attendance of one underground bishop, 14 priests and more than 3,000 lay Catholics.

Bishop Liu was born on May 13, 1912 in Biandukou Village, Renqiu District, Hebei. He entered Beijing Major Seminary in 1932, was ordained a priest in 1939 and consecrated a bishop in 1989. Bishop Liu studied medicine at Furen University, then continued his medical training in Anguo diocese.

. . . . [DEAD]
■ **Bishop LIU Shuhe** - see p.1
. . . . [DEAD]

■ Bishop Paul **SHI Chunjie**, the auxiliary bishop of Baoding, died in police custody in a government-run "old-age home" on November 3, 1991. Although reliable sources attributed Bishop Shi's death to a heart attack caused by maltreatment, the exact cause has never been known. The bishop, who was almost blind, had a history of serious illnesses including heart disease and possibly diabetes; a lack of proper medication may have contributed to his death. According to the Chinese, no charges were pending against Bishop Shi when he died. An official Chinese response to requests for information by the U.S. government (November 1991) listed him as having "never been accused of any offense."

According to an Asia Watch source, the whereabouts of Bishop Shi were unknown from the time he was secretly led away by Public Security Bureau personnel on December 15, 1990 until his death. He was probably held for part of the time in a "study camp" organized by the government.

On November 3, 1991, government personnel escorted members of Bishop Shi's family out of their village. They reappeared the next day with his body and orders to bury him within two days and to refrain from spreading news of his death. The attempt to avoid a large turnout backfired; some 1,500 people attended his funeral.

Bishop Shi lived in Xinli Village Church in Qingyuan County, Hebei Province, and was in charge of young seminarians and novice sisters in Baoding and Yixian dioceses. Born in January 1920, he was ordained a priest on June 1, 1947 and an auxiliary bishop on April 29, 1989. The official Chinese Catholic Church never recognized his consecration. Bishop Shi was arrested once before, in 1954, and served part of a 13-year sentence.

. . . . [DEAD]

■   Father **ZHANG Shentang**, a priest from Nanyang diocese in Henan Province, died from poisoning unconnected to his underground religious activities. At the time he was on parole from a 17-year prison term for printing religious books without permission, his deteriorating health having precipitated a transfer to house arrest and confinement to his village. Father Zhang had been arrested in the early 1980s.

. . . . [DEAD]

■   **Father ZHU Hongsheng** - see p.3
. . . . [DEAD]

Sentenced

■   Father **CHEN Yingkui**, arrested in 1991 in northern Hebei province, reportedly was sentenced to three years' "re-edcuation through labor". He is reportedly serving his sentence in Gaoyang County, Hebei.

■   Father **PEI Zhenping**, a young Trappist priest, who had trained outside the aegis of the official Chinese Catholic Church, was arrested on October 21, 1989. He had lived and worked in Youtong Village, Luancheng County, Shijiazhuang, Hebei Province. According to an Asia Watch source, Father Pei was sentenced to an unknown term of imprisonment and as of October 1993 was still being held. In a November 1991 response to requests for information by the U.S. government, however, Chinese officials claimed that Father Pei had "never been accused of any offense." The latter term is a misleading, non-legal one which does not preclude detention without trial or other restrictions on movement.

. . . . [? YRS]

■ Father **XU Guoxin**, from Langfang diocese in Hebei Province, was arrested in December 1991 and sentenced to three years' "labor re-education." No additional information is available.

. . . . [3 YRS]

Arrested/Sentence Unknown

■ Father **CHEN Yingkui**, from the Baoding area in Hebei Province, was arrested sometime in 1991. There is an unconfirmed report that he received a three-year sentence of re-education through labor.

■ Father Peter **HU Duoer**, 32, was arrested in December 1990 in Lianghuang Village, Xushui County, Hebei Province. According to an Asia Watch source, he was handcuffed by public security officials and treated very roughly before being locked up in a facility in Xushui. The charges against him are not known. Father Hu Duoer is the same person as Father **Hu Duo**, previously arrested on December 24, 1989 while visiting neighboring Shandong Province. Requests by the U.S. government for information about Father Hu's whereabouts elicited no response from Chinese officials (November 1991).

■ **JI Xiaoshang** and at least six other Catholics were arrested between late April and June 1992 in connection with the funeral of Bishop Fan Xueyan (see p.228). As of October 1992, the six others had been released, some after paying heavy fines. Ji, from Jiezhuang, was detained in June for holding a megaphone, and as of October 1992, he had not been released. **WEI Daquan**, from Song Village, was arrested and held for one week on a charge of impeding public affairs during Bishop Fan's mourning period. **TIAN Guochen**, from Wangting Village, was detained 40 days, fined 1,000 *yuan* ($175) and ordered to pay bail amounting to 600 *yuan* for asking what had caused Bishop Fan's death. Tian also had to prepare a banquet and offer gifts which cost him some 2,000 *yuan*. **SHE Sujie**, from Shenjiabi Village, was detained for one week for distributing funeral notices. **JIE Xiaoxin**, also from Jiezhuang Village, was held for two days, fined 1,000 *yuan* and ordered to pay 600 yuan for bail. **SU Lanmin**, from Donglu Village, was beaten during the 14 days he was held. His fine amounted to 400 *yuan*. **ZHANG Xiaoxi**, village unknown, was held for half a month.

■ Father **LIAO Haiqing**, 63, from Yujiang diocese in Jiangxi Province, was re-arrested by Public Security Bureau officials on August 16, 1992 while saying Mass in his home in Fuzhou, Jiangxi Province. At about 6:30 A.M., as more than 200 worshippers crowded in and around the house, some twenty police officers and Religious Affairs Bureau personnel forced their way in, demanding Father Liao leave with them immediately.

Worshippers told the officials to wait until the Mass was complete. Rather than comply, they interrupted the distribution of communion and later broke icons and confiscated religious articles. Earlier, on April 15, Fuzhou officials had warned Father Liao to stop his "private" meetings for religious activities. The arrest was presumably in response to his refusal. It was the fourth arrest for Father Liao who trained at Xujiahui Major Seminary in the 1950s. As a layman, he was arrested on two separate occasions prior to 1980 and was sentenced to terms of eight and five years. There is some indication that he was not released until 1980. After his release, Father Liao was ordained a priest. A year later, on November 19, 1981, he was again arrested and sentenced to another ten-year term. Held for at least part of his incarceration in Nanchang Prison No.4, he was released in July 1991.

■ Father **LIU Guangpin** - see p.395

■ **PEI Jieshu** and **PEI Shangchen**, two community leaders from Youtong village in Hebei Province, were arrested on October 23, 1989, according to an Asia Watch source. Both men were still in prison as of March 1993 despite an official Chinese response to U.S. government inquiries (November 1991) stating that Pei Shangchen had "never been accused of any offense."

■ Father **WANG Danian**, in his seventies, and two Catholic sisters were arrested in the area of Suzhou, Jiangsu Province in June or July 1992 and accused of "illegally doing missionary work." The two women were released by August 26, but as of July 1993, Father Wang continued to be held, either by the Changshu Public Security Bureau or in the city of Suzhou.

■ Father **XU [?]** - see p.395

■ Father **ZHU Ruci** - see p.395

■ Father **ZOU Xijin** - see p.395

Restricted

■ Father **AN Shi'an**, 79, the clandestine Vicar-General of Daming diocese, Hebei Province, is missing and there is legitimate concern that he is under some form of restricted movement. Arrested a few days after December 26, 1990, Father An, despite his two-year imprisonment, was never formally arrested or charged. In fact, an official Chinese response to inquiries by the U.S. government (November 1991), listed him as having "never been accused of any offense." According to an Asia Watch source, after his detention for unspecified reasons, Father An, ordained in 1942, was first sent for "re-education," probably to a "study camp" (see Han Dingxiang p.44). His post-camp whereabouts were never made public and the circumstances of his release, announced on December 21, 1992 by the then Chinese Minister of Public Security, are unknown.

■ Bishop **FAN Yufei**, 60, from Zhouzhi, Shaanxi Province, is out of prison but appears to be under a form of house arrest. The bishop had been arrested after saying Mass at his parish church in Daxingyingon on Easter Sunday, April 22, 1992 and held for five months. According to an Asia Watch source, Bishop Fan had been induced during his detention into signing a "statement of repentance" and renouncing his episcopal authority. After his release, realizing that he had been tricked, he repudiated the statement.

A group of eight priests arrested with Bishop Fan in April 1992 were also later released, according to the authorities, after "learning Communist thoughts at a place of green hills and clear waters," probably a guest house in the countryside near Baoji where they were forcibly detained. Throughout these "study seminars," the priests were held incommunicado, their whereabouts unknown. After their release, the eights priests were forced to report regularly to the police and seven of them were dismissed from the university where they all studied. Bishop Fan, who was ordained in 1982, had himself ordained some twenty priests in 1991, all of whom refused to work in the government-approved church system. The group detained were presumably from among these twenty.

■ Jesuit Auxiliary Bishop Joseph **FAN Zhongliang**, 73, acting bishop of Shanghai, was released from detention on August 19, 1991 and placed under house arrest on the outskirts of Shanghai. He is living with his niece. Bishop Fan is reportedly under constant surveillance by two policemen. He cannot travel and is subject to frequent and intense interrogation and intimidation. The Public Security Bureau questions him at least once or twice a month about where he goes, what he does and who he sees.

Bishop Fan and his assistant, **QIAN Zhijing**, were apprehended by public security officials on or about June 11, 1991 at a bus station. According to an Asia Watch source, they had been on their way to the coastal city of Wenzhou in eastern Zhejiang Province. Following Bishop Fan's detention, his house was searched and some of his belongings, including books, religious items and furniture, were confiscated. There had been speculation that the arrest was "a comment" on the announcement that the former bishop of Shanghai, Bishop Ignatius Gong Pinmei, had been secretly named a cardinal 12 years earlier. Bishop Gong, 90, who lives in the U.S., was formally elevated in Rome on June 28, 1991.

During an 18-month period just prior to his arrest, Bishop Fan was interrogated repeatedly, possibly in connection with his role as a vice-president of the November 1989 clandestine Bishops' Conference (*Reuters*, June 23, 1991). He had earlier been detained for 15 years, from 1967 to 1982, in a labor camp in western Qinghai Province. Bishop Fan became a priest in 1951 and was secretly ordained a bishop in 1985.

■ Father **GUO Fude** - see p.394

■ Bishop **GUO Wenzhi**, 73, bishop

of Harbin, Heilongjiang Province, cannot leave Qiqihar, his home village, according to an Asia Watch source. He was arrested there on December 14, 1989 in connection with the clandestine Bishops' Conference and released in March 1990. According to an official Chinese response to U.S. government inquiries (November 1991), Bishop Guo had "never been accused of any offense." Bishop Guo had been imprisoned twice before, first between 1954 and 1964, and again from 1966 until 1985, when he was interned in a Xinjiang Autonomous Region labor camp. Ordained in 1948 and consecrated a bishop in May 1989, he is thought to have resided in Hebei Province after his second release and to have taught foreign languages there.

■ Bishop **HOU Guoyang**, the underground bishop of Chongqing, Sichuan Province, was released in early 1991, but has had his movements restricted. According to an Asia Watch source, his arrest came in early January 1990, in part for his participation in the November 1989 clandestine Bishops' Conference. Other charges against Bishop Hou surfaced in the May 1990 issue of the magazine *Catholic Church in China* in which he was accused of inciting a small group to participate in demonstrations in Sichuan and of "collecting money to support the turmoil." Bishop Hou, who is not recognized as a bishop by the official Chinese church, but was ordained in 1988 by Bishop Fan Xueyan (see p.228), was further accused of publishing and distributing a "so-called Bible" and cautioned to cease his

"illegal activities." This warning marked the first time the Chinese government explicitly linked Catholics loyal to the Vatican to the pro-democracy movement, and Liu Bainian, a spokesman for the official Chinese Catholic Patriotic Association, went so far as to label Bishop Hou a fraud. In response to requests by the U.S. government for clarification of Hou's status (November 1991), Chinese officials said he had "never been accused of any offense."

■ Bishop Vincent **HUANG Shoucheng**, clandestine bishop of Fu'an diocese, Fujian Province, arrested on July 27, 1990, was placed under village restriction in March 1991. An official Chinese response to U.S. State Department inquiries (November 1991) listed Bishop Huang as having "never been accused of any offense." According to an Asia Watch source, two deacons arrested with Bishop Huang were released shortly after they were seized. The detentions were confirmed by the Director of the Fujian Religious Affairs Bureau who claimed those arrested had violated government regulations.

■ Bishop **JIANG Liren**, 80, from Hohhot, Inner Mongolia, secretly consecrated in late June 1989, was in prison from late 1989 until sometime in early 1991 in connection with the 1989 clandestine Bishops' Conference. A vicious campaign of character assassination by government cadres reportedly has succeeded in "destroying" him. According to an Asia Watch source, he is restricted to his own village and is under police surveillance. According to an official Chinese response to inquiries by the U.S. government (November 1991), Bishop Jiang had "never been accused of any offense."

■ Father Joseph **JIN Dechen**, the 72-year-old Vicar General of Nanyang diocese, Henan Province, arrested in December 1981 and sentenced on July 27, 1982 to a 15-year prison term and five years' subsequent deprivation of political rights, was released on parole in May 1992 and is confined to his village, Jinjiajiang, near Nanyang. An official Chinese response to requests for information by the U.S. government (November 1991) confirmed Father Jin's release. According to an Asia Watch source, he left prison in poor health. Father Jin reportedly had been held at the Third Provincial Prison in Yuxian, near Zhengzhou in Henan, on charges stemming from his objection to abortion and birth control. His first arrest, in 1958, resulted in a life sentence which was commuted; he was released in 1973.

■ Father Guiseppe **LI Fangchun**, 59, from Shanghai diocese, Henan Province, was arrested in February 1983 and sentenced to a 12-year term for refusing to renounce his loyalty to the Vatican. Other charges included probable connection with a "counterrevolutionary party" and spreading "counterrevolutionary propaganda." His release was one of the 18 announced by the Chinese in March 1993, but he reportedly had

been released some time prior to the announcement, probably in May 1992, at which time he was subject to restrictions on his movements. At the time, he was near death and could neither walk, speak nor even recognize people. Other than that he still suffers from a slight limp, he has since made a remarkable recovery. Ordained in the early 1950s, Father Li was first imprisoned in a labor camp from 1955 until 1979. At the time he was serving in Shangqiu diocese in Henan.

■ Bishop **LI Jingfeng**, 68, is gravely ill but is not permitted to leave the church compound in Fengxiang, Shaanxi Province or to receive visitors, according to repeated unconfirmed reports. His status is most clearly explained by the following report. Just after Easter 1992, public security officers arrived in the compound and told Bishop Li to come with them. He asked, "Am I compelled to go?" The answer was, "No, you're free, but you must come with us."

■ Bishop Joseph **LI Side**, the unofficial bishop of Tianjin since 1989, now in his sixties and in ill-health, was released in early May 1992 after several weeks in prison and is currently living under strict surveillance in Liangzhuang Village in mountainous Ji County. His arrest came on April 11, 1992, when he was invited to have "talks" with a government official. Bishop Li has been ordered not to go to the city and one of his auxiliaries has been installed as bishop by the official church. But Bishop Li's congregants still make the trip to Liangzhuang to worship at his temporary church.

Earlier, in June 1991, Bishop Li had been released after spending 18 months in detention without charge. He returned to Laoxikai (St. Joseph's) Cathedral in Tianjin on June 7, 1991 and openly presided at Masses starting on July 7. Although Bishop Li's secret consecration in 1982, which he later openly acknowledged, was not approved by Chinese authorities, his ordination as a priest was never officially questioned and he was thus able to return to religious duties. Prior to his 1991 release, Bishop Li had been taken on a "study tour" to visit churches in Jinan and Qingdao in Shandong Province, and after his second release, he was again taken on a similar tour. The official reason given for the travel was to acquaint the bishop with social changes. Unofficially, it is reported, the stratagem is one increasingly used by the authorities to tire out elderly churchmen.

Bishop Li's first detention was in connection with his role as a vice-president of the 1989 clandestine Bishops' Conference. He was arrested in the early hours of December 9, 1989 by a large contingent of public security personnel as he left his home to administer last rites. According to an Asia Watch source, Bishop Li was held in a city prison under very poor conditions, reportedly sharing a 30-square foot cell with 25 to 30 other prisoners. Food and sanitation were highly deficient. An official Chinese response to U.S. government inquiries about Bishop Li's first arrest listed him as having "never been accused of any

offense."

According to an Asia Watch source, the auxiliary bishop of Tianjin, **SHI Hongzhen**, is also closely watched and was under travel restrictions as of January 1994.

■ Bishop John Baptist **LIANG Xisheng**, underground bishop of Kaifeng diocese in Henan Province, arrested in October 1990 for "illegal religious activities," was released in February 1991. According to an Asia Watch source, he is restricted to his village. Bishop Liang, born in 1923, was ordained a priest in 1980 and a bishop in 1989.

■ Bishop Mathias LU **Zhensheng**, 73, the second bishop of Tianshui diocese in Gansu Province, is no longer in prison but his movements are restricted. He had been arrested in late December 1989 in connection with the founding of the 1989 clandestine Bishops' Conference. In response to U.S. government inquiries (November 1991), Chinese officials said Bishop Lu had "never been accused of any offense."

Bishop Lu was sentenced earlier, in 1984, to a ten-year prison term and four years' deprivation of political rights on a charge of engaging in "counterrevolutionary activities." The circumstances of his release from that sentence are not clear. Ordained a priest in 1981 and secretly consecrated a bishop in 1983 by Bishop Wang Milu (see p.240), Bishop Lu is not approved as a cleric by Chinese authorities.

■ Father **SHI Wande**, a priest from

Baoding who attended the November 1989 clandestine Bishops' Conference in Shaanxi Province, reportedly was arrested on December 9, 1989 in Xushui County about 43 miles southwest of Beijing. According to an official Chinese response to inquiries by the U.S. government (November 1991), Father Shi had "never been accused of any offense." Other than the Chinese report, there is no further information about Father Shi's whereabouts and there is apprehension that he is held against his will.

■ Father **SU Zhemin**, 60, accused of "organizing and taking part in illegal activities," was released on parole and is living in Baoding, Hebei Province. He is not free to move about. Father Su had been administratively sentenced on May 21, 1990 to three years' "labor re-education" by the Baoding City Labor Re-education Administrative Committee. According to an official Chinese response (November 1991) to requests for information by the U.S. government, in Father Su's case "legal responsibility was not pursued" - a commonly used euphemism for administrative punishments such as "labor re-education." As Vicar-General of Baoding diocese, Father Su took part in the 1989 clandestine Bishops' Conference in Shaanxi Province on behalf of Bishop Fan Xueyan (see p.228). Arrested on December 17, 1989, Father Su was initially held in Tangshan, where he reportedly was made to clean toilets, then moved to the northeast. According to an Asia Watch source, his family's efforts to visit him had been unsuccessful. Father

Su served two previous prison terms, one from 1959 to 1975 and another from 1982 to 1962. The latter also was an administratively imposed "re-education through labor" sentence.

■ Bishop Casimir **WANG Milu**, the "black bishop of Tianshui," Gansu Province, was released on parole in April 1993. He is at home in Ganggu district, Gansu, but may not freely move about. Bishop Wang, whose ordination is not recognized by the official Chinese Catholic Church, was arrested in 1983, then sentenced in 1985 by the Tianshui Intermediate People's Court to ten years in prison, four years' deprivation of political rights and confiscation of part of his property. An appeal to the Gansu High People's Court on April 29, 1985 failed, and on May 24 Bishop Wang was sent to a correctional facility, possibly a labor camp, in Gansu, to start serving his sentence. An Asia Watch source reported that he was held in a prison in Pingliang, Gansu, then transferred to a labor camp, Dashaping, in Lanzhou.

Bishop Wang was accused of "counterrevolutionary activities," including passing a list of twelve imprisoned priests to a visiting clergyman from Taiwan in November 1980, and visiting Bishop Fan Xueyan in Baoding in July 1980 and January 1981 in order to be secretly consecrated. Bishop Wang then received recognition of his consecration from the Vatican. Bishop Wang also was accused of other acts of "counter-revolutionary propaganda and incitement." He allegedly secretly ordained priests (four reportedly were named in the verdict); openly opposed the constitutional article prohibiting foreign domination of religious institutions; criticized the Catholic Patriotic Association, an official Chinese government body and, after a 1981 article in *Renmin Ribao* on Vatican interference in the internal affairs of China appeared, he further criticized government interference in religious practice.

Although he did not become a priest until 1980, Bishop Wang, born in 1939, was imprisoned during the Cultural Revolution for professing his faith. He was pardoned in 1979, but allegedly "continued his counter-revolutionary activities under the guise of religion." He was arrested again in 1981 and again released.

Bishop Wang reportedly was penalized several times during his last imprisonment for preaching the Gospel to other inmates.

■ Two brothers of Bishop Wang Milu (see above), Father **WANG Ruohan** and Father **WANG Ruowang**[2] from Tianshui, Gansu Province, arrested in connection with the 1989 clandestine Bishops' Conference, were released from prison after completing their sentences, one year each of "re-education through labor." In a contradictory account, Chinese officials informed the U.S. government that Father Wang Ruowang had "never been accused of any offense" (November 1991). Father Wang Ruowang had been arrested on December 9, 1989 in Xushui County, Hebei Province, and charged with "illegal religious

activities," then sent to a prison in Pingliang in Gansu. He was later detained for caring for Bishop Li Zhenrong during the latter's final illness in late 1991. In June 1991, Father Wang Ruowang was picked up on a bus as he was heading for Wenzhou in Zhejiang Province and forcibly returned to Gansu.

Father Wang Ruohan also was arrested in December 1989, but no further details about his subsequent activities are available. Both men are under strict restriction of movement and Father Wang Ruowang might at one time have had his residence permit confiscated and been refused permission to work.

■ Father Francis **WANG Yijun**, the 75-year-old vicar-general of Wenzhou diocese in Zhejiang Province, was released on parole on May 21, 1992. He is confined to his village, but is permitted to say Mass; however, he may not meet with foreigners. Father Wang was administratively sentenced on February 5, 1990 to three years' "re-education through labor" for failure to reform while serving a previous term. This administrative sentence followed immediately upon his release from a term of imprisonment which began with his arrest on May 19, 1981. According to the official notice, Father Wang was re-sentenced because "he refused to repent...continued to maintain illegal ties to the underground Catholic Church in Wenzhou...and instigated Christian believers against the religious policy and lawful decrees of the People's Government." This was Father Wang's third prison term. The first ran from 1957 until 1962 and was for "counterrevolutionary activities." In total, he was incarcerated for over 15 years.

■ Bishop John **YANG Shudao**, the clandestine bishop of Fuzhou, Fujian Province, arrested on February 28, 1988 at 8 A.M. in Liushan village, was released in February 1991 and is living in a church near Fuzhou. According to an Asia Watch source, he is still under surveillance and is under severe pressure to join the official church. Secretly consecrated in 1987, Bishop Yang served a previous prison term which terminated in 1980.

■ Father Mark **YUAN Wenzai**, 69, underground Vicar General of Haimen Diocese, Jiangsu Province, in July 1990 was placed under the custody of the patriotic bishop of the area, Monseigneur Yu Chengcai (in effect his jailer), and permitted to live at the church in Longshan, according to an Asia Watch source. As of March 1993, the arrangements had not changed. However, according to an official Chinese response to a U.S. government request for information (November 1991), Father Yuan had "never been accused of any offense." Father Yuan had been seized in early 1990 by the local Public Security Bureau and confined in the police station until his transfer to Longshan.

■ Father **ZHU Baoyu** of Nanyang diocese, Henan Province, reportedly has been released, probably on parole, and is restricted to his home village. Arrested in December 1981 for taking

Catholics on a pilgrimage to Sheshan, near Shanghai, he was sentenced in 1982 to ten years' imprisonment.

Current Status Unclear

Sentenced

■ Father **LI Xinsan**, from Anguo diocese in Hebei Province, is among 18 Catholics whose releases were announced by the Chinese government in March 1993. As of October 1993, however, he had not returned home. Father Li was sentenced to a three-year "re-education through labor" term and sent to a camp in Tangshan, Hebei. Arrested at the end of 1990 or the beginning of 1991, his offense was never specified.
. . . . [3 YRS]

■ Father **LI Zhongpei**, arrested on December 3, 1990 and sentenced to three years' "re-education through labor" at a camp in Tangshan, Hebei Province, is among those whose releases were announced by the Chinese government in March 1991. However, as of July 1993, he had not returned home.
. . . . [3 YRS]

■ Father **WANG Jiansheng**[2], 40, is among those whose releases the Chinese government announced in March 1993; as of October 1993, he had not returned home. Arrested on May 19, 1991, Father Wang was sentenced to three years' "re-education through labor" and sent to a Re-education Center in Xuanhua, Hebei

Province.

. . . . [3 YRS]

■ **ZHANG Guoyan**, a layman in his late thirties and son of Zhang Dapeng (see p.397) is among those whose releases were announced by the Chinese government in March 1993. As of October 1993, however, he had not returned home. For refusing to join the official Catholic Patriotic Association, Zhang Guoyan was administratively sentenced to three years' "labor re-education" sometime in 1991 or 1992. The date of his arrest is not known, but it probably occurred as part of the 1990 crackdown in Hebei Province.

. . . . [3 YRS]

■ **ZHANG Youzhong**, a layman arrested at the beginning of 1991 and sentenced to three years' imprisonment, is among those whose releases were announced by the Chinese government in March 1993; as of October 1993, however, he had not returned home.

. . . . [3 YRS]

■ **ZHAO Zhongyue** - see p.397

. . . . [? YRS]

Arrested

■ Father Joseph **CHEN Rongkui**, 28, from Yixiang diocese, Hebei Province, was arrested at the Dingxian railroad station on December 14, 1990. As of October 1993, he was reportedly still in detention. The charges against him are unknown.

■ Father Peter **CUI Xingang**, a 30-year-old parish priest from Donglu Village, Qingyuan County, Hebei, was arrested on July 28, 1991 at midnight. (Donglu is the site of a shrine frequented by Catholics on pilgrimage.) As of October 1993, Father Cui's whereabouts remained unknown.

■ Father **GAO Fangzhan**, 27, from Yixian diocese, Hebei Province, was arrested in May 1991 by plainclothes police just outside Shizhu Village in Dingxing County. As of October 1993, his whereabouts remained unknown.

■ Father **LIU Heping**[2], 28, was arrested on February 13, 1991 at his home in Shizhu Village, Dingxing County, Hebei Province. As of October 1993, his whereabouts remained unknown. Father Liu was arrested once before, on June 4, 1990, during a police raid in Zhaozhuang village, Hebei.

■ Father Paul **LIU Shimin**, 32, was arrested in Xiefangying, Xushui County, Hebei Province on December 14, 1990. As of October 1993, his whereabouts remained unknown.

■ **MA Shunbao**, a 42-year-old deacon, was arrested in Hebei Province on November 6, 1991. As of October 1993, his whereabouts remained unknown.

■ Father **MA Zhiyuan** and four seminarians were arrested on December 12, 1991 in Houzhuang, Xushui County, Hebei Province. As of October 1993, the whereabouts of the five remained unknown.

■ The whereabouts of Father **PEI Guojun,** Yixian diocese, Hebei Province, are unknown; there has been no news of him since January 29, 1991 and requests for information by the U.S. government elicited no response from Chinese officials (November 1991). Father Pei was arrested in connection with the November 1989 clandestine Bishops' Conference in Shaanxi Province.

■ **SHI Guohui,** a Catholic lay leader from Baoding, Hebei Province, apparently was arrested, probably in mid-December 1990. No further information is available.

■ Father **XIAO Shixiang,** 58, from Yixian diocese in Hebei Province, was arrested in a village in Dingxian on December 12, 1991 after he guided a retreat. Apparently the same priest as someone reported to have disappeared while on his way to Shandong Province on October 20, 1989, Father Xiao had not been heard of until his 1991 detention. As of October 1993, his whereabouts remained unknown.

2. Protestants

Died in Prison/Under Surveillance

■ **CUI Chaoshu,** an evangelist preacher, was seized by security officials at a house-church meeting in Huize County, Yunnan Province, sometime during the period 1990-92,

and was later beaten to death with a stick, according to an unofficial church source. The report has not yet been confirmed, nor is the precise date of the incident known. The source also reported that on a total of 74 occasions during the period in question, house church congregants in the county's Nagu, Yulu and Jiache townships were arrested by the police without warrants, then tied up, beaten with clubs and electric batons and heavily fined. In addition, the detainees' homes were searched and items of personal property, such as sewing machines and tape recorders, were confiscated. Moreover, local security authorities reportedly offered a bounty for the seizure, dead or alive, of **Wang Jiashui,** a local church pastor, and **He Chengzhou,** an evangelist. No further information on the various cases is currently available.

. . . . [DEAD?] [2 X ? YRS]

■ **LAI Manping** - see p.2

. . . . [DEAD]

■ **LIU Qinglin,** a traveling house-church evangelist from Zalantun, Inner Mongolia, who was administratively sentenced to three years' "re-education through labor," apparently died in prison shortly after sentencing in July 1989. He was 58 years old at the time. According to an Asia Watch source, Liu was arrested in mid-July 1989 for allegedly carrying out "unbridled witch-doctor activities," which actually included healing, and was charged with responsibility for the death of a child, a charge the child's parents disputed. He was also accused of being an untrained evangelist who had no official authorization to preach. At his arrest, Liu was questioned by 47 agents from the Public Security Bureau who brought him in for a "conversation."

Liu was arrested on two previous occasions, first in August 1987 when he was jailed for 15 days to correct his "mistaken perspective," and again in 1988. Meetings of his followers were disrupted by the Public Security Bureau, bibles were confiscated and Liu's application for land on which to build a church was ignored. From the time Liu began preaching in 1984, he reportedly converted over 3,000 people and established some 20 house churches.

. . . . [DEAD]

■ **ZHANG Yunpeng** - see p.272

Sentenced

■ **CHEN Xiangyun** (CHAN Syang-Ywin; also called CHEN Chen), a 74-year-old doctor practicing in Hong Kong, was sentenced in Meixian (his native place), Guangdong Province, on December 26, 1991 to a five-year prison term. He was charged with spying. On August 23, 1991, Dr. Chen flew to Meixian with two foreign English teachers who would be teaching at a university there. He carried a portable radio as a gift for a friend, Wang. On August 31, Dr. Chen was taken into custody at the airport, reportedly by Hong Kong police. According to an Asia Watch source, a shopkeeper to whom the men had taken the radio for help in operating it turned

them in.

On January 6, 1992, in the first indications they had of his whereabouts, Dr. Chen's family received an urgent call to come visit him. Prison authorities only permitted a visit of a few seconds, enough for the family to know that Dr. Chan was extremely emaciated, had lost all his hair and had to be supported by two guards. His condition reportedly was the result of severe beatings during interrogation. In mid-June 1992, when Dr. Chen's daughter tried to visit her father, she was denied permission because she was not a resident on the mainland. By February 1993, according to family members who had been able to visit irregularly, Dr Chen's health had improved.

Dr. Chen was in prison once before. According to family reports, he was sentenced to a 15-year term after the Korean War for being an intellectual and a Christian. He escaped to Hong Kong after serving eleven years. Mr. Wang reportedly was also arrested but nothing further is known about his case.

. . . . [5 YRS]

■ **CHEN Zhuman,** a 50-year-old peasant from Putian County, Fujian Province, was administratively sentenced in July 1992 to three years' "re-education through labor" for having "illegally" joined a local group of the New Testament Church in 1980 and communicating with its overseas members. Arrested on December 14, 1991, Chen was held at the Putian County Detention Center where, according to Amnesty International

(ASA 17/55/92), he was tortured and beaten during interrogation and left hanging upside down in a window frame for an extended period of time. Chen was later transferred to a prison in Quanzhou City, but the physical abuse continued. As a result of the repeated beatings by guards and other inmates, Chen has suffered a severe loss of hearing and his hands shake uncontrollably.

. . . . [3 YRS]

■ **LI Jiayao,** a shop owner and house church leader from Guangzhou City, born October 12, 1959, was administratively sentenced to three years' re-education through labor on May 23, 1992 for distributing Bibles and other unauthorized religious materials sent from overseas. On September 17, 1991, Li's van was intercepted by Public Security Bureau officials as he was driving along a Guangzhou street. Although no incriminating materials were found, Li was taken by the police to a local detention center. The following day, 50 police officers searched his home and confiscated 30 religious books along with Bibles, teaching materials, training tapes and personal belongings. Li's family was not notified of his detention until May 5, 1992, presumably after he had been charged. They were finally allowed to see him later the same month. Li is now doing hard labor at Chek Li Prison in Huanghua, western Guangzhou.

. . . . [3 YRS]

■ **WANG Xincai, ZHANG Yunpeng** and five others (names

unknown) - see p.272

unknown) - see p.272

. . . . [15, 14 YRS] [5 X ? YRS]

■ **ZHANG Lezhi,** a 32-year-old tradesman; **YAN Peizhi,** a farmer, 35; and a 50-year-old farmer named **XU Zhihe,** three Shandong Province Christians who had been arrested three months earlier, were sentenced in December 1992 by the Shouguang County Court to three-year sentences of "re-education through labor." The official charges against the men cited their "illegal" peaceful religious activities and their attempts to "restore and expand" the New Testament Church, an outlawed Protestant congregation to which they belonged. The three are reportedly now being held in the Chang Le County Labor Re-education Camp (Amnesty International, *ASA 17/23/93*). Zhang Lezhi had earlier spent two years in prison for his preaching activities; Yan and Xu had previously been detained for two months for the same offense.

Zhang, from Nine Lanes Village, was taken into custody by a plainclothes policeman on September 8, 1992. On the pretext of discussing a business matter, he was led from his market stall into a waiting jeep and taken to a local police station in handcuffs. The two others were arrested the following day and all were then transferred to the Shouguang City Detention Center. Their homes were searched, and Bibles, religious publications, personal letters and cassette tapes and recorders were confiscated. For protesting his innocence, Zhang Lezhi was handcuffed, assaulted with electric batons, had nine kilogram weights (later increased to 13 kilograms) tied to his legs and then had his hands and feet chained together for a period of three consecutive months. The chain was so short that he was bent over continuously at a 180° angle. In this position, Zhang was subjected to repeated beatings. When cold weather set in, he asked to be unchained so that he could put on additional clothing, but permission was denied. After sentencing, Zhang, Yan Peizhi and Xu Zhihe continued to suffer abuse from "common criminals" and were reportedly assigned the most onerous types of work by the authorities.

Five other members of the New Testament Church, from villages in Shouguang County, Shandong Province were also arrested in September 1992 but then released after periods of one to three months. They are **ZHENG Yulian**, Yan's 23-year-old wife; Xu's wife, **GUO Ruiping**; **ZHU Zizheng**, 30, a farmer; and **HU Jinting**, a 38-year-old farmer. All five were ill-treated in detention. Zhu Zizheng was reportedly forced to sit for an entire day on a so-called security chair *(anquan yi)*, a special seat fitted with spikes, and while on the chair he was beaten and had food forced into his mouth.

. . . . [3 X 3 YRS]

■ **ZHANG Ruiyu**, a 54-year-old teacher at the Physical Education Academy in Xianyu County, Fujian Province, and a house church member, reportedly was badly hurt on May 31, 1990 when Public Security Bureau officers raided her home and confiscated Bibles and religious literature. She was burned in the face with electric batons and beaten so badly that several of her teeth were broken. From then until her arrest on August 25, 1990, she reportedly was repeatedly harassed and beaten by Public Security Bureau officers. Held incommunicado, Zhang was finally charged on March 27, 1991 with "counterrevolutionary propaganda and incitement" and tried on April 9 and 10 for "holding illegal meetings, distributing seditious propaganda through cassette tapes, attacking the government and corresponding with foreigners." She was sentenced in September 1991 to a four-year term which she reportedly is serving in a women's prison in Fuzhou.

Zhang reportedly took part in the May-June 1989 demonstrations in Tiananmen Square. Her 1990 arrest was not her first. She was imprisoned twice before for a total of over seven years and was last released in 1989.

. . . . [4 YRS]

■ **ZHAO Donghai** - see p.273
. . . . [13 YRS]

■ **ZHENG Yunsu** and some 36 other leaders of the "Jesus Family" Christian sect in Duoyigou, Shandong Province, including Zheng's four sons, were arrested in May 1992 and sentenced in September to long prison terms. Zheng, the local leader, received a 12-year term which he is serving in a labor camp near Jinan, the regional capital, called the Shengjian Motor Factory. His oldest son, **ZHENG Jiping**, and his third son, **ZHENG Jikuo**, were each sentenced to nine years' imprisonment; the two others, **ZHENG X** and **ZHENG XX** (given names not known) received five-year terms. There is a possibility that one of them has since had his sentence reduced to three years. The other 31 leaders of the Jesus Family group were all administratively sentenced to three years of "labor re-education." According to an Asia Watch source, they are held in a labor camp near Duoyigou working in the coal mines. Zheng Yunsu, who is in his sixties, was also imprisoned for his religious beliefs during the Cultural Revolution.

Charges against the men included holding illegal religious gatherings, leading a "collective life," disturbing the social order, resisting arrest and beating up public security personnel. The latter charge probably referred to an attempt by a crowd of believers to prevent their church from being razed by the authorities. In June 1992, alarmed by the growth of the sect and the thousands who came to Duoyigou once a month to worship in two open courtyards, the Public Security Bureau broke up a meeting, bulldozed the church and confiscated furniture, long haired rabbits raised by the group and the cobblers' tools with which members earned a living. Government officials have admitted the razing but deny the confiscations. In addition, members of the Jesus Family, some of whom live communally, have been ordered not to participate in common meals even within a single household. As of July 1993, members of the community were continuing to suffer harassment, including being searched when they

went to worship and also sometimes having their money and goods confiscated.

[31 X 3 YRS] [2 X 5 YRS] [2 X 9 YRS] [12 YRS]

Arrested/Sentence Unknown

■ **DAI X** (given name not known), a bible distributor from Hubei Province, was arrested in June 1991. No further details are available.

■ **FAN Zhi, LENG Zhaoping, WANG Dabao, XU Hanrong, YANG Mingjen, ZENG Shaoying** and **ZHANG Guancui** were arrested in Yingshan County in August 1991 in connection with "illegal" religious activities. No further information is available about any of the detainees.

■ **MA Shuishen** - see p.45

■ **YANG Rongfu,** an Anhui Province house church member, was "arrested and taken away for no reason, with none of his family allowed to visit him," according to an Asia Watch source. No other information is available.

Restricted

■ **XIE Moshan,** now in his seventies, a well-known Protestant pastor, evangelist and author who spent 24 years in prison after 1956, was released on bail on July 23, 1992 after a second period in detention. His case remained under investigation, however, and he was placed under extremely strict surveillance. The authorities refused, pending closure of his case, to return to him money confiscated at the time of his detention, and as of October 1993 they had not returned his identity papers. According to one account, Xie was told to report to the Public Security Bureau each time he left home, even "when going out to buy vegetables," and he was prohibited from engaging in any religious activities. Another report indicated that he was forbidden to leave Shanghai and was required to report every Saturday from 9 to 11 A.M. to the security office of his local street committee.

Xie was seized on April 24, 1992 by two plainclothes Public Security officers while returning home by train to Shanghai from Guangzhou. His sister's home was searched four days later. Taken first to the Qingan branch of the Public Security Bureau and then to the Guangzhou Detention Center, Xie was searched and placed under administrative detention, the 8,700 *yuan* that he was carrying was confiscated by the police, and he was interrogated about why he was preaching outside his "home region" without permission. Officers wanted to know where he had been since his previous detention, which lasted from October 10, 1985 until October 1, 1986. They demanded to know what he was doing in Guangzhou, what his relationship was with "a certain foreign friend," and why he was carrying so much money; Xie explained that he intended to buy a tape recorder.

On May 2, the Shanghai PSB took

over Xie's case, escorted him back to that city and placed him in the Jing'an Detention Center. He was interrogated over matters including the printing of religious books in Fujian and Zhejiang provinces, and about baptisms and ordinations of elders and deacons that had recently been carried out on Hainan Island. On May 3, Xie was formally arrested and charged with "illegal itinerant evangelism" and "[committing offenses while] roaming around from place to place" (*liucuan huodong* - a term usually applied to itinerant robbers and swindlers). His family was notified of the arrest on May 8. Xie's first imprisonment, between 1956 and 1980, was on account of his refusal to join the (official Protestant) Three-Self Patriotic Movement.

3. Traditional Religious Sects

Peasant-based religious sects and mystical societies represent one of the most ancient and enduring aspects of Chinese cultural tradition. Proscribed by the Communist Party in 1949 as "reactionary" and "counterrevolutionary," the sects were driven completely underground during the 1950s and were believed, by the early 1980s, to have become virtually extinct. The loosening of Party control over the countryside that accompanied Deng Xiaoping's economic reforms breathed new life into the tradition, however, and by 1985 (according to the authorities), traditional or neo-traditional sects had reemerged "in every region and province of China with the exception of Tibet." This dramatic upsurge in sectarian activity has apparently continued to the present day, despite a severe and sustained government crackdown. Under a September 1983 amendment to the Criminal Law, the crime of "organizing and using a reactionary sect or secret society [fandong hui-daomen] for counterrevolutionary purposes" is punishable by death. On average, the typical sentencing range for traditional religious sect leaders in China lies somewhere between 10 years and life imprisonment.

Most of the following cases were found in two officially published sources. The first is a confidential Chinese government report, **Fandong Hui-Dao-Men Jianjie (An Introduction to the Reactionary Sects and Societies)**, compiled by the No.1 Bureau of the Ministry of Public Security and published by Qunzhong Chubanshe (Beijing: Masses Publishing House) in 1985. The report is marked: "Restricted Circulation: Public Security Organs Only" (Gong'an jiguan neibu faxing). Full translations of this document and numerous other case reports, together with an explanatory introduction, can be found in **Syncretic Sects and Secret Societies: Revival in the 1980s** (published in the quarterly journal Chinese Sociology and Anthropology, M.E. Sharpe, Armonk NY, Summer 1989; guest editor Robin Munro/Asia Watch). Page references to case reports in the English volume appear below as "SS p.(?)". The second main source is **Criminal Case-Studies Series (Vol.1: Crimes of Counterrevolution)**: see note on p.276, below. In the latter, the official editor censored most of the prisoners' middle names; these are denoted below by asterisks. Page references to case reports in the Chinese volume appear below as "CCS p.(?)". For further information on China's religious-sectarian tradition, see "Symposium: Syncretic Sects in Chinese society" (Parts 1 and 2), in **Modern China**, July and October 1982; and **The Flying Phoenix: Aspects of Chinese Sectarianism in Taiwan**, David K. Jordan and Daniel L. Overmyer (Princeton University Press, 1986). For a list of currently proscribed "reactionary sects" in China, see below, p.269.

Executed

■ **CAO Xiuhua**, 40, female, a native of Anqiu County, Shandong Province and leader of the *Qing Hua Sheng Jiao (Flowery Blue Saints)* sect, was arrested in August 1988 together with many of her followers. Although no allegations of violence were made against her, Cao was later sentenced to death on charges of "organizing and using a reactionary secret sect or society for counterrevolutionary purposes." According to the *1989 Shandong Yearbook,* Cao, a peasant, began her activities in 1982, when she proclaimed herself to be the "Third Virgin Daughter of the Jade Emperor" and to have "descended into the world to cure sicknesses." From then until the time of her arrest, she recruited almost 400 new followers into the sect and produced more than 5000 sectarian pamphlets. On August 1, 1988, she sent members to Beijing, Shenyang, Qingdao and Yantai to distribute the pamphlets, in readiness for the sect's proclamation (at 3:00 AM on August 8) of the founding of a "Saintly Dynasty." A nationwide manhunt was launched by the Ministry of Public Security after two sect members were intercepted carrying quantities of sectarian literature, and within two weeks the sect had been smashed. Other detained members (names unknown), including "Party, government and enterprise cadres and retired PLA officials, were all reportedly "punished by law," but none of the sentences were reported.
. . . . [EXECUTED]

■ **HU * ming, LIU * lin, SHEN * shu** and **ZHOU * zong**, all peasants aged between 46 and 65, were sentenced to death and executed, probably in 1983, for "organizing a reactionary sect or secret society for counterrevolutionary purposes." A fifth defendant, **PEI * lin**, who would now be 74, was sentenced to death with a two-year reprieve; it is not known if the sentence was commuted (to life imprisonment) after the probationary period. All five had already spent periods of between four and 20 years' imprisonment after 1953 on account of their membership in the *Yi Guan Dao (Way of Unity)* sect. After their release, from March 1980 onwards they secretly revived the proscribed sect's activities, recruiting more than 190 former members and publishing and distributing dozens of sectarian religious tracts. A restricted-circulation *(neibu)* official account of the case contained no indication that any of the defendants had either used or advocated violence. According to the account, a further 45 sect members (unnamed) received sentences of fixed-term imprisonment. The official account (CCS p.172) censored the prisoners' middle names and also the location of the alleged activities.
[DEATH W/REPRIEVE] [4 X EXECUTED]

■ **HUANG * ping, CUI * li, ZHAO * Tian, ZHAO * hong, LOU * rong** and **ZHOU * ling**, all peasants except for Cui (a brigade Party secretary) and Zhao * hong (a factory worker), were convicted in the early 1980s of "organizing a reactionary sect or secret society for counterrevolutionary

purposes." Huang was sentenced to death and executed; Cui and Zhao * tian were sentenced to death with a two-year reprieve (final outcome unknown); and the other three received fixed-term prison sentences. According to the authorities, Huang * ping, who had served a 15-year prison term after 1957 for membership of the *Tian Hua Dao (Way of Celestial Flowers)* sect, was released from prison in February 1980 and immediately resumed her sectarian activities by organizing a new branch of the *Tian Hua Dao*. To avoid rearrest, she named it the "World General Knowledge and Peace Society" and appointed herself as "First Secretary." Cui, however, was appointed as the sect's "Minister of Politics" and "State President," Zhao * hong was appointed as "Chief Delegate," Zhao * tian as "Minister of Defense," Lou as "Foreign Minister" and Zhou as "Minister of Public Security." The group recruited more than 100 members in seven villages across two communes. The official account (CCS p.178) censored the prisoners' middle names and also the location of the alleged activities.
[EXECUTED] [2 X DEATH W/REPRIEVE] [3 X ? YRS]

■ **LUO, WEI** and **SUN,** (given names not known), leaders of the *Yi Guan Dao (Way of Unity)* sect, were arrested in either Hunan or Hubei provinces sometime in the early 1980s on charges of "organizing and using a reactionary sect or secret society for counterrevolutionary purposes." Together with three other sect members, **LI¹, DING** and **LI²** (also

charged with "counterrevolution"-given names not known), they were tried and convicted sometime after September 1983. Although the sentences are not known, it is probable that all six sectarians were subsequently sentenced to death and executed.

According to an official report: "After Liberation, three former die-hards of the *Yi Guan Dao* named Luo, Wei and Sun were sentenced to terms of imprisonment for their crimes. Released after completion of sentence, they failed to repent their ways, and in the latter part of the 'Cultural Revolution' they once again began liaising together and scheming in secret to revive the counterrevolutionary activities of the *Yi Guan Dao*. Titling themselves as 'Ancients', 'Altar Chiefs' and so forth, they put forward the slogan: 'Grasp the key link, and rule through Buddha' *(zhua gang zhi fo)*. In addition, they planned to set up a 'Heavenly Appeal Center', an 'Administrative Law Court' and other reactionary organs.

"Collecting together all kinds of remnant *Yi Guan Dao* charts and certificates, and carrying these with them, they split up and roamed around nine different counties in Hubei and Hunan provinces, making secret contact and liaisons with former members of the *Yi Guan Dao*. They recruited more than 100 people altogether and appointed a total of 18 die-hard elements as Initiators and Deputy Ancients; they also collected, reproduced and circulated more than 30 different reactionary sectarian tracts, including the 'Cloth Bag Sutra' and the 'Maternal Edict'.

"Three men, named Li, Ding and Li, who had been made 'Deputy Ancients' and 'Initiators' of the sect, played an enthusiastic role in the counter-revolutionary activities led by Luo, Wei and Sun. They helped draft and revise such documents as the 'Great Oath and Confession' and the 'Red Sun's Cycle of Change'. Moreover, they followed Luo, Wei and Sun on a tour of the villages of Hubei and Hunan, preaching and disseminating the teachings of the *Yi Guan Dao,* and holding special initiation ceremonies for the new recruits, such as 'receiving the mandate', 'reviving the mandate' and 'taking the oath'.

"In the course of their sermons, Luo, Wei and Sun openly and publicly proclaimed: 'We must take down the Banner of the Proletariat and establish the Dharma-Dynasty of the Limitless Buddha'. Said they: 'We must comfort and pacify the new lands, and rectify the old rivers and mountains'. Also, they concocted and spread a number of rumors, inciting the masses to oppose the Party's policies, and engendering among people hostile sentiments towards the people's government. Everywhere they went, they created panic and alarm, seriously disrupting the daily lives and productive activities of the masses, and gravely threatening public order and stability.

"Luo, Wei and Sun were all remnant elements of the reactionary sects and societies who had failed to reform themselves properly through labor [i.e. during imprisonment]. Upon completing their sentences and securing their release, they continued to collude together in organizing and expanding their sectarian activities...The chief culprits in this case, they clamored and trumpeted for a restoration of the old social order, and seriously endangered the public peace. The three others, Li, Ding and Li, were active participants in the sect's criminal undertakings, and they became die-hard elements. They should all, therefore, in accordance with the criteria laid down in the [September 2, 1983] *Decision of the Standing Committee of the National People's Congress Regarding the Severe Punishment of Criminal Elements Who Seriously Endanger Public Security,* be convicted on charges of 'organizing a sect or society to carry out counter-revolutionary activities', and they may all be given punishments above the maximum level specified in the Criminal Law, up to and including imposition of the death penalty, in accordance with Article 1, Paragraph 5 of the *Decision.*" (SS p.97).

. . . . [6 X EXECUTED?]

■ **WANG * zhi, SUN * tang** now (if still alive) in his eighties, and **KONG * lin** (female), now in her forties, all peasants, were convicted in the late 1970s or early 1980s of "organizing a reactionary sect or secret society for counterrevolutionary purposes." Wang was sentenced to death and executed; the other two defendants were sentenced to unknown terms of imprisonment. According to the authorities, Wang, a follower from the 1960s onwards of *Yi Guan Dao (Way of Unity)* sect leader **Kong * zhu** (now deceased), in 1970 secretly established a new sect called the *Tian Bing Dizi Jun (Fraternal Army of the Soldiers of Heaven)*. After 1978, he and Sun recruited no less than 1,148 members into the sect, making this the largest case of officially-suppressed traditional Chinese sectarian activity so far monitored by Asia Watch.

An official account of the case, moreover, described the sect's religious beliefs and practices in such detail, particularly in references to the sect's adherence to the quasi-Buddhist notion of an imminent "Cataclysm of the Third Era" *(sanqi mojie)*, according to which the "world of illusion" will end after three cosmic *kalpas* - as if to make it clear the sect belonged firmly to the mainstream tradition of Chinese popular religious cults, a tradition extending back to approximately the sixth century AD. The official account contained no allegations or indications that the sect's leaders or members had ever engaged in or advocated violence. Allegedly, however, the sect "vilified Chinese Communist Party [members] as being 'devil people' *(moxing ren)* and viciously attacked the socialist system as being a 'realm of evil devils' *(wu mo shi)'*." The official account (CCS p.179) censored the prisoners' middle names and also the location of the alleged activities.

. . . . [EXECUTED] [2 X ? YRS]

Sentenced

■ **CHE** * **lun** (female), original name Wang * qin, a peasant, was sentenced to an unknown term of imprisonment, probably in 1982, on charges of "organizing a reactionary

sect or secret society for counter-revolutionary purposes." According to the authorities, Che joined the *Yi Shan Tang (One Benevolence Hall)* sect in the 1940s and was appointed as an Initiator *(dianchuanshi)* and as the sect's "Seventh Immortal Lady" *(Qi Xian Nü)*. In 1947, she established the *Guan Zhong Altar* branch, recruiting 350 members and appointing more than 40 new Altar Chiefs *(tanzhu)* and Initiators. After 1949, Che evaded the government's crackdown on traditional sects by changing her name, concealing her past and moving to a different county; eventually, she even secured "preferential treatment" (in land allocation, social welfare, etc.). from the government. Her past activities were finally uncovered by the government in 1981, after she secretly organized a branch of the *Xian Tian Dao (Way of the Prior Realm)* sect and recruited 105 members. The new group then "produced and distributed copies of the 'Water Sutra', the 'Five Impartialities Sutra' and other such reactionary texts, and made numerous [clandestine] speaking tours in which they attacked the Party's line and policies, thereby seriously disrupting production and disturbing the public order." The official account (CCS p.178) censored the prisoner's middle name and also the location of the alleged activities.

. . . . [? YRS]

■ **CHEN Ziran**, a leader of the *Pu Hua Men (Gate of Universal Change)*, was arrested in Jiujiang County, Jiangxi Province in the early 1980s. It is not known what sentence he received.

According to an official report, "Chen frequently instructed his disciples to post off reactionary letters to the Party Central Committee and to leading comrades of the provincial central committee. These letters slandered and vilified the socialist system by declaring: 'Things nowadays are worse than what they were under the KMT.' They uttered the profanity: 'Marx, Engels, Lenin and Stalin wrote reactionary works - they pulled the wool over the eyes of the Chinese people' (SS p.62).

. . . . [? YRS]

■   **CHENG Dingguo**, 70, Altar Chief *(tan zhu)* of a large branch of the *Lao Jun Dao (Way of the Old Master)* sect based in Luotian County, western Hubei Province, was arrested on January 15, 1989 together with **XU Yuanjie**, 72, a Palace General *(zhengdian jiangjun)* of the sect and **CHENG Guomin**, 56, a recent recruit. According to the *1990 Hubei Yearbook,* prior to their arrests, Cheng Dingguo and Xu Yuanjie, who had been sentenced in 1952 to 15 years' imprisonment for "reactionary sectarian activities," developed the sect's membership "across six counties and 13 townships, setting up 45 Main Altars and other centers of sect activity and compiling more than 20 different sectarian sutras, which they mimeographed and distributed."

Moreover, "Under the cloak of 'freedom of religious belief'...and by providing free medical services to the public and spouting such nonsense as 'by joining the sect one can avoid calamity' and 'after death one will ascend to heaven', they managed to recruit more than 2,400 members to the sect...and appointed 255 diehard sect members to such posts as 'Sage of the Transmigrations', 'Immortal Protector of the Dharma' and 'Saintly Inspirer of Benevolence'." According to the authorities, the sect "vainly conspired to overthrow the Chinese Communist Party and subvert the socialist system" and "establish the *Lao Jun Dao's* 'Buddhist Republic'." Altogether 19 other "diehard members" of the sect were arrested (names unknown) and 2,500 copies of sectarian sutras were seized. The fate of the three principal detainees is not known, but they could all have received the death penalty.

. . . . [3 X ? YRS/DP?]

■   **FAN Youjiang**, a leader of the *Pu Hua Men (Universal Transmigration Sect),* was arrested in Qichun County, Hubei Province in the early 1980s. It is not known what sentence he received. According to an official report, "Fan appointed his own son as 'Emperor', and then elevated his other followers to the position of 'Commanding Officer', 'General of the First Route Army', 'General of the Second Route Army', and so forth. He clamored: 'When the Emperor ascends the throne, the nation will be ours', and he coerced his disciples into taking the vow: 'We swear that once the Emperor is in power we will follow him always, never wavering in our allegiance'" (SS p.67).

. . . . [? YRS]

■   **FU Guomin**, a leader of the *Yi Guan Dao (Way of Unity)* sect, was arrested in Kunming, Yunnan Province in the early 1980s. It is not known what sentence he received. According to an official report, "After cracking the case, the authorities uncovered more than 1,160 copies of 328 different tracts and leaflets. Sect leader Fu Guomin had written and compiled documents entitled 'Why Choose the Way?', 'How to Cultivate the Way' and 'What are the Three Trials by Fire?' (SS p.76).

. . . . [? YRS]

■ **GAN Qixiang**, a leader of the *Tong Shan She (Society of Communal Benevolence)* sect, was arrested in the Zhenlong Commune of Xinyi County, Guangdong Province in the early 1980s. It is not known what sentence he received. According to an official report, "A 24-year-old woman named Liu Xiulin, an upper-middle school graduate and a commune member...felt depressed and dispirited as a result of a failed love affair. Gan Qixiang...came to see her and said: 'Join our society and practice self-cultivation, for through self-cultivation you will be able to develop virtue. That way, when you die your soul will go straight to heaven, and you won't have to worry about being sent to hell.' In addition, Gan raved to her that she should 'get betrothed to a spirit', and in this way he cajoled her into joining the sect" (SS p.58).

. . . . [? YRS]

■ **GONG Daqian**, an Ancient *(qianren)* in the *Yi Guan Dao (Way of Unity)* sect, was arrested in Kunming in 1982. It is not known what sentence he

received. According to an official report, "Out of a total of 93 people who had participated in the sect's activities, two were 'Ancients', 36 were 'Initiators', 20 were 'Altar Chiefs' and 26 were former disciples, amounting to 84 persons, or more than 90 percent of the overall membership" (SS p.52).

. . . . [? YRS]

■ **HE Xunzhen** and 12 other "leaders and diehard elements" of the *Xian Tian Dao (Way of the Prior Realm)* sect were arrested in August 1988 in Suichuan County, Jiangxi Province, together with "100 copies of reactionary sutras, several hundred items of sect paraphernalia, a variety of different charts and manuscripts and a quantity of ill-gotten cash, grain and tea-oil." It is not known what sentences He and the others received. According to an official press account, "The reactionary *Xian Tian Dao* has historical roots in Suichuan County reaching back almost a hundred years. The county was the site of the main lodge in Jiangxi Province of the sect's 'universal transmigration' school *(pu du pai)*. After Liberation, the people's government banned and eradicated this reactionary sectarian organization and dismantled its centers of activity. Since 1980, however, the sect has once again been recruiting new members, concocting rumors to disturb the masses, slandering China's present policies and committing other such crimes. Its scope of activities had grown to encompass 13 different temples altogether, spread across 11 of the townships in Suichuan county

including Caolin, Xixi and Nanjiang"
(*Fazhi Ribao*, August 27, 1988; in SS
p.31).

. . . . [13 X ? YRS]

■ **HUANG * cheng**, formerly a
peasant, now in his early seventies, was
sentenced to an unknown term of
imprisonment, probably in late 1983,
on charges of "organizing a reactionary
sect or secret society." According to
the authorities, Huang had been
sentenced in 1961 to an 18-year prison
term for being a leader of the *Zongjiao
Zhexue Yanjiu She (Religious
Philosophy Research Society)* sect.
After his release in 1979, he
immediately resumed his sectarian
activities, travelling around widely and
recruiting old former sect members,
especially two named **XIONG *** and
HUANG * lin (described only as "tried
separately," sentences unknown).
Among the "offenses" Huang allegedly
committed was to teach sect members
how to meditate *(da zuo)* and to give
lectures about a document known as the
"Heavenly Chart Sutra." The official
account (CCS p.188) censored the
prisoner's middle name and also the
location of the alleged activities.

. . . . [? YRS]

■ **JIANG Qianguo**, a resident of
Yueyang Municipality, Hunan
Province, and a Buddhist sectarian, was
sentenced after June 1989 on charges of
"using a reactionary secret sect or
society" *(fandong hui-dao-men)* to carry
out "counterrevolutionary activities,"
according to an Asia Watch source.
The charges related to his membership
of a Buddhist sectarian group and to his

involvement in the May-June 1989 pro-
democracy protest movement,
described by the authorities as
"participating in the turmoil." It is not
known what sentence Jiang received.

. . . . [? YRS]

■ **JIANG * wu, WANG * xiu,
WANG * yuan, WANG * qing**[1] and
SONG * you, all formerly peasants
and now, if still alive, in their eighties
or nineties, were sentenced to unknown
term of imprisonment, probably in late
1985. According to the authorities,
Jiang * wu in 1941 joined a Wutaishan-
based sect known as the *Xiang Shan Pu
Hua Fojiao Hui (Pro-Benevolence
Universal Change Buddhist Society)* -
another name for the *Jiu Gong Dao
(Way of Nine Palaces)* sect. Between
early 1983 and April 1985, he resumed
his sectarian activities, recruiting a total
of 10 new members and preaching
close observance of the traditional rites
and rituals of the *Jiu Gong Dao*.
Central to the sect's belief-system was
a conviction that the Buddha Maitreya
(Mi Le Fo) - the "Buddha of the Future
Era" - was about to descend to earth.
This was denounced by the authorities
as representing a "vicious attack on the
socialist system" and an attempt to
"place Buddha's law above the law of
the land." The official account (CCS
p.191) censored the prisoners' middle
names and also the location of the
alleged activities.

. . . . [5 X ? YRS]

■ **LI Chungfu** (Chongfu), the
61-year-old head of an alleged
"counterrevolutionary clique," was
arrested in April 1992 in Henan

Province by police and para-military troops together with 16 members of his organization (*Reuters*, November 2, 1992). According to an official Chinese magazine account (*Democracy and Law*, December 1991), Li, a peasant, had been planning for the past two years to overthrow the Communist Party and establish "a new imperial dynasty" with himself as emperor. Officials quoted in the magazine said that the existence of such a clique, which extended across two counties and included Communist Party officials, emphasized the need for constant vigilance.

. . . . [17 X ? YRS]

■ **LI Defeng**, a resident of Yueyang Municipality, Hunan Province, and a Buddhist sectarian, was sentenced after June 1989 on charges of "using a reactionary secret sect or society" (*fandong hui-dao-men*) to carry out "counterrevolutionary activities," according to an Asia Watch source. The charges related to his membership of a Buddhist sectarian group and to his involvement in the May-June 1989 pro-democracy protest movement, described by the authorities as "participating in the turmoil." It is not known what sentence Li received.

. . . . [? YRS]

■ **LI Huafang**, a leader of the *Ji Tan* (*Altar of Spirit-Writing*) sect, was arrested in Suichuan County, Jiangxi Province in the early 1980s. It is not known what sentence he received. According to an official report, "Li and other leaders of the sect collected more than 22,600 yuan from the masses in order to build and repair temples" (SS p.74).

. . . . [? YRS]

■ **LI Qiusheng**, a sect leader in Handan District, Hebei Province, was arrested in 1987. It is not known what sentence he received. According to an official press report, "Li and his cohorts, from 1979 onwards, managed to collect a total of more than 20,000 yuan in various sect fees and ceremonial contributions (*xie chang fei*)" The account continued, "Since 1983, [the district public security organs] have uncovered a total of 69 cases of sect and society revivalism. One 'emperor' has been ferreted out; 631 sect leaders engaged in active sabotage have been exposed; and 92 reactionary sect leaders and die-hard elements have been dealt with and punished....In the guise of engaging in commerce and trade, they carried out illicit liaison activities, disseminated the teachings of their sects and spread reactionary rumors. They held a total of 100 'emperor ceremonies' (*kai huang chang*), enlisted and appointed more than 1,500 sect leaders and initiated more than 5,200 ordinary disciples" (Hong Kong *Wen Hui Bao*, October 7, 1987; in SS p.27).

. . . . [? YRS]

■ **LI * shan**, now in his late sixties, and **LI * pu**, now in his fifties, both peasants, were sentenced to unknown terms of imprisonment sometime in the late 1970s or early 1980s on charges of "organizing a reactionary sect or secret society for counterrevolutionary purposes." According to the authorities, in 1949 both men joined the *Ren Xue Hao Dao (Way of Emulating Goodness)* sect, which was banned by the government in 1952. In 1972, the two set up a new branch of the sect, recruiting 15 members and preaching that "In 1984 *(Jiazi Nian)* a True Lord will appear in * City and establish a new dynasty." The two Lis also allegedly "slandered top Party leaders and attacked the government's birth-control policy." The official account (CCS p.182) censored the prisoners' middle names and also the location of the alleged activities.

. . . . [2 X ? YRS]

■ **LI Shufen** and three other leaders of the *Yi Guan Dao (Way of Unity)* sect were apparently seized in Yunnan Province in 1981 while on the run from the authorities. It is not known what sentences they received. According to an official report, "In April 1981 in Puning County, Yunnan, 'Initiator' Li Shufen of the *Yi Guan Dao* absconded from justice in an attempt to avoid punishment for his crimes. On hearing of this, two other 'Initiators' of the *Yi Guan Dao* in Kunming, named **ZHANG Shuying** and **ZHANG Caixian**, immediately procured for Criminal Li 20 yuan in cash and ration coupons for more than 400 catties of grain. Later on, in April and May of 1983, Zhang Caixian and others schemed to find work for **SU Ruying**, another *Yi Guan Dao* leader who was on the run, and arranged a hiding-place for him" (SS p.64).

. . . . [4 X ? YRS]

■ **LI Shuming**, a leader of the *Zhong*

Dao (Middle Way) sect, was arrested in Shaanxi Province in 1982. It is not known what sentence Li received. According to an official report, "Of the 38 principal members of this sect, 30 were found to be of 'Initiator' rank or above, and there were three 'Altar Chiefs'. All were time-served criminals who had either been released from prison already or else retained after completion of their sentences as labor-camp employees *(xingman liuchang jiuye)*" [The reference to "time-served criminals" almost certainly means that they had spent long periods in jail after 1949 on account of their sectarian activities. "Retained for employment" is a euphemism for the widely used practice in China of forcing time-served prisoners to remain as "workers" in the prison factory after completion of their sentences] (SS p.51).

. . . . [? YRS]

■ **LIAO Zhen'an**, described as a "reactionary sect leader," was listed in an official report of 1985 as "presently serving a prison sentence." It is not known what sentence Liao received or whether he is currently still in jail (SS p.83).

. . . . [? YRS]

■ **LIU * ying**, now 74, **LI * xin**, now 48, and **ZHENG * xin**, all peasants, were sentenced to unknown terms of imprisonment on charges of "organizing a reactionary sect or secret society for counterrevolutionary purposes," probably in 1984. According to the authorities, in 1973 the defendants joined a branch of the *Gui Yi Dao (Way of Returning to*

Unity) sect headed by **LIU** * **ting** (a former leader of the sect who was imprisoned for four years in the 1950s and who reportedly "died of illness in 1984" at the age of 81). Subsequently, the sect renamed itself as a branch of the *Tian Xian Dao (Way of Celestial Immortals)*. Over a 10-year period, the defendants recruited a total of 1,061 members in more than 40 villages across three counties, municipalities and districts. They convened more than 200 secret meetings of sect leaders, and allegedly made such statements as "The Chinese Communist Party is about to collapse, and it will then be time for a change of dynasty" and "When the final cataclysm comes, there will be mountains of corpses and bones and rivers of blood will flow." In addition, the group printed and distributed dozens of sectarian sutras and admonitory texts. The official account (CCS p.182) censored the prisoners' middle names and also the location of the alleged activities.

. . . . [3 X ? YRS]

■ **LU** * **gang**, **XIA** * **lan**, **LU** * **sen**, **LU** * **yi** and **LU** * **rui**, all peasants, were sentenced to unknown terms of imprisonment, probably in 1985 or 1986, on charges of "organizing a reactionary sect or secret society for counterrevolutionary purposes." According to the authorities, from 1983 onwards Lu * gang "enthusiastically carried out a restoration of the counter-revolutionary activities of the *Sheng Xian Dao (Way of Saints and Immortals)* sect. He and Xia undertook so-called "national and military inspection tours" around more than 10

townships and cities in two different provinces, preaching that "A world war will break out in 1986 or 1987 and half the world's population will die...after which the Lu family will ascend the throne." Lu * gang himself reportedly anticipated becoming "emperor" by the time he reached the age of 45. The official account (CCS p.183) censored the prisoners' middle names and also the location of the alleged activities.

. . . . [5 X ? YRS]

■ **LU Yongting**, an Initiator *(dianchuanshi)* in the *Guan Yin Fo Jiao (Buddhist Sect of the Goddess of Mercy)*, was arrested in Tanghe County, Henan Province in the early 1980s. It is not known what sentence he received. Allegations of a quasi-criminal nature, but still relating to free speech activities, were levelled against Lu. According to an official report, "Lu frequently posed as a spirit in order to treat the sick. When a male child was born to the family of sect member Wang Deyou, but fell ill six days later, Lu spouted nonsense about how the child would 'never survive to adulthood'. The credulous Wang failed to seek medical help for his new-born infant, with the result that it died some days later" (SS p.70).

. . . . [? YRS]

■ **LU Yunliang**, a sect leader, was arrested in Shangshui County, Henan Province in 1980. It is not known what sentence he received. According to an official report, "Lu installed himself as a 'Monarch', and then appointed both a 'State Empress' and a 'Supreme Commander of the Troops', in an attempt to restore the so-called 'Eastern Ming Kingdom'. In 1980, Lu and three of his cohorts went scurrying off to Beijing, to conduct an 'astrological inspection' in Tiananmen Square. They declared: 'Heaven's Moment *(tian shi)* is not yet ripe', adding that when the time came, they would 'enter the court and take over the throne'" (SS p.66).

. . . . [? YRS]

■ **LÜ * qin**, formerly a peasant, and **WANG * fan**, formerly a cadre in a materials supply company, both female and now in their sixties, and **WU * lin**, formerly a peasant, now in his forties, and **WANG * qing²**, formerly a retired Public Security Bureau cadre, now in his late sixties, were all sentenced to unknown terms of imprisonment sometime in the early 1980s, on charges of "using feudal superstition and organizing a reactionary sect or secret society for counterrevolutionary purposes." In 1968, the group became disciples of **Shi * ming** (died in 1980) a leader of the *Jiu Gong Dao (Way of Nine Palaces)* sect. They were taught by another sect leader, **Liu * feng** (also died in 1980) that a new historical era was about to begin, marked by "the advent of the White Dragon," and that the sect would magically "transport the soul of [sect member] Wang * an into the body of Deng **" [presumably, a reference to Chinese leader Deng Xiaoping.] In addition, the sect "carried out counterrevolutionary propaganda by frantically proclaiming that 'the Three Suns control the truth and the 10,000 faiths will fuse into one" [a reference to the ecumenical, "unitarian" faith of the traditional

sects.] The official account (CCS p.195) censored the prisoners' middle names and also the location of the alleged activities.

. . . . [4 X ? YRS]

■ **PAN Lianxiang**, a leader of the *Wan Quan Dao (Way of Myriad Fullnesses)*, was arrested in Zunyi County, Guizhou Province in the early 1980s. It is not known what sentence Pan received. According to an official report, "The sect wheedled more than 7,000 yuan and 14,400 catties of grain from people for the construction and repair of temples. On one occasion, they convened a 'Goddess of Mercy Meeting' that lasted for seven days and nights, presided over by specially invited Daoist priests. Each participating family had to contribute either two yuan or five catties of grain, and the total amount came to over 1,000 yuan and 7,000 catties of grain. There was extensive banqueting and drinking, resulting in a profligate misuse of resources. In addition, the sect's leader, Pan Lianxiang, wanted to build himself a stone mausoleum, so he got more than ten artisans to work on the project for nearly a two-month period, squandering in all more than 1,200 yuan and 1,200 catties of grain" (SS p.70).

. . . . [? YRS]

■ **TANG Tianxu**, a leader of the *Zhong Yong Dao (Way of the Golden Mean)* sect, was arrested in Kaijiang County, Sichuan Province in 1981. It is not known what sentence Tang received. According to an official report, "In June 1981, Tang convened a so-called 'Thunder Patriarch Assembly'. Binding together more than 10,000 sticks of incense, he created one great stick of 'heavenly incense', measuring four meters in length and four inches in diameter. Inciting more than 500 people from the areas of Kaijiang and Wanxian to gather around and watch, Tang flagrantly proclaimed: 'The sixty years of the *Jia Zi* cycle have now been fulfilled. There will be a great world war, and an emperor will emerge, a truly mandated Son of Heaven who shall ascend the throne'" (SS p.61).

. . . . [? YRS]

■ **WAN Yansheng**, from Hubei Province, and **ZONG Rongkun**, from either Hubei or Hunan provinces, both elderly men, were arrested in August 1988 on charges of leading the *Da Cheng Men (Mahayana Gate)* sect. It is not known what sentences they received. According to an official press report, "The order to ban and eradicate the *Da Cheng Men* was given in the 1950s. Over the past few years, however, a small number of stubborn adherents of the sect have been taking advantage of our policy of reform and opening-up in order to try to rekindle the sect from its ashes. A 69-year-old man named Wan Yansheng, from Wanjialou village in Shishou municipality, together with a 76-year-old man named Zong Rongkun, who resided in the local offices in Mount Bijia, in 1983 began to flaunt the banner of 'freedom of religious belief'. On pretexts such as 'adopting the prohibitions of vegetarianism' and 'cultivating the future life rather than

one's present existence', they conducted liaisons with a number of the sect's leaders in Shishou, Fengxian and Jinshi, and secretly recruited into the sect over 100 new members. All of this exerted an extremely bad influence among the masses." The account noted that "more than 100 sect members were ferreted out" during the crackdown (*Fazhi Ribao*, August 30, 1988; in SS p.32).

. . . . [2 X ? YRS]

■ **WANG Guixiang**, a leader of the *Sheng Dao (Way of the Saints)* sect, was arrested in the Shilin Commune of Hebi Municipality, Henan Province, probably in 1982 or 1983. It is not known what sentence Wang received. According to an official report, "A noteworthy aspect of the current wave of activity by the reactionary sects and societies is that, in order to cultivate their own 'successors', they have begun to compete with the authorities for the hearts and minds of the younger generation. Young people of around 16 and 17 years old, and even small children, are being drawn into membership of the sects....In Henan, a three-day-old infant named Zhang Junjie was inducted into the *Sheng Dao* (Way of the Saints) together with his mother (a commune member named Cui Yufen) by the sect's leader, Wang Guixiang" (SS p.53).

. . . . [? YRS]

■ **WANG Jiliang**, an Initiator in the *Fo Men (Buddha Gate)* sect, was arrested in Xiaba County, Henan Province in the early 1980s. It is not known what sentence he received.

According to an official report, "Hoping to exploit the prejudice found among certain sections of the masses in favor of male children and against female children, Wang spouted nonsensically that he was able to 'exchange the embryos' *(huan tai)*. This resulted in many commune couples failing to adopt the proper birth-control measures, and then, the woman having become pregnant, beseeching him to 'exchange the embryos'" (SS p.63).

. . . . [? YRS]

■ **WANG Wenchen**, a leader of the *Bai Yang Jiao (White Sun Sect)*, was arrested in Bayan County, Heilongjiang Province in the early 1980s. It is not known what sentence he received. According to an official report, "Wang Wenchen agitated and disturbed the masses with the rumor: 'You must all buy plenty of salt and matches, for when the Great Flood comes the roads will all be washed away, and it won't be possible to get any salt or matches brought in.' As a result of this inflammatory talk, the entire stock of edible salt and matches in the local mountainside brigade's supply-and-marketing store sold out almost immediately, and supplies of the goods to neighboring areas were also badly affected" (SS p.65).

. . . . [? YRS]

■ **WANG Xianyao**, a school teacher and a leader of the *Tian Guang Dao (Way of Celestial Light)* sect, was arrested in Heilongjiang Province sometime in the early 1980s. It is not known what sentence he received.

According to an official report, "Teacher Wang Xianyao from the Xingtong Middle School of Wanjinshan Commune in Baode County, Heilongjiang, was 32 years old and college-educated, but he ended up in the ranks of the *Tian Guang Dao*. Appointed to the post of 'Scribe' *(zhiwen)*, and serving as one of the so-called 'Ten Great Crown Princes', he soon became a die-hard element of the sect" (SS p.55).

. . . . [? YRS]

■ **WANG Yin**, a leader of the *Bai Yang Jiao (White Sun Sect)*, was arrested in Bayan County, Heilongjiang Province sometime in the early 1980s. It is not known what sentence he received. According to an official report, "Wang Yin flagrantly proclaimed: 'There will be terrible disasters over the next few years. If you believe in the Buddha you will be able to evade the Three Plagues and the Eight Misfortunes, and you'll be given a place next to Old Buddha himself. You can wear a Yellow Arm-Band, and when you die you'll go straight to heaven.' As a result of this inflammatory talk by Wang, more than a hundred people entered the ranks of the *Bai Yang Jiao*" (SS p.57).

. . . . [? YRS]

■ **WANG * hua, ZHANG * shan and LI * wen**, all formerly peasants, were sentenced to unknown terms of imprisonment on charges of "organizing a reactionary sect or secret society for counterrevolutionary purposes," probably in late 1983. According to the authorities, Wang and

Zhang, who had both joined the *Yi Guan Dao (Way of Unity)* prior to 1949, in the early 1980s "frequently staged memorial activities, such as burning paper slips and tending the grave, for He **, an arch-villain of the *Yi Guan Dao* who had been suppressed [i.e. executed] by the government." From 1981 onwards, the three men secretly revived the sect's activities, publishing and distributing a large quantity of sectarian literature and recruiting six new members. According to the authorities, "Wang * hua flagrantly proclaimed, 'I am the successor to the *Altar of Mercy and Benevolence (Ci Shan Tan)* [an old chapter of the *Yi Guan Dao*]...and I want to set a good example for all our brothers. Even if they arrest or execute me, I'll always be dedicated to the *Ci Shan Tang*'." The official account (CCS p.175) censored the prisoners' middle names and also the location of the alleged activities. If still alive, Wang and Zhang would now be in their eighties.
. . . . [3 X ? YRS]

■ **WEN Xinyuan,** a resident of Yueyang Municipality, Hunan Province, and a Buddhist sectarian, was sentenced after June 1989 on charges of "using a reactionary secret sect or society" *(fandong hui-dao-men)* to carry out "counterrevolutionary activities," according to an Asia Watch source. The charges related to his membership of a Buddhist sectarian group and to his involvement in the May-June 1989 pro-democracy protest movement, described by the authorities as "participating in the turmoil." It is not

known what sentence Wen received.
. . . . [? YRS]

■ **XI Jinxian,** leader of a branch of the *Yi Guan Dao (Way of Unity)* sect in Wuxi Municipality, Jiangsu Province, was arrested in 1987. No further details of the case are available, and it is not known what sentence Ji received. According to an official press account, "Over the past three years, [the provincial public security bureau] has dealt crushing blows against 28 different reactionary sect and society organizations. Throughout the province, altogether 237 cases involving the revival of sects and societies have been uncovered and smashed; a number of sect leaders and die-hard elements have been arrested, and several society Altars, Lodges and other bases of operation have been dismantled." The account continued: "A remorseless struggle is now being waged against these criminal activities. Wuxi Municipality has hit out against the revivalist activities of the *Yi Guan Dao* led by a man named Xi Jinxian. Tongshan County has investigated and crushed an attempted revival of the *Tai Shang Men (Gate of the Supreme Overlord)*, which extended over seven counties in the three provinces of Jiangsu, Shandong and Anhui and involved a conspiracy to carry out a counter-revolutionary revolt. Pi County has uncovered and smashed 17 cases of *Sheng Xian Dao (Way of Saints and Immortals)* revivalism. And Shuyang County has fought against the revival of the *Shen Men Dao* in its area" (*Zhongguo Fazhi Bao,* May 19, 1987; in SS p.24).

. . . . [? YRS]

■ **XIA Lihuai**, a resident of Yiyang District, Hunan Province, and a Buddhist sectarian, was sentenced after June 1989 on charges of "using a reactionary secret sect or society" *(fandong hui-dao-men)* to carry out "counterrevolutionary activities," according to an Asia Watch source. Xia's real offense was reportedly that he helped organize a memorial meeting after June 4 to commemorate the victims of the military crackdown on the pro-democracy movement. It is not known what sentence Xia received.

. . . . [? YRS]

■ **XIANG Enzhen**, a leader of the *Gui Gen Dao (Return-to-the-Root Sect)*, was arrested in the Nanzhao Commune of Zhenxiong County, Yunnan Province sometime in the early 1980s. It is not known what sentence he received. According to an official report, "Wang Zhaobi, a commune member, had a quarrel with his daughter-in-law, which later developed into a fight. On several occasions, he sought assistance from the brigade office and the courts, all to no avail. Taking advantage of the situation, a 'Supreme Navigator' *(dinghang)* in the *Gui Gen Dao,* a man named Xiang Enzhen, lured Wang into becoming a sect member and then persuaded him to leave his family and enter the Great Temple of the Arhats, so that he might observe vegetarianism and worship the Buddha" (SS p.58).

. . . . [? YRS]

■ **XUE Fuzhong**, a leader of the *Da Jiang Fo Guo (Great River Buddha Land)* sect, was arrested in Chaoyang County, Liaoning Province in the early 1980s. It is not known what sentence he received. According to an official report, "Xue instructed his cohorts to write out more than 30 reactionary leaflets, which were then posted up and distributed around Chaoyang County and Chaoyang municipality. The leaflets incited public discontent by saying: 'The common people are now being persecuted, and must unite together and place their reliance in the *Da Jiang Fo Guo.* We must struggle to redress the injustices against us, and we mustn't cease until we have driven back and defeated the officers of the Qing Dynasty's Manchu Army' (meaning: China's present Party and Government). Moreover, they vainly clamored that they would 'exploit the birth-control issue', in order to effect the overthrow of the socialist system and assist the founding of their own so-called 'Buddha Land'" (SS p.64).

. . . . [? YRS]

■ **YAN Guanbao**, a member of the *Hong San Jiao (Red Three Sect)*, was arrested in Jintan County, Jiangsu Province in the early 1980s. It is not known what sentence Yan received. According to an official report, "From 1979 onwards, Yan Guanbao hoodwinked a total of 17 different women into having illicit sex with him, all in the name of 'carrying out the *yin* assignation' *(zou yin chai)*, 'raising the ghost arrow' *(tiao gui jian)*, 'plucking the *yin* arrow' *(ba yin jian)* and 'stroking the happiness' *(mo xi)*" (SS p.72).

. . . . [? YRS]

■ **YANG Biao**, a leader of the *Yi Guan Dao (Way of Unity)* sect, was arrested in the region of Kunming, Yunnan Province in 1981. According to an official press report, "Out of 178 of the sect's disciples in the Kunming region, 116 (i.e. 65 percent of the total) were found to be former sect leaders and officials. These included seven 'Ancients' *(qianren)*, 47 'Initiators' *(dianchuanshi)*, 61 'Altar Chiefs' *(tanzhu)* and one 'Guarantor' *(yinbaoshi)*. A full 108 of them (61 percent) had been dealt with and punished by the authorities before: one person had been given a suspended sentence of death, six had received sentences of life imprisonment, 87 had been sentenced to fixed-term imprisonment and 15 to periods of criminal control *(juyi)*. Some had even joined in the sect's activities while still serving their prison sentences. The chief culprit in the case, the former 'Initiator' Yang Biao, had been arrested and sentenced three times in all since 1951, and had even had his sentence increased on one occasion. Released in April 1980, he began in May of the same year to conspire secretly with other former leaders of the *Yi Guan Dao,* in the hope of resuming the sect's counterrevolutionary sabotage activities."

The report added, " Yang viciously attacked the socialist system and maliciously incited his disciples by saying: 'Present-day society seems to be rotten to the core. The people at the top spend all their time competing for power and influence; those in the middle specialize in increasing their wealth and property by cunning; and those at the bottom excel only at stealing and pilfering from others. We must therefore carry out the universal transmigration of the myriad souls *(pu du zhong sheng).'* It is not known what sentence Yang Biao or any other members of the sect leadership received (SS p.51).

. . . . [? YRS]

■ **YANG Sende** (Desen) and **YANG Maicun**, both leaders of the *Hua Zhai Dao (Way of Flowers and Vegetarianism)* sect, were arrested in Lin County, Henan Province sometime in the early 1980s. It is not known what sentence they received. According to an official report, "The ringleader, a man named Yang Sende, was found to be a brigade leader and a member of the Party since 1946. Influenced by Yang, a total of 30 Communist Party members, 11 Youth League members, 24 state officials, six teachers from locally-run schools, 32 brigade and production team cadres and two doctors from the brigade medical station had all entered the ranks of the *Hua Zhai Dao*....Yang Maicun and Yang Desen [presumably an error or alternate name for "Yang Sende"] spread the rumor around that any ill person who joined their sect would be instantly cured, and that all healthy people would be able to evade illness by becoming members; they insisted that all those seeking medical help from them had first of all to join the sect" (SS p.54. and p.57).

. . . . [? YRS]

■ **YUAN Jingwu**, a leader of the *Fo Men (Buddha Gate)* sect, was arrested in Dancheng County, Henan Province in the early 1980s. It is not known what sentence he received. According to an official report, "Yuan fabricated and spread the rumor: 'A world war is about to begin... Jiang Jingguo will soon return.' Said he: 'The final cataclysm of the three eras is now imminent - there will be military chaos, great floods and fires, windstorms and plagues.' Moreover, 'When that time comes, the Five Ghosts will run amok in China, more than half of the population will die and the Communist Party's rule will then come to an end' (SS p.62).

. . . . [? YRS]

■ **ZENG Chuqiao**, a resident of Yiyang District, Hunan Province, and a Buddhist sectarian, was sentenced after June 1989 on charges of "using a reactionary secret sect or society" *(fandong hui-dao-men)* to carry out "counterrevolutionary activities," according to an Asia Watch source. Zeng was involved in helping organize a memorial meeting after June 4 to commemorate the victims of the military crackdown on the pro-democracy movement. It is not known what sentence he received.

. . . . [? YRS]

■ **ZENG Qifa**, an Initiator *(dianchuanshi)* in the *Yi Guan Dao (Way of Unity)* sect, was arrested in Shaanxi Province in the early 1980s. It is not known what sentence he received. According to an official report, "Zeng inflamed people's

thoughts by announcing: "After 1982 *Jia Zi* will reach completion, and the *Yi Guan Dao* will then send forth its light. Said Zeng: "X XX [presumably, Deng Xiaoping] will only rule for another two-and-a-half years. When X XX falls from power, it will be the turn of the *Yi Guan Dao* to rule China" (SS p.61).

. . . . [? YRS]

■ **ZHANG Desheng**, a leader of the *Tian Guang Dao (Way of Celestial Light)* sect, was arrested in Baoqing County, Heilongjiang Province in the early 1980s. It is not known what sentence Zhang received. According to an official report, "[The sect] had a regulation that each new member, upon his or her initiation, had to contribute a 59 yuan 'registration fee'. For one peasant family, all of whose members joined the sect together, the registration fees alone came to more than 350 yuan. By these means, the sect's leader, Zhang Desheng, swindled a total of more than 3,000 yuan from people. In Liu'an County, Anhui, the *Tian Guang Dao* stipulated that each new member had to pay a 35 yuan 'entry fee' upon joining the sect; and whenever a disciple introduced a new member, they were to be given a reward of 10 yuan" (SS p.68).

. . . . [? YRS]

■ **ZHANG Xiangyu**, a Qi Gong master and Beijing resident, arrested in April 1990, was sentenced to six years in prison. Zhang founded *The Nature Center Association*, one of many Chinese organizations promoting Qi Gong, an ancient healing and exercise art. Chinese authorities, concerned with its attraction for the masses and its "counterrevolutionary potential," have branded the art "superstitious" and therefore illegal; they accused Zhang of cheating people out of money.

. . . . [6 YRS]

■ **ZHAO Chunhuai**, a leader of the *Yi Guan Dao (Way of Unity)* sect in Tianjin, was arrested in the early 1980s. It is not known what sentence he received. According to an official report, "On many occasions Zhao openly distributed items of reactionary propaganda in the city's central square. Gathering crowds around himself, he attacked and vilified our Party and the socialist system, and clamored for a change of dynasty" (SS p.62).

. . . . [? YRS]

■ **ZHU Lianzheng**, a leader of the *Gui Gen Dao (Return-to-the-Root Sect)*, was arrested in Zunyi County, Guizhou Province in the early 1980s. It is not known what sentence he received. According to an official report, "Some of the sects openly hold meetings to demonstrate against the government, and even surround and besiege government officials who have been sent out to curb their activities. In Zunyi County, the *Gui Gen Dao* headed by Zhu Lianzheng conducted a large-scale 'Goddess of Mercy Meeting' at the Yaxi New Temple. Every day almost 100 people attended, burning incense and worshipping the Buddha, and attracting crowds of several hundred onlookers on each occasion. Their activities spread ever wider, with severe consequences for public order and social production.

After these sectarian activities had been firmly curtailed by the authorities, Zhu mustered a mob of people and created an unreasonable disturbance at the provincial Department of Public Security, and at the Zunyi district United Front department and the county's Bureau of Public Security. Declaring themselves to be Buddhists, and saying that their activities were quite lawful, they falsely accused the Yaxi District Police Station, which had seized and confiscated their various items of superstitious paraphernalia, of having carried out an 'act of looting'" (SS p.78).

. . . . [? YRS]

Presumed Arrested

■ **LUO Yiyuan**, a former "Commander of All the Troops" in the *Wu Liang Jin Gang Da Dao (Great Way of the Numberless Attendants of Buddha)* sect, was probably rearrested in the Zunyi District of Guizhou Province in 1979. According to an official report, "Luo, who had just been released from prison after serving a life sentence, subsequently reduced to fixed-term imprisonment, openly sought out a special official *(tepaiyuan)* of the public security bureau, in an attempt to get the original verdict upon him overturned. He also roped in his nephew, Chen Maocai, who was currently serving as a Party branch secretary, and got Chen to write up petition materials in support of his case. In addition, the 'general delegate' of this sect, a man named Dai Fangzhou, openly approached the Party branch secretary of the local commune office, creating a great rumpus by declaring that the label of counter-revolutionary that had been stuck on him had in fact been evilly concocted by the head of his production team, and demanding his 'rehabilitation'" (SS p.77).

. . . . [? YRS]

■ **ZHOU Jinfan** and **TAN Fangyou**, members of the *Huang Ji Dao (Sect of the Imperial Ultimate)*, were probably arrested in Lichuan County, Hubei Province in the early 1980s. It is not known what sentences the two sectarians received. According to an official report, "Zhou, a long-time sympathizer of the *Huang Ji Dao*, unearthed and retrieved a number of long-buried tracts, including the 'Garden of the Great Harvest' and 'Precious Confession of the Ten Catastrophes', and gave them all to a new sect member named Tan Fangyou to read. Tan carefully perused the texts and subsequently also acquired some new ones. From 1980 onwards, he copied out by hand a total of more than 20 volumes of such material, amounting to some several hundred thousand characters in all, and he distributed them in all directions. The sect's members were heard to declare: 'When you read the tracts of the *Huang Ji Jiao*, you feel as if a Buddha-Gem had formed within your heart, everything seems much clearer than before.' Said they: 'The final cataclysm of the three eras *(sanqi mojie)* [a folk Buddhist "end of the world" belief] is such a cruel and terrible event, how could anyone fail to believe in the

Huang Ji Jiao?' Some members and disciples become involved in the sect mainly as a means of cultivating their moral character and inner essence *(xiushen yangxing)*. Although already over 30 years old, they avoid matrimony, and instead devote themselves to practicing gymnastics and the martial arts, as a preparation for 'serving as bodyguards' in the *Huang Ji Jiao*" (SS p.76).

. . . . [2 X ? YRS]

List of Proscribed Sects

Bai Yang Jiao (White Sun Sect)

Chang Sheng Dao (Way of Eternal Life)

Da Dao Hui (Big Sword Society)

Da Jiang Fo Guo (Great-River Buddha Land)

Da Cheng Men (Mahayana Gate)

Da Tong Hui (Society of the Great Harmony)

Dong Ming Guo (Eastern Ming Kingdom)

Fo Dang/Fo Guo (Buddha Party/Buddha Nation)

Fo Men (Buddha Gate)

Fo Sheng Men (Buddha's Sacred Gate)

Guan Yin Fo Jiao (Buddhist Sect of the

Goddess of Mercy)

Guan Yin Hui (Society of the Goddess of Mercy)

Gui Gen Dao (Way of Returning to the Source)

Gui Gen Men (Gate of Returning to the Source)

Gui Xiang Dao (Way of Genuflection to Incense)

Gui Yi Dao (Way of Returning to Unity)

Hong San Jiao (Red Three Sect)

Hua Zhai Dao (Way of Flowers and Vegetarianism)

Huang Ji Dao (Way of the Imperial Ultimate)

Huang Ji Jiao (Sect of the Imperial Ultimate)

Huang Sha Hui (Yellow Sands Sect)

Ji Tan (Altar of Spirit-Writing)

Jiu Gen Dao (Way of the Old Source)

Jiu Gong Dao (Way of Nine Palaces)

Lao Jun Dao (Way of the Old Master)

Lao Ren Dao (Way of the Old People)

Ling Ling Jiao (Spirit-Spirit Sect)

Miao Dao (Way of the Temple)

Pu Du Jiao (Universal Transmigration Sect)

Pu Hua Men (Gate of Universal Change)

Pu Ji Tang (Hall of Universal Succor)

Ren Xue Hao Dao (Way of Emulating Goodness)

San Feng Dao (Way of Three Peaks)

Shen Men Dao (Way of the Spirit Gate)

Sheng Dao (Way of Saints)

Sheng Xian Dao (Way of Saints and Immortals)

Sheng Xian Jiao (Sect of Saints and Immortals)

Shou Shan Wan Long Tian Zhu Fo Jiao (Longevity Mountain and Myriad Prosperities Catholic-Buddhist Sect)

Si Fang Dao (Way of the Four Quarters)

Tai Shang Men (Gate of the Supreme Overlord)

Tian Bing Dizi Jun (Fraternal Army of the Soldiers of Heaven)

Tian Dao Hui (Society of Heaven's Way)

Tian De Sheng Jiao (Sect of the Saints of Heavenly Virtue)

Tian Di Fo Xian Hui (Heaven and

Earth Buddhist Immortals Sect)

Tian Guang Dao (Way of Celestial Light)

Tian Hua Dao (Way of Celestial Flowers)

Tian Ming Dao (Way of Celestial Brightness)

Tian Xian Dao (Way of Celestial Immortals)

Tong Shan She (Society of Communal Benevolence)

Triratna

Wan Quan Dao (Way of Myriad Fullnesses)

Wu Liang Jin Gang Da Dao (Great Way of the Numberless Attendants of Buddha)

Xi Tian Ling Shan Fo Men Jiao (Buddha-Gate Sect of the Spirit Mountain in the Western Paradise)

Xian Tian Dao (Way of the Prior Realm)

Xian Tian Da Dao (Great Way of the Prior Realm)

Yao Chi Dao (Way of the Jasper Pool

Yi Guan Dao (Way of Unity)

Yi Shan Tang (One Benevolence Hall)

Yu Xu Men (Gate of the Jade Void)

Yuan Chao Nong Fo He Guo (Yuan Dynasty Peasant Buddhist Republic)

Zhai Gong Jiao (Sect of Vegetarianism and Impartiality)

Zhen Kong Jiao (Sect of the True Void)

Zhong Dao (Middle Way)

Zhong Fang Dao (Way of the Middle Zone)

Zhong Xiao Tian Fu (Celestial House of Loyalty and Filial Piety)

Zhong Yong Dao (Way of the Golden Mean)

Zi Shen Guo (Zi Shen Nation)

Zongjiao Zhexue Yanjiu She (Religious Philosophy Research Society)

V. LONG-TERM PRISONERS

1. Sentenced Prior to 1989

Protestants

Sentence Known

■ **PEI Zhongxun** (CHUN Chul), a 75-year-old ethnic Korean evangelist from Shanghai, was arrested in August 1983 for "counterrevolutionary activities." During his interrogation he was accused by Public Security Bureau officers of spying for the Taiwanese government, but his imprisonment was in connection with his leadership of house churches in the Shanghai area and for accepting quantities of Bibles from overseas sources. Pei received a 15-year sentence which, according to an Asia Watch source, he is serving in Shanghai Prison No.2. According to his wife (*News Network International*, June 26, 1992), Pei is in "reasonably good health and spirits" despite chronic pain and swelling in his feet. He is allowed to receive medication and other provisions from home, is exempted from work and assigned to a private cell. Nevertheless, given his age and the fact that he still has more than five years to serve, she is concerned he may die in prison.

. . . . [15 YRS]

■ Of seven men from Lushan County, arrested in mid-1983 for "illegal" religious activities, one died in prison, one was still in detention as of January 1994, two have been released, and the whereabouts of three others are uncertain. **ZHANG Yunpeng**, from Zhaozhuang village, Houying Brigade, Zhanian Commune, received a 14-year sentence. He was 60 years old at the time, and he died in prison on January 24, 1990. **WANG Xincai**, 31, from Zhandeum Village, Fuling Brigade, Xinji Commune, was sentenced to 15 years in prison and is still being held; **CUI Zhengshan**, 37, who received a 12-year sentence, has been released, as has **QIN Zhenjun**, from Xinji Commune, aged 49, who served a nine-year term. **GENG Minxuan**, 58, from Sunzhang village, Malon Commune, received an 11-year sentence and may still be in prison. All were sentenced on June 2, 1984. All except **Qin Zhenjun** were deprived of their political rights for five years ; his were rescinded for four. There is no information about **XUE Guiwen**, 37, from Linzhuang Village, Xinhua

Brigade, Zhangdian Commune or **WANG Baoquan**, 67, of Second Street, Chengguan Township. All seven were accused of membership in an illegal evangelical group, planning to overthrow the Chinese government, links to foreign "reactionary" forces, receiving materials from overseas, disturbing the social order and disturbing and breaking up "normal" religious activities. Lushan Approximately one-third of Lushan County's population of some 400,000 is Christian.

[14, 15, 12, 9, 11 YRS] [2 X ? YRS]

■ **ZHAO Donghai,** a pastor and house church leader from Henan Province, was sentenced in 1982 or 1983 to a 13-year prison term for "counterrevolutionary activities." No further details are available.

. . . . [13 YRS]

Sentence Unknown

■ **DAN** * **dong,** now 54, formerly a peasant, and **LU ***, and **CHEN ***(no age or other details available), were sentenced to unknown terms of imprisonment, probably in late 1983, for leading a branch of the "Shouters" *(Huhan Pai)*, a Christian sect proscribed by the government. Dan * dong was convicted on charges of "counterrevolutionary propaganda and incitement"; the other two, described only as "already sentenced," were probably sentenced on the more serious charge of "organizing and leading a counterrevolutionary group." In February 1982, after attending a

meeting of the Shouters, the three men organized a branch group called the *Eternal Peace Shouters Church (Yongkang Huhan Zhumingzhong Jiaohui).*

According to the authorities, "On numerous occasions in public places, Dan * dong cursed the People's Government and the [official] Three Self Church. He incited people to 'arise and shout in struggle against the Three Self', clamoring that 'We can physically submit to the government, but it can never possess our souls' and that 'The earthly world will fall and the [spiritual] world will arise, and our Savior will descend to earth to put on trial the [present] lords and rulers.' In early 1983, Dan * dong and others allegedly "organized 'in the name of the Lord' more than 100 benighted and ignorant members of the masses to storm into a church building of the Three Self Patriotic Church on six separate occasions." As the official account reveals, "In May 1983, the People's Government ordered the 'Shouters Sect' to be banned and eradicated." Dan was then "placed under surveillance," but he continued to travel around neighboring districts and provinces "holding secret Shouter meetings and inciting members to 'Be strong and stay resolute'." According to the authorities, "His counter-revolutionary arrogance knew no bounds." The official account (CCS p.251) censored the prisoners' middle and last names and also the location of the alleged activities.

. . . . [3 X ? YRS]

■ **LI * shou** (age unknown) and **LI * shun**[1], now 41, formerly a peasant, were sentenced to unknown terms of imprisonment, probably in late 1983, in connection with their leadership of a Henan Province branch of the "Shouters," a Christian sect proscribed by the government. Li * shun was convicted on charges of "counter-revolutionary propaganda and incitement." The charges against Li * shou are not known, but he is said to have been the "sect leader" and thus was probably convicted on the more serious charge of "organizing and leading a counterrevolutionary group." According to the authorities, between 1980 and 1981, Li * shun, a sect elder *(zhanglao)*, grouped together more than 80 villagers and played them a tape-recording of sect leader Li * shou reading certain so-called "reactionary texts," including the *Gospel According to Saint Matthew* and a work entitled "Platform of the Seven Golden Lanterns." During this period, the group conducted more than 18 "reactionary meetings" in their county and Li * shou carried out "11 counter-revolutionary liaison trips to five neighboring towns and counties."

In 1982, Li * shou allegedly said at one of the meetings, "You must not listen to the government. For the church to unite with the government would be like committing the crime of adultery." In June 1983, following the arrest of a Shouters leader, Li allegedly declared at a "diehard sect-members" meeting: "Satan *([government note:]* meaning our Public Security Bureau) has now arisen, and we are now in a race against time with Satan....We must bring about the collapse of Satan's rule on this earth and build the Kingdom of Jesus instead....After victory, we shall live in God's eternal kingdom and rule by his side for a thousand years."

In 1983, Li * shun and other sect members took delivery of over 160 "reactionary 'Shouter' propaganda items" and distributed them widely. By then, he is said to have personally recruited more than 120 new members to the sect and helped others to recruit a further 100 members. As the official account reveals, "In [May] 1983, the government issued a proclamation formally banning the 'Shouters Sect'." Li * shou then went into hiding, and "recruited 54 new members in [Henan's] Yichuan and Fugou counties." The official account (CCS p.250) censored the prisoners' middle names and also the locations of most of the alleged activities.

. . . . [2 X ? YRS]

Political Prisoners

Sentence Known

■ **CAI Decheng**, a worker in a Xinxiang County (Henan Province) chemical fertilizer plant, and **GENG Qichang** were sentenced on December 31, 1983 by the Zhengzhou Intermediate People's Court at a public rally (Amnesty International from *Zhengzhou Radio*, January 3, 1984). According to the report, between January and April 1982, Cai wrote 70 "extremely reactionary counterrevolutionary banner slogans and big character posters" which he put up on walls, doors and trees in Xinxiang and Zhengzhou. He was charged with "counterrevolutionary propaganda and incitement" and sentenced to 15 years in prison and five years' subsequent deprivation of political rights. Geng was charged with concealing Cai's crime and sentenced to a three-year term from which he has presumably now been released. Cai's place of imprisonment is unknown.

. . . . [15 YRS]

■ **CHENG Xiaogang, SHI Dongting, ZHAO Fengxing** and **LI Guoquan**, from Jilin Province, were all sentenced to prison in the fall of 1983 for allegedly organizing a "counter-revolutionary clique," the *Preparatory Committee for Northeast China People's Autonomous Republic*; "making false charges against others"; and "plotting to overthrow the government" (Amnesty International from *Changchun Radio*, December 1, 1983). They were arrested in late 1981 or early 1982 and, according to the radio report, "admitted their guilt." Cheng received a 15-year term and five years subsequent deprivation of political rights. Shi and Zhao were sentenced respectively to 20 years and life and deprived of their political rights for life. The three reportedly are held in Changchun Municipal Prison. Li received a seven-year sentence and presumably has been released. Cheng was a teacher at a middle school affiliated to the former Northeast China Normal University; Shi worked at the Shengyang City No.1 Transport

Company; and Zhao was a worker at Jilin Province archives. No current information is available.

. . . . [15, 20 YRS] [LIFE]

■ **LIU De**, 32, a member of the editorial board of the *Jianna Literature and Arts Journal*, a literary magazine in Mianyang City, Sichuan Province, was sentenced to seven years' imprisonment and three years' deprivation of political rights by the Mianyang City Intermediate People's Court, an appeal to the Sichuan Province High People's Court having failed. The precise dates of Liu's arrest and trial are not known (Chinese officials gave no reply on his case in a November 1991 response to U.S. government requests for information on more than 800 prisoner cases), but he was probably first detained in January 1987 during a nationwide student protest movement. One official account, however, cited as the main reason for Liu's arrest statements he had made in mid-1985. The seven-year sentence was announced in February 1987. Government newspaper reports on May 2, 1987 claimed that Liu had "vilified the socialist system" by allegedly urging a crowd of students and teachers in a local technical high school to "join the struggle," so that within 15-20 years a new "-ism" (social philosophy) could emerge.

This was later confirmed in a restricted-circulation official account (CCS p.250), which said that on May 17, 1985 Liu gave a guest lecture at an industrial engineering college during which, "for more than two hours and in front of an audience of more than 100 people, he fabricated facts and turned the truth on its head by viciously attacking, vilifying, ridiculing and slandering China's socialist system, the Party and state leadership, and also a series of important decisions made by the Party since the [December 1978] 3rd Plenum." In the speech, Liu allegedly declared: "In 15 or 20 years from now, Communism will be replaced by a new ideology and a new political party will emerge to replace the Communist Party....I want to see with my own eyes the Communist Party's downfall." Liu should be due for release by January 1994.

. . . . [7 YRS]

■ **TANG Dadi,** an editor for *Xinhua*, the official Chinese news agency, was arrested in 1987 and sentenced to a seven-year prison term for allegedly providing information to a Japanese reporter. He reportedly is still in prison.

. . . . [7 YRS]

■ **ZHENG Qiuwu**, arrested in Hainan Island in 1986, was tried on charges of "organizing and leading a counter-revolutionary group" and sentenced to 14 years' imprisonment. He is currently being held in a special unit for political prisoners at Huaiji Prison, Guangdong Province. Zheng has been held in solitary confinement for most of the past seven years. The charges related to his leading role in a sizable, peaceful pro-democracy group that emerged on Hainan Island sometime prior to 1986. Among the "ideological heterodoxies" which Zheng was accused of committing was his

outspoken support for the idea of establishing stock markets in China, a notion that was officially condemned at the time but now forms a central part of the government's economic reform program. According to a former political inmate of Huaiji Prison, Zheng had by 1991 become mentally disturbed as a result of his prolonged solitary confinement.

. . . . [14 YRS]

Sentence Unknown

[NB: Most of the following cases were reported in an official, restricted-circulation (neibu) volume entitled **Criminal Case-Studies Series (Vol.1: Crimes of Counterrevolution)** *[Xingshi Fanzui Anli Congshu (Fangeming Zui)], compiled by the Supreme People's Procuratorate and published by Zhongguo Jiancha Chubanshe (Beijing), November 1992. In all cases, the detainees were listed as "convicted" but all sentencing details were omitted. The cases listed below solely concern freedom of speech or freedom of association-related activities, and are ones where the severity of the charges made it likely that long prison sentences were imposed and that those concerned are still behind bars. In most cases, the prisoners' middle or last names were censored by the editors; these omissions are denoted here by asterisks. Page references to case reports in the Chinese volume appear below as "CCS p.(?)".]*

■ **CHI * ting**, now 65, formerly a temporary worker, was sentenced to an unknown term of imprisonment on charges of "counterrevolutionary propaganda and incitement," probably in late 1983. According to the authorities, on January 23 and June 1, 1983, Chi publicly shouted "reactionary slogans" including "Down with the Communist Party" and "Support the KMT." After being seized by local security officials on the second occasion, he "continued to shout the above-mentioned counterrevolutionary slogans while being escorted to the local police station." Chi's subsequent trial probably coincided with the height of a major "crackdown on crime" campaign later that year, and it is thus likely that he received a heavy sentence as a result. The official account (CCS p.254) censored the prisoner's middle name and also the location of the alleged activities.

. . . . [? YRS]

■ **FU Bin**, now in his late thirties, formerly a worker at the Taiyuan No.1 Footwear Factory, Shanxi Province, was arrested on July 17, 1984 at his factory and later sentenced to an unknown prison term on charges of "counterrevolutionary propaganda and incitement." According to an official report (*1985 Shanxi Yearbook*, p.136), between July 1981 and February 1984, Fu posted up numerous "counter-revolutionary letters, flyers and banners" in 20 different sites along Taiyuan's Liberation Road and May 1st Road and at the Bell Tower; he also mailed out similar items across the country. According to the report,

"Criminal Fu's activities were protracted in duration and heinous in nature; his counterrevolutionary arrogance knew no bounds. It was one of the most serious cases to have occurred in our province for many years." Fu had signed the various "counterrevolutionary items" in the name of two separate organizations, the *"Jia-Li-Sen* Dare-to-Die Squad" (the name appears to be a transliteration of the English word "garrison") and the "Reclining Tiger Mountain Guerrilla Team" *(Wo Hu Shan Youji Dui)*. The authorities, however, determined that the organizations never in fact existed, so Fu was charged with making "counterrevolutionary propaganda" rather than "organizing a counter-revolutionary group." He was arrested after the police circulated a composite "suspect profile," which included details of the wanted dissident's "ideological tendencies," among major Taiyuan factories and work places.

. . . . [? YRS]

■ **HONG * ping**, a resident of Fuzhou Province, described in an official report as being the "chief criminal" behind a dissident group ¹ called the *Great Unity Party (Da Tong Dang)*, was sentenced to an unknown term of imprisonment, probably in 1984, on charges of "organizing and leading a counterrevolutionary group." Another member of the group, **WANG * bin**, was convicted on charges of "actively participating in a counter-revolutionary group" and was also sentenced to an unknown term of imprisonment. According to the authorities, Hong recruited Wang in

July 1983 after showing him the "Charter of the Great Unity Party" and appointed him as the party's "Municipal Committee Secretary." Wang then in turn recruited persons surnamed Liu, Qu, Wang and Xu as additional members (it is not known what punishment these four received) and "made to them the counter-revolutionary statement, 'Within 20 years, the Communist Party will be engulfed in chaos'." The official account (CCS p.165) censored both the prisoners' middle names and the location of the alleged activities.

. . . . [2 X ? YRS]

■ **JI** * **liang**, now 65, formerly a retired cadre who had worked in an electronics research institute, was sentenced to an unknown term of imprisonment on charges of "counter-revolutionary propaganda and incitement," probably in early 1986. According to the authorities, in March 1983 Ji wrote to several national and local newspapers opposing the official critique of the Cultural Revolution, calling for an end to the rehabilitation of those punished during that movement and warning that China was 'going capitalist'." Between July 1984 and June 1985, he allegedly wrote eight letters to numerous senior departments of the army and government, signed in the name of 'A Group of Political Deaf-mutes', which read, 'The power-faction led by Deng [Xiaoping] is engaging in plots and conspiracies'." Ji also called for a series of mass public discussion meetings to be held in Tiananmen Square and in provincial and municipal government offices to

debate the political situation in China. He also warned, "If the members of our group are arrested or assassinated, we will retaliate with 'an eye for an eye, a tooth for a tooth'." Finally, in September 1985, Ji "secretly distributed in public places in Beijing a total of 35 leaflets...which read, 'Let everyone unite to fight back the [official trend of] rehabilitating the capitalist-roaders; we must not abandon the cause half way.'" The official account (CCS p.262) censored the prisoner's middle name and also the location of the alleged activities.

. . . . [? YRS]

■ **LI** * **hong**, now 50, formerly a gas station worker, was sentenced to an unknown term of imprisonment on charges of "counterrevolutionary propaganda and incitement," probably in early 1981. According to the authorities, between December 1979 and November 1980, Li publicly posted up several dozen "counterrevolutionary banners" accusing Deng Xiaoping and other state leaders of being 'traitors to the proletariat, saboteurs of internationalism, running-dogs of imperialism, two-faced counter-revolutionaries, fascist elements and the Hitlers of the 1980s'." The official account (CCS p.264) censored the prisoner's middle name and also the location of the alleged activities.

. . . . [? YRS]

■ **LI** * **nian**[1], now 41, formerly a worker on a livestock farm, was sentenced to an additional unknown term of imprisonment on charges of "counterrevolutionary propaganda and incitement," probably in 1981. At the time, Li was already in prison serving a five-year sentence for robbery. According to the authorities, between December 1978 and March 1979, he posted up in the prisoners' dormitory of the No.4 Brigade of "** Labor-Reform Detachment" eight "counter-revolutionary banners" bearing the words "Down with * **," "Down with the Communist Party" and "Long Live Ch'iang [Kai-Shek]." Transferred the next month to the No.3 Brigade, Li repeated such acts twice during the following two years: "On May 16, 1981, while undergoing interrogation, Li posted up a counterrevolutionary slogan on the door of the [prison] latrine. His counterrevolutionary arrogance knew no bounds." The official account (CCS p.249) censored the prisoner's middle name and also the location of the alleged activities.

. . . . [? YRS]

■ **LIU * xin**, now in his fifties, formerly an unemployed worker, was sentenced to an unknown term of imprisonment on charges of "counter-revolutionary propaganda and incitement" sometime in the 1980s. According to the authorities, "From 1981 onwards, Liu wrote more than 80 counterrevolutionary letters and mailed then to over 20 work-units and districts. In the letters, he flagrantly vilified and disparaged China's people's democratic dictatorship and the socialist system, calling for workers and students to 'take to the streets' and stage strikes, class boycotts and work stoppages, and to cut off electricity supplies, and urging them to stick up

posters calling for the overthrow of the Communist Party all over the city. His counterrevolutionary arrogance knew no bounds." The official account (CCS p.245) censored the prisoner's middle name and also the location of the alleged activities.

. . . . [? YRS]

■ **LUO * xi** and **LIU * yang**, described in an official report as the "chief criminals" behind a dissident group known as the *China Youth Alliance (Zhongguo Qingnian Lianmeng)*, were sentenced to unknown terms of imprisonment, probably in 1983, on charges of "organizing and leading a counterrevolutionary group." Two other members of the political group (against which no allegations of violence were made), **GAO * shan**, a textiles factory technician, and **LIU * fang**, a technician in a wireless equipment factory, were convicted on charges of "actively participating in a counterrevolutionary group" and also sentenced to unknown terms of imprisonment. According to the authorities, in January 1982, Gao and Liu * fang were recruited into the dissident group by Liu * yang. The two then in turn recruited persons surnamed Liu and Jiang as additional members. (It is not known what punishment these two received.) On August 12, 1982, Gao and Liu * fang allegedly "held a meeting with Luo and Liu * yang at which they vented their hostile feelings towards the Chinese Communist Party and socialism....They then obtained from Luo and Liu * yang copies of the 'Charter of the China Youth Alliance (Draft)' and the 'Personnel Archives of the China Youth Alliance', and received verbal instructions on how to expand the organization and recruit new members." The official account (CCS p.163) censored both the prisoners' middle names and the location of the alleged activities.

. . . . [4 X ? YRS]

■ **NI * cai**, now 52, formerly an assistant engineer at a measuring instruments factory, was sentenced to an unknown term of imprisonment on charges of "counterrevolutionary propaganda and incitement," probably in early 1987. According to the authorities, from January to July 1986, Ni wrote numerous letters to national newspapers, colleges and universities, trade unions and other bodies criticizing as "outright revisionism and capitalism" the government's current policies and denouncing Deng Xiaoping and other leaders as "Party scabs and national traitors." In one letter, Ni proclaimed the founding of an alternative political group, the *Communist Party of China (Maoist) [Zhongguo Gongchandang (Mao)]*, and said that it had already held its "First National Congress." In the letter, he expressed "unbounded love and respect" for Chairman Mao and Premier Zhou Enlai.The official account (CCS p.266) censored the prisoner's middle name and also the location of the alleged activities.

. . . . [? YRS]

■ **PAN ***, now 33, formerly a cadre in an urban district civil affairs department, was sentenced to an unknown term of imprisonment on charges of "counterrevolutionary propaganda and incitement," probably in 1986. According to the authorities, "Between September 1985 and March 1986, Pan went to * University and, with the aim of inciting the students, wrote two pamphlets entitled *Vanguard of the Tides* and *Save the Country Through Democracy*. These articles wantonly disparaged the Chinese Communist Party and vilified the socialist system as 'a reactionary tyrannical power', inciting students by saying, 'If our words no longer have any effect, then we must move into action!'" Pan also made several photocopies of the two pamphlets and "secretly distributed them in more than ten higher colleges in Beijing, Shenyang and Harbin, and mailed copies to Hong Kong." He was arrested by the public security authorities on April 17, 1986. The official account (CCS p.243) censored the prisoner's last name and also the location of the alleged activities.

. . . . [? YRS]

■ **QI * long**, now 29, formerly a peasant, was sentenced to an unknown term of imprisonment on charges of "counterrevolutionary propaganda and incitement," probably in late 1985. According to the authorities, "On June 13, 1985, Qi wrote in his father's name a counterrevolutionary letter to army troops stationed on the frontline at Laoshan, Yunnan Province, which he mailed on July 30. Using extremely vicious language, he attacked the socialist system and incited the frontline troops by saying 'Don't lose your lives for the sake of the ruling elite's interests' and...'Your deaths would be futile and in vain'." The official account (CCS p.256) censored the prisoner's middle name and also the location of the alleged activities.

. . . . [? YRS]

■ **QIU * wen**, now 23, formerly a small private businessman, and **CHEN *2**, also now 23, formerly a worker at a measuring instruments factory, were sentenced to unknown terms of imprisonment on charges of "counter-revolutionary propaganda and incitement," probably in 1990. According to the authorities, "On December 22, 1989, Qiu drafted a counterrevolutionary letter entitled 'To Our Awakened Compatriots', in which he attacked and vilified the Party's leadership and the socialist system, vainly sought to incite discord between the [officially sanctioned] minority democratic-party groupings and the Communist Party, and incited students to overthrow the Communist Party, the people's democratic dictatorship and the socialist system." The next day, Chen * revised the document and signed it with the name "The Awakened Generation," and they then produced more than 40 copies. On December 27, the two allegedly travelled to * City and, "posing as students from Suzhou University, Nanjing University and Shanghai Normal University," they mailed 12 copies to government offices, higher colleges and newspaper offices in Beijing, Nanjing and Tianjin. On December 30, they then mailed an additional 13 copies to similar work-units in Shanghai and Guangzhou. The

official account (CCS p.245) censored the prisoners' middle name and also the location of the alleged activities.

. . . . [2 X ? YRS]

■ **ZHANG * hu**, now 44, **SONG * ze**, now 38, and **FENG * ji**, now 72, all formerly peasants, were sentenced to unknown terms of imprisonment on charges of "counterrevolutionary propaganda and incitement," probably in 1984. According to the authorities, from 1978 onwards Zhang had written numerous letters to the Taiwan government expressing support for the KMT and hoping for its return to power on the mainland. In March 1983, he and the other two men wrote more than 230 "counterrevolutionary leaflets," one hundred of which they posted up in * County town. In May of that year, they allegedly wrote a further 20 such items and posted 30 copies on trees along a main road. The official account (CCS p.247) censored the prisoner's middle name and also the location of the alleged activities.

. . . . [3 X ? YRS]

■ **ZHOU * jian**, now 40, formerly a peasant, was sentenced to an unknown term of imprisonment on charges of "counterrevolutionary propaganda and incitement," probably in 1981. According to the authorities, on the night of December 18, 1980, Zhou crept into a museum commemorating leaders of the Chinese revolution and tore up a copy of Chairman Mao's famous 1940 article "On New Democracy," after which he defaced several color photographs of Mao by scratching large crosses on them with a penknife. He also allegedly wrote out a "reactionary slogan" in red ink and posted it on the museum door. Later, Zhou noted in his diary: "This evening I did something which no one else in China has dared to do, something which will astound China and the world." He then fled to "* City" and posted up seven banners bearing the words "Down With Despot * **" [probably a reference to Hua Guofeng, then Communist Party leader.] After his arrest, Zhou is said to have "continued to spread reactionary ideas and incite unrest among the other prisoners," and to have "scrawled seven reactionary slogans in ballpoint ink on the detention center wall." The official account (CCS p.248) censored the prisoner's middle name and also the location of the alleged activities.

. . . . [? YRS]

■ **ZHOU * li**, now 41, formerly a peasant, was sentenced to an unknown term of imprisonment on charges of "counterrevolutionary propaganda and incitement," probably in 1986. According to the authorities, in October 1985, following a failed attempt to flee the country, Zhou was detained by the police in a "shelter for investigation" center. Embittered by this, Zhou then allegedly wrote out more than 500 "counterrevolutionary banners" bearing the words "Down With the Communist Party" and "Long Live Ch'iang Kai-Shek," and in January 1986 he distributed 522 "counterrevolutionary leaflets" outside government offices and hospitals in neighboring towns. The official account (CCS p.248) censored the prisoner's middle name and also the

location of the alleged activities.

. . . . [? YRS]

2. List of Long-Term Political and Religious Prisoners

Currently Serving Sentences of Ten Years or More

Confirmed

■ **CAI Decheng** - see p.274
. . . . [15 YRS]

■ **CHEN Lantao** - see p.82
. . . . [18 YRS]

■ **CHEN Yanbin** - see p.62
. . . . [15 YRS]

■ **CHEN Zhixiang** - see p.74
. . . . [10 YRS]

■ **CHEN Ziming** - see p.63
. . . . [13 YRS]

■ **CHENG Xiaogang** - see p.275
. . . . [15 YRS]

■ **CHI Shouzhu** - see p.104
. . . . [10 YRS]

■ **DING Junze** - see p.84
. . . . [12 YRS]

■ **DRADUL**[3] - see p.193
. . . . [16 YRS]

■ **GUO Yunqiao** - see p.98
. . . . [DEATH W/REPRIEVE]

■ **HAO Fuyuan** - see p.108
. . . . [10 YRS]

■ **HU Jian**[1] - see p.86
. . . . [10 YRS]

■ **HU Min** - see p.98
. . . . [15 YRS]

■ **HUANG Junjie** - see p.15, 95
. . . . [10 YRS]

■ **JAMPA NGODRUP** - see p.15, 194
. . . . [13 YRS]

■ **JAMPEL CHANGCHUP** - see p.173
. . . . [19 YRS]

■ **JAMPEL KHEDRUP** - see p.173
. . . . [18 YRS]

■ **JAMPEL LOBSANG** - see p.174
. . . . [10 YRS]

■ **JIANG Zhiqiang** - see p.76
. . . . [13 YRS]

■ **JIAO Zhijin** - see p.109
. . . . [15 YRS]

■ **JIGME GYATSO**[1] - see p.195
. . . . [LIFE]

■ **KAJIKHUMAR SHABDAN** - see p.222
. . . . [12 YRS]

■ **KUNCHOK LODROE** - see p.195
. . . . [13 YRS]

■ LAI Bihu - see p.112
. . . . [10 YRS]

■ LHUNDRUP DORJE - see p.195
. . . . [15 YRS]

■ LHUNDRUP TOGDEN - see p.185
. . . . [14 YRS]

■ LI Hongjiang - see p.92
. . . . [LIFE]

■ LI Wangyang - see p.99
. . . . [13 YRS]

■ LI Wei - see p.105
. . . . [13 YRS]

■ LI Xiaodong - see p.99
. . . . [13 YRS]

■ LI Yongsheng - see p.113
. . . . [12 YRS]

■ LIN Qiangguo - see p.112
. . . . [10 YRS]

■ LIU Baiqiang - see p.17, 96
. . . . [17 YRS]

■ LIU Heping[1] - see p.114
. . . . [12 YRS]

■ LIU Jian'an - see p.378
. . . . [10 YRS]

■ LIU Xin - see p.76
. . . . [15 YRS]

■ LOBSANG GELEK[2] - see p.188
. . . . [12 YRS]

■ LOBSANG PALDEN[4] - see p.178
. . . . [10 YRS]

■ LU Decheng - see p.101
. . . . [16 YRS]

■ LÜ Riying - see p.77
. . . . [13 YRS]

■ MAO Yuejin - see p.98
. . . . [15 YRS]

■ NAMAT ABDUMAT - see p.224
. . . . [15 YRS]

■ NGAWANG CHAMTSUL - see p.185
. . . . [15 YRS]

■ NGAWANG GYALTSEN[1] - see p.173
. . . . [17 YRS]

■ NGAWANG OEZER[2] - see p.173
. . . . [17 YRS]

■ NGAWANG PHULCHUNG - see
p.173
. . . . [19 YRS]

■ NGAWANG SUNGRAB - see p.170
. . . . [10 YRS]

■ NGAWANG TENSANG - see p.171
. . . . [10 YRS]

■ NGODRUP[2] - see p.197
. . . . [11 YRS]

■ PEI Zhongxun - see p.272
. . . . [15 YRS]

■ PHUNTSOG DORJE[2] - see p.198
. . . . [10 YRS]

■ PHUNTSOG GYALTSEN - see p.177
. . . . [12 YRS]

■ PHUNTSOG SAMTEN[2] - see p.185
. . . . [10 YRS]

■ QI Hongjun - see p.111
. . . . [12 YRS]

■ SHI Dongting - see p.275
. . . . [20 YRS]

■ SONAM DORJE[1] - see p.195
. . . . [13 YRS]

■ SONAM RINCHEN - see p.195
. . . . [13-15 YRS]

■ SUN Chuanheng - see p.93
. . . . [LIFE]

■ SUN Weibang - see p.109
. . . . [12 YRS]

■ SUN Xiongying - see p.73
. . . . [18 YRS]

■ TANAK JIGME SANGPO - see
p.198 . . . . [28 YRS]

■ TANG Guoliang - see p.112
. . . . [10 YRS]

■ TANG Yuanjuan - see p.105
. . . . [20 YRS]

■ TENDAR PHUNTSOG - see p.186
. . . . [10 YRS]

■ TENPA WANGDRAG[2] - see p.177
. . . . [14-15 YRS]

■ THUPTEN YESHE[1] - see p.196
. . . . [15 YRS]

■ TSERING NGODRUP - see p.201
. . . . [12 YRS]

■ TSERING PHUNTSOG[2] - see p.185
. . . . [13 YRS]
● WANG Juntao - see p.63   [13 YRS]
■ WANG Lianxi - see p.354
. . . . [LIFE]

■ WANG Xincai (and 5 others, sentences
unknown) - see p.272
. . . . [15 YRS]

■ WEI Shouzhong - see p.107
. . . . [15 YRS]

■ WU Jianmin - see p.103
. . . . [10 YRS]

■ WU Jianwei - see p.100
. . . . [14 YRS]

■ WU Shisen - see p.7
. . . . [LIFE]

■ XIONG Xiaohua - see p.100
. . . . [13 YRS]

■ YANG Jianwen - see p.72
. . . . [10 YRS]

■ YANG Lianzi - see p.73
. . . . [15 YRS]

■ YAO Guisheng - see p.355
. . . . [15 YRS]

■ YU Dongyue - see p.101
. . . . [20 YRS]

■ YU Zhenbin - see p.81
. . . . [12 YRS]

■ YU Zhijian - see p.101
. . . . [LIFE]

■ YULO DAWA TSERING - see p.179
. . . . [8-10 YRS]

■ ZHANG Jie[2] - see p.110
. . . . [18 YRS]

■ ZHANG Jingsheng[1] - see p.102
. . . . [13 YRS]

■ ZHANG Xiaoxu - see p.83
. . . . [15 YRS]

■ ZHANG Yafei - see p.62
. . . . [11 YRS]

■ ZHANG Yunpeng - see p.272
. . . . [14 YRS]

- **ZHAO Donghai** - see p.273
  . . . . [13 YRS]

- **ZHAO Fengxiang** - see p.275
  . . . . [LIFE]

- **ZHAO Junlu** - see p.108
  . . . . [10 YRS]

- **ZHAO Pinju** - see p.94
  . . . . [13 YRS]

- **ZHENG Hengkang** - see p.89
  . . . . [10 YRS]

- **ZHENG Qiuwu** - see p.276
  . . . . [14 YRS]

- **ZHENG Quanli** - see p.110
  . . . . [12 YRS]

- **ZHENG Yunsu** - see p.247
  . . . . [12 YRS]

- **ZHOU Hongbin** - see p.111
  . . . . [10 YRS]

- **ZHU Fangming** - see p.103
  . . . . [LIFE]

Probable

- **CHEN Jiahu** - see p.95
  . . . . [? YRS]

- **FU Bin** - see p.277
  . . . . [? YRS]

- **GAO * shan** - see p.279
  . . . . [? YRS]

- **HONG * ping** - see p.277
  . . . . [? YRS]

- **LI Xinfu** - see p.95
  . . . . [? YRS]

- **LIU * fang** - see p.279
  . . . . [? YRS]

- **LIU * yang** - see p.279
  . . . . [? YRS]

- **LUO * xi** - see p.279
  . . . . [? YRS]

- **WANG * bin** - see p.277
  . . . . [? YRS]

*[NB: Many prisoners convicted of "counterrevolution" in connection with their involvement in traditional religious "reactionary sects and societies" (**fandong hui-daomen**) are also believed to be currently serving sentences of 10 years or more. For a partial list of those arrested on such charges during the past decade but for whom specific sentencing details are not known, see pp.254-269.]*

APPENDICES

APPENDIX I: LIST OF KNOWN "COUNTER-REVOLUTIONARIES"

The following is a list of all persons known to have been tried, and believed still detained, on charges of "counterrevolution" in China today. In September 1993, Chinese officials stated that a total of 3,317 persons were currently being held after conviction on "counterrevolutionary" charges of all types. Although the following list accounts for only a portion of such cases, Asia Watch hopes, by releasing it, to begin the long-overdue process of eliciting from the Chinese authorities a full accounting of all sentenced "counterrevolutionaries."

CODE	CHARGE	STATUTE: SENTENCING RANGE
#1	"Colluding with foreign states to harm sovereignty or split the nation"	(DP = death penalty) Art. 91: 10 years to life/DP
#2	"Conspiring to subvert the government"	Art. 92: 10 years to life/DP
#3	"Instigating state personnel to defect to the enemy or rise in rebellion"	Art. 93: 10 years to life/DP
#4	"Defecting to the enemy and turning traitor	Art. 94: 3 years to life/DP
#5	"Participating in armed mass rebellion"	Art. 95: 3 years to life/DP
#6	"Participating in a mass prison raid or jailbreak"	Art. 96: 3 years to life/DP
#7	"Espionage"	Art. 97: 3 years to life/DP
#8	"Organizing or leading/actively participating in a counterrevolutionary group"	Art. 98: maximum life
#9	"Organizing and using reactionary sects or secret societies for counterrevolution"	Art. 99: maximum life/DP
#10	"Counterrevolutionary sabotage"	Art. 100: 3 years to life/DP
#11	"Counterrevolutionary injury/murder"	Art. 101: 3 years to life/DP
#12	"Counterrevolutionary propaganda and incitement	Art. 102: maximum life
#?	Unspecified "counterrevolutionary" charges	Arts.90-104: ? years/DP?
#DM	Demonstrators executed for alleged "counterrevolutionary" violence" during crackdown on 1989 democracy movement	

1. Key to "Counterrevolutionary" Charges

China's Criminal Law lists twelve main categories of "counterrevolutionary" offense, three of which concern activities solely involving exercise of the internationally guaranteed rights to freedom of speech and freedom of association. They are: the crime of "organizing or leading, or actively participating in, a counterrevolutionary group" (Article 98); the crime of "carrying out counterrevolutionary propaganda and incitement" (Article 102); and the crime of "organizing and using reactionary sects or secret societies for counterrevolutionary purposes" (Article 99). Although forming only a minority of the available "counterrevolutionary" charges, these three nonetheless account (according to the Chinese authorities) for the great majority of all cases sentenced by the courts since the early 1980s. All sentences passed by China's judicial authorities under these three articles of the Criminal Law are indefensible by international standards and constitute a violation of fundamental human rights. Similarly abusive is the common practice of "administratively" - i.e. without trial - sentencing dissidents to terms of "labor re-education." Such cases, a few of which are listed here for illustrative purposes, are unjustifiably excluded from the official government statistics.

Occasionally, "counterrevolutionaries" are also accused of recognized criminal offenses such as assault, rape or swindling property. In such cases, the defendant is usually charged under additional relevant articles of the Criminal Law and given a heavier ("combined") sentence. In other cases, those accused of using "counter-revolutionary groups," including both unauthorized political organizations and traditional religious "reactionary sects," for violent or other criminal purposes are charged solely under either Article 98 or Article 99; but this exceeds the proper legal scope of those provisions, which concern solely the political act of "organizing and using" such groups. (It is important to note that in China all "organized" or Triad-related crime is dealt with under other, so-called common criminal, statutes of the law.) Certain other charges, such as "counterrevolutionary assault or murder," are politically directed and legally quite redundant, since the acts in question could equally well be handled under existing common criminal statutes. Caution should also be observed in evaluating cases of alleged "counterrevolutionary sabotage," a charge laid against many pro-democracy detainees during the June 1989 crackdown. While the charge includes acknowledged violent offenses such as arson, it was also used to sentence dissidents who merely defaced public portraits of Chairman Mao or tore down government posters to prison terms of up to life imprisonment. In such cases, minor "common criminal" charges would clearly have sufficed for normal law-enforcement purposes.

Certain categories of "counterrevolutionary" crime, such as "armed mass rebellion," concern acts which would be recognized as criminal offenses under international law. Others, such as "colluding with foreign states to harm sovereignty or split the nation" (Article 91) and "conspiring to subvert the government" (Article 92), also resemble offenses recognized in other countries, for example "treason," "subversion" and "endangering national security." In practice, however, such charges are mainly applied, in the former case, against peaceful ethnic separatists or civil rights campaigners in Tibet, Inner Mongolia and Xinjiang; and in the latter, against peaceful pro-democracy dissidents in the ethnically Han areas. Similarly, the charge of "espionage" is sometimes indiscriminately applied, against, for example, Chinese or ethnic dissidents who merely provided information on human rights abuses to foreigners.

CODE	CHARGE	STATUTE: SENTENCING RANGE
X#1	"Stealing weapons"	Art. 112: max. life/DP
X#2	"Intentional injury"	Art. 134: max. 7 years/DP
X#3	"False accusation"	Art. 138: no fixed sentence
X#4	"Rape"	Art. 139: 3 years to life/DP
X#5	"Robbery"	Art. 150: 3 years to life/DP
X#6	"Disturbing social order"	Art. 158: max. 5 years
X#7	"Assembling a crowd to disturb order/ blocking or disrupting traffic/ obstructing security personnel"	Art. 159: max. 5 years
X#8	"Using superstition to rumor-monger or swindle"	Art. 165: max. 7 years
X#9	"Leaking state secrets"	Art. 186: max. 7 years/DP

2. Key to Additional Criminal Charges

For many sentenced "counterrevolutionaries," the judicial process culminates in a bullet to the back of the head; indeed, all but two of the twelve main "counter-revolutionary" charges are potentially punishable by the death penalty. In most cases, those so punished are prisoners convicted of violent or other recognized criminal activities; but the present list also includes the names of several dissidents who were executed for non-violent (i.e. freedom of speech and association-related) "counter-revolutionary" offenses. There are believed to have been many more such cases in China since the late 1970s than the few reported here - especially of prisoners (usually peasants) convicted of involvement in "reactionary" religious sects and societies.

Finally, in all alleged "counterrevolutionary" cases - aside from the fundamentally flawed nature of the charges themselves - a wide range of "fair trial" concerns also apply. A summary account of these is provided in the Introduction, above.

Page cross-references to the individual case accounts in this report are not included in the following list. For case details of the various prisoners listed, please refer to the INDEX. An **asterisk** appearing as part of a prisoner's name means that that part of the name was censored by the authorities in the official source which cited the case. Names listed in **italics** denote those prisoners for whom no separate case-entries appear elsewhere in this report; they are persons against whom allegations of violent or other acknowledged criminal acts (such as spying) were made by the authorities. Separate case-entries are provided, however, for certain "borderline" prisoners of the latter type, namely those who were in addition accused of pro-democracy or other free speech/freedom of association-related activities. (Examples include persons accused of "using counterrevolutionary groups/propaganda" for violent purposes, and those accused of "spying for Taiwan on the 1989 pro-democracy movement.") All such cases are included here so that the list may provide the fullest possible accounting of known sentenced "counterrevolutionaries" of all types in China today.

A. China

1. *Sentenced*

Non-Violent Cases

Sentence Known

CR #2

- **CHEN Ziming**
  . . . . [#2 #12: 13 YRS]

- **CHENG Xiaogang**
  . . . . [#2 #8/ X#3: 15 YRS]

- **LIU Gang**[1] . . . . . [#2: 6 YRS]

- **SHI Dongting**
  . . . . [#2 #8/ X#3: 20 YRS]

- **WANG Juntao**
  . . . . [#2 #12: 13 YRS]

- **ZHAO Fengxing**
  . . . . [#2 #8/ X#3: LIFE]

CR #8

- **AH Fang** . . . . . . [#8: 5 YRS]

- **AN Fuxing** . . . . . [#8: 5 YRS]

- **CHEN (Sun) Zhongming**
  . . . . [#8: 6 YRS]

- **CHEN Yanbin** . . [#8: 15 YRS]

- **JIAO Zhijin** . . . [#8: 15 YRS]

- **LENG Wanbao**
  . . . . [#8 #12: 8 YRS]

- **LI Wei** . . . . . [#8 #12: 13 YRS]

- **LIU Kai** . . . . [#8: 2 YRS]

- **TANG Weihua** . . . [#8: 2 YRS]

- **TANG Yuanjuan**
  . . . . [#8 #12: 20 YRS]

- **WANG Changhong**[1]
  . . . . [#8/ X#9?: 5 YRS]

- **WANG Ning**
  . . . . [#8 #12: 8 YRS]

- **YANG Tongyan**
  . . . . [#8: 10 YRS]

- **YU Zhenbin** . . . [#8: 12 YRS]

- **ZENG Yanzhuo** . . [#8: 4 YRS]

- **ZHANG Jie**[1] . . . . [#8: 5 YRS]

- **ZHANG Minpeng** . [#8: 5 YRS]

- **ZHANG Yafei** . . [#8: 11 YRS]

- **ZHENG Qiuwu** . [#8: 14 YRS]

- **ZHENG Quanli**
  . . . . [#8: 12 YRS]

- **ZHOU Min** . . . . . [#8: 6 YRS]

- ZHOU Yuan . . . . [#8: 5 YRS]

- ZHU Wenhua
. . . . [#8 #12: 6 YRS]

CR #9

- CUI * li
. . . . [#9: DEATH W/REPRIEVE]

- PEI * lin
. . . . [#9: DEATH W/REPRIEVE]

- ZHANG Xiangyu
. . . . [#9/ X#8?: 6 YRS]

- ZHAO * tian
. . . . [#9: DEATH W/REPRIEVE]

CR #10

- LU Decheng . . . [#10: 16 YRS]

- SUN Xiongying
. . . . [#10 #12: 18 YRS]

- YU Dongyue . . . [#10: 20 YRS]

- YU Zhijian . . . . . [#10: LIFE]

CR #12

- BAO Tong
. . . . [#12/ X#9: 7 YRS]

- CAI Decheng
. . . . [#12: 15 YRS]

- CAO Yingyun . . . [#12: ? YRS]

- CHEN Jie . . . . . [#12: 8 YRS]

- CHEN Lantao
. . . . [#12/ X#6/3: 18 YRS]

- CHEN Zhixiang
. . . . [#12: 10 YRS]

- CHI Shouzhu
. . . . [#12: 10 YRS]

- DING Junze . . . [#12: 12 YRS]

- DING Longhua
. . . . [#12: 6 YRS]

- Farmer X . . . . . [#12: 10 YRS]

- GE Hu . . . . [#12: 7 YRS]

- GUO Jinghua . . [#12: 5 YRS]

-
GYAGA . . . . . . [#12: 4 YRS]

- HAO Fuyuan . . . [#12: 10 YRS]

- HU Jian[1] . . . . . [#12: 10 YRS]

- HUANG Junjie
. . . . [#12: 10 YRS]

- JIANG Fuzhen
. . . . [#12: 8 YRS]

- JIANG Zhiqiang
. . . . [#12: 13 YRS]

- LI Baoqin . . . . . [#12: 5 YRS]

- LI Fufa . . . . . . [#12?: 7 YRS]

- LI Jie[1] . . . . [#12: 5 YRS]

- LI Nan . . . . [#12: 7 YRS]

- LI Wangyang
  . . . . [#12: 13 YRS]

- LI Xiaodong
  . . . . [#12: 13 YRS]

- LI Yongsheng
  . . . . [#12: 12 YRS]

- LI Zhenqi . . . . . [#12: 5 YRS]

- LI Zhongjie
  . . . . [#12: 5-6 YRS]

- LIAO Jia'an . . . [#12: 3 YRS]

- LIAO Yiwu . . . . [#12: 4 YRS]

- LIAO Zheng . . . [#12: 7 YRS]

- LIN Songlin . . . [#12: 8 YRS]

- LIU Baiqiang
  . . . . [#12/ X#5: 17 YRS]

- LIU De . . . . . . [#12: 7 YRS]

- LIU Heping[1] . . . [#12: 12 YRS]

- MA Xiaoyu
  . . . . [#12?/ X#?: 7 YRS]

- REN Wanding . . [#12: 7 YRS]

- SI Wei . . . . [#12: 4 YRS]

- SUN Sanbao . . . [#12?: 8 YRS]

- SUN Weibang

- . . . . [#12/ X#6/3: 12 YRS]

- SUN Zhenggang
  . . . . [#12: 5 YRS]

- Teacher LIU . . . [#12: 7 YRS]

- Teacher X . . . . . [#12: 12 YRS]

- TIAN Xiaoming
  . . . . [#12: 7 YRS]

- WANG Guoqing
  . . . . [#12: 5 YRS]

- WANG Xinlong
  . . . . [#12: 8 YRS]

- WEI Shouzhong
  . . . . [#12: 15 YRS]

- XIAO Bin[1] . . . [#12: 9.5 YRS]

- XU Boquan . . . . [#12: 8 YRS]

- XU Jianxiong
  . . . . [#12: 10 YRS]

- YANG Lianzi
  . . . . [#12: 15 YRS]

- YAO Huxian . . . [#12: 6 YRS]

- YU Zhuo . . . . . [#12: 2 YRS]

- ZHANG Jie[2] . . . [#12: 18 YRS]

- ZHANG Jingsheng[1]
  . . . . [#12: 13 YRS]

- ZHANG Ming[1] . . [#12: 10 YRS]

- ZHANG Ruiyu . [#12: 4 YRS]

- **ZHANG Weiping**
  . . . . [#12: 9 YRS]

- **ZHANG Xiaoxu**
  . . . . [#12: 15 YRS]

- **ZHANG Zongai**
  . . . . [#12: 5 YRS]

- **ZHAO Junlu** . . . [#12: 10 YRS]

- **ZHOU Feng** . . . [#12: 8 YRS]

- **ZHU Xiangzhong**
  . . . . [#12: 7 YRS]

CR #?

- **PEI Zhongxun**
  . . . . [#?: 15 YRS]

- **ZHAO Donghai**
  . . . . [#?: 13 YRS]

Sentence Unknown

CR #8

- **BAI Xiaomao** . . . [#8: ? YRS]

- **CHEN * chun** . . . [#8: ? YRS]

- **CHEN * feng** . . . [#8: ? YRS]

- **CHEN * juan** . . . [#8: ? YRS]

- **CHEN Jiahu** . . . . [#8: ? YRS]

- **CHEN Xuanliang**
  . . . . [#8? #12?: ? YRS]

- **DING Hancong**
  . . . . [#8?: ? YRS]

- **GAO * shan** . . . . [#8: ? YRS]

- **HONG * ping** . . . [#8: ? YRS]

- **HU Gang** . . . . . . [#8?: ? YRS]

- **JI Kunxing**
  . . . . [#8 #12?: ? YRS]

- **JIANG Fuxing** . . . [#8: ? YRS]

- **LI * dong** . . . . . . [#8: ? YRS]

- **LI * jin** . . . . [#8: ? YRS]

- **LI Fenglin**
  . . . . [#8? #12?: ? YRS]

- **LI Xinfu** . . . . [#8: ? YRS]

- **LIAO Baobin**
  . . . . [#8? #12?: ? YRS]

- **LIN * shou** . . . . . [#8: ? YRS]

- **LIU * fang** . . . . . [#8: ? YRS]

- **LIU * yang** . . . . . [#8: ? YRS]

- **LIU Bangming**
  . . . . [#8?: ? YRS]

- **LIU Chongyun**
  . . . . [#8?: ? YRS]

- **LIU Gui** . . . . . [#8?: 2.5 YRS?]

- LU Zhonghua . . . [#8?: ? YRS]

- LUO * xi . . . . . . [#8: ? YRS]

- PAN * hui . . . . . [#8: ? YRS]

- QU Biao
  . . . . [#8? #12?: ? YRS]

- RUAN * xue . . . . [#8: ? YRS]

- SHANG Jingzhong
  . . . . [#8 #12?: ? YRS]

- SHI Qing
  . . . . [#8 #12?: ? YRS]

- WANG * bin . . . . [#8: ? YRS]

- WANG * quan . . . [#8: ? YRS]

- WANG Yangli . . . [#8?: ? YRS]

- WANG Yuqing . . [#8?: ? YRS]

- WU Yingling . . . . [#8?: ? YRS]

- XIE * ying . . . . . [#8: ? YRS]

- XU Guocai
  . . . . [#8? #12: ? YRS]

- YAO Yuan
  . . . . [#8? #12?: ? YRS]

- YU * you . . . . . . [#8: ? YRS]

- YU Anmin . . . [#8 #12: ? YRS]

- ZENG Dazhao . . . [#8?: ? YRS]

- ZHANG Donghui
  . . . . [#8?: ? YRS]

- ZHANG Hanjiang
  . . . . [#8?: ? YRS]

- ZHANG Lin
  . . . . [#8? #12? : ? YRS]

- ZHANG Weidong
  . . . . [#8?: ? YRS]

CR #9

- BAO * ji . . . . . . [#9: ? YRS]

- CHE * lun . . . . . [#9: ? YRS]

- CHEN Ziran . . . . [#9: ? YRS]

- CHENG Dingguo
  . . . . [#9: ? YRS]

- CHENG Guomin . [#9: ? YRS]

- FAN Youjiang . . . [#9: ? YRS]

- FU Guomin . . . . . [#9: ? YRS]

- GAN Qixiang . . . [#9: ? YRS]

- GONG Daqian . . . [#9: ? YRS]

- HE Xunzhen . . . . [#9: ? YRS]

- HUANG * cheng . [#9: ? YRS]

- JIANG * wu . . . . [#9: ? YRS]

- JIANG Qianguo . . [#9: ? YRS]

- KONG * li . . . . . [#9: ? YRS]

- LI * pu . . . . [#9: ? YRS]

- LI * shan . . . . . . [#9: ? YRS]
- LI * wen . . . . . . [#9: ? YRS]
- LI * xin . . . . [#9: ? YRS]
- LI Chungfu . . . . . [#9: ? YRS]
- LI Defeng . . . . . . [#9: ? YRS]
- LI Huafang . . . . . [#9: ? YRS]
- LI Qiusheng . . . . [#9: ? YRS]
- LI Shufen . . . . . . [#9: ? YRS]
- LI Shuming . . . . . [#9: ? YRS]
- LIAO Zhen'an . . . [#9: ? YRS]
- LIU * ying . . . . . [#9: ? YRS]
- LOU * rong . . . . [#9: ? YRS]
- LU * gang . . . . . [#9: ? YRS]
- LU * rui . . . . [#9: ? YRS]
- LU * sen . . . . . . [#9: ? YRS]
- LU * yi . . . . [#9: ? YRS]
- LU Yongting . . . . [#9: ? YRS]
- LU Yunliang . . . . [#9: ? YRS]
- LÜ * qin . . . . . . [#9: ? YRS]
- LUO Yiyuan . . . . [#9: ? YRS]
- PAN Lianxiang . . [#9: ? YRS]
- SONG * you . . . . [#9: ? YRS]

- SU Ruying . . . . [#9: ? YRS]
- SUN * tang . . . . . [#9: ? YRS]
- TAN Fangyou . . . [#9: ? YRS]
- TANG Tianxu . . . [#9: ? YRS]
- WAN Yansheng . . [#9: ? YRS]
- WANG * fan . . . . [#9: ? YRS]
- WANG * hua . . . [#9: ? YRS]
- WANG * qing^1 . . . [#9: ? YRS]
- WANG * qing^2 . . . [#9: ? YRS]
- WANG * xiu . . . . [#9: ? YRS]
- WANG * yuan . . . [#9: ? YRS]
- WANG Guixiang . [#9: ? YRS]
- WANG Jiliang . . . [#9: ? YRS]
- WANG Wenchen . [#9: ? YRS]
- WANG Xianyao . . [#9: ? YRS]
- WANG XX . . . . . [#9: ? YRS]
- WANG Yin . . . . . [#9: ? YRS]
- WEN Xinyuan . . . [#9: ? YRS]
- WU * lin . . . . . . [#9: ? YRS]
- XI Jinxian . . . . . [#9: ? YRS]
- XIA * lan . . . . . . [#9: ? YRS]
- XIA Lihuai . . . . . [#9: ? YRS]

- XIANG Enzhen . . [#9: ? YRS]

- XU Yuanjie . . . . . [#9: ? YRS]

- XUE Fuzhong . . . [#9: ? YRS]

- YAN Guanbao . . . [#9: ? YRS]

- YANG Biao . . . . . [#9: ? YRS]

- YANG Maicun . . . [#9: ? YRS]

- YANG Sende . . . . [#9: ? YRS]

- YUAN Jingwu . . . [#9: ? YRS]

- ZENG Chuqiao . . [#9: ? YRS]

- ZENG Qifa . . . . . [#9: ? YRS]

- ZHANG * shan . . [#9: ? YRS]

- ZHANG Caixian
  . . . . [#9: ? YRS]

- ZHANG Desheng
  . . . . [#9: ? YRS]

- ZHANG Shuying
  . . . . [#9: ? YRS]

- ZHAO * hong . . . [#9: ? YRS]

- ZHAO Chunhuai . [#9: ? YRS]

- ZHENG * xin . . . [#9: ? YRS]

- ZHOU * ling . . . . [#9: ? YRS]

- ZHOU Jinfan . . . [#9: ? YRS]

- ZHU Lianzheng
  . . . . [#9: ? YRS]

- ZONG Rongkun . . [#9: ? YRS]

CR #12

- CHEN *2 . . . . . . [#12: ? YRS]

- CHEN Dao . . . . . [#12: ? YRS]

- CHI * ting . . . . . [#12: ? YRS]

- CUI Jiancheng
  . . . . [#12?: ? YRS]

- DAN * dong . . . . [#12: ? YRS]

- FENG * ji . . . . . [#12: ? YRS]

- FENG Zechao . . . [#12: ? YRS]

- FU Bin . . . . [#12: ? YRS]

- GAO Longfa . . . . [#12: ? YRS]

- JI * liang . . . . . . [#12: ? YRS]

- LI * hong . . . . . . [#12: ? YRS]

- LI * nian1 . . . . . . [#12: ? YRS]

- LI * nian2 . . . . . . [#12: ? YRS]

- LI * shou . . . . . . [#12: ? YRS]

- LI * shun1 . . . . . [#12: ? YRS]

- LI Nannan . . . . [#12?: ? YRS]

- LIN Ziyong . . . . [#12?: ? YRS]

- LIU * . . . . [#12: ? YRS]

- LIU * xin . . . . . . [#12: ? YRS]

- LIU Weipu . . . . . [#12: ? YRS]

- LIU Yi . . . . [#12: ? YRS]

- LU Zhanbiao
. . . . [#12?: ? YRS]

- LUO Ziren . . . . [#12?: ? YRS]

- NI * cai . . . . [#12: ? YRS]

- NIU Shengchang
. . . . [#12: ? YRS]

- OUYANG Xinming
. . . . [#12: ? YRS]

- PAN
. . . . [#12: ? YRS]

- PU Yong . . . . . . [#12: ? YRS]

- QI * long . . . . . . [#12: ? YRS]

- QIN Hubao . . . [#12: 10 YRS?]

- QIU * wen . . . . . [#12: ? YRS]

- SHEN Zhigao . . . [#12: ? YRS]

- SONG * ze . . . . . [#12: ? YRS]

- SUN Wufu . . . . [#12?: ? YRS]

- TANG Ping . . . . . [#12: ? YRS]

- WANG Cun . . . [#12?: ? YRS]

- WANG Gang . . . . [#12: ? YRS]

- WANG Haidong
. . . . [#12: ? YRS]

- WANG Jiaxiang
. . . . [#3? #12: ? YRS]

- WANG Xinlin . . . [#12: ? YRS]

- WANG Zhaoming
. . . . [#3? #12: ? YRS]

- WU Tongfan . . . . [#12: ? YRS]

- YANG Dongju . . . [#12: ? YRS]

- YANG Ensen . . . . [#12: ? YRS]

- YANG Fang . . . . [#12: ? YRS]

- YANG Hong . . . [#12?: ? YRS]

- ZHANG * hu . . . [#12: ? YRS]

- ZHANG Cheng
. . . . [#12?/ X#7?: ? YRS]

- ZHANG Shanguang
. . . . [#12: ? YRS]

- ZHANG Shen(g)ming
. . . . [#12/ X#3?: ? YRS]

- ZHAO Shujian
. . . . [#12: ? YRS]

- ZHOU * jian . . . . [#12: ? YRS]

- ZHOU * li . . . . . [#12: ? YRS]

- ZHOU Yiming . . . [#12: ? YRS]

- ZHU Yiqun . . . . . [#12: ? YRS]

- **ZHUANG Lixin**
. . . . [#12: ? YRS]

CR #?

- **ABDUWELI** . . . . [#?: ? YRS]

- **HAN Binglin** . . . . [#?: ? YRS]

- **HU Jian**[2] . . . . . . [#?: ? YRS]

- **LIU Ruilin** . . . . . [#?: ? YRS]

- **MA Xiaojun** . . . . [#?: ? YRS]

- **MUHTAR CHONG KADIR**
. . . . [#?: ? YRS]

- **SHADIKEJIANG** . [#?: ? YRS]

- **WANG Shuwei** . . [#?: ? YRS]

- **XIAO Han** . . . . . [#?: ? YRS]

Administratively Sentenced

[NB: This is the least complete part of the present list. Thousands of people are "administratively" sentenced without trial by the police to terms of up to three years' "labor re-education" every year. This includes an unknown number of "minor counter-revolutionaries," probably at least several hundred annually - that is, political dissidents whose cases usually remain entirely unknown to the outside world. Such cases, which are not included in the total

nationwide figure of "3,317 sentenced counterrevolutionaries" officially admitted to by the Chinese authorities, are seldom publicly reported and are thus especially hard to monitor.]

- **FU Shenqi** . . . . [3 YRS]

- **HUANG Shixu** . . . . . . [3 YRS]

- **LU Gang** . . . . [3 YRS]

- **SHAN Zhenheng** . . . . [? YRS]

- **ZHANG Xianliang** . . . [3 YRS]

Alleged Violent/Other Criminal Cases

Sentence Known

CR #2

- *WANG Hongwen*
. . . . [#2 #3 #8 #11 #12/ X#2:
DP/COMMUTED TO LIFE]

- *YAO Wenyuan*
. . . . [#2 #3 #8 #11 #12/ X#2:
DP/COMMUTED TO LIFE]

- *ZHANG Chunqiao*
. . . . [#2 #3 #8 #11 #12/ X#2:
DP/COMMUTED TO LIFE]

CR #6

- *Guo * hui*
. . . . . [#6 #10: DEATH W/REPRIEVE]

CR #7

- **CAI Weiguo** . . . . [#7: 5 YRS]

- **CHEN Guangliang** [#7: 7 YRS]

- **CHEN Xiangyun** . [#7: 5 YRS]

- *CHEN Xiaoli* . . . [#7: 20 YRS]

- *CU Chengyang* . . [#7: 12 YRS]

- **FENG Jun** . . [#7: 10-15 YRS]

- **GAO Xiaoshi** . . . . [#7: 7 YRS]

- *GUAN Jian* . . . . [#7: 20 YRS]

- **HE X** . . . . [#7: 6 YRS]

- **KAJIKHUMAR SHABDAN**
. . . . [#7: 12 OR 15 YRS]

- **LI Ziming** . . . . . [#7: 15 YRS]

- *LI li* . . . . [#7: 7 YRS]

- **LIANG Qiang** . . [#7: 15 YRS]

- **LIU Chunan** . . . [#7: 15 YRS]

- **LIU Jian'an** . . . [#7: 10 YRS]

- **LIU Weiguo** . . . . [#7: 7 YRS]

- **LU Zhengping** [#7: 10-15 YRS]

- **NG Kwai-kong** . . . [#7: 5 YRS]

- **OU Zongyou** . . . [#7: 15 YRS]

- **QIAN Rongmian** . [#7: 6 YRS]

- **QIU Lin** . . . . [#7: 10-15 YRS]

- **WANG Changhong**[2] [#7: 15 YRS]

- **WU Jidong** . . . . [#7: 10 YRS]

- **YANG Xiaohua** . . [#7: 8 YRS]

- **ZHANG Yi**[2] . . . [#7: 13 YRS]

- **ZHOU Yan** . . . . . . [#7: LIFE]

CR #8

- **GAO Xiaoliang** . . [#8: 9 YRS]

- **YAO Kaiwen** . . . [#8: 10 YRS]

CR #9

- **LU * xiang**[2]
. . . . [#9: DEATH W/REPRIEVE]

- **JI * wei**[2] [#9: DEATH W/REPRIEVE]

CR #10

- **NAMAT ABDUMAT**[12: 15 YRS]

CR #12

- **CHENG Yezi** . . . [#12: 5 YRS]

- **JI Heli** . . . . [#12: 8 YRS]

- **LIN Xiao'an** . . . [#12: 5 YRS]

- **YAN Qinren** . . . [#12: 5 YRS]

- **YUAN Chunyou** . [#12: 5 YRS]

- **ZHANG Yishan** . [#12: 12 YRS]

CR #?

- *CHI Qun* . . . . [#?: 18 YRS]

- *HUANG Zhaoqi* . . [#?: 18 YRS]

- *QI Benyu* . . . . [#?: 18 YRS]

- *XU Jingxian* . . . . . [#?: 18 YRS]

- *XU Zhaochang* . . . . [#?: LIFE]

Sentence Unknown

CR #2

- *CHE * ji* . . . . [#2: ? YRS]

- *CHEN Boda* . . . . . [#2: ? YRS]

- *LI * lian* . . . . [#2: ? YRS]

CR #3

- *JING ** . . . . [#3: ? YRS]

CR #4

- *CHEN * hua* . . . . [#4: ? YRS]

- *DUAN * xiang* . . . [#4: ? YRS]

- *GUO * kun* . . . . . [#4: ? YRS]

- *HAO * yun* . . . . . [#4: ? YRS]

- *KUANG * jing* . . . [#4: ? YRS]

- *LI * guang* . . . . . . [#4: ? YRS]

- *LIANG * jun* . . . . [#4: ? YRS]

- *LIN * qiu[1]* . . . . . [#4: ? YRS]

- *LIU * ming* . . . . . [#4: ? YRS]

- *NONG * shan* . . . . [#4: ? YRS]

- *QIAN * ding* . . . . [#4: ? YRS]

- *SHEN * ling* . . . . . [#4: ? YRS]

- *SHI * bao* . . . . . [#4: ? YRS]

- *SHI * hua* . . . . . . [#4: ? YRS]

- *TENG * yong* . . . . [#4: ? YRS]

- *WANG * kang* . . . [#4: ? YRS]

- *WENG * qiang* . . . [#4: ? YRS]

■ *XIA * gen* . . . . . . [#4: ? YRS]

■ *XU * cai* . . . . [#4: ? YRS]

■ *XU * zhong* . . . . . [#4: ? YRS]

■ *YAN * meng* . . . . . [#4: ? YRS]

■ *ZHANG * xin[1]* . . . [#4: ? YRS]

■ *ZHAO *[2]* . . . . . . [#4: ? YRS]

■ *ZHOU * tang* . . . . [#4: ? YRS]

■ *ZHOU * zhong* . . . [#4: ? YRS]

CR #5

■ *GU * shan* . . . . . . [#5: ? YRS]

■ *HU * di* . . . . [#5: ? YRS]

■ *RAN * fu* . . . . [#5: ? YRS]

■ *SHEN * qing* . . . . [#5: ? YRS]

■ *TAN * xiang* . . . . . [#5: ? YRS]

■ *WANG * sheng* . . . [#5: ? YRS]

■ *ZHANG * bing* . . . [#5: ? YRS]

■ *ZHANG * he* . . . . [#5: ? YRS]

■ *ZHOU * pei* . . . . . [#5: ? YRS]

CR #6

■ *DING * lai* . . . . . [#6: ? YRS]

■ *HUANG * rui* . . . . [#6: ? YRS]

■ *HUANG *[1]* . . . . . [#6: ? YRS]

■ *LIU * sheng* . . . . . [#6: ? YRS]

■ *LUO ** . . . . [#6: ? YRS]

■ *TANG ** . . . . [#6: ? YRS]

■ *TANG * ming* . . . . [#6: ? YRS]

■ *WANG ** . . . . . . [#6: ? YRS]

■ *XU ** . . . . [#6: ? YRS]

■ *YU * shun* . . . . . . [#6: ? YRS]

■ *ZHANG *[2]* . . . . . [#6: ? YRS]

■ *ZHAO * qiang* . . . [#6: ? YRS]

■ *ZHAO *[3]* . . . . . . [#6: ? YRS]

■ *ZHENG * long* . . . [#6: ? YRS]

CR #7

■ **AI * sha** [Kazakh] . [#7: ? YRS]

■ *BAI * hua* . . . . . . [#7: ? YRS]

■ **BAI Xinyu** . . . . . [#7: ? YRS]

■ *CAI ** . . . . [#7: ? YRS]

■ *CHEN * kun* . . . . [#7: ? YRS]

■ *CHEN Andong* . . . [#7: ? YRS]

■ *CHEN Hong[2]* . . . . [#7: ? YRS]

■ **CHEN Xuedeng** . . [#7: ? YRS]

■ **CHI Hecan** . . . . . [#7: ? YRS]

■ *DING* * . . . . [#7: ? YRS]

■ *DU Yongsheng* . . . [#7: ? YRS]

■ *GAO * xian* . . . . . [#7: ? YRS]

■ **HAXI *** [Kazakh] [#7: ? YRS]

■ *HAO* * . . . . [#7: ? YRS]

■ *HE * guo* . . . . . . [#7: ? YRS]

■ *HUANG Jun* . . . . . [#7: ? YRS]

■ *JIANG * kun* . . . . [#7: ? YRS]

■ *LI* * . . . . [#7: ? YRS]

■ *LI * hao* . . . . [#7: ? YRS]

■ *LI * qi* . . . . [#7: ? YRS]

■ *LI * quan²* . . . . . . [#7: ? YRS]

■ *LI * yun* . . . . [#7: ? YRS]

■ **LIANG C(h)aotian** [#7: ? YRS]

■ *LIN * qiu²* . . . . . . [#7: ? YRS]

■ *LIN * yin* . . . . . . [#7: ? YRS]

■ *LIN Tianlin* . . . . . [#7: ? YRS]

■ *LIN Weisheng* . . . . [#7: ? YRS]

■ **LIU Bihua** . . . . . [#7: ? YRS]

■ *LIU Li* . . . . [#7: ? YRS]

■ *LIU Weihong¹* . . . . [#7: ? YRS]

■ *LUO * shan* . . . . . [#7: ? YRS]

■ *LUO Zhongmin* . . . [#7: ? YRS]

■ *MA * di* . . . . [#7: ? YRS]

■ *MA * ying* . . . . . . [#7: ? YRS]

■ *MA Guirong* . . . . . [#7: ? YRS]

■ **MAIHAN ** [Kazakh]**
. . . . [#7: ? YRS]

■ **MUER *** [Kazakh]**
. . . . [#7: ? YRS]

■ *QIU * mei* . . . . . . [#7: ? YRS]

■ **QU Zuojie** . . . . . [#7: ? YRS]

■ *SHEN * qing* . . . . [#7: ? YRS]

■ *SHI * qiang* . . . . . [#7: ? YRS]

■ *SU * que* . . . . [#7: ? YRS]

■ *SUN * jiang* . . . . . [#7: ? YRS]

■ **SUN Daoshun** . . . [#7: ? YRS]

■ *TAN Jun* . . . . [#7: ? YRS]

■ **WANG Chengjin** . [#7: ? YRS]

■ **WANG Chengyin** . [#7: ? YRS]

■ **WANG Yusheng** . [#7: ? YRS]

■ **WANG Zhongyu** . [#7: ? YRS]

■ *WEI * qiang* . . . . . [#7: ? YRS]

- *WEI * qin* ...... [#7: ? YRS]

- *WU * jie* .... [#7: ? YRS]

- *WU Fuyuan* ..... [#7: ? YRS]

- **WUHE *** [Kazakh]
.... [#7: ? YRS]

- *XU * di* .... [#7: ? YRS]

- *XU * mei* ...... [#7: ? YRS]

- *XU Jian* .... [#7: ? YRS]

- **XU Jiansheng** ... [#7: ? YRS]

- *YAN Di* .... [#7: ? YRS]

- *YANG * kang* .... [#7: ? YRS]

- *YANG * pei* ..... [#7: ? YRS]

- *YANG Tao[1]* ..... [#7: ? YRS]

- *YE * fa* .... [#7: ? YRS]

- *YUE * lie* ...... [#7: ? YRS]

- *Zhang Ni** BI-TE*** (Caucasian name)
.... [#7: ? YRS]

- *ZHANG * qiu* .... [#7: ? YRS]

- *ZHANG * wen* ... [#7: ? YRS]

- *ZHANG * xin[2]* ... [#7: ? YRS]

- *ZHAO Zongxiang* .. [#7: ? YRS]

- *ZHENG Shousong* . [#7: ? YRS]

- *ZHOU Guoqiang[2]* . [#7: ? YRS]

- *ZHU *[1]* .... [#7: ? YRS]

- *ZHU Kexing* ..... [#7: ? YRS]

- *ZHUANG * xiong* . [#7: ? YRS]

- *ZHUANG * xiu* ... [#7: ? YRS]

CR #8

- **CAO * sheng** .... [#8: ? YRS]

- **CAO * you** ..... [#8: ? YRS]

- **CHEN * kang** ... [#8: ? YRS]

- **CHEN * long** .... [#8: ? YRS]

- **CHEN * qing** ... [#8: ? YRS]

- **CHEN *[1]** ...... [#8: ? YRS]

- **DAI * hua** ..... [#8: ? YRS]

- **DONG * fei** .... [#8: ? YRS]

- **DU * hong** ..... [#8: ? YRS]

- **FAN * an** ...... [#8: ? YRS]

- **FENG * ren** .... [#8: ? YRS]

- **GAO * heng** .... [#8: ? YRS]

- **GAO * hong** .... [#8: ? YRS]

- **GAO * nian** .... [#8: ? YRS]

- **GAO * qing** .... [#8: ? YRS]

- **GAO * zhi** . . . . . [#8: ? YRS]
- **HE * hua** . . . . . . [#8: ? YRS]
- **JI * wei[1]** . . . . [#8: ? YRS]
- **JIANG * feng** . . . [#8: ? YRS]
- **JIANG * fu** . . . . . [#8: ? YRS]
- **JIE *** . . . . [#8: ? YRS]
- **LEI * quan** . . . . . [#8: ? YRS]
- **LEI * tong** . . . . . [#8: ? YRS]
- **LI * chuan** . . . . . [#8: ? YRS]
- **LI * he** . . . . [#8: ? YRS]
- **LI * jun** . . . . [#8: ? YRS]
- **LI * luan** . . . . . . [#8: ? YRS]
- **LI * nian[2]** . . . . . . [#8: ? YRS]
- **LI * quan[1]** . . . . . [#8: ? YRS]
- **LI * rong** . . . . . . [#8: ? YRS]
- **LI * she** . . . . [#8: ? YRS]
- **LI * shun[2]** . . . . . [#8: ? YRS]
- **LI * wu** . . . . [#8: ? YRS]
- **LI * xiang** . . . . . [#8: ? YRS]
- **LI * yuan** . . . . . . [#8: ? YRS]
- **LI * zhong** . . . . . [#8: ? YRS]
- **LIANG * zhu** . . . [#8: ? YRS]
- **LIAO * bin** . . . . . [#8: ? YRS]
- **LIU * cheng** . . . . [#8: ? YRS]
- **LIU * jie** . . . . . . [#8: ? YRS]
- **LIU * tang** . . . . . [#8: ? YRS]
- **LU * dai** . . . . . . [#8: ? YRS]
- **LU * qian** . . . . . . [#8: ? YRS]
- **LU * sheng** . . . . . [#8: ? YRS]
- **LU * xiang[1]** . . . . . [#8: ? YRS]
- **MAO * bao** . . . . . [#8: ? YRS]
- **MIAO * sen** . . . . [#8: ? YRS]
- **OU * yan** . . . . . . [#8: ? YRS]
- **QIN * dai** . . . . . . [#8: ? YRS]
- **QIU Liangqing** . . [#8: ? YRS]
- **REN * li** . . . . [#8: ? YRS]
- **REN * ming** . . . . [#8: ? YRS]
- **REN Yuanqing** . . [#8: ? YRS]
- **SHEN * qi** . . . . . [#8: ? YRS]
- **SHI * chao** . . . . . [#8: ? YRS]
- **SHI * jun** . . . . . . [#8: ? YRS]
- **SHI * pin** . . . . . . [#8: ? YRS]
- **SONG *** . . . . . . [#8: ? YRS]
- **SONG * feng** . . . . [#8: ? YRS]

- TAN * yi . . . . . [#8: ? YRS]

- TANG * sheng . . . [#8: ? YRS]

- TIAN * fu . . . . . [#8: ? YRS]

- TIAN * zhen . . . . [#8: ? YRS]

- WANG * jie . . . . [#8: ? YRS]

- WANG * lian . . . [#8: ? YRS]

- WANG * liang . . . [#8: ? YRS]

- WANG * xin . . . . [#8: ? YRS]

- WANG * yan . . . [#8: ? YRS]

- WU * chun . . . . . [#8: ? YRS]

- WU * sheng . . . . [#8: ? YRS]

- XU * feng . . . . . . [#8: ? YRS]

- XU * gang . . . . . [#8: ? YRS]

- XU * zhi . . . . . . [#8: ? YRS]

- XUE * mei . . . . . [#8: ? YRS]

- YANG * bin . . . . [#8: ? YRS]

- YANG * jun . . . . [#8: ? YRS]

- YANG * min . . . . [#8: ? YRS]

- YANG * ming . . . [#8: ? YRS]

- YANG * ri . . . . . [#8: ? YRS]

- YIN * ai . . . . [#8: ? YRS]

- YING * chang . . . [#8: ? YRS]

- ZHANG * de . . . . [#8: ? YRS]

- ZHANG * hua . . . [#8: ? YRS]

- ZHANG * jian . . . [#8: ? YRS]

- ZHANG * ming . . [#8: ? YRS]

- ZHANG * ping . . [#8: ? YRS]

- ZHANG * yuan . . [#8: ? YRS]

- ZHANG Sanyi . . . [#8: ? YRS]

- ZHAO * fang . . . [#8: ? YRS]

- ZHAO * guo . . . . [#8: ? YRS]

- ZHONG * yi . . . . [#8: ? YRS]

CR #9

- AH Jin . . . . [#9/ X#2?: ? YRS]

- CHAI Zhizong [#9/ X#4?: ? YRS]

- DAI Xuanneng . . . [#9: ? YRS]

- GUO * xiang . . . . [#9: ? YRS]

- LI Guangchang . . [#9: ? YRS]

- LI * zhi . . . . [#9: ? YRS]

- LIANG Dianhua
  . . . . [#9/ X#4?: ? YRS]

- LIN Bingqi . . . . . [#9: ? YRS]

- LIN Yongkai . . . . [#9: ? YRS]

- LÜ * run . . . . . . [#9: ? YRS]

- SUN * lian . . . . . [#9: ? YRS]

- WANG Baorong
. . . . [#9/ X#4?: ? YRS]

- WANG * xing[1] . . . [#9: ? YRS]

- WANG * xing[2] . . . [#9: ? YRS]

- WANG * ying . . . [#9: ? YRS]

- WEI Zhijian . . . . [#9: ? YRS]

- WU Qixiang . . . . [#9: ? YRS]

- XU Shexiu . [#9/ #10?: ? YRS]

- ZHANG *[1] . . . . . [#9: ? YRS]

- ZHANG Fuzhi
. . . . [#9/ X#4?: ? YRS]

- ZHANG * hui . . . [#9: ? YRS]

- ZHANG Jingsheng[2]
. . . . [#9/ #10?: ? YRS]

- ZHAO *[1] . . . . . . [#9: ? YRS]

- ZHAO * rong . . . [#9: ? YRS]

- ZHENG * bao . . . [#9: ? YRS]

- ZHENG * huan . . [#9: ? YRS]

- ZHONG Chongzhen
. . . . [#9/ X#4?: ? YRS]

- ZHONG Qigan [#9/ X#4?: ? YRS]

- ZHOU Zhengwu . [#9: ? YRS]

CR #10

- *BAI * gui [Mongol]* [#10: ? YRS]

- *CHEN * jiao* . . . . [#10: ? YRS]

- *CHEN * liao* . . . . [#10: ? YRS]

- *CHEN * shu* . . . . . [#10: ? YRS]

- *DING * chang* . . . [#10: ? YRS]

- *GAO * * . . . . [#10: ? YRS]

- *GUO * hui* . . . . . [#10: ? YRS]

- *HUANG *[2]* . . . . . [#10: ? YRS]

- *LIU * chen* . . . . . [#10: ? YRS]

- *LIU * lu* . . . . [#10: ? YRS]

- *LU * * . . . . [#10: ? YRS]

- *QI * sheng* . . . . . . [#10: ? YRS]

- *SU * yu* . . . . [#10: ? YRS]

- *XU * chang* . . . . . [#10: ? YRS]

- *XUE * fu* . . . . . . [#10: ? YRS]

- *YANG *[1]* . . . . . . [#10: ? YRS]

- *YU * qiang* . . . . . [#10: ? YRS]

- *ZHANG * gong* . . . [#10: ? YRS]

- *ZHANG * qing* . . . [#10: ? YRS]

- *ZHANG * shou* . . . [#10: ? YRS]

- *ZHONG * long* . . . [#10: ? YRS]

- *ZHOU * ping* . . . . [#10: ? YRS]

CR #11

- *LI * jie* . . . . [#11: ? YRS]

- *WANG Baojiang* . . [#11: ? YRS]

- *ZHANG Benli* . . . . [#11: ? YRS]

- *ZHOU * long* . . . . [#11: ? YRS]

CR #12

- **CHENG * shan** . . [#12: ? YRS]

- **RUAN * qing** . . . [#12: ? YRS]

- **WU * quan** . . . . . [#12: ? YRS]

- **ZHONG * hua** . . . [#12: ? YRS]

CR #?

- *MA Tianshui*
. [#?: MENTALLY ILL/AWAITING TRIAL
(1982) ? YRS]

- *WANG * jin* . . . . . [#?: ? YRS]

- *XIE Jingyi* . . . . . . [#?: ? YRS]

- *ZHAO Dengcheng* [#?: 18 YRS?]

2. Arrested in 1992-93: Awaiting Trial/Sentence Unknown

Non-Violent Cases

- **AN Ning** . . . . [#8?: ? YRS]

- **CAO Jianyu** . . . . [#8?: ? YRS]

- **CHEN Qinglin** . . . [#8: ? YRS]

- **CHEN Wei**[1] . . . . . [#12: ? YRS]

- **DELGER** . . . . . . [#12: ? YRS]

- **DING Mao** . . . . . [#8?: ? YRS]

- **GAO Changyun** . . [#8?: ? YRS]

- **Gao Yuxiang** . . [#8 #12: ? YRS]

- **HE Quan** . . . . . . [#12: ? YRS]

- **HU Shenglun (Shigen)**
. . . . [#8 #12: ? YRS]

- **KANG Yuchun** [#8 #12: ? YRS]

- **LI Quanli** . . . . . . [#8: ? YRS]

- **LIU Baiyu** . . . . . [#8?: ? YRS]

- **LIU Jingsheng** . [#8 #12: ? YRS]

- **LIU Wensheng** . . . [#8?: ? YRS]

- **LU Mingxia** . . . . [#8?: ? YRS]

- **LU Yalin** . . . . . . [#8?: ? YRS]

- **LU Yanghua** . . . . [#8?: ? YRS]

- LU Zhigang . . [#8 #12: ? YRS]

- RUI Chaohuai . . . [#12: ? YRS]

- WANG Guoqi . . . [#8: ? YRS]

- WANG Jianping . . [#8?: ? YRS]

- WANG Peizhong
. . . . [#8 #12: ? YRS]

- WANG Tiancheng
. . . . [#8 #12: ? YRS]

- XING Hongwei . . [#12: ? YRS]

- XING Shimin . . . [#8?: ? YRS]

- XU Dongling . . . . [#12: ? YRS]

- XU Zhendong . . . [#8?: ? YRS]

- ZHANG Chunzhu [#12: ? YRS]

- ZHANG Guojun[1] . [#12: ? YRS]

- ZHANG Jian . . . . [#8?: ? YRS]

3. Executed

Non-Violent Cases

- CAO Xiuhua . [#9: EXECUTED]

- HU * ming . . [#9: EXECUTED]

- HUANG * ping
. . . . [#9: EXECUTED]

- LIU * lin . . . [#9: EXECUTED]

- SHEN * shu . [#9: EXECUTED]

- WANG * zhi . [#9: EXECUTED]

- ZHOU * zong [#9: EXECUTED]

Alleged Violent/Other Criminal Cases

- *BAI * hai* . . . [#10: EXECUTED]

- *BAI * hua* . . . [#10: EXECUTED]

- BAN Huijie . [#DM: EXECUTED]

- *BIAN * yu* . . . [#10: EXECUTED]

- BIAN Hanwu
. . . . [#DM: EXECUTED]

- CAI Hedai . . [#9: EXECUTED]

- *CHEN * dong* . [#10: EXECUTED]

- *CHEN * guang*
. . . . . . [#4/ X#2 X#1: EXECUTED]

- *CHEN * li* . . . [#5: EXECUTED]

- *CHEN * xin*
. . . . [#10/ X#5: EXECUTED]

- CHEN Guangping
. . . . [#DM: EXECUTED]

- CHEN Jian . [#DM: EXECUTED]

- CHEN XX . [#DM: EXECUTED]

- *GAO * li* . . . . [#10: EXECUTED]

- **GUO Zhenghua**
. . . . [#DM: EXECUTED]

- **HAN Weijun**
. . . . [#DM: EXECUTED]

- *HE * fei* . . . . [#10: EXECUTED]

- **HE Xiaokang**
. . . . [#DM: EXECUTED]

- *HE Xueyi*
. . . . [#8 #10 #11: EXECUTED]

- *HU * jie* . . . . [#10: EXECUTED]

- *KUANG * xiang* [#4: EXECUTED]

- *LI * ting* . [#10 #12: EXECUTED]

- **LI Wenbao** . [#DM: EXECUTED]

- *LIANG * * . . . . [#10: EXECUTED]

- **LIANG Hongchen**
. . . . [#DM: EXECUTED]

- **LIN Zhaorong**
. . . . [#DM: EXECUTED]

- **LIN Zhaorong**
. . . . [#DM: EXECUTED]

- *LIU * * . . . . . . [#11: EXECUTED]

- *LIU * xiang* . . [#11: EXECUTED]

- **LIU Baode** . [#DM: EXECUTED]

- *LU * gang* [#10 #11: EXECUTED]

- *LU * zhou*
. . . . . . [#10/ X#4 X#5: EXECUTED]

- *LÜ * * . . . . . . [#11: EXECUTED]

- *LÜ * fu* . . . . [#9: EXECUTED]

- **LUO Hongjun**
. . . . [#DM: EXECUTED]

- *MA * lu* . . . . [#10: EXECUTED]

- *MA * xin* . . . . [#10: EXECUTED]

- **MENG Duo** . [#DM: EXECUTED]

- **SHAO * wen** . [#9: EXECUTED]

- *SONG * lin* . . [#11: EXECUTED]

- *SUN * ping* . . [#10: EXECUTED]

- **SUN Baohe** [#DM: EXECUTED]

- *TAO Junguo*
. . . . [#8 #10 #11: EXECUTED]

- *WANG * feng*
. . . . [#10 #11: EXECUTED]

- *WANG * guang* [#10: EXECUTED]

- *WANG * wen* . [#11: EXECUTED]

- **WANG Guiyun**
. . . . [#9: EXECUTED]

- **WANG Hanwu**
. . . . [#DM: EXECUTED]

- **WANG Jun**[2]
. . . . [#DM: EXECUTED]

- **WANG XX** . . [#9: EXECUTED?]

- *WEI * li* . . . . [#10: EXECUTED]

- *WEI * shu*
. . . . [#8 #10 #12: EXECUTED]

- *XIE * min* . . . [#10: EXECUTED]

- *XIONG * heng*
. . . . [#10/ X#1: EXECUTED]

- **XU Guoming**
. . . . [#DM: EXECUTED]

- *YAN * shu* [#10 #11: EXECUTED]

- *YAN Qinggui*
. . . . [#8 #10 #11: EXECUTED]

- **YAN Xuerong**
. . . . [#DM: EXECUTED]

- *YANG *²* . . . . [#10: EXECUTED]

- **YU Chunting**
. . . . [#DM: EXECUTED]

- **YU Yongchuan**
. . . . [#DM: EXECUTED]

- *ZHANG * feng*
. . . . [#10: EXECUTED]

- *ZHANG * jun*
. . . . [#5: EXECUTED]

- *ZHANG * quan*
. . . . [#5 #8: EXECUTED]

- **ZHANG Wenkui**
. . . . [#DM: EXECUTED]

- *ZHAO * yun* . . [#5: EXECUTED]

- **ZHENG Lixi** . [#9: EXECUTED]

- **ZHONG Chongzhen**
. . . . [#9: EXECUTED]

- **ZHONG Qigan**
. . . . [#9: EXECUTED]

- *ZHOU * fu* . . [#11: EXECUTED]

- *ZHOU * gen* . [#5: EXECUTED]

- **ZHOU Jiguo**
. . . . [#DM: EXECUTED]

- **ZHOU Qi** . . [#DM: EXECUTED]

- **ZHOU Zhengxiang**
. . . . [#9: EXECUTED]

- *ZHU *²*
. . . . [#8 #10 #12: EXECUTED]

- **ZU Jianjun** . [#DM: EXECUTED]

B. Tibet

1. Sentenced

Non-Violent Cases

Sentence Known

CR #8

- **JAMPEL CHANGCHUP**
. . . . [#7 #8: 19 YRS]

- **JAMPEL KHEDRUP**
  . . . . [#7 #8: 18 YRS]

- **JAMPEL LOBSANG**
  . . . . [#7 #8: 10 YRS]

- **JAMPEL MONLAM**
  . . . . [#7 #8: 5 YRS]

- **JAMPEL TSERING**
  . . . . [#7 #8: 5 YRS]

- **NGAWANG GYALTSEN[1]**
  . . . . [#7 #8: 17 YRS]

- **NGAWANG KUNGA**
  . . . . [#7 #8: 5 YRS]

- **NGAWANG OEZER[2]**
  . . . . [#7 #8: 17 YRS]

- **NGAWANG PHULCHUNG**
  . . . . [#7 #8: 19 YRS]

- **NGAWANG RIGZIN**
  . . . . [#7 #8: 9 YRS]

CR #12 (Charge Confirmed or Presumed)

- **BUCHUNG** . . . . [#12: 5 YRS]

- **CHIME DROLKAR**
  . . . . [#12: 7 YRS]

- **CHOEDAK** . . . . [#12: 7 YRS]

- **CHUNGDAG[2]** . . [#12: 7 YRS]

- **DAMCHOE GYALTSEN**
  . . . . [#12: 4 YRS]

- **DAWA DROLMA[2]**
  . . . . [#12: 5 YRS]

- **DAWA TSERING[2]** [#12: 8 YRS]

- **DAWA[9]** . . . . . . [#12: 5 YRS]

- **DONDRUP DORJE** [#12: 5 YRS]

- **DORJE[4]** . . . . . [#12: 6-8 YRS]

- **DRADUL[3]** . . . . . [#12: 16 YRS]

- **DRAKPA TSULTRIM**
  . . . . [#12: 8 YRS]

- **DROLMA SANGPO**
  . . . . [#12: 3 YRS]

- **GELEK YONTEN** [#12: 7 YRS]

- **GYALTSEN CHOEDRON[1]**
  . . . . [#12: 4 YRS]

- **GYALTSEN CHOEZOM**
  . . . . [#12: 4 YRS]

- **GYALTSEN KELSANG[1]**

  . . . . [#12: 2 YRS]

- **GYALTSEN KUNSANG[1]**
  . . . . [#12: 4 YRS]

- **GYALTSEN LHAKSAM[1]**
  . . . . [#12: 7 YRS]

- **GYALTSEN LODROE[1]**
  . . . . [#12: 3 YRS]

- **GYALTSEN LUNGRING**
  . . . . [#12: 4 YRS]

- **GYALTSEN NYINYI**
  . . . . [#12: 4 YRS]
- **GYALTSEN SANGMO**
  . . . . [#12: 3 YRS]
- **GYALTSEN SHERAB**
  . . . . [#12: 5 YRS]
- **GYATSO DAMCHOE**
  . . . . [#12: 3 YRS]
- **GYATSO NGODRUP**
  . . . . [#12: 3 YRS]
- **JAMPA RANGDROL**
  . . . . [#12: 6 YRS]
- **JAMPA TENZIN²** [#12: 2 YRS]
- **JAMPA TSETEN** [#12: 7 YRS]
- **JAMPA¹** . . . . . . [#12: 4 YRS]
- **JAMPEL GENDUN**
  . . . . [#12: 9 YRS]
- **JAMPEL PHUNTSOG**
  . . . . [#12: 6 YRS]
- **JAMYANG KUNGA**
  . . . . [#12: 4 YRS]
- **JAMYANG SAMTEN**
  . . . . [#12: 5 YRS]
- **JIGME DORJE** . [#12: 3 YRS]
- **JIGME GYATSO¹** [#12: LIFE]
- **JIGME YANGCHEN**
  . . . . [#12: 7 YRS]

- **KELSANG DAWA²**
  . . . . [#12: 3 YRS]
- **KELSANG GYALTSEN**
  . . . . [#12: 6 YRS]
- **KHAMSANG GYALTSEN**
  . . . . [#12: 5 YRS]
- **KUNCHOK LODROE**
  . . . . [#12: 13 YRS]
- **KUNCHOK TSOMO**
  . . . . [#12: 3 YRS]
- **LEGDRUP** . . . . [#12: 3 YRS]
- **LHAGYAL** . . . . [#12: 4 YRS]
- **LHAKPA⁶** . . . . . [#12: 8 YRS]
- **LHUNDRUP DORJE**
  . . . . [#12: 15 YRS]
- **LHUNDRUP GADEN**
  . . [#12: 12½ YRS/MEDICAL PAROLE]
- **LHUNDRUP JINPA**
  . . . . [#12: 5 YRS]
- **LHUNDRUP TOGDEN**
  . . . . [#12: 14 YRS]
- **LOBSANG CHOEDRAG³**
  . . . . [#12: 5 YRS]
- **LOBSANG CHOEDRON²**
  . . . . [#12: 5 YRS]
- **LOBSANG CHOEDRON⁴**
  . . . . [#12: 4 YRS]

- **LOBSANG CHOEJOR**[1]
  . . . . [#12: 9 YRS]

- **LOBSANG CHOEKYI**
  . . . . [#12: 6 YRS]

- **LOBSANG DADAK**
  . . . . [#12: 9 YRS]

- **LOBSANG DARGYE**
  . . . . [#12: 7 YRS]

- **LOBSANG DORJE**
  . . . . [#12: 9 YRS]

- **LOBSANG DRADUL**
  . . . . [#12: 5 YRS]

- **LOBSANG DROLMA**[1]
  . . . . [#12: 5 YRS]

- **LOBSANG DROLMA**[2]
  . . . . [#12: 7 YRS]

- **LOBSANG GELEK**[1]
  . . . . [#12: 5 YRS]

- **LOBSANG GELEK**[2]
  . . . . [#12: 12 YRS]

- **LOBSANG GYATSO**[2]
  . . . . [#12: 3 YRS]

- **LOBSANG JAMPA**[1]
  . . . . [#12: 8 YRS]

- **LOBSANG KHEDRUP**
  . . . . [#12: 5 YRS]

- **LOBSANG LEGSHE**
  . . . . [#12: 5 YRS]

- **LOBSANG LHUNDRUP**[1]
  . . . . [#12: 3 YRS]

- **LOBSANG LHUNDRUP**[2]
  . . . . [#12: 7 YRS]

- **LOBSANG LHUNDRUP**[3]
  . . . . [#12: 7 YRS]

- **LOBSANG LUNGTOG**
  . . . . [#12: 7 YRS]

- **LOBSANG NYIMA**[1]
  . . . . [#12: 3 YRS]

- **LOBSANG PALDEN**[4]
  . . . . [#12: 10 YRS]

- **LOBSANG PHUNTSOG**
  . . . . [#12: 4 YRS]

- **LOBSANG SHERAB**[1]
  . . . . [#12: 8 YRS]

- **LOBSANG TASHI**[1]
  . . . . [#12: 7 YRS]

- **LOBSANG TASHI**[2]
  . . . . [#12: 5 YRS/LIFE?]

- **LOBSANG TENPA**[2]
  . . . . [#12: 8 YRS]

- **LOBSANG TENPA**[3]
  . . . . [#12: 3 YRS]

- **LOBSANG TRINLEY**[2]
  . . . . [#12: 4½ YRS]

- **LOBSANG TSONDRU**
  . . . . [#12: 6-7 YRS]

■ LOBSANG YARPHEL[1]
. . . . [#12: 7 YRS]

■ LOBSANG YESHE[1]
. . . . [#12: 5 YRS]

■ MIGMAR[3] . . . . [#12: 5 YRS]

■ NAMDROL LHAMO
. . . . [#12: 6 YRS]

■ NAMGYAL TASHI[1]
. . . . [#12: 8 YRS]

■ NGAGCHOE . . [#12: 5 YRS]

■ NGAWANG BUMCHOG
. . . . [#12: 5 YRS]

■ NGAWANG CHAMTSUL
. . . . [#7 #12: 15 YRS]

■ NGAWANG CHENDROL
. . . . [#12: 3 YRS]

■ NGAWANG CHOEJOR
. . . . [#12: 3 YRS]

■ NGAWANG CHOEKYI[2]
. . . . [#12: 5 YRS]

■ NGAWANG CHOEZOM[1]
. . . . [#12: 5 YRS]

■ NGAWANG CHOSHE
. . . . [#12: 3 YRS]

■ NGAWANG DAMCHOE
. . . . [#12: 4½ YRS]

■ NGAWANG DAWA
. . . . [#12: 6 YRS]

■ NGAWANG DECHOE
. . . . [#12: 3 YRS]

■ NGAWANG DEDROL[1]
. . . . [#12: 7 YRS]

■ NGAWANG DIPSEL
. . . . [#12: 4 YRS]

■ NGAWANG JANGCHEN
. . . . [#12: 5 YRS]

■ NGAWANG JIGME
. . . . [#12: 6 YRS]

■ NGAWANG KELDRON
. . . . [#12: 5 YRS]

■ NGAWANG KHEDRUP
. . . . [#12: 6 YRS]

■ NGAWANG KUNSANG
. . . . [#12: 6 YRS]

■ NGAWANG KYENMA
. . . . [#12: 4 YRS]

■ NGAWANG LEGSHE
. . . . [#12: 4 YRS]

■ NGAWANG LHAKSAM
. . . . [#12: 5 YRS]

■ NGAWANG LHUNDRUP[2]
. . . . [#12: 6 YRS]

■ NGAWANG LOCHOE
. . . . [#12: 5 YRS]

■ NGAWANG LUNGTOK
. . . . [#12: 5 YRS]

- **NGAWANG NAMDROL[1]**
  .... [#12: 7 YRS]

- **NGAWANG NAMGYAL[1]**
  .... [#12: 3 YRS]

- **NGAWANG NYIDROL**
  .... [#12: 3 YRS]

- **NGAWANG NYIMA[1]**
  .... [#12: 4 YRS]

- **NGAWANG OEZER[1]**
  .... [#12: 5 YRS]

- **NGAWANG PALDEN[1]**
  .... [#12: 4½ YRS]

- **NGAWANG PALDEN[2]**
  .... [#12: 3 YRS]

- **NGAWANG PEKAR**
  .... [#12: 8 YRS]

- **NGAWANG PELGON**
  .... [#12: 5 YRS]

- **NGAWANG PELKYI**
  .... [#12: 3 YRS]

- **NGAWANG PHUNTSOG**
  .... [#12: 7 YRS]

- **NGAWANG RAPJOR**
  .... [#12: 6 YRS]

- **NGAWANG RIGDROL**
  .... [#12: 6 YRS]

- **NGAWANG SAMTEN[2]**
  .... [#12: 4 YRS]

- **NGAWANG SANGDROL**
  .... [#12: 3 YRS]

- **NGAWANG SHENYEN**
  .... [#12: 6 YRS]

- **NGAWANG SHERAB[2]**
  .... [#12: 4½ YRS]

- **NGAWANG SONGSTEN**
  .... [#12: 7 YRS]

- **NGAWANG SOTHAR**
  .... [#12: 5 YRS]

- **NGAWANG SUNGRAB**
  .... [#12: 10 YRS]

- **NGAWANG TENDROL**
  .... [#12: 3 YRS]

- **NGAWANG TENKYI**
  .... [#12: 2 YRS]

- **NGAWANG TENRAB[1]**
  .... [#12: 7 YRS]

- **NGAWANG TENSANG**
  .... [#12: 10 YRS]

- **NGAWANG TENZIN[1]**
  .... [#12: 5 YRS]

- **NGAWANG TENZIN[3]**
  .... [#12: 8 YRS]

- **NGAWANG THONGLAM**
  .... [#12: 4½ YRS]

- **NGAWANG THUPTEN[2]**
  .... [#12: 4 YRS]

- **NGAWANG TSAMDROL**
  . . . . [#12: 5 YRS]

- **NGAWANG TSETEN**
  . . . . [#12: 3 YRS]

- **NGAWANG TSONDRU²**
  . . . . [#12: 4 YRS]

- **NGAWANG TSULTRIM²**
  . . . . [#12: 6 YRS]

- **NGAWANG YANGCHEN¹**
  . . . . [#12: 3 YRS]

- **NGAWANG YESHE**
  . . . . [#12: 3 YRS]

- **NGAWANG YUDRON¹**
  . . . . [#12: 3 YRS]

- **NGAWANG ZOEPA¹**
  . . . . [#12: 4½ YRS]

- **NGAWANG ZOEPA²**
  . . . . [#12: 5 YRS]

- **NGODRUP²** . . . [#12: 11 YRS]

- **NYIMA TSAMCHOE**
  . . . . [#12: 4 YRS]

- **OEZER CHOEKYI**
  . . . . [#12: 7 YRS]

- **PALDEN CHOEDRON**
  . . . . [#12: 7 YRS]

- **PEMA KELSANG**
  . . . . [#12: 4 YRS]

- **PENPA DRUGYAL**
  . . . . [#7? #12: 3 YRS]

- **PENPA TSERING²**
  . . . . [#12: 4 YRS]

- **PENPA WANGMO¹**
  . . . . [#12: 5 YRS]

- **PHUNTSOG CHANGSEM**
  . . . . [#12: 8 YRS]

- **PHUNTSOG CHOEKYI**
  . . . . [#12: 7 YRS]

- **PHUNTSOG DONDRUP**
  . . . . [#12: 4 YRS]

- **PHUNTSOG DORJE²**
  . . . . [#12: 10 YRS]

- **PHUNTSOG DRADAG**
  . . . . [#12: 4 YRS]

- **PHUNTSOG DRIME**
  . . . . [#12: 8 YRS]

- **PHUNTSOG GONPO**
  . . . . [#12: 5 YRS]

- **PHUNTSOG GYALTSEN**
  . . . . [#12: 12 YRS]

- **PHUNTSOG JORCHU**
  . . . . [#12: 5 YRS]

- **PHUNTSOG LEGSANG**
  . . . . [#12: 6 YRS]

- **PHUNTSOG LOCHOE**
  . . . . [#12: 7 YRS]

- **PHUNTSOG NAMGYAL**
  . . . . [#12: 6 YRS]

- **PHUNTSOG NYIDRON**
  . . . . [#12: 9 YRS]

- **PHUNTSOG PEMA**
  . . . . [#12: 8 YRS]

- **PHUNTSOG SAMTEN**[1]
  . . . . [#12: 6 YRS]

- **PHUNTSOG SAMTEN**[2]
  . . . . [#12: 10 YRS]

- **PHUNTSOG SEGYI**
  . . . . [#12: 8 YRS]

- **PHUNTSOG THUTOP**
  . . . . [#12: 5 YRS]

- **PHUNTSOG TSAMCHOE**
  . . . . [#12: 5 YRS]

- **PHUNTSOG TSERING**
  . . . . [#12: 5 YRS]

- **PHUNTSOG WANGDEN**
  . . . . [#12: 5 YRS]

- **PHUNTSOG YANGKYI**
  . . . . [#12: 5 YRS]

- **PHURBU TSERING**[2]
  . . . . [#12: 7 YRS]

- **PHURBU**[5] . . . . . [#12: 7 YRS]

- **PHURBU**[6] . . . . [#12: 4½ YRS]

- **RINCHEN CHOENYI**
  . . . . [#12: 7 YRS]

- **RINCHEN DAWA**[2]
  . . . . [#12: 5 YRS]

- **RINCHEN DROLMA**[1]
  . . . . [#12: 2 YRS]

- **RINCHEN SANGMO**
  . . . . [#12: 4 YRS]

- **SODOR** . . . . . . [#12: 7 YRS]

- **SONAM DORJE**[1]
  . . . . [#12: 13 YRS]

- **SONAM RINCHEN**
  . . . . [#12: 13 YRS]

- **SONAM TOPGYAL**[2]
  . . . . [#12: 5-6 YRS]

- **SOTOP** . . . . . . [#12: 7 YRS]

- **TANAK JIGME SANGPO**
  . . . . [#12: 28 YRS]

- **TAPSANG**[1] . . . . [#12: 5 YRS]

- **TASHI TSERING**
  . . . . [#12: 7 YRS]

- **TENDAR PHUNTSOG**
  . . . . [#12: 10 YRS]

- **TENPA PHULCHUNG**[2]
  . . . . [#12: 7 YRS]

- **TENPA WANGDRAG**[2]
  . . . . [#12: 14 YRS]

- **TENZIN CHOEPHEL**[2]
  . . . . [#12: 3 YRS]

- **TENZIN DRAKPA**
  . . . . [#12: 8 YRS]

- **TENZIN LOBSANG**
  . . . . [#12: 4½ YRS]

- **TENZIN PHUNTSOG**[1]
  . . . . [#12: 6 YRS]

- **TENZIN SAMPHEL**
  . . . . [#12: 3 YRS]

- **TENZIN THUPTEN**
  . . . . [#12: 4 YRS]

- **TENZIN TRINLEY**
  . . . . [#12: 3 YRS]

- **TENZIN WANGDU**
  . . . . [#12: 6 YRS]

- **TENZIN**[2] . . . . . [#12: 5 YRS]

- **THUPTEN KELSANG**[1]
  . . . . [#12: 6 YRS]

- **THUPTEN KELSANG**[2]
  . . . . [#12: 6 YRS]

- **THUPTEN KUNKYHEN**
  . . . . [#12: 3 YRS]

- **THUPTEN MONLAM**
  . . . . [#12: 4½ YRS]

- **THUPTEN NAMDROL**
  . . . . [#12: 9 YRS]

- **THUPTEN NAMLHA**
  . . . . [#12: 2 YRS]

- **THUPTEN PHUNTSOG**[1]
  . . . . [#12: 5 YRS]

- **THUPTEN TSONDRU**
  . . . . [#12: 4 YRS]

- **THUPTEN YESHE**[1]
  . . . . [#12: 15 YRS]

- **TRINLEY CHOEDRON**
  . . . . [#12: 3 YRS]

- **TRINLEY CHOEZOM**
  . . . . [#12: 5 YRS]

- **TRINLEY TENZIN**
  . . . . [#12: 3 YRS]

- **TSERING**[9] . . . . [#12: 7 YRS]

- **TSERING**[10] . . . . [#12: 6 YRS]

- **TSERING NGODRUP**
  . . . . [#7? #12: 12 YRS]

- **TSERING PHUNTSOG**[2]
  . . . . [#12: 13 YRS]

- **TSETEN DONDRUP**
  . . . . [#12: 7 YRS]

- **TSONDRU TENPHEL**
  . . . . [#12: 3 YRS]

- **TSULTRIM DONDEN**
  . . . . [#12: 4 YRS]

- **TSULTRIM SANGMO**
  . . . . [#12: 3 YRS]

- **UGYEN CHOEKYI**
  . . . . [#12: 3 YRS]

- **WANGDU**[2] . . . . [#12: 8 YRS]

- **YANGZOM**[3] . . . [#12: 7 YRS]

- **YESHE DRADUL**
  . . . . [#12: 6 YRS]

- **YESHE JAMYANG**
  . . . . [#12: 4 YRS]

- **YESHE KHEDRUP**
  . . . . [#12: 6 YRS]

- **YESHE NGAWANG**
  . . . . [#12: 6 YRS]

- **YESHE PALJOR**
  . . . . [#12: 5 YRS]

- **YULO DAWA TSERING**
  . . . . [#12: 8-10 YRS]

- **ZHILING** . . . . . [#12: 5 YRS]

  Sentence Unknown

  CR #12 (Charge Reported or Presumed)

- **BAGDRO**[1] . . . . . [#12: ? YRS]

- **CHIGCHEN** . . . . [#12: ? YRS]

- **DAWA NORBU** . . [#12: ? YRS]

- **DAWA SONAM** . . [#12: ? YRS]

- **DAWA**[1] . . . . [#12: ? YRS]

- **DAWA**[2] . . . . [#12: ? YRS]

- **DAWA**[3] . . . . [#12: ? YRS]

- **DELO** . . . . [#12: ? YRS]

- **DONDRUP**[2] . . . . [#12: ? YRS]

- **DONDUL** . . . . . . [#12: ? YRS]

- **DORJE TSOMO** . [#12: ? YRS]

- **DORJE**[2] . . . . [#12: ? YRS]

- **DORJE**[6] . . . . [#12: ? YRS]

- **GARCHU** . . . . . . [#12: ? YRS]

- **GELONG TSERING**
  . . . . [#12: ? YRS]

- **GYALTSEN CHOEZIN**
  . . . . [#12: ? YRS]

- **GYALTSEN KELSANG**[2]
  . . . . [#12: ? YRS]

- **GYALTSEN KUNGA**
  . . . . [#12: ? YRS]

- **GYALTSEN PELSANG**
  . . . . [#12: ? YRS]

- **GYALTSEN TSULTRIM**
  . . . . [#12: ? YRS]

- **GYATSO**[2] . . . . . . [#12: ? YRS]

- **HUACHEN KYAB**
  . . . . [#12: ? YRS]

- **INCHUNG** . . . . . [#12: ? YRS]

- **JAMPEL** . . . . . . [#12: ? YRS]

- **JAMYANG**[1] . . . . [#12: ? YRS]

- **JAMYANG**[2] . . . . [#12: ? YRS]

- **JAMYANG**[3] . . . . [#12: ? YRS]

- **JORDEN** . . . . . . [#12: ? YRS]

- **KAGYE** . . . . [#12: ? YRS]

- **KARMA**[1] . . . . . . [#12: ? YRS]

- **KARTSE** . . . . . . [#12: ? YRS]

- **KELSANG DAWA**[1]
  . . . . [#12: ? YRS]

- **KELSANG PHUNTSOG**
  . . . . [#12: ? YRS]

- **KELSANG TSERING**
  . . . . [#12: ? YRS]

- **KELSANG**[2] . . . . . [#12: ? YRS]

- **KHARMO** . . . . . [#12: ? YRS]

- **KUNCHOK TENZIN**
  . . . . [#12: ? YRS]

- **KUNSANG JAMPA**
  . . . . [#12: ? YRS]

- **KUNSANG**[1] . . . . [#12: ? YRS]

- **LI-ZE** . . . . [#12: ? YRS]

- **LOBSANG CHOEDRAG**[4]
  . . . . [#12: ? YRS]

- **LOBSANG CHOEDRON**[1]
  . . . . [#12: ? YRS]

- **LOBSANG DELEK**
  . . . . [#12: ? YRS]

- **LOBSANG GYALTSEN**[2]
  . . . . [#12: ? YRS]

- **LOBSANG JAMPEL**
  . . . . [#12: ? YRS]

- **LOBSANG NAMGYAL**
  . . . . [#12: ? YRS]

- **LOBSANG NGAWANG**[1]
  . . . . [#12: ? YRS]

- **LOBSANG PALDEN**[2]
  . . . . [#12: ? YRS]

- **LOBSANG PALDEN**[3]
  . . . . [#12: ? YRS]

- **LOBSANG TENZIN**[1]
  . . . . [#12: ? YRS]

- **LOBSANG TENZIN**[3]
  . . . . [#12: ? YRS]

- **LOBSANG THUPTEN**[1]
  . . . . [#12: ? YRS]

- **LOBSANG THUPTEN**[2]
  . . . . [#12: ? YRS]

- **LOBSANG TRINLEY**[1]
  . . . . [#12: ? YRS]

- **LOBSANG YONTEN**[2]
  . . . . [#12: ? YRS]

- **LODROE**[1] . . . . . [#12: ? YRS]

- **MIGMAR GYALTSEN**
  . . . . [#12: ? YRS]

- **MIGMAR TSERING**[2]
  . . . . [#12: ? YRS]

- **MIGMAR**[5] . . . . . [#12: ? YRS]

- **MONLAM GYATSO**
  . . . . [#12: ? YRS]

- **NAMGYAL CHOEWANG**
  . . . . [#12: ? YRS]

- **NGAWANG CHIME**
  . . . . [#12: ? YRS]

- **NGAWANG CHOEKYI**[1]
  . . . . [#12: ? YRS]

- **NGAWANG CHOKLANG**
  . . . . [#12: ? YRS]

- **NGAWANG DADROL**
  . . . . [#12: ? YRS]

- **NGAWANG DEBAM**
  . . . . [#12: ? YRS]

- **NGAWANG DEDROL**[2]
  . . . . [#12: ? YRS]

- **NGAWANG DORJE**
  . . . . [#12: ? YRS]

- **NGAWANG GYALTSEN**[2]
  . . . . [#12: ? YRS]

- **NGAWANG LAMCHUNG**
  . . . . [#12: ? YRS]

- **NGAWANG LHUNDRUP**[1]
  . . . . [#12: ? YRS]

- **NGAWANG LHUNDRUP**[3]
  . . . . [#12: ? YRS]

- **NGAWANG NYIMA**[2]
  . . . . [#12: ? YRS]

- **NGAWANG PEMO**[1]
  . . . . [#12: ? YRS]

- **NGAWANG SHERAB**[1]
  . . . . [#12: ? YRS]

- **NGAWANG TENGYE**
  . . . . [#12: ? YRS]

- **NGAWANG TENZIN**[2]
  . . . . [#12: ? YRS]

- **NGAWANG TENZIN**[4]
  . . . . [#12: ? YRS]

- **NGAWANG THUTOP**
  . . . . [#12: ? YRS]

- **NGAWANG TSEDROL**
  . . . . [#12: ? YRS]

- **NGAWANG WANGMO**[1]
  . . . . [#12: ? YRS]

- **NGAWANG YANGKYI**
  . . . . [#12: ? YRS]

- **NYIDROL** . . . . . [#12: ? YRS]

- **NYIMA**[5] . . . . [#12: ? YRS]

- **PASANG**[6] . . . . . . [#12: ? YRS]

- **PELKYI** . . . . [#12: ? YRS]

- **PEMA DROLKAR**[3]
  . . . . [#12: ? YRS]

- **PEMA OEZER**
  . . . . [#12: ? YRS]

- **PEMA YESHE**
  . . . . [#12: ? YRS]

- **PEPAR** . . . . [#12: ? YRS]

- **PHETHO** . . . . . . [#12: ? YRS]

- **PHUNTSOG CHENGA**
. . . . [#12: ? YRS]

- **PHUNTSOG JAMPA**
. . . . [#12: ? YRS]

- **PHUNTSOG TSUNGME**
. . . . [#12: ? YRS]

- **PHUNTSOG¹**
. . . . [#12: ? YRS]

- **PHURBU DROLKAR**
. . . . [#12: ? YRS]

- **SANGYE TENZIN**
. . . . [#12: ? YRS]

- **SHERAB NGAWANG**
. . . . [#12: ? YRS]

- **SHILOK²** . . . . . . [#12: ? YRS]

- **SHILOK³** . . . . . . [#12: ? YRS]

- **SICHOE DORJE**
. . . . [#12: ? YRS]

- **SONAM BAGDRO**
. . . . [#12: ? YRS]

- **SONAM DORJE⁴**
. . . . [#12: ? YRS]

- **SONAM DROLKAR¹**
. . . . [#12: ? YRS]

- **SONAM TENZIN**
. . . . [#12: ? YRS]

- **SONAM TSERING¹**
. . . . [#12: ? YRS]

- **TASHI DAWA**
. . . . [#12: ? YRS]

- **TATRU** . . . . [#12: ? YRS]

- **TENPA DARGYE**
. . . . [#12: ? YRS]

- **TENZIN CHOEDRAG**
. . . . [#12: ? YRS]

- **THUPTEN KUNGA**
. . . . [#12: ? YRS]

- **THUPTEN KUNPHEL**
. . . . [#12: ? YRS]

- **THUPTEN TSERING²**
. . . . [#12: ? YRS]

- **TSENDAK** . . . . . [#12: ? YRS]

- **TSENOR** . . . . . . [#12: ? YRS]

- **TSERING CHOEDRON¹**
. . . . [#12: ? YRS]

- **TSERING CHOEDRON²**
. . . . [#12: ? YRS]
- **TSERING DEKYI**
. . . . [#12: ? YRS]

- **TSERING DORJE²**
. . . . [#12: ? YRS]

- **TSERING GYALTSEN**
. . . . [#12: ? YRS]

- **TSERING PHUNTSOG¹**
. . . . [#12: ? YRS]

- **TSERING**[7] . . . . . [#12: ? YRS]

- **TSETEN NYIMA**
. . . . [#12: ? YRS]

- **TSETEN SAMDRUP**
. . . . [#12: ? YRS]
- **TSONDRU**[3] . . . . . [#12: ? YRS]

- **TSULTRIM NYIMA**
. . . . [#12: ? YRS]

- **WANG LANGJIE**
. . . . [#12: ? YRS]

- **YANGZOM**[1] . . . . [#12: ? YRS]

- **YESHE DROLMA**
. . . . [#12: ? YRS]

Alleged Violent/Other Criminal Cases

Sentence Known

CR #6

- **DONDRUP TSERING**
. . . . [#6?: DEATH W/REPRIEVE]

CR #7

- **JAMPA NGODRUP**
. . . . [#7: 13 YRS]

- **TAMDRIN SITHAR**
. . . . [#7: 12 YRS/PAROLED]

- **TENZIN PHUNTSOG**[2]
. . . . [#7: 5 YRS]

CR #11

- **LOBSANG TENZIN**[2]
. . . . [#11: LIFE]

- **GYALTSEN CHOEPHEL**
. . . . [#11: 15 YRS]

- **SONAM WANGDU1**
. . . . . [#11: LIFE/MEDICAL PAROLE]

- **TSERING DONDRUP**[1]
. . . . [#11: 10 YRS]

Sentence Unknown

- **SONAM WANGDU**[2] [#7: ? YRS]

2. Arrested in 1993: Awaiting Trial/Sentence Unknown

Non-Violent Cases

CR #12

- **ASHANG LA** . . [#12?: ? YRS]
- **BAGDRO**[2] . . . . [#12?: ? YRS]
- **CHANGLOCHEN**
. . . . [#12?: ? YRS]

- **CHIME** . . . . . [#12?: ? YRS]

- **CHIME WANGDU**
. . . . [#12?: ? YRS]

- **CHOENYI DROLMA**
. . . . [#12?: ? YRS]

- **CHOEPHEL** . . . [#12?: ? YRS]

- **DAKAR** . . . . . . [#12?: ? YRS]

- **DAWA DOL** . . . [#12?: ? YRS]

- **DAWA TSERING¹**
. . . . [#12?: ? YRS]

- **DAWA TSERING⁵**
. . . . [#12?: ? YRS]

- **DEKYI²** . . . . . . [#12?: ? YRS]

- **DEKYI³** . . . . . . [#12?: ? YRS]

- **DHONNOR** . . . . [#12?: ? YRS]

- **DILA** . . . . [#12?: ? YRS]

- **DODRONG NGAWANG DORJE**
. . . . [#12?: ? YRS]

- **DORJE¹** . . . . . . [#12?: ? YRS]

- **DORJE³** . . . . . . [#12?: ? YRS]

- **DRADUL¹** . . . . . [#12?: ? YRS]

- **DROLMA** . . . . . [#12?: ? YRS]

- **DUGBUNTHAR** . [#12?: ? YRS]

- **DUNGKAR TSO** [#12?: ? YRS]

- **GENDUN RINCHEN**
. . . . [#12?: ? YRS]

- **GYAGPA** . . . . . [#12?: ? YRS]

- **GYALPO¹** . . . . . [#12?: ? YRS]

- **GYALTSEN NORBU¹**
. . . . [#12?: ? YRS]

- **GYATSO¹** . . . . . [#12?: ? YRS]

- **JAMPA CHOEKYI**
. . . . [#12?: ? YRS]

- **JAMPA DEDROL**
. . . . [#12?: ? YRS]

- **JAMPA DROLKAR¹**
. . . . [#12?: ? YRS]

- **JAMPA GELEK**
. . . . [#12?: ? YRS]

- **JAMPA GYATSO**
. . . . [#12?: ? YRS]

- **JAMPEL DORJE**
. . . . [#12?: ? YRS]

- **KELSANG¹** . . . . [#12?: ? YRS]

- **KHYENRAB CHOEPEL**
. . . . [#12?: ? YRS]

- **KHYENRAB DRAGYE**
. . . . [#12?: ? YRS]

- **KHYENRAB TENDAR**
. . . . [#12?: ? YRS]

- **KUNCHOK TENPA**
. . . . [#12?: ? YRS]

- **LANGDOR** . . . . [#12?: ? YRS]

- **LHAKPA TSERING**[1]
. . . . [#12?: ? YRS]

- **LHAKPA**[1] . . . . . [#12?: ? YRS]

- **LHAKPA**[2] . . . . . [#12?: ? YRS]

- **LHAKPA**[3] . . . . . [#12?: ? YRS]

- **LHAKPA**[4] . . . . . [#12?: ? YRS]

- **LHASANG** . . . . [#12?: ? YRS]

- **LHASHAMHUA** [#12?: ? YRS]

- **LHATRIGYA** . . [#12?: ? YRS]

- **LOBSANG CHOEDRAG**[1]
. . . . [#12?: ? YRS]

- **LOBSANG CHOEDRAG**[2]
. . . . [#12?: ? YRS]

- **LOBSANG DAWA**[1]
. . . . [#12?: ? YRS]

- **LOBSANG DONYO**[1]
. . . . [#12?: ? YRS]

- **LOBSANG DONYO**[2]
. . . . [#12?: ? YRS]

- **LOBSANG GYALTSEN**[1]
. . . . [#12?: ? YRS]

- **LOBSANG GYALTSEN**[3]
. . . . [#12?: ? YRS]

- **LOBSANG PALDEN**[1]
. . . . [#12?: ? YRS]

- **LOBSANG SAMTEN**
. . . . [#12?: ? YRS]

- **LOBSANG TENPA**[1]
. . . . [#12?: ? YRS]

- **LOBSANG YONTEN**[1]
. . . . [#12?: ? YRS]

- **LOBSANG**[1]
. . . . [#12?: ? YRS]

- **LODROE PEMA**
. . . . [#12?: ? YRS]

- **LODROE PHUNTSOG**
. . . . [#12?: ? YRS]

- **LOTEN**[1] . . . . . . [#12?: ? YRS]

- **MENLHA KYAB**
. . . . [#12?: ? YRS]

- **MIGMAR TSERING**[1]
. . . . [#12?: ? YRS]

- **MIGMAR**[2] . . . . [#12?: ? YRS]

- **NAM LOYAK**
. . . . [#12?: ? YRS]

- **NAMGYAL CHOEDRON**
. . . . [#12?: ? YRS]

- **NGAGCHUNG**
. . . . [#12?: ? YRS]

- **NGAWANG CHOEDRAG**
. . . . [#12?: ? YRS]

- **NGAWANG CHOEDRON**[1]
. . . . [#12?: ? YRS]

- **NGAWANG CHOEDRON**[3]
  . . . . [#12?: ? YRS]

- **NGAWANG DONYO**
  . . . . [#12?: ? YRS]

- **NGAWANG DROLMA**[1]
  . . . . [#12?: ? YRS]

- **NGAWANG KARTSO**
  . . . . [#12?: ? YRS]

- **NGAWANG KELSANG**
  . . . . [#12?: ? YRS]

- **NGAWANG LAMCHEN**
  . . . . [#12?: ? YRS]

- **NGAWANG LOBSANG**
  . . . . [#12?: ? YRS]

- **NGAWANG LOSEL**
  . . . . [#12?: ? YRS]

- **NGAWANG RIKHAR**
  . . . . [#12?: ? YRS]

- **NGAWANG SANGYE**
  . . . . [#12?: ? YRS]

- **NGAWANG SONAM**
  . . . . [#12?: ? YRS]

- **NGAWANG THUPTEN**[1]
  . . . . [#12?: ? YRS]

- **NGAWANG TOPCHU**
  . . . . [#12?: ? YRS]

- **NGAWANG TSERING**
  . . . . [#12?: ? YRS]

- **NGAWANG TSONDRU**[1]
  . . . . [#12?: ? YRS]

- **NGAWANG TSULTRIM**[1]
  . . . . [#12?: ? YRS]

- **NORBU YANGCHEN**
  . . . . [#12?: ? YRS]

- **NORBU**[1] . . . . . [#12?: ? YRS]

- **NORBU**[2] . . . . . [#12?: ? YRS]

- **NORZANG** . . . . [#12?: ? YRS]

- **NORZIN** . . . . . [#12?: ? YRS]

- **NYIMA PHUNTSOG**
  . . . . [#12?: ? YRS]

- **NYIMA**[1] . . . . . . [#12?: ? YRS]

- **NYIMA**[2] . . . . . . [#12?: ? YRS]

- **PALDEN CHOEDRAG**
  . . . . [#12?: ? YRS]

- **PALDEN**[1] . . . . . [#12?: ? YRS]

- **PALJOR TSERING**
  . . . . [#12?: ? YRS]

- **PASANG**[1] . . . . . [#12?: ? YRS]

- **PASANG**[2] . . . . . [#12?: ? YRS]

- **PASANG**[4] . . . . . [#12?: ? YRS]

- **PASANG**[5] . . . . . [#12?: ? YRS]

- **PE-NGOE** . . . . . [#12?: ? YRS]

- **PEMA DORJE** . [#12?: ? YRS]

- **PEMA GYAL** .. [#12?: ? YRS]

- **PEMA NGODRUP**
  . . . . [#12?: ? YRS]

- **PEMA TSAMCHOE**
  . . . . [#12?: ? YRS]

- **PENDROL** . . . . [#12?: ? YRS]

- **PENDROL**[2] . . . . [#12?: ? YRS]

- **PENPA TSERING**[3]
  . . . . [#12?: ? YRS]

- **PENPA**[1] . . . . . . [#12?: ? YRS]

- **PENPA**[2] . . . . . . [#12?: ? YRS]

- **PHUNTSOG DROLMA**
  . . . . [#12?: ? YRS]

- **PHUNTSOG THOSAM**
  . . . . [#12?: ? YRS]

- **PHUNTSOG WANGDU**
  . . . . [#12?: ? YRS]

- **PHURBU NAMDROL**
  . . . . [#12?: ? YRS]

- **PHURBU TASHI**
  . . . . [#12?: ? YRS]

- **PHURBU TSERING**[1]
  . . . . [#12?: ? YRS]

- **PHURBU**[1] . . . . . [#12?: ? YRS]

- **RABGYAL** . . . . [#12?: ? YRS]

- **RIGZIN TSONDRU**
  . . . . [#12?: ? YRS]

- **RINCHEN DAWA**[1]
  . . . . [#12?: ? YRS]

- **RINCHEN NORBU**
  . . . . [#12?: ? YRS]

- **SAMDRUP TSERING**
  . . . . [#12?: ? YRS]

- **SHAWO DORJE**
  . . . . [#12?: ? YRS]

- **SHENYAN LOBSANG**
  . . . . [#12?: ? YRS]

- **SHERAB DROLMA**
  . . . . [#12?: ? YRS]

- **SISHIYI TSETEN DORJE**
  . . . . [#12?: ? YRS]

- **SONAM CHOEPHEL**[1]
  . . . . [#12?: ? YRS]

- **SONAM GYALPO**[1]
  . . . . [#12?: ? YRS]

- **SONAM GYALPO**[2]
  . . . . [#12?: ? YRS]

- **SONAM TASHI**
  . . . . [#12?: ? YRS]

- **SONAM TSERING**[1]
  . . . . [#12?: ? YRS]

- **SONAM TSERING**[2]
  . . . . [#12?: ? YRS]

- **SONAM TSERING**[3]
  . . . . [#12?: ? YRS]

- **SONAM TSETEN**
  . . . . [#12?: ? YRS]

- **SONAM**[1]
  . . . . [#12?: ? YRS]

- **TASHI CHUNGCHUNG**
  . . . . [#12?: ? YRS]

- **TASHI TOPGYAL**
  . . . . [#12?: ? YRS]

- **TASHI WANGDU**
  . . . . [#12?: ? YRS]

- **TENDAR**[1] . . . . . [#12?: ? YRS]

- **TENGYE** . . . . . [#12?: ? YRS]

- **TENPA** . . . . . . [#12?: ? YRS]

- **TENPA KELSANG**
  . . . . [#12?: ? YRS]

- **TENPA PHULCHUNG**[1]
  . . . . [#12?: ? YRS]

- **TENPA SONAM**
  . . . . [#12?: ? YRS]

- **TENPA WANGDRAG**[1]
  . . . . [#12?: ? YRS]

- **TENZIN CHOEDRAG**
  . . . . [#12?: ? YRS]

- **TENZIN CHOEKYI**[1]
  . . . . [#12?: ? YRS]

- **TENZIN CHOEKYI**[2]
  . . . . [#12?: ? YRS]

- **TENZIN DEKYONG**
  . . . . [#12?: ? YRS]

- **TENZIN DRADUL**
  . . . . [#12?: ? YRS]

- **TENZIN RABTEN**
  . . . . [#12?: ? YRS]

- **THAPKE** . . . . . [#12?: ? YRS]

- **THUBGO** . . . . . [#12?: ? YRS]

- **THUPTEN TSERING**[1]
  . . . . [#12?: ? YRS]

- **TOPGYAL**[1] . . . . [#12?: ? YRS]

- **TOPGYAL**[3] . . . . [#12?: ? YRS]

- **TOPJOR**[2] . . . . . [#12?: ? YRS]

- **TSAM-LA**[1] . . . . [#12?: ? YRS]

- **TSAMCHOE**[1] . . [#12?: ? YRS]

- **TSEGOEN GYAL**
  . . . . [#12?: ? YRS]

- **TSENYI** . . . . . . [#12?: ? YRS]

- **TSERING CHOEDRON**[3]
  . . . . [#12?: ? YRS]

- **TSERING CHOEKYI**
  . . . . [#12?: ? YRS]

- **TSERING DONDEN**
  . . . . [#12?: ? YRS]

- **TSERING YUDON**
  . . . . [#12?: ? YRS]

- **TSERING**[1] . . . . [#12?: ? YRS]

- **TSERING**[2] . . . . [#12?: ? YRS]

- **TSERING**[4] . . . . [#12?: ? YRS]

- **TSETEN DORJE**
. . . . [#12?: ? YRS]

- **TSETEN YARPHEL**
. . . . [#12?: ? YRS]

- **TSETHAR** . . . . [#12?: ? YRS]

- **TSEWANG PALDEN**
. . . . [#12?: ? YRS]

- **TSEWANG**[1] . . . [#12?: ? YRS]

- **TSULTRIM GYALTSEN**
. . . . [#12?: ? YRS]

- **TSULTRIM SHERAB**
. . . . [#12?: ? YRS]

- **TSULTRIM THARCHIN**
. . . . [#12?: ? YRS]

- **TSULTRIM TOPGYAL**
. . . . [#12?: ? YRS]

- **TSULTRIM ZOEPA**
. . . . [#12?: ? YRS]

- **WANGDEN** . . . [#12?: ? YRS]

- **WANGDU**[1] . . . . [#12?: ? YRS]

- **YANGCHEN**[1] . . [#12?: ? YRS]

- **YANGDRON** . . . [#12?: ? YRS]

- **YANGZOM**[2] . . . [#12?: ? YRS]

- **YESHE CHOEZANG**
. . . . [#12?: ? YRS]

- **YESHE GYALPO** [#12?: ? YRS]

- **YESHE JINPA** . [#12?: ? YRS]

- **YESHE KUNSANG**[#12?: ? YRS]

- **YESHE TSONDRU**[#12?: ? YRS]

- **YIDAN TSERING** [#12?: ? YRS]

- **ZOEPA CHOWANG**
. . . . [#12?: ? YRS]

3. Executed

Alleged Criminal Cases

- **DAWA5** . . . . [#6: EXECUTED]

- **MIGMAR TASHI**
. . . . [#6: EXECUTED]

APPENDIX II:
ALLEGED VIOLENT/OTHER CRIMINAL CASES

1. Pre-1989 Political Prisoners

Sentenced/Status Unclear

[NB: For details of the main documentary sources (referred to below as "SS" and "CCS") for the following cases, see notes on p.250 and p.276, above. Asterisks indicate where prisoners' middle or last names were censored in the official accounts.]

■ **CHENG * shan**, now 35, formerly a peasant, was sentenced to an unknown term of imprisonment on charges of "counterrevolutionary propaganda and incitement," probably in 1987. According to the authorities, from 1986 onwards Cheng wrote "counterrevolutionary articles" to local and provincial newspapers, including one entitled 'Second Manifesto of the *China Peace Party*', in which he allegedly urged the populace to take up weapons and overthrow the Communist Party. He is said to have called for an uprising in southern China in July 1986 and for the subsequent establishment of the *China Peace Party* as a ruling party based in the "new capital" of Xi'an. The official account (CCS p.244) censored the prisoner's middle name and also the location of the alleged activities.
. . . . [? YRS]

■ **GAO * heng**, an elderly peasant, was sentenced on charges of "organizing and leading a counter-revolutionary group" to an unknown term of imprisonment, probably in 1982, for forming a group called the *Republic of China's Mainland Army Unit No.6799 (Zhonghua Minguo Dalujun 6799 Budui)*. Gao allegedly formed the group in 1976 while serving a previous 10-year sentence on the same charge. Group members **ZHONG * yi, YING * chang, WU * sheng** and three men surnamed **Zhang, Jiang** and **Luo** were all tried separately on charges of "actively participating in a counterrevolutionary group" (sentences unknown). The group allegedly preached that the KMT was "about to launch an attack on the mainland" and that when the time came its members should "be ready to take up weapons to participate in the rebellion." The official account (CCS p.147) censored the prisoners' middle names and also the location of the alleged activities.
. . . . [7 X ? YRS]

■ **JIANG * feng**, a worker at a hydro-electric generating station, was sentenced on charges of "organizing and leading a counterrevolutionary group" to an unknown term of imprisonment, probably in 1983, for forming a dissident group called the *China Labor Party (Zhongguo Laodong Dang)*. Four other members, surnamed **Wang, Chen, Zhu** and **Lan**, were all "tried separately" (sentences unknown). According to the authorities, Jiang, a demobilized soldier, set up the party on February 15, 1982, "complete with a 'Politburo' and an spy body called the 'bureau of secrets'." The dissident party's motto allegedly was "Oppose the Communist Party and Save the Nation." After his plans were uncovered by the authorities, Jiang is said to have "conspired to flee and carry out revenge killings." The official account (CCS pp.142-3) censored the prisoners' middle names and the location of the alleged activities.

. . . . [5 X ? YRS]

■ LEI * quan, DU * hong, DONG * fei, MIAO * sen and LI * shun[2], all factory workers, and LU * qian and LEI * tong, both unemployed, were sentenced to unknown terms of imprisonment, probably in 1984, for forming a secret political group called the *China People's Heart Party (Zhongguo Min Xin Dang)*. Miao was convicted of "actively participating in a counterrevolutionary group," and the other six defendants were convicted on charges of "organizing and leading a counterrevolutionary group." According to the authorities, the party was formed in 1982 and recruited a total of 27 members. At the party's "First Congress" in February 1984, the leaders allegedly declared, "We must strike severely against [Communist Party members] and show no lenience. Those who should be killed must be killed, and those who should be beheaded must be beheaded." The official account (CCS p.145) censored the prisoners' middle names and the location of the alleged activities.

. . . . [7 X ? YRS]

■ LI * jun, CHEN * qing (professions unknown), CAO * sheng and FENG * ren, both unemployed, were sentenced to unknown terms of imprisonment, probably in 1981, for forming an organization called the *Anti-Communist Youth National Salvation Army (Fan-Gong Qingnian Jiu Guo Jun)*. Li and Chen were convicted on charges of "organizing and leading a counterrevolutionary group," and Cao and Feng were convicted of "actively participating in a counterrevolutionary group." According to the authorities, the group planned to stage incidents by using catapults to smash street lamps, and then carry out a jailbreak at the provincial No.2 Prison in order to release prisoners and recruit them into their "army." The official account (CCS pp.164-5) censored the prisoners' middle names and the location of the alleged activities.

. . . . [4 X ? YRS]

■ LI * quan[1], ZHAO * guo, SONG * , XUE * mei, ZHANG * de and SHI * pin, all peasants, were sentenced to unknown terms of imprisonment, probably in 1986, for forming an organization called the *Great Unity Party of World Loyalty, Filial Piety, Thriftiness and Righteousness (Shijie Zhong-Xiao-Jie-Yi Da Tong Dang)*. Li was convicted on charges of "organizing and leading a counter-revolutionary group" and "using feudal superstition for counterrevolutionary purposes"; the other five defendants were convicted of "actively participating in a counterrevolutionary group." Two others, JIANG * fu and

XU * zhi, were "tried separately" (sentences unknown). After the case was uncovered by the authorities, Li is said to have fled to Yunnan, Guizhou and Guangxi provinces, where he continued his activities, preaching that "a Wise One will appear on the Yunnan-Guizhou border with a five-cornered symbol on his hand...who will take over the empire." He dreamed that "a white-bearded old man gave me a precious sword," and said, "In future, when we fight, one swing of this sword and [our enemies'] heads will all fall."

By 1985, the group had recruited more than 30 members, and its slogans were "Overthrow the Communist Party," "Demand Democracy and Freedom" and "Take from the Rich to Give to the Poor." According to the authorities, the group planned to stage an armed uprising at 9:30 P.M. on August 15, 1985 (lunar calendar), in the aim of defeating the government's "one-child family" policy. The official account (CCS pp.154-7) censored the prisoners' middle names and the location of the alleged activities.

. . . . [8 X ? YRS]

■ LI * zhong, a peasant, TANG * sheng, a worker at a chemical fertilizer plant, and LI * yuan, a peasant, were all sentenced to unknown terms of imprisonment, probably in 1984, on charges of "organizing and leading a counterrevolutionary group" after they formed a secret political group called the *Upstanding Hall (Qi Li Tang)*. Three other members, YIN * ai, OU * yan, both workers, and LIAO * bin, were reportedly "tried separately" (sentences unknown), but the group is

said to have recruited "more than 140 members" in all, so the scale of arrests may have been much wider than was officially reported. The group's ideology incorporated occult Buddhist doctrines, but according to the authorities it was ultimately "dedicated to overthrowing the Communist Party" and among the aims of its manifesto was " to carry out training in the skills of killing the enemy." In April 1983, the group invested 6000 yuan to buy a shop called the "Welcoming Spring Store," which they planned to turn into a "general liaison center for the counterrevolutionary clique." The official account of the case (CCS pp.143-4) censored the prisoners' middle names and the location of the alleged activities.

. . . . [6 X ? YRS]

■ LIU * cheng, a worker at a pharmaceutical factory, and DAI * hua, a worker at a rubber factory, were sentenced on charges of "organizing and leading a counter-revolutionary group" to unknown terms of imprisonment, probably in 1982, after they formed an organization called the *Red Worker-Peasant-Soldier Alliance Party (Hongse Gong-Nong-Bing Lianmeng Dang)*. According to the authorities, the group, which was formed in July 1981, planned to steal money and weapons in order to stage an armed rebellion, and for this purpose had set up a "Dare-to-Die Squad." The official account (CCS pp.151-3) censored the prisoners' names and the location of the alleged activities.

. . . . [2 X ? YRS]

■ **LU * sheng**, a technician at a shipbuilding plant, **REN * ming**, a chemical factory worker, and **CHEN * kang**, a worker at a leather and metalware factory, were all sentenced to unknown terms of imprisonment, probably in 1985, on charges of "counterrevolution" for their involvement in a dissident group called the *China Scientific Socialism Grand Alliance - * City Group (Zhongguo Kexue Shehuizhuyi Da Tongmeng X Shi Xiaozu)*. Lu and Ren were convicted of "organizing and leading a counter-revolutionary group," and Chen was convicted of "actively participating in a counterrevolutionary group." According to the authorities, the group "conspired to convene a national conference in order to set up a nationwide counterrevolutionary organization." Moreover, the three men allegedly "planned to steal guns from the security section of a certain factory, to attack the public security organs and to set free prisoners and stage an urban rebellion." In February and March 1984, the group published a "reactionary" journal called *Compilation (Hui Ji)*, edited by Lu, which allegedly called for the overthrow of the Communist Party and the socialist system. At the same time, Ren * ming travelled to Zhejiang and Hunan provinces to make preparations, together with a man surnamed **Zheng** (tried in a separate case - sentence unknown), for the nationwide "counter-revolutionary conference." The official account (CCS pp.138-9) censored the prisoners' middle names and the location of the alleged activities.

. . . . [4 X ? YRS]

■ **LU * xiang¹, ZHAO * fang**, and **QIN * dai**, all peasants, and **LU * dai**, a coal mine worker, were sentenced to unknown terms of imprisonment, probably in 1986, for forming a political group called the *China Peasants and Workers National Party (Zhongguo Nong-Gong Minzu Dang)*. Lu * xiang¹ was convicted of "organizing and leading a counter-revolutionary group," and the other three were convicted of "actively participating in a counterrevolutionary group." Three other members, **CAO * you, LIU * jie** and **WANG * liang**, were tried separately (sentences unknown). According to the authorities, the group's manifesto read: "Our party's program is to thoroughly smash and overthrow both the new and the old bourgeois dictatorships, and to replace the current so-called socialism with military socialism. Our party's final aim is the establishment of military socialism." Between spring 1980 and winter 1984, the group recruited a total of 34 members across 18 counties and municipalities in four different provinces. Allegedly, the group called for a campaign of "guerilla warfare and civil war" against the Communist Party and aimed to set up a so-called *Ever-Triumphant Chinese National Republic (Zhonghua Minzu Sheng Qian Guo)*. The official account (CCS pp.139-41) censored the prisoners' middle names and the location of the alleged activities.

. . . . [7 X ? YRS]

■ **REN * li, WANG * lian, FAN * an** and **TIAN * fu**, all workers or unemployed persons, were sentenced to unknown terms of imprisonment, probably in 1983, on charges of "organizing and leading a counter-revolutionary group" called the *China Labor Party (Zhongguo Laodong Dang)*. Other members of the group, **LI * wu**, **YANG * min** and **JIE * **, were all "tried separately" (sentences unknown). According to the authorities, the defendants set up the secret party in February 1981 and decided also to form a "Chinese People's Army." Over the next year, the group held a series of "counterrevolutionary meetings" and allegedly made plans to rob banks and steal guns. After their arrest in April 1982, some members continued to try to recruit fellow-prisoners into the group. The official account (CCS pp.133-5) censored the prisoners' middle names and the location of the alleged activities.

. . . . [7 X ? YRS]

■ **RUAN * qing**, now 24, formerly an unemployed worker, was sentenced to an unknown term of imprisonment on charges of "counterrevolutionary propaganda and incitement," probably in 1987. According to the authorities, from 1983 onwards Ruan "listened to enemy Taiwan radio broadcasts...and became dissatisfied with the Party and government." In February 1986, he wrote a wallposter, signed in the name of the "Huatong Black River Clique," and displayed it on the gate of a leather factory. In subsequent posters, also displayed in public places, Ruan allegedly wrote that the Party's Crackdown on Crime campaign was an excuse to "execute young people" and he urged the general public "to take up

arms against the Communist Party." Ruan was said to have been caught by the authorities while attempting to escape to Taiwan. The official account (CCS p.347) censored the prisoner's middle name and also the location of the alleged activities.

. . . . [? YRS]

■ **SHEN * qi**, unemployed, was sentenced to an unknown term of imprisonment, probably in 1987, on charges of "organizing and leading a counterrevolutionary group" and "espionage" for forming a secret organization called the *Republican Party (Gong He Dang)*. Two others, surnamed **Tan** and **Lin**, were tried separately, as was an alleged "Taiwan spy" named **LI * nian²** (sentences unknown). According to the authorities, Shen formed the political party in July 1986 while being detained in a "shelter for investigation" center after a failed attempt to flee the country. The group's slogans reportedly were "Unite China Under the Three People's Principles" and "Overthrow the Chinese Communist Party." In addition, members allegedly planned to rob banks and steal weapons after their release from the holding center. A further allegation against Shen was that he had accepted a "spying mission" from fellow-prisoner Li * nian during his time in the holding center. The official account (CCS pp.148-9) censored the prisoners' middle names and the location of the alleged activities.

. . . . [4 X ? YRS]

■ **SHI * chao**, unemployed; **LI * he**,

a county forestry bureau cadre; **GAO * nian**, a peasant; **GAO * zhi**, a coal mine worker; **YANG * ri, LI * luan, GAO * qing, GAO * hong** (female) and **Yang * bin**, all peasants, were sentenced to unknown terms of imprisonment, probably in 1987, for forming a political group called the *General Uprising Headquarters of the China Egalitarian Republic (Zhong Gongping Guo Qiyi Zongbu).* Shi * chao was convicted of "organizing and leading a counterrevolutionary group," and the other eight defendants were all convicted of "actively participating in a counterrevolutionary group." According to the authorities, the dissident peasant party, which recruited a total of 54 members between July 1984 and July 1986, proclaimed: "Once the Communist Party steps down, it will be the turn of the Egalitarian Party. The Communist Party has been in power long enough, it's time for a change of dynasties." (Although no allegations of actual or planned violence were apparently made against the defendants, the case is included under the present heading because the group was evidently dedicated to staging an "uprising.") The official account (CCS pp.141-2) censored the prisoners' middle names and the location of the alleged activities.

. . . . [9 X ? YRS]

■ **SHI * jun**, a bus station ticket-seller, **CHEN *[1]**, an employee in a mining company, and **WU * chun**, a private stall-holder, were all sentenced to unknown terms of imprisonment, probably in 1983, on charges of "organizing and leading a counter-

revolutionary group." Other members of the group, **MAO * bao, YANG * jun** and **CHEN * long**, were "tried separately" (sentences unknown). According to the authorities, in February 1982 the defendants set up a "counterrevolutionary group" called the *People's Army (Renmin Jun),* which they planned to use the following month to break into a prison or labor camp and "release the prisoners and organize them into a Dare-to-Die Squad," for purposes of "staging a rebellion." They also allegedly planned to steal guns from a police station and rob banks to secure the group's operating expenses. The official account (CCS pp.130-2) censored the prisoners' middle names and the location of the alleged activities.

. . . . [6 X ? YRS]

■ **TAN * yi, HE * hua** (female) and **LIANG * zhu**, all peasants, were sentenced to unknown terms of imprisonment, probably in 1984, on charges of "organizing and leading a counterrevolutionary group" for forming a semi-occult, folk-Buddhist political group called the *Dark Army (Qing Jun).* Four other members, surnamed **Yue, Huang, Liang** and **Ma**, were "tried separately" (sentences unknown). According to the authorities, the group was set up in June 1979 and recruited in all more than 140 members from 18 neighboring townships and villages. It believed that a heavenly apocalypse would occur in 1984 that would bring Tan * yi to power as a new "emperor." At a secret conference in September 1980, the group "decided to develop the 'Dark Army' into a force of 830,000 soldiers and to appoint ten 'army commanders'." However, the official account (CCS pp.146-7), which censored the prisoners' middle names and the location of the alleged activities, gave no indication either that the planned "army" was anything more than a bizarre fantasy on the part of the group's leaders, or that they had any intention of actually staging an uprising against the authorities.

. . . . [7 X ? YRS]

■ WU * quan, now 55, formerly a cadre in the railroad public security bureau, was sentenced to an unknown term of imprisonment on charges of "counterrevolutionary propaganda and incitement," probably in late 1986. According to the authorities, "Between February 1978 and August 1986, Wu on six occasions wrote 10 counter-revolutionary banners bearing the words 'Down with Hua ** and Long live the Four' [presumably referring to former Party leader Hua Guofeng and the "Gang of Four"] and 'Down with the Communist Party', which he distributed and posted up...around the city." On March 16 and April 13, 1986, Wu allegedly mailed letters to the municipal Public Security Bureau threatening to blow up a local train station. The official account (CCS p.258) censored the prisoner's middle name and also the location of the alleged activities.

. . . . [? YRS]

■ XU * gang (profession unknown), LI * she and XU * feng, both peasants, and WANG * jie and WANG

* xin, both unemployed, were sentenced to unknown terms of imprisonment, probably in 1982, for their membership in a dissident organization called the China New Communist Party (Zhongguo Xin Gong Dang). Xu * gang, self-styled "chairman" of the party, was apparently convicted on charges of "organizing and leading a counter-revolutionary group," and the others were all convicted of "actively participating in a counterrevolutionary group." According to the authorities, the group made a failed attempt in early 1981 to illegally cross into the neighboring "X" country (name censored). In September of that year, they allegedly decided their aim should be "to wrest supreme state power by using the armed forces of 'X' country." The official account (CCS pp.162-3) censored the prisoners' middle names and the location of the alleged activities.

. . . . [5 X ? YRS]

■ ZHANG Sanyi, QIU Liangqing, TIAN * zhen, WANG * yan, LI * chuan and REN Yuanqing, described in an official report as being "remnant dregs of the Gang of Four," were sentenced to terms of up to 17 years' imprisonment by a Henan provincial Intermediate People's Court on charges of "organizing and leading a counter-revolutionary group." An additional 12 members of the group, the Chinese National United Front (Zhonghua Minzu Lianhe Zhenxian), were sentenced to unknown terms of imprisonment on charges of "actively participating in a counterrevolutionary group." (Their names are not known; according to an official 1992 volume, only eight additional members were convicted, but a 1984 newspaper account gave the total number of defendants in the case [including Zhang Sanyi *et al*] as "18.") During the Cultural Revolution, Zhang and the other "ringleaders" all rose to county or bureau-level leadership positions in the Communist Party.

Sacked from these posts after the fall of the "Gang of Four' in 1976, they are said to have "harbored dissatisfaction" with the authorities and in 1979 they "secretly set up the *Chinese National United Front,* recruiting altogether 22 members across six counties and municipalities in * Province and convening a total of 17 counterrevolutionary meetings." In addition, "Zhang and the others...schemed to distribute counter-revolutionary leaflets, to rob and steal weapons, and to assassinate people." (Neither of the official accounts, however, presented any further details or evidence to substantiate this latter charge.) According to the 1984 account, "They viciously attacked the Party's line, principles and policies since the [December 1978] 3rd Plenum of the 11th Central Committee and slandered and cursed the leading comrades of the Central Committee. They frantically clamored for the overthrow of the ruling party in China and for the 'reestablishment' of political power at all levels throughout the nation. Their reactionary mood was extremely arrogant" (CCS pp.129-30,

and *1985 Henan Yearbook* p.224).

. . [6 X ≤17 YRS] [12 X ? YRS]

■ **ZHANG Yishan**, leader of a secret dissident group called the *Popular Masses National Salvation Society (Minzhong Jiu Guo Hui),* was sentenced to 12 years' imprisonment sometime prior to 1989 on charges of "organizing and leading a counterrevolutionary group." Others sentenced on the same count include **JI Heli**, who received an eight-year prison term, and **YAN Qinren**, who received a five-year term. All three were also sentenced to four years' subsequent deprivation of political rights. Three other members of the group, **CHENG Yezi, LIN Xiao'an** and **YUAN Chunyou**, were each sentenced to five years' imprisonment on charges of "actively participating in a counterrevolutionary group," with two years' deprivation of political rights. A seventh defendant, **HONG Liang**, received a two-year prison term with one years' deprivation of rights. A detailed official account of the case (in *Jianchaguan Zha Ji [Random Notes of A Prosecutor],* Shanghai People's Press, May 1989, pp.7-12), failed to specify where or in which year the alleged activities occurred. According to the account, in the early 1960s Zhang Yishan had been a senior county-level official, and during the Cultural Revolution he rose to become a prefectural-level Communist Party deputy secretary; Ji Heli was his assistant. At the time of their alleged offenses (presumably, the mid- to late 1980s), both men had become private entrepreneurs and ran their own garment business. According to the official account, the dissident group had produced "its own political manifesto of nearly 10,000 words in length...which slandered and ridiculed the Communist Party...and called for the 'overthrow of the present regime and the establishment of a new political power'." The authorities alleged that Zhang Yishan, in a private meeting of the group, had proposed that members "carry out a bank robbery" in order to raise operating funds for their planned activities. No such attempt was actually made, however. Hong Liang is presumed released after completing his sentence; the four persons who received five-year sentences may also by now have been released.

..... [12, 8 YRS] [4 X 5 YRS]

■   ZHANG * hua, LI * xiang and ZHANG * ping, described in an official report as having been sentenced in the period 1977-82 to terms of between two and 10 years' imprisonment for common criminal offenses, were sentenced to additional unknown terms of imprisonment, probably in 1984, on charges of "organizing and leading a counter-revolutionary group" known variously as the New China Empire (Xin Hua Diguo) and National Preservation Party (Hu Guo Dang) while still in prison on the earlier counts. (Although the authorities made no allegations of violence against the group, the case is included under the present heading because all the detainees were currently serving prison sentences at the time of the alleged activities.)

On January 9, 1984, after being

transferred the previous year to a labor-reform farm, the prisoners set up the dissident group, according to the authorities. The group appears to have been based on traditional peasant "superstitious ideas." The three men "drafted a charter, set up rules of discipline and code names for the members, designed a "party flag"...and wrote an "Anthem for National Preservation" and a "Song of China." Also, "On January 11 [1984], Zhang * hua drafted four 'edicts' and declared the founding of the New China Empire and the National Preservation Party." The official account (CCS p.158) censored the prisoners' middle names and the location of the alleged activities.

.... [3 X ? YRS]

■   ZHANG * jian, SONG * feng, YANG * ming, LIU * tang, JI * wei[1] and LI * rong, all peasants, were sentenced to unknown terms of imprisonment, probably in 1984, on charges of "counterrevolution." Zhang was convicted of "organizing and leading a counterrevolutionary group," and the other five were convicted on multiple charges of "actively participating in a counterrevolutionary group," "incitement to rebellion" and "counterrevolutionary propaganda and incitement." According to the authorities, between January and June 1983 the defendants set up a secret organization called the New Central Committee of the Chinese Communist Party (Zhongguo Gongchandang Xin de Zhongyang Weiyuanhui). By September that year, they had allegedly "written 134 counterrevolutionary letters and mailed 97 of them to central Party leaders, Party secretaries of all the provinces, municipalities and autonomous regions, commanders of the eight Military Regions, Qinghua University, the Ministry of Petro-Chemical Industry and the Ministry of Public Security, and to the embassies or consulates in China of seven different foreign countries." The letters allegedly "incited [Party and military] leaders to stage an 'armed uprising' and called on students to boycott classes and workers to go on strike." The official account (CCS pp.132-3) censored the prisoners' names and the location of the alleged activities.

. . . . [6 X ? YRS]

■ **ZHANG * ming**, a schoolteacher, **ZHANG * yuan**, a technical college student, and **WANG * jin**, a worker at a water reservoir, were sentenced to unknown terms of imprisonment, probably in 1984, for forming a group called the *China Youth National Salvation Society (Zhongguo Qingnian Jiu Guo Hui)*. Zhang * ming was convicted on charges of "organizing and leading a counterrevolutionary group," and the other two were convicted of "actively participating in a counterrevolutionary group." According to the authorities, the group's manifesto "opposed the Party's policies since the [December 1978] 3rd Plenum, flagrantly vilified Party and state leaders...and clamored for 'the establishment of an armed force'." Moreover, the group allegedly said, "We must progressively stage jail breaks, in order to free our comrades." The official account (CCS pp.157-60)

censored the prisoners' middle names and the location of the alleged activities.

. . . . [3 X ? YRS]

■ **ZHONG * hua**, now 52, formerly a worker in a flour mill, was sentenced to an unknown term of imprisonment on charges of "counterrevolutionary propaganda and incitement," probably in 1987. According to the authorities, "Between November 1980 and October 1986, Zhong wrote or drafted 12 articles and pictures including 'Truth of the September 13 Incident', 'Reminiscences of Qing Dynasty Figures', 'A Record of Purchasing Heads', 'Appeal against the Injustice Done to "Bitter Love"' [a reference to a famous novella written by dissident author Bai Hua that was banned by the authorities in 1981] and 'News From the Western Hemisphere', and mailed them to Hong Kong, the Chinese National People's Political Consultative Conference, *People's Daily, Yangcheng Evening News* (a Guangzhou daily newspaper), *Shenzhen Special Zone Daily, Southern Magazine* and to municipal Party, government, labor union and Youth League offices. In them, he viciously attacked the Chinese Communist Party and slandered Party and state leaders, saying that he wanted to overthrow the people's democratic dictatorship, singing the praises of Jiang Qing [Chairman Mao's now-deceased widow] and expressing nostalgia for Ch'iang Kai-Shek. He complained that Lin Biao [Mao's designated successor, who died in a plane crash while allegedly fleeing to the Soviet Union] had been unjustly condemned, and clamored, 'We must offer a big price for the head of every mainland Chinese Communist cadre.' He also declared, 'We must unfold a vigorous armed struggle' to overthrow the people's democratic dictatorship. His counterrevolutionary arrogance knew no bounds." The official account (CCS p.243) censored the prisoner's middle name and also the location of the alleged activities.

. . . . [? YRS]

2. Traditional Religious Sects

Executed

■ **CAI Hedai**, a leader of the *Sheng Xian Jiao (Sect of Saints and Immortals)*, was arrested in Bo'ai County, Henan Province in the early 1980s. Although the sentence is not known, Cai was almost certainly executed. According to an official report, "A retired soldier named Li Shenglin developed an inflammation of the liver and sought medical assistance from a die-hard element of the *Sheng Xian Jiao* named Cai Hedai. Cai, however, proceeded to punch and beat Li up, and then later seized him by the throat and throttled the poor man to death" (SS p.70).

. . . . [EXECUTED]

■ **LÜ * fu, ZHANG *¹, LU * xiang², LÜ * run, ZHAO * rong** (female), **SUN * lian** and **GUO * xiang**, all peasants aged mostly in their

sixties or seventies, were convicted in the early 1980s of "organizing a reactionary sect or secret society for counterrevolutionary purposes." All except Guo had first joined the *Yi Guan Dao (Way of Unity)* in the 1930s and 1940s, and several had been imprisoned after 1949 for their sectarian activities. After their rearrest in the early 1980s, LÜ * fu was sentenced to death and executed, and Lu * xiang² was sentenced to death with a two-year reprieve (current status unknown). According to the authorities, the group, which recruited a total of 89 members in 57 villages and townships, preached that a cosmic apocalypse would occur in the year 1984 and the *Yi Guan Dao* would then take power in China. The leaders allegedly hoarded a large quantity of knives, hoes and clubs and planned to stage a violent uprising when the time came. The official account (CCS p.174) censored the prisoners' middle names and also the location of the alleged activities.

[EXECUTED] [DEATH W/REPRIEVE] [4 X ? YRS]

■ **SHAO * wen**, 27, formerly a worker in a transportation company, was sentenced to death and executed, probably in late 1984, on charges of "using feudal superstition and organizing a reactionary sect or secret society for counterrevolutionary purposes" after he led a group of 12 members of the *Yu Xu Men (Gate of the Jade Void)* sect in an attempted mass suicide by drowning. Eight of the group died, but Shao and the others were rescued from the water. According to the authorities, from 1978 onwards, Shao, who styled himself as the sect's "Deputy Pontiff," preached belief in the "Eternal Venerable Mother" *(Tian Sheng Lao Mu)*, the "Saintly Ancestral Buddha of the Southern Seas" *(Nan Hai Sheng Zong Fo)* and several other *Yu Xu Men* deities and declared that his disciples would "ascend to heaven after death." On August 16, 1984, upon learning that the Public Security Bureau had uncovered his "counterrevolutionary activities," Shao decided to lead his disciples in a "collective ascension to heaven" *(jiti sheng tian)* by committing suicide together with them. The following day they went to a village reservoir, tied their arms together and jumped into the water. The official account (CCS p.184) censored the prisoner's middle name and also the location of the alleged activities.

. . . . [EXECUTED]

■ **WANG XX**, a leader of the *Jiu Gong Dao (Way of Nine Palaces)* sect, was arrested sometime after 1978 on charges of "counterrevolutionary murder" and "organizing a reactionary sect or secret society for counter-revolutionary purposes." As regards the alleged violence, Wang had seriously injured a Party official, but in fact left him "crippled" rather than dead. Although the sentence is not known, it is probable that Wang was sentenced to death and executed.

According to an official report, "The father of commune-member Wang had been a leader of the *Jiu Gong Dao*. Shortly after Liberation, he was imprisoned for having used his reactionary sect as a means of sabotaging the Land Reform movement, and died of illness while undergoing reform through labor [imprisonment]. Steeped in his father's influence as a child, Wang himself went on in early 1978 to organize a branch of the *Tian Dao Hui (Society of Heaven's Way)*. He styled himself 'Society Master', and appointed men named Qiu and Hong as 'Second Master' and 'Temple Master' respectively; they recruited more than ten new members altogether. Wang frequently used to relate to them the contents of various enemy radio-broadcasts to which he had listened. In addition, he conspired with Qiu and Hong to concoct, by means of 'spirit writing' *(fu ji)*, a so-called 'Poem Bestowed by the Immortals'. In this, he concocted political rumors and slandered and abused the Party and the People's Government. He clamored, 'The Communist Party's rule won't last for much longer, for an Able One *(neng ren)* is about to appear'. Such statements greatly deceived the masses and disturbed their peace of mind.

"On top of this, Wang distorted the Party's policies by instigating the masses to forcibly divide up collective property. They dismantled tractors and other agricultural tools and machinery, and on the pretext that 'the *fengshui* is being disturbed', they sabotaged water conservancy installations and assembled a crowd to beat up officials of the Waterways Measurement department. When the brigade's Party secretary, Wu, went to investigate among the masses, Wang became fearful that his conspiracies would be exposed, so he hatched a wild scheme to assassinate

Wu. Fortunately, the masses heard the suspicious noise and came running to the rescue, but not before Wu had sustained a deep gash to his left arm, which left him crippled.

"Wang held the counter-revolutionary purpose of opposing the socialist system and the people's democratic dictatorship... He both organized and used a reactionary sect, disturbing people's minds with his 'Poem from the Immortals', sabotaging the policies and measures of the Party and government, disrupting agricultural production and injuring a rural cadre. His crimes were heinous...he should thus be convicted on the charges of 'counterrevolutionary murder' and 'organizing a reactionary sect or secret society for counterrevolutionary purposes'...and should be punished with extra severity" (SS p.96).

. . . . [EXECUTED?]

■   **ZHENG Lixi**, now 63, formerly leader of a "reactionary sectarian organization" called the *Yuan Chao Nong Fo He Guo (Yuan Dynasty Peasant Buddhist Republic)*, was arrested in May 1983, together with fellow sect-members **ZHENG * bao** (who would now be 82), **FANG * tong** (now 70) and **ZHENG * huan** (now 58), in Minhou County, Fujian Province. Zheng Lixi was later convicted on charges of "using feudal superstition for counterrevolutionary purposes" and also rape; he was sentenced to death and executed. The other three defendants (whose middle names were censored by the authorities) were convicted of "using feudal superstition for counter-

revolutionary purposes"; it is not known what sentences they received. Fang * tong was formerly a retired cadre in a supply-and-marketing cooperative; the other three were all peasants.

According to an official report,

Zheng proclaimed himself to be an 'Emperor' and the 'Tenth Great King of Heaven', and moreover appointed a total of 199 people to various posts including 'Prime Minister', 'State Patriarch' and 'Empress'. He wantonly declared: 'The Snake Spirit is now creating havoc, so the empire can know no peace'... 'The end of the world is nigh, the rule of the Communist Party will soon be over.' Raved he: 'This will be the final year of the Communist Dynasty. It won't survive into the coming year.' And also: 'We must annihilate the old dynasty and found a new one.' He planned to 'assume the throne' on the 17th of June of this year. The 'national flag' of the Yuan Chao Nong Fo He Guo carried the slogan: 'Oppose X, Oppose the Communist Party and Destroy the Imperial Government,' thus revealing the sect's counterrevolutionary ambitions.

The report added: *The sect concocted several official seals, inscribed with the characters: 'Truly-Mandated Son of Heaven' and 'Plenipotential Seal of the Yuan Dynasty'. They produced a 'Compilation of Synodal Decrees' and a 'Manifesto', and they created special sets of clothes, and various hats, boots and belts, all for the exclusive use of the 'Emperor' and his 'Empress'. On the pretext of 'catching ghosts', moreover, the sect appointed several of its die-hard elements to undergo special drill-training, as part of its doomed preparations for a counter-revolutionary insurrection.*

According to a second account, the sect "recruited members in six communes across three counties and municipalities, deceiving altogether 317 people" (SS p.67 and CCS p.168).

. . [2 X ? YRS/DP?] [EXECUTED]

■ **ZHONG Chongzhen and ZHONG Qigan** (father and son), peasants from Tangjian township in Shuyang County, Jiangsu Province who in 1974 founded a branch of the *Shen Men Dao (Way of the Spirit Gate)* sect, were arrested in 1986 and tried on September 30, 1987, on multiple charges of "organizing a reactionary sect or society for counter-revolutionary purposes," rape and swindling. Both men were sentenced to death and executed. According to an official report, prior to their arrests they recruited more than 300 followers and developed the sect across 12 townships and medium-sized cities. Reportedly,

The two Zhongs declared themselves to be 'Buddha Ancestor Spirits', 'Celestial Emperor Spirits' and 'True-Dragon Sons of Heaven', and they appointed a number of their disciples to such posts as 'Prime Minister', 'Secretary to the Celestial Emperor', 'The Nine Women', 'The Thirty-Six Younger Brothers' and 'The Immortals of the Eight Caves'.

In addition, they put forth the slogans,

"Cultivate the Way and become Buddhas and immortals - Entreat the masters and spirits to capture the demons and seize the foxes", and "Join the sect and you will be cured of all your illnesses." According to the authorities, "A small number of foolish and ignorant people were completely taken in by this." Moreover, they allegedly "raped, seduced or behaved indecently with as many as 14 different women." (See SS p.21 and *Zhongguo Fazhi Bao,* December 23, 1986. Also, an extremely detailed account of the case appears in *Zui'e de Guiji* ["The Tracks of Evil"], an anthology of criminal cases published by the People's Court Press, August 1991, pp.292-305.)

. . . . [2 X EXECUTED]

■ **ZHOU Zhengxiang**, a peasant from Baituo township in Xiangtan County, Hunan Province, and **WANG Guiyun**, a leader of the *Yi Guan Dao (Way of Unity)* sect, were executed on January 30, 1985 after conviction on charges of "using feudal superstition to carry out counterrevolutionary activities." According to an official press account,

From 1975 onwards, [Zhou] frequently spread about the rumor that he had received messages from a bird-sage, saying that the bird had addressed him as 'Emperor Zhou Zhengxiang'. In vain, he aspired to 'accede to the throne' in the year Jia Zi [i.e. 1984 according to the lunar calendar]. In the winter of 1976, Wang Guiyun, a counter-revolutionary element and an Altar Chief of the Yi Guan Dao, likewise proclaimed himself to be the 'Lord Buddha Maitreya'. Conspiring together, Wang and Zhou toured in succession more than 30 townships across the various counties and municipalities of Xiangtan, Xiangxiang, Zhuzhou and Changsha. Wang Guiyun distributed to upwards of 30 people a total of 40 photographs of himself, bearing the so-called Five-Character Truth of the Yi Guan Dao ('The Great and Incomparable Buddha Maitreya' - Wu Tai Fo Mi Le). By these means, they covertly expanded the society's membership.

In the course of their counter-revolutionary incitement and liaison activities, criminals Zhou and Wang on three occasions made supplication to the gods, conducted spirit-writing sessions (fu ji) and held official enfeoffment ceremonies. In all, they appointed around a dozen people to the following posts: 'Prime Minister of the Left' and 'Prime Minister of the Right', 'Grand Monarch', 'Commander', 'Military Counsellor', 'General', and 'Protector of the Dynasty'. Exploiting feudal superstition, moreover, Zhou Zhengxiang, in his capacity as 'emperor,' raped two female minors and seduced a large number of women. Criminals Zhou and Wang fraudulently obtained a large quantity of money and goods in the course of their counter-revolutionary activities. In accordance with the law, the Xiangtan Intermediate People's Court condemned both Zhou Zhengxiang and Wang Guiyun to death (Zhongguo Fazhi Bao, February 11, 1985).

. . . . [2 EXECUTED]

Sentenced/Status Unclear

■ **AH Jin**, described by the authorities as a "diehard element" of the *Hong San Jiao (Red Three Sect)*, was arrested in Wujiang County, Jiangsu Province in the early 1980s. It is not known what sentence he received. According to an official report, "A three-year-old girl named Guan Mingxue, from the Yonghu brigade of Hubin Commune, fell ill with meningitis. Ah Jin...attempted to 'cure' her by means of a so-called 'ghost catching ceremony' *(zhuo gui)*. On three occasions he made Guan drink a potion of incense ashes mixed with water. The time for prompt medical attention passed by, and the child died after fruitless attempts at emergency resuscitation" (SS p.71).

. . . . [? YRS]

■ **CHAI Zhizong**, a leader of a sect known as the "Triratna," was arrested in Anshan, Liaoning Province in late 1987. It is not known what sentence he received. According to an official press account,

Chai, a retired worker at Anshan city's (Tiedong) general barbershop, had at one time joined the Triratna before liberation. From 1984 to the first half of this year, he scraped people together, and recruited six disciples to spread feudal, superstitious and reactionary heresy. He also conducted promiscuity with his three women disciples, and turned his home into a lair for promiscuity and adultery.

In the name of practicing medicine, he pretended to be gods and ghosts to deceive the masses, and persecute the patients. In a short span of three years, he raped and threatened 16 women. At present this case is being tried." (*Liaoning Radio*, November 19, 1987, in SWB, November 25).

. . . . [? YRS/DP?]

■ **JI * wei²**, now 53, **ZHANG * hui**, now (if still alive) 85, **ZHAO *¹**, now 73, and **WANG * ying** now (if still alive) 85, all peasants, were convicted of "organizing a reactionary sect or secret society for counterrevolutionary purposes," probably in 1983. In December 1982, the group secretly formed a new branch of the *Xian Tian Dao (Way of the Prior Realm)* sect, and in due course recruited more than 230 members and set up more than 10 meeting centers. Ji, who was additionally convicted of rape, was sentenced to death with a two-year reprieve (final outcome unknown); the others received unknown terms of imprisonment. (While the rape charge may have been true in this case, it is also important to note that some traditional Chinese sects are characterized by relatively liberal, and occasionally promiscuous, sexual mores; official documents, moreover, indicate that rape charges are sometimes brought against sect leaders in cases which would elsewhere be viewed as involving consensual sex.) All but Ji had spent terms of three to 12 years in prison during the 1960s on account of their membership in traditional Chinese sects. The official account (CCS p.177) censored the

prisoners' middle names and also the location of the alleged activities.

[2 X ? YRS] [DEATH W/REPRIEVE]

■ **LI Guangchang** (also known as ZHENG Min), leader of a new sect called the *Zi Shen Guo (Zi Shen Nation)*, was arrested in spring 1986 together with several fellow sect-leaders and charged with "organizing and using a reactionary secret sect for counterrevolutionary purposes." It is not known what sentences any of the codefendants received, but it is probable that Li received the death penalty. The *Zi Shen Guo* was founded by Li and another peasant, **WEI Zhijian**, in 1981 in Shuitou township, Pingyang County, Zhejiang Province. By 1986, its membership and operations had extended to cover several counties in western Fujian Province, including Jiangle, Mingxi, Ninghua, Songxi and Jianning.

According to an official press report, at his first meeting with Wei, Li described the "origins" of his sect as follows: "You, my dear brother, are no doubt unfamiliar with the story of a man named Zhu Gang from the U.S., and another named *Wulinbietuo* from the USSR, who founded, in accordance with the last dying words of Sun Yatsen, the *Zi Shen Guo* society, and of how, together, they then set up in the Tongling region of Anhui Province a large underground military factory for the production of nuclear weapons. Well, these two persons enthroned me as Emperor and instructed me to go forth and establish myself as the ruler of China."

Later recruits to the sect's leadership included **LIN Bingqi**, **Lin Yongkai**, **WU Qixiang**, **DAI Xuanneng** and **ZHOU Zhengwu**, all peasants from Qingliu County who were also later arrested. According to the authorities, on Chinese New Year, 1986, the sect had planned to stage an armed uprising in Ninghua County, Fujian Province, but in a pre-emptive police raid on their headquarters (a Buddhist temple), a total of "33 sect leaders of regimental rank or above" were seized by the authorities. Li Guangchang was arrested two months later in Shandong Province (*Minzhu Yu Fazhi*, No.12, 1987).

. . . . [7 X ? YRS/DP?]

■ **LIANG Dianhua**, a leader of the *Xi Tian Ling Shan Fo Men Jiao (Buddha-Gate Sect of the Spirit Mountain in the Western Paradise)*, was arrested in Lishu County, Jilin Province in the early 1980s. It is not known what sentence Liang received. According to an official report, "Influenced by Liang Dianhua, commune members sold off all their mules, horses, pigs and other livestock, together with all their furniture and other goods, and then slaughtered their chickens, ducks and geese and uprooted their newly-sprouting crops, all in the anticipation that Criminal Liang would lead them to the 'Western Xia' land, where (said Liang) they would 'know happiness'." Declaring himself to be the 'Emperor and Master of the Law', Liang screamed for the overthrow of the People's Republic of China and called for the founding of a so-called 'Spirit Dynasty' which would 'set up its

capital at Chang An' [present-day Xi'an.] Flagrantly appointing officials and functionaries, he drew up a 'dynastic program', formulated 'rules of discipline', devised a 'commander's banner' and even composed a 'national anthem'. Furthermore, on the pretext of 'appointing empresses', he molested and raped a number of women."

Moreover, "Liang and his father cheated people out of more than 8,500 yuan, six wristwatches, and one bicycle. This was all done on such pretexts as 'performing spirit dancing' *(tiao shen)*, 'drawing magic diagrams' *(hua fu)*, 'traversing the *yin* to acquire longevity' *(guo yin jie shou)*, 'administering acupuncture', 'choosing the glued slips' *(chou tie)*, 'divining the fates' and 'purveying medicine'." In addition, "Liang appointed as his 'empress' a 20-year-old woman named Liu XX (the sister-in-law of sect member Ma Zixiang), on the pretext that Liu was 'possessed by spirits and immortals'. Gibbered Liang: 'To become an Empress you must first cross over into the immortal's body, so as to acquire the *yin* essence.' By this means, he tricked Liu into having illicit sexual intercourse with him on numerous different occasions" (SS pp.63, 67, 69 and 72).

. . . . [? YRS/DP?]

■ **WANG Baorong**, leader of the *Hong San Jiao (Red Three Sect)*, was arrested in Yancheng County, Jiangsu Province in the early 1980s. It is not known what sentence he received. According to an official report, "Wang spouted the absurd claim that his adopted daughter, a girl named Wang

Qiaoying, had been given to him by a 'spirit' to serve as his 'itinerant acolyte'. By this means, he succeeded in having his evil way with her over a long period of time. The girl's husband pursued Wang Baorong on many occasions, demanding the return of his wife. But Wang refused to let her out of his clutches, saying simply, 'She was given to me by a spirit' (SS p.72).

. . . . [? YRS]

■ WANG * xing[1], now 44, **Wang * xing**[2], now 33, and **LI * zhi**, now 43, all peasants, were sentenced to unknown terms of imprisonment, probably in late 1980, on charges of "participating in an armed mass rebellion" and "organizing a reactionary sect or secret society for counterrevolutionary purposes." According to the authorities, the three, all members of the *Huang Sha Hui (Yellow Sand Sect),* planned to incite a national rebellion against the Beijing government and reestablish the "Taiping Heavenly Kingdom" *(Taiping Tianguo).* After being surrounded by armed militia, the three allegedly violently resisted arrest and injured eight policemen. The official account (CCS p.185) censored the prisoners' middle names and also the location of the alleged activities.

. . . . [3 X ? YRS]

■ ZHANG Fuzhi, described by the authorities as the "chief criminal" of the *Shou Shan Wan Long Tian Zhu Fo Jiao (Longevity Mountain and Myriad Prosperities Catholic-Buddhist Sect),* was arrested in Anshan, Liaoning Province in the early 1980s. It is not

known what sentence he received. According to an official report, "Between 1978 and 1981, Zhang wheedled more than 4,000 yuan in cash from the masses, all in the name of collecting 'initiation fees', 'fees for the avoidance of heterodoxy' and such like." In addition, "Using such pretexts as the *'dharma-*crossing and breaching of the pass' *(fa du po guan)* and 'stealing away the true *yang' (dao qu zhen yang),* Zhang deceived and sexually abused a total of 18 female sect members, of whom two were minors" (SS p.69 and p.72).

. . . . [? YRS]

■ ZHANG Jingsheng[2], XU Shexiu and nine other sect members were arrested in Chengdu, Sichuan Province in June 1987. According to an official press account, "On 12 different occasions between 26 January and 8 June 1987, Zhang, Xu and the others distributed, in 11 districts and counties under the administration of Chengdu municipality, a total of over 15,000 counterrevolutionary leaflets, big-character posters and postal items, all printed by wood-block and bearing the titles 'Celestial House of Loyalty and Filial Piety' *(Zhong Xiao Tian Fu)* and 'Celestial Master Zhang' *(Zhang Tian Shi).* All these various documents viciously attacked the Four Cardinal Principles. Rarely since the founding of the PRC has so large a quantity of such material been found."

According to the account, Zhang confessed to having "organized a reactionary sect and used feudal superstition for the purpose of engaging in acts of counter-revolution." In addition, "he gave information leading to the prompt seizure by the authorities--from the home of his fellow-conspirator, Xu Shexiu, in the Tianhua township of Pujiang County-- of five reverse woodblocks for the production of counter-revolutionary leaflets; three wooden seals; over 300 still undistributed counter-revolutionary leaflets; 65 reactionary flags of a so-called 'People's Republic of Loyalty and Filial Piety' and a 'Celestial-House Nation of Loyalty and Piety'." The authorities charged that Zhang and Xu had "blindly schemed to carry out an armed rebellion in the near future, in the aim of 'founding a dynasty and ascending the throne'. Moreover, they had conspired to blow up the main bridges in the Xinjin, Qionglai and Pujiang counties of Chengdu municipality" (*Zhongguo Fazhi Bao*, July 6, 1987).

. . . . [2 X ? YRS/DP?]

■ **ZHENG** * **bao** and **FANG** * **tong** - see p.344

- see p.344

. . . . [2 X ? YRS]

3. Tibetans

Executed

■ **MIGMAR TASHI** and **DAWA**[5], originally arrested as "common criminals," were later tried as political criminals, sentenced to death and executed after allegedly planning an escape from Drapchi Prison. Their executions were announced on local television on May 18, 1990 (see Lhundrup Gaden, p.176). **DONDRUP TSERING**, who had allegedly also plotted to escape but who turned the other two in, received a death sentence with a two-year reprieve. There is no word as to what happened to him after the expiration of the reprieve.

[2 X EXECUTED] [DEATH W/REPRIEVE]

Sentenced

■ **DAWA**[10], 23, from Lhasa Kyire, arrested on June 6, 1989, was sentenced to an eight-year prison term by the Lhasa Municipal Court on September 12, 1989 for alleged "destruction of property" during the March 5, 1989 demonstrations in Lhasa (*Lhasa Radio*, September 12, 1989). He is being held in the Fifth Division of Drapchi Prison. According to *Tibet Daily* (September 18, 1989), Dawa, who worked as a stonemason on the construction team for the ancient buildings in the Lhasa Chengguan District, allegedly shouted "reactionary slogans" and threw stones at soldiers and at the doors and windows of the Tibet-Gansu Trade Building on March 5, 1989. The following day, he allegedly participated in the riots and "seriously disturbed the social order."

. . . . [8 YRS]

■ **DINGLING**, 17, from Lhasa, was sentenced by the Lhasa Municipal Chengguan District Court to a five-year prison term under Articles 150, 156, 64 and 14 of the Criminal Law for taking part in the riots in Lhasa on March 5-6, 1989. The date of sentencing is not clear. According to *Tibet Daily* (September 18, 1989), Dingling "deliberately damaged public and private property...and disturbed the social order. He shouted several reactionary slogans such as 'Tibetan independence'...and threw stones at Public Security officers." He was also accused of robbery.

. . . . [5 YRS]

■ **JAMPA NGODRUP** - see p.15, 194

. . . . [13 YRS]

■ **LOBSANG TENZIN**[2], a 25-year-old former Tibet University student from Lhasa, implicated as the "principal culprit" in the death of a People's Armed Police officer during the demonstrations in Lhasa on March 5, 1988 and arrested on March 19, had his death sentence commuted to life imprisonment in March 1991. He was one of two political prisoners in Drapchi Prison (see Tenpa Wangdrag[2], p.177) who, on March 31 1991, attempted unsuccessfully to hand then U.S. Ambassador James Lilley a letter protesting the torture and maltreatment of prisoners. The letter was snatched from Lilley's hand by the interpreter accompanying him.

. . . . [LIFE]

The two prisoners were immediately beaten and placed in unlit isolation cells. After protests by other inmates, five prisoners (see also Tenpa Phulchung[2] p.200, Lobsang Palden[4]

p.178, and Penpa[10] p.532) were moved on April 27 to Tibet Autonomous Region Prison No.2 at Powo Tramo County. The April 27 protest against moving the prisoners was violently suppressed. About twenty prisoners asked a guard about the missing men; the guard phoned for assistance and a large contingent of armed soldiers moved in. Each protestor was tied with rope. Four or five guards then beat each one unconscious, some several times. Prison staff were not permitted to intervene. Most of the protesting men were put in isolation cells, some in manacles. By June 1, when Lobsang Tenzin's manacles were removed, his health had been badly affected. His brother, who visited in October 1992, reported that both his memory and general physical condition were deteriorating.

Five others were implicated with Lobsang Tenzin in the death of the People's Armed Police officer. Three were charged as accomplices. **SONAM WANGDU**[1] (also known as SHOPRING, but usually as SHUKDEN), a 36-year-old businessman from Lhasa, received a life sentence but was later released on medical parole. He was so severely beaten after a December 15, 1990 prison protest marking the death in detention of Lhakpa Tsering[3] (see p.165), that a lower vertebra was crushed, causing severe nerve damage and paralysis from the waist down. One kidney also was badly damaged. Incontinent from bladder damage and confined to a wheelchair, Sonam Wangdu was released to home custody in February 1993. During his several hospital stays, the first in December 1991, after which he was returned to prison, basic medical expenses were borne by the state, but food and medicines not in stock had to be paid for by the family. Supporters outside Tibet were warned of the "dangers" of trying to send money to help. Sonam Wangdu was also severely beaten and tortured when first detained. For five consecutive days he was tied and suspended from the ceiling in the "airplane" position. Later he was made to walk back and forth with a concrete block balanced on his back; and he had to kneel on the roof of a prison greenhouse with his wrists bound behind him so that one hand was pulled down over his shoulder and the other was pulled up. When he fainted and tumbled from the roof, he hit a line of jagged rocks deliberately placed below. He was also brutally beaten while being returned to Gutsa Detention Center after his trial.

. . . . . [LIFE/MEDICAL PAROLE]

TSERING DONDRUP[1], a 33-year-old from Lhasa, who was a student of religion at the Academy of Tibetan Buddhism, was arrested March 19 and sentenced on January 19, 1989 to ten years in prison. He was another of the twenty Drapchi prisoners harshly disciplined in connection with the James Lilley affair. **GYALTSEN CHOEPHEL**, the third alleged accomplice, a 27-year-old Lhasa businessman, arrested March 13, 1988, received a fifteen-year sentence. He, too, was punished in the Lilley affair. Another inmate, **JAMPA CHOEPHEL** (lay name **BAGDRO**[3]), a 22-year-old

secretly accused of involvement in the incident and sentenced to a three-year-term, fled to India after his release. A Ganden monk, from Taktse County Tsang Ngog, he reportedly was so severely beaten, especially around the head, that he has difficulty walking and speaking. In addition to beatings, he was subjected to aerial suspension, repeated electric shocks, food deprivation, and he was handcuffed continuously for over thirty days. A sixth man, **TAMDRIN**[1], a 27-year-old Ganden monk, from Medro Gongkar, harshly disciplined in the Lilley affair, was accused but not charged with the policeman's death. Arrested April 18, he presumably was released after serving a five-year term. All the prisoners were sent to Drapchi after sentencing.

. . . . [15, 10 YRS]

In late May 1988, Asia Watch contacted the Chinese Embassy and wrote to China's Minister of Justice requesting permission to send observers to the men's trials. On June 3, the Embassy denied the request, stating that the matter was "purely China's internal affair in which no foreign country has the right to interfere." One session of the trial, on the morning of January 9, 1989, was described in the Tibetan exile press. During the session the defendants reportedly were asked to admit their guilt; the proceedings broke down after they refused to comply and instead made allegations of mistreatment and forced confessions. Soldiers not only prevented the defendants from speaking further but beat them for speaking at all. As the

Radio Lhasa broadcast made clear, the government considered their guilt established; the trial was simply a public formality.

■ **PASANG**[7], a 21-year-old laborer from Lhasa City, arrested March 8, 1989, was sentenced by the Lhasa Intermediate People's Court on September 12, 1989 for "burning, looting and rioting" during the March 1989 demonstrations in Lhasa and sent to Drapchi Prison. According to *Radio Lhasa* (September 13, 1989), he received a life term. However, another report lists his sentence as fifteen years which may represent a reduction. Or Pasang may be **JAGOE**, born in Lhasa Tromsigang, arrested in 1989 and sentenced to fifteen years in prison.

. . . . [15 YRS/LIFE?]

■ **PENPA TSERING**[1] (incorrectly referred to as TENPA TSERING) was arrested on October 16, 1987 for "disturbing public order during an anti-Chinese riot" in Lhasa on October 1, 1987 (*Xinhua*, March 11, 1988). Named as the "chief instigator and primary criminal" (in a case which included Jigme Gatso) Penpa Tsering, a 22-year-old Lhasa stonemason, received a ten-year sentence on June 19, 1988 for allegedly "burning and destroying" a Public Transport Vehicle. He is serving his sentence in Drapchi Prison.

. . . . [10 YRS]

■ **TENZIN PHUNTSOG**[2], a 39-year-old Sera monk, from Lhasa Ramoche, arrested June 12, 1989, allegedly participated with Tsering Ngodrup in the "espionage on behalf of the 'Ministry of Security of the Dalai clique,'" for which he received a five-year sentence and one year's deprivation of political rights on September 12, 1989. According to *Radio Lhasa*, in October 1988, Tenzin Phuntsog visited Dharamsala and arranged with the Security Office there to provide information on conditions in Tibet. "[They] sent what they obtained to the Ministry of Security of the Dalai clique through foreigners." "As secret agent [Tenzin Phuntsog] sincerely confessed his crimes and made contributions to the investigation into the case, he was given leniency." He is in Drapchi Prison.

. . . . [5 YRS]

■ **TENDAR**[3], a 19-year-old native of Medro Gongkar, is one of three Tibetans accused of taking part in violent demonstrations in Lhasa on March 8, 1989, and sentenced to prison terms on September 28, 1989 (FBIS, October 10, 1989). Tendar received a six-year term for allegedly stealing religious objects and chanting independence slogans. (In another report, a 27-year-old farmer named Tendar (also listed as TENRA and TENRAB), from Medro Gongkar County, Gyama Village No.10, was listed as being arrested on March 26, 1989. He is probably Tendar[3]). **DAWA TSERING**[3], a 26-year-old unemployed male from Lhasa, allegedly "participated positively in the troops of rioters, shouting reactionary slogans such as 'Tibetan independence,' as well as throwing stones at buildings and soldiers (*Tibet Daily*, October 5, 1989).

Held in Drapchi Prison, he was released upon completion of his four-year term. **DORJE**[5], a 26-year-old stonemason from Lhasa, arrested March 6, 1989, also received a four-year sentence in connection with the same incident and presumably has been released. He had been held in Drapchi Prison.

. . . . [6 YRS]

4. Pro-Democracy Movement (1989)

Executed

Beijing

■ Two peasants, **LIANG Hongchen**, 18, and **LI Wenbao**, 20, accused of stealing bicycles and money and "indulging in violence" following the military crackdown against the democracy movement on June 4, 1989, were sentenced to death on July 26, 1989 by the Beijing Intermediate People's Court (*Renmin Ribao*, July 26, 1989, in FBIS, July 28). Li and Liang had three days to appeal their sentences, but there were no subsequent reports to indicate they had been spared execution. Li was from Shunyi County, a suburb of Beijing; Liang was from a suburb of Shenyang, Liaoning Province.

. . . . [2 EXECUTED]

■ Seven people - **LIN Zhaorong**, **CHEN Jian**, **ZU Jianjun**, **WANG Hanwu**, **LUO Hongjun**, **ZHANG Wenkui** and **BAN Huijie** - were executed in Beijing on June 21, 1989. An eighth person, **WANG Lianxi**, a woman charged with setting fire to a bus, was apparently spared and sentenced to life in prison after her lawyer pleaded that she was retarded. All eight were sentenced to death by the Beijing Intermediate People's Court on June 17; their appeals to the Beijing Supreme People's Court were turned down. According to a *Beijing Radio* broadcast, Lin was a worker at Huimin Hospital in Beijing and had served a previous sentence of three years' forced labor for "hooliganism." He was accused of setting fire to a military vehicle on June 5. Luo was a ticket-seller for the Beijing Municipal Public Transportation Company; he was accused of beating up soldiers and knocking one of them unconscious (*Xinhua*, June 17 and 22, 1989; *Kyodo*, June 22, in FBIS June 19 and 22, 1989.) In a later report to the International Labor Organization, the Chinese government claimed Ban was executed for "very serious assault on women with aggravated circumstances" and Luo for "serious looting" (November 1990).

. . . . [7 EXECUTED]

■ **LIU Baode**, a "hooligan," was executed by shooting after his sentencing on November 30, 1989 by the Municipal Intermediate People's Court in Beijing. The sentence was announced in the official press without details as to the time and place of arrest or the alleged crime (*Beijing Ribao*, December 1, 1989, in FBIS, December 20, 1989). At the same time **SU Peng**, also allegedly a "hooligan," was sentenced to death; but again, the charges were not mentioned. Su's sentence was suspended for two years and he was deprived of his political rights for life. (According to a November 1991 response by Chinese officials to inquiries by the U.S. government, a person named Su Ping was released. It is most unlikely, however, that the two names refer to the same person.) Neither Liu's nor Su's connection to the pro-democracy movement is known, but the way in which their sentences were reported gave strong reason to suspect they were in fact pro-democracy activists.

. . . . [EXECUTED]

■ **ZHOU Jiguo**, a restaurant employee, and **MENG Duo**, 24, an unemployed worker, were tried and sentenced to death on December 8, 1989 by a Beijing court, on charges of murdering a policeman on June 4, 1989, according to a report in *Beijing Wanbao* (*AP*, December 8, 1989). A third co-defendant, **CHEN Yong**, a worker from Tangshan, Hebei Province, was sentenced to life imprisonment. The three allegedly attacked and killed Li Guorui, 20, a member of the People's Armed Police, at 5:00 A.M. on June 4 as government troops were converging on Tiananmen Square. According to *Beijing Ribao*, the sentences reflected the government's determination "to strike severe blows against the criminal activities of counterrevolutionary elements and to protect the security of the state." The report gave no indication as to whether the executions had been carried out, but since Li was

officially declared a "martyr," it is extremely unlikely reprieves were granted. According to the report, Meng had previously served time in a labor camp for theft.

. . . . [2 EXECUTED]

Hubei

■ **YU Chunting** and **GUO Zhenghua** were executed on July 29, 1989 after being sentenced to death by the Wuhan (Hubei Province) Intermediate People's Court. They were charged with murdering two civilians, stabbing a soldier and stealing his gun during the pro-democracy unrest in May in Wuhan (*Reuters* and UPI, July 31, 1989). The execution report appeared in *Guangming Ribao*, but no precise information on the murders was given. Yu had served a previous sentence in a labor camp; Guo was described as being a former criminal. **DENG Wenbin**, allegedly an accomplice, was sentenced to death but given a two-year reprieve. Two others were sentenced to life imprisonment and nine more were convicted on charges of assaulting police, damaging railway property and inciting people to attack Communist Party and government offices.

. . . . [2 EXECUTED]

Hunan

■ **CHEN XX,** a resident of Lian County in Guangdong Province, arrested in mid-June 1989 in Zhuzhou City, Hunan Province together with **YAO Guisheng** and **HU Nianyou**, was executed on December 3, 1989. Hu received a life term and Yao was sentenced to 15 years' imprisonment; both are currently being held in Longxi Prison (Provincial No.6). The three, who were accused of attempting to help members of the banned *Workers Autonomous Federation* (WAF) escape from Changsha, Hunan, after the June 4 crackdown, were tried by the Changsha Intermediate People's Court in either September or October 1989. The charges against Hu and Yao also included "robbery and assault."

During the later stages of the 1989 Democracy Movement, Hu reportedly went to Changsha, contacted the WAF and made contingency plans to assist leading members of that organization and of the Students Autonomous Federation to escape from China. In the course of a taxi journey between Changsha and Zhuzhou, Hu, Yao and other leading members of the WAF got into an argument with the taxi driver, who later denounced them to the police.

Yao Guisheng, 26, formerly a worker at the Hunan Knitting Mill, was head of the Changsha WAF's picket squad during the 1989 democracy movement. He reportedly suffered severe ill-treatment in Longxi Prison and as a result, by 1992, became mentally ill. Yao's family lives in Changsha's South Gate district. Hu, 28, is from Guangzhou City.

. . . . [EXECUTED]

■ HU Hongwei, MU Fei, OU Jie, OU Wenbing, PENG Wanjun and ZHANG Xin were sentenced to death by the People's Court of Changsha, Hunan Province in June 1989 for allegedly engaging in "beating, smashing and looting" (one of the official code-phrases for pro-democracy demonstrations), and were subsequently executed (*Hunan Radio*, June 22, 1989). A seventh defendant, LI Weihong (Weidong), a 26-year old worker in the Hunan Fire Fighting Equipment Factory, was given a two-year stay of execution. (A November 1991 official Chinese response to U.S. government inquiries confirmed that Li had been sentenced.)

Li allegedly participated in demonstrations during the 1989 pro-democracy movement, including one on the evening of April 22, when thousands of people in Changsha took to the streets to demonstrate and shout slogans. Some violence ensued, resulting in almost 40 shops being smashed and several dozen policemen injured. Arrested on his way home that evening, Li is currently serving his sentence in Yuanjiang Prison (Hunan Province No.1).

. . . . [6 EXECUTED]

Inner Mongolia

■ HAN Weijun was executed on March 14, 1991, for allegedly burning a Shanghai-brand army personnel carrier outside the main gate of People's University on June 4, 1989. With one exception, in May 1990, his was the only announced execution for involvement in the pro-democracy protests after the early months of the government crackdown. A large notice outside the Beijing Intermediate People's Court reported that Han had committed "serious crimes." The notice bore a large red check mark, indicating that the death sentence had been carried out. At the time of his execution, Han was described as a paroled robber allegedly once detained for "hooliganism," whose actions linked him to the "counterrevolutionary rebellion" of June 1989 (*South China Morning Post*, March 19, 1991).

Han Weijun, whose arrest under the name **HAN Yanjun** (the discrepancy in names is probably accounted for by a transcription error from the original radio report), was previously reported as having occurred in Chifeng City, Inner Mongolia on June 5, 1989 (*Inner Mongolia Radio*), was a Dongzhou City, Hebei Province native, 24 years old at the time of his execution. The severity of Han's sentence might have had to do with the allegation that, together with **ZHAO Guoliang** (see p.369), he covered for Chai Ling so she could leave Tiananmen Square. Other accusations against Han, who allegedly confessed "to setting up roadblocks and attacking troops in Tiananmen Square" as a backbone element of the Beijing "Dare-to-Die Corps," included spreading rumors that martial law troops "caused bloodshed" in Beijing and inciting rebellions in schools in Chifeng City after he arrived there on June 4 (FBIS, June 19, 1989).

. . . . [EXECUTED]

Shaanxi

■ **WANG Jun**[2], a railway worker, was sentenced to death on May 5, 1989 for allegedly "throwing bricks and stones at the police, setting fire to buses and cars and looting during riots in Xi'an" (*Xi Yu Yi Yuan*, 1989 No.5). There was no subsequent report of any reprieve.

. . . . [EXECUTED]

Shandong

■ Seventeen executions were carried out in Jinan, Shandong Province on June 20 or 21, 1989, after the condemned prisoners were paraded through the streets. According to a UPI report, nine more prisoners were given two-year deferrals of their death sentences. All had allegedly "seriously endangered public order." *Beijing Radio* said the trial was attended by 10,000 people. The evidence that the 17 executed were political prisoners is as follows. According to the UPI report, "An undetermined number of anti-government demonstrators were among 17 people put to death in the northeastern city of Jinan Wednesday for various crimes, the *Jinan Daily* reported." On June 22, 1989, moreover, Tokyo's NHK reported that according to *Beijing Radio*, "The Intermediate People's Court in Jinan...handed down [on June 21] death penalties, life imprisonment and penal servitude for definite terms respectively on 45 political offenders, who had caused great damage to public peace and order." Noted NHK, "Hence it is believed that the executed are 17 among those 45" (In FBIS, June 22,

1989).

. . . . [17 EXECUTED]

■ **SUN Baohe** was executed in Jinan, Shandong Province on October 14, 1989 after being convicted along with two others of burning a Shanghai-brand vehicle on June 6, 1989 (*Jinan Qunzhong Ribao*, October 15, 1989, in *Reuters*, October 20). Sun was labeled "the instigator." His co-defendants, **WANG Lixin**, a factory worker, and **WANG Yong[1]**, an office worker, each received ten-year prison terms.

. . . . [EXECUTED]

Shanghai

■ **XU Guoming**, a brewery worker, **BIAN Hanwu**, unemployed, and **YAN Xuerong**, a radio factory worker, were executed in Shanghai on June 21, 1989 after being sentenced to death by a Shanghai court for allegedly setting fire to a train that plowed through a group of demonstrators on June 6, 1989 at the Guangxin Road junction, killing six and injuring six others. The demonstrators were blocking the track to protest the massacre in Beijing. Warrants of arrest were issued on June 8, 1989 and the three were tried under Article 110 of China's criminal code. Their subsequent appeals were rejected.

. . . . [3 EXECUTED]

Sichuan

■ **YU Yongchuan**, described as one of a "gang of hooligans" who overturned a jeep and set in on fire on June 5, 1989, was executed in late May 1990, according to *Sichuan Ribao*

(*Reuters*, May 31, 1990). His sentence was announced at public meetings in Chengdu, probably to serve as a warning to those planning protests commemorating the first anniversary of the events of June 1989.

. . . . [EXECUTED]

■ **ZHOU Qi, HE Xiaokang** and **CHEN Guangping** were sentenced to death on November 7, 1989 by the Chengdu Intermediate People's Court (*Sichuan Provincial Radio*, in FBIS, November 9, 1989). The three were found guilty of engaging in "unbridled beating, smashing, looting and burning" during riots which raged through Chengdu for several days after the June 4 crackdown. The three men allegedly attacked the police, engaged in robbery, set fire to a movie theater and destroyed shops. (Three others, **WU Baiming, LI Ying** and **YANG Jin** were executed on charges of murder and theft ostensibly unrelated to the June pro-democracy events, although there may have been a connection.) All six appeals before the Sichuan Provincial High People's Court were rejected, and a public sentencing rally preceded the executions. Chengdu was the scene of a major conflict between police and demonstrators on June 4-6 in which as many as several dozen people were killed by security forces.

. . . . [3 EXECUTED]

■ **ZHOU Xiangcheng** and **WANG Guiyang**, peasants from Sichuan Province, were sentenced to death on July 1, 1989 by the Chengdu Intermediate People's Court after a public trial. They were convicted on arson charges for allegedly burning vehicles in Chengdu on June 5, 1989. Their appeals were turned down by the Sichuan High People's Court and the two were executed by firing squad on July 8. A third man, **HE Qiang** (Jiang), was sentenced to death but given a two-year reprieve (*Sichuan Ribao*, July 2, 1989, in *Reuters*, July 7.)

. . . . [2 EXECUTED]

Death with Reprieve

Workers and Peasants

Beijing

■ **DONG Shengkun**, 28 years old at the time of the alleged offense and formerly a worker at the Beijing No.2 Offset-Litho Printing Works, was convicted of arson sometime after June 1989 and sentenced to death with a two-year reprieve. Four others, **MIAO Deshun**, **WANG Guoqiang**, **SHI Guoquan** and **ZHAI Yicun**, were arrested at the same time; Dong, Miao and Wang were also accused of arson, while Shi and Zhai were accused of looting. In a response to U.S. government inquiries in November 1991, Chinese officials said Dong had been convicted but gave no details of the sentence; inquiries on the other four went unanswered, and it is not known what sentences they received.

According to an internal report by the Supreme People's Court (TC p.382), at 6:00 P.M. on June 4, 1989,

Dong Shengkun "seized the opportunity of the counterrevolutionary rebellion" to set fire to a People's Liberation Army truck at the southern end of Xingfu Street in the Chongwen District of Beijing. He then took a gasoline-soaked rag and set fire to the wheels of the vehicle, causing it to be completely destroyed. It is not known whether Dong's sentence was commuted to life imprisonment after the two-year probationary period or if the death sentence was carried out.

[4 X ? YRS] [DEATH W/REPRIEVE]

■ **GAO Zhiyuan** was sentenced to death with a two-year reprieve by a Beijing court. The date of sentencing is unknown as is Gao's subsequent fate. He surrendered to police in Lanzhou, Gansu Province, after a television report showed him burning a bus in Tiananmen Square during the 1989 demonstrations there. (Amnesty International, *ASA 17/17/91*.)

. . . . . . [DEATH W/REPRIEVE]

■ **LUAN Jikui** was sentenced to death by a Beijing court for arson, according to the Chinese government's report to the International Labor Organization (November 1990.) The sentence was subject to a two-year stay of execution. The date on which the stay expired is not known and there is no word on Luan's subsequent fate. Luan reportedly was arrested in Hebei Province for setting fire to military trucks in Beijing.

. . . . . . [DEATH W/REPRIEVE]

■ **SONG Yanlin**, arrested in Beijing (date unknown), was reportedly later sentenced to death with a two-year reprieve. Apart from a rather improbable report that Song was one of 400 prisoners allowed home on leave during the 1992 Chinese New Year festival period, no further details of the case are known.

. . . . . . [DEATH W/REPRIEVE]

■ **SU Peng** - see p.354

. . . . . . [DEATH W/REPRIEVE]

■ **SUN Hong**, a worker at a fluorescent light factory in Beijing, received the death penalty with a two-year stay of execution for "counterrevolutionary sabotage." He allegedly burned military vehicles and stole a gun on June 4-5, 1989 (*Beijing Ribao*, June 15, 1989). Sun, who was born in Beijing in 1970, was turned in to the authorities by an informer sometime before June 15, 1989. There is some doubt that he did anything more than hand his cigarette lighter to an unknown person at the scene of the burning.

. . . . . . [DEATH W/REPRIEVE]

Hubei

■ **DENG Wenbin** - see p.355

. . . . . . [DEATH W/REPRIEVE]

■ **WANG Shuxiang** - see p.9

. . . . . . [DEATH W/REPRIEVE]

Hunan

■ **CHEN Gang** - see p.97

. . . . . . [DEATH W/REPRIEVE]

■ **GUO Yunqiao** - see p.98

■ **LI Weihong (Weidong)** - see p.356

. . . . . . [DEATH W/REPRIEVE]

■ **WU Hepeng** - see p.369

. . . . . . [DEATH W/REPRIEVE]

■ **ZHU Yong** - see p.385

. . . . . . [DEATH W/REPRIEVE]

Sichuan

■ **HE Qiang** - see p.358

. . . . . . [DEATH W/REPRIEVE]

Sentenced

Students

Beijing

■ Three students, **CHEN Liangru, CHEN Yonghong** and **WANG Guangxin,** were tried and convicted of "armed robbery" in July 1989 by the Miyun County Court, Beijing (*Beijing Wanbao*, July 20, 1989). All three had joined the democracy movement in May 1989 and were arrested on May 25. Chen Liangru was sentenced in Miyun County Court, Beijing, to ten years' imprisonment; the other two received eight-year sentences. Requests by the U.S. government to Chinese authorities for information about Chen Liangru and Chen Yonghong elicited no response from the Chinese authorities (November 1991).

. . . . [8, 8, 10 YRS]

■ **LI Xiaolu, XIA Ming** and **YANG Jun,** all students at Beijing Normal

University, were arrested shortly after the Tiananmen crackdown for allegedly trying to hide a submachine gun on June 6, 1989. According to a November 1991 official Chinese response to inquiries by the U.S. government Li was sentenced to imprisonment - term unknown - and Xia and Yang were released. Asia Watch's information is that Yang received a one-year sentence and was expelled from school. According to *Beijing Ribao* (July 7, 1989), the three students were turned in by informers sometime after June 20, and another five people (see Ding Xu and Chen Qisheng p.381) were arrested for allegedly concealing stolen ammunition and guns.

. . . . [? YRS]

■ **WANG Yi**, a former student at the Beijing College of Broadcasting, was sentenced sometime after June 1989 to ten years' imprisonment for allegedly burning a military vehicle. He was held prior to trial in Qincheng Prison outside Beijing, but no information as to his current whereabouts is available. According to an Asia Watch source, his mother and father were forced to retire early because of their son's alleged crimes.

. . . . [10 YRS]

Workers and Peasants

Beijing

■ **CHENG Honglin** and **CHENG Hongli**, two brothers, and **LIU Changqing**, from Haiding district,

were sentenced to long prison terms for allegedly attacking police on June 3, 1989 in the area of the Qing Long Bridge (*Beijing Wanbao*, June 21, 1989). Cheng Honglin was sentenced to 12 years' imprisonment, and Cheng Hongli to seven years. Liu, charged with "hooliganism," received an eight-year sentence. The three men, all peasants, were arrested in Beijing in June 1989.

. . . . [7, 8, 12 YRS]

■ **GAO Tongxiang** and **WU Chunqi**, arrested in Beijing in connection with the burning of a People's Liberation Army vehicle, received long prison sentences. Wu is serving a life term; Gao, who was physically abused during his interrogation, received a ten-year term. The two are being held in Beijing No.1 Prison. Gao, who was born in 1956, was taken into custody in July 1989, just before Wu. Gao was formally arrested on December 28, 1990 and sentenced in February 1991. Although his trial was called "open" by the authorities, there were no family members present and no witnesses were called. At the appeal hearing, only the judges were present.

. . . . [10 YRS] [LIFE]

■ **LI Bing**, a leader of a "Beijing worker's independent organization," was sentenced to a seven-year prison term (International Labor Organization, November 1991). He was arrested in Beijing on June 21, 1989 for allegedly killing a soldier and trying to block military vehicles from entering Tiananmen Square on June 4 (*Beijing Ribao* and *Kyodo*, June 25, 1989, in

FBIS, June 26).

. . . . [7 YRS]

■ **LIANG Zenguo** was sentenced in Beijing to a 13-year term for looting, according to a government response to repeated inquiries on his case by the International Labor Organization (November 1990). There is no information as to the date of sentencing or the place of imprisonment; no biographical information is available. However, an earlier account (*Renmin Ribao*, June 23, 1989) which reported the June 10 arrest of a Beijing worker, **LIAN Zhenguo**, for looting, probably refers to the same person.

. . . . [13 YRS]

■ **LIU Zhenting**, a worker at the Beijing No.2 Automotive Assembly Plant, was sentenced to 17 years in prison. His family was warned that an appeal could result in a heavier sentence - even the death penalty. Arrested in June 1989, Liu was charged with setting fire to an army vehicle, forcibly taking a police helmet and looting. The first two charges resulted in a 14-year term; the looting charge drew another four years. The court ruled the total should not exceed 17 years.

. . . . [17 YRS]

■ **LIU Zhenxian**, a cake factory worker arrested after June 4, 1989, was sentenced, according to a November 1991 official response to inquiries by the U.S. government. Liu was arrested in early September 1989 for allegedly seizing a weapon on June 4 in Beijing (Amnesty International, *ASA 17/24/90*).

. . . . [? YRS]

■ **LIU Zihou**, 34, a staff member at the Beijing Aquatic Products Company, was tried on January 11, 1991 and received an eight-year sentence for the "serious crimes of participation in rebellion, arson and street blocking," according to a Chinese government reply to the International Labor Organization. Previously, a court spokeswoman had reported Liu as receiving "a relatively lenient sentence of several years in prison" (UPI, February 4, 1991). The January 10, 1991 notice outside the Beijing People's Intermediate People's Court confirmed that Liu had been "judged in conformity with the law for inciting armed rebellion" (*Agence France Presse*, January 11, 1991), in FBIS, same date), in effect, a charge of sedition. The U.S. government was also informed in November 1991 that he had been sentenced.

Liu was arrested on June 18, 1989, together with 15 others, "mostly vagrants and idlers," who were reportedly trying to flee China (*Xinhua*, in FBIS, June 19, 1989). He was accused of being the head of the "Capital Workers Special Picket Corps," an offshoot of the "Beijing Citizens Hunger Strike Corps." The group, which set up tent "freedom camps" at Tiananmen Square, was accused of burning military vehicles, setting up roadblocks to stop the army from enforcing martial law, and helping erect the "Goddess of Democracy" statue. According to a radio broadcast in Beijing, the group's members tried to flee Beijing after troops moved into the Square on June 3-4, 1989.

. . . . . . [8 YRS] [15 X ? YRS]

■ The trial of **MENG Fan(g)jun** and 13 other alleged "counter-revolutionaries," all of whom were charged with stealing guns from troops during the government crackdown against the pro-democracy movement on June 4, 1989, was broadcast live on Chinese television on September 8, 1989. Seven men, their heads shaven, received sentences ranging from two to thirteen years' imprisonment. **MENG** was sentenced to 13 years' imprisonment with three years' subsequent deprivation of political rights for allegedly stealing a machine gun from a burned-out tank and then hiding it at home. A November 1991 official response to U.S. government inquiries confirmed that he had been sentenced. Two brothers, also surnamed **MENG**, who helped him, were each jailed for 10 years. The sentences passed on the other seven are not known.

[7 X ? YRS] [2 X 10 YRS] [4 X 2-13 YRS] [13 YRS]

■ **MIAO Deshun, WANG Guoqiang, SHI Guoquan** and **ZHAI Yicun** - see p.359

. . . . [4 X ? YRS]

■ **NIU Shuiliang**, a Beijing city worker, was sentenced to twelve years' imprisonment for setting fire to army vehicles in June 1989.

. . . . [12 YRS]

■ **REN Yingjun** was sentenced sometime after June 1989 and **ZHAO Lisheng** was released, according to an official Chinese response to inquiries by the U.S. government (November 1991). The men, both peasants from the Fengtai district in Beijing, were arrested for throwing rocks at the headquarters of the Ministry of Radio, Television and Film in Beijing on June 4, 1989, according to a June 8, 1989 TV documentary, "The Facts about the Beijing Counterrevolutionary Riot." Ren, who reportedly refused his father's pleas to surrender, was turned in by informers.

. . . . [? YRS]

■ **SONG Kai**, a 34-year-old service worker at Yanjing Drugstore in the West District of Beijing, was arrested and sentenced, according to an official Chinese response to U.S. government inquiries (November 1991). He had turned himself in to the police, admitting only to minor misconduct, but was formally arrested on June 17, 1989 on charges of stopping and attacking soldiers on June 4 (*Beijing Wanbao*, July 6, 1989).

. . . . [? YRS]

■ **SONG Zhengsheng** and **GAO Liuyou** were tried in Beijing Intermediate People's Court for allegedly burning military vehicles. No further details are available (*Beijing Ribao*, July 1, 1989).

. . . . [2 X ? YRS]

■ **SUN Chuanheng** - see p.93

. . . . [LIFE]

■ **SUN Jizhong**, a brick factory worker, arrested in Beijing on September 28, 1989 after returning from North Korea, was later sentenced, according to an official Chinese response to U.S. government inquiries (November 1991). He was a member of a Beijing "Dare-to-Die" brigade, which on May 31, 1989 allegedly tried to block military trucks from entering the city. Sun fled to Tumen in Jilin Province, then crossed illegally into North Korea, according to a report in *Beijing Wanbao* (*Reuters*, October 12, 1989).

. . . . [? YRS]

■ **SUN Yancai** was sentenced in Beijing to life imprisonment on charges of looting, according to the Chinese government's report to the International Labor Organization (November 1990). A second defendant, **GONG Chuanchang** (Chuangchang) received a 15-year term for the same offense. Both men were arrested on June 10, 1989 (*Renmin Ribao*, June 23, 1989).

. . . . [15 YRS] [LIFE]

■ **UNCLE of LIU Xin** - Sentenced to life imprisonment, see p.76

. . . . [LIFE]

■ **WU Qiang**, a 22-year-old construction worker, was arrested in Beijing on July 2, 1989 and charged with stealing firearms. The Beijing Municipal People's Procuratorate claimed that on June 6, Wu threw bricks and soft drink bottles at three military vehicles; on the following day, according to the court, he looted firearms from a burned tank.

According to a report on *Beijing Radio*, Wu was to be "strictly punished" because he had refused to surrender.

. . . . [? YRS]

■ **YAN Heli**, 24, formerly a worker at the Beijing No.2 Machine Tool Factory, was reportedly sentenced in the summer of 1990 to five years' imprisonment on charges of "beating, smashing and looting." The charges related to his alleged involvement in the 1989 pro-democracy movement in Beijing.

. . . . [5 YRS]

■ **ZHANG Jianzhong**, 26, allegedly a member of the "Dare-to-Die Corps," and **BAI Xinyu**, 60, allegedly a former Taiwan soldier and KMT agent, were reportedly arrested in connection with the case of Dong Shengkun *et al* (see p.359). Zhang, a former Beijing worker and allegedly a bodyguard for leaders of the Beijing Students Autonomous Federation and for the broadcast station *Voice of the Student Movement*, was charged with mutilating the body of Liu Guogeng, a soldier killed in the army's June 4 assault on the student and worker demonstrators. A November 1991 official response to the U.S. government said, most implausibly, in view of the original charges, that "legal responsibility was not pursued" in Zhang's case.

Zhang was arrested prior to June 16, 1989 and allegedly confessed he was one of twenty "Dare-to-Die" members who took weapons from soldiers and gave half to student leaders (*Kuai Bao*, June 17, 1989, from a June 16, 1989 *Beijing Wanbao* report, cited in *Agence France Presse*). According to the report, Zhang also reportedly confessed that three soldiers were killed in the battle over the weapons. Furthermore, he allegedly told authorities that he saw demonstrators attack six soldiers and that students took weapons from the PLA soldiers and placed them under the Monument to the People's Heroes.

Bai, who was said by the authorities to have previously served a 15-year sentence for murder, allegedly burned a military vehicle on June 4, 1989. Two others arrested at the same time, **LI Wenbao** (see p.354) and **LIANG Hongchen** (see p.354), were later executed (UPI, June 27, 1989).

. . . . [2 X ? YRS]

■ **ZHANG Yansheng, BAI Fengying** and three other persons were arrested on June 21, 1989 and accused of "wildly attacking and destroying" the equipment of official reporters who were videotaping the events of June 4, 1989, at the Headquarters of the People's Armed Police (*Beijing Radio*, June 22, 1989, in FBIS, June 23). According to a November 1991 government response to inquiries by the U.S. government (November 1991), Zhang had been sentenced.

. . . . [5 X ? YRS]

■ **ZHAO Jianming**, arrested on June 10, 1989 for alleged involvement in the train-blocking incident in Shanghai on June June 6, was reportedly later sentenced to 12 years' imprisonment for "sabotaging public transport."

. . . . [12 YRS]

■ **ZHAO Pinju** - see p.94

. . . . [13 YRS]

Guangdong

■ **LI Jueming** and **LI Jinhua**, both unemployed workers, and **ZENG Weidong**, an unemployed peasant, were sentenced on October 9, 1989 by the Guangzhou Intermediate People's Court. They received prison terms of 18, 13 and 5 years for acts allegedly committed after June 4. An official Chinese response to inquiries by the U.S. government confirmed that Li Jinhua and Zeng were sentenced but gave no information about Li Jueming (November 1991). According to a report issued by *China News Agency* (October 9, 1989), Li Jueming and Li Jinhua "took advantage" of the student demonstrations in Guangzhou's Haizhu Square to intercept and damage a total of 15 vehicles, and to "openly insult" two young women who were passing by. Zeng was sentenced for going to Haizhu Square on the night of June 6 and for "joining a group of people who were waving the banner of 'Guangzhou Workers.'" It was also alleged that while there, he took part in acts of "beating, smashing and looting."

. . . . [5, 13, 18 YRS]

■ **NG Kwai-kong**, a 77-year-old Hong Kong man, was sentenced during the week ending April 6, 1991 to a five-year prison term on charges of spying for Taiwan. The trial took place in Shaoguan, Guangdong Province. Ng, a retired textile worker, was arrested in November 1990 while visiting his daughter (*South China Morning Post*,

April 6, 1991).

. . . . [5 YRS]

Guizhou

■ **GU Xinghua** (Xingchang) and **LI Xinhua**, two peasants from Xichai village, Qinshan district, Hezhang County, Guizhou Province, were arrested and accused of organizing the *People's Solidarity Party* (*Min-Gong*) in winter 1988 to carry out secret activities and undermine the socialist system. After the crackdown in June 1989, they allegedly planned military activities to "make weapons" (*Shijie Ribao*, December 23, 1989). Both men have been sentenced, according to a November 1991 response by Chinese authorities to U.S. government inquiries. No further information is available.

. . . . [2 X ? YRS]

■ A group of local farmers from Guizhou Province were arrested after forming a "dissident party" which allegedly aimed to topple the Communist Party. According to a report in *Renmin Gong'an Bao* (*People's Public Security News*), the dissident party planned to attack public security organizations' arsenals, blow up bridges and cut telephone lines on August 20, 1989, but the plot was detected and the party's leaders arrested on October 10 (FBIS, October 30, 1989). The sentences passed on the farmers, their names and the total number of detainees are all unknown.

. . . . [? X ? YRS]

Hebei

■ **LIU Yong**, a construction company worker from Tangshan, Hebei Province, was sentenced on December 9, 1989 to life imprisonment. He was allegedly involved in the killing of a soldier on June 4, 1989 (*Renmin Ribao*, December 9, 1989).

. . . . [LIFE]

■ **ZHANG Baoqing**, a peasant from Hebei Province who was working on a construction project in Beijing, is serving a five-year term for allegedly throwing rocks at martial law troops in June 1989. He was one of four or five charged with "hooliganism" and sentenced for his part in the incident.

. . . . [5 YRS]

Hubei

■ **HU Liangbin** (Lingbing on the International Labor Organization list), an unemployed worker, and **CHEN Wei[2]** and **JIN Tao** were all sentenced for pro-democracy activities in Wuhan, Hubei Province. According to the Chinese government's response to repeated ILO inquiries (November 1990), Hu received a life term for arson with aggravated circumstances; Chen received a three-year term for disturbing the peace; and Jin was sentenced to three years in prison for looting. Inquiries by the U.S. government to Chinese authorities about Chen's whereabouts elicited no response (November 1991). Jin and Chen presumably were released upon completion of their sentences. The three men were arrested in Wuhan on June 7, 1989 for allegedly overturning trucks, blocking traffic and setting fire to a public vehicle.

. . . . [LIFE]

Hunan

■ **JIANG Congzheng**, a worker at a Xiangtan, Hunan Province factory, in his twenties, was tried in early 1990 by the Xiangtan District Court on a charge of "gathering a crowd to create disturbances." He was sentenced to eight years' imprisonment. During the 1989 pro-democracy movement, Jiang allegedly took part in demonstrations and urged workers to go on strike. According to the authorities, he "sabotaged normal production activities in the factories," and after June 4, he "forcibly prevented workers from going on their shifts and insulted and intimidated those who chose to do so." Jiang was arrested in mid-June 1989.

. . . . [8 YRS]

■ **LI Dawei**, 31, a Xiangtan worker, was sentenced after June 1989 on charges of "disturbing social order," according to an Asia Watch source. It is not known what sentence Li received, or whether the charges involved any specific allegations of violence.

. . . . [? YRS]

■ **LIAO Zhijun**, a 26-year-old worker at the Changsha Pump Factory, Hunan Province, was sentenced in November 1989 by the Changsha Southern District Court to ten years' imprisonment on a charge of "robbery." On June 6, 1989, after the student movement was suppressed in Beijing, Liao allegedly "blocked traffic

in Dongfanghong Square and pretended to be a member of the Students Autonomous Federation picket squad, inciting some of the masses who didn't understand the true situation to join in. He also forced passing drivers to shout slogans" (*Hunan Ribao*, June 1989). Arrested on the spot and held first in Changsha No.1 Prison, Liao subsequently was transferred to Yuanjiang Prison (Provincial No.1).

. . . . [10 YRS]

■ **LIU Hui**, a 21-year-old unemployed resident of Changsha City, Hunan Province, was tried in mid-June 1989 by the Changsha City East District Court on a charge of robbery, and sentenced to five years' imprisonment. He was arrested on the evening of April 22, 1989 in connection with the so-called "beating, smashing, looting incident" which occurred in Changsha earlier that day.

. . . . [5 YRS]

■ **LIU Yuanyi**, 28, a Yueyang worker, was sentenced after June 1989 on charges of "disturbing social order," according to an Asia Watch source. It is not known what sentence Liu received, or whether the charges involved any specific allegations of violence.

. . . . [? YRS]

■ **PENG Aiguo**, a 20-year-old resident of Xiangtan City, Hunan Province, was tried soon after June 4, 1989 at the Yuhu District Court on a charge of "disturbing public order" and sentenced to six years' imprisonment. Arrested on May 22 for allegedly participating in the "Pingzheng Road Police Station Incident" (see p.561), Peng is serving his sentence in Lingling Prison (Provincial No.3).

. . . . [6 YRS]

■ **XIA Changchun**, a 24-year-old worker in the passenger transport section of the Hong Kong Affairs Bureau in Changsha, Hunan Province, was sentenced in June 1989 by the Changsha City Intermediate People's Court to 15 years' imprisonment on a charge of "hooliganism." He was arrested on the evening of April 22 and accused of "taking the lead in storming the municipal Public Security Bureau and stirring up chaos." Initially detained in Changsha No.2 Prison, Xia was later transferred to Yuanjiang Prison (Provincial No.1).

. . . . [15 YRS]

■ **YANG Zhicheng**, 29, a Xiangtan worker, was sentenced after June 1989 on charges of "disturbing social order," according to an Asia Watch source. It is not known what sentence Yang received, or whether the charges involved any specific allegations of violence.

. . . . [? YRS]

■ **YU Xudong**, a Changsha worker, was sentenced after June 1989 on charges of "disturbing social order," according to an Asia Watch source. It is not known what sentence Yu received, or whether the charges involved specific allegations of violence.

. . . . [? YRS]

■ **ZHANG Feilong**, 18, a worker at a factory in Shaoyang City, Hunan Province, was tried at the end of June 1989 by the Shaoyang City Intermediate People's Court on a charge of arson, and sentenced to six years' imprisonment. He had allegedly participated in many protest demonstrations and marches during the pro-democracy movement, including one on May 19, where, upon hearing the news of the declaration of martial law in Beijing, a large crowd of Shaoyang residents surged toward the city center and gathered in People's Square. Protesting against the Li Peng government's attempt to suppress the student movement, the crowd ended up burning several vehicles, including a government official's sedan, a police vehicle and two imported trucks. Zhang was arrested in mid-June and accused of having participated in the incident.

. . . . [6 YRS]

■ **ZHANG Song**, a 24-year-old resident of Changsha, Hunan Province, was tried in June 1989 on charges of "robbery" and sentenced to five years' imprisonment. Involved in demonstrations during the 1989 pro-democracy movement, Zhang was arrested on the evening of April 22 on charges of "beating, smashing and looting." He is being held in Longxi Prison (Provincial No.6).

. . . . [5 YRS]

■ **ZHANG Xiong** - see p.102

. . . . [5 YRS]

■ **ZHONG Donglin**, a 25-year-old worker at a factory in Shaoyang

Municipality, Hunan Province, was tried in 1989 by the Shaoyang Intermediate People's Court on a charge of arson and sentenced to ten years' imprisonment. Allegedly a participant in the "May 19" incident in Shaoyang during which some vehicles were set on fire, Zhong was arrested in July 1989.

. . . . [10 YRS]

■ **ZHU Zhengying, LIU Jiye, WU Hepeng** and six other workers or residents of Shaoyang City, Hunan Province, were sentenced in September 1989 by the Yueyang City (Hunan) Intermediate People's Court on charges of "arson," "hooliganism," and "counterrevolutionary propaganda and incitement." Wu received a suspended death sentence; Zhu received a sentence of life imprisonment; Liu received a sentence of five years; and the other six all received sentences upwards of five years' imprisonment. Originally held in Shaoyang City Jail, all nine were transferred to Longxi Prison (Provincial No.6).

During the 1989 pro-democracy movement, the men allegedly were active in student demonstrations and meetings. At the "May 19th Incident" in Shaoyang, they allegedly were present when two imported cars and a police car were burned and three cars were overturned. Only Wu, however, reportedly took part in the burning. The nine allegedly also were involved that evening when over 10,000 people stormed the Shaoyang municipal government offices, demanding that the city government declare its opposition to the declaration of martial law in

Beijing. The men's arrests, after June 4, 1989, were based on videotaped materials.

[5 YRS] [6 X 5+ YRS] [LIFE] [DEATH W/REPRIEVE]

Jiangsu

■ **FANG Xu, WANG Chunfu,** both workers, and **CHEN Minchun,** unemployed, were convicted for crimes allegedly committed during the pro-democracy demonstrations in Nanjing, Jiangsu Province, in May and June 1989 (*Jiangsu Fazhi Bao,* in FBIS, November 20, 1989). Fang and Wang, who allegedly had previous records for theft, were each sentenced to seven years' imprisonment by a Nanjing court. They allegedly forced two drivers from their vehicles on May 18, 1989 in Nanjing and wounded a passerby who tried to stop them. Fang also was convicted for attacking a street vendor with a knife the following day. Chen was sentenced to five years' imprisonment for "provoking" fights in a town market, resulting in injury to six people. He, too, allegedly had a criminal record.

. . . . [5 YRS] [2 X 7 YRS]

Inner Mongolia

■ **ZHAO Guoliang,** who reportedly "confessed to being a backbone element" of the Beijing Dare-to-Die Corps, was arrested by the Public Security Bureau in Chifeng City, Inner Mongolia on June 5, 1989. According to an *Inner Mongolia Radio* broadcast, Zhao, a 22-year-old self-employed garment seller from Wuhai City, kidnapped two public security personnel and "stormed" the Beijing Public Security Bureau. He also allegedly helped student leader Chai Ling leave Tiananmen Square on June 4, 1989. Along with Han Weijun, a worker who was later tried and executed, Zhao allegedly fled Beijing and travelled by train to Chifeng on June 4, allegedly to "incite rebellions in schools" (FBIS, June 19, 1989). Requests by the U.S. government for information about Zhao's whereabouts elicited no response from Chinese officials (November 1991).

. . . . [? YRS]

Shaanxi

■ **FAN Changjiang**, an unemployed man, and four others were tried and sentenced by the Xi'an (Shaanxi Province) Intermediate People's Court for their involvement in the April 21-22 violent clashes there. Fan, unemployed, was sentenced to 12 years' imprisonment for allegedly stealing audio tapes and looting a clothing store. The other four, **WANG Zunning** and **XIAO Sanfeng**, both peasants from Lantian County; **ZHAO Jian** (Junan) a temporary worker at the Xi'an Institute of Metallurgical and Architectural Engineering; and **SUN Chaohui**, a temporary worker in the Chengzhong office of the Employment Service Company of the Xi'an Survey and Drawing School, were all sentenced to terms of three to four years' imprisonment for allegedly "disrupting social order." An official Chinese response to U.S. government inquiries confirmed that Wang, Xiao

and Sun had been sentenced but elicited no information about Zhao (November 1991). It is presumed that those with three and four-year sentences were released upon completion of their terms.

. . . . [12 YRS]

■ **FENG Shuangqing**, a worker at a pharmaceutical plant in Xi'an, and four other people were sentenced to long terms of imprisonment by the Xi'an People's Court on September 23-24, 1989 (*Ming Bao*, September 26, 1989). All were accused of taking part in "riots" in Xi'an, Shaanxi Province, on April 21 and 22. According to *Xi'an Wanbao* (September 22, 1989), Feng received a five-year prison term; **ZHAO Ping**, a peasant, was sentenced to seven years; and **YU Yong**, a worker, was sentenced to ten years. **LIU Gang**[2], an unemployed worker and allegedly a "chief instigator," and a man named **SUN Guanghu** were both sentenced to life imprisonment for allegedly looting 13 shops, shouting "provocative slogans" and throwing stones at a bus.

In November 1991, Chinese authorities confirmed to the U.S. government that Feng, Liu, Sun, "TANG Yong" (probably Yu Yong) and "ZHAO Yangping" (probably Zhao Ping) had all been sentenced. Independent accounts of the violent clashes in Xi'an, in which numerous students were badly beaten by anti-riot police, indicate that the violence was mainly precipitated and carried out by the authorities, not by demonstrators.

. . . . [5, 7, 10 YRS] [2 X LIFE]

■ **RUI Chaoyang** and **ZHANG Bingbing** were sentenced to life and 16 years' imprisonment respectively for their part in the clashes that broke out in Xi'an on April 21 and 22, 1989 following a memorial service for deposed Communist Party Secretary Hu Yaobang. Rui was convicted of "hooliganism" *(Reuters,* August 17, 1989) and found guilty of breaking into a government compound, throwing stones at the police and smashing windows of a tourist bus. Zhang's sentence was confirmed in an official Chinese response to U.S. government inquiries (November 1991), but requests for information about Rui elicited no response. An account of both men's arrests and trials, reported on *Beijing Radio* on August 16, 1989, stated that Rui was a temporary worker at Xi'an's Huanbao Boiler Company; Zhang was a contract worker on the installation team of the Shaanxi Province No.3 Construction Company.
. . . . [16 YRS] [LIFE]

Shandong

■ **MENG Qingqin,** 52, an unemployed man from Longkou City in Shandong Province, was arrested shortly after the June 4, 1989 crackdown (according to one account, in Zhifu, Shandong Province on June 23). Tried by the Yantai Intermediate People's Court on July 24 on charges of "counterrevolutionary propaganda and incitement," he was sentenced to 10 years' imprisonment and four years' subsequent deprivation of political rights. (In a response to inquiries by the U.S. government in November

1991, Chinese officials confirmed that Meng had been sentenced, but no further information was provided.)

According to an officially published account, Meng (who allegedly had "been detained twice before by the public security organs for [economic] speculation and hooligan offenses"), on June 8, 1989 sent a single letter, signed in the name of "the people of Qingdao City," to the Shandong Students Autonomous Federation in which he "spread the rumor that martial law troops in Beijing had washed Tiananmen Square in blood and perpetrated terrible atrocities." The account continued: "He incited the students to take up arms and stage a countrywide uprising; occupy provincial and city television stations and Party Committee [offices]; and assassinate Party and state leaders and then set up a new central government, etc." Meng was convicted under Articles 102, 52 and 51 of the Criminal Law and reportedly did not lodge an appeal against his sentence *(1990 Yantai Yearbook,* p.231). (See also Amnesty International, *ASA 17/24/90.)*
. . . . [10 YRS]

■ **WANG Lixin** - see p.358
. . . . [10 YRS]

■ **WANG Yong**[1] - see p.358
. . . . [10 YRS]

Shanghai

■ **AI Qilong** and **YUAN Zhimin(g)** were sentenced in Shanghai to ten-year terms of imprisonment for allegedly sabotaging public transport and causing

serious damage, according to the Chinese government's response to requests for information by the International Labor Organization (November 1990). **ZHAO Zhimin** (Jianming on the ILO list) received a twelve-year term of imprisonment for the same offenses. **PENG Jiamin** (Jiapin) and **WEI Yinchun** (Yinchen on the ILO list) were sentenced to life terms. **SUN Manhong** (Mahong on the ILO list) received a five-year term. His sentencing and Peng's were confirmed by an official Chinese response to U.S. government inquiries in November 1991. All six men were charged with "smashing railway cars, setting fire to nine railway cars and six public security motor vehicles, turning over police boxes, beating up firemen to impede them from putting the fire out and fabricating rumors to mislead the people" (*Zhong Xin She*, June 10, 1989, in FBIS, June 12). According to deputy chief procurator Wang Shuquan, all pleaded guilty at their trial on June 18, 1989; however no sentences were announced at the time (see Yang Xiao p.576 and Zhu Qin p.583).
. . [5 YRS] [2 X 10 YRS] [LIFE]

On previous arrest lists, Asia Watch identified Sun Manhong and **SUN Jihong** (ZUN Jihong on the ILO list) as the same person; however, they were identified separately on the ILO list. Both men received five year sentences: Sun Jihong for arson; Sun Mahong for sabotaging transport equipment. Since the initial charges against the alleged perpetrator(s) cited activities that can be interpreted as arson and/or sabotage, Asia Watch still

cannot be certain if the cases are separate or the same one.

■ **CHEN Jinliang, MA Zhiqiang, SUN Xishen(g), YANG Jian, ZHANG Hongfu, LI Yi** and **WANG Baomei,** all members of the Shanghai Workers Autonomous Federation, were arrested on June 15, 1989 on charges similar to those for which the SWAF's leaders (see, for example, Li Zhibo p.162) were detained (*Renmin Ribao* June 11, 1989; *Jiefang Ribao* August 25, 1989). According to an official Chinese response to requests for information by the U.S. government (November 1991), Chen, Ma, Sun and Yang had been sentenced; Li and Wang had been released; and requests for information about Zhang elicited no response. In a reply to the International Labor Organization (March 1992), Chinese authorities further reported five-year sentences for Chen Jinliang and Ma Zhiqiang for "violating the criminal law by inciting and participating in the riots and by conspiring to overthrow the government" (*Renmin Ribao*, June 11, 1989), together with a seven-year term for Sun Xishen(g) "for the serious crimes of disturbing the traffic and hooliganism" (*Renmin Ribao*, June 11, 1989).

In 1992, Amnesty International reported that Ma Zhiqiang, in his late twenties, Yang Jian, Chen Jinliang and two others had been severely tortured in prison. After their arrests, they were held for one month at the Nanshiqu Detention Center in Shanghai, where the torture and threats began. They were accused of planning to murder a Party cadre and rob a bank, accusations for which there appears to have been no evidence. Ma not only was beaten but had his hands shackled behind his back so that the pain was intense, a common form of prison torture. All five men were finally charged with attempted murder and robbery and Ma, at least, was transferred to Shanghai No.1 Detention Center. In late spring 1990, the five were brought to trial but the court returned the case to the procuracy for further investigation.

Zhang Hongfu reportedly was released immediately after questioning by the police; and Yang Jian, Li Yi and Wang Baomei were also "released." It is not known how long any of the three were held and the discrepancy in reports about Yang may reflect a short prison term from which he had already been released by the time of the ILO report. According to earlier reports, Wang, along with Chen Shengfu and Cai Chaojun (see p.558) were instrumental in organizing the Workers Federation on May 25, 1989. Zhang, Sun and nine others allegedly planned the strikes and traffic disruption that took place on June 6 and urged people to organize to overthrow the government. Ma, Chen, Li and Yang allegedly planned to organize a *People's Party* committed to military struggle.

. . . . [2 X 5 YRS] [7 YRS]

■ On June 23, 1989, the Huangpu District People's Court sentenced fourteen members of a Shanghai "Dare-to-Die Corps" for allegedly obstructing traffic, deflating tires and beating drivers during demonstrations in Shanghai. **DAI Zhong** was sentenced

to a term of three to seven years in prison; **ZHAN Xinhuo** (Xinguo) and **YUAN Zhiqiang** (**YAN Zhiqiang**) were sentenced to eight years' imprisonment and deprived of their political rights for one year; **CHEN Honggen** was sentenced to an eleven-year term and deprived of his political rights for two years; and **TANG Jianzhang** was sentenced to thirteen years in prison and deprived of his political rights for three years (*Shanghai Radio*, June 24, 1989, in FBIS, June 27). A Chinese response to U.S. government requests for information (November 1991) confirmed that Dai, Yuan, Tang, and Chen were sentenced.

[3-7 YRS] [2 X 8 YRS] [11, 13 YRS]

■ **DONG Langjun** (Liangjun), an unemployed worker, was arrested and sentenced according to an official Chinese response to inquiries by the U.S. government (November 1991). However, according to the Chinese government's response to International Labor Organization inquiries (November 1990), he was "never arrested" nor did he ever "come before judicial authorities," often a euphemism for an administrative sentence of "re-education through labor." Dong was one of nine "ruffians" (see Jiang Deyin p.564) detained in connection with protests in Shanghai. On June 8-9, 1989 he allegedly "stormed the Huangpu District Party Committee and government organs" and the "police substations in People's Square and Nanjing Road."

. . . . [? YRS]

■ **FU Liyong**, a worker, **HE Heng** and **HU Jiahao** have been sentenced, according to an official Chinese response to requests for information by the U.S. government (November 1991). All three were arrested in Shanghai on June 7 or 8 for protest activities on June 6, 1989. They allegedly blocked traffic, deflated the tires of five vehicles and beat up drivers (*Jiefang Ribao*, August 23, 1989).

. . . . [3 X ? YRS]

■ **GAO Guihong**, 26, and **WANG Xia** were sentenced on June 29, 1989 by the Shanghai Railway Transportation Court to five and four years' imprisonment respectively for disrupting traffic during demonstrations in Shanghai on June 5 and 6 (*Shanghai Radio*, in FBIS, July 7, 1989). An official Chinese response to requests for information by the U.S. government (November 1991) confirmed the men were sentenced; Wang presumably was released upon completion of his term. Gao, self-employed, was charged with gathering crowds to stop three passenger trains at a railway crossing near Guangxin Road and with stopping motor vehicles near the same spot. He reportedly had been detained twice before for "scuffling." Wang, a worker at the Shanghai No.7 Weaving Mill, was accused of inciting people to sit on railway tracks during a demonstration in Shanghai at noon on June 6, 1989 and of "inciting" onlookers to assault public security personnel who tried to maintain order. According to the broadcast, Wang had previously served time in "re-education through labor"

for "hooliganism."

. . . . [5 YRS]

■ **JIANG Xidi** and **ZHANG (YANG) Jinfa**, two Shanghai workers accused of joining the "counter-revolutionary riot" on June 4, 1989, reportedly were sentenced for "taking advantage of the turmoil to damage property, cause trouble and disrupt the social order." Jiang, who was found guilty of beating two train drivers, received a 12-year sentence and four years' suspension of political rights. Zhang received an 11-year sentence and three years' deprivation of political rights for "hooliganism and disrupting the public order." An official Chinese response to requests for information about Zhang from the U.S. government (November 1991) stated that Yang Jinfa was sentenced. It also noted that **ZHANG Jinhe** was sentenced. Zhang Jinfa and Yang Jinfa are one person, and it is possible that another name given, Zhang Jinhe, also refers to the same person. If not, there is no information which would help identify Zhang Jinhe (*Jiefang Ribao*, July 15, 1989).

. . . . [11, 12 YRS]

■ On June 23, 1989, the Yangpu District People's Court, at a public meeting in the Shanghai Electric Plant, sentenced six defendants (see Song Ruiying p.375 and Yu Jiasong p.579) to prison terms for "inciting the masses," "sabotaging vehicles," "gathering together a bunch of hoodlums to make trouble" and "obstructing public order" during the first ten days of June 1989. **LIU Yajie**, a young worker at a Shanghai Harbor Bureau plant, was sentenced to five years in prison with deprivation of political rights for one year, for "gathering together hoodlums to disrupt traffic order." On June 7, 1989, Liu allegedly joined the "flying motorcycles" near Shanghai's Tongji University and shouted "reactionary slogans" on some main avenues; early on June 8, he allegedly let the air out of the tires of a trolley bus, thus blocking traffic. An official Chinese response to U.S. government inquiries (November 1991) confirmed that Liu had been sentenced.

. . . . [5 YRS] [5 X ? YRS]

■ **SONG Ruiying** (Ruiyang), an inspector at Shanghai's Xinhu Steel Plant, was sentenced by the Yangpu District People's Court at a public meeting in the Shanghai Electric Plant to five years' imprisonment and one year's deprivation of political rights for "gathering together hoodlums to disrupt traffic order" (see Liu Yajie p.374 and Yu Jiasong p.579). During a demonstration on June 8, 1989 at a Shanghai road junction, Song allegedly used a microphone to urge spectators to "intercept motor vehicles" and let the air out of their tires; she herself disabled three vehicles. Song was also accused of "falsely claiming that her son was killed in Beijing" and of "bringing hammers and other tools from home for others to use in committing crimes." Prior to the June events, Song accumulated "many disciplinary sanctions for violating work discipline." Chinese authorities acknowledged to the International Labor Organization (November 1990) that Song was sentenced for sabotaging transport equipment; and an official Chinese response to U.S. government inquiries (November 1991) confirmed that she was sentenced.

. . . . [5 YRS]

■ **YANG Tingfen**, a railroad worker in the East Shanghai Work Area, arrested for allegedly helping student demonstrators block and damage military railroad tracks on June 5, 1989 (*Jiefang Ribao*, August 23, 1989), was sentenced to prison according to an official Chinese response to requests for information by the U.S. government (November 1991). No further details are available.

. . . . [? YRS]

■ **ZHANG Renfu**, a worker at the Shanghai Aquatic Products cold storage plant; **ZHENG Liang**; **ZHANG (ZHONG) Quancheng** and six other unemployed members of the "illegal" Shanghai Patriotic Workers' Support Group (SPWSG), organized May 24, 1989, were sentenced to terms of two to eight years' imprisonment. Zhang Renfu and Zheng Liang received five-year terms for sabotaging transport equipment, according to a report to the International Labor Organization (November 1990) by Chinese authorities; however, Zhang Quancheng, they said, was "never arrested" nor did he "come before judicial authorities." He was probably sentenced administratively to "re-education through labor" and presumably was released upon completion of his term. That Zhang

Renfu and Zheng were sentenced was confirmed in a response by Chinese officials to requests for information from U.S. government (November 1991). Requests for information about Zhang Quancheng elicited no response. Dates of sentencing are unknown, but the arrests probably occurred in mid-June 1989; film of Zhang Renfu's interrogation was shown on June 16 on "Morning News," a *Beijing Television* program.

In addition to the above charges, Zhang Renfu, a founder of the SPWSG, and Zheng were found guilty of organizing illegal demonstrations, spreading political rumors and setting up roadblocks, thus disrupting traffic and social order. A later ILO report (March 1992) said Zhang "violated the criminal law by inciting and participating in riots and by conspiring to overthrow the government." Charges against other members included robbing drivers of money and property, "stabbing and wounding People's Armed Police on patrol, making speeches and shouting reactionary slogans on the Bund and in People's Park." In addition to their membership in the SPWSG, Zhang Renfu and Zheng were members of the Shanghai Workers Autonomous Federation. In all, sixty-six members of illegal organizations in Shanghai reportedly were detained; 26 of them were formally arrested (fbis, November 22, 1989).

[2 X 5 YRS] [8 X 2-8 YRS] [16 X ? YRS]

Shanxi?

■ PANG Fuzhong, a peasant, was sentenced to ten years' imprisonment for burning military vehicles on June 4, 1989. It is unclear if Pang, who was arrested in Beijing on June 14, 1989, is from Shanxi or Shandong Province. An early *Beijing Ribao* (June 15, 1989) reported he was from Shanxi; later reports listed him as being from Shandong.

. . . . [10 YRS]

Sichuan

■ According to *Agence France Presse*, **CHENG Yong, NI Erfu** and **ZHANG You** were sentenced to life imprisonment on July 8, 1989 in Chengdu, Sichuan Province. Chinese authorities reported to the International Labor Organization (November 1990) that Zhang was found guilty of arson, looting and disturbing the public peace. The charges against the others, apart from alleged participation in the riots which swept Chengdu after the Beijing massacre, are unknown. At the men's trials, the death sentences of two others, **WANG Guiyang** (see p.358) and **ZHOU Xiangcheng** (see p.358) were upheld. A contradictory report from the Chinese authorities to the U.S. government (November 1991) said that Zhang You was still "under investigation." There was no response to inquiries about Ni Erfu.

. . . . [3 X LIFE]

■ **DAI Weiping** was tried and sentenced sometime after June 1989, according to an official Chinese response to inquiries from the U.S. government (November 1991). The length of his term and place of imprisonment were not reported. An earlier account (*China News Service*, October 29, 1989), reported that Dai and three others were arrested in October 1989 in Chongqing, Sichuan Province for allegedly belonging to a dissident ring, the *Chongqing Patriotic and Democratic Alliance*. The organization allegedly was formed on May 21, 1989, and continued its activities even after the government's military suppression of the pro-democracy movement in Beijing. After June 4, Dai and his followers "held secret meetings, planned the formation of 'underground armed forces,' attempted to seize and steal firearms and ammunition and even tried to seek support from overseas forces." No other details about the men were given, but the Hong Kong press, quoting provincial sources, said that the *Chongqing Patriotic Democratic Association* was a workers' organization with some support from the unemployed. The Chinese government report stated that it was "one of the most important counter-revolutionary groups"; other sources say it was certainly one of the largest.

. . . . [? YRS]

Alleged Taiwan Agents

■ **CHEN Guangliang,** 48, a private doctor in Shaoyang City, Hunan Province, and **LIU Chunan,** a 65-year-old retired teacher from Shaoyang City, were sentenced in March 1990 by the Yueyang City Intermediate People's Court in Hunan on charges of "counter-revolutionary espionage." Chen was

sentenced to a seven-year term; Liu received a 15-year sentence. Both men, who were arrested in December 1989, are held in Longxi Prison (Provincial No.6). Some years earlier, Chen and Liu allegedly had joined a Taiwanese "spy organization" and engaged in intelligence collection. During the 1989 pro-democracy movement, together with Liu and others, Chen, according to Chinese authorities, "went all over the place stirring up chaos in a vain attempt to create even more chaos." Liu allegedly "during the 1989 pro-democracy movement, stirred up the wind and lit fires, created chaos and radioed information about the chaos to a Taiwanese spy organization."

. . . . [7, 15 YRS]

■ **GAO Xiaoshi** (Xiaosheng), 32, who allegedly confessed to collecting information about the pro-democracy movement and passing it on to Taiwan intelligence authorities, was sentenced in December 1989 to seven years' imprisonment and four years' subsequent deprivation of political rights. The sentence was passed by the Yinchuan Intermediate People's Court, Ningxia Hui Autonomous Region. Gao allegedly was recruited by the KMT (KMT) military intelligence agency in 1988 while abroad and was accused of returning to China in October of that year to engage in activities that seriously endangered China's security (FBIS, December 29, 1989). An additional report of the arrest in Shanghai on June 20, 1990, of an alleged "Chinese National Agent," **QIAO Xiaoshi**, may in fact be a reference to Gao Xiaoshi.

.... [7 YRS]

■ **HE X** (given name not known), a businesswoman, was sentenced to a six-year prison term on November 8, 1991 in Guangzhou, Guangdong Province, on charges of spying for the Republic of China (*Xinhua, Reuters,* November 9, 1991). Between March 1989 and April 1990, she allegedly reported to Taiwanese agents in Japan on the state of Chinese politics, economics and social order between March 1989 and April 1990, reportedly receiving $322 for information about the unrest leading to the events of June 4, 1989 in Tiananmen Square. According to *Xinhua,* two men were arrested in Jiangxi Province on similar charges.

.... [6 YRS]

■ **LI Zimin**, a 40-year-old private businessman in Hengyang City, Hunan Province, was sentenced at the end of 1990 by the Hengyang City Intermediate People's Court to 15 years' imprisonment on a charge of "espionage." He allegedly participated in the 1989 pro-democracy movement and "stirred up trouble everywhere." Li was also accused of sending coded intelligence messages to "the enemy" (Taiwan). Arrested in June 1990, he is held in Hengyang Prison (Provincial No.2).

.... [15 YRS]

■ **LIU Jian'an**, a 40-year-old teacher at No.23 or No.25 Middle School in Changsha, Hunan Province, was sentenced on December 7, 1989 by the Changsha Intermediate People's Court to ten years' imprisonment with two years' subsequent deprivation of political rights (FBIS, December 14, 1989). (His trial was prominently announced together with that of **Zhang Jingsheng**, a Hunan pro-democracy veteran who was sentenced to 13 years' imprisonment for his role in the 1989 democracy movement.) Liu allegedly started listening to "the enemy radio" of Taiwan in May 1989 and tried to maintain contact with the station. According to *Hunan Ribao,* Liu was accused of writing 16 "counter-revolutionary letters to KMT secret agents" and of "organizing, publishing and distributing reactionary books." Arrested in June 1989, he is serving his sentence in Yuanjiang Prison (Provincial No.1). Liu is a graduate of Hunan Normal University's history department.

.... [10 YRS]

■ **LIU Weiguo**, a 38-year-old worker in Leiyang City, Hunan Province, and **WANG Yusheng** (Rusheng), a 40-year-old private businessman in Hengyang City, Hunan, were arrested in June 1990 as Taiwan spies. Wang allegedly joined a KMT Military Intelligence Bureau unit in 1985 and returned to the mainland as a spy in October 1986. Liu allegedly joined the intelligence organization in 1989 at the time of the pro-democracy "turmoil," collected information for the KMT and stole Chinese government documents. According to a *Hunan Provincial Radio* report (FBIS, July 9, 1990), both men "confessed" their activities after authorities purportedly seized incriminating espionage equipment. Liu also was accused of trying to storm the municipal government offices and of sabotaging his factory's production, and was sentenced at the end of 1990 by the Hengyang City Intermediate People's Court to a seven-year term. The charge was "espionage." Wang's sentence is not known. According to the report, the two men were held in Hengyang Prison (Provincial No.2).

. . . . [? YRS] [7 YRS]

■ **OU Zongyou,** a 46-year-old self-employed painter, was sentenced to 15 years' imprisonment by a Guiyang (Guizhou Province) court on charges of spying for Taiwan and of stirring up anti-government unrest during the "counterrevolutionary rebellion." According to *Xinhua,* Ou was arrested on June 22, 1989 in Guiyang for spreading rumors, slandering the Chinese Communist Party, collecting banned publications and taking pictures of "anti-state demonstrations." He allegedly was a member of Taiwan's Military Intelligence Bureau and had received espionage training in Hong Kong. Requests by the U.S. government for information concerning Ou elicited no response from Chinese officials (November 1991).

. . . . [15 YRS]

■ **QIAN Rongmian, LIANG Qiang** and **WANG Changhong**[2], accused of being Taiwan agents, were given heavy sentences on January 4, 1990 (*Xinhua,* January 4, in *Shijie Ribao,* January 4, 1990) by the Beijing Intermediate People's Court (*Beijing Television,* January 4, in FBIS, January 5, 1990).

Liang, 36, a Beijing factory cadre, who was sentenced to 15 years' imprisonment and three years' subsequent deprivation of political rights, allegedly joined the KMT's Mainland Work spy unit in October 1986 and returned to Beijing in November of that year. Authorities claimed that during April and May 1989, he collected intelligence in Beijing and wrote reactionary articles for the Beijing Students Autonomous Federation and the Beijing Workers Autonomous Federation with the aim of inciting students and others to rebel. At the time of his arrest on May 27, 1989, he allegedly was preparing a manifesto for a new *China Solidarity Party.* Wang, a 38-year-old Beijing factory worker cadre arrested on June 20, 1989, also received a 15-year sentence and three years' deprivation of political rights. He allegedly joined the Taiwan spy network in January 1989, arriving in Beijing on assignment on April 17. During the uprising, Wang allegedly recruited Qian as a spy. Qian, also a Beijing factory cadre, received a six-year sentence and was deprived of his political rights for one year. He was arrested in Zhangjiakou on June 23, 1989.

. . . . . . [6 YRS] [2 X 15 YRS]

■ **YANG Xiaohua,** a 30-year-old former member of the Yichang City song and dance company, was arrested by officers of the State Security Bureau on July 26, 1989 in Yichang City, Hubei Province, on charges of spying for Taiwan. On September 28, Yang was tried and sentenced to eight years' imprisonment (*1990 Hubei Yearbook,* p.134, and *Hubei Radio*). According to the authorities, Yang was recruited by Taiwan's intelligence service while on one of several trips abroad. During the student demonstrations of May and June 1989, he allegedly wrote propaganda materials and mixed with students from Yichang city in order to "instigate them to storm local party and government organs." He also allegedly "conspired to distribute reactionary propaganda materials, in an attempt to extend the scope of the [social and political] chaos." A search of Yang's home allegedly turned up evidence of his espionage activities.

.... [8 YRS]

■ **ZHANG Yi**[2] and **WU Jidong**, Guangzhou (Guangdong Province) residents and alleged Taiwan agents, were sentenced for spying on October 23, 1989 by the Guangzhou Municipal Intermediate People's Court. They were arrested around June 20, 1989. Wu, 23, an employee of a Guangzhou guest house, received a ten-year sentence and three years' deprivation of political rights. Zhang, an unemployed 25-year-old, received a thirteen-year term and four years' deprivation of political rights. Both men allegedly joined the KMT spy organization in October 1988. Authorities claimed that during May and June 1989, Zhang and Wu used a secret code to report to the KMT organization on the Beijing and Guangzhou student movements (*Guangdong Provincial Radio*, February 3, 1990, in FBIS, February 5).

.... [10, 13 YRS]

■ **ZHOU Yan (ZHAN Yan)** and

four others accused of spying for Taiwan, were sentenced on February 21, 1990 by the Shanghai Intermediate People's Court. Zhou, the alleged leader of the spy group, received a life sentence with permanent deprivation of political rights; and **CAI Weiguo (CAO Weiguo)**, was sentenced to a five-year prison term. Three others, presumably **QIU Lin** (Liu), **LU Zhengping** (Zhengqing) and **FENG Jun** (Jin), all charged with espionage in the same case (*Shanghai Radio*, January 13, 1990, in FBIS, January 16), received sentences ranging from ten to 15 years.

Zhou, 23, a worker at the Shanghai Joint Woolen Knitwear Company, allegedly joined the Taiwan secret service in March 1988 when he became acquainted with a Taiwanese spy in Japan. Authorities claimed he was given funds for espionage activities, recruited Cai and others in September 1988 and Lu and Feng in February 1989, and then passed on information about the post-June 4 Shanghai disturbances allegedly collected by Lu, Feng and others. Qiu, 30, described as deputy general manager of the Qingyi Trading Company in Beijing and a former Shanghai reporter (*Renmin Ribao Hai Wai Ban*, June 13, 1989), was arrested on June 7, 1989 for alleged active involvement in "a reactionary salon." He allegedly became a secret agent in June 1988, covertly entering China the following September. Qiu allegedly was assigned to collect intelligence and recruit new agents, for which purposes, it was claimed, he was provided funds for cameras, video-cassette recorders and secret writing instruments. He was said to have actively collected intelligence during the "turmoil," the official term for the pro-democracy movement, in Shanghai in spring and summer 1989.

[5 YRS] [3 X 10-15 YRS] [LIFE]

Arrested/Sentence Unknown

Students and Intellectuals

■ **HU Jinping**, a member of the Autonomous Federation of University Students from Outside Beijing, was arrested on June 6 or 7, 1989 for allegedly setting fire to military vehicles (*Beijing Wanbao*, June 7, 1989).

■ **LI Jiangfeng**, 21, a student at the Beijing University of Science and Technology, was arrested on June 15, 1989 in Hebei and accused of being a leading member of the Beijing Students Autonomous Federation. He was taken into custody by the Qinhuangdao City Public Security Bureau and charged with burning six military vehicles in Beijing. Hebei officials turned him over to the Beijing Public Security Bureau.

■ **YAN Jiazhi** and **ZHONG Liang** - see p.385

■ **YANG Yijun**, 21, accused of setting ablaze 21 military vehicles during the "counterrevolutionary rebellion" in Beijing, was arrested by the Qinhuangdao City Public Security Department on June 15, 1989. He was a student at a college associated with the Capital Iron and Steel Company, Beijing, and lived in Machangdian Village, Niutouya Township, Funing County. Yang fled to Hebei Province after June 4, 1989 and was turned over to the Beijing Public Security Bureau after his arrest. There has been no further news of Yang since his arrest.

Workers and Peasants

Beijing

■ **BAI Wenbo** was arrested on June 11, 1989 for allegedly burning a military vehicle and giving a "counter-revolutionary speech" (*Beijing Ribao*, June 13, 1989). No further details are available.

■ **GAN Huijie** was arrested in Beijing on June 3, 1989 for allegedly attacking members of the armed forces (*Renmin Ribao*, June 23, 1989. No other information is available on the case.

■ **GAO Hao** was arrested in Shanghai on November 7, 1989 for burning military vehicles during the "counterrevolutionary rebellion" in Beijing (*Washington Post*, December 3, 1989). Other than that he was seized at the Shanghai railroad station, no further information is available.

■ **HE Wensheng** and **CHEN Qisheng** were arrested sometime after June 11, 1989 for allegedly hiding a submachine gun stolen from martial law troops on June 6, 1989 (*Beijing Ribao*, July 4, 1989). Both men were members of the Black Panther Shock Brigade of the Beijing Citizens Autonomous Federation. Requests by the U.S. government for information about Chen elicited no response from Chinese authorities (November 1991). Others arrested in connection with the same case included **DING Xu**, a 24-year-old Dongfang Car Rental Company worker, **WANG Jinlong** and **PENG X** (given name not known). Although the latter three were charged with violating Article 163 of the Criminal Code, their surrender reportedly earned them lenient treatment.

■ **HUANG Lianxi**, arrested in Beijing on June 6, 1989, allegedly set fire to the seats of a trolley bus (*Renmin Ribao*, June 12, 1989). No additional information is available.

■ **HUO Liansheng**, 23, a peasant from Miyun County east of Beijing, was arrested on June 4, 1989 and accused of stealing a gun (*Beijing Wanbao*, June 10, 1989).

■ **JIN Peilin**, a self-employed 43-year-old from the Dongcheng district of Beijing, was arrested on June 20, 1989 for allegedly attacking soldiers, according to an Asia Watch source. Jin, when he appeared on *Beijing Television* (June 20), reportedly showed clear signs of physical torture.

■ **JING Weidong** and **SUN Guozhong** (Ruozhong on the International Labor Organization list), both peasants from Yuegezhuang, Fangshan County near Beijing, and one other unnamed person, were detained on June 17, 1989 in Beijing for allegedly shooting at the PLA from their truck as they sped through a Beijing checkpoint. A PLA guard, Deng Zhigang, reportedly was wounded in the head and thigh (*Renmin Ribao*, June 19, 1989). According to a Chinese government reply to the ILO (November 1990), neither Jing nor Sun was ever arrested or had come before the judicial authorities. This may well mean they were sentenced administratively to terms of "re-education through labor." Requests by the U.S. government for information about Jing and Sun elicited no response (November 1991).

■ **LI Jiang**, a "key" member of the "Dare-to-Die" team of the Beijing Workers Autonomous Federation (BWAF), allegedly turned himself in to the police after seeing himself on a June 11, 1989, TV videotape "standing on top of a tank and assaulting PLA soldiers." He was accused of burning a tank and three military vehicles in Tiananmen Square on June 4 (*Zhongguo Ribao*, June 19, 1989). According to the Chinese government's reply to the International Labor Organization (November 1990), Li was never arrested or brought before the judicial authorities. It is possible that he was instead sentenced administratively to "re-education through labor."

■ **LI Shiqian**, a worker at a farm in

Beijiao, near Beijing, was shown on state television on June 22, 1989 with a pistol that his son had allegedly taken from a soldier and used during the student demonstrations in Tiananmen Square. Li was reportedly deputy leader of a "Dare-to-Die" team and played a liaison role between the students and "an independent worker's union." His father was arrested on June 20 for allegedly hiding the pistol, some walkie-talkies the sum of 7,500 *yuan*. Li, who fled Tiananmen Square on June 4 and allegedly buried the articles on the grounds of the farm (*Beijing Ribao*, June 23, 1989), was arrested on June 13. Public security officials attempted many times to "persuade" Li to turn over the articles, but he allegedly reburied them in another place where they were later found by the authorities. Requests by the U.S. government for information about Li Shiqian elicited no response from Chinese authorities (November 1991).

■ **LI Shuntang, LIU Xiaojin(g), YANG Junzhong, ZHOU Wanshui, LU Xiaochun** and **YU Yongjie** went on trial in Beijing on January 15, 1991. They were accused of arson, looting, larceny and blocking traffic in connection with pro-democracy activities in Beijing in June 1989 (*New York Times*, January 16, 1991). No details of the sentencing are available.

■ **MENG Jinquan**, 22, accused of burning seven military vehicles, looting a machine gun and raping a woman during the "counterrevolutionary rebellion" in Beijing, was arrested by the Wanzhuang Security Inspection Station of the Langfang City Public Security Department on June 15, 1989 (*Beijing Radio*, June 20, 1989 in FBIS June 27). No further information on the case is available.

■ **YANG Yongqian** was arrested in early June 1989 for allegedly attacking government buildings and beating a policeman, presumably in Beijing (China Concern Group, Hong Kong University). No additional information is available.

■ **YU Tieliang**, unemployed, who allegedly attacked soldiers and burned vehicles on June 3, 1989; and **YU Peiming**, 59, a Beijing steel worker who gave a speech in the Liuliqiao area allegedly criticizing Party leaders and inciting people to overthrow the government, were arrested *on June 11 (Beijing Ribao,* June 13, 1989). Requests by the U.S. government for information about Yu Peiming elicited no response from Chinese officials (November 1991).

■ **ZHANG Chunhui**, a 24-year-old temporary worker, and **JIANG Shan** and **XIN Yajiang**, both unemployed, were arrested in Beijing on June 26, 1989, by the Public Security Bureau and the People's Armed Police (*Fazhi Ribao*, June 29, 1989). Accused of killing a People's Armed Policeman, Lin Yanpo, during the "turmoil" in Beijing (*Reuters*, June 30, 1989), they were described as "rioters... always scurrying into Tiananmen Square to agitate and stir up trouble." Zhang allegedly made a full confession, but no further information is available.

■ **ZHANG Guojun**[2]; **SUN Yanru** (possibly a woman); **LI Huanxin**, a worker at the Zhongmei Model Flour Factory; **XIE Nanfang**, a driver at the Capital Bus Company; **HE Yongpei**, a worker at the Wangfujing Art Store; **GAO Hong**, a service worker at the Yongdingmen Motel; **CHEN Yonggang**, an operator at the Dongdan Telephone Bureau, and five other people (names unknown) were arrested on June 12, 1989 in Daxing County near Beijing. They were accused of destroying military vehicles, attacking the police and spreading rumors (*Beijing Ribao*, June 14, 1989). According to an official Chinese response to inquiries by the U.S. government (November 1991), He Yongpei was later released. Although there was no reply to requests for information on Li Huanxin, a person named **LI Hongxin** (about whom no inquiries had been made) was listed as released. The names may refer to the same person.

■ **ZHAO Yasui**, 28, was arrested in Beijing for allegedly beating soldiers and stealing a rifle (*Beijing Wanbao*, in UPI, July 8, 1989). No further information is available.

■ **ZHAO Yude**, described as a "ruffian" (*Hebei Ribao*, July 12, 1989), was accused of attacking public security cadres in Beijing and arrested by the Public Security Bureau of Jixian County, Hebei Province, around July 6, 1989. No further information is available.

Guizhou

■ **BAI Daoqian**, a Guizhou Province native, was arrested in Kunming, Yunnan Province, sometime between June 9 and June 12, 1989. According to a spokesperson for the Kunming Public Security Bureau, Bai Daoqian, who was described as "a murderer" wanted by police in Guizhou, fled to Beijing prior to the June 4 crackdown, joined the Beijing Residents' "Dare-to-Die" team and then participated in the "counter-revolutionary rebellion" on June 3-4. He later fled to Kunming and joined the Kunming Citizens Autonomous Federation. The official account gave no details, however, of the alleged murder incident. In a November 1991 Chinese government reply to U.S. government inquiries, a person named Bai Daoxian (whom the U.S. side had not asked about) was listed as being "currently under investigation." This was probably a reference to the same person, although no details of the charges or case disposition were revealed.

Hebei

■ **LU Zhongshu**, a "ruffian" from Guan County, Hebei Province, was arrested in Beijing on June 6, 1989 and charged with burning army trucks and armored vehicles (*Renmin Ribao*, June 12, 1989). Requests to Chinese authorities by the International Labor Organization (February 1990) for information about the case elicited no response.

■ **YANG Jianhua** was arrested by the authorities sometime before July 12, 1989 in the Dachang Hui Nationality Autonomous County, Hebei Province, for allegedly burning 30 military vehicles during the "counter-revolutionary rebellion" in Beijing (*Hebei Ribao*, July 12, 1989). Subsequent details of the case are unknown.

Heilongjiang

■ **LIU Yihai**, a worker from Trucking Unit No. 5 of the Harbin City (Heilongjiang Province) Bus Transport Company, was among 33 people arrested on June 6, 1989 by the Harbin Public Security Bureau. According to a *Jinhua Radio* broadcast, Liu was accused of being part of a group of 38 "unlawful elements" who allegedly shouted at students, threw sand and rocks at trucks and tried to protest in front of the Harbin Public Security Bureau. A report in *Heilongjiang Ribao* (June 9, 1989) said the group appeared at Harbin Civil Engineering College, Harbin Shipbuilding College and Harbin Engineering College at 11 P.M. one night, "seriously disturbing students' sleep." According to the report, Liu, who allegedly had a criminal record for pickpocketing, confessed to joining in the incident in order to "vent his spite upon the government." In addition, he had allegedly robbed trucks in the Nangang District of Harbin City "because he hated the government." Requests by the U.S. government for further information on Liu's case elicited no response from Chinese officials (November 1991).

■ **XIAO Zhongwu** and **QU Yutang** were arrested in Harbin, Heilongjiang Province on June 10, 1989 for allegedly inciting passengers to destroy a bus (*Renmin Ribao*, June 21, 1989). Subsequent inquiries by the U.S. government on the two men's case elicited no response from Chinese officials (November 1991).

Hunan

■ **ZHU Yong**, a member of the Standing Committee of the Beijing-based Workers Autonomous Federation from Outside Beijing; **YAN Jiazhi**, principal of the Xintian County School of Agricultural Technology; and **ZHONG Liang**, leader of the "illegal" *China Democratic Party*, were all arrested in connection with "counter-revolutionary activities" in Hunan Province (*Hunan Ribao*, August 5, 1989). Nothing is known of what subsequently happened to them. Zhu, arrested by the Public Security Bureau in Changde City, allegedly participated in the "turmoil" and helped beat two policemen to death. There is serious concern that he may have been either executed or sentenced to death with a two-year reprieve. Yan was arrested in Hunan's Lingling district and accused of printing and distributing "counter-revolutionary posters" and inciting his students to make trouble. Zhong was picked up in Changsha City after being listed on a "wanted notice."

Jiangsu

■ **QI Minglian**, a worker, was arrested in Jiangsu Province after returning home from Beijing where he allegedly stole military property during the crackdown on June 3-4, 1989. He was among 3,782 people officially reported arrested in Jiangsu Province in connection with the pro-democracy movement. Requests by the U.S. government for further information on Qi's case elicited no response from Chinese officials (November 1991).

Liaoning

■ **ZHAO Jun[2]**, an unemployed 17-year-old, was detained on June 23, 1989 by the Dadong district Public Security Sub-bureau in Shenyang, Liaoning Province, for allegedly participating in smashing and burning vehicles and "other counter-revolutionary activities" (China Concern Group, Hong Kong University; Amnesty International, *ASA 17/24/90*).

Shandong

■ **LUAN Zhetang**, a worker at the Jining Textile Machinery Plant in Shandong, was arrested around June 7, 1989 at the Tianjin Railroad Station. He was accused of smashing and burning military vehicles, beating the corpses of dead soldiers and taking advantage of the disturbances in Beijing on June 4, 1989 to steal money.

Shanghai

■ **CHEN Deqing** was arrested for blocking and attacking trains in Shanghai on June 6, 1989. According to a report in *Jiefang Ribao* (August 23, 1989), Chen joined with others from Shanghai to show support for pro-democracy demonstrators in Beijing. No further information about his case is available.

■ **GU Hao**, arrested at the Shanghai Railway Station on November 7, 1989, was accused of burning military vehicles in Beijing around June 4, 1989 (Amnesty International, *ASA 17/24/90*). Nothing is known of his current status.

■ **HU Kesheng** was arrested on June 7 or 8, 1989 in Shanghai on charges of forcibly stopping a truck and attempting to use it as a roadblock. **DONG Jin** was arrested on the same day for allegedly deflating the tires of a vehicle in order to block a road. **HU Linyong, KONG Qiming, XU Guibao, SHEN Minggui**, and **LIU Ronglin (LI Ronglin)** were arrested on June 5 or 6, 1989 for allegedly causing destruction to vehicles (*Renmin Ribao*, June 21, 1989). Liu Ronglin, for example, was accused of slashing the tires on three vehicles. According to an official Chinese response to requests for information by the U.S. government (November 1991), Xu Guibao was released and Liu Ronglin was "not pursued for legal responsibility," often a euphemism for an administrative sentence of "re-education through labor." He was presumably released after completing his sentence. Requests for information about Hu and Dong elicited no response, and there is no news on the status of the other cases.

Shanxi

■ **KANG Yaoqing**, a worker from Shanxi Province, was arrested in Beijing sometime after June 4, 1989 for allegedly smashing and burning military vehicles. There has been no further news on his case.

Sichuan

■ **LI Yujun**, a peasant from Heping village, Shapingba Hualongqiao, Chongqing; **TANG Zhonghua**; **XIAO Hua**, a peasant from Nancong County; **YU Zhuanliu**, from Chongqing; and **ZHOU Bing**, a peasant from Ba County, who were all described as "lawless elements," were arrested on the evening of June 5, 1989 in the Shapingba-Sanjiaopai district of Chongqing, Sichuan Province. They allegedly broke into and smashed eight trucks, taxis and cars. Tang allegedly had previously served a term of "re-education through labor"; Yu had allegedly served a term of administrative detention. **LUO Qianbi** and **YANG Qun**, two "rumor-mongers," were arrested separately on June 8 and 9, 1989 by the Shapingba, Chongqing Public Security Bureau in connection with the same incident. Luo, a worker at the Chongqing Dye Factory, allegedly led a group in trying to break into the Public Security Bureau on June 6, 1989 to demand the release of Li and the other above-mentioned "lawless elements." Yang, a worker at the Southwest No.3 Pharmaceutical Factory, was accused of going to Chongqing University to incite students

to attack the Public Security Bureau. She also allegedly urged students to go to the factories and enlist workers in this effort. Both women allegedly admitted their wrongdoing and promised to "abide by the law...and refrain from disturbing public order" (Amnesty International, *ASA 17/24/90*). Requests by the U.S. government for further information on Luo's and Yang's cases elicited no response from Chinese officials (November 1991).

■ **WANG Yongqian** was arrested in Chengdu, Sichuan Province along with 40 others on June 15 or 16, 1989, for allegedly surrounding Chengdu city hall on the afternoon of June 6, 1989, shouting "counterrevolutionary slogans," throwing rocks, burning bottles and instigating the masses to beat police and soldiers (*Chengdu Xinhua Shi*, June 16, 1989, in *Dongfang Ribao*, June 17, 1989).

■ **YAN(G) Qingzhong** was reportedly arrested (location unknown) for taking part in "looting and arson" after June 4, 1989. According to a Chinese government reply to the International Labor Organization in November 1991, however, one "Yan Quingzhong" from Sichuan Province, presumably the same person, was "never brought to court." This may mean that he instead received a sentence of "labor re-education."

Zhejiang

■ **CHEN Yunbiao**, a peasant from Zhejiang Province, was arrested at the Beijing railroad station prior to June

13, 1989. He allegedly stole military uniforms and other military supplies during the "counterrevolutionary rebellion." There has been no further news on his case.

Alleged Taiwan Agents

■ **BAI Xinyu** - see p.364

■ **LIANG C(h)aotian** was arrested as an alleged KMT secret agent in November 1989 in Yunnan Province and reportedly confessed to his crimes. According to *Xinhua* (January 13, 1990, in FBIS January 16, 1990), Liang, a native of Longchun County, Yunnan, collaborated with the U.S.-based *Chinese Alliance for Democracy* in carrying out sabotage. Liang allegedly joined the Mainland Task Force of the KMT in 1981. Authorities claimed that at the end of 1986, in collaboration with **Wang Bingzhang** and **Ke Lisi**, both then leading members in the *Chinese Alliance for Democracy*, Lian directed and organized the task force's Northern Burma Branch. He allegedly sent people into Yunnan to conduct espionage activities. Officials purported that, in a plot to enlarge the pro-democracy "disturbances," he distributed "reactionary propaganda materials."

■ **QU Zuojie**, a 26-year-old Shenyang (Liaoning Province) worker and alleged Taiwan agent, reportedly turned himself in to the authorities on May 25, 1989. He was alleged to have joined the KMT intelligence organization in March 1989 and to have been sent back to China from Hong Kong to "support" the student movement in spring 1989 (*Renmin Ribao Hai Wai Ban*, June 23, 1989).

■ **WAN Zhongyu, WANG Chengjin** and **WANG Chengyin** were arrested by the Kunming (Yunnan Province) State Security Bureau and accused of spying for Taiwan (*Zhongxin Shi*, August 24, 1990). According to the report, Wan, a 28-year-old factory worker, and Wang Chengjin, 33, who resigned from his factory position prior to his arrest, were recruited as agents while overseas in the spring of 1989. After their "training," Wan allegedly was appointed chief of the Kunming post of the KMT Mainland Working Committee and Wang Chengjin was appointed his deputy. Wang Chengyin, a 31-year-old factory worker, was purportedly recruited by his brother when he returned to Kunming. All three were accused of supplying information to "someone outside the country" and of plotting to establish an underground organization to create turmoil when the opportunity to do so arose. Wan and the Wang brothers reportedly admitted their activities after authorities seized their "spy apparatus."

■ **XU Jiansheng** and eight other people were arrested (probably in August 1990) in connection with four separate spy cases; all allegedly were scheming to "create turmoil on the mainland"; and all reportedly pleaded guilty (*Xinhua*, August 18, 1990, in FBIS, August 20). According to the official report, "their tasks were to recruit new agents, develop the so-called democracy movement, establish underground organizations, distribute video tapes and publications and smuggle arms and radio equipment into the mainland to stir up big turmoil." State television showed videotapes, apparently taken by secret police cameras, of the alleged spies. Xu, a native of Chenghai County in Guangdong Province, allegedly joined a KMT spy organization in 1989. Chinese officials claimed he trained in Taiwan, then returned to China to establish spy strongholds and organize underground armed forces.

SUN Daoshun, a native of Lianjiang County in Fujian Province, allegedly joined the KMT Military Intelligence Bureau in 1989. Authorities reported that he recruited **LIU Bihua, CHI Hecan** and **CHEN Xuedeng**, who were instructed to "look for an opportunity to launch so-called 'democracy movement' activities...." They allegedly distributed videotapes and printed matter in order to instigate turmoil. **ZHAN Taixing**, originally from Qionghai County in Hainan Province, allegedly joined the KMT Military Intelligence Bureau in 1986, then returned to the mainland purportedly to establish the "nuclear armed unit behind enemy lines" and an underground organization called *Union of Hainan Youth for National Salvation*. Zhan also was accused of shipping arms from Taiwan in an attempt to create "large-scale unrest." **ZHOU Changzhou** and **WANG Qianyang** allegedly were two of Zhan's recruits. **BAI Xue**, from Kaifeng in Henan Province, allegedly joined the same organization in 1987, returning to China to look for opportunities to instigate turmoil.

APPENDIX III: RELEASES

APPENDIX III: RELEASES

1. Release Confirmed or Reported

Catholics

■ Bishop Peter **CHEN Jianzhang**, bishop of Baoding, Hebei Province since 1988, was finally allowed home on November 13, 1993. Another elderly churchman, Bishop **SHI Enxiang** (see p.395) was released and returned home at the same time. On November 17, 1990, Bishop Chen "disappeared" from his residence in Xiefangying, Xushui County and was not seen for the next three years. He reportedly was first held in a "study camp" with some 20 others, then moved to an "old-age home," probably in a remote village in Laiyuan County, approximately a year later. Some time after April 1992, he was moved again to an unknown location, where he may have been held under "strict residential surveillance," a form of control used for "those who do not seriously endanger society and should not be put under arrest." Other reports allege he was actually sentenced to a three-year "labor re-education" sentence and released at its conclusion.

An official Chinese response to requests for information by the U.S. government (November 1991) listed Bishop Chen as having "never been accused of any offense" (a misleading, non-legal term which does not preclude detention without trial or other restrictions on movement). Despite government assurances that Bishop Chen had never been accused of wrongdoing and was therefore free, as of July 1993, family and friends had been unable to contact him. In an attempt to prove that he was alive and well, in February 1993 Chinese authorities gave a photograph of the bishop, taken in October 1992, to his family. However, when relatives asked where the bishop was, the officials replied, "His place has to be kept secret." According to unofficial church sources, the late Bishop Liu Shuhe (see p.1) reported that in early 1992, when he and Bishop Chen were being held together in a remote abandoned barracks, watched over by two guards, conditions were so poor that both bishops' frail health deteriorated drastically. On April 19, 1992, Bishop Chen persuaded Bishop Liu to escape and seek medical help. Before his death, the latter gave directions for finding Bishop Chen, but when searchers arrived, there was no sign of him.

Upon their release in November 1993, Bishop Chen and Bishop Shi immediately resumed their pastoral duties, and on November 17-18, they presided over "a solemn celebration" of the establishment of the church in the Baoding diocese. Some 10,000 Catholics, five bishops and fifty priests reportedly participated. A severe diabetic, Bishop Chen is completely paralyzed on his right side as a result of a cerebral hemorrhage and is unable to care for himself. Ordained in 1947 and consecrated a bishop in 1983, he was sentenced to life imprisonment in 1954, released on parole in 1980, arrested again in 1981 and then freed in 1987. Of his 73 years, Bishop Chen has spent over 30 in prison.

■ Father Gabriel **CHEN Tianxiang**, 81, was arrested November 19, 1981 in Shanghai and tried in February or March 1983 at which time he was sentenced to a 12-year prison term. In 1988 or 1989, he was released, reportedly because his health was deteriorating. According to an Asia Watch source, the charges against Father Chen, a Jesuit, had to do with his participation in the "Zhu Hongsheng counterrevolutionary clique" (see p.3), with baptizing several communist cadres while in detention and with the unauthorized saying of Mass after his release from a previous sentence. Father Chen's earlier arrest was in July 1955, but he was not sentenced until 1960 to a 15-year term. Later, his sentence was extended by three years for reasons unknown. Before his release in 1979, Father Chen served part of that sentence in the Sulphate Factory in Nanchang and part in a labor camp. His current whereabouts are unknown; no recent information is available.

■ Father Joseph **DONG Zhenlu**, in his sixties, and Father **PEI**, about 40, both from Zhengding diocese in Hebei Province, were released, one on December 15, 1992, the other on December 28. They were then sent back to Hebei. Both priests had been picked up by public security officers at a hostel in Guangzhou sometime between the evening of November 17 and noon on November 18, 1992. They had planned to meet church contacts to discuss recent developments in their diocese. Neither priest had affiliated with the official Catholic Patriotic Association.

■ Father **GAO Yihua**, 30, a priest from Changle County, Fujian Province, arrested September 14, 1988, was released a month or two after his detention, according to an Asia Watch source.

■ Father **GUO Bole**, from Shanghai, arrested on July 22, 1992, was held by the Changshu (Jiangsu Province) Public Security Bureau for two months. He was detained for "illegal" preaching, saying Mass at a family's home and possibly because he organized a summer vacation catechism class (*Gong Jiao Bao*, September 11, 1992), Father Guo, now in his mid to late-fifties, has consistently refused to join the official Chinese Catholic Church. For this recalcitrance and for other religious activities, he has spent many years in Chinese labor camps in Qinghai Province. Father Guo was ordained on July 3, 1982.

- Father **GUO Fude**, 69-year-old member of the religious order "Society of the Divine Word" who was ordained in 1947, is probably not in detention, according to an Asia Watch source, but the circumstances of his release are unknown. By the time he was re-arrested, in the spring of 1982, Father Guo had already spent 22 years in prison. At his trial in 1983, he was sentenced to a further twelve-year term, reduced on appeal to seven, for publicly preaching in support of the Pope. At least part of Father Guo's imprisonment was spent in a labor camp in his native Shandong Province

- Father **GUO Qiushan** - see p.395

- Father **GUO Shichun** - see p.395

- Father **GUO X** (given name not known) - see p.395

- **HOU Chongyan** - see p.398

- Father **HUO Bingzhang**, retired vicar-general of Baoding diocese, died on February 19, 1992. The circumstances surrounding the death of the 82-year-old priest are not clear, but he probably died of cancer. Arrested in 1981, Father Huo was sentenced in 1983 to ten years in prison on a charge of "colluding with foreign forces to jeopardize the sovereignty and security of the motherland." He had been released in 1987 and was staying at a shrine in Donglu village, Hebei Province, a site frequented by Catholics on pilgrimage. An official Chinese response to inquiries by the U.S. government (November 1991),

confirmed the release. In an earlier episode in the late 1960s or early 1970s, Father Huo spent some three years in prison.

- **LI Yongfu**, a layman from Tianjin diocese, arrested in connection with the clandestine Bishops' Conference in November 1989, was held briefly and released. According to an official Chinese response to inquiries from the U.S. government (November 1991), Li had "never been accused of any offense."

- **LIN Shanming**, a 26-year-old seminarian from Pingtung County in Fujian, and **LIN Wenming**, 25, possibly a seminarian from Fuqing County, arrested on September 14, 1988, have both been released.

- Bishop Peter **LIU Guandong**, 73, from Qingyuan County in Hebei Province, was released from prison on May 21, 1992 and after initially being restricted to his village is now free to move about. He is recognized as a priest but not as a bishop by the official Chinese Catholic Church. As clandestine bishop of Yixian diocese in Hebei, Bishop Liu was arrested when he appeared as requested at the Baoding Public Security Bureau. He was administratively sentenced on May 21, 1990 to three years' "re-education through labor" part of which he served at a "farm" in Qingyuan County near Tangshan in Hebei where he reportedly collected garbage. Charges against Bishop Liu included "planning, organizing and forming illegal organizations" and "taking part in illegal activities." Both accusations referred to his part in convening the clandestine Bishops' Conference held in Shaanxi Province in November 1989. Bishop Liu had been de facto president. Between his arrest and sentencing, Bishop Liu's home was raided and books and money confiscated.According to a court document, Bishop Liu's first arrest came in 1955. Released in 1957, he was convicted the

■ Father **LU Jenun [SP?]**, 27, from Baoding diocese, Hebei Province, was arrested on February 6, 1990 and freed 15-20 days later. The circumstances surrounding his arrest and subsequent release are unknown.

■ **QIAN Zhijing** - see p.236

■ Bishop Cosmas **SHI Enxiang**, the 71-year-old auxiliary bishop of Yixian diocese, Hebei Province, was arrested sometime in mid-December 1990, held by the Xushui County Security Bureau and sent for "study" sessions for about a month, possibly in Handan. He then disappeared and was not heard of until November 13, 1993, when he reportedly was finally released and allowed to return to his home. Another elderly churchman, Bishop CHEN Jianzhang (see p.392) was released and returned home at the same time. For most of the previous three years, Bishop Shi was probably held at a "labor re-education farm" in Hebei. According to an official Chinese response to inquiries by the U.S. government (November 1991), Bishop Shi was "never accused of any offense." Bishop Shi, who is ailing,

was ordained on June 1, 1947 and consecrated a bishop in April 1982.

■ **WANG Chengqun**, a lay Catholic, was released in late May or early June 1993. He had been taken in for "shelter and investigation" by the Baoding (Hebei Province) Public Security Bureau on December 27, 1992.

■ **WANG Gengsheng**, a seminarian from Xianxian diocese, Hebei Province, was briefly detained for helping care for then ailing Bishop Li Zhenrong (see p.230), who died shortly after his arrest in late 1991. He had eluded police for two years, ever since the November 1989 clandestine Bishops' Conference in Shaanxi Province. Others involved in Bishop Li's care may also have been detained, including a doctor and his wife. The former helped hide the bishop's identity.

■ Father **WANG Yijun** - see p.241

■ Bishop James **XIE Shiguang**, 74, clandestine bishop of Xiapu diocese, Fujian Province; Father **ZHU Rutan** (previously identified only as Father Zhu); and Father **ZHENG Xinzong** (previously identified as Father Zheng), both also from Xiapu, were released on January 28, 1992. The releases were confirmed by an Asia Watch source. Premier Li Peng reportedly told President George Bush that they had breached Chinese law but were repentant. Their release was widely reported to have been an "offering" in exchange for President Bush's agreement to a bilateral meeting at the

United Nations on January 31, 1991. Whether there are conditions attached to any of the men's releases is not known.

Father **GUO Qiushan**, Father **GUO Shichun**, and Father **GUO X** (given name not known) have been released on bail for health reasons but are confined to house arrest in their respective villages. Father **ZHU Ruci**, chancellor of Xiapu diocese; Father **LIU Guangpin**, in charge of financial affairs for Xiapu diocese; Father **ZOU Xijin**, director of studies for clandestinely approved seminaries in Xiapu diocese; and Father **XU** are believed to be still in custody. In response to U.S. government inquiries, Chinese officials gave no information on Fathers Zhu, Zou and Xu, and said only that Father Liu was "under investigation" (November 1991).

The ten Catholic clergymen were arrested on July 27, 1990 in Fu'an City, Fujian, at a meeting on church affairs at Loujiang Church. The Director of the Fujian Religious Affairs Bureau confirmed the arrests, claiming those arrested had violated government regulations.

■ Bishop **YANG Libo**, the 77 year-old bishop of Lanzhou diocese in Gansu Province, was released on parole but without recanting his views on December 8, 1992. His situation is unclear. He may have been sent back to his home in the town of Zhangye, northern Gansu, some 90 kilometers from the cathedral in Lanzhou. Arrested there in late December 1989, in mid-1990 Bishop Yang was

administratively sentenced to three years' "re-education through labor," which he served in the Pingantai Re-education Center in Lanzhou. According to an official Chinese response to U.S. government inquiries (November 1991), in the case of Bishop Yang, who is not recognized as a cleric by Chinese authorities, "no legal responsibility was pursued" - a commonly-used euphemism for "labor re-education."

According to an Asia Watch source, Bishop Yang, who was ordained in 1949 and secretly consecrated in 1981, was accused of gathering a large number of worshippers for services in the Ganquanzi Church in Shandan County and of appointing twelve people as Catholic leaders. In addition, he took part in the 1989 clandestine Bishops' Conference and has "resisted reform." Bishop Yang was sentenced four times between 1952-1987 for counterrevolutionary crimes, spending all told over 28 years in prison. After his release from a labor camp in 1980, he was not permitted to resettle in his house in Lanzhou. For three years, until he was re-arrested in 1983, Bishop Yang was an "illegal" person.

■ Bishop Bartholomew **YU Chengti**, 72, (previously reported as Yu Chengdi), clandestine bishop of Hanzhong diocese, Shaanxi Province, was free to move about as of May 1993. An earlier account (April 1992) reported that he had not been heard from since his November 1991 release. Bishop Yu first "disappeared" from his residence in early August 1991. All those who normally worked for him also "disappeared," including his younger brother, Father **YU Chengxin**. There was speculation that all were confined in a "labor re-education" camp and released at the same time as the bishop. In a response to U.S. government inquiries (November 1991), Chinese officials said that Bishop Yu and Father Yu had "never been accused of any offense."

Bishop Yu and his brother were arrested for the first time in December 1989 or January 1990 in conjunction with the November 1989 clandestine Bishops' Conference. The bishop was released from a Xi'an prison sometime before January 1991 and ordered not to leave Chenggu; Father Yu was released at the same time and under the same conditions. Bishop Yu joined the church some 20 years ago.

■ **ZHANG Dapeng,** a Catholic layman from Baoding, Hebei Province, was released from "labor re-education" in July 1993. Despite government reports that Zhang's wife, **ZHAO Zhongyue**, was released at the same time, her actual status remains unclear. Both were first arrested in mid-December 1990; Zhang received a three-year sentence of "labor re-education" at that time, while Zhao was released after three months in detention. According to an Asia Watch source, however, Zhao Zhongyue was re-arrested sometime in 1992 and later sentenced to three years of "labor re-education." During the period between her two arrests and prior to Zhang Dapeng's sentencing, Zhao was not permitted to return to work and was

forced to pay for her husband's food and lodging in police detention. Several other unofficial church figures who had received administrative sentences and were listed as released by the government in March 1993, had also reportedly not returned home as of May 1993.

■ Father Anthony **ZHANG Gangyi**, an 84-year-old Shaanxi Province native, who had been confined to a village in Sanyuan diocese, Shaanxi, is free to move about, according to an Asia Watch source. He was released from prison on June 6, 1990 because of his deteriorating health. After his return to China in 1949, Father Zhang spent more than 30 non-consecutive years in prison. He was last detained for "political reasons" - he allegedly said "something wrong" at a religious meeting - at 2 A.M. on December 11, 1989, briefly released, then re-arrested on December 28 and incarcerated in a Xi'an municipal prison. In response to U.S. government inquiries, Chinese officials said in November 1991 that Father Zhang had "never been accused of any offense."

Prior to his work as a parish priest at Zhangerce Church, a regional pilgrimage center in Sanyuan County, Shaanxi, Father Zhang was a chaplain in Italy in World War II. When he re-visited there in 1987, he received a Heroes of the Resistance medal.

■ **ZHANG Li[1],** of Yixian diocese, Hebei Province, arrested on July 25, 1992 in Xuanhua for illegal preaching, was released after several months in detention.

■ **ZHANG Weiming** was one of those whose releases, conditions unknown, the Chinese government announced in March 1993. According to an Asia Watch source, his actual date of release was on January 17. Zhang was detained on December 14, 1990 at 7 P.M. with his wife, **HOU Chongyan**, according to a March 25, 1991 letter from Hou written after her release on February 11, 1991. She and Zhang, who had been sentenced to "re-education through labor," were stopped on the street, forced into a car and taken to a small motel. The following day, they were transferred to a western suburb of Baoding, Hebei Province and kept for ten days in a boarding house owned by the No.604 Factory. Six people guarded Hou, who by then was separated from her husband. Another transfer followed, this time for fifty days, to a boarding house owned by the No.543 factory. Guards were with Hou at all times. Nineteen other people, detained at the same time, were released almost immediately.

Two days after the couple was seized, members of the Public Security Bureau attempted a secret break-in of their apartment, but were discovered by a relative. The police, who were gloved, searched and photographed the apartment and confiscated eight categories of items, including religious books and magazines, photographs of a priest's funeral Mass, letters and bank statements.

When Hou was released she was warned by Shi Jianzheng of the Public Security Bureau not to write her children, who were studying outside China. She also was told, "You are not allowed to sue us. Even if you do, we are not afraid. You have to be prepared to report whenever we call you." She was later informed that her husband "was held for political as well as religious reasons." A letter from Zhang to his sons (There are minor discrepancies between Zhang's and his wife's letters. He says their arrests came on December 9 and that his wife was imprisoned for three months.) added the information that an "uncle and aunt" were also arrested. He went on to say that he expected to be imprisoned for a long time because "I am a Catholic intellectual" and "I once wrote to President Bush." The method they are using, he said at the time, was to keep him imprisoned secretly, neither declaring him guilty nor innocent. He characterized the prison conditions as wretched and went on to say that in spite of severe medical problems, including a prior heart attack, severe ulcers and arthritis, it was extremely difficult to see a doctor. He was not permitted to write letters as other prisoners were, nor could he learn the condition of his elderly sister. Zhang warned his sons not to attempt to come back to China since their letters to him were confiscated and the police questioned him intently about their contents.

In a letter dated February 29, 1992, Hou wrote that she was finally able to visit her husband after a lapse of 14 months, and was permitted monthly visits but could not collect his salary. She said she expected Zhang's release on December 15, 1992. According to an Asia Watch source,

Zhang and Hou obtained Chinese passports and visited their sons in the U.S.

■ **ZHANG Youshen,** a layman administratively sentenced without trial to three years' "re-education through labor" on July 2, 1991 for writing an unpublished article, "Criticism of the Chinese Catholic Patriotic Association," about the official organization he had refused to join, was released in March 1993. A leader of the Catholic community in Baoding, Hebei Province, the 65-year-old retired editor from the Huadong Bu Di Yi Jiaopian Chang (Chemical Industry Department No.1 Film Factory), was held in the Hengshui Labor Camp in Hebei. According to his trial document, Zhang was officially charged with "counterrevolutionary activity" for attacking the Communist Party and the Chinese government in his article. According to an Asia Watch source, Zhang, a graduate of Beijing University's philosophy department, wrote the article out of his "deep interest in religion and philosophy" and not because he was prompted to do so by another party. The article was found by the authorities after Zhang lent it to someone; that person was then unexpectedly arrested and the article was found in his home during a search.

In March 1991, the police came to Zhang Youshen's home and ordered him to accompany them to the Public Security Bureau. Later that same day, his family was informed that he was being detained for "shelter for investigation" *(shourong shencha)*. In April, the police searched Zhang's home, looking for any reference material he might have used while writing his article. They confiscated prayer books and hymnals. Because these religious materials were printed by the underground church, they were branded by the authorities as "illegal printed matter." Although the family was never notified of Zhang's place of detention, they knew he was being held for "shelter and investigation" in the Baoding Detention Station, together with five young criminals who had already been charged. No family visits were permitted until Zhang was moved in July 1991. Food in detention was poor and insufficient and Zhang's health deteriorated. On orders from the guards, other prisoners would not talk with him, and initially he was not even permitted to write letters home. At the "labor re-education" camp, Zhang worked in the fields, was housed in a small room with three young prisoners and was permitted family visits twice a month in the presence of a police officer.

Protestants

■ **BAI Shuqian,** an elderly house church member from Ye County, Henan Province, who had been sentenced to a 12-year prison term on September 12, 1984, was released on July 28, 1992. His early release, ostensibly for "good behavior," came immediately after he was confined to a prison hospital with a pulmonary infection. He was detained on July 29, 1993 for association with the Shouters, an "illegal" religious sect; for holding banned religious meetings; and for receiving religious literature from abroad. Bai, aged 54 at the time of his arrest, was held first at Ye Country Prison and was moved after sentencing to Henan Provincial Prison No.4 in Kaifeng.

■ **CHANG Lubin,** a 37-year-old American citizen working as a computer engineer for Hewlett Packard in Singapore, was arrested on September 8, 1992 during a raid on a church meeting in Guofa Village, Wuyang District, Henan Province. Two other foreigners, both women, one from Malaysia and one from Singapore were released after four days. Chang was held for 16 days before being released, partly because he was not carrying his U.S. passport at the time of the raid. (See also **Ma Shuishen,** p.45.)

■ **Sister CHEN,** a leader of a mission team in Shaanxi Province, was arrested on December 28, 1989, detained for three months and then released.

■ **CUI Zhengshan,** see p.272

■ **DING Hai,** a 31-year-old Protestant lay leader from Henan Province, arrested before June 1990 for possessing video equipment without the requisite license, was released in March 1992 for "good conduct." She had been sentenced administratively in November 1989 to a three-year term of "re-education through labor."

■ **David DONG,** a 19-year-old student arrested on December 20, 1991

in Kunming, Yunnan Province for receiving Christian literature from an American, was released in February 1992. Prior to his release, Public Security Bureau officers confiscated some of his possessions and boarded up his apartment.

■ **LI Tianen,** a house church leader based in Shanghai and detained in early 1992, was released that March. Earlier, on October 29, 1990, he was arrested in Mudanjiang, Heilongjiang Province for leading an evangelism course for some 100 pastors.

■ **LIANG Sanying,** a house church leader from either Henan or Shaanxi Province, was detained for at least ten days in the spring of 1990.

■ **LIN Xianggao (Samuel Lam),** the 69-year-old pastor of the Damazhan Church in Guangzhou, has been under renewed pressure to register his church with the official Three-Self Patriotic Association. On July 5, 1993, for example, he received a visit from Public Security officers who told him that his church was illegal (*South China Morning Post*, July 8, 1993). Over a year ago, Pastor Lin was subject to constant pressure lasting over two months. On March 28 1992, after interrogation, he refused to register. A few days earlier, on March 23, the Public Security Bureau interrogated him for three hours. On March 24, his church was ransacked and foreign religious literature confiscated. Even earlier, on March 17, he was brought in for questioning. On March 19, he was visited at his church and warned that he had been violating the law and the church would be closed. More interrogations followed in March and April. In May, the pressure for registration eased. According to the *Far Eastern Economic Review* (April 8, 1993), although some 200 people attend Pastor Lin's church each Sunday, a half-dozen public security agents sit near the entrance taking note of the participants.

Earlier, on February 22, 1990, Pastor Lin was detained, then released two days later after continuous interrogation during which he agreed to close his church. During his brief period of incarceration, Pastor Lin's house and church were searched and religious publications and video and recording equipment confiscated. Lin was first detained in September 1955. Released after 16 months, he was re-arrested and sentenced to a 20-year term; his release came on May 29, 1978. Lin taught English before resuming preaching a year later. In 1988, he was warned by the Public Security Bureau to stop his activities.

When Liu Wenyan, Director of Religious Affairs in Guangdong Province, wanted to know why Lin had to practice religion on his own when there were already sufficient churches for him to attend, Lin replied that his faith was controlled by God, not the government -- joining the official church would cede control over what he could preach, what topics were prohibited and how long his sermons might run (*New York Times*, June 28, 1991).

On October 19 at 5 P.M., one of Lin's co-workers was detained until 2 A.M. Public Security Bureau officials told him they had been watching him for some time and they were aware of a trip he had made into the countryside to preach. At the same time, they confiscated 15,000 bibles from his home.

■ **LIU Huanwen**[1], a seminarian in his late twenties, arrested during the height of the 1989 pro-democracy demonstrations in Tiananmen Square for carrying a six-foot wooden crucifix, was released in April 1992. He had been administratively sentenced in November 1990 to two years' "re-education through labor."

■ **MAI Furen**, in his late seventies, was unexpectedly released from prison in April 1991, according to an Asia Watch source. However, a prison document dated March 24, 1991 indicated that Mai was actually granted parole by the Guangdong Reform-Through-Labor Department for medical reasons, and could be jailed again. Another report indicated he was freed through an administrative order of the Ministry of Justice, in coordination with the Ministry of Public Security, because of his advanced age. He left prison with chronic bronchitis and in a generally weakened condition. Mai was one of three house church leaders sentenced in January 1986 (see Sun Ludian, p.402, and Song Yude p.402). He received a 12-year prison term on charges of "counterrevolutionary propaganda and incitement" for connections to the Little Flock church, a Protestant evangelical group, and for distributing bibles. A native of Shantou, Guangdong Province, Mai was first detained in September 1983 and held after sentencing in the Meixian Labor Reform Camp in northern Guangdong.

- **MAO Wenke**, an itinerant woman preacher in her thirties, was detained in Hunan Province in September 1992 after meeting with Shen Tong (see p.452), a U.S.-based student dissident who had briefly returned to China that August. Although released a week later on medical bail, Mao (listed in the 1992 Asia Watch report *Anthems of Defeat* as Mao **Yong**ke), was informed by the police that she might still face trial. Originally a Chinese language teacher at the Xiangtan Physical Education College and currently unemployed, Mao had been active for several years in the underground "house church" movement. In 1987, she began travelling around several southern provinces, including Jiangsu, Zhejiang and Hunan, preaching the gospel, and after the June 1989 government crackdown, she visited prisons to visit and appeal for the release of several pro-democracy activists. Prior to her latest detention, Mao had been harassed and interrogated on several different occasions for her church work and accused of "using religion as a cloak for political activities."

- **SONG Tianying**, daughter of renowned evangelist Dr. John Sung, was released on September 8, 1990 after spending 44 days in police custody for "vagrancy." The charges related to an itinerant mission she

undertook in east China; her arrest came on July 27 while addressing a religious meeting in Zhangzhou, Fujian Province. During the time Song was held, prominent house church leaders in the area had their homes searched. Two were detained briefly; several hundred bibles were confiscated; and twenty churches were closed. Prior to this arrest, Song had spent over twenty years in prison for her religious beliefs.

- **SONG Yude**, a 39-year-old evangelical minister and house church leader from Baimiao Village in the Yuehe District of Tongbo County, Henan Province, was released from prison in early April 1992. He was convicted on January 29, 1986, one of three sentenced that month (see Mai Furen see p.401 and Sun Ludian p.402) and given an eight-year term and three years' deprivation of political rights (which he still faces) under Article 102 of the Criminal Code, for allegedly distributing reactionary religious publications, conducting illegal religious meetings and slandering the Three-Self Patriotic Movement (TSPM). According to the charges, Song's activities, including the establishment of a network of illegal house churches in Henan and Hubei, constituted "counterrevolutionary propaganda and incitement." In April 1986, his appeal was rejected. Arrested on July 16, 1984 for refusing to join the official TSPM, Song was held in Tongbo Detention Center until his trial.

- **SUN Ludian**, 67, of Shantou in Guangdong Province, who was sentenced in January 1986 (see Mai

Furen p.401, and Song Yude p.402) to nine years' imprisonment for "counter-revolutionary propaganda and incitement," was released on bail in May 1991. According to one account, he was freed under an administrative order of the Ministry of Justice in coordination with the Ministry of Security. First arrested in September 1983 on charges related to his maintenance of illegal overseas connections, including membership in the Little Flock church, a Protestant evangelical group, Sun was held in Meixian Labor Reform Camp in northern Guangdong. During his incarceration, he reportedly was very ill; his present health status is not known.

- **QIN Zhenjun**, see p.272

- **WEI Xiangzhi**, a Shaanxi Province evangelist, arrested on August 10, 1990, was released on September 26 after she was interrogated by the Public Security Bureau.

- **XIE Moshan** - see p.248

- **XU Yongze,** 52, from Nanyang, Zhenping County, Henan Province, was released after completing his sentence (*China News and Church Report*, September 12, 1991). On April 26, 1991, he was taken to a local Public Security office and detained an additional month. Sent home in May, he was placed under close surveillance. According to an Asia Watch source, Xu's release came when a guarantor agreed to be responsible for keeping him from resuming his religious activities. Arrested on April 16, 1988 in Yuetan Park in Beijing, reportedly by the Ministry of State Security, Xu was subsequently sentenced to three years' imprisonment. In spite of serious illness, he was detained in Zhenping County Prison. In addition to his preaching, which he began in 1968, Xu trained young evangelists. The group, the New Birth Christian Movement, many of whose members reportedly have been arrested or detained, has expanded to other provinces and has established over 3,000 house churches. Xu was first arrested in August 1982 and was held without trial in a labor camp. He reportedly escaped sometime that year and immediately resumed his rural missionary work, managing to evade arrest until he journeyed to Beijing in the hopes of meeting Billy Graham.

- **YANG Xinfei,** a 66-year-old house church leader, arrested September 19, 1990 in Xiamen, Fujian Province, was released in early 1991. At the time of her arrest, Yang's house was ransacked and stacks of bibles, allegedly "used by overseas hostile forces as tools to deceive mainland believers," were confiscated. Ordered to write a "confession admitting her mistakes, to disassociate herself from the house church movement and to join the Three-Self Patriotic Movement," and to provide a list of all Chinese and foreigners who had attended her church, she refused. This was not Yang's first arrest. During the twenty-year period 1957-77, she spent time in prison.

■ ẒHANG Yongliang, a 51-year-old pastor and house church leader from Fangsheng in Henan Province, arrested in September 1990 and sentenced in late 1991 to three years' "re-education through labor," was unexpectedly released in early 1992. He had been held in Nanyang, Henan. According to an Asia Watch source, Zhang, charged with "maintaining contact with an overseas Christian organization" and receiving bibles from abroad, was severely beaten in prison. Prior to his conversion in the mid-1970s, Zhang was a Chinese Communist Party cadre. He was imprisoned for several years in the early 1980s for itinerant preaching.

At least six other leaders from Zhang's church were arrested and detained at the time of his arrest. They are presumed to have been released.

■ ZHU Mei, born May 12, 1919 in Nantong, Jiangsu Province, a retired primary school teacher and an active member of an independent Protestant Church in Shanghai, was released on bail for medical reasons in early April 1992. Prior to her return home, she spent two months in a Shanghai hospital (Amnesty International, *ASA 17/55/92*). After her arrest on June 3, 1987, Zhu was incarcerated in Shanghai No.1 Prison (Tilanqiao Prison). On November 1987, she was sentenced in secret to a five-year term by the Shanghai Intermediate People's Court for "harboring a counter-revolutionary element," probably her son whom she had encouraged to escape. He was wanted for demonstrating for religious freedom in November 1986 and for publishing a

family history which included a record of involvement in freedom of religion issues. Zhu was imprisoned once before, for six years during the Cultural Revolution, for religious activism.

Reports of Zhu's ill-treatment have surfaced several times. She allegedly was beaten with electric batons at the time of her arrest, then on different occasions in 1987 for failing, while ill, to complete her work assignments (Amnesty International *ASA 17/24/91*). During one beating, her right knee was broken and she reportedly still has trouble walking. Other prison conditions, including an insufficient diet and long work hours, also contributed to her declining health.

Students, Intellectuals and Officials

■ AN Qingguo, 32, editor at Sichuan People's Publishing House and an editorial team leader for the Sichuan Press social science program, *Toward the Future*, has been released, according to an official Chinese response to inquiries from the U.S. government (November 1991). His arrest had been reported in April 1990 *(Jiushi Niandai)*.

■ BAI Nanfeng, an economist with the Research Institute for the Reform of the Economic Structure (RIRES), an institute associated with Zhao Ziyang, was freed sometime in December 1990, according to a report by *AP* (January 8, 1991). He had spent 18 months in detention after an armed soldier and four plainclothes policemen escorted him from his home on June 18, 1989.

Bai is the author of *Richly Endowed Poverty* and one of the signers of the May 19, 1989 "Six Point Declaration." He is the brother of **BAI Nansheng** (see below).

■ **BAI Nansheng**, deputy director of the Social Research Office of the Rural Development Research Institute and one of the signers of the May 19, 1989 "Six Point Declaration," was released sometime in August 1990 (*South China Morning Post*, September 7, 1990). After Bai's arrest at his sister's house on July 10, 1989, he was held incommunicado in Qincheng Prison until his release. Bai has been given permission to do research work; he is the brother of **BAI Nanfeng** (see above).

■ **BI Yimin**, a former editor at *Beijing Economic Weekly*, arrested in August 1989, was released in January 1991. He has lost his job.

■ **BAO Zunxin**, 55, a former magazine editor and associate research fellow at the Institute of History of the Chinese Academy of Social Sciences, was released early, on November 15, 1992, because he had "shown repentance," according to *Xinhua*. He had been sentenced on January 26, 1991 to five years in prison and two years' deprivation of political rights for "instigating and participating in the turmoil and riots aimed at overthrowing the government" (*Reuters*, November 25, 1992). Bao was tried January 15, 1991 at the Beijing Intermediate People's Court after notification on November 24, 1990 that he had been

charged with "agitating counter-revolutionary propaganda" (UPI, January 15, 1991; *Hong Kong Standard*, November 29, 1990). A philosopher and leading intellectual, Bao, an Anhui Province native, was arrested at home on July 7, 1989 shortly after the authorities' issuance of secret warrants in June 1989 (*Bai Xing*, May 1990, in FBIS, May 14, 1990). His name appeared on a government "wanted list" dated September 1989, under the heading: "Major criminals on Ministry of Public Security wanted lists who have now either been caught or have turned themselves in."

Bao reportedly was held in Qincheng prison; however, according to an Asia Watch source, he was seen in September 1990 in an army hospital. "Small, frail and in poor health before his imprisonment, he looked no more than 70 pounds, scrunched in a wheelchair." According to a second source, Bao made several suicide attempts after discovering that the authorities had used statements made by him in prison as the basis for arresting several other pro-democracy figures. He is said by the source to have developed signs of mental illness and to require daily medication for heart disease and high blood pressure. Sometime in September or October 1991, Bao had part of his cancerous colon surgically removed after which he returned to solitary confinement at Beijing Prison No.2. Early in 1992 and again in October, he was admitted to the prison hospital. Repeated requests by family members for treatment outside prison were refused at those times.

Bao was prominently mentioned in Mayor Chen Xitong's June 30, 1989 report, "Checking the Turmoil and Quelling the Counterrevolutionary Rebellion." Chen singled out Bao for his involvement in the production of several major pro-democracy texts: the May 13, 1989 big-character poster, "We Can No Longer Remain Silent"; the May 14 "Our urgent appeal concerning the current situation," jointly made by 12 intellectuals; and the "May 17 Declaration." Bao also had argued strongly against the imposition of martial law and had tried to organize his fellow intellectuals to form an independent organization and to support demonstrating students.

Between February and May 1989, Bao authored several pro-democracy petitions which were circulated among intellectuals for signature. A February 28, 1989 petition demanded the release of political prisoners, including Democracy Wall activist Wei Jingsheng (see p.507). One in mid-April, called on the government to rescind its decision to restructure the subsequently shuttered Shanghai liberal newspaper, *Shijie Jingji Daobao (World Economic Herald)*. The "May 17 Manifesto" was the last petition which Bao helped write. The document, which equated Deng Xiaoping with past Chinese tyrants, read in part,

The Qing Dynasty died 76 years ago, but China still has an emperor without an emperor's title - a senile and fatuous autocrat. Down with autocracy. The autocrats can come to no good end. Rule by old men must die.

During the first half of the 1980s, Bao was acting chief editor of the journal, *Dushu (Reading)*, which advocated intellectual freedom and openness to the West. From 1983 to 1987, he was editor-in-chief of the book series *Weilai (Future)*, also known as *Zouxiang Weilai (Toward the Future)*, a series which introduced new concepts in western social science and humanities to its Chinese readers. A number of leading younger intellectuals, now in exile, sat on its editorial board.

Bao was dismissed from his post and expelled from the party on August 9, 1989 for "stubbornly clinging to bourgeois liberalization (and) fanning...the recent students' unrest..." In July 1989, his works and those of nine other authors were banned by the State Press and Publications Administration. As of June 1993, he still could not publish.

■ **CAI Feng**, a physics student in the 1986 entering class at Central-South Industrial University in Hunan Province, was released after being held for several months in early 1990. At the time, students at the university had planned to hold a demonstration celebrating the uprising in Romania but were stopped by large numbers of Public Security Bureau officials. Despite the police presence, over a period of several days, campus banners and posters proclaiming the glories of socialism were plastered with graffiti. Cai was arrested in connection with these events as a member of a "counterrevolutionary student organization." Earlier, Cai had attended the "Conference on the 70th Anniversary of the May 4 Movement" held by *China Youth* magazine and made a "very radical" speech. During the pro-democracy movement, Cai was active in his school's Students Autonomous Federation. Even before the student movement broke out, he had advocated "immediately taking to the streets."

■ **CAO Siyuan**, 44, a senior advisor to former Party Secretary-General Zhao Ziyang, was one of 211 dissidents "excused from investigation, given lenient treatment and released," according to *Xinhua* (May 10, 1990). At his release, he requested a written statement of innocence, but was refused. Within days, he was informed of his forthcoming expulsion from the Chinese Communist Party. Cao protested, as Party rules allowed, insisting that he had not been found guilty of any crimes. He received no response and since his release, has been quietly but closely watched by security authorities.

The Stone Company, which instigated the expulsion, also violated a state regulation in refusing to pay Cao after his release and denying back salary for the period he was detained. According to a 1984 document, "Opinions on Government Employees' Salary During Their Detention for Investigation," issued by the Labor and Personnel Ministry:

Government employees, when they are detained for investigation, should receive 75 percent of their salary...; the reduced part can be paid back to

them when they are released without criminal charge or administrative punishment...

"They didn't succeed in drowning him legally, so they are now strangling him economically," a family member said.

After his release, Cao tried to revive the Siyuan Bankruptcy Consulting Firm which had had its registration canceled for its contacts with him. In August 1990, the firm got a new license, but it has made little money. Cao, who has to support his family of four - his wife, daughter and mother - finds himself unable to make ends meet.

One of the prime movers behind an attempt, in May 1989, to convene an emergency session of the National People's Congress to press for the repeal of martial law in Beijing, Cao was arrested on June 3, 1989 in Beijing and charged with "counterrevolution." He reportedly was held in Qincheng Prison. Cao was an advocate of constitutional and electoral reform and the chief architect of China's bankruptcy law. An economist, political theorist and legislative draftsman, he was also director of the Stone Corporation's Institute for Social Development Research.

■ **CHEN Ding** - See p.97

■ **CHEN Guangke**, in his forties, originally a cadre at one of the offices of *Hunan Ribao*, was arrested after June 4, held for almost a year, then released in mid-1990. During the 1989 pro-democracy movement, Chen participated in protest activities and wrote several articles in support of the student movement.

■ **CHEN Guojin**, a 22-year-old student in the Chinese department of Loudi Teachers Training College in Hunan Province, was released in May 1990 from detention in Loudi Jail. He was arrested shortly after June 8, 1989. He had convened a large mourning ceremony for the dead of Beijing at an area sports arena, given a speech in which he condemned the communist government and followed it with a march, and on June 8, organized a second march, blocked traffic and organized a strike among steel workers. As an office-holder in the college's Students Autonomous Federation and the organizer and Commander-in-Chief of the Loudi Students Autonomous Federation, Chen organized student demonstrations and petitioning activities and carried out liaison work with students from other provinces. Chen was also involved in the 1986 student movement at Loudi.

■ **CHEN Hanhua**, a biology teacher at Central China Teachers College in Wuhan, Hubei Province, was released after ten days in detention. She had been arrested in connection with the attempted escape of Wang Juntao (see p.70).

■ **CHEN Hong[1]**, a journalist at *Zhongguo Ribao*, was arrested in 1989, held for a few weeks and released.

■ **CHEN Jianxing**, 28, was released in November 1990, according to an Asia Watch source. An official Chinese response to U.S. government inquiries confirmed that he had been sentenced (November 1991). A member of one of the minor officially tolerated Chinese democratic parties and a strong advocate of the multi-party system, Chen was arrested in August or September 1989 upon his return to Beijing Foreign Languages Institute where he was a graduate student. He was held at Banbuqiao Detention Center and Qincheng Prison. As of July 1993, Chen was working at a company in Guangzhou.

■ **CHEN Jianyong** - see p.495

■ **CHEN Lai**, a student at Beijing Teachers College, was convicted and released on January 26, 1991 (*AP*, January 26, 1991). Chen was listed as facing trial on charges of "counter-revolutionary sabotage" but was convicted only of minor crimes. He was expelled from school; and for at least a year following his release, was unable to find a job. As of August 1993, his situation was unknown.

■ **CHEN Lebo** and **RUAN Jiangning**, both journalists, have been released (*Reuters*, September 25, 1990). No dates were given. Chen, now in his forties, was director of the domestic economic section of the progressive Shanghai newspaper, *Shijie Jingji Daobao (World Economic Herald);* Ruan was deputy director of the newspaper's Beijing office. The newspaper was prevented from publishing in May 1989 and was closed down later that year. Its chief editor,

QIN Benli, under house arrest from June 1989 until he died on April 15, 1991, was never charged. Chen was accused of joining the pro-democracy movement and engaging in "counter-revolutionary propaganda," according to *Shijie Ribao* (*World Journal*, October 19, 1989). He reportedly signed a petition to the authorities in Beijing. Ruan also was charged with engaging in "counterrevolutionary propaganda." He was in Tiananmen Square throughout June 3-4, 1989 and reportedly conducted interviews there. Chen and Ruan were held incommunicado at No.1 Detention Center in Shanghai; Chen reportedly was beaten during incarceration.

- **CHEN Peisi**, a noted comedian who was arrested around July 25, 1989 for involvement in the democracy movement (*Press Freedom Herald*, No.5, July 27, 1989) was released, possibly as early as February 1990.

- **CHEN Po**, formerly a lecturer in either history or international politics at Beijing University, was released without trial on January 26, 1991 (*AP*, January 26, 1991). However, he had his Beijing residence card, permitting employment and residency in Beijing, rescinded by the Beijing Public Security Bureau and he lost his university position. As of January 1992, Chen was supporting himself through temporary work at a private research institute. During the 18 months he was in detention, his wife filed for divorce and his parents broke off relations with him. Chen, in his late thirties, reportedly was active in getting students out on the Beijing streets at the start of demonstrations in April 1989. He was taken in for questioning in July 1989 and formally arrested in January 1991 on a charge of "counter-revolutionary propaganda and incitement." According to *Xinhua* (UPI, January 26, 1991), Chen, along with 17 others, was found to have "committed only minor crimes and [to] have shown repentance and performed meritorious service."

- **CHEN Pokong**, 30, a teacher from Zhongshan University in Guangzhou and honorary president and advisor to the Guangzhou Students Autonomous Federation, was released on July 1, 1992 after completing a three-year term for "counterrevolutionary propaganda and incitement" (*South China Morning Post*, July 14, 1992). The federation led protests in May-June 1989 which effectively closed the city's bridges and stalled traffic. Chen founded a Chinese political party, the *China Social Democratic Party*, and issued a manifesto calling for democracy, human rights, the rule of law and a free press. He was arrested in August 1989 and charged in February 1990. In an official response to U.S. government requests for information, Chinese authorities confirmed that Chen was sentenced (November 1991).

- **CHEN Qiwei**, 33, a vice-director of the Economics Department at East China Normal University in Shanghai, was one of the 97 prisoners whose release was announced on June 6, 1990. He had been arrested in August 1989 and held incommunicado in the

Shanghai No.1 Detention Center. A deputy head of the *Shanghai Social Scientists Federation*, a group formed during the pro-democracy movement, Chen wrote articles and gave lectures promoting the idea that political reform should precede economic change.

■ **CHEN Xiaoguan**. a lecturer at the University of Politics and Law, was detained for over a year in connection with the 1989 pro-democracy movement. He has been released and is in financial straits.

■ **CHEN Xiaoping**, 29, a constitutional law expert who worked to revamp China's constitution and was outspoken in support of constitutionally guaranteed basic freedoms, was convicted of sedition on February 12, 1991 by the Beijing Intermediate People's Court. According to *Xinhua*, the official Chinese news agency (*AP*, February 12, 1991), he was exempted from punishment "for voluntarily giving himself up to police and showing willingness to repent." According to an *AP* source, Chen, a native of Hengyang, Hunan Province, did not admit guilt; rather he told the court during his February 5 trial that he would have liked to overthrow the "corrupt government."

Almost as soon as he was released, Chen was advised that he had lost his lecturer's job at the University of Politics and Law in Beijing, his right to reside in Beijing and his Party membership. He had to return to his family in rural Hunan Province (*South China Morning Post*, May 9, 1991), but after some months returned to live on the university campus with full knowledge of university authorities. The arrangement was temporary while Chen tried to recover his Beijing residence permit. Financial support came from family and friends while Chen continued writing on constitutional law. He is in poor health.

A graduate of Beijing University's Law Department, Chen emerged as a leader of the 1989 pro-democracy movement. He was instrumental in forming the Beijing Citizens Autonomous Union and often was seen using a bullhorn to exhort Beijing citizens to support the student protestors. His arrest came shortly after June 4, 1989. Earlier, in late 1986 and early 1987, he was active in student protests, at which time he criticized a government ban on demonstrations as unconstitutional. As punishment he was denied a prestigious job with the Legal Commission of the Standing Committee of the National People's Congress.

■ The situation of **CHEN Xuedong**, a leader of the Nanjing Students Autonomous Federation, is still unclear. According to an Amnesty International report, he was secretly tried in January 1991 and sentenced to two years in prison. According to another unconfirmed report, he was released in July 1991 after serving out his term. An official Chinese response to inquiries from the U.S. government listed him as released (November 1991), but gave no indication as to whether he had been tried. Chen, a physics student at Nanjing University, was accused of setting up a "demonstration headquarters" and "broadcasting station" in Nanjing and of inciting workers to strike. He allegedly "organized several demonstrations, shouted reactionary slogans and wrote counterrevolutionary posters" (UPI, June 15, 1989). On June 14, 1989, state television reported Chen's June 13 arrest.

■ **CHENG Jian'an** and **ZHANG Jianjing** were released on July 26, 1991 after serving two years in a shared dark cell in Qincheng Prison on charges of organizing a "counter-revolutionary rebellion." They then left Beijing. According to a *Reuters* report (July 28, 1991), the two were able to talk together prior to their trials. After they were sentenced they reportedly were able to receive reading matter from their families and to study English.

■ **DAI Miaoqi**, a 35-year-old teacher at Shaoyang Teachers Training College in Hunan Province, has been released. He was sentenced in 1990 by the Shaoyang Intermediate People's Court to three years of "criminal control" on charges of "counterrevolutionary propaganda and incitement." Dai had joined the pro-democracy movement during its early stages and was arrested shortly after June 4, 1989. In sympathy with the Beijing students' hunger strike, Dai led a student sit-in at the main gate of the Shaoyang government offices. He also wrote a number of "reactionary articles" asserting that the government had forfeited its own legal status through its actions.

■ **DAI Qing**, China's best-known

woman journalist and a regular columnist for *Guangming Ribao*, a Beijing daily formerly popular among intellectuals, was formally dismissed by her newspaper in February 1993 (*South China Morning Post*, February 16, 1993), almost three years after she was released from prison. She was told she had relinquished her right of re-employment when she was forced to resign in order to accept a Neiman Foundation fellowship at Harvard University in 1991. Dai has challenged the February decision, claiming it contradicted the government's announcement that overseas students should be given job preference when they returned to China. In addition, the ban on Dai's works, issued after the crackdown on dissidents in 1989, is still in effect.

Dai has had a series of difficulties since her release from prison on May 9, 1990. She was one of two dissidents forcibly abducted to prevent her meeting with then U.S. Assistant Secretary of State for Human Rights Richard Schifter, who had accompanied then Secretary of State James Baker on his November 1991 visit to Beijing. Her newspaper, which had revoked her reporter's license, suddenly informed her she had an out-of-town assignment in Qinghuangdao to write about a glass factory. When she refused to fall for the ruse, she was forcibly removed from a downtown Beijing hotel and taken to Beidaihe, a summer resort 180 miles east of Beijing, where she was held for four days. For three days, Dai was not permitted to use a telephone. Only when she threatened a hunger strike was she permitted to contact her husband (*Washington Post*, November 21, 1991).

One of her reasons for requesting a meeting was her failure to obtain a passport to accept the Neiman Foundation fellowship which was to have commenced in September 1991. It took until December 16 for her to finally receive the document. Up until then, *Guangming Ribao* blocked her request, insisting she first quit her job. Newspaper authorities then told Harvard she was no longer a journalist. In an unusual step, the university held her place open until the start of the second semester.

Dai encountered further difficulties at the end of her first semester when she tried to return to China for the summer. Her journey was interrupted on May 30, 1992 in Hong Kong when Chinese airline officials refused to permit her to board a flight for Beijing. Only after the personal intervention of Premier Li Peng was she permitted to enter China on June 7.

When Dai was released from prison in 1990 without charge, Public Security authorities concluded she had made the mistake of "supporting and taking part in political turmoil" and should be "dealt with" by the unit to which she belonged (*Ming Bao*, May 19, 1990, in FBIS, May 22). Dai, who after her release, published a lengthy article, "My Imprisonment," maintained she was treated well in prison, but her hopes of resuming her newspaper job were quashed early on (FBIS, May 17, 1990). She was told by her office to "stay at home to study ideology and take a rest."

During the pro-democracy movement, Dai helped rally other journalists to the support of Qin Benli (see Wang Ruowang p.463), the popular Shanghai editor. Just before President Gorbachev's visit, she went to Tiananmen Square to try to persuade students to leave, saying she feared a government crackdown. Beijing mayor Chen Xitong's June 1989 report listing intellectuals and activists considered by the authorities to have engaged in serious anti-government activity, mentioned Dai by name. She was accused of slandering the government and of belonging to an illegal organization; and she was criticized for resigning from the Communist Party on June 4, 1989 and for signing an appeal in the May 15, 1989 *Guangming Ribao* asking the government to recognize the legality of the student movement. Dai, 50, was arrested on July 14, 1989, held first in Qincheng Prison, then moved in February 1990 to a police "guest house."

Dai has been honored abroad. In May 1992, she received the Golden Pen of Freedom from the International Federation of Newspaper Publishers. In April 1993, she received the Golden Environmental Prize from a U.S. organization for her work in highlighting the dangers of the projected Three Gorges hydroelectric dam on the Yangtze River.

■ **DAN Bin**, formerly a Henan University student, was held for six months in Qincheng Prison in connection with the 1989 pro-democracy movement. Other than that he has been released, no details are available.

■ **DAN Jing**, a female journalist for *Xinhua* arrested in Changsha, Hunan Province, on June 7, 1989, reportedly was released in 1991. It is unclear whether she had been sentenced.

■ **DING Xiaoping** and **ZHANG Wei**[2] were released on January 27, 1991 without ever having been charged, according to an Asia Watch source. Ding, 29, formerly a graduate student at Beijing University and first coordinator of its Preparatory Committee, left Qincheng Prison too ill to work. Zhang also was held in Qincheng.

■ **DONG Huaimin** - see p.93

■ **DONG Xiang**, a member of a youth theater and a friend of Wang Peigong with whom he was arrested, was released on March 8, 1991 (*AP*, March 9, 1991). He had been detained for over a year. According to the report, Wang's wife had given money to Dong to help student leader Wuerkaixi escape. Wuerkaixi had stayed briefly at Dong's house.

■ **DUAN Xiaoguang** has been released from prison and works as an Associate Professor at Nanjing University's Department of Philosophy, according to an Asia Watch source. Duan, in his early thirties, was seized by the authorities in Shenzhen around August 30, 1989 while attempting to leave for Hong Kong. His arrest was ordered directly by the Ministry of Public Security in Beijing. On September 22 at 9:00 P.M., the authorities searched his room at the university without warning. Although Duan was never formally charged, the authorities considered him one of the organizers and planners of the peaceful Nanjing demonstrations, and more than just a local leader. During his incarceration Duan was held incommunicado at the Nanjing Detention Center.

■ **FAN Zhe**, a 71-year-old retired engineer from Anhui Province, who was arrested in July 1991, was released at the end of November (Amnesty International *ASA 17/22/92*). A former employee at the Tongling Locomotive Works, reportedly in poor health, Fan had been held without charge for his activities in Shanghai. He allegedly distributed leaflets and hung out a large banner criticizing the Communist Party.

■ **FAN Zhong**, a student in the 1986 entering class at Central-South Industrial University, Hunan Province, was "exempted from criminal sanctions" and released in December 1991 by the Changsha City (Hunan) Western District Court. Accused of "disrupting social order," he was arrested on June 17 or 29, 1989. First held in Changsha No.2 Prison, then moved in mid-July to Changsha No.1 Prison, Cell 6, Fan was severely mistreated. On several occasions, he was manacled to a "shackle board" *(menbanliao)* and he was subjected to electric shocks. His health deteriorated to the point where he lost his perceptive faculties and physical coordination.

Before the 1989 pro-democracy movement, Fan was chairman of his school's student union and vice-chairman of the Hunan Students Union, both government-approved posts. During the 1989 movement, he helped found the Hunan Students Autonomous Federation which he later co-chaired. On May 16, Fan was general commander of a mass hunger strike in front of the Hunan provincial government offices. He also helped plan a June 8 memorial meeting. In fall 1992 Fan left China, and he now lives in a western country.

■ **FANG Ke**, 34, was released in October or November 1990 (Amnesty International, *ASA 17/07/91*). According to a *Beijing Television* broadcast (FBIS, June 15, 1989), he had turned himself in to authorities in his native city of Wuhan, Hubei Province on June 12, 1989. A member of the Standing Committee of the Beijing Students Autonomous Federation, Fang was a doctoral candidate in philosophy at Beijing People's College and a teacher at a university in Wuhan.

■ **FEI Yuan**, a leading member of the Chen Ziming-Wang Juntao group (see p.63 and p.70), has been released, according to an official Chinese response to U.S. government inquiries (November 1991). His release came despite the description of him in the prosecution's indictment against Luo Haixing, Li Peicheng and Li Longqing (see p.443) as the one who masterminded the unsuccessful effort to help Chen and Wang escape. The indictment stated that Fei had been "dealt with separately" by the authorities. At the time of the 1989 demonstrations, Fei was deputy director of *Jingjixue Zhoubao (Economics Weekly)*, a lecturer at the Institute of Finance and Economics and a member of the Beijing Social and Economic Sciences Research Institute (SERI).

■ **FENG Chuan** - see p.88

■ **FENG Gang**, a 35-year-old radio announcer for *Guizhou Provincial Television*, was released in January or February 1991, according to Asia Watch sources. An official Chinese response to U.S. government inquiries provided confirmation (November 1991). As one of the major organizers of pro-democracy protests in Guiyang, the capital of Guizhou Province, Feng reportedly made several public speeches and led the May 1989 demonstrations there. After June 4, he recorded *Voice of America* broadcasts, then played the tape in front of the *Guizhou Provincial Television* and Broadcasting Department. Prior to his arrest at the end of July 1989, Feng had been warned by friends that he was on the wanted list, but he refused to go into hiding or attempt to escape. Reportedly tortured while in prison, he has suffered some undiagnosed mental illness. After his release, Feng worked as a bartender. According to an Asia Watch source, his work unit put him on half pay and took away his housing.

■ **FENG Qingnian**, a Jiangsu Engineering College student, was detained for more than a year in connection with the 1989 pro-democracy movement. No other details, other than that he has been released, are available.

■ Four students from Shanghai's Fudan University reportedly were released, according to the school's vice-president (*Hong Kong Standard*, December 19, 1990.) All were accused of engaging in "counterrevolutionary criminal activities," such as setting up roadblocks. There is no additional information.

■ **FU Weidong**, **SHI Li**, **LIU Hongli**, **XIE Qian**, **HANG Guangsheng** and **LU Guofu** were released in January 1992, according to an Asia Watch source. No further information is available, and it is unclear whether the six served sentences or were released without charge.

■ **GAO Ertai**, a 58-year-old Jiangsu Province artist and a theorist specializing in aesthetics, arrested on September 9, 1989, was released less than five months later and, fearful of re-arrest, fled China in the summer of 1992 (*South China Morning Post*, May 1, 1993). At the time of his arrest, Gao was a professor at Sichuan Normal University in Chengdu whose transfer to Nanjing University's Chinese department had been approved. After his release, he was not permitted to resume teaching in Chengdu nor could he proceed to Nanjing, and he was refused permission to accept a fellowship at Harvard University.

In the late 1950s, accused as a rightist, Gao was sent to a forced labor camp in the remote northwest. Recruited by an army post in close proximity to the prison camp to draw propaganda posters, he was able to survive the 1960-62 famine which decimated the prison population. He was punished again during the Cultural Revolution; his wife, sent to the countryside to do physical labor, died. Gao was criticized in 1983 during the Anti-Spiritual Pollution Campaign for his views on alienation and humanism. He was forbidden to teach, advise graduate students or publish. In the late 1980s, several of his books were banned. In addition to his other talents, Gao, born in October 1935, is a poet.

■ **GAO Honggang**, who entered Beijing University in 1985, was sentenced to three years in prison for "robbery" in connection with the 1989 pro-democracy movement. Released in May 1992, he has been employed as a "temporary worker."

■ **GAO Peiqi**, a highly decorated police lieutenant who served six months in prison reportedly for assisting the escape of pro-democracy activists, fled China on March 21, 1992. He had worked in Shenzhen, the special economic zone bordering Hong Kong. Gao was never charged after his 1990 arrest, but was fired from the force after his 1991 release (*AP*, July 21, 1992).

■ **GAO Shan**, a 37-year-old economist and deputy director of the Chinese Communist Party's Research

Institute for the Reform of the Political Structure of the Communist Party Central Committee, was released from Qincheng Prison on January 28, 1993, according to a government announcement. He was sentenced to a four-year term for "leaking state secrets" at a closed trial before the Beijing Intermediate People's Court on August 6, 1992, over three years after he was arrested on May 28, 1989, and eight months after formal charges were brought in January 1992. An economist and graduate of Beijing Normal University, Gao had been accused in Beijing Mayor Chen Xitong's June 30, 1989 speech to the National People's Congress Standing Committee of leaking information about the impending imposition of martial law by Politburo decree. The reference was to a meeting on May 19, 1989 attended by about 20 leading members of state research institutes, including Gao, which called for an emergency meeting of the Standing Committee in an attempt to block the order.

From 1982 until he joined the Research Institute for the Reform of the Political Structure, Gao was a member of the Rural Development Research Group. He also acted as adviser to the Research Institute for the Reform of the Economic Structure and was a close associate of Bao Tong (see p.61), former chief advisor to Zhao Ziyang.

■ **GAO Shuxiang**, a well-known reformer and former manager of a collective enterprise, a "Labor-Service Company," in Hengyang City, Hunan Province, was released from prison in late June 1992 on "medical parole"

(baowai jiuyi). He was never brought to trial, but had been indicted by the procuracy four times. Each time, the court rejected the case for lack of evidence. According to an Asia Watch source, he was suspected of providing funds to the pro-democracy movement. Gao, about 40, was first detained in Beijing shortly after June 4, 1989. A month later, he was either released and then voluntarily returned to Hengyang, or he was escorted back in custody. Arrested upon his return and charged with embezzling public funds from the collective, Gao was held incommunicado in Wanjiawan Prison. During his incarceration, he was so severely beaten by Yang Zhanglong, an investigator for the Hengyang South District Procuracy, that he is now deaf in one ear. At the time of his beating, Gao received no medical treatment. In addition, he suffers from severe hepatitis and a serious prison-induced skin problem. He is without work.

Formerly a cadre in the Hengyang Petroleum Company, where his wife still works, Gao gained a reputation as a pioneering figure in the economic reforms in Hengyang through his success in running the collective labor-personnel services firm. Prior to his arrest, the authorities, reportedly angered by his attempted reforms, tried to charge him with economic crimes.

■ **GAO XIN**, 35, a former lecturer at Beijing Normal University and chief editor of its newspaper, *Shida Zhoubao*, was arrested in June 1989 and released to house arrest on December 16. He was detained again on May 30, 1990 and held for 18 days after he, **ZHOU Duo** (see p.493) and **HOU Dejian** (see p.421) scheduled a joint news conference for May 31 at which they planned to issue an open letter to the Chinese government appealing for amnesty for political prisoners and, in particular, for the release of **LIU Xiaobo** (released after conviction in early 1991; see p.438). The four, Hou, Zhou, Gao and Liu, had begun a second hunger strike on June 2, 1989 in support of student demands; they were also the ones chiefly responsible for negotiating the peaceful withdrawal of students from Tiananmen Square in the early morning of June 4, 1989.

In March 1991, Gao accepted an invitation to Harvard University as a visiting scholar. His was the first case in which a well-known intellectual imprisoned for 1989 pro-democracy activities was officially permitted to go abroad (*Ming Bao*, March 11, 1991, in FBIS, same day).

■ **GAO Xu**, formerly a computer student at Shanxi University, was released from prison after ten months in detention and went to work at the Taiyuan Masses Machinery Factory. As the student representative from his school, Gao was sent to Beijing during the 1989 pro-democracy movement. On June 4, 1989, he was tied to a pillar at the Great Hall of the People, on one side of Tiananmen Square, and severely beaten by martial law troops. At Minzu Palace he was beaten again, then transferred to Qincheng Prison and finally to a detention center in Taiyuan, Shanxi. There, guards kept awake by his howls of pain, severely beat him

with a bench until it broke. Gao reportedly is almost blind in one eye and suffers from persistent headaches.

■ **GONG Yanming**, a 38-year-old general manager at the Yinhai Company, a subsidiary of Hunan Province General Import-Export Corporation, was released as innocent at the end of 1990. During the 1989 pro-democracy movement, Gong allegedly supported the students and encouraged cadres and officials of his company to participate in protest demonstrations. Placed under investigation after June 4, he was arrested in July on charges of economic impropriety, then charged with corruption. In May 1991, an article in *Zhongguo Qingnian Bao* denounced the injustice done to Gong and asserted that "political scores" should not be settled against people under the guise of accusing them of "economic offenses."

■ **GONG Zizhen**, a law department graduate student at the University of Politics and Law when he was arrested in connection with the 1989 pro-democracy movement, has been released. As of March 1993, he was working for a company in Beijing.

■ **GU Bin**, an alleged ringleader of the Shanghai human rights group, *Zhongguo Renquan Wenti Yanjiuhui (Study Group on Human Rights in China)* (see Yang Zhou p.478), was released, according to an Asia Watch source. An earlier report by Chinese authorities to the U.S. government listed him as "under investigation" (November 1991). Gu, 26, who claimed he had participated in the 1986 student protests while studying in the electrical engineering department at the Chemical Industry Technical School in Shanghai, was detained for questioning on April 5, 1991.

■ **GUO Haifeng**, sentenced to four years in prison and one year's deprivation of political rights on January 26, 1991 by the Beijing Intermediate People's Court, was released on parole on February 17, 1993. The decision was made by the Kaifeng Intermediate People's Court in Henan Province on the basis of Guo's having "observed prison regulations" (*Xinhua*, February 17, 1993).

Guo was convicted on charges of "counterrevolutionary sabotage" for attempting to set fire to an armed vehicle (*Washington Post*, January 27, 1991). Guo and three other activists (see Yao Junling p.479, Chen Lai p.408 and Li Chenghuan p.500), went on trial on January 9, 1991 according to notices posted outside the court (*AP*, January 10, 1991). The court did not notify families of the trials, which recessed after a brief session, and relatives had to search for lawyers who would attend the sentencing and help file appeals (*AP*, January 11, 1991).

The 27-year-old Guo, a student at Beijing University and at one time chairman of the Beijing Students Autonomous Federation, was seized by troops in front of Zhongnanhai, the residence compound of China's leaders, around 2 A.M. on June 4, 1989, shortly after the arrival in Tiananmen Square of vanguard contingents of the People's Liberation Army (PLA) (*Beijing Radio*,

June 10, 1989). According to the report, Guo was captured "on the spot by the martial law enforcement troops while he and a gang of ruffians were trying to set fire to an army unit's armored vehicle." He reportedly was badly beaten after his arrest. An official press report said Guo had intended to set fire to the former imperial gate in Tiananmen Square on which Mao's portrait is mounted (*Reuters*, January 9, 1991). On April 22, 1989, Guo and two other students (see Zhang Zhiyong p.490 and Zhou Yongjun p.494) knelt on the steps of the Great Hall of the People in an effort to submit a seven-point petition to the government calling for the posthumous rehabilitation of Hu Yaobang, former Secretary-General of the Party. Guo also participated in the April 29, 1989, "dialogue meeting" with government spokesman Yuan Mu.

■ **GUO Ruiping** - see p.246

■ **GUO Wenshen**, a 24-year-old security guard, formerly from Hong Kong, was released on June 23, 1989 after allegedly confessing to illegally bringing Hong Kong newspaper clippings about the June 4 massacre into China. He reportedly was arrested on June 11, 1989 for allegedly putting up "counterrevolutionary posters" and distributing "counterrevolutionary newspapers" in Shaoguan, Guangdong Province, and for telling students at his old junior high school there that 7,000 students were killed by the PLA in Tiananmen Square (*Beijing Radio*, June 13, 1989; *Wen Wei Bao*, June 14, 1989; *Ming Bao*, June 17, 1989). A

Ming Bao reporter learned of Guo's detention from a relative of Guo's, who read a report of his arrest in *Yangchen Wanbao*. Guo's family, who remained in Guangdong when Guo left for Hong Kong over ten years ago, had appealed to Chinese authorities for leniency. According to them, Guo has minor "mental" problems. In response to U.S. government inquiries, Chinese officials said in November 1991 that Guo Wenshen had "never been accused of any offense."

■ **GUO Xiaopu**, a fourth year Beijing University geology student; **GUO Shanghua**, a second year student in the economic administration department; and **WANG Wei**[1] (see p.465), now at work in the university's technology company, were all released (*Beijing Radio*, in FBIS, April 6, 1990). No further information is available.

■ **GUO Xin**, formerly a Shanxi University student, has been released from prison and is "waiting for work." He was detained for a year in connection with his pro-democracy activities which included commanding a march on May 20, 1989.

■ **GUO Yanjun**, a journalist working for the *Fazhi Ribao (Law Daily)*, has been released, according to an Asia Watch source. Guo was arrested in Beijing, reportedly in July 1989. He allegedly served as a go-between for students and authorities and was accused of "spreading rumors."

■ **GUO Yanqiu**, an editor at *Zhongguo Funü Bao*, has been released

from prison, according to an Asia Watch source. No further details are available.

■ **HAN DONGFANG, QIAN Yumin, LIU Qiang, HE Lili, CHEN Jingwen, ZHANG Jinli, ZHOU Guoqiang** and **SONG Jie**, all former members of the Beijing Workers Autonomous Federation (BWAF), were detained by the police on June 2 and 3, 1992, and held for several days for planning to gather quietly in a park to commemorate the June 4, 1989 crackdown. All had spent time in prison after June 4, 1989 for their dissident labor-organizing activities during the pro-democracy movement. On June 4, **MEN Xinxi**, a dissident artist involved in the 1978-81 Democracy Wall movement, was picked up at Han's house and held at a local police lockup for more than a month. **ZHOU Guoqiang** (see p.51), 34, who has a BA degree in law from a "spare-time" university, had planned to lead the vigil, but public security officials warned him several times to cancel the event, eventually insisting he sign a letter accepting responsibility even if he did not attend (UPI, June 6, 1992).

As for the other detainees, **Zhang Jinli**, a 31-year-old housing maintenance worker, was originally held nine months without charge. Song graduated in 1989 from Beijing Technical University. Originally arrested on June 9, 1989, he was charged with recording tapes in Tiananmen Square between May and June 4, but was released without charge after six months. He has been employed as a financial planner in the Beijing Subway Research Institute.

Liu Qiang, a 27-year-old leader of the BWAF who appeared on the government's June 14, 1989 list of "most wanted" workers, had been released some time after November 1991 (*AP*, January 25, 1992), having spent over two years in prison without ever being charged. According to a report to the International Labor Organization (November 1991), when Liu was released, he was "declared innocent of all criminal responsibility." The Chinese response to inquiries by the U.S. government (November 1991) confirmed the release. A former worker at the Beijing No.3209 Printing Factory, Liu reportedly was held at Taoran Ting 7th Detention Center in the Xuanwu district of south Beijing (Amnesty International, *ASA 17/73/90*). State television showed him being hauled off a train during his arrest in Inner Mongolia on June 14, 1989. He had been accused of "distributing knives stolen from military vehicles to his pickets, instigating his followers to take iron bars from the railings on both sides of Tiananmen Square, ordering the preparation of a number of gasoline bombs, participating in a secret meeting with leaders of the Beijing Students Autonomous Federation, and leading pickets in setting fire to 12 military vehicles and two tanks in frenzied beating, smashing, and looting."

Qian Yumin, a former railway worker and a leading member of the Beijing Workers Autonomous Federation, was detained on May 29,

1989, but according to an official Chinese response to International Labor Organization inquiries (November 1991), he was "released immediately after questioning by the police."

HE Lili, 30, one of the three "most wanted workers" on the Chinese government's June 14, 1989 list and formerly a lecturer at the Workers University of the Beijing Bureau of Machinery Industry, was "released following re-education or absolved of criminal responsibility by the courts," according to a Chinese response to International Labor Organization inquiries (November 1991).

- **HAN Lifa** - see p.11

- **HAO Mingzhao,** a student in the entering class of 1985 in the geology department of Central-South Industrial University, Hunan Province, was detained for several months after June 1989 and then released and expelled from college. Hao was first detained in June 1989, shortly after turning himself in to the Public Security Bureau in compliance with the provincial government's "Registration Order" for members of the Hunan Students Autonomous Federation, of which he had been a Standing Committee member. He started planning pro-democracy demonstrations in mid-April 1989, and was a steering committee member of the Changsha "May 4th Joint Demonstration." In addition, he helped organize and gave a speech at the city's "June 8 memorial meeting." Originally chairman of the official student union at his school, in

1988, in protest against the government's "campaign against bourgeois liberalization," Hao changed his name and went to Mt. Emei to become a monk, but was later brought back by school authorities.

■ **HE Libin**, **GUO Yue** and **ZHANG Jianchao**, all probably students, were arrested for helping plan a memorial meeting in Wuhan, Hubei Province on June 4, 1989, commemorating those who died that day in Beijing (Amnesty International, ASA 17/66/90). **LI Haitao** (presumably released; see p.547) was sentenced in connection with the same event and **MIN Dongxiao** (MIN Yue) was arrested for making "counter-revolutionary speeches" in the streets of Wuhan. According to an official Chinese response to U.S. government requests for information, Zhang and He have been released; there was no reply to inquiries about Guo; and Min was listed as having "never been accused of any offense."

■ **HE Nan**, a 34-year-old cadre in a Changsha (Hunan Province) municipal construction firm, was "released on bail for medical treatment" in August 1990 after developing kidney stones. Arrested in late 1989, He Nan allegedly "spread rumors all over the place" during the pro-democracy movement and later "reproduced and distributed videotapes which had been made overseas and smuggled into China concerning the June 4 incident."

■ **HE Weiling**, a faculty member

from Beijing University's chemistry department, has been released, according to an official Chinese response to inquiries by the U.S. government (November 1991). He had been arrested near his home sometime in the middle of May 1989. Before returning to China, He served as a delegate in the United State from RIRES and from the Kang Hua Company. He also was associated with an agricultural development group and reportedly was a friend of Deng Pufang, former director of the Kang Hua Company and the son of Deng Xiaoping. He Weiling went to Tiananmen Square in late May 1989 to tell students to stop demonstrating so as not to provide the conservative faction of the Chinese Communist Party with a pretext for carrying out a crackdown, and to urge students to rethink their strategy. He reportedly tried to persuade the students to call off their hunger strike on condition that the government agree to retract the controversial *Renmin Ribao* editorial of April 26, 1989, "Resolutely Oppose the Turmoil."

■ **HOU Dejian**, the 33-year-old Taiwan-born pop singer, was released by Chinese authorities around June 18, 1990, after a three-week detention to prevent a joint news conference with **ZHOU Duo** (see p.493) and **GAO Xin** (see p.416). Hou was taken to Fujian, escorted to sea on a Chinese coastal patrol craft and transferred to the Taiwanese authorities on June 20, 1990. He had defected to the People's Republic in 1983. Hou was quoted as saying in an interview in Taiwan's *United Daily News* that Chinese authorities had given him two choices: prison or Taiwan. During his detention, Hou was asked to sign a statement admitting his "counterrevolutionary activities" and to retract statements he had earlier made to the press. But he refused, he said, to make a false confession. Taiwanese authorities have permitted Hou to remain there. However, he was tried on September 17, 1990, on charges of illegally entering the country and was given a seven-month prison sentence, suspended for three years (*Shijie Ribao*, September 19, 1990).

Hou had taken refuge in the Australian Embassy for two months after the 1989 Beijing crackdown, but re-emerged in August 1989 after the Chinese government guaranteed he would not be prosecuted.

■ **HOU Jie**, a 27-year-old journalist at *Beijing Ribao*, arrested prior to June 18, 1989, was released in 1990, according to an Asia Watch source. He is no longer permitted to work as a journalist.

■ **HOU Wenyin**, formerly a law student at Shanxi University, was detained for ten months for writing a letter to Jiang Zemin criticizing the government's crackdown on June 4, 1989. He was permitted to return to school and graduate; and he was given a job assignment but is not permitted to teach.

■ **HOU Xiaotian**, the 29-year-old wife of the well-known dissident Wang Juntao (see p.70) (sentenced to 13 years' imprisonment in February 1991),

was finally issued a passport in July 1993 after a wait of 18 months and arrived in the United States for a six-month visit in October 1993. During the elapsed time, the only response by Chinese authorities to her request to be permitted to take up a scholarship offer at Columbia University in New York was to inform her she had not served her country for five years after graduation and, therefore, did not qualify for study abroad. When she changed her application to request permission for a family visit in Denmark, she received no response. Hou is now in the United States.

A tireless campaigner on her husband's behalf, Hou has subjected herself to great personal risk, constant surveillance and harassment. Warned not to talk with foreign journalists, Hou has persisted for which she has been punished by having her prison visits curtailed. Nevertheless, due primarily to her efforts in publicizing his condition, Wang finally was transferred from solitary confinement to a prison hospital and then to one outside the prison system. Efforts to act as his agent in his suits against Qincheng Prison, the Public Security Bureau and *Xinhua* have been less successful. An August 20, 1992, application to demonstrate in relation to the suits resulted in Hou's disappearing for four days. Police took her to Yanshan Sanatorium in Changping County, some 40 kilometers from Beijing, to "talk over the situation."

Hou was also one of two women abducted to prevent a meeting with then U.S. Assistant Secretary of State for Human Rights, Richard Schifter, who accompanied then Secretary of State James A. Baker on his November 1991 visit to Beijing. She was held for a day and a half. Earlier, on January 11, 1991, she was detained for eleven hours after a Hong Kong newspaper reported she planned to hold a news conference calling for justice for her husband. In prison herself for four months in 1990, Hou then had to be treated in a Beijing hospital for chronic ailments contracted when crowded cell conditions necessitated her sleeping on the concrete floor. And her outspokenness on behalf of her husband cost Hou her state job and housing.

■ **HU Hao**, a student in the entering class of 1985 in Hunan Medical University, was released in early 1990. A member of the Standing Committee of the Hunan Students Autonomous Federation and director of its secretariat, Hu escaped to the countryside after June 4, 1989, but was later arrested and held in Changsha No.1 Prison, Cell 19.

■ **HU Ji**, who allegedly gave speeches in Xin Cheng Square in Xi'an in support of demonstrating students, was released in late November 1990 (Amnesty International, *ASA 17/07/91*). He reportedly was arrested on September 16, 1989 and held incommunicado in a building which was not a regular prison. Ji had been a professor of history at the Communication University in Xi'an and before that at Northwest University. He is the author of two books on Shaanxi Province history and served as Secretary of the Tang Dynasty Historical Studies Society.

■ **HU Jinting** - see p.246

■ **HU Lei**, formerly a student in the Chinese department at Central China Teachers University, was detained on May 18, 1990 in connection with the 1989 pro-democracy movement. Other than that he was released seven months later, no further information is available.

■ **HU Xiaoxin**, a Hubei Medical College student arrested in May 1990 for having joined a "counter-revolutionary clique" in Wuhan, was released some seven months later. As of March 1993, he was unable to find employment.

■ **HUANG Teh-Pei** (Peter T.P. Huang), a Taiwanese reporter for the *Independent Evening Post* in Taibei, who was arrested on July 3, 1989, around the same time as student leader Wang Dan (see p.459), was released on July 11. He had been picked up by police in front of the Beijing Hotel shortly after his alleged return from a secret meeting with Wang.

■ **HUANG Yongshan**, 28, was released from prison sometime toward the end of 1990, according to an Asia Watch source. He was arrested in July 1989, when he returned to Beijing after accompanying Chen Yizi, the former director of RIRES, to south China in preparation for Chen's successful bid to flee the country. A member of RIRES since 1987, Huang is a specialist in macro-economic research. Prior to the

1989 pro-democracy movement, he had joined the 1987 demonstration as a student leader. There had been reports that Huang was tortured in prison.

■ **HUANG Zheng**, a 23-year-old cadre at a Hunan Province import-export corporation, was "released on bail for medical treatment" in 1991. As of May 1992, his case had not been formally concluded, and he was subject to re-arrest and trial at any time. Huang was arrested in early 1990 for alleged "political offenses" believed to be related to the pro-democracy movement. He was detained in Changsha No.1 Jail.

■ **JI Futang**, a business management graduate student at Liaoning University's Economic Management College, and a member of the Shenyang Students Autonomous Federation, allegedly registered "on his own initiative" with the Shenyang sub-bureau of the Huangpu District Public Security Bureau on June 17, 1989. Ji reportedly agreed when he registered "to explicitly answer all related questions about his participation in the Federation," whose "illegal activities" he allegedly participated in starting on May 17. The Shenyang Public Security Bureau reportedly was "pleased with his confession." According to an official Chinese response to inquiries by the U.S. government, Ji has been released (November 1991).

■ **JIA Yonghua**, from Shanxi Province, was arrested and released in connection with the 1989 pro-democracy movement. There is no additional information available.

■ **JIANG Fengshan**, 37, formerly a teacher in the philosophy department of Xiangtan University, Hunan Province, administratively sentenced in early 1990 by the Xiangtan City Public Security Bureau to three years' re-education through labor, has been released. During the 1989 pro-democracy movement, Jiang gave public speeches on several occasions. He allegedly supported the students in "creating a disturbance," and after June 4, stirred up the workers to go on strike and block traffic. Jiang was arrested in July 1989 and held in the Xiangtan City Jail. After his release, the government reportedly had him fired from any job he managed to find.

■ **JIANG Guolian**, 43, head of the Chemical Industry Section of Dajiang Applied High Technology Research Institute (Dajiang Institute) in Hubei Province, was "exempted from criminal punishment" for his part in concealing Wang Juntao (sentenced in January 1991 to 13 years in prison as a "black hand" dissident; see p.70) during his attempt to escape from China. Such a verdict means the prisoner does not go to trial, but is considered guilty, has a criminal record and encounters all the attendant problems such as job dismissal and loss of housing. However, a list presented by Chinese officials in response to inquiries from the U.S. government (November 1991) simply recorded him as released. Jiang, who turned himself in on November 21, 1989, was formally arrested between January 5-8, 1990, indicted on February 16, 1990 and released on April 19, 1991. For information about others involved in the case, see: Chen Zhiyang p.137, Xiao Yuan p.472, Liu Danhong p.434, and Wu Litang p.551.

■ **JIANG Qisheng**, a graduate of the Beijing Institute of Aeronautics and a doctoral candidate in philosophy at People's University, was released, according to an official Chinese response to inquiries by the U.S. government (November 1991). Arrested in Beijing in September 1989, Jiang was released one year and five months later and ordered to withdraw from school. As of March 1993, he was without work. Jiang was a member of the Standing Committee of the Beijing Students Autonomous Federation's Dialogue Delegation, which negotiated with government authorities during the pro-democracy movement (Amnesty International, *ASA 17/24/90*).

■ **JIANG Rongsheng**, formerly a doctoral student at Qufu Teachers College (Anhui Province) where he participated in the 1989 pro-democracy movement, was released from prison at the end of 1990. According to an Asia Watch source, Jiang's "body and mind were harmed" during his prison stay; as of March 1993 he was unemployed.

■ **JIN Yan**, an employee at the Children's Film Studio, who was arrested sometime prior to October 15, 1989 and returned to Beijing under police escort, has been released, according to an Asia Watch source. She was detained in Guangzhou after the government secretly videotaped her making a one-hour public speech protesting the June 4 massacre. Provincial authorities said Jin had fled to Guangzhou to "evade justice."

■ **JING Wenqing** may be the same as **JING Wenqian**. When the U.S. government in November 1991 made an official inquiry about the former, who had been the secretary of the Beijing Students Autonomous Federation and a graduate student at Beijing Teachers Training University, the Chinese government responded that a person named Jing Wenqian had been released. According to Asia Watch information, Jing Wenqing, 26, was originally held in Paoju Lane Detention Center, had been sentenced to between three and five years' imprisonment. He was arrested on June 15, 1989 for allegedly inciting people to intercept, burn and smash 31 military vehicles near the Majia Overpass in the Haidian District in Beijing.

■ **KE Yunlu**, a writer who signed the "May 16 Declaration," was arrested in Shanxi Province in July of 1989; he reportedly was released on bail prior to the 1990 Chinese New Year to await trial. According to an official Chinese reply to U.S. government inquiries (November 1991), Ke had "never been accused of any offense." A colleague of **ZHAO Yu** (see p.492), Ke was the author of the popular 1985-86 television series *Xinxing (New Star)*, about a newly appointed reform-minded official.

■ **KONG Xianfeng** and **XUE Jian'an** were sentenced on January 5, 1991 by the Beijing Intermediate People's Court. Kong, whose sentencing was confirmed in an official Chinese response to U.S. government inquiries (November 1991), received a three-year sentence with one year's subsequent deprivation of political rights. Held at the notorious Lingyuan Prison and reportedly tortured (see Liu Gang p.65), he is known to have been released. Xue, a teacher at Beijing Light Industries College, sentenced to a two-year prison term and one year's deprivation of political rights, is now in Canada. Charges against both men included assembling crowds, undermining public order and impeding the advance of martial law troops in Beijing.

■ **LAN Ma** - see p.88

■ **LEI Shaojun**, 30, formerly a teacher in the department of social sciences at Central-South Industrial University, Hunan Province, is now in the U.S. He had been working in a trading company in Shenzhen until April 1992, but departed when public security officials began questioning him.

After the events of June 4, 1989, at a meeting in his school to mourn "the perished of Beijing," Lei announced he was resigning from the Communist Party. Arrested in December 1989 and detained in secret, he was sentenced in June 1990 by the Changsha Intermediate People's Court to two

years' "control" *(guanzhi)* on a charge of "counterrevolutionary propaganda and incitement." Lei later returned to work, but was "subject to control and supervision" *(jianguan)*.

■ **LEUNG Wai-man,** a 32-year-old Hong Kong resident and accredited journalist in Beijing for the Hong Kong *Express,* was deported from China in early November 1992, and banned from re-entering the country for two years. Leung, while covering the Chinese Communist Party's 14th Congress and visits to Beijing by the governor of Hong Kong and the Japanese Emperor, had allegedly bribed a government employee named **WU Shisen** (see p.7) in order to obtain a "most confidential document." The document in question was Jiang Zemin's keynote speech to the Party Congress (*International Herald Tribune*, November 2, 1992), which Leung then forwarded to her editor's office in Hong Kong. Arrested on October 24, 1992 as she was preparing to return to Hong Kong, Leung was held incommunicado for a week and then expelled from the country. In explaining their decision not to prosecute, Chinese authorities said Liu had "confessed her guilt and demonstrated a good attitude" (*South China Morning Post,* November 2, 1992). According to the report, Leung admitted she paid a large sum of money for the speech and that she had also obtained "many internal secrets" from the same government official. The Chinese government's definition of "state secrets" is, however, notoriously vague and inclusive. In this case, the

Jiang Zemin speech was scheduled to be made public only days after the alleged incident.

■ **LI Cuiping**, Secretary-General of the Autonomous Federation of Students from Outside Beijing, was arrested in Baoding in Hebei Province, south of Beijing (*Hebei Ribao*, July 12, 1989). According to an Asia Watch source, she was released from Qincheng Prison and allowed to graduate from Beijing Medical College, then was sent to work in a hospital in Liaoning Province. According to an official Chinese response to U.S. government inquiries, one "Li Zhiping" - a possible reference to Li Cuiping - had been released by November 1991.

■ There are conflicting reports concerning **LI Datong**, a journalist and head of the Schools' Department of *Zhongguo Qingnian Bao (China Youth Daily)*. According to one report, Li, who allegedly represented journalists requesting a meeting with the Communist Party's Propaganda Department in May 1989, was arrested before July 1989 and is out of custody (Hong Kong Journalists Association). According to an Asia Watch source, Li probably was never arrested, but has lost his job. Although he has not been required to move, he must now pay "market rates" for his housing instead of the low rate to which he was entitled as a member of his work unit.

■ **LI Guiren**, an editor and publisher from Xi'an, Shaanxi Province, 50 years old, was released on bail for medical treatment on February 18, 1993 (*Xinhua*, February 18, 1993). He was not due to be released until June 25, 1994, but had been critically ill for over a year, in an emaciated condition and unable to stand. The Chinese government ignored year-long family and international appeals, including one in December 1992 to Politburo member Qiao Shi, for proper diagnosis and treatment in a modern hospital facility.

Six months after Li's release, in May 1993, he was still too weak to withstand the heart and gallstone surgery he desperately needs. And he cannot afford to be hospitalized. The Shaanxi People's Publishing House which took over his original work unit refused to pay his salary while he was in prison. Officials there have unequivocally stated that he has been fired and that the unit will assume no responsibility for his medical bills or living expenses. Li claims that since he had been illegally detained and never admitted guilt, he is entitled to welfare benefits. In the meantime, according to an Asia Watch source, Li's angina "breaks out" several times a day and he is in a "emergency" situation. He can only take three or four paces and lies in bed worried that he will have to be hospitalized at any moment. Since Li's release he has had at least two official visits, one from prison wardens and one from the Public Security Bureau. Prison authorities wanted Li's doctor's current report on his health, which Li refused to relinquish, telling them they had no right to make the request. The PSB came to warn him not to go outside or receive visitors between June 3 and 5.

Li first complained of heart palpitations on three separate occasions in the winter of 1991. He received no medical attention. In February 1992, pleas for his hospitalization were rejected by the vice-governor of the province, Xu Shanlin and the provincial Party Secretary, Zhang Boxing. In March, after international calls for Li's hospitalization reached Chinese regional and national officials, two members of the secret police visited city and party officials in Xi'an and prison officials at Shaanxi No.1 Prison in Fuping County where Li was being held, to determine how news of his medical condition had reached western humanitarian organizations. As a result, in April, Li was transferred to Shaanxi No.2 Prison in Weinan, but received no better medical care. He received some medication which was ineffective but was denied a special diet despite his abdominal pains and despite the loss in prison of what were left of his teeth. Just prior to his release, Li required intravenous feeding.

During all this time, Li's family were permitted only one short visit a month. Reading matter was restricted to what was officially approved. Despite his condition, Li was beaten on at least one occasion and was shackled at least once for three days. And, he shared a cell for the first two years of his imprisonment with "common" criminals in the Fifth Branch Detention Center of the Xi'an Public Security Bureau.

Li was sentenced to a five-year term for "counterrevolutionary propaganda and incitement" in February 1991. He had been tried almost one year earlier, on March 1, 1990 by the Xi'an First Criminal Court, and his subsequent appeal rejected. When Li was detained, on June 26, 1989, one day after he had been formally dismissed from his post, for trying to organize a strike of publishing house employees (*Shaanxi Legal Weekly*, July 12, 1989), he was editor-in-chief of Hua Yue Publishing House, a publishing arm of Shaanxi Province People's Press. The day after the June 4 military crackdown in Beijing, he called a meeting in Xi'an of his work unit, told its members of the "hundreds of thousands of soldiers [who] had perpetrated a terrible massacre in Beijing" and urged workers to sign a protest petition and strike. Li also was accused of organizing four demonstrations during May 1989, of writing "provocative slogans" calling for the removal of Li Peng and Deng Xiaoping, of "promoting chaos" and of sending a telegram to Zhao Ziyang urging that the People's Liberation Army not be used against demonstrators. The copy of his telegram, which he posted on the wall of the Hua Yue building, was later labeled an outlawed *da zi bao* (big character poster) by the state prosecutor. The publishing house has been shut down.

Although virtually unknown outside China, Li is well-known and widely respected within Chinese literary circles. Over the course of his career, he has been a consistent champion of intellectual freedom. His stance, that Marxism is not incompatible with freedom of expression, first earned him trouble in the early eighties. People's

University denied him a degree in literary criticism for holding "politically untenable ideas."

Even as a teenager in 1957, Li was branded a "rightist" by Chinese authorities. After the 1983-84 Anti-Spiritual Pollution Campaign, organized to rid Chinese culture of western influences, he wrote a long article in *Wen Xue Jia (Literati)*, a magazine he had founded, defending his ideas. The issue was banned. In the very last issue, before the authorities shut it down in 1987, Li published his graduate thesis. In Xi'an, where the magazine was published, every single copy was confiscated and burned.

Undaunted, Li, through a series of articles and letters in *Renmin Ribao* and *Guangming Ribao* in 1988-89, continued to champion the idea that working through the Communist Party would bring democratization and a free press to China. In 1988 he wrote the preface for *Story of a Chinese Who Doesn't Know How to Tell Lies*, by the well-known dissident Liu Binyan, now in exile in the U.S. The book of literary reportage, fictionalized stories based on facts, was banned in Xi'an because of Li's praise for Liu in the preface.

Li is also esteemed by his colleagues for his unrepentant stance. To this day he continues to resist ideological re-education. In his defense statement, secretly recorded at his trial and smuggled out of China, Li acknowledged his activities but emphatically denied he ever intended to overthrow the government of China. He insisted his trial was illegal and history would judge his efforts on behalf of the people.

Li is a graduate of Shaanxi Normal College and worked in the countryside as a teacher during the Cultural Revolution.

■ **LI Guofeng**, former curator of the Shaanxi Provincial Government archives, was arrested in June 1989 for anti-government activities. Held in the Fifth Branch Detention Center of the Xi'an Public Security Bureau, he was released in May 1990.

■ **LI Haiwen**, a student at South China Engineering University, arrested in connection with the 1989 pro-democracy movement, has been released. No other details are available.

■ **LI Honglin**, 68, formerly a research fellow at the Fujian Academy of Social Sciences, who was released from prison on May 7, 1990 (*Xinhua*, May 10, 1990), on March 24, 1993 was finally able to obtain the letter of recommendation from his former unit which enabled him to apply for a passport (*Ming Bao*, March 25, 1993, in FBIS, March 26). He arrived in Hong Kong on July 8 on his way to the U.S. to join his family. Although Li's wife received her passport in 1992, Li had not been able to take up invitations from Princeton and Columbia Universities, nor had he been able to visit his son and granddaughter in the U.S. According to the Ministry of Public Security, Li's application, in principle, raised no problems (*South China Morning Post*, December 11, 1992); however, the delay was never explained. Li's daughter, also an employee at the Fujian Academy of Social Sciences, has been refused permission to leave China. In early 1992, a Chinese official assured then U.S. Secretary of State James Baker that those without pending charges could apply to go abroad.

Li, arrested at his home in Fuzhou, Fujian on July 6, 1989 by ten armed police carrying search and detention warrants issued by the Public Security Bureau of Fujian Province, was detained for ten months. Since his release, he has not been able to continue his research but has received his salary.

Li was an advocate of political and economic reforms and is the author of *The Storm of Theory*, summarizing the debate on socialism in China, and *Four "Isms" in China*, which argued that the country's problematic social system resulted from the concurrent existence of feudalism, capitalism, socialism and communism. He had been head of the Research Institute of the History of the Chinese Communist Party at the Chinese Museum of History and had been deputy director of the Bureau of Theory in the Communist Party's Propaganda Department. Li was briefly president of the Fujian Academy of Social Sciences but resigned during the Anti-Bourgeois Liberalization Campaign of 1986-87. In 1986, he was a Henry Luce fellow at Princeton. Li was one of 42 intellectuals who signed a letter to the Central Committee of the Communist Party on February 26, 1989 calling for the release of political prisoners, and was one of 11 prominent intellectuals who signed the May 11, 1989 "Urgent Appeal on the Current Situation." He also attempted to negotiate a dialogue between student leaders and the Chinese government.

■ **LI Hui**, a student leader accused of being a "counterrevolutionary rebel," was released, according to an official Chinese response to inquiries by the U.S. government (November 1991). He was arrested in early June 1989 in Tianjin and turned over to the Beijing Municipal Public Security Bureau on June 15. According to a report in *Tianjin Ribao* (June 17, 1989), Li was the "general commander of the west line of Tiananmen Square under the Beijing Students Autonomous Federation." He allegedly took part in blocking military vehicles and organized a propaganda team to go to Jinan, Shandong Province and Wuhan, Hubei Province to "stage counter-revolutionary instigation." On June 6, 1989, Li and seven others arrived in Tianjin and allegedly began distributing leaflets about "the true situation of the June 4 massacre." Forty-five others were arrested in Tianjin during June 1989, according to the report.

■ **LI Jing** - see p.144, 145

■ **LI Jinjin**, born September 7, 1955, a prominent legal scholar and advisor to the Beijing Workers Autonomous Federation, was released on April 30, 1991 and reportedly was "exempted from prosecution." No official announcement was made and Li returned to Wuhan, Hubei Province where the family resided. After his release, Li went to work at a debt-collection agency because his unit refused to take him back. In early 1993, he went to the U.S. as a visiting scholar.

Until student demonstrations started in April 1989, Li had been head of the official Graduate Students Union at Beijing University. A doctoral student in constitutional law there, he was to present his dissertation proposal on June 3, 1989. According to an Asia Watch source, Li was arrested at gunpoint on June 12, 1989 at his home. From there, he was transferred to Paoju Detention Center in Beijing, then to Banbuqiao Prison and finally to Qincheng. Family members had been permitted to drop off packages for him until late August 1989. From then until his release, he was permitted no family visits.

Li did his undergraduate work at the South-Central Institute of Politics and Law in Wuhan and was a lecturer there. He has authored several articles on administrative justice and constitutional law. Li served in the army and at the Public Security Bureau before attending college.

- **LI Kezhou**, formerly a graduate student at Beijing University, was sentenced to a three-year prison term and was released upon its completion, according to an Asia Watch source. An official Chinese response to U.S. government inquiries confirmed that he had been sentenced (November 1991). Li was arrested after announcing that an opposition party existed in China. It appears as if the "party" consisted only of Li.

- **LI Nanyou**, 51, deputy director of the Books and Editorial Department of the World Knowledge Publishing House in Beijing and signatory to the "May 17 Declaration," was released along with 210 other intellectuals and students in May 1990 (*Xinhua*, May 10, 1990). He was arrested on June 19, 1989 and while in prison lost sight in one eye. Li's work unit has not permitted him to return to his job, and in 1992 he was expelled from the Communist Party. It was recommended that he be dismissed from his post; his pre-June 1989 salary, the equivalent of that of an associate professor's, was sharply reduced; and his wife's work situation at a state-run enterprise, was affected adversely.

A native of Shanghai and the son of Li Xuedan, a revolutionary martyr, Li Nanyou refuses to agree that the 1989 pro-democracy movement was "turmoil and counterrevolutionary"; he prefers that history be the judge (*Ming Bao*, October 13, 1992, in FBIS, October 14).

- **LI Peng**[1], a cadre in the Beijing Municipality's Industry and Commerce Department, was released after serving a two-year sentence in Qincheng Prison.

- According to an Asia Watch source, **LI Qian (LI Zhanlai)**, a Zhejiang Agricultural University student whose name appeared on a Zhejiang Public Security wanted list, was arrested. In response to inquiries from the U.S. government (November 1991), Chinese officials list a **LI Qiang** as released. Both names may refer to one person.

■ **LI Shaojun** (pen-name **LI Aiju**), a student in the entering class of 1985 in the physics department of Hunan Normal University, is now living outside China. During the 1989 pro-democracy movement, Li served as vice-head of the Finance Department of the Hunan Students Autonomous Federation and was one of the chief organizers of the June 8 "Mourning Meeting." After June 4, he fled to Guangzhou, but returned home to Hengyang, Hunan, only to be arrested in August 1989 and detained in Changsha No.1 Prison, Cell 23. Li was released in December but arrested again in April 1990 at his uncle's home in Guangzhou. He was sent back to Changsha and held for over two months before being "educated" and released.

■ **LI Shaoyu**, 40, an assistant researcher in the Industrial and Economics Department at the Sichuan Academy of Social Sciences, has been released, according to an official Chinese response to U.S. government inquiries (November 1991). He reportedly was arrested sometime before April 1990.

■ **LI Shengping**, a researcher at the Marxist-Leninist Institute (a division of the Chinese Academy of Social Sciences) and the Economics and Technology Institute, and deputy editor of an anthology of twentieth century literature, was released in May 1990 and permitted to return to work at his old institute. That he was released was confirmed in an official Chinese response to U.S. government inquiries (November 1991). Li's arrest by the State Security Bureau was in connection with his association with Yan Mingfu, a close associate of Zhao Ziyang and one of the few party members who initially lost his job and was not permitted to re-register as a party member, but was later "rehabilitated." Li, whose pro-democracy activities extend back to the 1978-79 Democracy Wall Movement, and Yan had gone together to Tiananmen Square to urge the student hunger strikers to leave.

■ **LI Xiaofeng** - see p.144, 145

■ **LI Yawei** - see p.88

■ **LI Yuhua**, 21, a student in the Chinese Department at Changde Teachers College, Hunan Province, has been released. Arrested in July 1989, he was sentenced in January 1990 by the Changde City Intermediate People's Court to two years' imprisonment on a charge of "counterrevolutionary propaganda and incitement." In April, he was sent to Longxi Prison (Provincial No.6) to serve his term.

During the 1989 pro-democracy movement, Li was vice chairman of the Changde Autonomous Union of (Students in) Institutions of Higher Education. He allegedly organized student demonstrations, conducted a sit-in for almost 20 days in front of the municipal government offices and on June 5 organized a traffic blockage by students and city residents thereby "creating great economic losses."

■ **LI Zhiguo**, arrested by the Shanghai Public Security Bureau on

June 10, 1989 as the "ringleader of a counterrevolutionary clique" *(Beijing Radio*, in FBIS, June 12, 1989) has been released, according to an official Chinese response to requests for information by the U.S. government (November 1991). In March 1989, Li reportedly established an organization named the *Freedom Society*, through which he advocated the overthrow of the government and the founding of a "Kingdom of Greater Freedom." He allegedly "sent letters of comfort to trouble-making students in various localities and instigated them to fight the reactionary government to the end." He urged that a military camp be set up and he created a national flag, emblem, flower and currency for the new kingdom.

■ **LIAN Shengde**, 24 or 25, who served briefly as Provisional Deputy Commander-in-Chief of the Tiananmen Square Command Center just after the May 20, 1989 declaration of martial law, was released in December 1990 and dismissed from Chinese Airlines College, according to an Asia Watch source. He had been arrested in Shenzhen on August 10, 1989. Requests by the U.S. government for information about Lian, however, elicited no response from Chinese officials (November 1991). A student at Shenzhen University, Lian was a senior leader of the Autonomous Federation of Students from Outside Beijing and a Command Center Standing Committee member.

■ **LIANG Yu**, who was a graduate student at Qinghua when he was arrested in connection with the 1989 pro-democracy movement, was held briefly in Qincheng Prison, then permitted to return to his studies. However, when he graduated, Liang was assigned to work in a Beijing factory.

■ **LIN Buxiang**, formerly a student at Beijing University, was held for more than a year in connection with the 1989 pro-democracy movement, then released and expelled from school.

■ **LIN Guizhen**, 26, forcibly repatriated to China from Japan in August 1991, was sent without trial to a "re-education" camp in her hometown of Fuzhou in Fujian Province, accused of "counterrevolutionary activities." Chinese provincial and local officials, who at first refused comment, finally acknowledged on February 21, 1992 that Lin had spent six months of her one-year sentence in the camp. The Chinese Embassy in Tokyo in acknowledging the report, said Lin's "re-education" related to her "anti-social tendencies." A spokesman said Lin had never been involved in "counterrevolutionary activities" but had left home because of family problems. He further acknowledged that after her release on January 16, her re-education continued at home *(AP*, February 21, 1992). Ambassador Yang Zhenya, in acknowledging Lin's detention, said it resulted from her violation of China's emigration laws (UPI, February 21, 1992). The Japanese government, which said it had been assured that Lin would be "treated fairly" when it abruptly repatriated her, promised an investigation, but nothing came of it.

Lin's saga came to light when a Japanese television reporter visited China in an effort to film her story and discovered from her parents that she was in a labor camp. Returning to Japan, he notified her lawyer. According to him, Lin, who had taken part in marches in Fuzhou and feared persecution, hid out with friends after June 4, then boarded a boat for Okinawa. With 230 others, she was interned in Nagasaki after she arrived in Japan on September 27, 1989 and applied for refugee status. Denied asylum on the grounds she was an economic, not a political, refugee, Lin was deported on August 13, in the middle of two appeal processes. She was arrested by Public Security Bureau officers two days after she arrived home.

Both lawsuits continued after Lin was repatriated. One asked for annulment of the order of deportation because of procedural irregularities; the other asked for annulment of the Justice Ministry's refusal to entertain her application for refugee status. Lin eventually lost both suits.

- **LIN Shengli** - see p.435

- **LIU ANPING**, a performance artist branded as a leader of the 1989 pro-democracy demonstrations in Hangzhou, Zhejiang Province, was imprisoned for a year and then released. No further details are known.

- **LIU Danhong**, a 25-year-old woman from Qiqihar, Heilongjiang Province and a resident of Hubei Province, was released in June 1991, according to an Asia Watch source. An official Chinese response to U.S. government inquiries (November 1991) also listed Liu as released. She was sent to her home in Wuhan, Hubei Province but has not been able to find work. Her former job, as business manager at the now defunct Beijing Human Resources Evaluation and Testing Center, an organization connected to Wang Juntao and Chen Ziming's (see p.63) Beijing Social and Economic Sciences Research Institute (SERI), no longer exists. Liu, a university graduate, was detained in November or December 1989, officially arrested between January 5-8, 1990 and indicted, along with four others (see Wu Litang p.551, Jiang Guolian p.424 and Liu Hanyi p.436), on February 16, 1990 for attempting to help Wang Juntao (sentenced to 13 years' imprisonment as a "black hand" counterrevolutionary) escape from China. The four other defendants were sentenced to terms of up to two years; Liu Danhong was mentioned in their April 19, 1991 official criminal verdicts as being "prosecuted separately." For information about others involved in the case see Xiao Yuan p.472 and Chen Zhiyang p.137.

- **LIU Di**, 39, a former editor of the unofficial Democracy Wall (1978-81) journals, *Beijing Spring* and *Today*, was released after over a year in Qincheng Prison for his role in the 1989 pro-democracy movement. He had been arrested in his Beijing home in July 1989 by the State Security

Bureau. Liu was picked up again on February 29, 1992 for attending a birthday party honoring another released dissident, **ZHANG Qianjin**, and again released. He has been unable to find work.

Liu's first arrest, in 1977 in Taishan, Shandong Province, was for his alleged involvement in the April 5, 1976 "Tiananmen Incident," for which he was imprisoned for eighteen months. Although the "incident" was re-evaluated in 1979, Liu was unable to enter a university or obtain a good job. Until 1988, when he was employed by Chen Ziming (see p.63) as an editor at *Jingjixue Zhoubao (Economics Weekly)*, he worked as a paralegal dealing with divorce cases.

- **LIU Feng, LIN Shengli**, and **ZHANG Wei**[1], all students from Henan Province, were arrested on August 11, 1989 by the Zhengzhou People's Procuratorate, according to an August 22 *Henan Radio* broadcast (FBIS, August 23, 1989). In a November 1991 official response to U.S. government inquiries, Lin was said to have been released and Liu sentenced. According to an earlier official report, however, Liu was freed on June 20, 1991 after serving two years for "jeopardizing social order."

Lin Shengli, 21, a law student at Zhengzhou University, was one of the founders of two "illegal organizations," the Autonomous Federation of Zhengzhou Universities and Colleges and the Autonomous Committee of Zhengzhou University, of which he was also the chairman. He was accused of organizing a "massive" demonstration

in Zhengzhou on May 22, 1989; of setting up a radio station, *Voice of Democracy*, at Zhengzhou University; and of leading students to factories around Zhengzhou on June 4 to deliver "counterrevolutionary speeches" and urge workers to strike. Detained on June 13, 1989 while distributing so-called "reactionary leaflets" at the Xinan County Hotel, he was not formally arrested until two months later.

According to the radio report, Zhang Wei, 22, was a freshman in the journalism department of Zhengzhou University. On June 5, 1989, the day after the crackdown in Beijing, Zhang, together with a law student referred to only as **YANG X**, gave "inflammatory speeches" at Erxi Pagoda in Zhengzhou. The following day, Zhang set up a temporary radio station and began broadcasting news material taken from the *Voice of America*. Reports such as "What Really Happened in Beijing," were also aired. The radio station, named *Voice of Truth*, continued to operate for three days. Then on June 9, 1989, Zhang and Yang X put up posters throughout Zhengzhou University Campus "slandering principal party and state leaders." Zhang was detained on June 22 and later charged with "counter-revolutionary propaganda and incitement." It is not known what became of Yang X. It is unclear if Zhang is the student released in Beijing on January 27, 1991 without having been charged.

Liu Feng, 19, originally detained in Xinxiang, Henan, was a second-year student of public health at the Henan

University of Medicine. A native of Jiaozuo City, he was accused of organizing demonstrations and holding a leadership position in the Zhengzhou College Students Autonomous Federation. The radio report said he led hundreds of Zhengzhou students on a bus trip to Tiananmen Square and helped organize the Henan students there. Back in Zhengzhou on June 6, Liu allegedly organized more than 300 students in a siege at the University of Medicine's administration building. In the course of the demonstration, the assistant to the president of the college reportedly was wounded in the head. Liu was charged with "counter-revolutionary propaganda" and "disturbing public order."

■ **LIU Fuan**, a student in the department of basic science at Beijing Medical University, reportedly was released on January 25, 1990 (Amnesty International, *ASA 17/24/90*). He was arrested in Hebei by the Zhangjiakou City Public Security Bureau sometime in mid-June 1989, according to *Hebei Ribao* (June 17, 1989). Liu allegedly was a leader of the student movement in Beijing and reportedly organized assistance for Tiananmen Square hunger-strikers (see Zhao Yiqiang on p.134).

■ **LIU Hanyi**, 43, and **TONG Chongwu**, born 1951 in Ningbo, Zhejiang Province, the office/business manager and accountant respectively at the Wuhan City (Hubei Province) Dajiang Applied High Technology Research Institute (Dajiang Institute), arrested for helping conceal Wang

Juntao (sentenced in January 1991 to 13 years in prison as a "black hand" dissident), have been released, according to information supplied to the U.S. government by Chinese officials (November 1991). The men were formally arrested between January 5-8, 1990, indicted along with Wu Litang (see p.551), Liu Danhong (p.434) and Jiang Guolian (p.424) on February 16, 1990 and tried on April 19, 1991. Liu Hanyi, who was seized on October 19, 1989 at the Changsha Railway Station while escorting Wang Juntao (see p.70) to a rendezvous with Fei Yuan (never prosecuted), received a term of one year and nine months, expiring on July 19, 1991; Tong, also detained on October 19, was sentenced to a term of one year and six months which expired on April 20, 1991.

■ **LIU Jiaming (LU Jieming)** - see p.135

■ **LIU Jian**[3], a Standing Committee member of the Beijing Students Autonomous Federation was released, according to an official Chinese response to inquiries by the U.S. government (November 1991). He was arrested on June 15, 1989 by the Xianghe County, Hebei Province, Public Security Department for "taking part in the counterrevolutionary rebellion in Beijing" (*Beijing Domestic Service*, June 20, 1989, in FBIS, June 27, 1989).

■ **LIU Jianqiang** - see p.129

■ **LIU Jianjun**, admitted to graduate school at Fudan University just prior to his arrest, was released from prison in early 1990 and expelled. His student status was later restored. During the 1989 pro-democracy movement, Liu was the chairman of his school's Autonomous Student Federation and allegedly organized demonstrations during which students from several dozen suburban campuses marched to the Hunan Provincial government offices. Students at Liu's school also were responsible for arranging the June 8, 1989 Mourning Meeting. Arrested either before June 17 or in September 1989, Liu was held in Changsha No.1 Prison and in Changsha County Jail. He had been a student in the entering class of 1985 in the agricultural machinery department of Hunan Agricultural Academy.

■ **LIU Jianqiang** - see p.129

■ **LIU Jihua**, a resident of Chongqing, was arrested in 1990 and sentenced to three years' imprisonment for "counterrevolutionary propaganda and incitement" on account of his peaceful pro-democracy activities. After serving his sentence at the Sichuan Provincial No.2 Prison (also known as the Sichuan New Life *Laodong* Factory), Liu was released in June 1993.

■ **LIU Mianli**, 32 years old, a teacher at the Loudi Teachers Training College, Hunan Province, was released after having been held for more than two years, starting in July 1989, in Loudi Jail. He allegedly had written "reactionary articles" during the 1989 pro-democracy movement, given numerous public speeches and called upon students to take a confrontational stance toward the government which, he believed, was the only way to "win back justice." Several days after June 4, Liu, along with some students, reportedly took to the streets shouting such slogans as "Down with Li Peng." An alternate account reported that the person referred to was not named Liu Mianli and was not arrested in connection with the 1989 pro-democracy movement.

■ **LIU Suli**, 34, a lecturer in public administration at the University of Politics and Law in Beijing and a senior associate at SERI (Beijing Social and Economic Sciences Research Institute), was released without trial on January 26, 1991 (*AP*, January 26, 1991), then fired from his job. *Xinhua* (UPI, January 26, 1991) reported that Liu was found to have "committed only minor crimes and to have shown repentance and performed meritorious services." According to friends of Liu's family, his wife had received official notification, dated November 24, 1990, from the Beijing Procuratorate of the charges, "instigating and spreading counterrevolutionary propaganda" (UPI, November 27, 1990). On June 10, 1989, Liu, along with **CHEN Xiaoping** (see p.410), went into hiding in Wenzhou, Zhejiang Province, but returned to Beijing several days later. On June 17, according to *Shijie Ribao* (December 9, 1990), Liu was arrested.

Liu served as head of the Liaison Department of the Beijing United Consultative Committee on Tiananmen Square. According to his wife, he "insisted on principles of peace, reason and non-violence" (*Hong Kong Standard*, November 29, 1990). A native of Xuzhou, Jiangsu Province, Liu is the father of an nine-year-old boy.

- **LIU Taiheng** - see p.88

- **LIU Xiangqian**, from Wuhan, Hubei Province, was sentenced to a two-year term for his involvement in the 1989 pro-democracy movement. He had been a graduate student at the Central China Normal College at the time of his arrest on May 1, 1990, but was expelled after his release.

- **LIU Xiaobo**, 35, the controversial literary critic and author convicted of "counterrevolutionary propaganda and incitement" on January 26, 1991, but exempted from punishment, was finally given permission in late December 1992 to go to Australia as a visiting scholar on the faculty of Asian studies at Australian National University in Canberra. By May 1993, he was back in Beijing.

Liu went on trial January 16, 1991 (*Reuters*, January 18, 1991), according to the notice posted at the Beijing Intermediate People's Court (UPI, January 15, 1991), two months after his wife received notification of his arrest (*South China Morning Post*, November 28, 1990). According to *Xinhua* (*Washington Post*, January 27, 1991), although Liu "committed serious crimes [he] acknowledged them, showed repentance and performed some major meritorious services." According to the *New York Times* (January 27,

1991), he may have been released in response to international, and particularly, U.S. pressure. However, although Liu retained the right to live in Beijing, he lost his university position (*South China Morning Post*, May 9, 1991). Two years after the crackdown in Beijing he was still attacked in the official press as a "counter-culture advocate" and he was under intense police surveillance until late 1992. As late as June 1993, Liu still could not publish in China.

Liu, described by some students as their "spiritual tutor" (*Reuters*, January 18, 1991), was arrested on June 6, 1989; the arrest was not announced until June 23. At that time, state radio, television and print media said Liu had close ties to Hu Ping, head of the U.S. based organization, *Chinese Alliance for Democracy*, which publishes the journal *China Spring*. Although Liu did not advocate violence, and indeed urged students and others to return weapons obtained on the night of June 3-4, 1989, he was accused by the authorities of "instigating and participating in the rioting" and of supporting armed resistance.

On April 26, 1989, Liu returned from the United States, where he had been a visiting scholar at Columbia University's East Asian Institute, to take part in the democracy movement. He was one of four men (see Gao Xin p.416) who started a second hunger strike on June 2, 1989 at the base of Tiananmen Square's Monument to the People's Heroes. In a declaration issued that night, the four stated: "Through our hunger strike, we want also to tell the people that what the government media refers to as a small bunch of troublemakers is in fact the whole nation. We may not be students, but we are citizens whose sense of duty makes us support the democracy movement started by the college students...." The four successfully negotiated the withdrawal of students from Tiananmen Square just before dawn on June 4, 1989, which may be the "meritorious services" alluded to in the *Xinhua* report. Two of the men involved were released in 1990; the third was deported.

By the time of his arrest, Liu, like many other activists, was advocating multiparty democracy, freedom of expression and association, and strict implementation of the Chinese constitution, which guarantees most basic rights. After the crackdown, he was reviled continuously by the Chinese media. In an article entitled "The 'Black Hands' Make Clear Their Position - Exposing the Fugitive 'Elite' of Turmoil," reprinted in *Renmin Ribao*, Liu was accused of returning to China under the auspices of the "China Democracy and Unity League" (presumably, a reference to the *Chinese Alliance for Democracy*) in order to "participate in plotting the turmoil," and of stating, in an "instigation" speech at Beijing Normal University, "I am not afraid of being blamed as a 'black hand.' On the contrary, I feel proud of it...." Another alleged comment, "We must organize an armed force among the people to materialize Zhao Ziyang's comeback," also was used against him (UPI, January 16, 1991).

A native of Jilin Province and a graduate of Jilin University, Liu was a faculty member in the Chinese department at Beijing Normal University. His 1988 doctoral degree on the aesthetics of Chinese literature is from the latter university. Liu had strongly criticized some of the older Chinese intellectuals, particularly in "Contemporary Chinese Intellectuals and Politics," an article published when Liu arrived in New York in 1989.

Liu was held in Qincheng Prison for over 19 months. His family was permitted one visit, during the Chinese New Year, late January 1990. He is married to Tao Li, a teacher at the Beijing Language Institute. They have a young son.

■ **LIU Xiaofeng**, deputy director of the Research Institute for the Reform of the Economic Structure (RIRES), an institute associated with Zhao Ziyang, has been released from prison without trial. Arrested after the June 4 crackdown, he reportedly was detained for approximately one year in Qincheng Prison where he was investigated for "economic crimes" and badly beaten. Members of RIRES, along with some staff members of the Rural Development Research Institute, were involved in late May 1989 in an important drive to convene an emergency session of the Standing Committee of the National People's Congress in an attempt to repeal martial law.

Liu was the former head of the student association at Beijing University, a member of the Communist Youth League and one-time mayor of Ge'ermu in Qinghai

Province.

■ **LIU Yijun** and **LIN Lin**, refused asylum by Hong Kong and threatened with repatriation to China, were accepted for resettlement in Canada and arrived in Vancouver on September 17, 1992. Liu, a 29-year-old dissident poet, editor and journalist active in the 1989 pro-democracy movement; and Lin, 24, a computer programmer who had provided Liu with shelter in Shenzhen, spent nine months in jail in Hong Kong as alleged illegal immigrants (*South China Morning Post*, September 17, 1992) before they were permitted to emigrate. According to Liu, she first started her dissident activities in 1987 with a campaign in *Hot Island World*, a Hainan magazine at which she worked, urging writers to expose "conservative forces." During her coverage of events at Tiananmen Square in 1989, she wrote 54 poems in classical Chinese, collectively called *The Blood and Tears in the Red Capital*. One poem, widely circulated in leaflet form, attracted the attention of Chinese authorities, and upon her return to Hainan, Liu was arrested. She reportedly was told to sign a prepared confession accepting a "re-education through labor" sentence and treatment for alleged mental illness. Escaping from her captors, Liu went to Shenzhen, where she reportedly was discovered and blackmailed. On December 17, 1991, she left for Hong Kong with Lin, who had already "confessed" her presence in Tiananmen Square but had never been detained.

■ **LIU Zhongtao (CHEN Le)** - see

p.139

■ **LONG Jianhua**, formerly a student in the entering class of 1986 in the foreign languages department at Hunan Normal University, was released after six months of "re-education" and went to teach middle school in a village in his native Xiangxi Autonomous Prefecture, Hunan Province. He had been arrested in March 1990 after he made up his bed to look like a coffin, then hung on it a portrait of Hu Yaobang edged in black silk.

This was not Long's first arrest. During the 1989 pro-democracy movement, he was involved in the early activities of the Democracy Salon, the planning of the May 4 Joint Demonstration, the organization of the Joint Action Provisional Committee of [Hunan] Institutions of Higher Education and the establishment of the Hunan Students Autonomous Federation. He also was vice-chairman of his school's autonomous student union and wrote posters, banners and other propaganda materials. After June 4, Long fled. He was arrested in mid-September and held in Changsha No.1 Prison, Cell 3. In December 1990, he was declared innocent and released. Long then returned to school and, until his re-arrest, continued his studies.

■ **LONG Xianping**, a 35-year-old English teacher in the foreign languages department at Xiangtan University, Hunan Province, was released after serving two years in Changsha Prison. According to one account, she was arrested in September 1989 and in mid-1990 sentenced to three years' imprisonment by the Xiangtan City Intermediate People's Court on a charge of "counter-revolutionary propaganda and incitement." Another source reported that Long was arrested on June 19, 1989 and sentenced in late 1989 to two years' imprisonment.

Long reportedly was not active during the 1989 pro-democracy movement until the events of June 4, after which she organized mourning activities by students at Xiangtan University, made speeches, participated in student protests and tried to organize strikes in factories. Long is married and has a four or five-year-old child.

- **LU Jiamin**, 45, an associate professor of politics at China Labor College, (an institution for training cadres of the official labor organization, the All-China Federation of Trade Unions), and secretary-general of the Labor Movement Society, was released on January 26, 1991 without trial. He and 17 others (see Liu Suli p.437, Chen Po p.409, Xiong Yan p.474 and Zhou Yongjun p.494) were found to have "committed only minor crimes and (to) have shown repentance and performed meritorious services" (*Xinhua*, in UPI, January 26, 1991). Lu was originally charged with "counter-revolutionary propaganda and agitation" (*South China Morning Post*, December 3, 1990). According to a *Shijie Ribao* report (December 4, 1990), the warrant for his indictment was issued by the Beijing People's Procuratorate and delivered by the Beijing Public Security

Bureau. Lu was due for release in late September 1990, according to the report, but his unrepentant attitude, evident in his alleged statement that he would never regret participation in the pro-democracy movement, reportedly resulted in his indictment.

According to Lu's wife, **Zhang Kangkang**, the well-known writer, Lu was held in Qincheng Prison, Beijing, from July 11, 1989 until his release (*Zhengming*, August 1990). He reportedly was allowed visits from relatives during the 1990 Spring Festival.

After Lu's release, he was unemployed for some months until finally being permitted to work in a library. In mid-February 1993, Chinese authorities finally informed Lu that they were restoring his salary and other benefits and that he would be permitted to conduct research at his former institution, but would not be permitted to teach.

Lu was imprisoned once before, for a three-year period which started in 1969. He was an editor of the unofficial journal *Beijing Spring* during the 1978-79 Democracy Wall movement.

- **LU Liling** and **SUN Li**, two Beijing intellectuals previously reported arrested in late June 1989 (Amnesty International, *ASA 17/66/89*), have been released, according to an unconfirmed report. Lu, a 35-year-old woman, formerly was a member of the editorial department of *Development and Reform*, the journal of the Research Institute for the Reform of the Economic Structure (RIRES). She was arrested in late June 1989. Sun is a graduate of the Institute of Sociology at Beijing University and was a staffer at the Institute.

■ **LU Shengqun**, 37, a sales and marketing official at the Hunan Province Light Industrial Institute, was arrested in early July 1989 and held for several months before being released. After June 4, he helped leaders of the Hunan Students Autonomous Federation hide from authorities, then escape to Guangzhou and other places.

■ **LU Weimin** (also known as **LI Jie**[2]) and **SONG Lin** reportedly were released sometime in June 1990 (Amnesty International, *ASA 17/60/90*). An official Chinese response to inquiries by the U.S. government (November 1991) confirmed their releases. Lu, a 36-year-old critic, author and lecturer in the Chinese Department at East China Normal University in Shanghai, was arrested on September 6, 1989 in Shanghai. He allegedly took a leading role in student protests there. Song, a 34-year-old poet and professor of Chinese literature at the same university, was arrested the same day in Fuzhou. He led a march of students and workers on June 9, 1989 in Shanghai to protest the killings in Beijing. Interviewed under a pseudonym several days later, Song said, "Some people think the time for peaceful action is over and we should go on to acts of sabotage; but I think the better attitude is one of passive non-cooperation." Song had been warned in mid-June 1989 that he was on a wanted list.

■ **LU Yongxiang**, a writer who had been detained in connection with the pro-democracy movement, has been released, according to an Asia Watch source. No additional details are available.

■ **LUO Anyi**, deputy head of the director's office in the Research Institute for the Reform of the Economic Structure (RIRES) and in charge of its personnel files, was released from Qincheng prison probably in September 1990 and placed under house arrest. **YANG Xiao**[2], another RIRES member, received the same treatment (Amnesty International, *ASA 17/66/91*). According to an official Chinese response to inquiries by the U.S. government, a person named Yang Xiao was released (November 1991), but that may refer to a person with the same name from Shanghai (see p.576). If so, inquiries about Yang Xiao[2] have gone unanswered.

Luo, who joined RIRES in 1985, had previously worked in Guizhou Province. During the Cultural Revolution he was a Red Guard "faction leader" and was imprisoned for ten years. He reportedly was arrested in 1976 after the first Tiananmen incident and then again in 1980-81. Yang, a 28-year-old graduate of Beijing University's Sociology department and secretary to Chen Yizi (head of RIRES, escaped from China shortly after June 4, 1989) performed work at RIRES that brought him into close contact with student activists.

■ **LUO Chengxun** - see p.443

- **LUO Haixing, LI Peicheng** and **LI Longqing** (in Cantonese, **Lo Hoi-sing, Lai Pui-sing** and **Li Lung-hing**), all Hong Kong residents implicated in Chen Ziming's (see p.63) attempted escape from China, were released from prison before completing their terms. Luo, 42 years old at the time, went free on medical parole for treatment outside the country on September 9, 1991 after John Major, Great Britain's Prime Minister, visited China. In excellent health, Luo told reporters that what he did was a matter of principle and he would do it again if the chance arose (*Hong Kong Standard*, September 11, 1991). He is not permitted to return to China. Li Peicheng and Li Longqing were released over eight months later, on May 25, 1992, also on medical parole, and were deported from China.

The Chinese government has consistently maintained that Hong Kong residents arrested in China for criminal offenses should be dealt with in accordance with Chinese law. Accordingly, the three were tried by the Guangzhou Intermediate People's Court on February 26, 1991 for "harboring criminal elements." On March 4, 1991, the court sentenced Luo and Li Peicheng to five years' imprisonment and Li Longqing to a term of four years. Although the court said Luo's "cooperative" attitude mitigated his punishment, the five-year sentence was unexpectedly harsh when compared with those of other prominent pro-democracy activists. The Guangdong Higher People's Court rejected Luo's appeal on March 22, but did not give reasons or notify his

family (*South China Morning Post*, March 28, 1991). Luo's wife said the purpose of the appeal was not to obtain a more lenient sentence but to expose the irregularities of legal procedures in China (*South China Morning Post*, March 27, 1991.) Luo then appealed to the Supreme People's Court. After his first appeal, Luo was moved to Guangzhou No.2 Detention Center. According to an Asia Watch source, prior to the move he made nylon flowers for export. When orders for a shipment arrived, Luo was taken from his cell in Guangzhou No.1 Detention Center to the prison factory.

The trial court ruled that all three men were part of an "underground railroad" effort to assist the unsuccessful escape of Chen Ziming (see p.63), condemned to 13 years' imprisonment by Beijing as one of the "black hand" organizers of the democracy movement. Luo allegedly carried information about Chen's hiding place between persons in Guangzhou and the *Hong Kong Alliance in Support of the Patriotic Democratic Movement in China*, an umbrella organization for pro-democracy groups in Hong Kong. Li Peicheng and Li Longqing, allegedly paid by the underground railroad to help dissidents evade a nation-wide dragnet, were accused of acting on Luo's information to try and assist Chen.

The trials lasted a total of two and one-half hours. With the exception of Luo's younger brother, who, after negotiations, was able to hear the proceedings from the public gallery, the authorities did not permit family members to attend the trials. It was the first occasion the brothers had had to see each other since Luo was picked up on October 14, 1989 by border guards in Shenzhen. He was not formally arrested until December 18. Luo, who holds a Hong Kong British passport, is originally from Guilin, Guangxi Zhuang Autonomous Region. Luo's case was originally handled not by the Guangzhou Public Security Bureau, but by a special group sent to Guangzhou directly by the Ministry of State Security to track down "pro-democrats on the run" (*Ming Bao*, December 22, 1989, in FBIS December 22.) All three cases were handed back to the Guangzhou authorities sometime in April 1990 (*Hong Kong Standard*, June 26, 1990, in FBIS, same date.)

From 1986 until March 1989, when he began to operate his own import-export business, Luo was the Beijing representative of the Hong Kong Trade Development Council in Beijing. He is the son of **LUO Chengxun**, also known as **LUO Fu**, former editor-in-chief of the Hong Kong newspaper *Xin Wan Bao*. In 1983, Luo Chengxun was sentenced by the Beijing Municipal Court to ten years' imprisonment for allegedly spying for the United States, but was quickly released and kept under house arrest in Beijing. From July 1991 until his son's release, Luo Chengxun was allowed to visit once a month. He himself finally was able to return to Hong Kong in January 1993 (*Reuters*, January 22, 1993).

Li Peicheng, 34, entered China on October 12, 1989 and was picked up in Zhanjiang, Guangdong Province, the following day. A junior high school graduate and native of Dongwan City, Li allegedly made five separate trips to help 17 dissidents escape, for which he reportedly earned $17,300. According to the bill of prosecution, his arrest was authorized on December 16, 1989 and he was formally arrested on December 18. Li is originally from Dongwan in Guangdong Province. Li Longqing, 33, originally from Xinhui County, Guangdong, is a junior high school graduate and worker. He was detained on December 5, 1989 in Shenzhen while visiting his wife in the hospital after she gave birth. On January 25, 1990, his arrest was authorized; on February 12, 1990, he was formally arrested. Li allegedly earned $12,000 for helping 14 people escape. At no time during their imprisonments in Huaiji Prison, over a year of which was spent in solitary confinement, was either Li permitted visitors.

■ **LUO Yuping**, daughter of former Chief of General Staff Luo Ruiqing, arrested in July 1989 for allegedly supporting the pro-democracy movement and leaking military secrets to students, has been released from prison but discharged from the army. Luo, 41, was a writer (pen-name **DIAN Dian**) and a medical officer at the PLA General Staff Headquarters Clinic. According to a report in Hong Kong's *Ming Bao* (FBIS, April 27, 1990), she was released "through the back door" after her mother solicited help from old friends.

■ **MA Lianggang**, formerly a student at Anhui University; **SHEN Liangqing**, a government cadre (possibly a procuratorial official); and **HUANG Jinwan** (also known as Huang Xiuming), a company manager, all of whom were arrested in mid-1992 in connection with their alleged membership in an underground dissident organization, reportedly were released on medical parole on September 8, 1993. **TIAN Yang**, arrested at the same time, is said to have been released somewhat earlier. The four had been detained for over a year, having been picked up in May or June 1992. According to an official Chinese response to a U.S. government inquiries (November 1991), Ma, described in an Anhui broadcast (July 29, 1989) as being a "key member" of the Hefei Independent Student Union, had been sentenced to prison in connection with the 1989 democracy movement. Other than that he was arrested in Haikou, Hainan Province prior to July 19, 1989, no further information is available about this earlier incident.

■ **MA Shaofang, ZHANG Ming**[2] and **WANG Youcai**, all sentenced on January 5, 1991 by the Beijing Intermediate People's Court, have been released. Zhang, one of those who was severely tortured in Lingyuan Prison (see Liu Gang p.65), was released in the spring of 1992; Wang, who was released early because he had "shown repentance," on November 29, 1991; and Ma in May 1992. All three were on the list of "21 Most Wanted Students" issued by the Chinese authorities shortly after the June 1989 crackdown; the three were the first "most wanted" student leaders to be

tried.

After his release, Ma began working as a vice-president for a trading company in Beijing. On April 22, 1993, while on his way to Guangzhou for a meeting about attracting Taiwanese investment, he was detained while going through security at the Beijing airport. The police then took him by train to his hometown in Jiangdu County, Jiangsu Province. Ma is under surveillance there and may not return to Beijing (*South China Morning Post*, April 26, 1993). No reason for the action was ever given. In an open letter, Ma has protested the extension of his deprivation of political rights, the loss of his work and his enforced exile. Zhang has gone into business with friends.

Three other defendants, probably workers, were sentenced at the same time (see Kong Xianfeng p.426) and an additional two students, **LI Yuqi**, the Beijing Students Autonomous Federation leader at Qinghua University, and **PANG Zhihong**, a 25-year-old student at Liaoning Railway College, who allegedly repented, were convicted of minor crimes (*New York Times*, January 6, 1991) but "exempted from criminal punishment" (*Xinhua* in *Reuters*, January 5, 1991). Pang was dismissed from college and has had trouble finding work. Li, a chemistry student from Beijing, was first held with non-political offenders in Changping Prison in a suburb of Beijing. After his release he could not find work.

Zhang, a 27-year-old Qinghua University automotive engineering student and No. 19 on the "most wanted" list, was sentenced to three years in prison and one year's deprivation of political rights, as was Ma, a 28-year-old former student at the Beijing Film Academy, who was No. 10. Wang, a 24-year-old Beijing University physics graduate and No. 15 on the list, was handed a four-year term with one year's deprivation of political rights. Fan Shumi, a spokesperson for the Beijing Intermediate People's Court, said Zhang was tried in open court (*AP*, December 4, 1990) and the *Washington Post* (January 6, 1991) reported *Xinhua* as saying that more than 60 Beijing residents, as well as relatives of the defendant, were present when the sentence was announced. Foreign journalists and international observers were barred from the trial.

Zhang reportedly went on trial November 27, 1990. According to an official notice posted outside Beijing Intermediate People's Court on November 28 (*Reuters*, November 28, 1990), Zhang, a Jilin native and a key figure in the Beijing Student Autonomous Federation, was charged with "counterrevolutionary propaganda and incitement." According to a report in *Xinhua* (*Washington Post*, January 6, 1991), all defendants were tried separately, so the exact trial dates of the others are not known (*Reuters*, January 5, 1991).

All those sentenced as well as the two who were released, were accused of "inciting subversion against the people's government and the [attempt at] overthrowing the socialist system during the 1989 turmoil and rebellion."

Some of the prisoners, though the report did not specify which ones, also were found guilty of "organizing and directing" attempts to impede members of the armed forces charged with enforcing martial law in Beijing; others were guilty of "assembling crowds to disturb public traffic and seriously undermining public order."

Zhang reportedly was arrested before September 13, 1989 in Shenzhen while trying to escape to Hong Kong (*Ming Bao*, June 20, 1990, in FBIS, June 20). He was held in Qincheng Prison before sentencing. Wang, at one-time general-secretary of the Beijing Students Autonomous Federation, was arrested sometime between June and September 1989. He had attempted to organize continued student resistance in Shanghai after the June 3-4, 1989 crackdown in Beijing, according to *Renmin Ribao* (September 24, 1989). Wang also was mentioned in "Facts about the Shanghai Riot," an article published in *Wen Wei Bao* on June 28, 1989 which condemned many leading dissidents. Ma, a native of Jiangsu Province and an associate of student leader Wuerkaixi in the Beijing Students Autonomous Federation, reportedly turned himself in to the authorities on June 17 in Guangzhou. His arrest followed a June 13, 1989 state television broadcast of "wanted posters" for the 21 leaders of the student movement. Ma allegedly made speeches during the protests and with three other student leaders held a May 21, 1989 meeting with government representatives. He, too, was detained in Qincheng Prison. Other than that Pang was a student at Qinghai

University, there is no information available about him or about Li.

- **MA Ziyi**, 38, a lecturer in the history department of East China Normal University, was released, according to an official Chinese response to U.S. government inquiries (November 1991). She was arrested shortly after July 2, 1989, when Wang Dan was captured. Wang allegedly used Ma's apartment as shelter for a short period prior to his arrest. Ma allegedly also helped shelter Bao Zunxin (see p.405).

- **MAO Genwei** - see p.77

- Two Shanghai poets, **MENG Lang** (MENG Junliang), born August 16, 1961, and **MO Mo (ZHU Weiguo)**, born 1964, were arrested on April 17, 1992 by officers of the Public Security Bureau armed with search warrants and then held for six weeks. Both men had their homes searched and numerous books, manuscripts, personal writings and notes confiscated. According to a copy of the search record, more than 100 items, most of which were poetry magazines and books produced in China and abroad, were confiscated from Meng Lang's house alone. The reason for the two men's detention appears to have been their involvement in an unofficial literary magazine, *Modern Chinese Poetry (Xian Dai Han Shi)*. Four issues of the quarterly, the purpose of which was to promote and develop contemporary Chinese poetry, had been published under a rotating executive editorship. At the time of their arrests, Meng Lang and Mo Mo

were two of four editors in the process of preparing the fifth issue. A previous editor had been questioned but never detained.

Although Meng Lang has received little official recognition, among his contemporaries he is considered to be one of the foremost of an important new school of Chinese poets. A graduate of the precision instrumentation department of the Shanghai College of Mechanical Engineering, Meng worked for four years at his specialty before turning full time to literature. Among his many activities, Meng edited works of Chinese avant-garde literature and critique at the Shenzhen University Editing and Publishing Center, helped to edit a (still-unpublished) general collection of unofficial modern Chinese poetry, and established several unofficial literary publications. From 1982 until 1987, Meng worked at the Shanghai Optical Instruments Factory, for the last two years as a divisional deputy manager and communications director. No additional information about his colleague, Mo Mo is available.

- **MAO Wenke** - see p.402

- **MO Lihua**, 34, formerly a teacher at Shaoyang Teachers College, Hunan Province, was released in mid-1991 on parole. Arrested on June 14, 1989, she was sentenced on December 21 by the Shaoyang City Intermediate People's Court to three years' imprisonment on charges of "counterrevolutionary propaganda and incitement," then sent to Changsha Prison. During the 1989 pro-democracy movement, Mo allegedly supported the student demonstrations. On June 5, she delivered a speech at a mourning ceremony in Shaoyang People's Square denouncing the June 4 crackdown in Beijing as "a bloody repression of the people by a fascist government."

Mo was fired from her college teaching position a couple of months before her release, but when she decided to head south in search of work, government officials informed her she was not allowed to leave the school where she was living with her husband and seven-year-old daughter. She was especially forbidden to travel to other parts of the country, and also was required to receive permission from authorities even to visit friends and relatives in Shaoyang. Mo is now in Hong Kong.

■ **PENG Rong**, 27, a Beijing University biophysics major, **ZHOU Jian (ZOU Jian)**, a biology major, and **LI Hai**, of the philosophy department, have all been released. At his release, on May 26, 1992, Peng was exiled to his native place, Zhuzhou, in Hunan Province. Sentenced on February 25, 1992, according to a notice posted outside the Beijing Intermediate People's Court, Peng received a two-year term dated from the time he was first detained, May 25, 1990. Peng went on trial Christmas Day 1991 on charges of "counterrevolutionary propaganda and incitement" and "colluding with hostile foreign forces." The latter charge had to do with Peng's alleged contacts with overseas Chinese and foreigners. According to a *Reuters*

report (December 30, 1991), Peng's lawyers, who had originally intended to enter a not guilty plea, changed their minds after considerable pressure from government officials.

Peng was arrested, after police searched his dormitory room, for collaborating with other Beijing University students and with two from Wuhan (Hubei Province) University, probably Zou and Li, to commemorate the first anniversary of the June 4 crackdown. In an on-campus speech, Peng called on the West to lift economic sanctions, arguing that sanctions impeded an "open door" policy and democratic reform. Along with Li and Zhou, he also conducted and published by means of a signed poster, an "illegal" poll of student attitudes toward another round of protests. It indicated that most had become apolitical, depressed and withdrawn after the 1989 crackdown. During the student movement, Peng commanded the Beijing Students Autonomous Federation security forces which were charged with guarding the movement's leaders. He also allegedly led student marchers and made fiery speeches for which he was placed under surveillance.

Li was released on June 8, 1991 according to a report in *A Changing China* (Fall 1991). At the time, he was physically weak and suffering from poor-sanitation-related skin ailments. During Li's 18 months in detention, Chinese authorities denied his family permission to visit. Zhou was listed as released by Chinese authorities in response to requests for information by the U.S. government (November 1991).

According to an Asia Watch source, he was arrested in Wuhan on May 15, 1990 for distributing leaflets and released on December 15.

■ **PENG Xiaoyong**, 29, formerly a doctoral student in Shanghai's Jiaotong University and a member of the Standing Committee of the Shanghai Students Autonomous Federation, was released after 14 months in detention. When the time came for university officials to allocate work, they ordered that he not be sent to a large city. Assigned to a job in the mountains of Sichuan Province, Peng refused and headed south (presumably to Guangzhou) to find work on his own.

■ **PENG Yuzhang**, a retired professor from Hunan University in his late sixties, was released from prison on grounds of mental illness, then committed to a psychiatric asylum. As of April 1993, however, he was reportedly living at home. Arrested in June 1989, Peng allegedly participated in sit-ins and hunger strikes during the pro-democracy movement. While detained in Changsha No.1 Prison, Cell 24, he was punished for shouting demands to be released, and was placed on a "shackle board" *(menbanliao)* for more than three months, after which he was severely emaciated and unable to walk unassisted.

■ **QI Lin**, formerly an assistant foreign editor at *Beijing Ribao*, was released on temporary medical parole on June 29, 1992 apparently because prison officials were afraid he might become terminally ill in jail. He is an insulin-dependent diabetic and had become unconscious several times during his detention. Qi was arrested on July 11, 1991, tried twice secretly, once on January 30, 1992 in Beijing People's Intermediate People's Court and again on February 15 by a higher court. He received a four-year sentence on April 8, 1992 for allegedly "leaking state secrets," to a Taiwanese newspaper. The secret referred to the fact that the relevant Party committee had been divided as to whether to subject Hu Jiwei, former editor of *Renmin Ribao*, to disciplinary action for his involvement in a May 1989 effort to invalidate the martial law order for Beijing by convening a special session of the National People's Congress. According to the verdict, law officers had obtained material evidence - two fountain pens - testimony from witnesses and from high-tech forensic research establishing Qi's guilt.

Apprehended at his home in Beijing on July 11, 1991 by the Public Security Bureau, Qi was formally arrested on July 23. At the time of his apprehension, he was severely hurt and lost a great deal of blood. The circumstances surrounding the incident are not known. At the same time, Qi's home was searched and his wife, **Li Jingyin**, a secondary school teacher, interrogated.

Qi, a 1989 graduate of the journalism department of People's University and the 1988 winner of an "outstanding young journalist" award, was active during the 1989 pro-democracy movement, helping stage a May 18 protest by *Beijing*

Ribao and *Beijing Wanbao* newsmen outside the Beijing Municipal Building. On May 23, he marched again. He also submitted a letter charging Chen Xitong, mayor of Beijing, and Li Ximing, the party secretary, with lying to the public about the movement of martial law troops and demanded they admit their mistakes. On June 4, 1989, Qi reportedly witnessed many deaths and documented them through photographs. Earlier, from mid-April on, as he delivered food and water to students in Tiananmen Square, he also took documentary photos; and he encouraged his newspaper to run stories about the movement. From mid-1989 until his arrest, despite financial hardship, Qi continued to criticize the government, to document events linked with the pro-democracy movement and to organize meetings from his home. After June 4, Qi was subject to intense investigation and placed on Party probation for two years.

Since his release, Qi, 36, ousted from his job and disqualified as a journalist, has been too weak to look for work and he and his wife have had trouble meeting his high medical bills (*South China Morning Post*, February 9, 1993). With the indictment against him still standing, Qi cannot go abroad for medical treatment.

■ **QIAN Liyun** - see p.60

■ **QIN Guodong (CHEUN Kwom-tung)**, 21, a medical student, and **LIANG Xihua (LIANG Zaohua or LEUNG Tso-wah)**, a 23-year-old student of international finance at Jinan University in Guangzhou, both residents of Macao, were released on August 23, 1989 after having been detained incommunicado for almost a month. Along with **CHEN Zewei (CHAN Chak-wai)**, 30, they were suspected of trying to help a student leader, **ZHENG Xuguang** (see p.31, 445), sentenced in January 1991, escape from China. On July 26, 1989, Chen, Qin and Liang traveled from their homes in Macao, where they were on vacation, to Guangzhou. They were taken into custody on July 27 by a special team sent to Guangzhou from the national office of the Public Security Bureau. On August 11, their families received anonymous telephone calls reporting that the three had been detained. Chen, a second-year Chinese major at Jinan University and vice-chairman of the Macao student union, was released on June 18, 1990 and returned to his family in Macao (*Ming Bao*, June 20, 1990, in FBIS, June 20).

■ **QIN Weidong (QIN(G) Weizhong)**, a student at the Beijing University of Science and Technology and a leader of a Students Autonomous Federation organized by Beijing Medical University, was released, according to an official Chinese response to U.S. government inquiries (November 1991). He was arrested on June 24, 1989 in Zhangjiakou (*Hebei Ribao*, July 12, 1989; *Shijiazhuang Radio*, in FBIS, July 31).

■ **REN Tao**, a 22-year-old student at Beijing Broadcasting College and a member of the Beijing Students Autonomous Federation, was released, according to an official Chinese response to inquiries by the U.S. government (November 1991). He was arrested sometime in June 1989 while travelling to the countryside allegedly to spread the news of the uprising in Beijing to rural areas (Amnesty International, *ASA 17/24/90*).

■ **REN Zhihua**, a student from Hunan Province, was detained soon after the June 1989 crackdown and then released after a few months.

■ **SHA Yuguang**, 47, an accountant at the Beijing Wireless Factory who was detained by the police on May 29, 1992 while on his way home from work, was released on July 10 pending further investigation. He was then informed, however, that he would have to submit regular reports to the police about his various meetings with friends. Two members of an underground pro-democracy group, probably Hu Shenglun and Gao Yuxiang (see p.20), had reportedly been staying at Sha's home at the time they were arrested, and a quantity of pro-democracy literature had been found in the house. After his release, Sha was suspended without pay from his work unit. A veteran activist from the 1978-81 Democracy Wall period, he had edited an unofficial pro-democracy journal called *Zhonghua Si Wu (China, April 5th)*.

■ **SHANG Hongke**, a former student from the Party History department at People's University, who walked into the university's archives building on June 1, 1992 and then reportedly disappeared, abandoning his bicycle in front of the building, was released sometime prior to mid-September that year, according to an Asia Watch source. Although nothing definite is known either about his detention or his release, Shang is thought to have been detained in connection with the government's mid-1992 crackdown on underground pro-democracy groups. Although Shang had never been arrested before June 1992, because of his participation in the 1989 pro-democracy movement he had neither been permitted to graduate from college nor allocated a job. After traveling to Hainan Province in search of work, he later returned to Beijing and occupied a dormitory room at the university (*Wah Kiu Yat Po*, June 11, 14, 19, 24, 1992). At the time of his arrest, Shang was an employee at a joint investment firm run by the renowned economist Cao Siyuan.

■ **SHAO Jiang**, 24, a member of the Standing Committee of the Beijing Students Autonomous Federation and deputy-general of the Beijing University Self-Rule Preparatory Committee, was released from prison in February 1991, having been "exempt from criminal prosecution." In an official response to inquiries by the U.S. government, Chinese authorities confirmed the release. He had been arrested on September 1, 1989 on the border between Zhuhai and Macao (*Zhong Xin She*, September 3, 1989). When Shao attempted to go to Taiwan for the anniversary of his grandmother's funeral in October 1991, his application was rejected on the grounds that as a leader of a "counter-revolutionary organization," he was a security risk (Article 5(8) of the Chinese Immigration Regulation Law). Shao was further informed that although he had never been charged, there were problems with his thought and he could harm his country. According to Shao, at the time of his release he was told he would enjoy all the rights of a Chinese citizen and there would be no problem if he wished to travel abroad. As of May 1993, Shao, a mathematics major at Beijing University before his arrest and expulsion, was working as a salesman in a computer company in Guangzhou.

- **SHE Sujie** - see p.234

- **SHEN Lie**, a 22-year-old computer programming software specialist and a member of the Standing Committee of the Shanghai Students Autonomous Federation, was released from detention, according to an official Chinese response to inquiries from the U.S. government (November 1991). He is now in Arizona. Shen, a former student at Shanghai Industrial College, class of 1987, from Ningbo, Zhejiang Province, had been held without trial in a Shanghai prison. He was arrested sometime after September 1989, after his name appeared on the August 19 government "most wanted" list.

The other Shanghai student leaders also were released. **HE Dongdong**, **LI Dianyuan** and **LI Hongbo**, students from Shanghai Communications University, and **HE Zhe**, a student from Shanghai Marine Transport College, were all arrested sometime after June 4, 1989. Li Dianyuan, a 27-year-old graduate student, went to Changsha, Hunan Province, at the end of May 1989. Once there, he contacted the Hunan Students Autonomous Federation, assisted in its work and helped organize the June 8 mourning ceremony in Changsha. Arrested at his home in Shaoyang, Li was held for several months in Changsha's No.1 Detention Center, then transferred back to Shanghai. In June 1990, the Shanghai Intermediate People's Court sentenced him to a three-year term on the charge of "counterrevolutionary propaganda and incitement." **QIU Xiaoping**, another Shanghai leader and a graduate student in international law at the Shanghai Academy of Social Sciences Institute of Law and head of the graduate students' association there, who reportedly organized protest activities in Shanghai in May-June 1989, was detained in the city's Hongqiao district for ten months and expelled from school. He Zhe, 24, from Yiyang, Hunan Province, was a student of industrial management projects, class of 1985. Qiu, 39, is from Zhenjiang in Jiangsu Province. Shen, He Dongdong, Li Duanyuan and Qiu were all members of the Standing Committee of the Shanghai Students Autonomous Federation.

- **SHEN Tong**, a student activist who fled China several days after the June 4, 1989 crackdown in Tiananmen Square, was arrested in Beijing on September 1, 1992, hours before a news conference which he had scheduled to announce the formation of a Beijing branch of his Boston-based

Democracy for China Fund, and held for 54 days in a hotel room. On October 24, he was permitted to meet with his mother and other family members and then put on a plane back to the U.S. Shen, a Chinese citizen, had entered China on a tourist visa on July 29 to meet with underground Chinese activists and set up the fund's branch office, which, he said, would be organized in accordance with Chinese law and registered with all relevant bodies. In deporting him, the Foreign Ministry characterized his activities as "anti-government," "illegal" and "incompatible with his status as a tourist." A number of pro-democracy students, intellectuals and workers who had met with Shen were later arrested by the authorities, and several of them had either been tried (see **Qi Dafeng, Lu Gang, Huang Shixu**) or were awaiting trial (see **An Ning, Meng Zhongwei**) as of November 1993.

■ **SHEN Yinhan,** 30, a leading member of the Beijing Workers Autonomous Federation and a university graduate, has been released, according to an official Chinese response to inquiries by the U.S. government (November 1991). He reportedly had been imprisoned in Paoju Detention Center. Before 1989, Shen was chairman of the official workers' union of the Bureau of Civil Aviation (Amnesty International, *ASA 17/24/90*). (NB: A "Chen Yinshan" listed in a November 1990 Chinese government reply to the ILO was almost certainly a misspelling for Shen Yinhan).

■ **SHI Binhai** - see p.143

■ **SHI Guanghua** - see p.88

■ **SONG Bin** - see p.471

■ **SONG Min,** a history major at Beijing Normal University and a graduate of the Institute of Aviation, arrested together with a classmate in Xiangxi, Hunan Province, was released, according to an official Chinese response to requests for information by the U.S. government (November 1991). Song had gone into hiding around May 20, 1989.

■ **SONG Mitu,** 31, and **WANG Hongming,** 24, both leaders of the Shanghai Students Autonomous Federation, "registered" themselves with the Public Security Bureau in Jiading County on June 14, 1989 (*Shanghai Radio,* June 16, 1989, in FBIS, June 20). Wang was a student in the Department of Precision Mechanical Engineering at the Shanghai University of Science and Technology. Song, formerly a research student, graduated from the university's Department of Radio Engineering in 1982. The two reportedly "confessed" to taking part in numerous pro-democracy meetings and to inciting students to demonstrate in the streets.

It is possible that the name of **WANG Yongming,** who was listed as released in an official Chinese response to inquiries from the U.S. government (November 1991), in fact refers to Wang Hongming. If not, then the latter's status remains to be clarified.

No information was forthcoming on the status of Song Mitu, but it is believed that no 1989 student activists remained imprisoned in Shanghai as of December 1993.

■ **SONG Qu** - see p.88

■ **SONG Wei** - see p.88

■ **SONG Shaowen**, a student from Yantai, Shandong Province, arrested in connection with a demonstration to commemorate the June 4, 1989 crackdown in Beijing, has been released. Other than that he was never formally charged, the report gave no additional details.

■ **SONG Xiaoyong**, a 25-year-old naval officer who received a two-year prison sentence after June 1989 and was released in early 1991, and **XING Li**, a 27-year-old Shanghai student leader, escaped from China with the help of an underground pro-democracy network (*AP*, October 16, 1991). The *AP* source provided a copy of a January 24, 1990 document from a People's Liberation Army political branch in Fujian which accused Song of "not having complete trust in the Communist Party," but no other information about his activity is known. Xing reportedly organized street demonstrations in Shanghai. After the June 1989 crackdown, he was placed under house arrest and forbidden to work.

■ **SONG Yuchuan**, born in 1950, was released in the fall of 1991 after serving a two-year sentence for stealing

weapons from martial law troops. He was tried on June 19, 1990, almost a year after his arrest in early August 1989 for failing to turn in a burned-out gun. Song reportedly kept the gun as evidence that the PLA shot innocent citizens.

A graduate of the Chinese Academy of Social Science's Institute of Journalism from which he earned an MA in 1986, Song, prior to his arrest, was a lecturer at the Chinese Academy of Social Science's Graduate School, Department of Public Communication, as well as a journalist at *Renmin Ribao*. He has been dismissed from his positions and his Party membership has been canceled. Earlier, during the Cultural Revolution, Song was sent as a laborer to Shaanxi Province.

■ **SU Ding**, 32, Dean of the East-West Art Institute of the Sichuan Academy of Social Sciences, who was reported to have been formally charged by the Sichuan Provincial Government with political crimes allegedly committed during the 1989 pro-democracy movement, was released in late May 1990. According to an Asia Watch source, Su made speeches, participated in demonstrations and attended meetings, all of which were branded as "anti-Party." A specialist in aesthetics and literary theory, he was arrested in late August 1989 in Beijing while buying an international air ticket. He had been invited to serve as a visiting scholar at Arizona State University and his travel documents were all in order. In spring 1989, Su was forced by Sichuan Party authorities to write a series of "self-criticisms" for having recommended for publication a book which was later denounced as "anti-Party." Through this and similar acts, Su acquired the taint of "bourgeois liberalization." During his time in detention, Su was held incommunicado and his arrest was never made public.

■ **SUI Jin**, a graduate student at the Beijing Aviation Academy, was released in April 1990 after some four months in prison. He had been arrested on December 31, 1989 for putting up a poster on campus on December 26 about the downfall of the communist regime in Romania.

■ **SUN Jianwei**, from Shandong Province, was 18 years old when he was arrested and held in Qincheng Prison. At his release after one-half year, he was permitted to return to his studies at Qinghua.

■ **SUN Lijuan** - see p.82

■ Amnesty International *(ASA 17/24/90)* has reported the following releases: **SUN Liwan**, a violinist at China Central Ballet, arrested in June 1989 and detained for several weeks or months; **BAO Jian**, a student at the Beijing Conservatory of Music detained in June 1989 and released in late 1989 or early 1990; **CHENG Hong**, 29, a woman journalist with *China Daily*, arrested in June 1989 for contacting foreigners; and **GUO Xiaolin**, a poet arrested in July 1989 and released sometime toward the end of the year.

■ **SUN Xingwu**, 22, a physics student from Fudan University arrested on June 21, 1989, was released in May 1990 from the Shanghai No.1 Detention Center, according to an Asia Watch source. In September or October he escaped to Hong Kong but was forcibly repatriated to China, arrested for illegally crossing the border and held in detention at the same center for four months. Sun was judged "exempt from prosecution" and released in April or May 1991. Although he had already graduated from Fudan, Sun was not allocated work. He subsequently found his own in a computer company in Shenzhen.

■ **TAN Li**, a 20-year-old student in the entering class of 1986 in the foreign languages department of Hunan Normal University, and **ZHANG Xiaoyan**, a 21-year-old student in the same department, were tried in June 1990 by the Changsha Intermediate People's Court on charges of "counter-revolutionary propaganda and incitement." Tan received a one-year prison sentence, was sent to Changsha Prison, and is now free. Zhang was exempted from criminal sanctions and released. Both women were held in the same cell in Changsha No.1 Prison before their trial.

During the 1989 pro-democracy movement, Zhang participated in her department's (unofficial) Democratic Propaganda Team. She reportedly gave speeches both on and off campus and wrote "reactionary articles and wall posters." Zhang, together with Tan, allegedly wrote and posted on a wall on campus a big-character poster which read: "Down with the Communist

Party." Tan was arrested in November 1989 after being thoroughly investigated, and Zhang was arrested late that year.

■ **TAN Liliang**, a 28-year-old-teacher at Hunan's Loudi Teachers College and a graduate of the education department of Hunan Normal University, was released from reform through labor at Longxi Prison (Provincial No.6). He was sentenced in early 1990 by the Loudi Prefecture Intermediate People's Court to two years' imprisonment on a charge of "counterrevolutionary propaganda and incitement." During the 1989 pro-democracy movement, Tan allegedly organized class boycotts and student demonstrations and planned a "long-term resistance struggle" with Hunan Normal University students. After his release, he reportedly changed jobs at least 20 different times, because the government had him fired from any work he found.

■ **TANG Boqiao**, originally a student in the entering class of 1986 in the politics department at Hunan Normal University, and former chairman of the Hunan Students Autonomous Federation, was admitted to the U.S. as a political refugee in April 1992. His pro-democracy activities pre-date the 1989 movement. On its eve, he helped organize a Democracy Salon, within his school and later helped extend it to all institutions of higher education in Changsha. In late April, Tang took part in the Committee to Prepare Demonstrations and Meetings in Commemoration of the 70th

Anniversary of the May 4 Movement. After a demonstration and rally on May 4, he helped found the Joint Action Provisional Committee of Hunan Institutions of Higher Education and served as its provisional chairman.

On May 14, Tang went to Beijing to observe and participate in the Beijing student movement, returning on the evening of May 19. On May 22 he took part in the re-organization of the Hunan Students Autonomous Federation, serving as chairman. On May 24, he directed a city-wide protest demonstration; on May 28 he drafted a "pledge of loyalty" for the students. On June 8, Tang and **ZHANG Lixin** (also released) presided over a pro-democracy meeting of 140,000 persons to mourn the dead of Beijing. On June 27, 28 and 29, *Hunan Television* repeatedly broadcast a province-wide "wanted notice" for Tang.

In the early morning of July 13, Tang was arrested in Jiangmen City in Guangdong. After interrogation in two Guangdong counties, he was returned to Hunan, and on July 17, 1990, was tried by the Changsha City Intermediate People's Court and sentenced to three years' imprisonment with two years' subsequent deprivation of political rights on charges of "counter-revolutionary propaganda and incitement." In November 1989, Tang was sent to Hunan's Longxi Prison (Provincial No.6). He was paroled on February 12, 1991 and subsequently escaped abroad. *Anthems of Defeat*, an Asia Watch work, was in large part Tang's work.

Tang has reported that he was

severely beaten by armed police officers at the time of his arrest, and that he suffered various forms of ill-treatment at several different institutions in Hunan. He was beaten, shocked with electric batons, shackled and confined in a tiny punishment cell.

■ **TANG Hua**, in his thirties, the deputy editor of *Young People*, a magazine published by the Hunan Provincial Communist Youth League, was released after being held and investigated for more than one-and-a-half years. Accused of "spreading rumors" in order "to attack the Party and government," of publishing articles in *Young People* "championing democracy and science," and of helping student leaders with strategies for the pro-democracy movement, he was arrested after June 4, 1989.

■ **TANG Min**, a 36-year-old Fujian writer, who was tried in December 1989 in Xiamen for criminal libel but not sentenced until January 1990, was released from prison on December 25, 1990, according to an Asia Watch source. In addition to a prison sentence, she reportedly paid a stiff fine, 2,000 *yuan*. Tang allegedly slandered a military officer's widow and two other people in a 1986 satirical short story, "The Mysterious Miasma of Taimu Shan," which satirized the downfall of the Gang of Four. According to an article in *Xiamen Ribao* (January 12, 1990), Tang's story falsely alleged that a militia commander, his wife and his wife's uncle "ran roughshod over the community" and that after the commander's death he was transformed into a cow with whom his widow fell in love.

The source reported that discrepancies between the story's content as written and as presented in Tang's indictment were numerous and reflected the state's interest in establishing libel. The names of the principals were changed; Tang's sympathetic portrayals of their characters were altered to read as metaphors for total evil and inhumanity; and the commander's actual transformation into a cow was substituted for the community's unfounded belief in such a metamorphosis. At Tang's trial, although ample testimony as to the commander's misdeeds was submitted and no motive for libel was established, the judge concluded that Tang's story "had had a dampening effect on all the base level cadres of the area" and was indeed libelous. At the time of sentencing, Tang's case had been pending for two years. Her imprisonment and fine were probably motivated by her role as a mediator between students and officials during student demonstrations in Fuzhou.

■ **TANG Zhibin**, 30 years old, formerly a reporter for *Young People*, the journal of the Hunan Provincial Communist Youth League, was arrested at the end of 1989 and released in mid-1990. However, he was fired from his official position and has had trouble finding work. During the 1989 pro-democracy movement, Tang allegedly joined the students in demonstrations and sit-down protests. According to the authorities, he was "appointed as an adviser" by the students and "his ideology went into reverse."

■ **TIAN Boping**, a student at Loudi Normal College *(Loudi Shi-Zhuan)*, Hunan Province, was detained after June 4, 1989 and held for more than a year before being released.

■ **TIAN Changle**, a student at Hunan Normal University, was detained after June 4, 1989 and held for over a year before being released.

■ **TIAN Qing**, distinguished music historian and Deputy Director of the Research Institute of Music in the Chinese Academy of Arts, Beijing, was released in early 1991. He was arrested on September 23, 1989, and held incommunicado in the Erlong Detention Center in western Beijing. Tian, a Tianjin native in his early forties, had been under investigation since he was denounced for giving a lecture on June 4, 1989 at the Shanghai Music Conservatory in which he described the events he witnessed in Beijing on June 3.

■ **TU Haiying**, a 46-year-old lecturer at the Acoustics Research Institute of Shaanxi Teachers University and a Xi'an intellectual, was released in March 1991. He had been held in the Fifth Branch Detention Center of the Xi'an Public Security Bureau. Arrested in July or August 1989, Tu had made speeches at student rallies, wrote and posted big-character posters on the

campus and served as an inspiration to students in Xi'an.

■ **TU Qiusheng** - see p.144, 145

■ **WAN Jinxin** (previously listed as **WAN Xinjin**), 33, a lecturer at the Research Institute of Ancient Law Documents of the University of Politics and Law and a leader of the Beijing Citizens Autonomous Federation, was released in February 1991 and dismissed from his job. An official Chinese response to U.S. government inquiries confirmed the release (November 1991). According to one report, Wan turned himself in to the police, apparently on June 17, 1989, in Pingdu County, Shandong Province. According to another report, a **WAN Jinjin** (Qiangjin), also a law lecturer, was arrested on campus. Both reports probably refer to the same person. Wan was accused of organizing a citizens' federation, making "inflammatory speeches" and "fabricating rumors." Authorities described him as one of seven "ringleaders" of illegal organizations arrested in Shandong in mid-June 1989 (*Beijing Ribao*, June 25, 1989, FBIS, June 23, 1989).

■ Five poets arrested in Chengdu, Sichuan Province in March 1990 for making a secret videotape commemorating the June 4 massacre were released without charge at the end of February 1992. The group's leader, **LIAO Yiwu** (see p.88), received a four-year sentence and is still in jail. The five released are **Wan Xia**, a 31-year-old with a heart condition who held no formal job prior to his arrest;

LI Yawei, a 30-year-old middle school teacher; LIU Taiheng, 37; WANG Qing (pen name BA Tie), a 37-year-old office worker; and XUN Mingjun, 29, also an office worker. According to the authorities, the five, who were held with Liao Yiwu in the Chongqing Detention Center, had "made mistakes, but were not guilty of crimes."

Other friends of the poets detained in March 1990 were reportedly released after a few weeks (*South China Morning Post*, March 6, 1992). They are believed to include LAN Ma; SONG Wei, in his thirties; his brother SONG Qu; ZHOU Lunzuo, a Chongqing native and twin brother of ZHOU Lunyou (see p.555) who served a three-year sentence for dissident activities; SHI Guanghua; and FENG Chuan, who taught at Sichuan University. All seven were members of *Fei Fei*, an "underground" poetry society based in Chengdu. According to a Chinese poet living in exile in the U.S., all group members were accused of participating in the 1989 pro-democracy movement (*Shijie Ribao*, September 1, 1990) and of "belonging to the 'decadent school' of writing and publishing 'subversive poetry'." In addition to the distribution of the tapes, the group had been printing poetry broadsheets, some of which surfaced in Beijing.

In a November 1991 response to U.S. government inquiries, Chinese authorities listed Zhou Lunzuo and Song Wei as having "never been accused of any offense." Liao Yiwu, ZENG Lei, Wan Xia, Li Yawei, Wang Qin, and Liu Taiheng were all listed as still "under investigation"; and Shi Guanghua was listed as released. Inquiries about Song Qu and Lan Ma elicited no response, and the current status of Zeng Lei is not known.

■ WANG Chengzong - see p.144, 145

■ WANG Dan, 24, one of the top student leaders of the pro-democracy movement in Beijing, an organizer of the Beijing Students Autonomous Federation and No.1 on the list of "most wanted" students, was released on parole on February 17, 1993. The decision reportedly was made by the Beijing Intermediate People's Court on the basis of Wang's having "observed prison regulations" (*Xinhua*, February 17, 1993). Wang has told reporters he has no regrets and he has pledged to continue to fight for democracy in China. There has been no response to Wang's request to resume his studies at Beijing University. As of January 1994, he was taking a correspondence course in history offered by the University of California at Berkeley. Less than a month after his release, Wang was ordered to Hainan for three weeks to avoid press attention during meetings of the National People's Congress and the Chinese People's Political Consultative Conference.

According to a report in the *South China Morning Post* (April 3, 1993), when he attempted to return to Beijing prior to the Congress' conclusion, Wang was held in Guangzhou for two days. In response, he staged a four-hour hunger strike. Later, when he applied to the Xinjiekou Public Security office, which is in charge of his case, to go to Guangzhou and Shandong, his request for Shandong was granted but that for Guangzhou refused. Wang's parole conditions require him to remain in Beijing. Yet on the fourth anniversary of the crackdown in Beijing, Wang planned to be at a "health resort" in Beihai, Guangxi Province for treatment of his prison-contracted pharyngitis. He could not explain why such treatment was unavailable in Beijing (*Hong Kong Standard*, May 31, 1993). According to a report in *Newsweek* (June 7, 1993), Wang has said he fears being arrested at any time. And, he says, he will not leave China to study overseas for fear of becoming stateless (*Hong Kong Standard*, August 23, 1993).

Wang was sentenced on January 26, 1991 to four years in prison and one year's deprivation of political rights (UPI, January 26, 1991). His appeal was turned down (*Reuters*, April 17, 1991) and he was moved to Beijing Prison No.2, a "reform through labor" camp, at the end of July 1991 (*Beijing Review*, September 16-21, 1991). Wang said the worst of his imprisonment was a four-month period of solitary confinement which started on April 4, 1991.

Before his release, Wang shared a cell with five common criminals, the only prisoners with whom he was permitted contact. Two of his cellmates were assigned to watch him. Wang was not required to perform physical labor and was not permitted to take part in the activities organized for prisoners. He reportedly wrote essays on liberty during his spare time and did not

"admit guilt," although he did admit he broke Chinese law for which he accepted full responsibility. One report quoted a prison official as saying about Wang that it was not easy to "reform his ideology." Wang was permitted to write two letters a month and to receive a closely monitored monthly half-hour visit from family members. They were permitted to bring books written in Chinese, which had to be approved by a censor. From the time of his arrest until Chinese New Year 1990, no visits at all were permitted. Wang did exercise regularly; his diet consisted largely of cornbread and cabbage soup. Sometime in October 1991, he was permitted to buy at his own expense the official *Renmin Ribao*. Prior to that, the only newspaper he was permitted was *Beijing Ribao* (*Reuters*, November 5, 1991.) Wang also watched national news broadcasts. At his release, he said his health was "mediocre."

Wang, who went on trial on January 23, 1991 according to a notice posted outside the Beijing Intermediate People's Court, was charged with "counterrevolutionary propaganda and incitement" (*AP*, January 22, 1991.) The proceedings reportedly lasted only three hours; and Wang's parents were not notified of the date until the morning of the trial (*Washington Post*, January 27, 1991.) The *New York Times* (January 28, 1991) reported that Wang neither admitted "counterrevolutionary propaganda and incitement" nor did he say that the student movement had been a mistake. According to *Xinhua* (January 27, 1991), however, he "committed serious crimes but has shown repentance such as confessing his own crimes and exposing others." Wang's lawyer, from the Beijing No.1 Law Office, was selected for him by the government. She said she could defend Wang only on the basis that he was guilty.

Family friends reported that a notice of indictment had been sent by the Beijing Public Security Bureau to Wang's family, including his father, an assistant professor of geology at Beijing University, and his mother, a researcher at the Chinese Revolutionary History Museum, on November 23, 1990. They were informed that only family members would be permitted to attend his trial (UPI, December 5, 1990).

Wang, a native of Jilin Province and a history major at Beijing University, was arrested on July 2, 1989 after meeting a Taiwanese journalist to ask for help in fleeing China; his arrest was officially acknowledged in August 1989. As of mid-1990, he reportedly was held in solitary confinement in Qincheng Prison and was required to write confessional materials every day. At the time, he was permitted to write letters and friends were permitted to deliver clothes. One friend of Wang's reportedly received a postcard from him in early 1990 urging the recipient to "keep up the effort."

Before the crackdown, Wang studied recent political developments in Eastern Europe and wrote an article advocating similar reforms for China. In 1988-89, he was a key organizer of 17 open-air "democracy salons" during which those attending were urged to discuss controversial subjects. Officials

cited these as evidence that Wang agitated the unrest. They also accused him of doing the bidding of dissident astrophysicist Fang Lizhi (UPI, January 23, 1991). In the same dispatch, UPI reported on a May 1989 article by Wang:

We make no attempt to conceal the aim of the current student movement, which is to exert pressure on the government to promote the progress of democracy. People's yearning for democracy, science, human rights, freedom, reason, and equality, which lack a fundamental basis in China, have once again been aroused.

■ **WANG Du**, a 33-year-old non-conformist painter who spent nine months in prison, was released on June 19, 1990 in Guangdong Province. Arrested in Guangzhou on September 27, 1989, Du was charged on April 21, 1990 with engaging in "counter-revolutionary propaganda and incitement." He had spoken out at a demonstration in Guangzhou during the 1989 pro-democracy protests (*Agence France Presse*, April 27 and June 20, 1990, in FBIS, April 30 and June 20, 1990).

■ **WANG Jianxin**, deputy director of the Historical Preservation and Museum Science section of Northwest University in Xi'an, has been released, according to an official Chinese response to U.S. government requests for information (November 1991). He was arrested on campus sometime during the first half of September 1989. Wang, who helped organize a May 17,

1989 student protest demonstration in Xi'an, reportedly went into hiding in early June 1989. He allegedly had written an independent wall-poster account of the April 22 clash between Xi'an police and student demonstrators which blamed the police for the violence. He also wrote letters to Deng Xiaoping, Li Peng, Zhao Ziyang and the Supreme People's Court and Procuracy calling for a government investigation into the causes of the "April 22 Massacre" in Xi'an. Wang was held incommunicado until his release.

■ **WANG Jie**, detained in February or March 1990, was held briefly, then placed under surveillance for a year-and-a-half, and dismissed from his job at the Party Cadres School. He had been one of the staff at *Today*, an underground magazine in circulation during the Democracy Wall period. Wang is a Beijing resident.

■ **WANG Jisheng**, 22, a student at Yueyang Engineering Academy, Hunan Province, has been released from Longxi Prison (Provincial No.6). Arrested in July 1989, he was sentenced that November by the Yueyang City Intermediate People's Court to one year's imprisonment on a charge of "disrupting social order." During the 1989 pro-democracy movement, Wang allegedly organized the Yueyang Students Autonomous Federation and served on its Standing Committee. He reportedly organized student demonstrations and held a sit-in in front of the Yueyang City government offices.

■ **WANG Li**, formerly an economics student at Nanjing University, was arrested in February 1991, released that June and expelled from school. He had been accused of joining a "counter-revolutionary clique," the *United Democratic Front (Minzhu Lianhe Zhenxian)*. As of March 1993, Wang, born in 1970, was living in Nanjing but was unemployed.

■ **WANG Lian(g)ping, CHEN Shengzhi, XU Houqiang, LI Gang, ZHANG Yu, LIU Junguo, TAN Wenzhe** and **HUANG Guoqiang**, a group of Guangdong students who were detained in the aftermath of the pro-democracy crackdown, have been released, according to an Asia Watch source. Few details as to the dates of their detentions and releases or the putative charges against them are known. Liu, detained only briefly, escaped to Hong Kong. Wang, formerly a student at South China Normal University and a Standing Committee member of the Guangzhou Patriotic Students Association, who was accused of instigating "troubles," reportedly was treated leniently after repenting his actions (*Agence France Presse*, FBIS, June 29, 1990). However, he was expelled from college and went to teach in Hainan Province.

■ **WANG Luxiang**, 33, a prominent signatory of the "May 16 declaration" and co-author of the controversial television series, *River Elegy (He Shang)*, was never re-arrested, contrary to earlier reports. His only arrest came in June 1989 and he was released after being held more than a year. Wang, a native of Jiangsu Province, was a philosophy post-graduate at Beijing University. He had taught at Beijing Normal University before joining *Central Television* but upon his release was dismissed from his job.

River Elegy depicted China as subject to periodic political upheavals like the ebb and flow of the Yellow River, and it highlighted the differences between the "transparency" of democracy and the "opacity" of autocracy. The series' main author, Su Xiaokang, escaped from China in August 1989 and lives in the U.S.

■ **WANG Peigong**, a renowned playwright in his late forties, was convicted and released on March 8, 1991 (*Reuters*, March 10, 1991) after spending almost 21 months in isolation in Qincheng Prison. Arrested in Guiyang, probably on June 30, 1989, Wang was kept for three days at a detention center there, then moved to Paoju for one week, and finally to Qincheng. He reportedly was charged on June 7, 1990, with "counter-revolutionary activity and the harboring of student leader Wuerkaixi" (*Hong Kong Asia Television*, June 7, 1990 in FBIS, same date). Police allegedly discovered documents belonging to Wuerkaixi at Wang's Beijing home. Although Wang was never tried, a police report at his release said that investigation had established his guilt. He was exempted from prosecution because of his "good attitude" (*AP*, March 9, 1991).

Wang, who publicly renounced his membership in the Communist Party to show support for the democracy movement, wrote a play called *WM* about the Cultural Revolution. In it he described the ordeal of young urban men and women sent to the countryside to learn from the peasants. The work was banned in 1985 and according to a report in *Shijie Ribao* (February 27, 1991), the propaganda department had told all news media to continue to criticize *WM*.

■ **WANG Qing** - see p.88

■ **WANG Qing** - see p.88

■ **WANG Ruowang[1]**, the 74-year-old journalist, satirical essayist and veteran critic of the Chinese government, finally obtained a passport from the Chinese government and entered the U.S. in August 1992. Since his arrival, along with his wife **FENG Suying (YANG Zhi)**, he has continued to speak out about the Chinese government's repression of dissidents and the need to topple the present regime. He last went public when two close friends were arrested in China in March 1993, criticizing China's policy of continuing to detain less well-known activists while freeing famous ones, and in an open letter to the National People's Congress, he called for amnesty for all political and religious prisoners. Wang also urged legislators to remove constitutional clauses, such as the "four cardinal principles" and phrases such as "counterrevolutionary" and "proletarian dictatorship," which contradicted reform and opening to the outside (*South China Morning Post*, March 18, 1993). His request to attend the congress session as a "special guest" was turned down on the grounds that all guest seats had been allotted.

Although Wang and Feng were last detained by Public Security Bureau officials in 1991, once on September 16 for ten hours, and once on April 18 for thirty hours of interrogation (see Yang Zhou p.478), they were under constant surveillance up to the time they were permitted to start passport application procedures on May 27, 1992. Until then, despite his unexpected release without charge on October 29, 1990 after 16 months in incommunicado detention, Wang's case was still under investigation. He had been advised not to talk to foreign reporters or write for overseas publications. And he was prevented from accepting an appointment from Columbia University in New York. Petty harassment also continued. In April 1991, Wang's telephone line was disconnected, and he was one of three dissidents attacked in the official party newspaper as a "counter-culture advocate" (*Reuters*, May 5, 1991). Feng was also criticized for failing to keep her husband in line, a guarantee she made when he was released from prison.

The couple's April 18 detention probably was related to Wang's involvement in an underground publication in Shanghai promoting human rights and democracy and to a laudatory article he wrote mourning the death of **QIN Benli**, the crusading former editor of *Shijie Jingji Daobao (World Economic Herald)*, who died on April 15. (Just two weeks before Qin, 73, died in Shanghai's Huadong Hospital, he was officially censured and put on probation for two years by the Communist Party. The disciplinary action resulted from the role *Shijie*

Jingji Daobao and its staff played in the 1989 pro-democracy movement prior to the paper's enforced closure by order of then Shanghai party leader, Jiang Zemin. Qin was never arrested for his 1989 pro-democracy activities. Earlier, during the 1967-77 Cultural Revolution, he was sent to a farm for six years; during the 1957 "anti-rightist" campaign, he was purged.) In the article, Wang advocated clemency and an official party funeral for Qin (*South China Morning Post*, April 22, 1991). In addition, according to an article in a Hong Kong magazine, *The Nineties*, Wang secretly visited Qin in the hospital.

Wang went into hiding on June 14, 1989 but returned to Shanghai on July 18 to face his accusers. He was placed under house arrest on July 19; on September 8, 1989, he was incarcerated in a detention center in Shanghai and accused of "counter-revolutionary propaganda and incitement."

According to the *New York Times* (November 1, 1990), Chinese officials denounced Wang as "a representative of bourgeois liberalization" and accused him of helping to "inspire and spread the protests in Shanghai." On October 20, 1989, two articles sharply critical of Wang appeared in Shanghai's *Wen Wei Bao* and *Jiefang Ribao*. His activities during the pro-democracy movement were listed as listening to the *Voice of America* and spreading rumors based on its broadcasts; writing articles in support of the student hunger-strike and giving "counter-revolutionary" speeches in Shanghai's People's Square; publishing articles in the Hong Kong press; writing an open letter to Deng Xiaoping in late April 1989 expressing support for the student protestors; and participating in a demonstration march in May 1989 in support of the student movement. He also was castigated in the Shanghai press for having said of the movement: "I am very happy. It is a wonderful sight. The long-awaited day has finally arrived." A similar attack on Wang was published in *Renmin Ribao* in January 1990. Another attack, appearing in *Beijing Turmoil*, a 1990 government-sponsored publication, accused Wang of giving interviews to foreign reporters and wearing a sign which said "Save the country, save the people, save the students."

Wang was a member of the Communist Party from 1937 until early 1987, when, in the wake of the large-scale student demonstrations of the preceding winter, he was expelled along with dissident intellectuals Fang Lizhi and Liu Binyan. Reportedly, Deng Xiaoping personally ordered Wang's expulsion. Earlier, in 1957, Wang was branded a "rightist" and expelled from the Party for five years; for his activities during the Cultural Revolution, he was imprisoned for four years.

During Wang's stay in the U.S., he has had successful cataract surgery on both eyes.

- **WANG Shengli** - see p.5

- **WANG Wei[2]**, arrested on June 2, 1989 on charges of disturbing the social order, may be the same person as Wang Wei[1] (see p.419), who was listed

as released in an official Chinese response to U.S. government inquiries (November 1991). With **SUN Weibang** (see p.109), Wang took charge of the Beijing Students Autonomous Federation broadcasting station.

- **WANG Xiaoping**, an editor at the Worker's Publishing House, has been released, according to an official Chinese response to U.S. government inquiries (November 1991). He was arrested in mid-October 1989. No further information is available.

- **WANG Xing** (Xixing), a student from Harbin residing in Beijing, was released in 1991, according to an Asia Watch source. At his release, he reportedly was extremely ill with tuberculosis, but as of March 1993 was known to be working in the northeast. No other details about his current circumstances are available. In late May 1989, Wang was commander-in-chief at Tiananmen Square.

- **WANG Xuezhi[2]**, a former teacher at the South China University of Science and Engineering, arrested for participating in the pro-democracy movement, has been allowed to leave China in order to be re-united with his French wife (*Reuters*, June 25, 1990). According to *Shijie Ribao* (June 26, 1990), Wang was never charged, although the authorities accused him of having "plotted turmoil" in Guangzhou.

- **WANG Yan**, an associate of escaped political scientist Yan Jiaqi, arrested probably around July 4 or 5,

1989, reportedly was released from detention in December 1989.

■ **WANG Yang**[2], who drove the Taiwanese journalist, **HUANG Teh-pei** (Peter T.P. Huang), to a secret meeting with student leader Wang Dan (see p.459), was released after 45 days. He was arrested on July 2, 1989 by the State Security Bureau in Beijing, and according to his own post-release report, was beaten in detention. Wang, now in Australia, was detained in Changping County Detention Center.

■ **WANG Yong**[2] and **REN Hepeng** were released, according to an official Chinese response to requests for information by the U.S. government (November 1991). They had been arrested in early June 1989 for allegedly obstructing military vehicles, shouting "counterrevolutionaryslogans" and attacking soldiers on June 3-4 in Beijing (*Beijing Ribao*, June 15, 1989).

■ **WANG Yongfa**, a 38-year-old teacher at the No.1 Middle School in Lanshan County, Lingling Prefecture, Hunan Province, was finally released in February 1992. Arrested in October 1989, he was declared innocent at his trial in February 1990 and ordered freed. However, he was then administratively sentenced by the Lanshan County Public Security Bureau to two to three years' "re-education through labor." A university graduate, Wang had allegedly distributed handbills and organized street demonstrations by the students during the 1989 pro-democracy movement.

■ **WANG Yu**, a teacher in the Chinese department at Hunan University, was detained for two months after he called on his students to remember those who died and were injured in June 1989. Following his release, he was hospitalized with hepatitis.

■ **WANG Zhengyun**, one of the students on the Chinese government's June 1989 "21 Most Wanted" list, reportedly was arrested sometime during the week of July 10, 1989 in Yunnan Province (*Agence France Presse*). According to an official Chinese response to inquiries from the U.S. government (November 1991), he has been released. Wang, 21, a native of Yunnan and a student at the Central Institute of Nationalities in Beijing, is a member of an ethnic minority.

■ **WANG Zhihong** - see p.63

■ **WANG Zhihua**, a former graduate student in the Chinese department at Beijing Normal University, was released from detention in May 1990, according to an Asia Watch source. Expelled from school, he was returned to his home in Hangzhou, Zhejiang Province without a job assignment. Wang is probably the person marked as already arrested on a "most wanted" list issued by the Ministry of Public Security in September 1989.

■ **WANG Zhixin**, secretary general of the Beijing Students Autonomous Federation and No.12 on the Chinese government's list of "most wanted" students, was held for half a year and released without charge. An official Chinese response to U.S. government inquiries confirmed the release (November 1991). Wang, formerly a student at the University of Politics and Law, was arrested in March 1991 after alluding capture for more than a year and a half; he reportedly was charged with "counterrevolutionary propaganda and incitement." During his imprisonment in Qincheng Prison, Wang was in isolation.

■ **WANG Ziqiang**, in his late twenties, and **YANG Guansan**, a graduate of Beijing Economics Institute and Deputy Director of the Social Survey Department which conducted public opinion polls, were released, according to an official Chinese response to U.S. government inquiries (November 1991). Wang and Yang were among over ten members of the Research Institute for the Reform of the Economic Structure (RIRES), an institute associated with Zhao Ziyang, who were arrested after the June 4 crackdown and reportedly detained in Qincheng Prison. Members of RIRES, along with some staff members of the Rural Development Research Institute, were involved in late May 1989 in an important drive to convene an emergency session of the Standing Committee of the National People's Congress in an attempt to repeal martial law.

Yang, in his mid-thirties, was arrested on July 13, 1989. At the time, he was part of an international research project on "Perceptions of Justice in East and West" which was developing a common public opinion survey instrument on social justice. Yang's work at RIRES involved contacts with students interviewed there over a period of several years. Wang worked closely with Yang.

■ **WEI Daquan** - see p.234

■ **WEI Nan**, formerly a self-financed student in the construction department at Hunan University, was released in July 1990 after which he enrolled as a student at Changsha's Communications Academy. Expelled from Beijing University during the 1987 student movement, Wei became a leader of the Hunan University autonomous student union during the 1989 pro-democracy movement. He was arrested after June 4, held in Changsha No.1 Prison, released in December, then arrested again in April 1990.

■ **WEN Yuankai**, 46, a prominent biophysicist and reformist from the prestigious China University of Science and Technology in Hefei, Anhui Province, finally received approval from the Chinese government to take up a six-month fellowship at the California Institute of Technology's Molecular Bio-Technology Center (*South China Morning Post*, June 12, 1992). He first applied for permission in September 1991; on June 11, 1992, he submitted a formal request for a passport.

Before he left for the U.S., Wen, in a test case, sought guarantees that he would be allowed to return to China and, once home, would be permitted to pursue all his professional and business activities. Over 200 students wrote in support of his request to return to the university.

Wen also asked that three technical books he wrote be removed from the Central Committee's blacklist and that his positions in social and academic bodies be restored. He still may not teach, conduct research or advise graduate students. An attempt, attributed to Wen, to team up computer and pharmaceutical companies with university facilities to manufacture health and anti-aging products has been dissolved. An internal police document outlining the possibility that political dissidents might use private-venture profits to fund political opposition could be responsible for the rupture (*Reuters*, June 2, 1991). Wen does not have the personal funds with which to finance his own research.

Wen has contended that since he was never formally charged, there is no legal basis for the restrictions placed on his activities. Rather, he has said, the three publishers involved, the Science and Technology Presses of Anhui, Jiangxi and Guangxi, are afraid of the political stigma attached to publishing his works. One of the banned books, *On Computer-Aided Drug Molecular Design*, is considered a ground-breaking study. The university has agreed that Wen may teach when he returns to China, but, it argued, permission to retain a laboratory and to have graduate students, must be obtained from higher-level authorities.

Soon after his detention, in August 1989, Wen lost his official position as the Deputy Director of Anhui Province Education Committee and was then expelled from the Communist Party for "adhering to the stand of bourgeois liberalization and openly declaring opposition to the four cardinal principles" (*Ming Bao*, January 24, 1990, in FBIS, January 29, 1990). After June 1989, criticisms of his reformist ideas appeared in Communist Party documents and internal news reports at least 17 times, according to one of his friends. Chen Xitong, mayor of Beijing, explicitly criticized him on June 30, 1989 for his appeals to the government to recognize the pro-democracy movement as "patriotic." Wen also was expelled from the Anhui Society of Chemists and Chemical Engineers.

In his appearance at Tiananmen Square during the 1989 demonstrations, Wen tried to persuade the students to leave. But his activities pre-dated the pro-democracy movement. As the major mover of reform in the field of science and technology, he worked closely with another dissident intellectual, Yan Jiaqi, now in exile, to support Zhao Ziyang's economic reform campaign.

Before his release in December 1990 (*Shijie Ribao*, December 24, 1990), Wen spent 15 months incommunicado in the "reception center" of the local office of the People's Armed Police. And before that, the Anhui Provincial Public Security Bureau placed him under house arrest, detaining him at an unknown corner on campus, where he reportedly was engaged in "thorough self-censorship" (*Shijie Ribao*, December 10, 1990). He was not free to leave the campus, nor could he give lectures.

The China University of Science and Technology was the birthplace of the 1986-87 student protest movement. At that time, Fang Lizhi, China's leading dissident and Wen's close friend, was the university's chancellor. Wen himself had studied abroad but returned to China to devote himself to reform. His campaign speeches all over the country made him known among university students as a "youth mentor."

■ **WU Fangli**, 21, a student at Xiangtan University in Hunan Province, arrested in June 1989, was released at the end of the year. He had been head of the college's student propaganda section during the pro-democracy movement and allegedly led student demonstrations, gave speeches and went to factories to urge workers to strike. After June 4, Wu went to the Xiangtan Iron and Steel Plant and other large-scale local enterprises to provide accurate news about the massacre in Beijing and to call upon workers to stage a total strike.

■ **WU Gaoshen**, a teacher at Taizhou Commercial College in Zhejiang Province, was sentenced to a two-year term for organizing demonstrations and giving speeches in connection with the 1989 pro-democracy movement. Other than that he has been released, no additional information is available.

■ **WU Jiaxiang**, a 37-year-old economic researcher and poet from Anhui Province, was released the same day he was sentenced by the Beijing Intermediate People's Court to a three-year prison term. When he was finally tried in a brief hearing on August 25, 1992, he had already spent more than three years in detention and so was released on bail. He has to report to the Beijing police on a regular basis, however (*South China Morning Post*, August 26, 1992). Another report in South China Morning Post on January 29, 1993, said that he was offered a job as an economic researcher in a state-run company in Jinan, Shandong Province, but turned it down to stay in Beijing because his wife is employed there, and because of concerns for his daughter's education.

According to an Asia Watch source, during his prison stay at Qincheng, Wu displayed the initial signs of a mental breakdown, his overall health gradually deteriorated and he suffered from severe insomnia. Two weeks after his release, on September 5, Wu was taken to 301 Military Hospital unconscious from an overdose of sleeping pills. According to a family member, he was disoriented after his long incarceration, most of it in isolation, and needed the pills to help him sleep (*South China Morning Post*, September 9, 1992). Wu was permitted no visitors from July 1989 until January 1991. Before all visitation privileges were rescinded again in December 1991, permission had been granted for one or more supervised home visits of thirty minutes duration.

Wu was charged at the end of February 1991 with "counterrevolutionary incitement and propaganda," and his case transferred to the Beijing Municipal People's Procuratorate. Accused of drafting defamatory and slanderous speeches and slogans against Chinese leaders and the party during the 1989 pro-democracy movement, he was first detained for questioning on July 17, 1989 by the Beijing Public Security Bureau. In December 1990, he was discharged from his work unit and formally arrested.

From 1988 until the June 1989 crackdown, Wu was a member of the Research Office of the Communist Party's Central Committee. He was associated with ousted Party Secretary General Zhao Ziyang and his close advisor, Bao Tong. Holder of a masters degree in economics from Beijing University, Wu advocated the application to China of Samuel Huntington's "new authoritarianism" theory. This concept, which would have involved the creation of a structure for centralizing power in the hands of one person, was popular among certain reform-minded intellectuals prior to June 4, 1989.

Wu was not involved in the 1989 protests. He did, however, support the reforms and took a position against force. It has been reported that the reason for Wu's arrest was a letter he wrote to Deng Xiaoping asking him to step down.

Wu's wife, **Li Manying**, is an editor in the technical advice department at *Zhongguo Keji Bao (China Technology Daily)*. They have a seven-year-old daughter. Faced with Wu's high medical bills and the cancellation of his government pension, the family's livelihood is increasingly precarious.

■ **WU Rangyuan**, 46, formerly a research fellow at the Chinese Academy of Social Sciences, Institute of Semiconductivity, was released sometime before August 22, 1990 (Amnesty International, *ASA 17/93/90*). She was arrested on June 9, 1989 for allegedly spreading rumors and instigating people to burn vehicles in Beijing in early June 1989 (*Beijing Ribao*, June 17, 1989).

■ **WU Wei**[1], a writer and assistant to Bao Tong (see p.61), was detained for several weeks around June 4, 1989, then released, according to an Asia Watch source.

■ **WU Xiaoyong**, the producer and allegedly the scriptwriter of an unauthorized radio program which announced on June 4, 1989 that thousands had been killed in the military crackdown in Beijing and that the event was "a gross violation of human rights and the most barbarous suppression of the people," reportedly was secretly tried and sentenced to 12 years' imprisonment (*China Daily News*, July 14, 1989; *Shijie Ribao*, August 19, 1989; Amnesty International, July 1990). Although the sentencing was unconfirmed, it is known that Wu was quietly released from Qincheng Prison, probably in mid-September in the custody of his father, State Council Vice Premier Wu Xueqian, for treatment of a chronic stomach ailment (*Hong Kong Standard*, October 18, 1990, in FBIS, same day). A former University of Missouri student, Wu Xiaoyong was suspended from his job on June 5, 1989, and arrested at the end of August (*Zhengming*, March 1990). He had been Deputy Director of the English language service at Radio Beijing.

■ **WU Xuecan**, 42-year-old former senior editor and journalist at *People's Daily Overseas Edition*, was released on September 17, 1993, three months before his four-year sentence was due to expire. The conditions attached to his release are not known. At the time, in July, when Chinese officials made the decision for early release, Wu was so notified but given no reason. "Perhaps I am useful to them," he said when he returned to his Beijing home. In addition to his health problems including severe digestive ailments and failing eyesight, Wu left prison jobless, having been fired from *Renmin Ribao*. He said he had no idea what he would do, but did know the profession of journalism was closed to him because of his "political unreliability." Nevertheless, Wu, who also lost his party membership, maintained that his actions during the 1989 pro-democracy movement in Beijing were legal.

Formally indicted on December 3, 1991, Wu went on trial December 28, 1991 on a charge of "counter-revolutionary agitation and propaganda" for encouraging liberal ideas and splitting the party. He was not sentenced by the Beijing People's Intermediate People's Court until February 25, 1992. Originally held in Qincheng Prison, Wu was then transferred to Beijing No.2 Prison. He did no regular labor, but on occasion, in his cell, he was given a large bag of garments sewn by other prisoners. His job was to remove the stray threads, his weak eyesight making it impossible for him to continue to make buttonholes as he did when he first arrived at No.2 Prison.

Wu had been arrested in December 1989 when he was spotted at a pier in Sanya city, Hainan Province. His July 6 wanted notice instructed "public security bureaus at all levels to immediately search for and apprehend" him and "upon discovery" to take him in for "shelter and investigation." Wu's main crime, according to the notice, was to publish an unauthorized "special issue" *(hao wai)* of *Renmin Ribao* on May 19. In that edition, Wu discussed the disagreements between top Party officials and called for the dismissal of Li Peng. **SONG Bin** and **ZHANG Shuxian**, two reporters arrested in connection with the "special issue," were released on bail in 1991. Wu also led the Beijing demonstration by *Renmin Ribao* journalists and in late May 1989, during three days when censorship was relaxed, wrote freely of the major events occurring in China.

Considered politically reliable during the Cultural Revolution, Wu was plucked from the navy and sent to Zhongshan University as a "worker, peasant, soldier student." After graduation in 1976 and before his employment at *Renmin Ribao*, Wu worked at the People's Press. He is a native of Binhai County in Jiangsu Province.

■ **WU Yunxue**, a sophomore in

applied physics at Beijing University, has been released, according to an official Chinese response to inquiries by the U.S. government (November 1991). He reportedly was detained prior to October 1989 for his work on the communications staff of the Beijing University Autonomous Student Union (Amnesty International, *ASA 17/24/90*).

■ **XIA Ming** and **YANG Jun** - see p.360

■ **XIANG Hong**, a cadre in the Communist Youth League's Municipal Committee in Chongqing, Sichuan Province, was arrested in connection with pro-democracy events. Other than that he was subsequently released, no information is available.

■ **XIAO Feng**[2], 55, formerly general manager of the Hunan Province General Import-Export Corporation, was released on bail in 1990 for medical treatment. After June 4, 1989, he was accused of having "donated company funds to the students" during the pro-democracy movement and of subsequently helping the students to conceal the money. Xiao was suspended from work and placed under investigation, then arrested in early 1990.

■ **XIAO Xuehui** was released in February 1991 and sentenced to two years' deprivation of political rights. The 43-year-old author, a lecturer in the philosophy department at Southwestern Nationalities University in Chengdu and a leading member of the Sichuan Association of Ethical Studies, has not been permitted to continue teaching. Xiao was arrested in 1989 for her alleged role in leading student protests in Chengdu and charged with "counterrevolutionary propaganda and incitement." According to *Jiushi Niandai* (April 1990), she was detained in Xindu, where repeated beatings worsened her already serious liver and kidney problems.

■ **XIAO Yong** - see p.79

■ **XIAO Yuan**, arrested on July 12, 1989 in connection with concealing Wang Juntao (sentenced in January 1991 to 13 years in prison as a "black hand" dissident) during his attempted escape from China, was released around July 7, 1992 after serving a three-year term (*South China Morning Post*, July 14, 1992). As of March 1993, he was working in a company in Beihai, Guangxi Province. Xiao served his sentence at a labor reform factory in Wuhan. His sentencing was first revealed in the verdict against others involved in the case (see: Chen Zhiyang p.137, Jiang Guolian p.424 Liu Danhong p.434, Liu Hanyi p.436 and Wu Litang p.551) and confirmed by an official Chinese response to inquiries by the U.S. government (November 1991). Xiao, a 40-year-old native of Chengdu, Sichuan Province and a member of the Science and Technology Institute of the Central China Teachers University, Wuhan, for which he ran a company, was formally charged in September 1989 and indicted in January 1990 for "concealing a wanted criminal."

■ **XIE Changfa**, a 35-year-old cadre who worked in succession at the Changsha (Hunan Province) Steel Factory, the Changsha city government, and as a township head in Liuyang County, Hunan, has been released. He was arrested in July 1989 and held in Changsha No.1 Prison, Cell 13, then administratively sentenced in early 1990 to two years' "re-education through labor." During the 1989 pro-democracy movement, Xie allegedly gave speeches in Liuyang, Ningxiang, Wangcheng, Changsha and other places. One speech that he delivered in Liuyang County allegedly had a "particularly bad influence."

■ **XIE Xuanjun**, a co-author of *River Elegy* who turned himself in to the authorities after his name appeared on a "most wanted" list shortly after the June 4 crackdown, reportedly was released in February or March 1990. He had remained in the capital after the crackdown because of his wife's advanced pregnancy. Prior to June 1989, Xie and Wang Luxiang (see p.462) travelled throughout China making speeches critical of the political system.

■ **XIE Zhenrong** (TSE Chun-wing), arrested in Guangzhou in July 1989 after a failed attempt to help student leader **ZHENG Xuguang** (see p.31, 445) escape, was released from Guangzhou No. 1 Detention Center on September 27, 1990. Xie allegedly was involved in the "underground railroad," a Hong Kong-based network which secretly helped over 100 pro-democracy activists escape from China.

■ **XIN Zuoliang**, formerly a student at South China Engineering College, was released after being held for nine months in connection with 1989 pro-democracy activities. As of May 1993, he was unable to find work.

■ **XIONG Wei**, a 24-year-old student at Qinghua University's department of radio and No.20 on the "21 most wanted" list, was one of the 97 prisoners whose release was announced on June 6, 1990. Xiong, in the company of his mother, turned himself in on June 14, 1989. The next day, national television showed him being questioned by police. Xiong, a native of Yincheng, Hubei Province, reportedly had coordinated the medical teams helping those who, from May 13 to May 19, 1989, staged the hunger strike in Tiananmen Square. He also was involved in an attempt to send an appeal from hunger strikers to the United Nations and to the Red Cross. Xiong was probably detained in Qincheng Prison.

■ **XIONG Wenzhao**, a teacher of constitutional law at the Central Minorities Institute's Department of Law, was released with 96 others on June 12, 1990, according to an Asia Watch source. He was never charged nor was any reason for his detention given. A condition of his release was that he participate regularly in a study group organized to help him realize his errors. Xiong, born in 1959, was permitted to return to the college but was forbidden to write or publish. He has been informed that he will not be promoted nor can he expect to improve his housing situation, one room. During Xiong's detention, family members were permitted to collect his salary. Later he received a 60 percent pay cut to compensate for his prison expenses. For awhile he received no salary, then 60 percent was restored. Although Xiong's wife is employed in another department at the Central Minorities Institute, his parents have had to help financially. In addition, Xiong was dismissed from the Chinese Communist Party

Xiong was detained on August 24, 1989, approximately one week after his wife gave birth. This was after being assured by his work unit that he would not be punished. After his arrest, his apartment was searched and letters from friends overseas and a letter to a foreign friend describing June 4 were seized. During Xiong's detention in Banbuqiao, his family received at least one letter from him but were not permitted to visit or send clothing.

Xiong completed B.A. and M.A. degrees at the University of Politics and Law in 1985 and 1987. He helped to organize a Teachers Support Group there, gave lectures on the constitution and freedom, supported the students and actively discussed politics and freedom.

■ **XIONG Yan**, 29, a political science graduate of Hunan Normal University and a post-graduate law student at Beijing University prior to his dismissal, was released without trial on January 26, 1991 (*AP*, January 26,

1991). Stripped of all academic degrees, denied identification papers and too seriously ill with kidney disease to work, he and his wife lived on her small earnings until Xiong fled China on June 5, 1992. At that time, the Chinese government had begun a sweep of underground dissident groups, one of which Xiong had founded to pressure the government for political reform. His wife (see Qian Liyun p.60), arrested in September 1992 in connection with Shen Tong's (see p.452) attempts to form a Beijing Branch of his Boston-based *Democracy for China Fund*, was freed after two months. Xiong has been granted political asylum in the U.S.

A Beijing Students Autonomous Federation member and No. 21 on the government's 21 "most wanted" student list, Xiong was seized on a train at the Fengzhen station in Inner Mongolia on June 13, 1989. According to the *South China Morning Post* (June 15, 1989), he was one of a number of student leaders who met with Premier Li Peng on May 18, 1989. At that meeting, Xiong was quoted as saying, "We believe, no matter whether the government does or not, that history will recognize this movement as a patriotic and democratic movement....The people want to see whether the government is really a people's government or not." A native of Shuangfeng, Hunan Province, Xiong was held with other political offenders in Qincheng Prison. According to the *1990 Datong Yearbook*, Xiong's name was also placed on a special "most wanted" list issued by the Ministry of State Security shortly after June 4,

1989.

- **XU Qinxian**, head of the Beijing-based 38th Group Army, reportedly was released in June or July 1990 and forced to retire from the military without a pension. He reportedly was court-martialled and given a "stiff sentence" in autumn 1989 for failing to enforce martial law (*South China Morning Post*, December 28, 1989, in FBIS, same day). According to a report in *Shijie Ribao* (July 25, 1990), the decision was made by Deng Xiaoping for political reasons related to restructuring of the military leadership. Xu, reportedly the son of the late vice-minister of defense, Xu Guangda, was said to have checked into a hospital soon after the declaration of martial law on May 20, 1989, claiming that he could not carry out orders to suppress demonstrators (FBIS, January 19, 1990). According to Yang Baibing, then Chief Political Commissar of the PLA another 110 officers and 1400 enlisted men also refused to take orders or left their posts during the People's Liberation Army crackdown (*South China Morning Post*, December 28, 1989).

- **XU Quan**, formerly a student at Qufu Normal College in Shandong Province, was detained for more than a year in connection with the 1989 pro-democracy movement. No further information is available.

- **XU Xiaowei**, 33, former deputy secretary-general at *Shijie Jingji Daobao (World Economic Herald)*, and head of the newspaper's Guangzhou office, was released (*Reuters*, September 25, 1990) after being held incommunicado at Shanghai No.1 Detention Center for more than a year. Detained on June 30, 1989, he was officially arrested on charges of "counterrevolutionary propaganda and incitement" on December 20. According to an August 15, 1990 People's Procuracy, Shanghai Branch, Decision Not to Prosecute, Xu, a college graduate from Wuxi City, Jiangsu Province, "on the evening of May 21, 1989...in order to prepare the content of the slogans for the march on the following day to be held by *Shijie Jingji Daobao*, telephoned the paper's Beijing office reporter, Zhang Weiguo. Zhang told Xu four reactionary slogans and then he told them to Qiu Xiaoping. Also on the next morning he asked a worker at the paper, Wang Peipeng, to write the four reactionary slogans on banners." The document added that although Xu's actions violated the law, they did not constitute the crime of "counterrevolutionary propaganda."

- **XU Yiruo**, a former political prisoner, left China in the summer of 1993 and now lives in a Western country. A Qingdao, Shandong Province native and an ardent Catholic, he was first arrested in Qingdao after the crackdown in Beijing and held for seven weeks for his role as deputy head of Qingdao University's Student Autonomous Federation. During the 1989 pro-democracy movement, Xu, then a freshman in the Chinese language department, traveled to Beijing to support the student hunger strikers. While there, he joined the

Autonomous Federation of Students from Outside Beijing. After his release, although on probation, Xu was permitted to return to the university. In March 1991, when the former head of the Qingdao University student association was arrested, Xu stowed away to Hong Kong, but was repatriated after 15 days. He was sent to a prison farm for a brief period, then returned to Qingdao just prior to the second anniversary of the Tiananmen Square crackdown.

On June 4, 1991, Xu put up two small posters on campus. One started with a poem: *It is two years since that bloody June Fourth. Today I stand back and my heart shrivels.* Arrested four days later, after police checked the handwriting of all Qingdao University students, he was interrogated and confined under house arrest. Managing to escape, Xu fled to Beijing. From there, he called human rights groups in Hong Kong and London, but after one such phone call, stepped out of the phone booth into the arms of waiting police officers (*New York Times*, July 19, 1993. The rights group, although identified by NYT as Asia Watch, was actually Amnesty International). Sent back to Shandong, Xu spent four months in Qingdao No.1 Prison in a cell 8 feet by 10 feet which he shared with 11 "common" criminals. They all worked making Christmas lights for export, sometimes for 20 hours a day. Beatings were common. After three months, in October 1991, Xu was sentenced administratively to two year's "re-education through labor" on a charge of writing reactionary articles. Sent to Shandong No.1 Re-education

through Labor camp, he worked a daily 12-hour shift in Zibo mine, with one Sunday off every two weeks.

Xu, born August 5, 1969, was released in February 1993, five months before his sentence was due to expire. Prohibited from returning to the university, prevented from finding work and with the Public Security Bureau and his neighborhood street committee monitoring all his activities, Xu again fled the country and gained political asylum.

■ **XUN Mingjun** - see p.88

■ **YAN(G) Jinchao, YANG Hongzhe, CHEN Menghui** and three workers (see Zhang Zhiyong[2]), all from Ningxia Hui Autonomous Region, have been released. "After investigation and education, they acknowledged their criminal behavior during the period of turmoil and demonstrated their repentance" (*Reuters*, January 3, 1991, from *Ningxia Ribao* reaching Beijing same day); the Yinchuan People's Court and the Yinchuan Public Security Bureau thus decided to be lenient. According to police officials in the regional capital of Yinchuan who announced the releases, as of January 1991 no one arrested in connection with the pro-democracy protests was detained there. Yang Jinchao's release was confirmed by an official Chinese response to U.S. government inquiries (November 1991).

Yang Jinchao, 21, a Ningxia University student, and Chen Menghui and Yang Hongzhe, students at Ningxia Teachers College, were arrested on July 21, 1989 in Yinchuan City,

Ningxia for "counterrevolutionary incitement." Chen, 21, and Yang Hongzhe, 21, were accused of writing articles and wallposters "wickedly slandering the Communist Party." Yang Jinchao, who apparently returned to Ningxia from Beijing on June 4, 1989, was accused of spreading "false" rumors about the Beijing military crackdown in Ningxia (*Ningxia Ribao*, July 28, 1989, in *Ming Bao*, August 2, 1989) and, on the basis of *Voice of America* broadcasts and other foreign media reports, about the imposition of martial law in Beijing. He also was accused of forming an illegal students' union on June 5, 1989 and of inciting students to boycott exams and classes. On June 6 in Yinchuan, he allegedly led an "anti-government demonstration of more than 20,000 persons."

■ **YANG Baikui**, 30, an associate of wanted political scientist Yan Jiaqi (who escaped from China through Hong Kong in the summer of 1989, was released on May 10, 1990. Yang was arrested, probably around July 4 or 5, 1989, for allegedly advising student leaders during the pro-democracy protests and for signing one of the petitions addressed to the government during that time. For such activities, he was fired from his job as a researcher at the Institute of Political Science in the Chinese Academy of Social Sciences. Yang is an administrative law specialist who studied at Beijing University in the late 1970s and early 1980s.

■ **YANG Chang**, a 24-year-old resident of Guangzhou, Guangdong Province, and formerly a student at Jinan University, was released in mid-1990. During the 1989 pro-democracy movement, he allegedly carried out liaison activities between the students autonomous associations of various colleges and universities in the interior of China, including those in Changsha, Hunan Province. After June 4, Yang helped student activists escape arrest and go into hiding. He himself was arrested in August 1989 and held first in Guangzhou and then in Changsha.

■ **YANG Jun** - see p.360

■ **YANG Lang**, vice-director of the reporters' section of *Zhongguo Qingnian Bao*, has been released, according to information supplied by an Asia Watch source in June 1990. Alleged to have led the United Association of Capital (i.e., Beijing) Intellectuals and to have been a key organizer in rallying support for the student movement, Yang was arrested sometime before October 1989 (*Zhengming*, October 1989).

■ **YANG Lujun**, a researcher at the Asian Institute of the Shanghai Academy of Social Sciences, was one of the 97 reportedly released on June 6, 1990. He had been arrested in August 1989 and held incommunicado in Shanghai No.1 Detention Center. Yang allegedly was actively involved in the democracy movement and visited Hong Kong in May 1989 where he signed a protest petition.

■ **YANG Tao**[2], a history major at

Beijing University and one of the 21 "most wanted" student leaders, was quietly released sometime in August 1990, according to students and teachers at the university (*Reuters*, September 12, 1990). However, official spokespersons at the State Education Department and at his school denied knowledge of his release. The 19-year-old Yang, who was held for 13 months in Qincheng Prison, reportedly was expelled from school and barred from entering any Chinese university. He was banished to his home town of Fuzhou, the capital of Fujian Province, where he experienced difficulty finding work. Yang, who was head of Beijing University's Autonomous Student Union, was labeled an "instigator of the counterrevolutionary rebellion" at the time of his arrest in Lanzhou, Gansu Province on June 17, 1989. He was further accused of "advocating bourgeois liberalization" and of "wantonly attacking Marxism."

■ **YANG Wei**[1], 36, was released in Shanghai on February 12, 1991. According to a Shanghai Foreign Affairs official (*AP* February 14, 1991), he showed "understanding of his crimes." Arrested on July 18, 1989 in Shanghai, Yang allegedly incited students and made reports to a "counterrevolutionary organization" (*Reuters*, February 12, 1991). A Sichuan native, he had been a graduate student in molecular biology at the University of Arizona but left the United States in late 1986 for China and was arrested in January 1987 for his alleged role in the December 1986 student demonstrations. At the same

time, he was accused of involvement in the U.S. based organization, *Chinese Alliance for Democracy*, which publishes the journal *China Spring*. Sentenced to two years in prison, Yang was released in January 1989. His political rights had been suspended for an additional year, however, and he was unable to return to the United States to continue his studies. In connection with his second arrest, the government news agency, *Xinhua*, claimed on July 18, 1989 that Yang refused to "show penitence" after his release and continued to make speeches and incite students to oppose the government. Yang is now in the United States.

■ **YANG Zhou**, a veteran dissident and co-organizer of the Shanghai-based *China Study Group on Human Rights,* was taken into custody for questioning along with another activist, **Qin Yongmin** (see p.7). on November 14, 1993 after taking part in a dissident meeting in Beijing to discuss a "Peace Charter" promoting non-violent political reform in China. Both men were initially held at Beijing's Paoju Lane Detention Center, then transferred to police holding centers in their home towns. In early January 1993, Yang was freed, but Qin remained in detention in Wuhan.

Yang has been jailed for dissident activities several times before. He first served a three-year prison term from 1979 to 1981, after attempting to set up a human rights organization during the Democracy Wall period (*Ming Bao*, in *Shijie Ribao*, June 4, 1991; see also **Yang Qinheng** *et al*, p.50). On April

18, 1991, he was seized along with another dissident, Gu Bin (see p.417) by the Public Security Bureau and held for "shelter and investigation" at Shanghai No.1 Detention Center for over a year. Ten other members of the Shanghai rights group were also detained at that time. In addition to being charged as a ringleader, Yang, in his fifties, was accused of sending a registered letter in July 1990 to Party leader Jiang Zemin appealing for an amnesty for all political prisoners, a genuine multi-party system and true freedom of expression as guaranteed by the Chinese constitution. The letter was privately circulated by group members; however, plans to distribute a regular newsletter *Luntan (Forum)*, a compilation of human rights articles culled from the Hong Kong press, never materialized. After the government intercepted the letter, the group's equipment and mailing list were confiscated, together with Yang's notebooks, articles and poetry.

On February 28, 1992, Yang's wife, **Li Guoping**, a practicing lawyer for five years, had her lawyer's license revoked and confiscated by the Shanghai Judicial Department for her activities on her husband's behalf. She appealed to the Ministry of Justice for a review, and when on May 14 the ministry upheld the original decision, she initiated legal action via the Shanghai Intermediate People's Court. The suit was accepted, but according to an Asia Watch source, Li was later disbarred for life. After her husband's detention, Li had written herself a letter of introduction from the Nanpu Law Firm, where she worked, to the Public

Security Bureau's Political Security Unit, in an effort to find out about her husband's situation; she also wrote an article for a Hong Kong newspaper on his case. When finally granted an interview with Yang, she informed the authorities that she was a family member, but they then revoked her license, saying that publishing abroad and "using deceit" to visit a PSB organ was a "serious matter."

■ **YAO Junling**, a student at Beijing Physical Education College charged with "counterrevolutionary sabotage" (see Guo Haifeng p.418), was sentenced to two years in prison and one year's deprivation of political rights on January 26, 1991 by the Beijing Intermediate People's Court (*New York Times*, January 27, 1991). An official Chinese response to U.S. government inquiries confirmed that he had been sentenced (November 1991). After his release, Yan was unable to find work.

■ **YAO Wei**, a student at Hunan University, was released without criminal prosecution after being detained for three months. In May 1989, Yao took part in a "lie-in" on the railway tracks at Changsha Station organized to demonstrate opposition to the government (see Zhong Hua p.554).

■ **YAO Yongzhan** (also known as **ZHANG Cai**; in Cantonese, **YIU Yung-Chin**), 21, was released on June 5, 1990. A leader of the Shanghai Students Autonomous Federation, Yao was arrested on June 11, 1989 as he was about to depart from Shanghai Airport on a flight to Hong Kong. He was held for most of his time in custody at Shanghai No.1 Detention Center. At a press conference following his return to Hong Kong, Yao condemned the military crackdown in China and called for the immediate release of all political prisoners. He acknowledged his part in organizing mass protests in Shanghai and his leading role in the outlawed Shanghai Students Autonomous Federation. He also commented on the deleterious effect prison conditions had on his health. Yao, attributing his freedom to changes in the international situation, said that contrary to official statements that "all released dissidents had pleaded guilty, voluntarily confessed their wrongdoing and expressed a willingness to repent," he had neither confessed nor repented while in jail (*South China Morning Post*, June 8, 1990). Yao had been under investigation for violating local laws, including "carrying banned material." He was charged with "counter-revolutionary propaganda activities aimed at inciting the public" and was originally expected to stand trial as a Chinese national. Yao is now in the United States.

■ **YE Maoqiang**, a leading member of the Shanghai Students Autonomous Federation and a lecturer at the Fudan University Center of Culture and Media Studies, was released on August 15, 1990 (Amnesty International, *ASA 17/73/90*). Chinese officials, in a response to inquiries by the U.S. government, confirmed his status

(November 1991). Considered by many the most influential leader of the democracy movement in Shanghai, Ye organized an intellectual group, *Seven Gentlemen of Fudan (Fudan Qi Junzi)*, to prepare the groundwork for the 1989 pro-democracy movement there. He was arrested on July 21, 1989.

■ **YE Wenfu**, a poet and army officer, was released during the last week in December 1989, according to a January 8, 1990 *AP* report. An official at the Coal Mining Management College where Ye worked, confirmed the account. During the pro-democracy movement, Ye, who was arrested some time in July 1989, joined student demonstrators in Tiananmen Square. On May 18, 1989 he dedicated a poem, "Bitter Love," to the protestors, then announced his intention of resigning from the Communist Party. He also signed the May 16, 1989 declaration issued by the Beijing Union of Intellectuals calling on the government to accept student demands.

Ye was born in Hubei Province in 1944 and joined the PLA when he was 20. Four years later, he started writing poetry and had his first works published in *PLA News* and *PLA Literature*. In 1978, Ye's first book of poems, *The Love of Mountains*, was published. In 1980, he won the Award for an Outstanding Modern Poem by a Chinese Poet; and in 1981 he published "General You Shouldn't Do That," a long poem depicting corruption and malpractice within upper levels of the military. In response, 25 generals requested his sacking. Ye was imprisoned briefly in 1983 during the Anti-Bourgeois Pollution Campaign; in 1986 he was forced to resign from the army.

■ **YI Danxuan**, a student at Guangdong Province Commercial Institute in Guangzhou and a member of the Guangzhou Students Autonomous Federation, was released on August 6, 1991 after serving two years of a three-year sentence on charges of "counterrevolutionary sabotage." Arrested in Guangzhou in July 1989, Yi allegedly led a blockade of the city's main bridges after the news of the June 3-4 crackdown in Beijing reached Guangzhou. He also was accused of aiding a Beijing student leader, **ZHENG Xuguang** (see p.31, 445), in an attempted escape (*AP*, August 13, 1991). An official Chinese response to U.S. government requests for information about Yi confirmed that he had been sentenced (November 1991). According to an Asia Watch source, Yi was in poor health and did not receive proper medical attention during his prison term. His present medical condition is unknown.

■ **YI Gai**, formerly a student in the music department at Hunan Normal University, was released in March 1990 and has had trouble finding work. Arrested after June 4, 1989, he was held in Changsha No.1 Prison for eight months. During the 1989 pro-democracy movement, Yi served as head of the Hunan Students Autonomous Federation Liaison Department with responsibility for

liaison work between the autonomous student unions of the various schools. He also wrote a "Report of an Investigation into the Hunan Student Movement" [*Hunan xueyun kaocha baogao*], deliberately mimicking the title of Mao's famous "Report of an Investigation into the Hunan Peasant Movement." Yi had been jailed for political reasons once before, also for eight months. While he was serving in the army, a military court ordered his incarceration.

■ **YIN Jin**, the 34-year-old former head of the Shanxi bureau of *Hainan Jingji Bao* arrested in July 1989 and sentenced without trial to three years' "labor re-education," escaped to Taiwan in July or August 1993. As of January 1994, he was still being held in the Xinzhu Processing Center for Mainland People. Released in January 1992 after serving more than thirteen months in a detention center and eighteen months at a labor-reform farm, Yin escaped to Hong Kong in May 1992, but after only a few days, he was returned to China. According to the decision of the Taiyuan Labor Re-education Administrative Committee (dated July 23, 1990):

[Yin] participated and supported rigorous activities...produced and distributed flyers...[and] instigated riots. He ordered others to organize illegal gatherings...gave inciting speeches...encouraged students to go on hunger strikes and instigated the press to support the students....After he was detained, his attitude was rude. He insisted on his counterrevolutionary

principles. He continued to attack important members of the party and the country.

According to other accounts, Yin wrote articles and petitions in support of press freedom and in support of the striking students in Beijing. His greatest offense was to read a letter addressed to the National People's Congress in the main square in Taiyuan. The letter, reportedly written in blood, demanded that Li Peng be fired. Yin suffered severely in prison. According to his own account:

The prison conditions were absolutely inhumane. I was locked up without fresh air or sunlight, and not even given enough time to go to the bathroom. Physical abuses in Chinese prisons are routine. I was severely beaten, handcuffed, shackled to an iron-weight over a hundred pounds, and thrown into a cold, wet and dark cell. This mistreatment caused permanent damage to my nerve system, complete decay of my teeth and [temporary] paralysis from the waist down. And the worst of all, they took away my dignity.

Yin still has bouts of severe pain and cannot afford medical treatment; and beatings by the Taiwan police reportedly have exacerbated his prison-induced injuries. According to Yin, one of the beatings came at the hands of the head of the detention center, who used a club to beat Yao's waist and buttocks and was joined by other officials and guards when Yin refused to lie down with his head against the wall. The

incident, on September 22, 1989, started after a television crew, invited to do a story on the humane treatment of prisoners who were to be executed the following day, left. The condemned men, angry when the "fantastic" meal, ostensibly prepared for them, was denied them, protested through singing. Others joined in and the beating began.

While in prison, Yin brought legal action in the Taiyuan Intermediate People's Court against the Municipal Public Security Bureau (PSB) for illegally ordering his arrest - a wanted notice had been issued without the requisite approval - and illegally holding him without trial for 13 months. He also brought suit in the Taiyuan Municipality People's Procuratorate against the head and deputy head of the PSB detention center and the director of the PSB's Fifth Division for violating his democratic rights and his person and for dereliction of duty.

In April 1993, Yin attempted to sue a senior Party official for slander and for abusing his power (*Agence France Presse*, April 9, 1993, in FBIS, same day). The official had called Yin a "hooligan" and the "dregs of society" for taking part in the 1989 pro-democracy movement. When the Shanxi Provincial Higher People's Court refused to accept the suit, Yin applied to demonstrate in Taiyuan, the provincial capital of Shanxi, so as to publicize his grievance. He said he was left without the means to support himself, his mother, wife and small daughter because his status as a political prisoner prevented any publication from hiring him. In the summer of 1992, Yin peddled ice popsicles on the street but was often chased away by law-enforcement officials on the pretexts of security and sanitation. He has appealed to the U.N. for financial help. (See also **Guo Chengdong** *et al,* p.?.)

■ **YU Fangqiang** (Fangqing), a student at Beijing Science and Engineering University and a "major participant" in the pro-democracy movement, was arrested in his native city of Xintai, Shandong Province on June 17, 1989 (*Shandong Provincial Radio*, June 22, 1989, in FBIS, June 23). According to an official Chinese response to U.S. government inquiries (November 1991), there is a "**YU Wangqiang**" who was released. This may be a reference to Yu Fangqiang.

■ According to an Asia Watch source, **YU Guolu**, a 33-year-old member of the Research Institute for Economic, Technological and Social Development, a division of the Sociology and Economics Research Institute, has been released. Yu was briefly detained in June 1989 and then re-arrested later in 1989 in Beijing, following the arrest of his brother-in-law, Chen Ziming (sentenced to a 13-year term as a "black hand.") Yu and his wife, **CHEN Zhihua**, a former employee at the same institute, who was detained briefly, have lost their jobs and have no steady source of income. They have one child.

■ **YU Haocheng**, a 65-year-old legal scholar and former director of the China Legal System and

Social-Development Research Institute, was freed sometime in late December 1990 (*AP*, January 8, 1991). He is at home in Beijing but reportedly is suffering from heart disease and gallstones. Yu's repeated applications for a passport so he might accept invitations from abroad have all been turned down, most recently in fall 1993 (see p.54). He reportedly is considered a security risk because of his previous work as director of the Public Security Department's Masses (Qunzhong) Publishing House. Yu has not worked there since 1987. He was fired during the Anti-Bourgeois Liberalization campaign for allegedly publishing "questionable" books and advocating political and legal reforms. Despite his "retirement," essentially forced, Yu has been demoted, which means minimally a decrease in his pension and the loss of his telephone.

In addition, Yu has been subject to petty harassments, such as having his name removed from a *Who's Who of Social Scientists in China* and being prohibited from delivering papers at academic conferences. The Chinese Law Society and the Chinese Society of Political Science canceled his memberships. He was unable to publish under his own name. When he finally did, in December 1992, for the magazine *Future and Development*, the magazine was shut down. In his article, Yu accused "a few leading cadres" of fearing democracy and warned that failure to liberalize could threaten the party's monopoly of power. Some of Yu's confiscated manuscripts have yet to be returned to him. Despite the harassment, Yu has continued to speak out. In an article in June 1993, he said China has no freedom of thought because of the ideology imposed on the legal system. Listing rights supposedly protected by the constitution, Yu went on to allege that they were all routinely violated because legislation which would protect them was lacking.

The Public Security Bureau arrested Yu on June 27, 1989 and took him away in handcuffs from his home in Beijing. He was held at the Ministry of State Security's "reception center" at Shunyi, near Beijing. *Shijie Ribao* (January 17, 1991) reported he was confined to one room and a Public Security Bureau guard was with him at all times. Yu's family was permitted to visit; toward the end of his detention, family members could bring food and reading matter other than the official journals *Hongqi (Red Flag)* and *Renmin Ribao*, which had been his only reading.

On May 14, 1989, Yu joined 11 other intellectuals in a public appeal to the government to declare the student movement a "patriotic democracy movement." His name was included on a Politburo list of about 40 of Zhao Ziyang's supporters who were collectively referred to as the "Anti-Party Coalition." He was criticized by name in Beijing Mayor Chen Xitong's speech of June 30, 1989 for allegedly advocating bourgeois-liberalization and "plotting and instigating the counterrevolutionary rebellion."

Yu was declared a "rightist" and imprisoned in solitary confinement during the Cultural Revolution. In 1988, Yu helped publish *New*

Enlightenment, a magazine calling for political change. It was shut down after three issues (*AP*, January 8, 1991). At various times, Yu has been director of the Legal Institute of the Capital Iron and Steel Works, general editor of the periodical *The Science of Law*, a member of the Standing Committee of the Chinese Political Science Association and an official of the Chinese Association for Legal Science.

- **YU Shiwen**, 23, who disappeared in mid-July 1989 from Zhongshan University in Guangzhou probably was released in November 1990. According to an Asia Watch source, Yu's family was not notified until a month and a half after he was seized that he had been detained for "creating turmoil." In July 1990, one year after his detention, Yu was formally arrested. A philosophy major, class of 1990, Yu was active in the short-lived 1986-1987 democracy movement, helping to organize student demonstrations in Guangzhou. Later he established a university-based "Democracy Salon." During the 1989 pro-democracy movement, Yu was chairman of the student association at his university. He helped organize peaceful rallies and demonstrations on campus and in the city. Even after the crackdown in Beijing, Yu continued to organize protests.

Yu's parents were denied permission to visit him until May 29, 1990 and even then, consent was granted only with the proviso that they "would try to persuade [him] to admit that he had committed a crime." During the visit, Yu's parents were further advised that should Yu continue "his refusal to cooperate," he would be put on trial. Other than the one brief prison visit, no direct communication between Yu and his family was permitted.

■ **YU Zhaohui**, a student in the entering class of 1985 in the department of general medicine of Hunan Medical University, was released in November 1989, presumably because he "informed and established merit" while in jail. During the latter part of the 1989 pro-democracy movement, Yu served as special assistant to the chairman of the Hunan Students Autonomous Federation. On June 14, he fled with **TANG Boqiao** (see p.456) and others to Guangdong Province but was arrested after returning to Changsha and held in Changsha No.1 Prison, Cell 27.

■ **YUAN Yue**, a People's University Party history major from Jiangsu Province, who participated in the 1989 pro-democracy movement, was released from prison in October 1990. No other details are available.

■ **YUE Weipeng**, a student in the entering class of 1985 in the Chinese department of Hunan Hydraulic Power Normal University, was released in December 1989 and assigned as a teacher to a remote county in Gansu Province. During the 1989 pro-democracy movement, he had participated in a Democracy Salon and in the founding of the Provisional Committee on May 4. Yue was also a member of the Standing Committee of the Hunan Students Autonomous Federation and a leader of the student movement at his school. Arrested after June 4, he was held in Changsha No.1 Prison, Cell 24.

■ **ZANG Yongli**, a student at Beijing Normal College and head of a "Dare-to-Die" team during the 1989 pro-democracy movement, was detained for more than a year, then exempt from prosecution.

■ **ZENG Guangli**, formerly an economics student at Beijing University, has been released, according to information supplied to the U.S. government by Chinese officials (November 1991). He had been arrested on May 25, 1990 in connection with the distribution of pamphlets in Wuhan, Hubei Province. Zeng also was involved in the "counterrevolutionary activities" committed by **PENG Rong**, but the nature and extent of Zeng's involvement is unknown.

■ **ZENG Lei** - see p.88

■ **ZENG Ming**, a 29-year-old teacher at Central-South Industrial University, Hunan Province, has been released, but the government has had him fired from any work he has managed to find. Zeng was sentenced in May 1990 by the Changsha Intermediate People's Court to a half-year prison term on a charge of "counterrevolutionary propaganda and incitement." During the 1989 pro-democracy movement, Zeng secretly cooperated with student activists, and after June 4 he allegedly denounced the government and demanded that Li Peng be punished. He was arrested in December 1989 after arousing suspicion for his attitude during the Romanian Revolution.

■ **ZHAI Weimin**, a 23-year-old student leader who ranked sixth on the Chinese government's list of "21 most wanted" students and was sentenced to a prison term of three-and-a-half years, was released on September 13, 1993 reportedly after completing his term. He is believed to have returned from a prison in Henan Province to his home in Xian County, Henan. According to a notice posted outside the Beijing Intermediate People's Court on February 25, 1992, Zhai was found guilty of "counterrevolutionary propaganda and incitement." He went on trial on November 29, 1991 (*South China Morning Post*, December 7, 1991). Until his arrest, variously reported as March or May 1990, Zhai, who was enrolled in the Beijing Economics Institute, continued his work on behalf of democracy and a multi-party system through an underground group, the *Democratic Front for the Salvation of China*, organized in early 1990. Details of the underground group, which did not repudiate socialism or the Communist Party, were first disclosed to Western journalists by Zhai at a secret news conference held in Beijing in March 1990. Zhai said that the month before, in February 1990, more than sixty people participated in a secret conference held by the Democratic Front in Beijing.

Four others, **LIU Tianhua** (see) and **FANG Quan** (see), students at Beijing Economics College; an unnamed cadre; and **DAI Zhiyi**, a business man, were arrested in connection with the same case. Dai, who reportedly harbored Zhai and was "under investigation" by the authorities (according to a November 1991 official Chinese response to U.S. government inquiries), was released some time after November 1991 (*AP*, January 25, 1992). A **DAI Zhihi**, confirmed as released in February 1992 but with no identifying information, may be Dai Zhiyi. The others were held in Qincheng Prison along with Zhai. Requests by the U.S. government for information about Liu and Fang elicited no response from Chinese officials (November 1991), but there is an unconfirmed report they have been released.

■ **ZHAN Weiou** - see p.79

■ **ZHANG Bingjiu**, 42, was picked up by the Beijing Public Security Bureau in June 1991 and detained for four months in a military compound near Beijing. He had spent two years in hiding, from June 4, 1989 to June 2, 1991. After his release, Zhang, who holds a PhD in economic theory from Beijing University, was dismissed from his job in the office of the university's Director of Education and forced to move out of university housing. His Beijing residence card, permitting him to live and work in Beijing, was rescinded. To survive, Zhang moved from one friend's house to another managing some income from sporadic translating work.

■ **ZHANG Cunyong**, 27, an instructor in the department of management, Beijing University of Science and Technology, and **HOU Xiangjun** were released, according to an official Chinese response to inquiries by the U.S. government (November 1991). It is unclear what happened to Zhang's sister who was arrested with the men on June 15, 1989. Zhang was active in the democracy movement prior to the June 4 crackdown; afterwards he edited and printed information about the repression. His sister and Hou allegedly assisted in the printing.

■ **ZHANG Guangzhong**, who formerly worked in the office of the manager of Shanghai Masses Vehicle Factory, was arrested in 1989 and charged with "counterrevolutionary propaganda and incitement." He was held for 13 months and dismissed from his job. Earlier, in the second half of 1988, Zhang did free lance work, writing for several Hong Kong newspapers including *Ming Bao* and *Hsing Tao Ji Pao*.

■ **ZHANG Guoshou**, a student demonstrator, was released on June 8, 1991 according to a report in *A Changing China* (Fall 1991). At the time, he was physically weak and suffering from poor-sanitation-related skin ailments. During his 18 months in detention, Li's family was denied permission to visit. No further information is available.

■ **ZHANG Jianhua** - see p.159

■ **ZHANG Lixin**, 25, a student at Beijing Normal University and the leader of a Beijing Students Autonomous Federation propaganda team that went to the south, was released in mid-1990. He had been arrested at the end of June 1989 at a friend's house in Xiangtan City, Hunan Province, held at Changsha No.1 Prison and later transferred to Beijing. A member of the Standing Committee of the BSAF and the leader of its picket squad, Zhang had gone from Shanghai to Changsha in late May or early June 1989 to contact the Hunan SAF. On June 8, together with **TANG Boqiao** (see p.456), he presided over a mourning ceremony held at the Changsha Railway Station.

■ **ZHANG Qianjin, ZHAO Xin, LI Xiang, CHEN Wei, WANG Tao, WEN Ning, LIU Di** - see p.26

■ **ZHANG Rujun** - see p.11

■ **ZHANG Shu**, a reporter for *Renmin Ribao Hai Wai Ban*, was released in 1990. He reportedly was arrested after June 24, 1989, along with six printers from the paper, for blocking military vehicles. Zhang wrote a special edition of *Renmin Ribao* after the executions of three workers in Shanghai (June 21, 1989). In that edition, he described the Politburo meeting during which Communist Party Secretary Zhao Ziyang was removed from office. Although it was never actually printed, the edition was photocopied and circulated. Zhang allegedly also helped organize demonstrations by other *Renmin Ribao* journalists. There is no word as to the whereabouts of the printers.

■ **ZHANG Shuxian** - see p.471

■ **ZHANG Wei[3]**, an economic official in his thirties, reportedly placed under house arrest after he resigned his job to protest the imposition of martial law in Beijing, has been released. Zhang was chairman of the Tianjin Economic and Technological Zone.

■ **ZHANG Weiguo**, the 37-year-old journalist and former Beijing bureau chief for the crusading *Shijie Jingji Daobao (World Economic Herald)*, was finally permitted to leave China on January 31, 1993 to take up a year's fellowship at the Center for Chinese Studies at the University of California, Berkeley. After his February 12, 1991 release following twenty months in prison, Zhang continued to be harassed by Shanghai authorities. The most serious incident occurred on July 30, 1991 when he was arrested, then held in an army camp in Shanghai for 23 days. On June 27, after Zhang's apartment was staked out by police and he had been questioned extensively about his foreign contacts, he went into hiding at the home of relatives in Yingshan Village, near Hangzhou, Zhejiang Province. At 2 A.M., thirty police officers broke down the door, handcuffed Zhang and escorted him back to Shanghai where he was held incommunicado. During his internment, he was questioned extensively about an alleged growing network of

underground organizations, about information he allegedly had of a Hong Kong pro-democracy group operating in Shanghai and about his contacts with foreigners, including reporters. He also reportedly was queried about a letter he wrote to Wan Li, head of the National People's Congress criticizing China's lack of legal protections.

At his release, which came only after his mother guaranteed that he would not leave Shanghai, Zhang was told his case had not yet been cleared up, therefore, not only could he not leave Shanghai, he had to report to the police whenever they asked. He was told he could be re-arrested anytime. Technically, he was on bail awaiting trial, a status which was not abrogated until the end of 1992 just before his passport application was accepted.

Earlier, on May 29, 1991 and again on May 30, Zhang was questioned for eight hours about his relationship with Gu Bin (see p.417) and *Luntan (Forum)*, the journal the Shanghai-based *Study Group on Human Rights in China* had planned to publish. He also was quizzed about his contacts with foreign reporters and about his plan to compile a selection of the writings and speeches of **Qin Benli**, the deceased crusading editor of *Shijie Jingji Daobao*. Authorities demanded Zhang hand over the manuscript. As a condition, Zhang insisted the police hand over his confiscated prison diaries; to date they have refused.

Zhang also experienced work difficulties after his first release from prison. Not permitted to work as a journalist, his unit, the Shanghai Academy of Social Sciences, ordered him to accept a job at the Jinshan Petrochemical Company, forty-five miles from Shanghai. Should he refuse, which he did, his salary was to be suspended. That did not happen until September 1992; then in November, Zhang was formally expelled from the academy. He earned his living as an independent freelance writer, appearing in print in Hong Kong and Taiwan, sometimes under a pseudonym. Zhang was harassed in other ways. In a BBC interview in May 1991, he complained that although theoretically he could practice his basic rights as a citizen, in reality he was denied the ability to exercise them.

Zhang was seized on June 20, 1989 in Jingshan near Shanghai; he was formally arrested on September 20, 1989. First held in a detention center on the outskirts of Shanghai, he was then moved to Shanghai No.1 Detention Center where he shared a cell with common criminals, 15 prisoners to a space 15 square meters. (Zhang angered Shanghai officials by describing prison conditions in an interview in *Ming Bao*, a Hong Kong paper, on April 8, 1991). He developed a heart problem soon after his arrest. After his release, Zhang spoke out publicly about his lack of access to a lawyer and about the fact that at no time was he furnished with "the most basic pieces of evidence or judicial documents."

Zhang reportedly played a key role in organizing and feeding pro-democracy information to the *Herald*, one of China's most liberal newspapers. A lawyer, he also tried to institute legal proceedings to protest the way in which the newspaper was closed down in May 1989 by then Shanghai Party Secretary Jiang Zemin. At the time of his release, a Shanghai official said Zhang had "written big character posters everywhere."

According to a Shanghai Foreign Affairs official (*AP*, February 14, 1991), Zhang was released because he showed "understanding of his crimes." The Shanghai Procuratorate reportedly told him (*South China Morning Post*, February 13, 1991) they had evidence that in late May 1989, he had fabricated "revolutionary slogans charging that the Li Peng-Yang Shangkun clique was attempting a coup, and that he had tried unsuccessfully to ensure that these slogans would be used during anti-governmentdemonstrations...While these deeds were against the law, they did not constitute the crime of making counterrevolutionary propaganda and instigation."

■ **ZHANG Xiaojun**, 24, formerly a teacher at Taoyuan Normal College in Changde, Hunan Province, was released, but the government subsequently had him fired from any job he managed to find. Formerly the Secretary of the Young Communist League at Taoyuan Normal College, Zhang allegedly organized student demonstrations during the 1989 pro-democracy movement. He was arrested in October 1989 and sentenced in April 1990 by the Changde City Intermediate People's Court to two years' imprisonment on a charge of "counterrevolutionary propaganda and incitement." In July, Zhang was sent to

Longxi Prison (Provincial No.6) for reform through labor.

■ **ZHANG Xiaoxi** - see p.234

■ **ZHANG Yuxiang, WANG Zhan, ZHAN Weiou** and **XIAO Yong** - see p.79

■ Lieutenant Colonel **ZHANG Zhenglong**, who authored a controversial history of the Chinese military and was arrested in August 1990, was reportedly later released. His book, *White Snow, Red Blood*, officially published in August 1989, however, remains banned (*Christian Science Monitor*, September 27, 1990). Zhang was reportedly detained on orders from the Politburo for his expose of "Red Army atrocities and tactical blunders by Mao Zedong during the civil war in the 1940s." The book was denounced at a Politburo meeting in the spring of 1990 for "denying the justice of a revolutionary war" and "seriously exposing the dark side of the PLA." The book is considered a symbol of opposition to current hardline Chinese leaders both within and outside the military.

White Snow, Red Blood, using Communist Party documents and reports from party survivors, tells the story of the siege of Changchun, a city in northeastern China, during which, according to Zhang, many city residents died of starvation. "Hundreds of thousands of Chinese people were killed by [other] Chinese people. Why was this? Was this for socialism? Was this for the Communist Party? Was it worth it?" he asks in the book (*AP,*

November 13, 1990 in *Shijie Ribao*, November 14, 1990).

Zhang, born in 1947 in Liaoning Province, Benxi County, Caohekou District, comes from a family of railroad workers. Two years after his 1966 high school graduation, he was sent to the countryside to work. Joining the army in 1969, he eventually rose to the rank of Lieutenant Colonel in the propaganda section, Shenyang Military District (*Shijie Ribao*, November 16, 1990). Zhang's previous prize-winning works, fictionalized stories based on fact - known as "reportage" in China - were published in *Jiefang Jun Wenyi (Army Literature)* and *Kun Lun*, another army publication.

■ **ZHANG Zhiyong**[1], a student of international relations at Beijing University, was released in January 1991, according to an Asia Watch source. He was expelled from school and as of March 1993 was working in a company in Tianjin. In November 1991, an official Chinese response to U.S. government inquiries reported that Zhang had been sentenced, but the prison term was not disclosed.

Along with his younger brother, Zhang was arrested at Nanjing University shortly after June 4, 1989. He was one of three students (see Guo Haifeng p.418 and Zhou Yongjun see p.494) who knelt on the steps of the Great Hall of the People on April 22, 1989 in an attempt to deliver a petition to the government. Zhang reportedly also took part in the Tiananmen Square hunger strike, was involved in an effort to invite Mikhail Gorbachev to meet with the student protestors during the

Soviet leader's state visit to Beijing in mid-May 1989, and served as a special advisor to Chai Ling, head of the General Command of Tiananmen Square, in late May. After June 4, Zhang fled to his hometown in Anhui Province, then went with his younger brother to Nanjing University, where the latter was a student (*Zhengming*, April 1990). There is no information as to the whereabouts of Zhang's brother.

■ **ZHANG Zhong**, a retired deputy factory manager and amateur history writer, was released on August 9, 1990 (Amnesty International, *ASA 17/73/90*). He had been detained on September 22, 1989 for "shelter and investigation," a form of detention which does not require charges. Zhang allegedly had written an "anonymous" letter to the Communist Party in which he made "serious political mistakes."

■ **ZHANG Zhongli**, a Chinese historian arrested after June 4, 1989, was released prior to June 1990, according to an Asia Watch source.

■ **ZHAO Changqing**, in his first year in the history department at Sichuan Normal University when he was arrested in connection with the 1989 pro-democracy movement, was held in Qincheng Prison for over a year, then released.

■ **ZHAO Guangyu**, a student in his late twenties at the Beijing Institute of Atmospheric Physics, has been released, according to an official Chinese response to inquiries by the U.S. government (November 1991). He

reportedly was detained for questioning in late June 1989 for allegedly putting up posters during the protests in Beijing (Amnesty International, *ASA 17/24/90*).

■ **ZHAO Jinwu**, a Shanxi University student, was detained for seven months for his role in the Taiyuan pro-democracy demonstrations and for helping to bring news of the June 3-4, 1989 events in Beijing to Taiyuan. He was reportedly part of a group (the "Shaanxi Planning Committee" - see **Ge Hu**, p.86) who planned to organize an unofficial broadcast entitled "The Truth about June 3-4 in Beijing."

■ **ZHAO Shaoruo**, a student, has been released, according to an official Chinese response to requests for information by the U.S. government (November 1991). He had been detained in August 1989 for carrying a coffin during the protest march by the Central Academy of Fine Arts.

■ **ZHAO Tiguo**, a member of the executive committee of Beijing University's Independent Student Union and chief commander of the university's pickets, has been released, according to an official Chinese response to inquiries by the U.S. government (November 1991). An Asia Watch source has reported that after Zhao left Qincheng Prison, he was permitted to continue his studies at Beijing University, but at graduation was sent to the Daqing oilfields in Heilongjiang Province to work.

■ **ZHAO Xiaoming** (pen name **BEI Ming**), the 36-year-old wife of the well-known writer **ZHENG Yi**, arrested for participating in the 1989 pro-democracy movement, was released in early 1990 after nine months in solitary confinement. She then went into hiding, continuing to stay underground even after she left China in mid-1992. In the meantime, Zheng, a Chongqing, Sichuan Province native who had settled in Shanxi Province, hid for 43 months until the pair finally were granted asylum and came to the U.S. on January 6, 1993. During April and May 1989, Zhao, an active member of the Association of Beijing Intellectuals, and her husband published *News Briefings*, up-to-date summaries of pro-democracy activities in Tiananmen Square. Zheng, on the wanted list for signing the "May 16 Manifesto," a petition that called Deng Xiaoping "a senile and fatuous autocrat," also helped organize street protests by students and intellectuals. He was one of the principal organizers of the *Joint Liaison Group of All Circles in the Capital*. After he surfaced, in May 1992, Zheng published detailed documentary evidence of widespread cannibalism in Guangxi Province during the 1966-76 Cultural Revolution. He is the author of *Old Well*, a novel made into an award-winning movie, and of numerous other short stories, novels and historical non-fiction.

Born on March 10, 1947, Zheng was sent to Shanxi in 1968 during the Cultural Revolution to work as a peasant and a coal miner. In 1978, he passed the first college entrance examinations held in China for ten years and entered the Chinese department at Jinzhong Normal College. After graduation, he edited the magazine *Jinzhong Arts and Literature* and in 1962 was employed as a writer-in-residence by the Shanxi provincial branch of the *Chinese Writers Association*. During this period, Zheng founded and became deputy editor of the literary review *Huang He (Yellow River)*.

■ **ZHAO Yiqiang** - see p.135

■ **ZHAO Yu**, a member of the Shanxi Province Writers Association and author of an exposé about competitive sport in China, *Qiang Guo Meng (Dream of a Strong Country)*, disappeared shortly after June 4, 1989; he reportedly was arrested on July 4 (*Shijie Ribao*, February 12, 1990), imprisoned for three months, then conditionally released. According to an Asia Watch source, Zhao went back to his hometown, Changzhi in Shanxi, but had to report to the Public Security Bureau whenever he intended to travel. According to a November 1991 official Chinese reply to U.S. government inquiries, Zhao had "never been accused of any offense." A signatory of the "May 16 Declaration" and head of the intellectuals' contingent in Tiananmen Square, Zhao encouraged other writers to participate in demonstrations there.

■ **ZHAO Zhizhong**, a 26-year-old teacher in Beijing Central Cultural College, arrested in June 1989, was released that December. According to an Asia Watch source, he was tortured in prison.

■ **ZHENG Di**, the 33-year-old deputy chief editor of the magazine *Jingjixue Zhoubao (Economics Weekly)*, produced under the auspices of the Social and Economic Sciences Research Institute (SERI), has been released, according to an official Chinese response to U.S. government inquiries (November 1991). He was arrested on October 19, 1989 while trying to flee the country. A graduate of Beijing University's economics department, Zheng's official job was as a teacher, and although he has not been fired, he has not been assigned work, nor is he permitted employment as a journalist.

■ **ZHENG Mingxia**, chief of finance of the student movement, was arrested sometime after the June 1989 crackdown, probably in mid-July in Beijing (*Xinhua*, July 22, 1989). At the time of her arrest, Zheng allegedly was carrying 21,000 *yuan* and the equivalent of 10,000 *yuan* in foreign currencies obtained during a trip to Jiangsu Province. It is possible that **CHEN Mingxiao** on the list submitted by Chinese authorities in response to inquiries by the U.S. government (November 1991) is Zheng Mingxia. If so, she has been released.

■ **ZHENG Yulian** - see p.246

■ **ZHOU Duo**, 45, left China for the United States on December 1, 1992 to accept a visiting scholar position at Harvard University. (He returned to China in December 1993.) It had taken almost two years to obtain a passport. In an interview with *Kyodo News Service* (November 14, 1992, in FBIS,

November 16), Zhou said one reason for taking the position had to do with the difficulty he faced working in China without access to libraries and research materials. First arrested on July 10, 1989 in southern China, Zhou was released on May 10, 1990 along with 210 others. At the time of his arrest, he was head of two departments at the Stone Corporation, Strategic Planning and Public Relations. Before joining Stone, Zhou lectured on sociology at Beijing University and before that he taught at the Communist Youth League's cadre training institute. Stone's Institute for Social Development was implicated in the petition drive to block martial law in Beijing in May 1989.

After his release, Zhou was jobless, having been fired from the Stone Corporation. He tired earning his living through private enterprise (*Washington Post*, June 2, 1991) but the authorities, reluctant to permit the development of a financial base for a dissident movement, interfered (*Reuters*, June 2, 1991). His partner in a resort project was pressured to withdraw; Zhou himself was forced out of a research project (see Wen Yuankai p.467).

On May 30, 1990, three weeks after his release, Zhou was again taken into custody and held for 18 days (see Gao Xin p.416).

■ **ZHOU Fengsuo**, 23, a physics major at Qinghua University and a member of the Standing Committee of the Beijing Students Autonomous Federation, was one of the 97 prisoners released by the authorities on June 6,

1990. Zhou, who was on the list of 21 "most wanted" student leaders, was arrested near Xi'an on June 13, 1989, shortly after being informed on by his elder sister and brother-in-law. Zhou was dismissed from school and has had difficulty finding work.

■ **ZHOU Lunzuo** - see p.88

■ **ZHOU Yongjun** (wrongly spelled as "Yongun" on an International Labor Organization list), formerly a fourth year student at the University of Politics and Law in Beijing, arrested sometime in June 1989, was released without trial (*AP* January 26, 1991). He reportedly had been charged with "counterrevolutionary propaganda" (UPI, November 27, 1990) but was found to have "committed only minor crimes and to have shown repentance and performed meritorious service" (*Xinhua*, in UPI, January 26, 1991). According to the ILO report (November 1991), he was declared innocent of all criminal responsibility. A 23-year-old Sichuan native, Zhou was imprisoned in Qincheng Prison in Beijing (*Shijie Ribao*, April 12, 1990; *Xin Bao*, April 12, 1990) until his release. Until he fled China in late April 1992, Zhou worked in a trading company in Shenzhen.

Zhou was a founding member of the Beijing Students Autonomous Federation. He was one of the students who, on April 22, 1989, knelt for several hours on the steps of the Great Hall of the People and asked to be allowed to hand over a petition to the authorities. (See Guo Haifeng p.418 and Zhang Zhiyong p.490) On April 23, 1989, Zhou was elected as the first chairman of the Beijing Students Autonomous Federation, which represented 21 universities and colleges in the capital. He was dismissed from this post on April 28 after he declined to support the April 27 demonstration march protesting the *Renmin Ribao* editorial of the previous day, which condemned the student movement as "turmoil" and a "planned conspiracy." The protest march drew massive public support. Zhou continued to play an active role in the pro-democracy movement, however, taking part in the Tiananmen Square hunger strike and later serving as a legal adviser to the Beijing Workers Autonomous Federation.

■ **ZHOU Zhirong**, a 32-year-old teacher at Xiangtan No.2 Middle School, Hunan Province, and a graduate of the Geography Department of Hunan Normal University, was released from prison either in February or March 1993. As of May, he was working in Guangdong Province at a poorly paid factory job. In December 1989, Zhou was sentenced by the Xiangtan City Intermediate People's Court to a seven-year prison term on charges of "counterrevolutionary propaganda and incitement" Sometime later, the sentence was reduced to five years. In September 1989, Zhou went of his own accord to the Public Security Department. Held first in Xiangtan Jail, he was subjected to psychological and physical abuse. Later, while in Longxi Prison (Provincial No.6), Zhou was accused of organizing "counterrevolutionary meetings." He was secretly transferred on the evening of February 12, 1991 to Lingling Prison (Provincial No.3) and put in solitary confinement. Following a three-month period on a "shackle board", Zhou showed signs of psychological disturbance.

Zhou was a 1980 student leader of the Hunan Normal College free election campaign and, as a result, spent time in prison. He allegedly gave speeches at public gatherings during the 1989 pro-democracy movement. After June 4, he conducted a lone sit-in in front of the Xiangtan municipal government offices wearing a black coat with the character for "sadness" written on the front and one for "mourning" written on the back.

Zhou's widowed mother is bed-ridden. His younger brother, who had his leg injured in an accident, looked after her while Zhou was in prison. When Zhou's friends sent small sums of money to help her, they were interrogated by police and told to stop.

■ **ZHU Guoqiang**, a former student of about 24 years old, who had been seized by the police in a bookstore in Changsha, Hunan Province on or about September 15, 1992 and taken away for questioning in connection with his meetings with U.S.-based student dissident Shen Tong (see p.452), was released sometime during the second week in February 1993. Zhu's arrest occurred after a plainclothes security officer, posing as an agent for a pro-democracy escape network, had visited the woman friend of a leader of the *All China People's Autonomous Federation*, a Hunan-based

pro-democracy underground network. When the security officer asked her where the leader might be found, she said she herself didn't know, but that Zhu Guoqiang might know. Zhu was arrested the following day and held for the next five months in Changsha City No.1 Jail, run by Section 4 of the Changsha Municipal Public Security Bureau. Ill-treated in prison, Zhu was in extremely poor health at the time of his release. Originally from Shenyang in northeastern China, Zhu played a minor role in the 1989 movement.

The privately owned bookstore in Changsha, Hunan Province, *Tongren Shuju (Colleagues Press)*, where Zhu Guoqiang was picked up, was closed down by the authorities in late October and its staff and management subject to lengthy questioning and harassment. **CHEN Jianyong**, a physics graduate from Beijing University and an employee of the bookstore, was taken into custody in November and released during the second week in February 1993. Earlier, because of participation in the 1989 pro-democracy movement, he had been forced to withdraw from school. **XIE Changzhong**, a non-employee supporter of the store, was arrested around the same time and released at the end of March. He is the younger brother of XIE Changfa (see p.473), who served a "labor re-education" sentence for his part in the 1989 pro-democracy movement in Hunan.

■ **ZHU Limin**, a Beijing junior high school student arrested in June 1989 on charges of throwing rocks at martial law troops, was held for four months and released.

■ **ZHU Wenli**, 22, head of the social section of the Beijing Students Autonomous Federation, was arrested in Shenyang, Liaoning Province on June 12, 1989. According to *Liaoning Radio*, Zhu was captured by a staff member of the Heping Hotel in Shenyang after he tried to register at the hotel with a false identity card. The chief of the reception desk called security officials, who found "materials for propagating counterrevolutionary rebellion," a dagger and 1,400 *yuan* in his bag. Official reports claimed that Zhu, who was unemployed and allegedly had been detained on numerous occasions prior to June 12, confessed his part in a team organized to block military vehicles. Zhu lived at the Tonghe Forestry Farm in Weike Forest, Heilongjiang.

According to an official Chinese response (November 1991) to U.S. government inquiries concerning his whereabouts, Zhu has been released. However, in a similar response to the International Labor Organization (November 15, 1991), Chinese authorities stated that Zhu had "never been brought to court" - a probable reference to an administrative sentence of "labor re-education."

■ ZHU Zizheng - see p.246

■ **ZOU Xiaotong, LIU Xiangyang, PAN Gequan** (Mingquan), **SUN Jian, ZHANG Rensheng** and **ZHENG Hua**, students and staff members at Wuhan University, arrested after June 4, have been released, according to an official Chinese response to U.S. government inquiries (November 1991). In addition, six other members of the university community in Wuhan, Hubei Province were reported to be "under supervision" and **LI Haitao** (see p.547), who was sentenced has presumably been released. Liu and Zou, both students in Wuhan University's Chinese department, reportedly were arrested in June in Wuhan. (Zou Xiaotong may be the same person as **ZH(O)U Xiaotong**). Zhang, also a Chinese department student, writers section, was arrested on June 21 at his home in Guangxi Province. Pan and Sun, philosophy department students, were arrested in June, Pan in late June at his home in Suzhou, and Sun on June 14. Zheng, a philosophy department member, was arrested in Wuhan in July (Amnesty International, *ASA 17/24/90*).

Workers and Peasants

■ **BAI Chunxiang** - see p.93

■ **CAI Jinxuan** - see p.103

■ **CHEN Erjin**, a 48-year-old native of Yunnan Province, was arrested in late April 1981 and tried on March 7, 1982 in Kunming for plotting to create a "counterrevolutionary party." He was sentenced to ten years' imprisonment and five years' subsequent deprivation of political rights. Chen was due for release in April 1991, and an official Chinese response to U.S. government requests for information confirmed that he was no longer in prison by November of that year. He eventually resurfaced in Beijing, and as of November 1993 he was working in a Japanese joint venture company there.

Before his arrest, Chen, whose formal schooling ended after fifth grade, worked first as a peasant and then as an unskilled laborer. Later he attended a teacher-training college, graduating in 1966. He was active as a Red Guard leader during the Cultural Revolution, then worked as a teacher, and in the 1970s he was a statistician in a coal mine. During the period 1975-76, Chen wrote a major work of dissent entitled "On Proletarian -Democratic Revolution," but its submission for publication in 1976 resulted in his arrest. He served ten months in prison, during which time he was beaten and tortured but refused to renounce his views. After his release, the verdict against him was reversed and he was officially declared a "victim of the Gang of Four." His manuscript was ultimately published in 1979 by Xu Wenli's *April Fifth Forum*, perhaps the most influential of the Democracy Wall *samizdat*-style journals. In it, Chen argued on Marxist principles against a "bureaucratic monopoly power elite" (the Communist Party) and for a "proletarian-democratic revolution" which would combine Maoist anti-bureaucratism with U.S.-style separation of powers and entail the creation of a two-party system. Chen gave no known interviews to foreign journalists or commentators during the Democracy Wall movement. As a result he was not well known outside China during the movement, nor is he now. Chen is married and has three children.

■ **CHEN Shuai**, a 26-year-old worker at No.1 *Xinhua* Factory in Changsha, Hunan Province, was arrested after June 4, and in 1990 was tried by the Changsha Intermediate People's Court on charges of "counter-revolutionary propaganda and incitement." Sentenced to two years' imprisonment, he was released at the expiration of his term. After the Beijing students began their hunger strike, Chen and several other local workers organized the Changsha Workers Autonomous Federation, for which he served as spokesman until his withdrawal from all public activities.

■ **CHENG Qiyang (CHANG Qiyang** on the ILO list) was released, according to an official Chinese response to inquiries from the U.S. government (November 1990). An earlier report to the International Labor Organization that he had never been arrested nor had he ever come before judicial authorities is not inconsistent. Cheng was one of three men (see Zhu Genhao p.582 and Liu Jian[2] p.125) detained between June 6 and June 9, 1989 and accused of setting up roadblocks in Shanghai, instigating others to do the same and attempting to "stop and overturn police cars." Cheng also was accused of letting the air out of the tires of 36 vehicles during a demonstration to protest the Beijing massacre. In all, 130 "lawless elements" were arrested in Shanghai for "disrupting traffic and obstructing official business" between June 6 and 9.

■ **CHENG Zhizhong**, a 20-year-old bus driver charged with throwing rocks at martial law troops, was released in November 1989 after having been detained four months.

■ **CUI Ruilin**, a private shopkeeper, was released in January 1990 after seven months in prison. He was arrested in June 1989 on suspicion of "setting fire to an army vehicle."

■ **DAI Yue** - see p.156

■ **DENG Keming**, a 21-year-old temporary worker from Sichuan Province, has been released and reportedly is wandering jobless from place to place. He had been sentenced in July 1989 to a two-year prison term by the Changsha (Hunan Province) Eastern District (Basic-Level People's) Court on charges of "beating, smashing, and looting" in connection with the 1989 pro-democracy movement. Deng, who formerly worked at the Changsha Measuring Instruments Factory, was arrested the evening of April 22. After sentencing, he was sent for "re-education through labor" to Longxi Prison (Provincial No.6) in Hunan. During his term, Deng's wrist was broken.

■ **DUAN Juan**, a 19-year-old woman, and **XIONG Changping**, 21, both self-employed small traders from Chongqing, Sichuan Province, have been released, according to an official Chinese response to U.S. government inquiries (November 1991). Earlier accounts reported each was sentenced to 15 years' imprisonment for engaging in "counterrevolutionary incitement." Duan and Xiong were arrested May 5, 1989 (*Chongqing Ribao*, May 7, 1989) after returning from Beijing and making speeches at Chongqing University telling students what was going on in the capital and encouraging them to boycott classes. Duan reportedly was beaten during interrogation at the Songshan "shelter and investigation" center because she refused to "confess" (Amnesty International, *ASA 17/40/90*).

■ Seven pro-democracy dissidents, held at Tianjin No.1 Prison before they were released, included Tianjin Democratic Revival Association members **FANG Jun**, four years reduced to two-and-a-half; **CHEN Wei**[3], a two-year term; and **XU Wenjie**, a two-year non-custodial sentence. Tianjin Workers Autonomous Federation members included **LU Yao**, three years; **CHEN Gang**[3], two years; **WEI Minghua**; and **WANG Yawen**.

■ **FENG Guowei** - see p.157

■ **HE Qiu**, 43, formerly a Guangzhou shipyard worker, arrested in April 1981 and sentenced on May 29, 1982 to ten years' imprisonment for "counterrevolutionary offenses," was released in late 1991. An official response to U.S. government requests for information only confirmed that he was sentenced (November 1991).

He Qiu reportedly went with Fu Shenqi (see p.10), a worker and Democracy Wall activist from Shanghai, to Beijing to discuss with authorities there the right of citizens to publish unofficial magazines. Starting in 1978, He was editor of several such journals, *Road of the People*; *Free Exchange*; and *Responsibility*, the organ of the unofficial *All-China Association of the Democratic Press*, and he was one of the first to stand as an unofficial candidate in the winter of 1980 for election from his work unit to a local People's Congress. He Qiu was first imprisoned between 1973 and 1976, allegedly for having "mischievous ideas," after a letter to his brother criticizing China's policies was intercepted by the security police.

■ **HE Qunyin**, a "core member" of the Beijing Workers Autonomous Federation was "released immediately after questioning by the police," according to a Chinese report to the International Labor Organization (March 1992). He was captured in Xi'an on June 14, 1989, for allegedly taking part in a May 28 protest outside Beijing police headquarters that had been organized to demand the release of detained workers. Liu also was accused of attacking army troops.

■ **HE Yongpei** - see p.384

■ **HU Hai,** a 58-year-old peasant from Liuzhuang Township, Henan Province was conditionally released in mid-January 1993 (Amnesty International, *ASA 17/04/93*. Although the conditions are uncertain, it is probable that he is out on bail pending a re-trial. Hu was sentenced in November 1991 by the Weihui City People's Court to a three-year term. The charges included "disturbing the social order" by "inciting the masses" to complain to authorities "unreasonably causing trouble and seriously disrupting the functioning of government work." For several months prior to his arrest in May 1991, Hu had taken part in petitioning provincial and central authorities to act to lower excessive local taxes imposed in 1990 by Liuzhuang officials. The petitions were unsuccessful. Late in 1992, the Supreme People's Court ordered the Xinxiang City Intermediate People's Court to re-try the case in accordance with Article 149 of the Criminal Procedure Law. Under Article 41, Chinese citizens are guaranteed the right to petition higher authorities to redress abuses of power, neglect of duty and illegal actions by government officials. Citizens are also guaranteed the right to sue for monetary compensation for losses incurred as a result of officials' actions.

■ **HU Shikuan**, a peasant from Henan Province, was arrested in June 1989 in Beijing for setting fire to an army vehicle. He was released nine months later, in March 1990.

■ **HUANG Shunsheng**, a paper factory worker, arrested in Beijing in June 1989 on charges of "setting up roadblocks and hindering army vehicles from advancing," was released after four months in detention.

■ **JIA Changling** - see p.157

■ **JIANG Bing**, 27, a special (vocational) middle school graduate from Chongqing, Sichuan Province, was arrested in fall 1990 (probably September) and sentenced to three years' imprisonment for "counter-revolutionary propaganda and incitement" after writing a letter to the British Broadcasting Corporation's Beijing bureau setting forth his views on democracy. Jiang, who was released on September 21, 1993, served his sentence at the Sichuan No.2 Prison in Chongqing (also known as the Sichuan New Life *Laodong* Factory).

■ **JIANG Zhi'an** - see p.156

■ **LAN Xiaohua**, a young man from Sichuan, was arrested sometime in 1989 after writing a letter to the U.S. Embassy in Beijing entitled "A Denunciation of the Eight Major Crimes of the Chinese Communist Party." Later sentenced to three years' imprisonment, he served the entire term in Chongqing Municipal Jail and was released in 1992.

■ **LI Chenghuan**, identified as an unemployed worker by Chinese sources, was convicted and released on January 26, 1991, according to a same day *AP* report. Li reportedly faced trial on charges of "counterrevolutionary sabotage," but was "exempt from criminal punishment."

■ **LI Chunguo**, a worker, arrested in June 1989 for throwing rocks at martial law troops, was released five months later.

■ **LI Hongxin** (Huanxin)- see p.384

■ **LI Jie** - see p.103

■ **LI Jun**, a worker at the Xi'an Special Industrial Art Factory, and **LI Zehua**, a Shaanxi Steel Company worker, turned themselves in to the police after the violent clashes in Xi'an on April 22, 1989. For so doing, they were "exempted from criminal punishment"; it is not clear if the two were placed under any other form of restriction (Amnesty International, *ASA 17/24/90*).

■ **LI Lin** and **LI Zhi**, two brothers who fled to Hong Kong in July 1989, were arrested on February 16, 1991 when they returned home to Hengyang, Hunan Province. This was in spite of general assurances from the top party leadership that returning dissidents would not be punished, and specific reassurances by local public security officials in Hunan Province that the brothers could return home safely. During interrogation, they were held incommunicado, beaten, punched and prodded repeatedly with electric batons. After a campaign of international pressure on their behalf, the two brothers were sentenced on July 9, 1991 to five-and-a-half-month prison terms, backdated to February 15, on charges of "illegally crossing the border." They were released on July 15, shortly after which they were allowed to return to Hong Kong. They now live in the United States together with Li Lin's wife and young child.

The chief of Hengyang People's Court denied any inconsistency between the blanket assurance given by Party General Secretary Jiang Zemin and the arrest of the brothers. According to the official, "Pro-democracy dissidents who have not broken any law will not be arrested, but those who have made criminal offenses should be given appropriate punishment" (*Hong Kong Standard*, June 14, 1991). Li Lin, 31, a steel worker and a "core" leader in the Hunan Workers Autonomous Federation, left for China just before the Lunar New Year in February. His brother, a 23-year-old pop singer who was also active in the 1989 protests in Changsha, followed after receiving a phone call from Guangzhou that it was safe to do so. The two men had been granted temporary residence in Hong Kong, where Li Lin worked as a mechanic at Kowloon Motors and Li Zhi was employed in a cosmetics factory. Li Lin had been formally expelled by the party committee in Hengyang, the Hunan provincial capital, for renouncing his party membership on June 4, 1989.

■ **LI Yi** - see p.372

■ **LI Zhifu** has been released, according to a Chinese response to International Labor Organization inquiries (March 1992). There is no identifying information of any kind in the report, nor had information about him been requested by the ILO.

■ **LI Zixi** (Zhixi), a worker at the Politics and Law University Press arrested sometime in early July 1989 after having been in hiding for over a month, was released in early 1991 and dismissed from his job, according to an Asia Watch source. Earlier requests by the U.S. government to Chinese officials for information elicited no

response (November 1991). According to a *Beijing Ribao* (July 1989) report, Li allegedly helped organize the Beijing University Teachers Hunger Strike Team, acted as Supplies Team leader for the Beijing Workers Autonomous Federation and "called for the overthrow of the Communist Party." An article in *Renmin Ribao* in late August accused Li, who is in his early forties, of "inciting, with ulterior motives, the military officers who were guarding Xinhuamen (i.e. the government seat in Beijing) to turn around their guns."

■ **LIU Jianguo**, a worker at Beijing Aviation College, arrested in June 1989 and charged with surrounding martial law troops, was released in November that same year.

■ **LIU Jingyang**, a peasant from Hebei Province, was arrested in July 1989 for inciting a group of construction workers to go on strike. He was released in November that same year.

■ **LIU Peigang,** a teacher of politics at the Attached Special Middle School of *Tianjin Television* who led a group called the Tianjin Democratic Revival Association *(Tianjin Minzhu Zhenxing Hui)* during the May 1989 protests, was released in August 1993. Arrested on June 9, 1989, Liu was later tried on charges of belonging to a "counter-revolutionary organization" and sentenced to six year's imprisonment. A worker named **LI Zhenqi**, also a member of the TDRA, was also tried on similar charges and sentenced to five years' imprisonment. Both men were sent to serve their sentences at Tianjin No.1 Prison. Despite his shorter sentence, Li has not yet been released.

■ **LIU Qing**, the prominent Democracy Wall activist, arrived in the U.S. on July 14, 1992. After numerous administrative roadblocks by Chinese officials and several appeals by the U.S. government, the Chinese authorities finally permitted Liu and his wife to leave. Released from prison on December 11, 1989, Liu was re-arrested in mid-May 1990, then re-released on November 3, 1990. At the time of his first release, Liu was sent into internal exile and given work in Mian County, Shaanxi Province, his official place of registration. However, he returned to Beijing, where he had lived prior to his arrest, to visit his mother and to marry. The real reason for Liu's second arrest and subsequent release probably had to do with the then up-coming anniversary of June 4 and the Asian Games slated for Beijing that September; the ostensible one was lack of a valid Beijing residence permit (*Reuters*, May 23, 1990).

Liu, a Nanjing University graduate and former machine-tool operator, was one of the chief editors of *April Fifth Forum*, one of the foremost journals of the 1978-81 democracy movement. He was arrested on November 11, 1979 for producing and distributing transcripts of the secret trial of Wei Jingsheng (see p.507), sentenced to a 15-year prison term in 1979. Liu initially spent five months in solitary in Beijing's Banbuqiao Detention Center

where he developed rheumatism due to the extreme cold and dampness. In April 1980, he was moved to a shared cell, but shortly thereafter was assigned, without trial, to a labor camp in Shaanxi Province for three years' "re-education through labor." Toward the end of that period, Liu smuggled out a long and detailed manuscript, *Prison Notes,* documenting his experiences within the Chinese penal system. Only then, in 1982, was he formally charged, secretly tried and given a seven-year criminal sentence on top of the three years he had already served. Throughout his imprisonment, the last five years of which were in Weinan No.2 Prison in Shaanxi, Liu was punished severely for refusing to confess and recant. According to his own account, he was beaten, starved, often allowed neither to exercise nor to talk. Every day for four years he was made to sit rigid and still on a low stool. Throughout his imprisonment, Liu was denied visits from family members.

■ **LIU Shanqing (LAU Shan Ching)**, a 40-year-old Hong Kong citizen, was released on December 26, 1991 after serving his full ten-year sentence in Guangzhou, Guangdong Province for activities in connection with the Democracy Wall movement. Because he had been deprived of his political rights for three years, the Chinese government could have prevented him from returning home until the end of 1994. At his release, Liu, a computer sales engineer and University of Hong Kong graduate, insisted that he had done nothing subversive and said he would continue to support the development of democracy in China. In an interview (*Wall Street Journal*, February 11, 1992), he said he was kept "in captivity" in three different prisons, the last Huaiji Prison, a solitary confinement reform-through-labor farm in the Zhaoqing area of northwest Guangdong. Because Liu refused to repent, he was not eligible for early release.

According to Liu, "They treated us inhumanely. All the time they told me, 'If you don't change, there's no chance to come back'" (*Reuters*, December 29, 1991). Liu said he was not tortured but was kept in virtual solitary confinement. His daily activities were limited to one hour's exercise, cooking and reading official newspapers. While in isolation, Liu was "supervised" by an inmate who by following him everywhere, even to the bathroom, earned a shortened sentence.

The hardest, Liu said, were the two times he was put into a dark cell, once for 20 days during his first year when he was still in Mei County Prison. He had refused to plead guilty in a year-end report and to accept ideological reform. The other punishment occurred when Liu gave his parents a copy of the prosecutor's indictment and was put into the dark cell for a month. During those times, Liu was chained at the feet; there was nothing to do and nobody came for 24 hours at a stretch. The only light came through a small hole in the ceiling. Although, Liu said, he tried to keep track of the days, he became "muddled." He tried pasting rice grains

on the wall to help remember, but often forget whether he had done so or not.

Liu was arrested in secret when he went to China on Christmas Day 1981 to visit the families of Democracy Wall prisoners. During his first seven nights in prison he was interrogated until dawn. Then interrogation continued for nine more months during which time he was held in isolation. In 1985, Liu wrote a 300 word confession of his "counterrevolutionary activities" (*South China Morning Post*, December 30, 1991. In return, he was given a radio that received BBC broadcasts. A year later he recanted and was thrown into solitary. The 100 odd prisoners in his squad were informed he was not allowed to talk with anyone.

Liu's detention did not come to light until his father made inquiries in Guangzhou on March 13, 1982; even then, the older Liu was not informed of his son's whereabouts. The "Committee for the Rescue of Liu Shanqing," formed in Hong Kong by Liu's friends, finally received a letter from the Hong Kong government to the effect that Liu was considered a Chinese national and was being detained for engaging in "unlawful" deeds. After further visits from his father in June 1982 and May 1983, officials of the Guangzhou Intermediate People's Court informed Liu senior that Liu Shanqing had been tried and sentenced under Articles 90, 52 and 102 of the Criminal Code. In a letter to the Students Union of the Chinese University of Hong Kong, dated August 10, 1983, the Chinese authorities declared that the trial had been "public," although neither Liu's family nor his friends had been

informed of the event in advance. The
letter went on to say that Liu had been
convicted on February 7, 1983 of
collaborating with "counterrevolutionary elements" to "attack the
socialist system and the people's
democratic dictatorship" and of
"violating the laws and regulations of
the country."

■ **LIU Xinfang**, a worker arrested in
connection with the 1989
pro-democracy movement and held in
Qincheng Prison, has been released.
No other details are available.

■ **LIU Yubin**[1], 30, has been released
from a two-year prison term. He was
arrested in June 1989 for organizing an
independent workers union at the
Shijiazhuang Pharmaceutical factory in
Hebei Province.

■ **LIU Zhongtao**, also known as
CHEN Le, a worker at the Hunan
Rubber Factory and an auditor in the
history department at Hunan Normal
University, was released from prison in
early 1990. On the eve of the 1989
pro-democracy movement, Liu took
part in a Democracy Salon; on May 4,
he took part in organizing a Provisional
Committee composed of representatives
from various schools. Relieved of his
position on the committee because his
status was "not genuine" (i.e. he was
not a real student), Liu went on to
serve as special assistant to one of the
chairmen of the Students Autonomous
Federation. After June 4, he planned
the establishment of a "Democracy
Movement Lecture Center," but was
arrested either in June or August 1989.

During part of his incarceration in
Changsha No.1 Prison, Cell 17, Liu
went on a hunger strike.

■ **PAN Mingdong**, a 40-year-old
private businessman and former boxing
coach with the Hunan Province
Physical Education Commission, was
released in 1991 from the Xinkaipu
Labor Re-education Center (Hunan
Switchgear Factory) in Changsha,
Hunan, where he had been detained
since October 1989 on suspicion of
drafting a "Declaration of Hunan
Autonomy." The document, issued on
June 8, 1989 by the *Preparatory
Commission for Patriotic
Self-Governance by the People of
Hunan*, had called for military rebellion
against the Li Peng government.
Because the authorities could find no
proof that Pan had authored the
declaration, he received only a two-
year term of "labor re-education." His
father, posthumously rehabilitated, had
been executed in the 1950s as a
"counterrevolutionary" for opposing
Chairman Mao's line.

■ **PENG Shangzhi** - see p.150

■ **TANG Yixin**, **WANG Hong**[2], and
YANG Rong, all young employees of
the Hunan Province Electrical Battery
Plant, were re-arrested in mid-April
1990 after posting a slogan banner in
public and distributing protest leaflets
in advance of the first anniversary of
the June 4 crackdown. Their
underground printing plant was
discovered by authorities and
destroyed, and they were accused by
the government of engaging in

"counterrevolutionary propaganda" activities and of possibly forming a "counterrevolutionary organization." The three were released after three months, in July 1990.

In 1989, the men were active in the Changsha Workers Autonomous Federation, organizing many factory strikes. They were arrested after June 4 that year, held for several months at Changsha No.1 Prison, and then released as innocent. After they were freed from their first arrest, Yang, Wang, and Tang continued to carry out underground pro-democracy activities, which included publishing a journal and a newspaper.

■ **TIAN Wei**, a driver and member of the Flying Tiger Brigade, has been released, according to an official Chinese response to inquiries from the U.S. government (November 1991). An earlier report to the International Labor Organization that he never was arrested nor had he ever come before judicial authorities (November 1990), is, therefore, problematic. Tian, from Shanghai, was detained on June 12, 1989, according to the International Confederation of Free Trade Unions; the June 4 Monitoring Group (January 8, 1991) lists his arrest date as December 6, 1989 in Beijing.

■ **WANG Baikun**, identified as a leader of a "Dare-to-Die Corps" brigade providing security for students during the "period of turmoil" (*Washington Post*, December 3, 1989), has been released, according to an official Chinese response to inquiries by the U.S. government (November

1991). His arrest came on November 16, 1989; the date of his release is unknown.

■ **WANG Baomei** - see p.372

■ **WANG Bo**, a worker from Shibalipu, Beijing, arrested in June 1989 and sentenced to four years in prison, was released on June 11, 1993.

■ **WANG Changan**, 22, a worker, was arrested after turning himself in to local authorities on June 23, 1989 in Jinan. He was accused of setting up barricades on roads and railway tracks and of organizing the Jinan Autonomous Residents Union (*Agence France Presse*, June 24, 1989, in FBIS, June 26). According to an official Chinese response to U.S. government inquiries (November 1991), Wang has been released.

■ **WANG Fushun**, **YANG Hengwu** and **LI Meihu**, a self-employed transport worker, were never arrested nor did they ever come before judicial authorities, according to the Chinese government's report to the International Labor Organization (November 1990). An official Chinese response to U.S. government inquiries listed Wang as released but supplied no information about Yang or Li (November 1991). It is a reasonable assumption the three received "labor re-education" terms, an administrative sentence which carries no criminal "charge." Since "re-education" terms usually do not exceed three years, Yang and Li have probably now been released.

Wang, Yang and Li turned themselves in on June 10, 1989 in Beijing and confessed to blocking roads with vehicles on June 3. As a result, 32 military vehicles were halted and 20 others burned (Amnesty International, *ASA 17/24/90*).

■ **WANG Jianmin**, a 34-year-old worker at the Changcheng Hotel, arrested in June 1989, was released one month later for lack of evidence. According to an Asia Watch source, when Wang returned to work he still had bruises and injuries over his back and chest from his prison stay. His knees were bruised and swollen from long periods of kneeling. At the time of Wang's last report to the authorities, he was warned against telling anyone he had been beaten and he was further cautioned about what he might say "on the outside" or else he "would bear responsibility for the consequences."

■ **WANG Wang**, arrested along with eight other leaders of the Shanghai Workers Autonomous Federation on June 9, 1989, was "released immediately after questioning by the police" according to a Chinese reply to International Labor Organization inquiries (March 1992). Requests by the U.S. government (November 1991) for information about Wang elicited no response from Chinese officials. According to a *Beijing Radio* broadcast (FBIS, June 12, 1989), Wang and the others were accused of holding secret meetings, spreading rumors, distributing leaflets, advocating strikes, chanting reactionary slogans, advocating the overthrow of the government, setting up roadblocks and disrupting traffic. Allegedly, "they also vilified the Shanghai Council of Trade Unions as being totally paralyzed.

■ **WANG Xizhe,** formerly a factory worker in Guangzhou, Guangdong Province was released on parole on February 3, 1993 after serving nearly 12 years of a 14-year sentence. He must report regularly to the police for the next two years and faces four and a half years' deprivation of political rights. According to *Xinhua*, Wang was released early because he "obeyed prison regulations... and had a good attitude." In accordance with Article 73 of the PRC Criminal Code, the judicial department concerned submitted the proposal for parole to the Zhaqing City Intermediate People's Court which ratified it.

After his release, Wang, insisting he would rather go back to prison than give up personal freedoms (*South China Morning Post*, June 30, 1993), continued to talk to foreign journalists and to publish articles in the Hong Kong press. Chinese officials reminded Wang he is still on parole and reportedly demanded he cease his press activities and warned him to refrain from starting a private business. On July 3, Wang was intercepted on his way to work and forced to take a tour of southern China including the Zhuhai Special Economic Zone. Police originally told Wang's wife he would be gone for a week on a "study and inspection tour" (*AP*, July 7, 1993), but he was sent home after four days with no official explanation of the purpose or the foreshortening.

After 1988, Wang was held in punitive solitary confinement in a special compound for political prisoners, but his prison conditions improved shortly after the release of the 1991 *Chinese White Paper on Human Rights*. When Wang left prison, however, he was forced to leave behind the books and essays he wrote while in confinement (*South China Morning Post*, February 4, 1993). At the time of his release, Wang defended his political beliefs and re-affirmed that what he had done was "worthwhile." In a letter of appeal to the Supreme People's Court, he insisted that he was not guilty and demanded his thorough rehabilitation. He said he would take legal action against those who made false charges against him and would demand damages for political, economic and mental loses. This latest appeal is but one in a series. After Wang was confined in solitary, he wrote an appeal letter a month - some 50 all together. He never received any replies.

Wang was arrested on April 20, 1981 and sentenced on June 1, 1982 on charges of "counterrevolutionary propaganda" and sedition, of forming a "counterrevolutionary group" and of inciting the masses to defy the state and to disobey the state's decrees (*Ming Bao*, March 17, 1993). The severity of his sentence, which was served in Huaiji County Labor Reform Camp in Guangdong Province, was thought to be partly attributable to his campaign to secure the release of Liu Qing (see p.502). Earlier, Wang was a co-author of a renowned pro-democracy article, "On Socialist Democracy and the Legal System," which was pasted up as a wall-poster in Guangzhou in 1974. Together with others involved in the article, he served several years in prison for his audacity in challenging the highly repressive system in place in China during Mao's last years. Released in 1979, Wang played a major role in the Democracy Wall movement, assisting in the production of *April Fifth Forum* and editing his own journal, *Study Bulletin*. As part of his activities for the "National Committee for the Release of Liu Qing," Wang noted in an open letter to the National People's Congress that China's constitution guaranteed Liu's right to publish the transcript of Wei Jingsheng's (see below) trial. Other articles and wall posters by Wang denounced the Mao personality cult, protested against arbitrary Party control of society and pleaded for democracy and self-government. Wang is married and has one son.

■ **WEI Jingsheng,** the 43-year-old renowned Democracy Wall dissident who had already served fourteen-and-a-half years of a 15-year sentence, was unexpectedly released on parole on September 14, 1993. Six days later, on September 20, he was finally permitted to return to his parents' home. Until then, the No.1 Section of the Beijing Public Security Bureau, which deals with political dissidents, kept him at a location they tried to keep secret, the Mingyuan Hotel, a government guest house. When finally able to talk with reporters, Wei said "I have no regrets about the time I spent in prison because it was for the interests of the whole country," (*Washington Post*, September

21, 1993). He said he believed he had done nothing wrong, he had not changed his political views a bit and he still planned to fight for democracy. But because he is on parole and forbidden to take part in political activities for the next three years, he refused to elaborate. In detailing the conditions of his probation, Wei did say "I cannot vote, I have no freedom of expression, I cannot form any kind of organization, even doing business is not allowed (*New York Times*, September 21, 1993). He did confirm that he had been beaten in prison, had suffered "mental torment," had lost all but a dozen or so of his teeth and was suffering from prison-induced heart and lung problems.

According to Wei's account, he spent five years in prisons in the Beijing area, three-and-one-half of them in Beijing Prison No.1, and five years in Qinghai labor camps, including the 10,000 prisoner Tanggemu Labor Reform Camp (Qinghai No.13 *Laogai* Detachment). The last four years he was at the Nanpu New Life Salt Camp in Tangshan, Hebei Province, reportedly one of the largest and most profitable of the forced-labor camps in the Chinese prison system. According to a description in a confidential prison magazine, Nanpu is "the largest coastal salt-farm in the whole of Asia."

At no time was Wei in a cell with other prisoners. At Nanpu, his cell measured two meters by two-and-a-half meters. A door opened into a guards' room and a 15-square meter yard was attached. Wei was not permitted to leave the unit, nor could he speak with anyone but his guards. Throughout his ordeal, he was deprived of reading materials, including even government newspapers. Although Wei reportedly was released by order of the Tangshan Intermediate People's Court because he "had shown a good attitude," and "followed prison regulations," in March 1993, Minister of Justice Cai Cheng described Wei's behavior in prison as only "fair" and said he had little chance of early release because of his steady opposition to the government (*South China Morning Post*, March 26, 1993).

In an obvious bid to influence Western public opinion, Chinese authorities released a videotape taken of Wei as he "toured" Tangshan on January 13, 1993. On the tape, released to CNN (*Baltimore Sun*, March 26, 1993), Wei was shown visiting tourist spots, a department store and a book store, seeing a dentist, buying small items and sharing a meal with accompanying police officers. Back in his cell, Wei was taped watching TV. Another tape, made in the fall of 1992, showed Wei on a trip to Beijing, reportedly undertaken to show him how China has changed since his arrest.

Formerly an electrician in the Beijing Zoo, Wei, an Anhui Province native, was arrested on March 29, 1979 and sentenced in October of that year on charges of passing "military secrets" to a foreign journalist in Beijing and engaging in "counterrevolutionary propaganda and incitement." The so-called "military secret" was information which had already been broadcast on Chinese television concerning China's December 1978 invasion of Vietnam; the charge of "counterrevolutionary propaganda" referred solely to Wei's advocacy of peaceful and nonviolent political change. In his journal, *Explorations*, a small mimeographed magazine which first appeared in the winter of 1978, he published extracts from an Amnesty International report on Chinese political prisoners. He also wrote several controversial articles, the most famous of which was "The Fifth Modernization," his clarion call for democracy. In December 1978, the article in its entirety was pasted up on Beijing's Democracy Wall. The following March, along with other Democracy Wall writers, Wei was denounced by Deng Xiaoping. Wei responded by writing and circulating an article entitled "Democracy, or New Autocracy?", in which he warned that Deng was fast becoming a Mao-style dictator.

According to an Asia Watch source, "Ordinary police and prison guards had no authority over [Wei]....He was watched over by a team of special security officers. No single official was allowed to be alone with him. His condition was reported directly to Deng Xiaoping's office. Deng decided personally on everything related to Wei." In March 1993, at the start of his fifteenth year in prison, Wei was co-recipient with Nelson Mandela of a major U.S. human rights award, the Gleitsman Foundation's International Activist Award. After his release, many of Wei's prison letters and a number of more recent political commentaries by him were published in newspapers and magazines around the world. In early December 1993,

following publication of an article by Wei in the *New York Times* in which he sharply criticized China's leaders for widespread violation of human rights, he was informed by Public Security Bureau officials that under the terms of his prison parole he was banned from publishing any articles either at home or abroad. Wei ignored the ban.

■ **WU Zhijun** - see p.149

■ **XU Guibao** - see p.386

■ **XU Shuiliang**, 41, formerly a worker in a pharmaceutical factory in Nanjing, was released in May 1991 and is living in Hangzhou, Zhejiang Province. In response to U.S. government inquiries (November 1991), Chinese officials confirmed that he had been released. Xu was arrested in July 1981 in Nanjing and subsequently sentenced to 15 years' imprisonment which he reportedly served in Laohuqiao Prison in Nanjing. The date of his trial is not known and the charges against him were never made public, but he was identified in the court judgement against Xu Wenli (see below) as a key member of the latter's "counterrevolutionary group."

A prominent theoretician of the Democracy Wall movement, Xu contributed a series of trenchant pro-democracy articles to the unofficial press. He was previously detained for three years starting in 1975 for putting up wallposters in the streets of Nanjing criticizing China's "bureaucratic elite" and the unfair system of official privileges. Held for several years without charge at that time, Xu was released in 1979 and quickly became active in the Democracy Wall movement.

■ **XU Wenli**, China's "Special Prisoner 01," now 49, was released on parole on May 26, 1993. *Xinhua*, the official Chinese news agency reported that "Xu was sentenced by the Beijing Municipal Higher People's Court for illegally organizing a clique to overthrow the government" and that parole was granted "for performing very well and obeying prison regulations." Xu, who had completed twelve years of a fifteen-year sentence, eleven of them in solitary confinement, laughed when he heard the report. He also said he committed no crime, "because what I did was for my country and my people" (*Reuters*, May 26, 1993). Although reports of Xu's imminent release circulated for more than a week, he was told of it only one hour before he actually could leave.

Imprisoned for dissident activities during the 1979 Democracy Wall movement, Xu experienced severe medical problems while in prison. He was denied laboratory tests for a urinary blockage after medical staff at Beijing Prison No.1 dismissed his complaints following a perfunctory examination (*Far Eastern Economic Review*, May 7, 1992). Permission for that examination was obtained only after worldwide publicity about his severe infection. Xu had been getting weaker and weaker. "Horrendous prison conditions" (*Hong Kong Standard* (February 27, 1992), including insufficient food, prolonged solitary confinement in a tiny punishment cell, lack of medical treatment and lack of sanitation including permission to wash only once a month, all contributed to his decline. Xu has lost most of his teeth and his hair has turned white.

Xu, from Anqing in Anhui Province, spent the first three years of his sentence in solitary confinement in a six square meter cell. In late 1985, he managed to smuggle out a detailed account, *My Defense Statement*, dated December 1984, about his arrest, trial and general treatment in prison, including his 200 interrogation sessions. Following the document's publication in the West in 1986, Xu was moved to another windowless cell measuring only three square meters, where he spent another three and a half years. Family visits were denied and radio, newspapers and television banned. Transferred to a larger but still solitary cell, Xu was monitored around the clock by a video camera. He was permitted to leave his quarters only to relieve himself and he was declared ineligible for "labor reform" because he had never "confessed" to his "crimes."

When Xu's wife was permitted to see him in early 1989, Xu could barely speak; he spent most of that half-hour in uncontrollable tears. A reporter from the *South China Morning Post* visiting Beijing No.1 Prison in September 1989 was told by the deputy governor, Song Wenbo, that Xu was still in solitary confinement. Solitude, declared Song, was "beneficial to Xu's individual reform."

On November 28, 1990, Xu's wife appealed for his release on humanitarian grounds. She reported he was malnourished and showed signs of lymphatic tuberculosis. The lumps on his neck had not been diagnosed, she added, because he refused to permit the prison doctor to take a blood sample, fearing contamination from a re-used needle (*Hong Kong Standard*, November 29, 1990). Nevertheless, an anti-tubercular medication was prescribed; a doctor Kang consulted agreed the symptoms could indicate tuberculosis.

Xu, who describes himself as "just a small electrician who puts out fires," helped launch *April Fifth Forum*, a major dissident journal, and in November 1979 he put up a poster on the Xidan Democracy Wall. He wrote a 20-point list of suggestions to the Central Committee of the Chinese Communist Party, circulated a private newsletter, gave numerous interviews to foreign journalists and television stations emphasizing the need for democracy in a Marxist society and published several articles in Hong Kong under a pseudonym. Regarded as a moderate within the movement, Xu publicly protested the arrests of Wei Jingsheng (see p.507) and Liu Qing (see p.502), and in the summer of 1980 was the chief organizer of the unofficial North-China Association of the Democratic Press. He was arrested on October 4, 1981 and sentenced on June 8, 1982. Fifty people attended his trial, but the audience was hand-picked by the authorities, and all those without an official pass, including Xu's wife, **Kang Tong**, were denied admission.

The precise official terms of Xu's parole are not known, but his original sentence included four years'

subsequent "deprivation of political rights."

■ **YANG Hui**, a worker from Xiangtan City, Hunan who enrolled in a part-time correspondence college course prior to the 1989 protest movement, was arrested after June 4 and held for almost a year before being released.

■ **YANG Xiuping** - see p.156

■ **YAO Tiansheng** - see p.11

■ **YOU Dianqi** ("Diangsi" on an International Labor Organization report), a "core member" of the Beijing Workers Autonomous Federation, was "released immediately after questioning by the police," according to a Chinese response to ILO inquiries (March 1992). Requests by the U.S. government for information went unanswered (November 1991). You was captured in Xi'an on June 14, 1989, according to a UPI report. He allegedly took part in a May 28 protest outside Beijing police headquarters organized to demand the release of detained workers, and he was accused of attacking army troops.

■ **Manager ZHANG** (given name not known), in his forties, formerly a manager of the Changsha Municipal Heavy Machinery Plant, Hunan Province, was released from detention and as of May 1992 was unemployed. Arrested soon after June 4, 1989 and detained for several months, Zhang allegedly had supported students' and workers' strike activities. According to the authorities, "on several occasions he gave banquets for students and local residents who had come to the factory to make disturbances, which had an extremely bad effect."

■ **ZHANG Hongyu** - see p.372

■ **ZHANG Shaoying** - see p.149

■ **ZHANG Yuxiang (MENG Tianye)** - see p.79

■ **ZHANG Zhenmin**, a worker at a plant associated with the Harbin City Printing and Dyeing Mill, arrested along with ten other members of a Dare-to-Die youth team in Taiping, has been released, according to an official Chinese response to inquiries from the U.S. government (November 1991). It is not known what happened to other team members, all of whom were arrested on or before June 8, 1989. All those involved allegedly "made trouble and disturbed the social order in the name of supporting and mourning those who died in Beijing." They rode through the streets shouting "Long live Dao Qiang Pao" (Knife, gun, artillery), the name of a gang responsible for acts of murder and arson. Zhang, a Harbin native described as a key leader of the group, reportedly stayed away from work for long periods of time; the other team members were described as "jobless and ill-behaved loafers" (Amnesty International, *ASA 17/24/90*).

■ **ZHANG Zhiyong**[2], a worker; **YAO Yong**, a peasant; and **WEI Pizhi**, who was unemployed at the time of his arrest, were released in late 1990 or early 1991 (see Yang Jinchao p.476).

"After investigation and education, they acknowledged their criminal behavior during the period of turmoil and demonstrated their repentance" (*Reuters*, January 3, 1991 from *Ningxia Daily* reaching Beijing January 3, 1991); therefore the Yinchuan People's Court, Ningxia Hui Autonomous Region, and the Yinchuan Public Security Bureau decided to be lenient.

■ **ZHANG Zhonghui**, a 16-year-old who worked in a factory in Changsha, Hunan Province, was released as not guilty at the end of 1990. Arrested with several others in June 1989 and accused of theft, Zhang was formally charged in early 1990. He was publicly tried for the first time in May 1990. Although the trial was suspended for lack of sufficient evidence, Zhang remained in detention. In late 1990, his family finally petitioned the government, at the same time making public the results of fingerprint tests demonstrating Zhang's innocence. Workers at the factory where Zhang had worked immediately protested and the accusations against him were swiftly withdrawn. It has been reported that the real reason Zhang and the others were arrested was that they had offended the son of the factory security chief.

■ **ZHAO Lisheng** - see p.363

■ **ZHAO Ping**, a 26-year-old worker in the Beijing Zhongguancun Kefu Computer Company, arrested in June 1989, was released that November. According to an Asia Watch source, he was tortured while in prison.

■ **ZHOU Yong** - see p.103

■ **ZHOU Shaowu**, a young worker who had been imprisoned after the June 1989 crackdown, went to Tiananmen Square with his girlfriend on June 4, 1992, and was again arrested, this time in connection with a government crackdown against underground pro-democracy groups. (See Hu Shenglun p.20). He was held at the Beijing East District PSB Jail for approximately forty days and then released. According to official accounts (*Beijing Television*, June 14, 1989; FBIS, June 15, 1989), Zhou, a former worker at the Ningguo County Ferro-Alloy Plant in Anhui Province, was first arrested on June 10, 1989 in Shanghai in possession of various "reactionary materials" including a proposal to establish an organization called the *League of Democratic Parties*. Between May 18, 1989 when he arrived in Beijing, until his departure from the city on June 2, Zhou was active in the Beijing Students Autonomous Federation, serving as a liaison between students and workers in the square. After reaching Shanghai on June 6, he allegedly made contact with "other illegal organizations" and was then arrested. According to a Chinese government reply to the International Labor Organization's Freedom of Association Committee (November 11, 1991), Zhou was eventually either "released after re-education or absolved of criminal responsibility by the court."

■ **ZHU Jianbin**, a 37-year-old former Wuhan steel worker and co-founder of the unofficial journal, *Sound of the Bell*, was released from prison around August 1992 after serving eleven years. He reportedly has returned to Wuhan, Hebei Province and is working. According to Chinese authorities, Zhu was originally sentenced in April 1981 to a six-year prison term, but when he broke prison regulations he had his sentence increased. In August 1980, after signing a petition calling for the release of Liu Qing (see p.502), and meeting with other activists in southern China to form the *All-China Association of the Democratic Press*, Zhu was briefly detained, then was rearrested in April 1981. The author of a major dissident article, "The Intermediate Formation and its Developmental Tendencies," which argued that China was an anomalous society caught between feudalism, capitalism and socialism, Zhu was detained solely for his peaceful exercise of the right to free expression.

■ **ZHU Lianyi** - see p.563

Occupation unknown

■ **CHEN Ren, HU Bosen, JU Hongnian, SHEN Zhixiang, YU Rongfu** and **ZHONG Manxiang**, were listed by the Chinese authorities as released (November 1991), in response to a U.S. government request for information about some 800 dissidents. The six names were not included on the U.S. list, however, and nothing further is known about any of them.

■ **CHEN Yongfa** was released after serving a three-year sentence in connection with the 1989 pro-democracy movement. No additional information is available.

■ According to an Asia Watch source, **GUI Chongwu**, arrested in connection with Wang Juntao's (see p.70) attempted escape from China, served a sentence of one-and-a-half years and was released.

■ **JIANG Zhu**, who reportedly surrendered to the Public Security Bureau in Luanping, Hebei Province (*Hebei Ribao*, July 11, 1989), has been released, according to an official Chinese response to inquiries by the U.S. government (November 1991). He allegedly was involved in "illegal organizations" in either Hebei or Beijing.

■ **SHI Jiangang**, a "major participant" in the pro-democracy movement, was arrested at a relative's home in Shandong Province on June 10, 1989 by the Laoling City Public Security Bureau (*Shandong Provincial Radio*, June 22, 1989, in FBIS, June 23). According to an official Chinese response to U.S. government inquiries (November 1991), he has been released. No other information is available.

■ After **SUN Xiaojun** completed a two-year term for his activities in connection with the 1989 pro-democracy movement, he continued his organizational efforts. Fearful of being detained again, he escaped from China.

■ **WANG Yongwing** - see p.453

■ **ZHANG Shaoying** - see p.149

■ **ZIE Zi** (probably a misspelling for XIE Zi) was released, according to a March 1992 Amnesty International report. There is no further information on the case.

Ethnic Nationals

■ **AMA PHURBU**, a 57-year-old Lhasa businesswoman, sentenced without trial on September 16, 1990 to a three-year "labor re-education" term for "political activities," was released on April 28, 1992, six months before the end of her term. Detained on October 31, 1989 for allegedly organizing memorial prayers for those killed during earlier demonstrations, she was held first in Yitrutu, a part of Sangyip, then moved to Gutsa Detention Center. Other members of Ama Phurbu's family also have been imprisoned. One son is Gyaltsen Choephel (see p.352); another son was briefly detained in April or May 1991 during a round-up of activists likely to protest China's fortieth anniversary celebration of the "liberation" of Tibet. An unconfirmed account from June 1990 reported that in that same year, members of Ama Phurbu's family were placed, at least temporarily, in preventative detention (*Tibet Information Network*).

■ **BAATAR** and **BAO Hongguang (ULAN GEREL)**, 36-year-old Hohhot, Inner Mongolia natives and leaders of the 1981 student protest against Han Chinese domination, were released on parole, Baatar early in 1993 and Bao in early 1992. Baatar's family is his guarantor. The two men were sentenced to eight years' imprisonment in the spring or summer of 1988, having been arrested sometime between August 10-15, 1987 after escaping to Outer Mongolia, where they were refused political asylum and then extradited back to China. Arrested near the border, the two were beaten by army troops, and Baatar had his arm broken by rifle butts when he refused to kneel in a gesture of submission. Baatar graduated from the department of economics of the University of Inner Mongolia in 1982 and was assigned to work for the Xilin Gol League's planning commission. Bao is a 1982 graduate of the Engineering College of Inner Mongolia.

■ **BAGDRO**[4], 21, from Lhokha Namgyal Shol, arrested in 1990 and sentenced in 1991 to a two-year prison term, was released from Sangyip Prison, probably around March 1992.

■ **BUZANG**, a 23-year-old born in Phenpo Lhundrup County, arrested in 1989 and sentenced to a prison term of one-and-a-half years, was released from Sangyip Prison.

■ **CHIME TSERING** - see p.190

■ Four of five nuns from Shungsep Nunnery who were sentenced without trial to three years' "labor re-education" at a public sentencing rally on September 24, 1989, **CHOENYI LHAMO**, 19, from Nyemo Dzong; **SONAM CHOEDRON**[2], 22, from Chushul Ratoe; **KUNCHOK**

DROLMA, sometimes written GONJO DROLMA, 29, from Lhokha Gongkar; and Rigzin Choedron, have been released. The release of the fifth, **TASHI CHOEZOM**, is presumed. Rigzin Choedron died in October 1992, following her release (see p.166). According to a *Tibet Information Network* report (May 23, 1993), Kunchok Drolma was severely tortured and suspended by ropes for long periods during her first three years in prison. According to one source, she "remained under torture and had no peace for a single minute" during her time in prison. She was "beaten up with her arms tied up and subjected to intensive interrogation" (*Tibet Information Network*, October 1993). One other nun, **RINCHEN CHOENYI**, (lay name MIGMAR[12], also referred to as RICHOE), 20, from Chushul, sentenced to a seven-year term on October 5, 1989, was still in Drapchi Prison as of January 1994 and had been expelled from her nunnery. She was arrested once before for her alleged participation in protest demonstrations on June 1, 1988. Her release, on that occasion, for an "improved attitude towards her crime," was accompanied by her "written guarantee" to mend her ways and not to demonstrate again (Amnesty International, *ASA 17/10/90*).

All six nuns allegedly shouted "reactionary" pro-independence slogans on the Barkhor on September 22, just two days before they were sentenced (*Tibet Daily*, September 25, 1989). According to the newspaper account, "In order to safeguard the unity of the homeland and to severely punish those lawless people...who intended to split the homeland, the Lhasa Public Security Bureau on September 24 denounced six nuns who openly took part in activities on September 22 aimed at splitting the homeland....The nuns were hysterically shouting several reactionary slogans such as 'Tibetan independence.' They were swollen with arrogance and were caught in the act by the cadres and policemen...with the suddenness of a thunderbolt."

■ **CHUNGDAG**[3], a 21-year-old native of Lhasa Thelpung Gang, arrested in 1989, was released after completing a two-year sentence in Sangyip Prison. No other information is available.

■ **CHUNGDAG**[4], 20, born in Lhasa Kyire, arrested in 1989, was released after completing a one-year sentence in Sangyip Prison. No other details are available.

■ **DADRON**[2] (possibly a contraction for DAWA DROLMA[3]), a 14-year-old from Lhasa, in Sangyip Prison in late 1991, was released upon completion of her term.

■ **DAMCHOE PEMO**, a 26-year-old trader and native of Nyemo, arrested, reportedly by members of the State Security Bureau, at 4 P.M. on May 20, 1993 on suspicion of being a member of the *Snowland Youth Association*, a pro-independence organization, was released on October 29 from Seitru Prison. Five months pregnant at the time of her arrest, Damchoe Pemo miscarried after nine days during which

she was forced to stand for a 12-hour stretch, denied sleep for a period of 48 hours, tortured with electric batons and deprived of food. A nurse was permitted to visit her following the miscarriage, but at most, Damchoe Pemo visited a hospital only briefly even though her condition was described as critical. Damchoe Pemo's arrest came five days after that of her uncle Lobsang Gyaltsen[3] (see p.42), also suspected of belonging to a pro-independence organization. Although her home, in the Barkhor area of Lhasa, was searched by seventeen police officers after her uncle's arrest, it is believed no incriminating evidence was found. According to Amnesty International (*ASA 17/35/93*, August 13, 1993), **TASHI TOPGYAL**, 30, Damchoe Pemo's husband and also a trader, was detained on June 23, 1993. Nothing further is known about his arrest or place of detention.

Damchoe Pemo reportedly was arrested once before, probably in March 1989 for involvement in a demonstration, and held two years.

■ **DAWA**[11], a 19-year-old from Lhasa Rabsel, arrested on March 5, 1989 and sentenced to a three-year prison term, has been released. Held first in Sangyip, he finished his term in Trisam Prison.

■ **DAWA**[12], born in 1936, a native of Lhasa Tsemonling and formerly a monk at Sera Monastery, was released after three years in Gutsa Detention Center. He had been arrested in March 1988, probably for his involvement in a March 5 demonstration. Beaten during his prison stay, he had to be hospitalized for a period of six months just prior to release. Dawa was arrested twice before, and beaten each time. His first arrest came during a 1981 fact-finding mission. When the mission delegates approached the Potala, he allegedly shouted independence slogans. The second detention, lasting six months, started on August 28, 1986, and was for possession of anti-Chinese documents. Dawa is the uncle of Sonam Lhamo (see p.530), who demonstrated and was arrested with Ngawang Tsepak (see p.529).

■ **DAWA DONDRUP**, a 30-year-old native of Khangma, Shigatse Prefecture, arrested on March 7, 1989 and released after serving a two-year administrative sentence in Sangyip Prison, died at the age of 31 on November 9, 1992 in his home in Lhasa Shol. His death, reportedly from kidney failure, came a year and eight months after his March 7, 1991 release. It is strongly suspected that Dawa Dondrup's death resulted from beatings and maltreatment sustained in prison. According to one source, "at the time of his release he was in very bad health. His kidney and bladder were damaged and he could not retain urine. Later he managed to get an x-ray of his back, which showed that the main rib was broken on the lower side."

Dawa Dondrup reportedly was beaten unconscious several times, in the police station after his arrest for participating in the major Lhasa demonstrations, and again in the detention center to which he was moved. According to one source, during the four months and eleven days between his arrest and his September 17, 1989 sentencing, during which time no one knew where he was, Dawa Dondrup was subjected to harsh interrogation sessions which included "the sustained use of different implements...including wooden sticks, iron rods, gun butts, ropes and chairs." In addition, "he received no proper medication during his detention, he was not given proper food and he was forced to work while his health was bad." It is suspected that Dawa Dondrup received especially brutal treatment in prison because he had been a soldier, having served for four years starting in 1979, during which time he was regarded as politically reliable and a model soldier (*Tibet Information Network*, October 1993).

■ **DAWA KYIZOM**, a 20-year-old student at Lhasa Middle School No.1, from Lhasa Kyire, was released on medical parole in the custody of her mother on October 24, 1992. Since her sentence was to run through November 22, 1993, she presumably is no longer on parole. Dawa Kyizom reportedly has "serious rheumatic heart disease" and the release permitted her to enter a hospital outside the prison system. It also made her parents financially responsible for her care. Contradictory reports at that time of her release placed her in Trisam, after transfer from Gutsa Detention Center. Dawa Kyizom's three-year "re-education through labor" sentence for "counterrevolutionary propaganda" was in connection with her giving a forbidden Tibetan flag to a 26-year-old Gyumed monk, lay name Tsering Dorje[2] (see p.207), who then reportedly flew it over the roof of his temple in Lhasa on October 1, China's National Day. She reportedly confessed under police interrogation. At the time Dawa Kyizom was arrested, 9:30 A.M. on October 26, 1990, she lived in Lhasa Thepung Gang with her mother Samten Wangmo and her father Shidam (*Tibet Information Network*, February 20, 1991).

■ **DAWA SANGPO**, 18, from Lhasa, arrested in 1989 and sentenced to a one-year term, has been released from Sangyip Prison. No other information is available.

■ **DAWA TSERING**[3] - see p.353

■ **DAWA TSERING**[4], a 15-year-old from Lhasa, held in Sangyip Prison as of late 1991, was released upon completion of his term.

■ **DONDEN**, a 21-year-old monk from Lhokha Gongkar, Namgyal Shol, arrested in 1989 and sentenced to a one-and-a-half year term, has been released from Sangyip Prison. No other information is available.

■ **DORJE DRADUL**, 59, from Lhasa Banakshol, arrested at home on March 15, 1993, was released on April 6. He had had a stomach operation one month prior to his detention which required a special diet administered on an hourly basis. At the time he was seized and taken to a Public Security Office for intense interrogation, his

home was searched, and cassettes, a history book, and documents which he had written were taken. On March 21, police officers returned to his home, asked his wife, **KELSANG YANGCHEN**, for a photograph of him taken in India with a "foreigner," and took her in for two weeks of questioning. The arrests of **LOTEN**[1], 51, a Gyumed monk, and **NYIMA**[2], a 28-year-old Ganden monk from Gyama, followed, the latter on April 2 and the former several days before. Loten, previously imprisoned for three years, had been released around the end of December 1992 and expelled from his monastery.

■ **DORJE WANGDU**, 33, administratively sentenced on September 26, 1991 to three years "labor re-education" for "counterrevolutionary activities," among them suggesting to friends that they wear Tibetan clothes on a Chinese holiday, was released before the expiration of his term. According to an official document headed Lhasa Municipal People's Government, Committee of Re-education Through Labor, which was obtained by the *Tibet Information Network* (February 20, 1991), three additional reasons for his sentence were given. They had to do with giving Buddhist objects, "symbols of personal protection," to some monks at Ganden Monastery on February 22, 1991; possessing "reactionary leaflets" and "once taking a copy of a reactionary poster with red stamps on it from Muru Monastery and saying he was going to put it up at an important time." When Dorje Wangdu was arrested on April 22, he was running an electronics repair shop. He is the brother of Lobsang Tenzin[2] (see p.351), sentenced to life imprisonment in connection with the death of a policeman.

- **DRAKPA TENGYE** - see p.178

- **DROLMA YANGZOM**, a 30-year-old Lhasa woman, arrested first in 1987 and held two months in Gutsa Detention Center, was arrested again in 1989, detained four months in Sangyip Prison, then released.

- **GENDUN RINCHEN**, 46, a Tibetan tourist guide for China International Travel Service (CITS) arrested during the night of May 13, 1993, by the State Security Bureau, and his neighbor, **LOBSANG YONTEN**[1] (lay name TSASUR CHOEZEY), a 61-year-old former monk at Loseling College at Drepung Monastery, who had been seized two days earlier, were unexpectedly freed on January 10 and January 11, 1994, respectively. Lobsang Yonten had previously been imprisoned from 1960 to 1986. Although the two men were held incommunicado and in solitary confinement at Seitru, a part of the Sangyip Prison Complex in the suburbs of Lhasa, for eight months, initial reports indicated that, in a departure from the authorities' normal practice in the case of Tibetan dissidents, they had not been tortured or ill-treated in detention.

Just prior to their arrests, the two reportedly had planned to present a European Community delegation, due to arrive in Lhasa May 16, with a name list of Tibetan political prisoners and letters of appeal describing the state of human rights and prison conditions in Tibet. On May 25, the Chinese Foreign Minister denied that the arrests were related to the delegation's visit and insisted that the two had "stolen a large amount of state secrets" and "engaged in separatist activities which directly threatened China's national security." (In Chinese judicial practice, any information not published openly by the state can be retrospectively deemed a "state secret.") In August, the Deputy Party Secretary in Lhasa reiterated the accusation to a visiting American senator, adding that Gendun Rinchen had "coaxed people to overthrow our present system" and "favored the independence of Tibet." The normal penalty for "supplying state secrets to foreigners" ranges from several years' to life imprisonment, and in "especially heinous cases," the death penalty may be applied.

Gendun Rinchen is from Markham in Kham. From the age of ten until 1987, he lived in India with his parents, working his last ten years there as a mechanical engineer. Before taking a job with CITS, he was employed by Lhasa Travel Agency. According to reports from those who knew him, Gendun Rinchen was deeply concerned about the state of human rights in Tibet and had attempted to alert international public opinion to conditions within Tibet. Lobsang Yonten, at the time of his arrest, earned his living by teaching private classes in Tibetan. Following their arrests, some 110 people inside Tibet, including a number of Communist Party and government officials, reportedly signed a total of twenty-two separate petitions calling upon the United Nations to press the Chinese authorities to release the two men. Initial reports of their releases gave no indication as to whether or not all charges had been dropped, or if they were only conditional or temporary in nature.

■ **GONG LA**, a female second-year student at Tibet University when she was arrested, reportedly was so severely injured by prison guards while in custody that she had to be hospitalized in Worker's Hospital, probably sometime in August or September 1989 (*Reuters*, October 22, 1989). The nature of her injuries is unclear, but initial reports said that she had been crippled and that one kidney had been seriously impaired. Her family was required to meet all her medical expenses, and had to agree to return her to police custody if and when she recovered. A native of Dayab in Chamdo, Gong La was arrested in her dormitory room sometime after the imposition of martial law; her arrest was confirmed by the president of Tibet University, Tsewang Gyurme, who added that she had been expelled from the university and banned from engaging in further study or being appointed to a government post. Her offense, putting up posters calling for Tibetan independence, earned her an administrative sentence of three years' "labor re-education." Her present whereabouts are unknown.

■ Of the six nuns, two from Phabongkha Nunnery, and four from Chubsang Nunnery, arrested for demonstrating in Lhasa on April 24, 1988 and sent to Gutsa Detention Center, at least five have been released. **GYALTSEN CHOEDRON**[2], from Lhokha, and **GYALTSEN LOCHOE**, (also known as GYALTSEN LODROE[2]; lay name **ZOMKYI**), from Taktse County, both 20 years old, from Chubsang Nunnery, were regularly beaten during their four or five-month detentions as were the others. **GYALTSEN TENZIN**, (lay name TSERING DROLMA), 20, from Kham Paldar, held five months, was expelled from Chubsang after her release. She has since escaped to India. **GYALTSEN CHOEKYI**[1], (lay name DAWA DROLMA[4]), 26, a Phabongkha nun, from Lhokha, detained until January 19, 1989, is the sister of Kelsang Pema (see p.535). **TENZIN WANGMO**[1], 20, from Taktse, detained for five months, may have been re-arrested on August 21, 1990. It is not clear with which nunnery she was affiliated.

According to a statement given to a British TV reporter by one of the demonstrators, "Six of us demonstrated peacefully in the Barkhor and shouted 'Long live the Dalai Lama,' 'Get rid of the Chinese,' and 'We don't want to live under Chinese rule any more.' We distributed leaflets. We walked around the Barkhor twice and were arrested....In prison we were interrogated and beaten many times."

■ **GYALTSEN JAMPA** and **GYALTSEN LHADRON**, 25, nuns

from Chubsang Nunnery, held in Gutsa Detention Center, are known to have been released. Other than that Gyaltsen Lhadron was expelled from her nunnery, no other information about either of them is available.

- **GYALTSEN MONLAM** - see p.16, 180

- **GYALTSEN NGODRUP**, a 19-year-old nun from Garu Nunnery, possibly from Taktse Shen Tseto, has been released from prison; in February 1990, she was expelled from her nunnery. No other information is available.

- Six Garu nuns were arrested on December 19, 1987 after a demonstration, and held in Gutsa Detention Center for one month and six days. All were expelled from Garu Nunnery on February 11, 1990. Three of the six, **GYALTSEN NORBU**[2], 20, from Phenpo; **NGAWANG ZOMPA**, 20; and **NGAWANG DROLMA**[2], 20, from Phenpo, were never re-arrested.

One of the six, **GYALTSEN WANGCHUK**, was re-arrested with five or six other Garu nuns, in connection with a demonstration on December 10, 1988 and held in Gutsa Detention Center. All the arrestees have been released; and all were expelled from the nunnery on February 11, 1990. Gyaltsen Wangchuk, 20, from Phenpo Lungshoe, received a two-year sentence. She reportedly suffered a broken hip from beatings and torture and was forced to give blood while imprisoned. The others,

held for periods ranging from seven to nine months, included **GYALTSEN TENDAR**, a 30-year-old Garu nun from Phenpo; **GYALTSEN WANGMO**[1], in her twenties, from Damshung; **LOBSANG WANGMO**, a Garu nun in her twenties, from Damshung; and **NGAWANG LHAKDRON**[1], a 20-year-old from Lhasa. **PHUNTSOG PALDEN**, a Michungri nun in her twenties, born in Drigung, also was arrested on December 10, held in Gutsa for one month, and released. For information about Gyaltsen Choezang, also arrested on December 10, 1988, see Gyaltsen Drolma (p.585).

Two of the original six arrested, **GYALTSEN CHOETSO** and **GYALTSEN DEKYI**, 30, were among fourteen Garu nuns, arrested after a demonstration on April 17, 1988, and sent to Gutsa Detention Center for periods ranging from two to ten months. While there, they were all subjected to systematic torture including severe beatings with sticks, gun butts and chairs; to assaults with electric batons on most parts of their bodies; and to kicks and punches Kung Fu style. During some of the sessions, the nuns were forced to strip. Some of them received shocks from an electrical contraption that rendered them unconscious or sent them into convulsions. Prison guards even deliberately provoked a dog into attacking **NGAWANG CHOENYI**, 26, from Phenpo, and allowed it to repeatedly bite her. **GYALTSEN CHOEKYI**[2], (lay name **DAWA DROLMA**[5]), 20, from Ngangrey, reportedly was tried on January 10,

1989 but released twenty days later. Gyaltsen Choetso, 26, from Taktse County, not only experienced "routine" torture, but was attacked by a dog and was made to stand barefoot on ice for an hour. She has some permanent hearing impairment, reportedly from blows to her head and from the electric shocks. Although Gyaltsen Choetso was held only ten months in connection with her April 1988 arrest, she was formally arrested and charged on May 25, 1988 and tried on January 10, 1989. For further information about Gyaltsen Lhazom, 25, from Nyangrey, one of the fourteen arrested, see Gyaltsen Drolma (p.585). Others arrested on April 17, 1988 included **GYALTSEN TSEDON**, 22, from Phenpo; **NGAWANG YANGCHEN**[2], 19, from Medro Gongkar or Dripung; **NGAWANG TSEDON**, 20, from Lhokha; **NGAWANG SANGMO**, 20, from Phenpo; **GYALTSEN DECHEN**, 30, from Phenpo, arrested April 30; and **NGAWANG PEMO**[2], 20.

A year later, on February 1, 1990, Gyaltsen Choekyi managed to escape arrest at Garu when nine nuns were seized. Forewarned, she ran away three days earlier. Gyaltsen Dechen, Ngawang Choenyi; Gyaltsen Choetso; **NGAWANG CHOEZOM**[2], 26, from Phenpo Lhundrup; **GYALTSEN WANGMO**[2], 30, from Taktse County; and **NGAWANG PEZOM**, 26, from Medro Gongkar, were all arrested and held for several months in Gutsa during which time they were beaten and tortured. Other Garu nuns reported that those who were arrested in February had put up posters in the nunnery compound during the time that a "work

team" conducting screening and "re-education" was in residence. In addition to those already named, others known to have been expelled from the nunnery include Gyaltsen Choetso, Gyaltsen Dekyi, Gyaltsen Dechen, Gyaltsen Pezom, Gyaltsen Wangmo, Ngawang Choenyi and Ngawang Choezom.

■ **GYALTSEN YANGCHEN**, an 18-year-old Garu nun born in Phenpo, was arrested on January 21, 1991 and detained for three months in Gutsa Detention Center before being released. No other information is available.

■ **HUCHUNTEGUS** - see p.216

■ **JAMPA CHOEPHEL** - see p.351

■ Three Ani Tsangkhung nuns, **JAMPA DROLKAR**[2], in her twenties, **GYALTSEN KUNSANG**[2], and **NAMDROL TENPA**, 19, arrested between mid-January and early February 1991 for "splittist activities" at the time of the awarding of the Nobel Peace Prize to the Dalai Lama in December 1989, have been released. Jampa Drolkar, from Medro Gongkar, spent some four months in Gutsa Detention Center; Namdrol Tenpa, from Peleg in Toelung Dechen County, some five months. Gyaltsen Kunsang, in her twenties, also from Toelung, received a one-year sentence. Namdrol Tenpa has since escaped to India.

■ **JAMPA PHUNTSOG**[1], a 20-year-old native of Lhasa, arrested on March 6, 1988, offense unknown, reportedly was released from prison after having served a term of approximately one-and-a-half years.

- **JAMPA PHUNTSOG**[2], a 64-year-old Namgyal monk, from Phenpo Lhundrup County, arrested on March 17, 1988 for allegedly staging a solo demonstration on March 3 during the Monlam festival and for speaking out for Tibetan independence, was released after serving a three-year sentence in Seitru Prison. He reportedly was beaten and tortured with an electric baton when taken into custody. All told, Jampa Phuntsog spent 26 years in prison (*Tibet Bulletin*, December 1991) including two other terms, one between 1959 and 1978, and another from March 1979 until 1985.

- **JAMPEL NYIMA**, a 26-year-old Drepung monk from Damphag, reportedly arrested in August 1991, possibly at the same time as two other Drepung monks, **NGAWANG SANGPO** and **NGAWANG GOMCHEN**, was released from Gutsa Detention Center. No reason for his arrest was ever given. Jampel Nyima had been arrested previously - date unknown - released in February 1990, expelled from his monastery, and probably sent to the countryside. The two others, both 20 years old and both from Medro, reportedly were also sent to Gutsa. Their present whereabouts are unknown; they may still be in prison.

- **JAMYANG**[7], a 30-year-old native of Lhasa, arrested in 1989 and sentenced to a two-year term, has been released from Sangyip Prison. No other information is available.

- **JIGME WANGCHEN**, 35, a monk from the Jokhang Temple in Lhasa, arrested on March 8, 1988 and sentenced to a three-year prison term, has been released. Held for three months in Seitru, he was moved to Sangyip Prison where he took part in the May 20, 1991 protest (see p.186). He was then moved back to Seitru and from there to Trisam.

- **JIYANG Hung**, a 24-year-old Mongol woman who worked at the Ih Ju League's Party School, Inner Mongolia, is no longer under house arrest where she was placed, as were 25 others, on or about May 15, 1991, for her participation in the Ih Ju League's *National Culture Society* (see **Huchuntegus**, p.216). She was a member of its Provisional Council and formerly was a student in the law department at Inner Mongolia University.

- **KARMA**[2], a 22-year-old Sera Monk, from Phenpo, arrested for demonstrating on March 20, 1992, was held in Gutsa (length of detention unknown) before being released.

- **KARMA DONDRUP**, a 20-year-old, born in Kham Nangchen, arrested in 1989 and sentenced to two years' imprisonment, was released from Sangyip Prison in 1991.

- **KHEDRUP**, a 25-year-old monk from Toelung Gongkar, held in

Drapchi Prison as of late 1991, has been released.

■ **LEGTSOG** - see p.169

■ **LHAKDRON**, a female in her twenties, from Lhasa, arrested on March 7, 1989 for allegedly participating in a demonstration earlier that day, and sentenced to a two-year prison term, has been released. She is the daughter of Choezed Tenpa Choephel (see p.163).

■ **LHAKPA**[7], a 20-year-old Lhasa native, arrested in 1989 and sentenced to two years in prison, has been released from Sangyip. No other information is available.

■ **LHAKPA TSAMCHOE**[1], a 13-year-old female from a tailoring cooperative in Lhasa Ramchoe, arrested on March 8, 1990 (or possibly March 1989) for demonstrating, and held in Sangyip over four months, was released, dismissed from the cooperative, and barred from employment. Badly beaten when she was taken into detention, Lhakpa Tsamchoe was immediately hospitalized for fifteen days. Upon release, she was placed in an adult work gang cleaning septic tanks. Lhakpa Tsamchoe reportedly is left with some lameness in her left arm and leg.

■ **LHAKPA TSAMCHOE**[2], a 30-year-old woman, born in Lhasa, was arrested in 1988 and detained for six months in Gutsa Detention Center before being released. No other information is available.

■ **LHAKPA TSERING**[4], a 30-year-old security officer at the Lhasa Central Bank and a native of Lhasa, arrested in 1988, has been released after serving two-and-a-half years in Gutsa Detention Center. He was accused of writing "reactionary" posters and leaflets and putting them up while on patrol in February and March 1988 (*Lhasa Radio*, September 29, 1988).

■ **LHAKPA TSERING**[5], a 30-year-old native of Dhode, arrested in 1989 and sentenced to a two-year term, has been released from Sangyip Prison.

■ **LHAKPA TSERING**[6], a 21-year-old native of Toelung, arrested in 1989 and sentenced to a two-year term has been released from Sangyip Prison. No other information is available.

■ **LHAKSAM** - see p.195

■ **LHAMO TSERING**, a Lhasa businesswoman in her thirties, arrested in 1989 and sentenced to two years in prison, was released on March 19, 1991.

■ **LHUNDRUP GADEN** - see p.176

■ **LOBSANG CHOEJOR**[3] - see p.539 and p.15, 194

■ **LOBSANG DAWA**[2], a 26-year-old monk from Sogtsang Monastery, arrested on August 8, 1990 and released August 12, 1991, escaped Ngaba, his native place, in mid-1992. At the time, he was under police surveillance. According to his own testimony, Lobsang Dawa was detained for "breaking down the signboards of the main Chinese administrative office in Thangkar and for putting up wall posters condemning Chinese policies in Tibet on July 20, 1990. Some of the posters read: 'Our land is being destroyed by outsiders who have taken away all our riches. We will not bear this anymore.' 'Long live Tibet.'" Once seized, Lobsang Dawa was transported to the police station in Thangkar where he was handcuffed and placed in solitary confinement. During interrogation he admitted that on May 17, 1990, he had worked together with two other monks, **JIGME GYATSO[2]** and **NGAWANG GYATSO[2]**, but that he had been the one to plan everything and to write the posters. The two others were arrested the following day, August 9.

All three monks were displayed at two rallies, a public one in Thangkar and one at the monastery where their teacher announced their expulsions. They were then transferred to Zhoghe Detention Center. On February 7, 1991, the Intermediate People's Court sentenced Lobsang Dawa to a one-year term and an additional year's deprivation of political rights for having violated Article 102 (2) of the Criminal Law by "inciting anti-progressive elements against the People's Republic of China." Only officials and police officers attended the proceedings. His colleagues were released from detention without ever coming to trial. Once tried and transferred to Zhoghe Prison, Lobsang Dawa was not permitted to engage in the normal prison routine, including scheduled work, exercise and cleaning.

- **LOBSANG JINPA**, 21, from Sera Monastery, in Gutsa Detention Center in late 1991, has been released. No other information is available.

- **LOBSANG NORBU** (also known as **TENZIN WANGCHUK[2]**), an Amdo monk, was arrested on July 8, 1991 and held until April 23, 1992. According to his own report, he was seized at a gas pump west of Lhasa because of suspected involvement in activities supporting Tibetan independence. During the first three months of his detention at Sangyip prison, he was severely tortured.

- **LOBSANG RAPJOR**, a 20-year-old Chamdo monk, arrested in December 1989 and sentenced to a one-and-a-half-year-term, has been released from a prison in Chamdo.

- **LOBSANG TENZIN[4]**, a 23-year-old Tashi Choeling monk, arrested on September 14, 1990 (probably a Tibetan date) and sentenced to two years in prison, has been released. He was last in Trisam Prison.

- **LOBSANG THAPKE**, a 21-year-old Sera monk, from Phenpo Lhundrup County, was released from Gutsa Detention Center following his second arrest, date unknown. He had earlier served a two-year sentence at Drapchi Prison for participating in a March 5, 1988 demonstration. Arrest date was March 7.

- **LOBSANG THARCHIN**, a 30-year-old Lhasa native, arrested in 1989 and sentenced to a two-year term, has been released from Sangyip Prison.

■ **LOBSANG TSERING** (also known as LHO TSERING), a 48-year-old originally from Karze, arrested while traveling between Lhasa and Shigatse, was released on December 12, 1990. His arrest did not come to light until October 1990 when Lobsang Tsering's home in Lhasa was raided by the police in the presence of his wife. They told her he had been arrested for printing and distributing religious literature. Five others held in connection with the distribution, **NAMGYAL**, 53; **BUTRU**; **THUPTEN**[3]; **TENZIN GYATSO**; and **PALDEN TSERING**, were released within six months of their arrests. Butru was arrested in Lhasa; the others, arrested in Karze, were held at the district prison there. This was not the first time Lobsang Tsering was detained. He served eight years after the 1959 occupation of Tibet by Chinese forces, during which time he was severely "struggled" against.

■ **LOBSANG WANGCHUK**, a 25-year-old Drepung monk, reportedly imprisoned for four or five months after taking part in the March 1988 demonstrations in Lhasa, was admitted to the Lhasa Worker's Hospital in January 1992 for chronic kidney failure. It is known that his condition, which may have been related to treatment received in prison, improved.

■ **LOBSANG WANGYAL**, a 57-year-old native of Lhasa Banakshol, arrested in 1989 and sentenced to a

one-year term, has been released from Sangyip Prison.

■ **LOBSANG YARPHEL**[2], a 41-year-old native of Drayap, arrested in May 1989, spent nineteen months in prison in Chamdo before he was released.

■ **LODEN TENDAR**, a 49-year-old monk from either Shidhe Gon or Drepung Monastery, originally from Lhasa, sentenced to three years' imprisonment, has been released. Other than that he was in Gutsa Detention Center in late 1991, nothing further is known about his arrest date, imprisonment or his alleged offense.

■ **LOTEN**[2], a 19-year-old native of Lhasa Kyire, arrested on March 5, 1989 and sentenced to a three-year prison term, has been released. He was transferred to Trisam Prison to complete his sentence after initially being detained in Sangyip.

■ **LOTSE**, a 20-year-old native of Markham County, arrested in 1989 and sentenced to a two-year prison term, has been released from Sangyip.

■ **MIGMAR**[8], a 39-year-old resident of Lhasa, held in Gutsa Detention Center as of late 1991, has been released. The date of his arrest, his alleged offense and his prison sentence are not known.

■ **MIGMAR**[9], a 22-year-old student from Lhasa Paljor Khangsar, was in Gutsa Detention Center as of February 22, 1992, but reportedly was held only briefly. She had been detained once before, for two days, for allegedly "carrying" political posters. In that incident, on December 11, 1990, Migmar and three others, including **PHURBU DROLMA** (also known as **PHURDREN** or **PHURDRON**), 20, a student from Lhasa Kushu Dongpo, were putting up posters and scattering leaflets on the main road in the Tibetan quarter when the police appeared. The women reportedly told the officers that they had found the leaflets in front of the Jokhang and thought that they had better carry them away. It is unclear if Phurbu Drolma served a two-year sentence in connection with the 1990 incident or if she were held only briefly at that time and later re-arrested. She spent all but the last month of her term in Gutsa Detention Center and was released from Trisam Prison (*Tibet Information Network*).

- **MIGMAR TSERING**[3], 20, from Lhasa Ramchoe, arrested from his home on March 8, 1990, has been released but is barred from employment. According to family members, he was badly beaten in prison and has suffered memory loss from the blows to his head. "If you ask him to get something, he forgets by the time he can go next door," said one relative.

- Several members of a pro-independence group, the *Young Lions*, arrested November 4, 1989, have been released. **MIGMAR TSERING**[4], a 20-year-old, born in Lhasa Tromsigang, served a one-half-year prison term in Drapchi. **LHAKPA TSERING**[7], a 14-year-old Lhasa native, was released after serving a two-year sentence in Drapchi. Two other students associated with the group, **PENPA TSERING**[3] (see p.201) and **TASHI WANGDU** are still unaccounted for. In December 1989, the Lhasa People's Procuratorate sent **PHURBU**[9], another Lhasa middle school student allegedly involved with the group, to a "relevant department to undergo re-education through labor." At the time, *Lhasa Radio* (December 8, 1989), stressed that his offenses "were not serious" because he was not a leader in the group. Since "labor re-education" sentences usually run no more than three years, it is presumed Phurbu has been released. For further information see p.165.

- **MYHA**, a 20-year-old native of Kantse, arrested in 1988 and detained for eleven months in Gutsa Detention Center, has been released. No other information is available.

- A father and three sons, **NAMGYAL TASHI**[2], 56; **RIGSAM**, 21; **RIGCHO**, 25; and **RIGYO**, arrested after pro-independence materials were found in a raid, have all been released. Rigsam and Rigcho were monks at Samye Monastery and allegedly took part in a demonstration there on May 23, 1991 at which time a Tibetan flag was hoisted. Namgyal Tashi was visiting at the monastery at the time. The whereabouts of two others implicated in the same case are unclear. They are **SHERAB** and **LHAGYAL**[2]. It is possible that Lhagyal[2] and Lhagyal[1] (p.187) are the same person.

■ **NGARI**, a 40-year-old monk, born in Lhokha, arrested in March 1988 and detained for five months, has been released. No further information is available.

■ **NGAWANG CHOEDRON**[2], (also referred to as **NGAWANG TSULTRIM**[3]; lay name **TSENYI LHAMO**), 27, a Chubsang nun from Medro Gongkar Gyama, and another nun **LOBSANG DROLMA**[3], arrested for demonstrating and chanting reactionary slogans in Lhasa on October 15, 1989, were sentenced to three years' "labor re-education." Released on October 15, 1992 from Trisam Prison, after transfer from Gutsa, Ngawang Tsultrim was expelled from her nunnery. Lobsang Drolma is presumed also to have been released.

■ **NGAWANG RANGDROL**, a 20-year-old Samye monk from Yamdrog Nakar, sentenced to three years in prison for allegedly writing "Tibetan Independence" on the wall of a tea house, probably in connection with a demonstration, was released on April 7, 1992. He fled Tibet in October 1992. After he was arrested, along with **TENDAR**[2], 16, from Dranang, both men were taken to a room in a Samye hotel, interrogated, beaten and released shortly thereafter. Ngawang Rangdrol was quickly re-arrested and held for eleven months at the Lhokha jail. During that time he was beaten once more and forced to give blood twice. At Drapchi Prison, where he was next sent, he was forced to give blood once more and was badly beaten in connection with his participation in a

prison demonstrating protesting the death of Lhakpa Tsering[3] (see p.165).

■ **NGAWANG TENRAB**[2], a 24-year-old monk, born in Phenpo Lhundrup County, arrested on March 8, 1989, served a one-year sentence in Sangyip Prison before he was released. Other than that he may be a Tsuglhakhang monk, no other information is available.

■ Four Drepung monks, arrested in March 1988 and released after completing their sentences, were then expelled from their monastery. **NGAWANG TOPCHEN**, 22, from Phenpo Lhundrup, was arrested on March 6 for participating in demonstrations, for boycotting the Monlam festival in March 1988 which had been organized by the Chinese to show that conditions in Lhasa were "normal," and for putting up posters in the monastery from September 27, 1987 until he was arrested. According to testimony given by Ngawang Topchen in exile, he was initially taken to Gutsa, then moved to Sangyip Prison where he spent ten months, during which time he was so severely beaten that some of his ribs were broken. As a result of improper healing, they are permanently deformed. In addition, Ngawang Topchen was forced to break his Buddhist vows by killing pigs. **NGAWANG GENDUN**, (lay name **DAWA**[13]), 31, from Chushul County, Gampa Jangthang, arrested on March 20, entered the monastery in 1984, and was treasurer or senior secretary until his expulsion. He served a two-year prison term. **NGAWANG**

NAMGYAL[2], (lay name TASHI TSETEN), 31, a supervisor monk, from Toelung Dechen, Gurum Chu, arrested on March 6, served a three-year term. He is the brother of Ngawang Phulchung (see p.173), also a Drepung monk, serving a long-term sentence in Drapchi. For details about the fourth monk, see Ngawang Pekar (p.172).

■ **NGAWANG LHAMO** - see p.585

■ **NGAWANG TSENYI**, an 18-year-old Garu nun born in Phenpo, was arrested on January 23, 1991 and detained in Gutsa Detention Center for three months before being released.

■ Among a group of at least nine nuns sentenced without trial on September 11, 1989, seven Chubsang nuns and one Shungsep nun are known to have been released. The eight were sentenced by the Lhasa Municipal Management Committee for Re-education Through Labor to terms of two or three years' "re-education" for "daring to openly disobey martial law regulations." They had been arrested on September 2 for allegedly chanting "splittist" pro-independence slogans at a dramatic production presented at the Norbulingka in connection with the traditional Shoton Festival (*Tibet Daily*, September 14, 1989). According to the account, their "secretly plotted" fifteen minute "frenzied" demonstration interrupted a Tibetan opera which was attended by high-ranking officials.

NGAWANG TSEPAK, 20, who completed her two-year term on September 2, 1991 and fled to India, gave a detailed account of the nuns' prison treatment (*Tibet Information Network*, December 11, 1991). According to her report, they were handcuffed in the park and driven to Gutsa Detention Center. Once there, they were stripped naked, their hands were tied behind them and they were suspended from trees in the prison courtyard in the "airplane" position, with their arms behind their backs and over their heads. Asked to give the names of others involved, they were beaten or given electric shocks on various parts of their bodies, including the insides of their mouths, until they complied. Both male and female guards took part in the assault, according to the informant. Ngawang Tsepak estimated that she was suspended for three hours until both her shoulders were dislocated. No medical treatment was provided. She was later hospitalized, possibly in connection with an injury she sustained when kicked in the lower left abdomen while hanging.

Ngawang Tsepak also corroborated earlier accounts, in April and May 1990, of forced blood extraction from prisoners in Gutsa (*Tibet Information Network*, August 1991). In November or December 1990, after more than a quart of blood was removed, she herself became ill and shook continuously. She was hospitalized for three months. A native of Dro village in Medro Gongkar, Ngawang Tsepak worked as a farm laborer before she joined the Chubsang nunnery in 1989.

In August 1990, Ngawang Tsepak and five others were beaten with a plastic stool and a belt for singing a pro-independence song. They were then moved to a smaller cell and beaten again. For the next year, the six, including the informant and **DAWA LHAZOM**, 18, from either Zogang County or Phenpo Kyelung; **NGAWANG CHOEKYI**[3] (lay name DECHEN DROLMA), 21, from Toelung Gurum; **LOBSANG CHOEDRON**[3] (lay name PASANG DROLMA), 19, from Chushul Nyethang; and **SONAM LHAMO**, 19, from Lhokha Tachi, remained in the small cell under a stricter than usual regime. All except Sonam Lhamo, who received a two-year sentence, served three-year terms; all were expelled from the nunnery. Some time before they were released, Lobsang Choedron and Ngawang Choekyi were transferred to Trisam. Dawa Lhazom reportedly was severely beaten again, probably in connection with a May 23, 1991 prison protest. As a result, her face was swollen and her body covered with bruises.

Others from Chubsang sentenced to three-year-terms and expelled from the nunnery included **NGAWANG CHOEZOM**[3], 29, from Lhokha Chonggye, transferred from Gutsa to Trisam; and **PHUNTSOG TENDROL** (lay name MIGMAR[10]), 25, from Nyethang Ratoe. The Shungsep nun, **PASANG WANGMO**, about 19, reportedly was also tortured and expelled, but released shortly after her detention.

NGAWANG PEMA, a nun from either Shungsep or Chubsang nunnery, was sentenced with the nine nuns above. It is quite possible that she is the same person as Ngawang Pemo[2] (see p.522), a 20-year-old Garu nun, born in Toelung, arrested on April 17, 1988 for allegedly taking part in a demonstration with another Garu nun, Gyaltsen Dekyi (see p.521), placed in Gutsa Detention Center, and released on June 17, 1989. There are numbers of cases of nuns demonstrating soon after their releases from prison. Additionally, nuns who are banned from one nunnery may join another, which may account for the discrepancy in this case. Ngawang Pema's current whereabouts are unknown, but her release is presumed.

■   **NGAWANG YANGDRON**, a 14-year-old girl from Lhasa, was arrested on August 21, 1990 and detained for five or six months in Gutsa before being released. Her arrest may have been in connection with the arrests of sixteen demonstrators, mostly nuns, at the Norbulingka that same day.

■   **NGAWANG YUDRON**[2], a 46-year-old Lhasa businesswoman, sentenced to a seven-year sentence in Drapchi Prison for demonstrating in March 1989, reportedly was released halfway through her term. She had been arrested on April 1. Her son, Migmar Tenzin, 25, lost his job as an electronics technician for the Tibet Autonomous Regional Government because of his mother's separatist activities. The April 6, 1991 letter notifying him of his dismissal, explicitly stated his own conduct was good.

■ **NGODRUP WANGMO**, from Lhasa Ramoche, arrested from her home at midnight on May 13, 1993 in connection with the arrests of Lobsang Yonten and Gendun Rinchen (see p.519), was questioned and released that same evening. She had been detained on suspicion of stealing state secrets.

■ **NORBU**[4], 26, from Phenpo, detained on July 17, 1990 (probably a Tibetan date) and sentenced to a two-year term, has been released. He was last held at Trisam Prison.

■ **NYIMA**[6], a 23-year-old from Lhasa, arrested in 1989, was released from Sangyip Prison after serving a one-year term. No additional information is available.

■ **NYIMA KELSANG**, a 20-year-old native of Lhasa, arrested in 1989 and sentenced to three years in prison, was released from Sangyip Prison after the completion of his term. No other information is available.

■ **NYIMA TASHI**, a 20-year-old native of Lhasa, arrested in 1989 and sentenced to three years in prison, was released from Sangyip Prison after the completion of his term. No other information is available.

■ **NYIMA TENZIN**, a 29-year-old associated with the Lhasa Medical and Astronomy Institute, from Medro Gongkar, detained on July 19, 1990 (probably a Tibetan date) and sentenced to a two-year term, has been released. He was last held at Trisam Prison.

■ **NYIMA TSAM**, an 18-year-old woman, born in Lhasa, was arrested in 1988 and detained for six months in Gutsa Detention Center before being released. No other information is available.

■ **OEZER**, a 20-year-old native of Markham County, arrested in March 1988, was released after eleven months. No additional information is available.

■ **PALDEN GYATSO**, a 60-year-old monk from Drepung Monastery and a native of Shekar, was released from Drapchi Prison in August 1992 and fled Tibet. He had been sentenced on April 19, 1984 to nine years in prison and two years' subsequent deprivation of political rights for distributing "counterrevolutionary propaganda." Arrested on August 26, 1983 for allegedly passing a written appeal for Tibetan independence to a group of Beijing-based foreign correspondents in Tibet on an arranged visit, he also, in speaking with some of the thirteen visitors about Tibetan hopes for the return of the Dalai Lama, allegedly said that he was awaited "as the thirsty await water" (*Tibetan Review*, August 1983). Palden Gyatso was further accused of putting up pro-independence posters on March 9, 1982 and of having written a "reactionary" letter meant for the Dalai Lama. This was a second prison term for Palden Gyatso. For participating in the 1959 rebellion, he served 15 years, 1960 to 1975.

■ **PASANG**[8] a 20-year-old woman born in Lhasa, was arrested in 1987 and detained for two months in Gutsa Detention Center before being released. No other information is available.

■ **PASANG**[9], a 19-year-old native of Lhasa, Chagshing, arrested in 1989 and sentenced to two years in prison, which he served in Sangyip, has been released. No other information is available.

■ **PASANG DAWA**, a 20-year-old native of Lhasa, arrested in 1989 and sentenced to three years in prison, was released from Sangyip Prison at the completion of his term.

■ **PASANG GYALPO**, a 20-year-old native of Lhasa, arrested in 1989 and sentenced to a one-year term, has been released from Sangyip Prison. No other information is available.

■ **PASANG TSERING**, a 19-year-old student from Lhasa, arrested on March 7, 1989 and held in Gutsa and Sangyip, was released after four months. He had been arrested once before, on March 3, 1988 for taking part in demonstrations. Detained three months in Gutsa, he was expelled from school and barred from normal employment.

■ **PEDON**, a woman in her thirties, from Lhasa, was arrested in 1988 and detained for six months in Gutsa Detention Center before being released. No other information is available.

■ **PEMA CHOEDRON**, a 20-year-old Ani Tsangkhung nun from Toelung Gongkar, held in Gutsa Detention

Center, has been released. The date of her arrest and her alleged offense are unknown.

■ **PEMA DROLKAR**[4], a woman in her twenties, born in Lhasa, was arrested in 1988 and detained for two months in Gutsa Detention Center before being released. No other information is available.

■ **PEMA NORBU**, about 20 years old, from Medro County Drigung, arrested in 1989 and sentenced to a two-year term, has been released from Sangyip Prison.

■ **PEMA YANGCHEN**, a 40-year-old woman born in Lhasa, was arrested in 1987 and detained for over two months in Gutsa Detention Center before being released. No other information is available.

■ **PENPA**[10], a 25-year-old painter (probably refers to Thangka painting, a traditional Tibetan art form), born in Lhasa Tsemonling, arrested for his participation in the March 5, 1989 protests in Lhasa, was released on November 23, 1992. The sentence, three years' imprisonment and one year's deprivation of political rights, was handed down on July 29, 1989 but not made public until August 6. A *Xinhua* account (August 6, 1989), reported that "Criminal (Penpa) actively participated in various tumultuous counterrevolutionary activities. He took the lead in shouting reactionary slogans, waving the 'banner of the snow mountains and lions' and willfully destroying public property."

Originally held in Drapchi Prison, Penpa was one of five prisoners moved after the "Lilley Affair" (see Tenpa Wangdrag[2] p.177). Penpa may be the **BU PENPA** (Bu means boy), who according to an unconfirmed report, had his sentence extended by five years and was moved from Outridu (a section of Sangyip Prison Complex) to Drapchi (*Tibet Information Network*, August 31, 1991) and then to Powo Nyingtri. If Penpa is Bu Penpa, then the report about a sentence extension was incorrect.

■ **PENPA**[11] (also called ZHALU PENPA), a 26-year-old monk from the Tsuglhakhang, born in Tsang Zhalu, arrested on March 8, 1988, was released after one year in Sangyip Prison and expelled from his monastery.

■ **PENPA TASHI**, a 20-year-old native of Lhasa, arrested in 1989 and sentenced to a two-year prison term, has been released from Sangyip Prison. No other information is available.

■ **PENPA WANGMO**[2] (lay name PENPA DROEN), an 18-year old nun from Shungsep Nunnery, from Lhokha, arrested in 1989 and sentenced to a three-year prison term, has been released from Drapchi Prison.

■ **PHUNTSOG**[2], about 20, from Toelung Dechen County, arrested in 1989 and sentenced to a two-year prison term, has been released from Sangyip Prison. No other information is available.

■ **PHUNTSOG**[3], a 23-year-old Tsemonling monk from Medro Gongkar, detained on September 14, 1990 (probably a Tibetan date approximately equivalent to November 1) and sentenced to a two-year term, has been released. He was last held at Trisam Prison.

■ **PHUNTSOG**[4], a 20-year-old native of Lhasa Ramchoe, arrested in 1988, was detained one-and-a-half years in Gutsa Detention Center before his release. No additional information is available.

■ **PHUNTSOG**[5], a 21-year-old monk from the Tsuglhakhang, born in Medro Gongkar County, was arrested on March 8, 1989 and sentenced to a three-year term. He has been released from Sangyip Prison.

■ Of the six Tibetan nuns and two Tibetan lay women charged with staging an illegal demonstration calling for Tibetan independence on October 14, 1989 in central Lhasa, two, arrested for participating in a later demonstration, are still in prison (see Phuntsog Nyidron, p.184). The other four nuns, all from Michungri Nunnery, administratively sentenced without trial on October 18, 1989 to terms of three years' "labor re-education" by the extra-judicial Labor Re-education Administrative Committee (*Tibet Daily*, October 18, 1989, in FBIS, November 1, 1989), have been released from Trisam Prison after initial detention in Gutsa. Included are: **PHUNTSOG SANGYE**, (lay name **TENZIN SELDRON**), a 19-year-old from Toelung Gurum; **TENZIN WANGMO**[2], (lay name PHUNTSOG LAMDRON, also known as TAPSANG[2]), a 20-year-old from Toelung Gurum; **KELSANG WANGMO**, (lay name PED-CHOE), a 21-year-old from Nyethang; and **TENZIN CHOEKYI**[3], (lay name TSETEN[3]), a 20-year-old from Chushul. Two lay women, **KELSANG DROLKAR**[1] and **TSICHOE**, who allegedly shouted "reactionary" slogans during the demonstration, were sentenced to two and three years respectively in "labor re-education" camps and are presumed to have been released.

■ **PHUNTSOG TSEYANG** (lay name PENPA[12]), an 18-year old Michungri nun from Phenpo Nyarong, arrested on August 14, 1991, sentenced to two years' imprisonment, part of which she served in Trisam, was released upon completion of her term. Although she was assured at the time of her discharge that she could return to her nunnery, the presence of a "work team" made that impossible and she escaped to India. Other nuns have confirmed that they were refused permission to return to their nunneries after they served out their sentences (see Rigzin Tsondru p.38).

Phuntsog Tseyang was one of three monks and three nuns who staged a demonstration on the Barkhor in Lhasa. Two monks and two nuns managed to escape, but Phuntsog Tseyang and the other monk, from Sera Monastery, were taken to the People's Armed Police Station with their "hands folded up their backs to the fullest extent and

their heads touching their knees." Instead of being escorted inside, the two were "savagely beaten," Phuntsog Tseyang until she lost consciousness. They then were taken by jeep directly to Gutsa Detention Center (*Tibet Information Network*, September 4, 1991).

■ **PHURBU**[7], 27, from Toelung, and **PHUNTSOG DARGYE** (lay name LOYAK[1]), 29, from Medro Gongkar Thankgya, both Dralhaluphug monks, were sentenced to three and two-year prison terms respectively. Despite the fact that Phurbu's sentence may have been increased to four-and-a-half years, then reduced by two months, he is recorded as released, as is Phuntsog Dargye. The latter reportedly was released on April 4, 1992 and expelled from his monastery. Arrested on the morning of March 6 or April 25, 1990 (the discrepancy may reflect the difference between Tibetan and western dates), the two monks were sent to Sangyip Prison and later transferred to Trisam. Phuntsog Dargye, arrested once before, on March 5, 1988, and imprisoned in Sangyip for four months, fled Tibet in mid-1992.

■ Of the Ani Tsangkhung nuns who were arrested June 10, 1991 for demonstrating around the Jokhang Temple in Lhasa, five have been reported released and one other was presumably released after serving her term. During at least part of their detention, they were held in Trisam Prison and before that probably in Gutsa Detention Center. Those whose releases were reported included

PHUNTSOG WANGMO (lay name KARMA CHOEDRON), 22, from Toelung; NGAWANG WANGMO[2] (lay name LHAKPA[9]), 23, from Lhokha; PHURBU CHOEDRON, (lay name NGAWANG), 22, from Toelung Dechen; NGAWANG LHAKDRON[2] (lay name PEMA DROLKAR[5]), a 26-year-old from Toelung; and NGAWANG YANGCHEN[1] (lay name PEMA DECHEN), 23, from Toelung Gongkar. With the exception of Ngawang Yangchen, all received two-year sentences; she was reportedly sentenced to three years, and if the report is accurate, she was released early. NGAWANG PHURDRON[2] (lay name TSAMCHOE[3]), 22, from Medro Gongkar, presumably was released. Two others NGAWANG CHOEKYI[4], 27, from Lhokha Dranang and PHURBU TSAMCHOE, from Toelung might also have been arrested in connection with the demonstration, or they may be alternate names for two of the nuns above.

■ PHURBU[8], a 20-year-old Tsomolung monk, arrested in December 1990, was released from Trisam Prison after serving a two-year sentence.

■ PHURBU TSERING[3], a 21-year-old native of Lhasa, arrested sometime in 1989 and sentenced to a two-year prison term, was released from Sangyip Prison in 1991.

■ PHURBU TSERING[4], (also known as PHURTSE), a 25-year-old painter from Lhasa, arrested in 1989, served a three-year prison term in

Drapchi and Trisam before being released.

■ RINCHEN KUNSANG, (also known as RIGZIN KUNSANG), a 20-year-old nun and native of Nyemo, arrested for demonstrating in Lhasa on May 17, 1988, was released on or about July 7, 1988 and expelled from her nunnery in January or February 1990. According to an account by one of the participants, "On May 17, fifteen of us demonstrated outside the Tsuglhakhang. We shouted, 'Tibet is independent,' 'Long live the Dalai Lama' and 'Release all prisoners.' We were arrested on that very day on the Barkhor. The demonstrators were detained for over one month and twenty days. For the first four weeks that we were in [detention in Gutsa], we were questioned continuously."

The account continued, "One day, two Tibetan policemen made us stand in a line and then they took us one by one into a room. DEKYI CHOEDRON [released July 7, 1988] was the first to be taken into the room and KELSANG PEMA (lay name YANGZOM[4]) was second. In the room, they stripped off all our clothes. Then they made us lie face down on the floor. They beat us from head to foot. I couldn't count how many times. Then they made us stand up while they pushed their electric batons into the vagina and the anus. I don't know how many times" (Tibet Information Network). Kelsang Pema, a 25-year-old Shungsep nun, born in Lhokha, also was released on July 7. Made to undergo "re-education" at the nunnery between August and October 1989, she was nevertheless expelled along with 42 other nuns in February 1990. Kelsang Pema is the sister of Gyaltsen Choekyi[1] (see p.520). Others arrested at the same time included **TENZIN CHOEDRON, TSEWANG CHOEDRON, KELSANG CHOEDREN, SHERAB CHOEDRON, URGYEN DROLMA, LOBSANG DROLMA[3], KELSANG PALMO, TENZIN CHOEZOM** and **SONAM[3]**.

■ **RIGZIN**, a 24-year-old monk from the Jokhang (Tsuglhakhang) Temple in Lhasa, born in Taktse County, was released after one year in Sangyip Prison. He had been arrested on March 8, 1989.

■ **SAMDRUP[2]**, about 20 years old, from Lhasa Chagshing, who was arrested in 1989, was released after serving a three-year sentence in Sangyip prison.

■ Among seven Shungsep nuns arrested for demonstrating on the Barkhor on either June 30 or July 25, 1990 (Tibetan dates, probably corresponding to September 14 by the western calendar), two have been reported released and two others were presumably released upon completion of their terms. Those confirmed released are **SAMTEN DAWA** (lay name DAWA[17]), 23, who had received either a two or three-year term; and **CHIME YUDRON**, 17, who was sentenced to three years. Both are from Lhokha Dranang. **DAWA YANGZOM**, 24, from Lhokha and **TSERING YANGZOM[3]**, a 19-year-old from Yamdrog Gang, were sentenced

to three years in prison and presumably have been released. All were originally held in Gutsa Detention Center. All but Tsering Yangzom were known to have been transferred to Trisam sometime after February 1992. She alone is known to have been expelled from the nunnery.

■ **SAMTEN GYATSO** - see p.195

■ **SAMTSE**, a 43-year-old native of Drayap, arrested in November 1989 and held for one-and-a-half years in Chamdo Prison, has been released.

■ **SONAM CHOEDRON[3]** (also known as GANDEN KHANGSAR AMA-LA) was sentenced to a prison term of two years on February 8, 1991 on charges of "counterrevolutionary propaganda and incitement." Along with Tseten Norgye (p.540) and Thupten Tsering[4] (p.538), both of whom were released after serving four-year terms, she was accused of creating and distributing pro-independence leaflets. Sonam Choedron was first detained on April 20, 1989, but was not formally arrested until November 10. She reportedly was released in April 1991 after having completed her term. Her daughter, **NYIMA[7]**, who apparently was never charged in connection with the same events, was released at the same time (*Tibet Information Network*, August 10, 1991).

■ **SONAM TSERING[4]**, a 21-year-old from Toelung Dechen County, arrested in 1989, spent one-and-a-half-years in Sangyip Prison prior to his release.

- **SONAM WANGDU[1]** - see p.351

- **SOZHI TSUNMA**, a 20-year-old woman born in Lhasa, was arrested in 1987 and detained for two months in Gutsa Detention Center before being released. No other information is available.

- **TAMDRIN[2]**, a 14-year-old monk, from Medro Gongkar County, arrested sometime in 1990, has been released. No other information is available.

- **TAMDRIN SITHAR**, a middle school teacher and member of the Kunsang-tse family, now in his sixties, was released on parole from Drapchi Prison before the expiration of his sentence. He had been arrested on August 26, 1983 and sentenced in September 1984 to a twelve-year prison term, reportedly for being a spy for the Dalai Lama, a charge that indicated he probably had in his possession printed political materials from Dharamsala, the seat of the Tibetan government in exile. Tamdrin Sithar was imprisoned once before, from 1971 to 1975 for "underground activities."

- **TASHI[2]**, an 18-year-old from Lhasa, was released from Sangyip Prison upon completion of his three-year term. Other than that he had been arrested in 1989, no further information is available.

- **TASHI DONDRUP[1]**, (also known by the Chinese name LAO BE), a 20-year-old native of Lhasa Tsemonling,

arrested on March 5, 1989 and subsequently sentenced to three years in prison, has been released. First held in Sangyip Prison, he was later transferred to Trisam.

- **TASHI DONDRUP[2]**, (also known as MALI, probably a Chinese name), a 20-year-old native of Amdo, arrested in 1989 and sentenced to a three-year prison term, has been released from Sangyip Prison.

- **TASHI DROLMA[2]**, a woman in her twenties, from Kham Markham, arrested carrying pro-independence leaflets and audio cassettes on March 7, 1988, was released after one year and four months in prison. Detained first in Pema Shen for nine days, then for six weeks in Sethog Chang in Chamdo, she was finally moved to Gutsa Detention Center. After her escape to India, Tashi Drolma recounted her treatment, including four months in an isolation cell, and that of some other Gutsa prisoners. Eight times during the winter of 1988-89, she and the others were forced to stand for twelve hours at a time in several inches of water deliberately poured on the cement floor of their cell (*Tibet Information Network*, August 17, 1990).

- **TASHI LHAMO**, a 30-year-old native of Amdo, detained in Sangyip Prison in 1989 "for examination," after "participating in the rebellious activities" of March 1989, was "set free in 1989," according to a July 10, 1991 letter from the Chinese Ambassador to France to the Strasbourg Council (*Tibetan Review*,

November 1991). She had been arrested once before, on September 27, 1987, for reasons unknown.

■   **TENCHOE**, a 19-year-old native of Lhasa Chagshing, arrested in 1989 and sentenced to a three-year prison term, has been released from Sangyip Prison. No additional information is available.

■   **TENPA DADAK**, from Jamyang Kyil, was held for four days during April 1992 after speaking out at a meeting in Jamyang Kyil. He reportedly opposed the Chinese policy which was to be implemented by the Lhasa East Neighborhood Committee.

■   **TENZIN**[3], a 60-year-old native of Drapchi, was arrested in 1988 and detained for ten months in Gutsa Detention Center before being released. No other information is available.

■   **TENZIN CHOEPHEL**[2] - see p.168

■   **TENZIN WANGCHUK**[1], a 22-year-old from Lhasa, who was held in Gutsa Detention Center as of late 1991, has been released. No other information is available.

■   **TENZIN WANGYAL**, a 22-year-old job-seeker from Lhasa, arrested in 1989 and sentenced to a two-and-a-half or three-year term, was released from Drapchi Prison.

■   **THUPTEN**[2], a 20-year-old native of Medro Gongkar, arrested on March 6, 1988, reportedly was released after

serving a sentence of approximately one-and-a-half years. No other information is available.

■   **THUPTEN GYURMED**, an unemployed 18-year-old Lhasa worker, in Drapchi Prison as of late 1991 serving a three-year term, has been released.

■   **THUPTEN PHUNTSOG**[2], a monk about 20 years old, born in Toelung Dechen County, arrested in 1987 and sentenced to two years in Sangyip Prison, has been released. No other information is available.

■   **THUPTEN TSERING**[4], 44, a temporary technician at the West Power House in Lhasa, the alleged leader of the *Sub-committee for Tibetan Independence* (see Tseten Norgye p.540, and Sonam Choedron[3], p.536), sentenced on February 8, 1991 to a four-year prison term, was released upon its completion. He had been detained on April 20, 1989 and formally arrested on November 10, 1989 on charges of "distributing counterrevolutionary propaganda." According to court documents, he received a "reactionary document advocating independence" from a monk at Dralhaluphug, and in July 1988 asked a colleague to make a stencil of it. Thupten Tsering then made "over twenty copies," adding the group's name before he gave them out for distribution. In October 1988, he allegedly prepared copies of another leaflet, and later was involved in the preparation of two more. Thupten Tsering was the first known

Communist Party member in Tibet to have become a political prisoner. He had been held in Gutsa.

■ **THUPTEN YESHE**[2], a 17-year-old monk from Lhasa, arrested sometime in 1990, has been released. No additional information is available.

■ **THUGA**, a 20-year-old native of Kantse, arrested in 1989 and sentenced to a three-year term, was released upon its completion from Sangyip Prison. No other information is available.

■ **TING SE CHUN DADHUL** (the first three syllables are Chinese), about 20 years old, born in Lhasa Town-3, has been released from prison. No further information about his arrest and imprisonment are known.

■ **T S A M - L A**[2], a L h a s a businesswoman in her thirties, died on August 25, 1991, some months after her early release, on March 5, 1991, from a three-year prison sentence. The exact cause of death is not known, but it is known that Tsam-la sustained damage to her internal organs, probably from repeated and brutal prison beatings, kicks, and assaults with electric batons. She had been sent to the hospital for exploratory surgery shortly before her release, which supposedly was for "good behavior," but more likely was because prison authorities did not want her to die in prison. Tsam-la's arrest came on December 10, 1988 after she allegedly hit security force members on the hands and arms with an iron bar to

deflect their aim as they fired on demonstrators.

■ **TSAM-LA**[3], a 20-year-old nun from Chubsang Nunnery, has been released from Gutsa, expelled from her nunnery, and sent back to Toelung, her native place. A cell-mate reported she became ill as a result of forced blood extraction while in prison.

■ **TSEDOR**, a 24-year-old native of Dakyab County, arrested in 1989 and sentenced to a one-and-a-half-year term, has been released from Sangyip Prison.

■ **TSEGYAL** (also listed as TSEGYEY), a 20-year-old from Lhasa, arrested in 1989 and sentenced to three years in prison, has been released from Trisam Prison. He had been transferred there from Sangyip.

■ **TSENOR**, a 20-year-old native of Lhasa, arrested in 1989 and sentenced to a one-year term, has been released from Sangyip Prison.

■ Five monks from Ratoe Monastery were arrested on either October 4 or 5, 1988 for allegedly participating in a series of anti-Chinese demonstrations at Ratoe Monastery beginning on September 29, 1988. They reportedly were severely beaten at the time of their arrests and during interrogation (*Tibet Information Network*, August 30, 1991). **TSERING DONDRUP**[2], 21, from Chushul, allegedly the leader of the demonstrations, was led away in handcuffs on October 4 while other monks were pushed aside at gunpoint.

He spent three months in prison in Chushul. **LOBSANG**[2], arrested October 5, accused of putting dynamite under cars, is presumed to have been released after completing a three-year term in Outridu, a section of Sangyip Prison Complex. **LOBSANG CHOEJOR**[3], 30, from Chushul Ratoe, arrested October 5, was released from Trisam Prison after serving a three-year sentence. He may have been the one who gave Jampa Ngodrup (see p.15, 194) the list of those arrested in connection with the March 5, 1988 demonstration in Lhasa. **MIGMAR TENZIN** was arrested again on March 26, 1990 and served one-and-a-half years in Sangyip before he was released. **TSERING NORBU**, re-arrested with Migmar Tenzin and held in Sangyip, was released after one month.

■   **TSERING DORJE**[3], a 27-year-old from Lhasa, by one report a businessman, by another an employee at the Grain Store Office, was released in 1991 after serving a three-year sentence in Drapchi Prison for "damaging public property." According to one source, he was arrested on March 7, 1988; according to another, he was arrested on the night of September 28, 1987, released, then re-arrested in March 1988 and sentenced on January 19, 1989.

■   **TSERING DORJE**[4], a 29-year-old native of Lhasa, Tengye Ling, arrested in 1989 and sentenced to a three-year prison term, has been released. Other than that he was first held in Sangyip

Prison and possibly moved to Trisam, no other information is available.

■   **TSERING PALDEN**[3] (Died) - see p.209

■   **TSETEN**[4], a woman in her twenties, from Dib, was arrested in 1988 and detained for four months in Gutsa Detention Center before being released. No other information is available.

■   **TSETEN DROLKAR**, a 19-year-old woman born in Taktse County, arrested on January 21, 1991 and detained in Gutsa Detention Center for four months, has been released. No other information is available.

■   **TSETEN NORGYE**, a 51-year-old receptionist at the Banakshol Guest House, from Banakshol Lhasa, was arrested on April 23, 1989 as a pro-independence leader, formally charged "according to the law" on November 10, 1989, summoned to trial on February 6, 1991 and tried on February 8 after only two days to prepare his case. He was sentenced in late February to four years in prison and released on March 22, 1993. According to a summary of an official announcement (*Tibet Information Network*, February 13, 1991), Tseten Norgye, originally from Gyantse, was accused of joining an "anti-government organization in 1988, the previously unknown *Uprising Group for Tibetan Independence*...and engaging in collecting information for the Dalai Lama Group." He reportedly distributed   "counterrevolutionary" literature produced on a mimeograph machine at his workplace. Tseten Norgye allegedly "learned the documents by heart and spread their contents by word of mouth." However, the procuracy statement only charged him under Article 102, as an accessory to a joint crime, that of "inciting the overthrow of the political power of the dictatorship of the proletariat and the socialist system."

The police learned of Tseten Norgye's activities through an informer. His arrest, along with the arrests of a number of other Tibetans, came in a raid on his home by seven police officers. He was initially held incommunicado in Lhasa's Chakpori Prison, believed to be a detention center run by either the Army or the People's Armed Police, and reportedly was badly beaten, tortured and possibly blinded in one eye during interrogation there. After he was moved to Drapchi Prison, Tseten Norgye's conditions improved and he was allowed visits from his family. A previous prison sentence, variously reported as twelve or twenty years, ended in 1985. Others involved in the case were tried at the same time (see Thupten Tsering[4], p.538 and Sonam Choedron[3], p.536).

■ **TSETEN TASHI**, a 23-year-old Dakyab County native, arrested in 1989 and sentenced to a two-year term, has been released from Sangyip Prison. No other information is available.

■ **TSEWANG**[2], an 18-year-old native of Lhasa, Chagshing, arrested in 1989, was held in Sangyip Prison for

one year, then released. No additional information is available.

■ **TSEWANG DORJE**, a 27-year-old native of Chamdo Pashod County, who worked in Lhasa as a painter, has been released from Trisam Prison. Arrested on December 18, 1989 and initially sent to Sangyip Prison, he served a three-year term.

■ **TSEYANG**, (probably a contraction of TSERING YANGZOM[2]) a 14-year-old Lhasa female, held in Sangyip Prison as of late 1991, has been released.

■ **TSOGYE DROLMA**, a 60-year-old Lhasa woman, was arrested in 1988 and detained for ten months in Gutsa Detention Center before being released. No additional information is available.

■ **TSULTRIM JAMPA** - see p.190

■ **YANGCHEN**[3], a 17-year-old from Lhasa; **YANGCHEN DROLKAR**, 25, from Nagchu; **KELSANG DROLKAR**[2], 20, from Nagchu; **LHAKPA**[8], 19, from Lhasa; and **MIGMAR**[11], a 12-year-old from Gyaltse, members of a carpet weaving cooperative, arrested on March 6, 1989, were held in Gutsa Detention Center after taking part in demonstrations. All five were expelled from the cooperative after their releases. According to what little else is known, Migmar, held for two months, was beaten at the time of her detention, and Yangchen has fled to India.

■ **YESHE ZOEPA**, a 26-year-old unofficial monk from Ganden Monastery, imprisoned for demonstrating on December 10, 1988, was released early for "working hard" during the two years and three months he served of his three-year term. He left Tibet in November 1991. Yeshe Zoepa was one of twelve beaten at the police station near the Barkhor immediately after they were seized. Moved almost immediately to Gutsa, they were beaten again. During interrogation the prisoners were asked to name others involved and when they refused, shocked, sometimes into unconsciousness. They also were beaten with sticks and broom handles; kicked; and hung up with their hands tied in front, sometimes from a tree, sometimes from a window mullion (*Tibet Information Network*, December 29, 1991).

■ **YUDRON**, a Lhasa woman in her twenties, was arrested in 1988 and detained for six months in Gutsa Detention Center before being released. No other information is available.

■ **YUGA**[1], a 20-year-old native of Kantse, arrested in 1989 and sentenced to a two-and-a-half-year prison term, has been released from Sangyip Prison. In addition, **YUGA**[2], the same age and from the same place, received a three-year sentence and also was released from Sangyip. So far as is known they are two different people.

■ **ZOEPA**; **GENDUN**, 30; and **TASHI GYATSO**[2], 30, monks from Labrang Tashi Khyil Monastery, and **LOBSANG GYATSO**[3], 30; **TASHI GYATSO**[3], 24; and **KUNCHOK GYATSO**, from Gesar (Zorge) Monastery, affiliated with Labrang, have all been released from Minkye Prison in southern Gansu Province (called Amdo by Tibetans). They were arrested in September 1987 for listening to a tape of the Dalai Lama officiating at an important religious ceremony, the Kalachakra Initiation. Lobsang Gyatso, from Zorge in Amdo, sentenced to a four-year term, was released in September 1991 and restricted to his monastery for an indefinite period. He was required to report to local police authorities every seven days; could not leave the area without permission and could not be away more than seven days. Tashi Gyatso was released in September 1988 after serving one year; he faced the same restrictions. The others were released after a fifteen-day detention period.

2. *Release Presumed*

Catholics

- **CHEN Youping**, a member of the religious community of Liushan village, Fujian Province, has been released, according to an unconfirmed report. He was arrested in the village on February 29, 1988.

- Father **CHEN Yunshang** - see p.3

- The status of Father **FENG Yongbing**, 36, from Changle County, Fujian Province, arrested on September 14, 1988 is unclear. There is an unconfirmed report that he has been released.

- Father **LIN Jiale**, from Fuzhou, Fujian Province, has probably been released. According to an Asia Watch source, there is no additional information available about his arrest or the conditions of his release.

- Father **LIU Shizhong**, from Fuzhou, Fujian Province, reportedly was released from detention. There is no confirmation of the report and no additional information is available.

- The whereabouts of Father **SUN Ximan**, Tianshui diocese, Gansu Province, are unclear, but there are unconfirmed reports that he may have been released. According to an Asia Watch source, Father Sun was arrested in connection with the 1989 clandestine Bishops' Conference. In a contradictory account, Chinese authorities told the U.S. government in November 1991 that Father Sun had "never been accused of any offense."

- The status of **WANG Jingjing**, a member of the religious community of Liushan village, Fujian Province, is unclear. There is an unconfirmed report that he has been released. Wang was arrested in his village on February 28, 1988 at 8 A.M.

- **WANG Tianzhang**, a deacon from Lanzhou diocese, Gansu Province has probably been released, but his present circumstances are unknown. He was arrested on December 16, 1989 in connection with the 1989 clandestine Bishops' Conference. In response to U.S. government inquiries, Chinese officials said in November 1991 that Wang had "never been accused of any offense."

- **WANG Tongsheng** (Tongshang), a 56-year-old Catholic layman, held at the Re-education Center in Chengde, Hebei Province, was one of those whose releases were announced by the Chinese government in March 1993. As of October 1993, he had not returned home, but it is presumed he was released upon completion of his term. Wang was last arrested on December 23, 1990 and subsequently sentenced to three years' "re-education through labor." He is probably the deacon and community leader previously identified as Wang Tongshan, arrested once before in December 1989, released, then picked up again and sent to a "study camp," probably in Tangshan, Hebei.

■ The status of Father **WANG Yiqi**, a member of the religious community of Liushan village, Fujian Province, is unclear. There is an unconfirmed report that he has been released. No further information is available.

■ Father **WEI Jingyi**, a priest in his mid-thirties, from Yixian diocese, Hebei Province, was one of those whose releases were announced by the Chinese government in March 1993. As of July 1993, he had not returned home, but it is presumed he was released upon completion of his term. Father Wei had been sentenced in March 1991 to three years' "re-education through labor" in connection with the November 1989 clandestine Bishops' Conference in Shaanxi Province. He was arrested in August 1990 in Harbin, Heilongjiang, where he had previously served. An official Chinese response in November 1991 to U.S. government requests for information in effect confirmed the sentence, stating that Father Wei was "not found legally responsible," a commonly-used euphemism for administrative sentencing. Father Wei's ordination, in Baoding, Hebei Province, in the early 1980s, has never been recognized by the official Chinese Catholic Church, and Father Wei has refused, for his part, to have anything to do with the official Chinese church.

■ The whereabouts of Father **ZHANG Xiaocheng**, Tianshui diocese, Gansu Province, who was arrested in connection with the 1989 clandestine Bishops' Conference, are uncertain, but an Asia Watch source has reported that

he may have been released. In response to U.S. government inquiries, Chinese officials said in November 1991 that Father Zhang had "never been accused of any offense."

Protestants

■ **DU Zhangji**, a house church leader from Henan Province, was sentenced in 1985 to four years' imprisonment for opposing the official Three-Self Patriotic Movement. There has been no confirmation of his presumed release.

■ **HE Suolie,** a house church leader from Henan Province, arrested in 1985 for allegedly opposing the official Three-Self Patriotic Movement, was sentenced to an eight-year prison term and was due for release in 1993. No other information is available.

■ **KANG Manshuang,** a house church leader from Henan Province, was sentenced in 1985 to a five-year term for opposing the official Three-Self Patriotic Movement. There has been no confirmation of his presumed release.

■ **XU Guoxing**, a house church leader in Shanghai, born March 16, 1955, was sentenced administratively to three years' "re-education through labor." Arrested first on March 14, 1989, released without charge on June 16 after intensive interrogation, then re-arrested on November 6, 1989 by the Shanghai Municipal Public Security Bureau and sentenced on November 18, 1990, he was accused of setting up illegal churches in Shanghai and in Anhui, Zhejiang and Jiangsu provinces. He also "broke social order by stirring up trouble and creating conflicts," "interfering with and damaging the regular order of religious activities." Xu was at Da Feng Labor Farm in northern Jiangsu Province. It is presumed he was released in late 1992 after having completed his sentence.

According to an Asia Watch source, family members were told by prison camp officials to petition for his release. The family refused. They did not want it to appear as if he was repentant and would forego preaching. It is, the source continued, Xu's life work which he refuses to have restricted by government prohibitions on the content of sermons. Rather, the family said, he will preach the Gospel according to the Bible. Xu's father, mother and brother were permitted prison visits. During the two years, 1980-82, Xu spent in language school in the U.S., he was baptized in a Baptist church. However, he has no denominational or foreign affiliations.

Students, Intellectuals and Officials

■ **CHEN Tianlai**, a 24-year-old unemployed high school graduate and resident of Dongan County in Hunan Province, was administratively sentenced by the Lingling Prefecture Public Security Bureau in November 1989 to three years' "re-education through labor." He presumably was released upon completion of his term. During the 1989 pro-democracy movement, Chen "infiltrated the ranks of the students," took to the streets to create disturbances, and spread "rumors" and "superstitions."

■ **CHEN Xiangping**, a 31-year-old cadre who worked for the Changde City government in Hunan Province, was administratively sentenced to two years' "re-education through labor" by the Changde City Public Security Bureau in November 1989. He presumably was released upon completion of his term. Chen allegedly "showed dissatisfaction" with the Party during the 1989 pro-democracy movement.

■ **Chen Ziming's cousin** (name unknown, see p.63) who was a teacher and the oldest of three people arrested for hiding Chen, was sentenced to two years' "re-education through labor" (*Shijie Ribao*, December 7, 1990). It is presumed he was released upon completion of his term. According to an Asia Watch source, the men were arrested at the same time as Chen (sentenced to a thirteen-year prison term as a pro-democracy "black hand") at their home in Zhanjiang, Guangdong Province, where Chen reportedly had been hiding.

■ **DENG Yuanguo**, a 32-year-old teacher at the Huaihua No.1 Middle School in Hunan Province, was sentenced to two years' "re-education through labor." He was arrested following the failure of the August 19, 1991 coup in the Soviet Union, after making statements calling for the Soviet Communist Party to step down. Deng had previously been detained for "shelter and investigation" for publicly supporting the May 1989 student protest movement.

■ **FANG Quan** - see p.486

■ **GAO Jun**, a 22-year-old student in the Labor Personnel Institute at People's University in Beijing, and a member of the Beijing Students Autonomous Federation, reportedly was arrested in June 1989 in Shanghai. Gao went out to market and disappeared. The following month, the Public Service Bureau informed the university that he had been arrested. It is possible that **one "GU Jun,"** in whose case "legal responsibility was not pursued" (according to an official Chinese response in November 1991 to inquiries by the U.S. government) is in fact Gao Jun. If so, he probably served an administrative sentence of "re-education through labor" and has been released. If Gu Jun is another dissident, then Gao's status remains unclear.

■ **GENG Qichang** - see p.274

■ **HE Bowei**, a 22-year-old student in the Chinese department at Hunan Normal University, Hunan Province, was sentenced in April 1990 by the Changsha Western District Court to a two-year prison term on a charge of "disrupting social order." He was arrested in July 1989, and presumably was released upon completion of his term. During the 1989 pro-democracy movement, He Bowei organized and became leader of a "Dare-to-Die" squad, later renamed the "Blood Song squad," at his school.

■ **HE Hua** - see p.81

■ **HU Junda**, a 35-year-old lecturer at the Xiangtan Electrical Machinery Specialized School, Hunan Province, was administratively sentenced by the Xiangtan City Public Security Bureau to three years' 're-education through labor, after having been detained in Xiangtan Prison for ten months. He presumably was released upon completion of his term. Hu allegedly wrote "counterrevolutionary articles" during the 1989 pro-democracy movement, encouraged students to create disturbances, and stirred up workers to go on strike. After June 4, he fled to Shenzhen, then swam to Hong Kong from Shekou, but was arrested later after voluntarily returning to the mainland.

■ **HU Ruoyang** and **XIAO Feng**[1] - see p.65

■ **LI Baoming**, a 27-year-old teacher at Tianjin University, was one of eight arrested in Tianjin on March 25, 1991, according to a report in the *South China Morning Post* (August 27, 1991). As the leader of the *89 Alliance*, a pro-democracy group, he was sentenced to 18 months" "re-education through labor." Presumably he has been released. The others, held only a month, were expelled from school or dismissed from their jobs. The *89 Alliance*, established in September 1989 by Nankai University students at the time Li was a law student there, had over one hundred members including students, teachers and government workers, by the time it was discovered.

In addition to meetings, members wrote analyses of the democracy movement's failure and of China's social structure, and distributed their articles and leaflets to a select readership. Most members of the group were from Tianjin, but some participants came from Shanghai, Beijing, Yunnan, Fujian and Liaoning.

■ **LI Dejun**, 30, a college graduate and teacher at Canhekou Peasants' Middle School in Benxi County, Liaoning Province, sentenced to three years' imprisonment on charges of "counterrevolutionary propaganda and incitement," presumably was released upon completion of his term. An official Chinese response to inquiries by the U.S. government confirmed that he had been sentenced (November 1991). Li, arrested in late July 1989, according to a report in *Liaoning Ribao* (July 20, 1989), allegedly sent letters to 13 different colleges and universities and on May 18, 1989 put up a big-character poster at the Canhekou railroad station saying, "Support the petition of college student hunger strikers." The report alleged that Li incited workers and peasants to co-operate with students to establish a multi-party system in China, "energetically advocated bourgeois liberalization, lavished praise on Fang Lizhi and others and viciously attacked party leadership."

Li was held under appalling conditions in Lingyuan Prison in Liaoning, where along with other political prisoners, he was subject to inhuman torture, solitary confinement and other brutalities. In attempts to alleviate their conditions and focus international attention on their plights, Li and other inmates at Lingyuan went on hunger strikes at least twice, for which they were severely punished. (For details see Tang Yuanjuan p.105.)

■ **LI Gangyi**, 58, formerly a section chief in the PRC State Council's Rare Earths Leadership Group Office, was sentenced to two years' imprisonment after June 1989 on charges of "concealing a weapon." According to an internal report by the Supreme People's Court (TC p.375), the weapon, a type-56 assault rifle, was stolen from a burned-out armored personnel carrier by Li's sons, **Li Bing** and **Li Manrong**, on June 4, 1989. Li Gangyi then hid the rifle in his home until June 14, when it was discovered by the Public Security Bureau. The report stated that the two sons had been "dealt with separately," but gave no indication of the sentences they received. It is likely however, that Li Bing is the same person as someone of that name (see p.361) who was announced elsewhere as having been sentenced to seven years' imprisonment. (The report, by *Beijing Radio,* originally accused Li Bing of having killed a soldier and blocked military vehicles, but this charge was presumably later replaced by a lesser one.) Li Gangyi is presumed to have been released after serving his sentence.

■ **LI Guoquan** - see p.275

■ **LI Haitao**, 34, was sentenced to a four-year prison term by the Wuhan (Hubei Province) Intermediate People's Court on August 29, 1990 for "counterrevolutionary propaganda and incitement" and for disrupting transportation by organizing a May 16, 1989 sit-in on the Yangzi River Bridge. Students from six area colleges participated. The agitation and propaganda charges referred to Li's public disagreement with the authorities' suppression of pro-democracy students in Beijing and to his organizing a memorial service on June 6, 1989 at Wuhan University for those killed in Beijing. Li also was charged with helping Chai Ling record her secret tape on June 8, 1989. In it, she emphatically denounced the June 4 massacre. On June 9, Li allegedly assisted in copying the tape and in disseminating it at Wuhan University and at the Zhongnan Shopping Mall. According to the indictment of the Procuratorate, "As a result, Chai Ling's reactionary recording was spread to such places as Hong Kong, Taiwan, and Japan, creating an extremely bad impression" (FBIS, November 8, 1990; *Baixing*, November 1, 1990). According to Amnesty International (*ASA 17/63/90*), Li, who was the first of those whose names appeared on a wanted list to be tried, appealed his sentence to the Hubei Provincial High Court. An official Chinese response to U.S. government inquiries confirmed that Li was imprisoned (November 1991). He presumably was released upon completion of his term.

As chairman of the Autonomous Union of Wuhan University Postgraduate Students, Li helped organize a student sit-down in front of the Hubei provincial government gate

on May 16. On May 26, he chaired a joint meeting to work out a plan to coordinate student efforts throughout the city. A sit-down demonstration followed that evening. On June 4, when Li led the students into the street to demonstrate, he allegedly said, "The Li Peng government has completely torn off its hypocritical mask. We should no longer have any illusions about this government."

Li, a 34-year-old native of Luchuan County, Guangxi Zhuang Autonomous Region, a Wuhan University doctoral candidate in philosophy, and editor of the journal *French Studies*, was arrested on June 16, 1989 by the Wuhan Public Security Bureau. Proceedings were instituted against him on July 22, 1990. He reportedly was imprisoned at Wuhan's No.1 Detention Center. At least eight other students and staff from Wuhan University also were arrested (see He Libin p.421, and Liao Baobin p.159).

■ **LI Jiawei**, a member of the Sichuan Academy of Social Sciences and an editor at its publishing house, and **ZHANG Li**[2], former director and examining editor at the same academy, were found guilty of "dereliction of duty" for authorizing the publication of *The Complete Biography of Du Yuesheng*. (Du was a gangster in Shanghai in the 1930s who provided important support for Chiang Kai-shek.) The case was heard in criminal proceedings in the Sicheng District People's Court in Chengdu. Zhang was sentenced to one year in prison and one year's probation; Li received a three-year sentence and four years' probation. That they were sentenced was confirmed by the Chinese government in response to requests for information by the U.S. government (November 1991). The relative leniency of the sentences, under Articles 187, 67 and 68 of the Criminal Code, was explained by their "relatively good attitude in pleading guilty, and their active redemption of the harm done to society by recalling all counterrevolutionary books that had been published and sold" (*Zhong Xin She*, March 26, 1990, in FBIS, April 13, 1990). According to an August 28, 1989 *Chengdu Radio* report (FBIS August 30, 1989), the two men were expelled from the Communist Party and accused of "seriously violating political discipline" and "departing from the orientation of socialist publication." It is presumed that both Li and Zhang were released after completing their terms.

■ **LI Jinge** - see p.80

■ A man named **LI Lei** was reportedly detained for three months in Shanghai in the winter of 1989 on account of pro-democracy activities. He is presumed to have subsequently been freed.

■ **LI Meihu** - see p.505

■ **LIAN Danming (LI Dangming)**, a student in Xi'an, Shaanxi Province, was tried and sentenced after June 1989, according to a November 1991 official Chinese response to inquiries by the U.S. government. An Asia Watch source reported that Lian

received a four-year prison term and was originally held in the "Fifth Branch" (possibly the PSB Dept. No.5) detention center. Neither the date of arrest or sentencing is known.

■ **LIANG Xiang**, former governor of Hainan Province and a vice-secretary of the Chinese Communist Party in Hainan, was permitted to go to Shenzhen to live sometime in April 1991, after applying via a special-case investigation unit, (*Shijie Ribao*, May 4, 1991). He had been confined to a guest house in Haikou following his arrest on alleged corruption charges. Later, after a minor stroke while in custody, Liang was moved to a hospital, then sent to recover at Pan Oulianhua Mountain. It is believed his detention stemmed from his close connection with Zhao Ziyang, the deposed Secretary General of the Chinese Communist Party (*Shijie Ribao*, March 1, 1991).

■ **LIU De** - see p.275

■ **LIU Fuan** and **LIU Jiaming** - see p.134

■ **LIU Tianhua** - see p.486

■ **LIU Yunshen**, a 58-year-old former teacher in Liaoyang, Liaoning Province, arrested in June 1989, was sentenced to four years in prison on charges of "counterrevolutionary propaganda and incitement." He was held in Lingyuan Prison and presumably was released upon completion of his term. So far as is known, Liu was not involved in any of the hunger strikes in the facility. (For details see Tang Yuanjuan p.105.)

■ **LONG Xiaohu**, 30, a cadre in the Hunan Provincial Foreign Affairs Office, a graduate of People's University, and reportedly the grandson of the KMT governor-general of Long Yung, Yunnan Province, was arrested on the evening of June 3, 1989 and held at the public security branch station in Changsha's Eastern District, Hunan Province. He was later secretly sent for two years' "re-education through labor." It is presumed he was released after completing his sentence.

Long allegedly did liaison work for the students during the 1989 pro-democracy movement. After June 4, he left China legally, but returned in May 1990 at the invitation of the State Physical Education Commission and the PRC Asian Games Committee to attend the opening ceremonies of the Asian Games. It was then that he was accused of hiding four blank passports and almost HK$100,000 for the purpose of "rescuing student leaders."

■ **MA Hongliang**, a leader of the Shaanxi Province Students Autonomous Federation and a student at the Xi'an Institute of Metallurgy, was sentenced to four years' imprisonment for "counterrevolutionary propaganda and incitement" (*South China Morning Post*, March 19, 1991). His sentence was confirmed by an official Chinese response to inquiries by the U.S. government (November 1991); he reportedly was sent to Shaanxi No.2 Prison in Weinan after sentencing and presumably was released upon

completion of his term. Ma was arrested on June 7, 1989. A *Xi'an Radio* broadcast on June 12, 1989, suggested that he had engaged only in peaceful protests. He allegedly incited people against the provincial government, plotted to set up a radio station at Tiancheng Square in Xi'an to spread rumors and "poison people's minds," sabotaged traffic and instigated students and shopkeepers to strike. Ma was active in Xi'an from mid-April 1989 until the end of the protests.

■ **MAO Genhong** - see p.77

■ **MIN Hexun**, approximately 29 years old, a teacher in the politics department of Yueyang Teachers Training College, Hunan Province, was tried in early 1990 by the Yueyang Intermediate People's Court on charges of "counterrevolutionary propaganda and incitement" and sentenced to three years' imprisonment. Arrested in July 1989, he was held in Hengyang Prison (Provincial No.2) and presumably was released upon completion of his term. Min allegedly supported the student demonstrations in 1989 and wrote a large number of "reactionary articles" urging workers to stage protest strikes. These were said by the authorities to have "exerted an extremely bad influence." In addition to his other activities, Min reportedly was involved in the "Yin Zhenggao Affair" (see Xie Yang p.552).

■ **QIN Dong**, pen name of a 30-year-old journalist for a local newspaper in Hunan Province, was tried in 1990 by the Changsha (Hunan) Intermediate

People's Court on a charge of "counterrevolutionary propaganda and incitement" and sentenced to four years' imprisonment. An enthusiastic participant in the 1989 pro-democracy movement, Qin was arrested soon after June 4 and accused of having "written reactionary articles." He was held in Lingling Prison (Provincial No.3) and presumably was released upon completion of his term.

■ **WEI Xi**, 28, formerly an art teacher at Funing County Teachers Training College, Hebei Province, was sentenced to two years' imprisonment for "counterrevolutionary propaganda and incitement" after June 1989. According to an internal report by the Supreme People's Court (TC p.381), on June 6, 1989, Wei posted up a series of "counterrevolutionary banners" on his college campus denouncing the military crackdown on the pro-democracy movement in Beijing and declaring June 4 to be "China's National Day of Shame." On June 15, Wei turned himself in to the authorities and hence received "lenient treatment." He is presumed to have been released after serving his sentence. The report added that Wei had "incited one of his students," **SHAO Haiwen**, to "stencil and reproduce 128 reactionary leaflets, which they then distributed around campus." Shao was said to have been "dealt with separately," but it is not whether she too was subsequently sentenced.

■ **QING Yi**, a 30-year-old teacher at No.1 Middle School, Yongzhou City in Lingling, Hunan Province, was administratively sentenced in December 1989 by the Yongzhou City Public Security Bureau to two years' "re-education through labor." He presumably was released upon completion of his term. Qing, a technical college graduate, allegedly committed serious political errors during the 1989 pro-democracy movement by writing "articles of counterrevolutionary propaganda" and organizing student demonstrations. He was arrested in September that year.

■ **WANG Zhan** - see p.79

■ **WU Haizen** (Haizhen), 34, a lecturer on the foreign language faculty of the Yunnan Education Institute and at the Yunnan Student Federation, was sentenced to three years' imprisonment in late 1989 or early 1990 on charges of engaging in "anti-government propaganda." He presumably was released upon completion of his term. That he was sentenced was confirmed by Chinese officials in a reply to U.S. government inquiries (November 1991). Wu was arrested together with two others (see Yang Hong p.123) on June 13, 1989 in Kunming, Yunnan Province for giving "dozens of speeches attacking party and government leaders" to students and factory workers.

■ **WU Litang**, reportedly detained on October 20, 1989, was arrested between January 5-8, 1990, indicted on February 16, 1990 with four others, "publicly" tried on April 19, 1991 by the Wuhan City (Hubei Province) Intermediate People's Court with three others and sentenced to a two-year term expiring on October 19, 1991. An official Chinese reply to inquiries by the U.S. government confirmed the sentencing (November 1991); Asia Watch has not been able to confirm his release. Wu, the 43-year-old former director of the Wuhan City Dajiang Applied High Technology Research Institute (Dajiang Institute) helped conceal Wang Juntao (sentenced in January 1991 to 13 years in prison as a "black hand" dissident) from July to October 1989, during his attempt to escape from China. According to Wu's indictment, "after the case was broken, U.S. $1,800, 18,600 in *Renmin Bi Exchange Certificates* and other things used in Wang Juntao's escape were recovered from [Wu's] home." For information about others involved in the case, see: Chen Zhiyang p.137; Jiang Guolian p.424; Liu Hanyi p.436; Liu Danhong p.434 and Xiao Yuan p.472.

■ **XIAO Huidu**, a 34-year-old teacher at No.1 Middle School, Huaihua County, Hunan Province, was administratively sentenced in early 1990 to two years' "re-education through labor." He presumably was released upon completion of his term. During the 1989 pro-democracy movement, Xiao, a graduate of Hunan Normal University, allegedly was involved with students from outside the area, helping them "make chaos" *(dongluan)* and writing "reactionary slogans." He was arrested in October 1989.

■ **XIAO Ming**, a 35-year-old teacher in the philosophy department at Xiangtan University, Hunan Province, was sentenced in mid-1990 by the Xiangtan City Intermediate People's Court to two years' imprisonment on a charge of "counterrevolutionary propaganda and incitement." Sent to Yuanjiang Prison (Provincial No.1) for labor reform, he presumably was released upon completion of his term. During the 1989 pro-democracy movement, Xiao allegedly wrote "reactionary articles" and stirred up the students to demonstrate. After June 4, he gave several speeches "viciously attacking the Party and the government" and was arrested in July.

■ **XIE Yang** and several other officials in the pioneering administration of Yin Zhenggao, the vice-mayor of Yueyang City, Hunan Province, who were implicated in the "Yin Zhenggao Affair," were reportedly sentenced to prison for their involvement in the 1989 pro-democracy movement. Xie, the 32-year-old secretary of the Yueyang Communist League received a two-year term and presumably was released upon its completion. (See also **Min Hexun**, p.550.) Charged with "counterrevolutionary propaganda and incitement," Xie was sentenced by the Yueyang City Intermediate People's Court in early 1990 and served his sentence at Hengyang Prison (Hunan Provincial No.2 Prison). Xie had publicly declared his support for the students and helped organize their demonstrations. He also made speeches at several institutes of higher learning.

Yin Zhenggao had demanded clean government and accountability on the part of his subordinates and had denounced his superior, the Mayor, at a municipal Party meeting. As a result, he was turned out of office and, along with several of his closest colleagues, placed under house arrest.

■ A man named **XU Zhigang** was reportedly detained for six months in Shanghai in the winter of 1989 on account of pro-democracy activities. He is presumed to have subsequently been released.

■ **XUE Deyun**, a poet from Guizhou Province who wrote under the name **MA Zhe**, was arrested in Beijing on December 12, 1986, for participation in student protest demonstrations held earlier that day. He was accused of inciting students to continue demonstrating, of calling for the abrogation of official regulations restricting public demonstrations and for "abolition of the Chinese Communist Party's leadership." He allegedly came to Beijing Normal University "to peddle illegal printed materials" and "to preach the bourgeois view on democracy and freedom under the pretext of discussing poems with students." It is not known whether Xue was ever tried, or if he is currently still detained. Officially described as "unemployed," Xue was a member of the Guizhou-based *Enlightenment Society*, an unofficial but influential group of poets and literary and political theorists which was active during the 1978-81 Democracy Wall movement. Requests by the U.S. government for information concerning Xue's whereabouts (November 1991) elicited no information from Chinese officials.

■ **YAN Fangbo**, 17, a student at a middle school in Longshan County, Xiangxi Autonomous Prefecture, Hunan Province, was administratively sentenced in early 1990 to two years' "re-education through labor." Arrested late in 1989, he presumably was released upon completion of his term. During the 1989 pro-democracy movement, Yan organized street demonstrations by middle school students and made contact with Hunan Normal University students who had come to Longshan County. He also was accused of posting "reactionary slogans."

■ **ZENG Zhaohui**, 22, a student in the entering class of 1987 at Hengyang Industrial College, was tried in early 1990 by the Hengyang (Hunan Province) Intermediate People's Court on charges of "counterrevolutionary propaganda and incitement" and sentenced to three years' imprisonment. He was held for a while in Longxi Prison (Provincial No.6), and presumably was released upon completion of his term. Two other students from the Hengyang Industrial College were also arrested, but their names and present circumstances are not known.

During the 1989 pro-democracy movement, Zeng served as chairman of the Hengyang Students Autonomous Federation. He organized street demonstrations and gatherings, and led a group of students in a 10-day sit-in protest outside the city government offices. Zeng was arrested in July that year.

- **ZHANG Ronghe**, 17, a student at a middle school in Linfeng County, Changde, Hunan Province, was administratively sentenced at the end of 1989 to two years' "re-education through labor." He presumably was released upon completion of his term. During the 1989 pro-democracy movement, Zhang allegedly posted big-character posters, disseminated "reactionary" speech and organized student demonstrations. He was arrested after June 4.

- **ZHANG Xu**, a Tianjin junior high school student at the time of the 1989 uprising in Beijing, was sentenced to a one-year "re-education through labor" term from which he presumably has been released. After he returned from Tiananmen Square with eight university students, Zheng reportedly was arrested on the Beijing University campus and accused of being a pickpocket.

- **ZHAO Gang**[2], a 26-year-old former Beijing Normal College student arrested in July 1989, received a four-year sentence in connection with the pro-democracy movement. He presumably was released upon completion of his term.

- **ZHAO Muyu**, a 28-year-old-teacher at the No.1 Middle School, Jinshi City, Changde Prefecture, Hunan Province, was administratively sentenced in December 1989 to two years' re-education through labor. He presumably was released upon completion of his term. During the 1989 pro-democracy movement, Zhao allegedly stirred up the students to demonstrate and wrote articles attacking the government. He was arrested after June 4.

- **ZHENG Jinhe**, a teacher and Communist Youth League Committee Secretary at the No.1 Middle School, Yongzhou City, Lingling Prefecture, Hunan Province, was administratively sentenced in December 1989 to two years' "re-education through labor" on the grounds of "counterrevolutionary error." He presumably was released upon completion of his term. During the 1989 pro-democracy movement, Zheng allegedly secretly supported the students in joint demonstrations with Lingling Teachers College. The date of his arrest is not known.

- **ZHONG Hua**, 24, a student in the class of 1986 in the environmental engineering department at Hunan University, secretly arrested in March 1990, was sentenced in July 1990 by the Changsha City (Hunan Province) Western District Court to three years' imprisonment on a charge of "disrupting traffic order." He presumably was released upon completion of his term. During the 1989 pro-democracy movement, Zhong was the head of the picket squad of the school's autonomous student union. At the end of May, he organized a student "lie-in" on the railway tracks at Changsha Station to block the trains and thus demonstrate opposition to the government. After June 4, Zhong was able to continue his studies at the university until his reaction to the failure of the Romanian Revolution "brought him to the attention of authorities."

- **ZHONG Minghui**, 30, a teacher at a middle school in Jinshi City, Changde Prefecture, Hunan Province, was administratively sentenced at the end of 1989 by the Jinshi City Public Security Bureau to three years' "re-education through labor." He presumably was released upon completion of his term. During the 1989 pro-democracy movement, Zhong allegedly wrote "reactionary articles" and spread "rumors," creating a very "bad influence." He was detained after June 4.

- **ZHOU Liwu**, a 27-year-old teacher at the Hunan No.2 School of Light Industry and a graduate of the philosophy department of Xiangtan University, was sentenced in early 1990 by the Changsha Intermediate People's Court to a two-year prison term on a charge of "counterrevolutionary propaganda and incitement." Zhou, who has never admitted guilt, was sent to Longxi Prison (Provincial No.6). He presumably was released upon completion of his sentence. During the 1989 pro-democracy movement, Zhou allegedly wrote "reactionary articles," planned student demonstrations and made public speeches attacking the Party and the government. He was arrested after June 4 1989.

- **ZHOU Lunyou**, a key member of an avant-garde underground poets'

society, *Fei Fei*, in Chengdu, Sichuan Province, was sentenced in March or April 1990 to three years' imprisonment on charges of illegal publishing and "counterrevolutionary incitement." Arrested in his hometown of Xichang on August 15, 1989, he presumably was released upon completion of his term. In an official Chinese response to U.S. government inquiries (November 1991), "legal responsibility was not pursued" in Zhou's case, a commonly used euphemism for administrative detention. According to the Hong Kong magazine *Zhengming* (December 1990), Zhou was first detained in Xichang, then imprisoned at the Obian Tea-Farming Labor Reform Center in northwest Sichuan. Some thirteen other members of the society were also arrested (see Liao Yiwu p.88); most have now been released.

Before Zhou became a full-time underground writer and publisher, he was a librarian at the Agricultural Professional School in Xichang. He also was one of the chief editors of an official publication, *Sichuan Poetry*. Just prior to the 1989 pro-democracy uprising, Zhou and his twin brother, Zhou Lunzuo (see p.459), lectured in universities throughout China. Their critical speeches excited many students and led to criticism by the Sichuan Provincial government and the *Chongqing Evening News*. Zhou Lunyou arrived in Beijing at the height of the protests, but failing to make connections with principals there, returned to Chengdu to "start a revolution." Zhou had been arrested once before, in 1985 in Wuhan, Hubei, after having given a series of talks at universities on the Yangzi River. According to **Zhou Yaqing**, Zhou's wife, Zhou continued to write poetry in prison despite his deteriorating physical condition, the result of torture and poor living conditions. Some of his prison poems found their way to Beijing.

From 1985 to 1989, the *Fei Fei* society published four poetry collections comprised of works by several dozen young poets. A fifth was in the planning stages when Zhou was arrested.

■ **ZHOU Yongping**, about 37, a teacher in Beijing University's sociology department, was arrested in Shenzhen but probably released in June or July 1989 (Amnesty International, *ASA 17/24/90*).

Workers, Peasants and Business Persons

■ **AN Baojing**, 32, a "principal member" of the Xi'an Workers Picket Corps and the Workers Autonomous Federation of Shaanxi Province, was arrested prior to June 25, 1989 and "brought to justice." According to an official Chinese response to inquiries by the U.S. government (November 1991), "legal responsibility was not pursued" in An's case, a commonly used euphemism for an administrative sentence of "re-education through labor." A Chinese government report to the International Labor Organization (November 1991) indicated that An "had his sentence remitted or was released after re-education."

An was accused, along with several others (see Zhao Demin p.556), of setting up both the Picket Corps and the WAF in late May 1989 and of "instigating" a group of people to stage demonstrations in Xi'an City by "yelling reactionary slogans and spreading reactionary leaflets." He also was accused of blocking traffic and manning barricades on June 4, 5 and 6.

■ **BAI Dongping**, a 27-year-old Beijing train attendant, member of the standing committee of the *Beijing Workers Autonomous Federation* and a liaison officer of the federation's registration and reception section, was "released after re-education or had his sentence remitted," according to an official Chinese response to the International Labor Organization (November 1990). Bai was detained briefly on May 28, 1989, then released after 3,000 people demonstrated outside the Beijing Public Security Bureau headquarters and the Ministry of Public Security. He was reportedly rearrested in Zhongjiang County, Sichuan Province on June 17, 1989 while on the run, and was later accused of participating in the "counter-revolutionary rebellion."

■ **BAO Hongjian, CHANG Ximing** (Zimin on an International Labor Organization list), **REN Xiyin** (Xijing on the ILO list), **XU Ying** and **ZHAO Demin**, five "principal members" of the Xi'an Workers Picket Corps, were arrested prior to June 25, 1989 and "brought to justice." According to an ILO report (November 1990), Chinese authorities said the five either had their sentences remitted or were released after "re-education through labor." Zhao was accused of setting up the organization in late May and of "instigating" a group of people to stage demonstrations in Xi'an City by "yelling reactionary slogans and spreading reactionary leaflets." He also was accused of blocking traffic and manning barricades on June 4, 5 and 6, 1989. The four others were similarly charged. According to a *Shaanxi Provincial Radio* report (June 25, 1989, in FBIS, June 27), "the six criminals (see An Baojing p.556) candidly confessed their illegal acts committed since the second half of May." All were members of the WAF of the province of Shaanxi.

■ **BOSS WU** (name unknown), about 40, originally the owner of the Wusepan (Five-Colored Dish) Restaurant on May 1st Road East, about 100 meters from the main entrance to the Hunan provincial government offices, was sentenced in 1990 by the Changsha Eastern District Public Security Bureau to three years' "re-education through labor." He was held in the Changsha Xinkaipu Labor Re-education Center and presumably was released upon completion of his term. During the 1989 Democracy Movement, Wu and his family, moved by the "righteous actions" of the students, put up a sign reading, "Students Eat Free." From the time martial law was declared in Beijing until the restaurant was forcibly closed by the government in early June, it provided almost 60,000 *yuan* worth of free food to the students. "Everyone in

Changsha knew about it. After June 4, the government played a trick. On the one hand, they published a notice in the newspapers canceling the restaurant's business license and wrote a criticism, making it look as if the sanction would only go that far. On the other hand, they secretly arrested Wu and held him for a long time [prior to sentencing]."

■ **BU Hengbin**, a farmer, and **CAO Mingfu**, a worker at the Xiaosuzhou Food Factory, were "not found legally responsible," according to an official Chinese response to U.S. government inquiries (November 1991). The term is usually a euphemism for an administratively imposed sentence of "re-education through labor." Since re-education sentences usually do not exceed three years, it is presumed both men have been released. Bu and Cao were arrested in Nanjing, Jiangsu Province, prior to May 25, 1989. Police objected to banners they carried in a demonstration there.

■ **BU Yunhui**, 24, a peasant in Group 6 (a village subdivision) of Tiepuling village, Yiyang County, Hunan Province, was sentenced in early 1990 to three years' imprisonment by the Changsha Eastern District Court on a charge of "disrupting traffic order." He presumably was released upon completion of his term. During the 1989 Democracy Movement, Bu allegedly took part in several demonstrations in Yiyang City and Changsha. On June 6, while he was lying down on the railroad tracks in Changsha station, he was threatened by public security cadres and, becoming angry, shouted slogans. Arrested on the spot and held in Changsha No.1 Jail, Bu was one of 31 workers and unemployed workers identified in *Hunan Daily* (June 1989) as "criminal elements who participated in turmoil."

■ **CAI Chaojun(g)**, an unemployed worker named by the Shanghai Municipal Public Security Bureau as the founder of the Shanghai Workers Autonomous Federation, was sentenced to a prison term, according to a response by Chinese officials to requests for information by the U.S. government (November 1991). The Chinese reply to the International Labor Organization (November 1991) listed his term as four years and his offense as disrupting traffic. He presumably was released after completing his time. An earlier account said Cai was arrested on June 9, 1989 for taking part in demonstrations and erecting roadblocks between June 3 and June 5. According to the Hong Kong paper *Zhongguo Tongxun* (August 16, 1989), authorities in Shanghai discovered that Cai, who reportedly had just been released from a labor camp, was the founder of the Shanghai Workers Voluntary Supporting Group, which on May 17, 1989 became the Shanghai Workers Autonomous Federation (SWAF). *Wen Wei Bao* described how eleven illegal Shanghai organizations were broken up and 99 people arrested after the SWAF was banned on June 9, 1989. In its January 1990 reply to the International Labor Organization, Chinese authorities claimed the "Shanghai Workers

Autonomous Federation's program provided for the organization of a workers' strike, the build up of its own armed force, and the overthrow of the government and abolishment of the socialist system."

■ **CAI Weixing**, a 25-year-old worker formerly employed at the Changsha Power Machinery Factory in Hunan Province, was sentenced in December 1989 by the Changsha Eastern District Court to four years' imprisonment. He was held in Longxi Prison (Provincial No.6) and presumably was released upon completion of his term. Cai, who reportedly participated in demonstrations during the 1989 pro-democracy movement, was arrested on April 22 for allegedly "stirring up the masses to beat, smash, and loot."

■ **CAO Zihui** (Qihui), a worker at the Beijing Motor Vehicle and Motorcycle Plant, arrested on June 7, 1989 in Tianjin, was "not found legally responsible," according to an official Chinese response to inquiries from the U.S. government (November 1991). The term is a euphemism for an administrative sentence of "re-education through labor," which usually does not exceed three years and from which Cao presumably has been released. A report in *Tianjin Ribao* said Cao, a member of the "Northeast Tigers Dare-to-Die Team," had seized two soldiers from the People's Liberation Army and brought them to Tiananmen Square "for publicity." An earlier report said after his arrest, he was handed over to the Beijing Public Security Bureau along with 46 other "counterrevolutionaries."

■ **CHAO Binglin**, a 30-year-old Shenyang, Liaoning Province native, arrested in June 1990 and sentenced to two years in prison on charges of "counterrevolutionary propaganda and incitement," presumably was released upon completion of his term. He was held in Lingyuan Prison. So far as is known, Chao was not involved in any of the hunger strikes in the facility. (For details see Tang Yuanjuan on p.105.)

■ **CHEN Shengfu**, a leader of the Shanghai Workers Autonomous Federation, had his sentence remitted or was released after "re-education through labor," according to the Chinese government's response to inquiries by the International Labor Organization (November 1990). He was one among a group of nine (see, for example, Li Zhibo p.162) arrested on June 9, 1989 for holding secret meetings, spreading rumors, distributing leaflets, advocating strikes, chanting reactionary slogans, advocating the overthrow of the government, setting up roadblocks, and disrupting traffic (*Beijing Radio* in FBIS, June 12, 1989). Allegedly, "they also vilified the Shanghai Council of Trade Unions as being totally paralyzed."

■ **CHEN Wei**[2] - see p.366

■ **CHEN Yueming**, 24, a resident of Changsha City, Hunan Province, where he ran a motor vehicle spare-parts business, was tried by the Changsha Intermediate People's Court on a charge of "counterrevolutionary propaganda and incitement" and sentenced to three years' imprisonment. He had been arrested in September 1990 for his involvement in secret underground pro-democracy work between 1989 and 1990. Chen was held in Lingling Prison (Provincial No.3) and presumably was released upon completion of his term.

■ **CHENG Fulai**, a Beijing worker arrested in June 1989 and charged with throwing rocks at martial law enforcement troops, was administratively sentenced to two years' re-education through labor in November 1989. He presumably was released upon completion of his term.

■ **DAI Dingxiang** - see p.98

■ **DENG Jun**, **WU Wei**[2], **XIONG Hanjun** (previously listed as **Xiong Jianjun**) and **FU Guanghui**, all workers in the Changde City Water Supply Plant in Hunan Province, and all in their thirties, were sentenced in November 1989 by the Changde City Public Security Bureau to two or three years' "re-education through labor." All presumably were released after completing their sentences. During the 1989 pro-democracy movement, the four men organized a Workers Autonomous Organization and agitated for strikes, which led to a brief shutoff of Changde's water supply. They were arrested shortly after June 4.

■ **DENG Liming**, a 29-year-old worker in Shaoyang City, Hunan Province, was sentenced in December 1989 by the Shaoyang City Public Security Bureau to three years' "re-education through labor." He presumably was released upon completion of his term. Deng was arrested in July 1989 for "creating disturbances" in Shaoyang during the pro-democracy movement. He allegedly disseminated "reactionary speech," posted big-character posters, and stirred up the masses to "wreck."

■ **DENG XX** (nicknamed "Shorty"), a 23-year-old private businessman from Changsha, Hunan Province, was tried for robbery by the Changsha City East District Court in mid-June 1989 and sentenced to a four-year prison term. He was arrested on the evening of April 22 in connection with the so-called "beating, smashing, and looting incident" which had occurred earlier that day. Deng presumably was released upon completion of his term.

■ **DONG Huaimin**, **WANG Zhongxian** and **WEI Ren**, all of whom were tried and sentenced on charges of "counterrevolutionary propaganda and incitement" by the Beijing Intermediate People's Court on February 25, 1992, are now presumed released after completing their terms. Two others tried at the same time, **Wang Guoqing** and **Li Baoqin** (see p.93), both received five-year terms and remain in prison. Dong Huaimin was jailed for four years; and Wang Zhongxian and Wei Ren received three-year terms (*Da*

Gong Bao, February 28, 1992, in FBIS, same date). Two others, **WANG Lidong**, who apparently was arrested in 1990, and **BAI Chunxiang**, were also convicted, but Wang received a two-year sentence and is presumed released, while Bai, for reasons unknown, was "exempt from criminal punishment." Wang Zhongxian, a worker now in his fifties, was arrested on or around June 9, 1989 for his involvement in the Beijing Workers Autonomous Federation and for continuing to operate the group's underground press after June 4. He was held at Paoju Detention Center, Banbuqiao Jail and Qincheng Prison, but his situation as of July 1993 was unknown. Wang's wife, arrested with him, was also later released. Prior to 1989, Wang worked at his own plastics factory in Guan County, Hebei Province.

Dong Huaimin (pen name **Pan Ni**), 47, was released on July 12, 1993, then returned to Jiaxing, his wife's hometown. Expelled from his unit after his trial, Dong had no job to which he could return. His wife, Wei Hongjun, works in the library of the Jiaxing Agricultural School in Zhejiang. But her pay is insufficient to maintain the couple and their 17-year-old daughter. Dong, who served his sentence in Yuhang County Prison in Zhejiang Province, was a "special commentator" in May 1989 for the Beijing Workers Autonomous Federation, collecting and editing articles for broadcast over the BWAF's station in Tiananmen Square. Later charged with "counter-revolutionary propaganda and incitement," he was interrogated in Beijing's Paoju Detention Center, and later transferred to the infamous "K-Block" of Banbuqiao Jail. He was subjected to such severe torture and ill-treatment there that, even prior to sentencing, he is said to have "resembled an emaciated old man." According to the source, "His hair was long and tangled, his nails were half an inch long and he was wearing a dirty little coat. He couldn't raise his arm above his shoulder." A guard, disliking a rebellious poem Dong had written on the cell walls, shackled his hands behind his back *(bei chui)* for eighteen days, so that he could neither feed nor wash himself.

A poet and political science teacher in the Jiaxing Nursing School in Zhejiang, Dong was secretly tried and convicted of counterrevolutionary incitement. Prior to trial, there was no notification to his wife or to any other relatives, nor were they permitted to attend. According to the sentencing document, Dong had his sentence reduced to four years because he saved a People's Liberation Army (PLA) lieutenant on June 4, 1989. A member of the PLA prior to the Cultural Revolution, Dong served in the Beijing Defense District, but was imprisoned for opposing a Cultural Revolution leader. After his release in 1967, he retired from the army and taught Marxist ideology. At the start of the 1989 protests, Dong was on his way to Beijing at the invitation of *Guangming Ribao* to edit an article on the "new authoritarianism." In Shanghai, he accidentally ran into student demonstrators. Joining the '89

movement, he proceeded to Beijing where he organized a Democracy Forum in front of the History Museum bordering Tiananmen Square. Still later he established a group called *Young China*. One of Dong's broadcast articles, "Taking the Bastille in the 1980s," was condemned by *Renmin Ribao* as a "heavily weighted bomb of the counterrevolutionary rebellion."

- **DOU Linhuai** - see p.92

- **DU Wenge** - see p.577

- **FAN Yuntie**, a 32-year-old peasant from Jinshi City, Hunan Province, was sentenced by the Jinshi City Public Security Bureau in November 1989 to two years' "re-education through labor." He presumably was released upon completion of his term. During the 1989 pro-democracy movement, Fan "infiltrated the ranks of the students" and created opportunities to "make disturbances." After June 4, he allegedly hid "reactionary elements."

- **FENG Ming**, in his twenties and a resident of Xiangtan City, Hunan Province, was tried as a "common criminal" in late 1989 by the Yuhu District Court, Xiangtan, and sentenced to a three-year prison term. He presumably was released upon its completion. Feng was arrested for allegedly participating in an incident on May 22 during which a group of people reportedly "burst into" the Pingzheng Road Police Station in Yuhu.

- **FU Guangrong**, a 27-year-old unemployed resident of Zhuzhou City,

Hunan Province, was sentenced by the Zhuzhou City Public Security Bureau to three years' "re-education through labor." He presumably was released upon completion of his term. During the 1989 pro-democracy movement, Fu allegedly spread "rumors all over the place" and directed the students to "create disturbances." Later, he helped students hide.

■ **FU Zhaoqin**, a peasant from Taojiang County, Hunan Province, was sentenced by a court in Yiyang City to four years' imprisonment on a charge of disrupting social order during the 1989 student movement. Held in Yiyang City Jail after his arrest in mid-June, he was then transferred to Yuanjiang Prison (Provincial No.1) and presumably released upon completion of his term. Fu was accused of "pretending to be a responsible person in the Hunan Students Autonomous Federation, stirring up disturbances, disrupting public order, and humiliating public security cadres."

■ **GAO Bingkun**, a 37-year-old unemployed resident of Changsha's Southern District, was sentenced by the Changsha (Hunan Province) Southern District (Basic-Level People's) Court in early 1990 to four years' imprisonment on a charge of "disrupting traffic order." He was imprisoned in Yuanjiang Prison (Provincial No.1) and presumably was released upon completion of his term. Arrested on June 6, 1989, and held first in Changsha No.1 Prison, Gao allegedly organized a mass "lie-in" on the railroad tracks shortly after June 4,

"causing the No.48 train from Guangzhou to Beijing to stop for over 10 hours."

■ **GAO Jin(g)tang**, a worker at the Zhejiang Clothing Research Institute, and **LI Xiaohu** were sentenced to three-year terms of imprisonment for disturbing the public peace, according to the Chinese government's reply to repeated International Labor Organization inquiries (November 1990). In a reply to U.S. government inquiries, Chinese officials confirmed that both men were sentenced (November 1991). It is presumed they were released upon completion of their terms. The men, "leading" members of the Hangzhou Workers Autonomous Federation, were arrested on June 10, 1989 along with five others (see Zhu Guanghua p.582) (*Beijing Ribao*, June 13, 1989). On the same day, the Hangzhou Public Security Bureau banned the Hangzhou Workers Autonomous Federation for "deliberately creating chaos." According to an official Chinese report, on June 7, 1989 members of the Hangzhou Workers Autonomous Federation, "taking advantage of the social turmoil...seized traffic boxes (and) put up the slogan 'fighting for democracy, freedom and human rights.'" They made "reactionary speeches" and "slandered the government by calling it a 'puppet regime.'" Furthermore, in its January 1990 reply to the International Labor Organization, the Chinese government accused the Hangzhou Workers Autonomous Federation of "adopting two-faced tactics," namely: "overtly advocating the elimination of corruption, the suppression of autocracy and the promotion of socialist democratic reform; covertly proclaiming its intention of overthrowing the dictatorship of the people and abolishing the leading role of the Communist Party."

■ **GAO Yunming**, 32, a worker in the Mutual Inductance Instrument Factory in Shenyang, Liaoning Province, was among 37 "lawless persons" arrested for fighting in Shenyang on June 8 (*Xinhua* radio broadcast, June 9, 1989). According to the report, twenty-nine of the 37 "will be released after re-education." Gao originally was to be tried, but according to the Chinese government's report to the International Labor Organization (November 1990), he had his sentence remitted or was released after "re-education through labor."

■ **GONG Chencheng** (Xiancheng), a key member of the Shanghai Patriotic Workers Support Group and a member of the Shanghai Workers Autonomous Federation, was exempted from punishment by the court because he turned himself in to the Huangpu Public Security Bureau (FBIS, November 22, 1989). The Chinese report to the International Labor Organization (November 1990) that Gong's sentence was remitted or that he was "released after re-education," implied that the charges against him were not dismissed; that at the least a record of his "crime" exists, and he may even have served a "re-education through labor" sentence.

■ **GUO Yaxiong**, a native of Hunan Province who allegedly drafted a "Declaration of the Dragon" (see Tian Bomin p.93) and "distributed it here and there in an effort to egg on people to make trouble," was accused of organizing assault teams. According to a Chinese report to the International Labor Organization (November 1991), he received a three-year prison term for "disrupting traffic," presumably he was released upon its completion. Guo was arrested on June 8, 1989 along with four other members of the Beijing Workers Autonomous Federation (BWAF) (*Beijing Television*, June 14, 1989). They reportedly were turned in by informers and accused of "instigating some thugs to beat, smash, loot and burn military vehicles...in the early hours of June 4, 1989." The only other named arrestee, **ZHU Lianyi**, a worker from the Third Urban Construction Company in Beijing, was "declared innocent of all criminal responsibility and released," (ILO, November 1991). Zhu allegedly joined the BWAF on May 18 and was in charge of setting up its printing workshop (*Beijing Wanbao*, June 22, 1989). When officers of the Public Security Bureau cracked down on the print shop, they allegedly seized military supplies captured by BWAF members during their "smashing and looting."

■ **HE Jianming** - see p.98

■ **HE Zhaohui** - see p.103

■ **HU Yuchang**, a worker at the Shanxi Xinhua Printing Company, was sentenced to one year's "re-education through labor," in connection with the 1989 pro-democracy movement. He presumably has been released.

■ **HUANG Yongxiang** - see p.140

■ **JIANG Deyin**, a Dongchang Loading and Unloading Company worker, had his sentence remitted or was released from "re-education through labor," according to the Chinese government's response to International Labor Organization inquiries (November 1990). He was one of nine "ruffians" (see Dong Langjun p.373) arrested in connection with protests in Shanghai.

■ **JIN Tao** - see p.366

■ **LI Jian**[2], a self-employed farm laborer from Shanghai, sentenced to three-and-a-half years' imprisonment for allegedly shouting "counter-revolutionary slogans," deflating tires and blocking traffic on June 5, 1989 (*Jiefang Ribao*, July 15, 1989), presumably was released upon completion of his term. An official Chinese response to inquiries by the U.S. government (November 1991) listed two people named Li Jian. One was listed as sentenced; the other as released. Asia Watch listed a third Li Jian. It is not possible to determine with certainty which dissident received what treatment.

■ Six leaders of the Changsha *Workers Autonomous Federation* who had been arrested on or before June 16, 1989 - **LI Jian**[3], the group's founder and first chairman; **HE Zhaohui**,

vice-chairman of the standing committee; **LU Zhaixing**; **ZHANG Xudong**, a founder, vice-chairman and a member of the standing committee; **ZHOU Yong**, a founder and chairman; and **LIU Xingqi** - were all released from prison as of November 1993. A seventh WAF leader, **ZHOU Min**, (see p.103) was sentenced to six years' imprisonment and is currently being held at the Hunan Province No.1 Prison at Yuanjiang. The six now freed were charged after June 1989 with "counterrevolutionary propaganda, blocking traffic and instigating strikes" (*People's Daily Overseas Edition*, June 20, 1989) and received sentences of up to four years' imprisonment. Three others, **CAI Jinxuan**, Standing Committee member and deputy picket leader; **LI Jie**[3]; and **WANG Changhuai** (presumed released after serving a three-year sentence - see Zhang Jingsheng p.102) all surrendered to the public security authorities after June 4, 1989. The Changsha WAF, founded on May 20, 1989, was banned on June 12.

Li Jian, a 25-year-old worker at the Changsha Zhengyuan Power Equipment Parts Factory, was sentenced in April 1990 by the Changsha City Intermediate People's Court to three years' imprisonment on a charge of being a member of a "counterrevolutionary group." In response to an inquiry from the International Labor Organization (ILO, November 1990), the Chinese government confirmed that he was arrested and that his sentence was for "disturbing the peace." Li was detained first in Changsha No.1 Prison and later in Yuanjiang Prison (Provincial No.1). He was presumably released upon completion of his term. On May 18, 1989, Li Jian, masquerading as LI Ming[2], a political education student from Hunan University, allegedly took part in "storming" the provincial government building. With Zhou Yong, Lu and Li Jie, he raised a banner reading "Workers on Hunger Strike," organized the Workers' Hunger Strike Team and helped stage a hunger strike at the building's gate. On May 21, Li Jian and Zhou Yong called on all the workers of Changsha to participate in a general strike. The Changsha WAF also organized transportation tie-ups which succeeded in paralyzing city traffic for three days. Production was halted at some dozen enterprises, including the Changsha Automobile Electrical Equipment Factory, the Changsha Down Factory and the Changsha Cigarette Factory. "In the Changsha [Cigarette] Factory alone, this caused more than 1 million *yuan* in economic losses."

He Zhaohui, a 24-year-old worker for the Changsha Railway Passenger Transport Section whose family resides in Chenjia Wan in Chenzhou, Hunan, was sentenced in June 1990 by the Changsha Eastern District Court to four years' imprisonment on a charge of "disturbing social order." The sentence also was confirmed in a Chinese government response to ILO inquiries (November 1990); and in an official Chinese response to the U.S. government in November 1991. He allegedly organized strikes by railroad workers and posted slogans and big-character posters. He Zhaohui was

detained first in Changsha No.1 Prison, then moved to Longxi Prison (Provincial No.6), and presumably released upon completion of his term.

Lu Zhaixing (LIU Zhaixing on previous arrest lists), 27, a worker in the Changsha Knitwear Factory, was sentenced in April 1990 by the Changsha Eastern District Court to three years' imprisonment on a charge of "disrupting public order." Arrested at home on June 15, 1989, he was first held in Changsha No.1 Prison, moved to Yuanjiang Prison (Provincial No.1) and presumably released upon completion of his sentence. A contradictory Chinese government report, given to the ILO (November 1991), stated Lu had had his sentence remitted or was released after "re-education through labor."

Zhang Xudong, a 32-year-old worker at the Changsha North District Hong Qiang Power Machinery Plant, was sentenced in mid-1990 by the Changsha Intermediate People's Court to four years' imprisonment on a charge of "counterrevolutionary propaganda and incitement." The sentence was confirmed in a Chinese government response to an ILO inquiry in January 1992, but the report said he was convicted for "disturbing the peace." Zhang, whose family lives in Chongsheng Alley in Changsha's North District, wore leg irons and handcuffs the entire ten months he was held at Changsha No.1 Prison. He presumably was released upon completion of his sentence.

Zhou Yong, a 30-year-old worker at the Changsha No.2 Pneumatic Tool Plant, arrested for the second time in

June 1989, was acquitted and released in early 1990 for having "performed meritorious service." Zhou was first detained on May 28 with other WAF leaders who had participated in sit-in protests, but was set free after students marched to protest the arrests. Zhou's second release was confirmed in a Chinese government report to the ILO (November 1991) listing him as having had his sentence remitted or having been released after "re-education through labor." Liu Xingqi, a 24-year-old worker at the Changsha Lightbulb Factory, held in Changsha No.1 Prison, was given a three-year prison sentence, according to a Chinese government response to the ILO (November 1990). He presumably was released upon its completion. Li Jie, 27, a worker in Department 3416 of the Ministry of Aeronautics, was released in June 1990 after being detained in Changsha No.1 Prison. Cai Jinxuan, 24, a worker at the Changsha Textile Mill, was held in the Changsha No.1 Prison until his release in April 1990.

Among other activities, Li Jie allegedly participated in sit-ins and organized demonstrations and strikes. Cai helped organize worker strikes and printed propaganda materials. Liu organized strikes and meetings and took part in organizing the memorial rally. Zhou Yong allegedly led workers in sit-in protests and demonstration marches and instigated workers to strike in several dozen factories in the Changsha area. Zhang reportedly organized worker demonstrations and strikes. Lu allegedly organized demonstrations and strikes by workers at the Knitwear Factory.

■ **LI Jianzhong**, a worker from Shaoyang City, Hunan, who made a living pushing carts, was sentenced to three and a half years' imprisonment after June 1989 for allegedly "disrupting traffic" during the protest movement. He is presumed to have been released after completing his term.

■ **LI Mingxian**, a 31-year-old jobless worker from Gaixian County who was arrested on June 16, 1989 in Fushun City, Liaoning Province, has had his sentence remitted or was released after "re-education though labor," according to the Chinese government's report to the International Labor Organization (November 1990). Li allegedly entered Beijing on May 13, 1989, joined the "counterrevolutionary rebellion at the Shengli Hotel" and participated in "the counterrevolutionary activities of beating soldiers and smashing army vehicles on June 3-4." Described as an ex-criminal, Li was first captured in Beijing, but escaped and fled to Fushun via Yingkou (FBIS, June 16, 1989).

■ **LI Nianbing, YU Chunsheng, WAN Yong, WAN Guoping** and **WANG Zhongshou** were sentenced in southern Jiangxi Province during the week of July 17, 1989 for "serious" public order offenses committed in the square of the provincial capital, Nanchang, during a demonstration there on May 4, 1989 marking the seventieth anniversary of the May 4th Movement. According to the July 20,

1989 *Jiangxi Ribao*, the five blocked traffic, smashed and overturned vehicles, set fire to property and attacked people. Li, a worker, was jailed for four years. Yu, identified only as a company employee, Wan Yong, jobless, and Wan Guoping, a worker, were jailed for three years. Wang Zhongshou, self-employed, received a two-year sentence. It is presumed all were released upon completion of their terms.

■ **LI Shusen**, a 38-year-old worker from Jinxi Municipality, Liaoning Province, arrested in June 1989, was sentenced to four years in prison on charges of "counterrevolutionary propaganda and incitement." He was held in Lingyuan Prison and presumably was released upon completion of his term. So far as is known, Li was not involved in any of the hunger strikes in the facility. (For details see Tang Yuanjuan p.105.)

■ **LI Suping** - see p.87

■ **LI Xin**, a 25-year-old worker whose family lives on Kui'e North Road in Changsha, Hunan Province, was sentenced in December 1989 by the Changsha Northern District (Basic-Level People's) Court to a term of three years' imprisonment on a charge of "disturbing social order." During the 1989 pro-democracy movement, Li allegedly was deputy head of the picket squad *(jiucha dui)* of the Changsha Workers Autonomous Federation. He was arrested in June that year, held in Yuanjiang Prison

(Provincial No.1) and presumably released after completing his term.

■ **LI Zhongmin**, a teacher until 1988 at a Youth Palace attached to the Changchun No.1 Motor Works in Jilin Province, was arrested in June 1989 and sentenced in November 1990 to two years' imprisonment and one year's deprivation of political rights for "taking an active part in a counter-revolutionary group." Li, who was a member of a workers' discussion club formed by **Tang Yuanjuan** (currently serving a 20-year sentence for "counterrevolution" - see p.105), is presumed to have been released after serving his term. Born in 1955 in Nongan County, Jilin Prison, Li left the Changchun No.1 Motor Works in 1988 to work in Shenzhen.

LIANG Liwei, an assistant engineer at the boiler testing laboratory, received a three-year prison sentence and one year's deprivation of political rights for "counter-revolutionary propaganda and incitement," also in connection with his membership of Tang Yuanjuan's workers' group. He too is presumed released. Born in 1961 in Gaixian County, Liaoning Province, Liang graduated from the Northeastern Institute of Electric Power in 1983.

■ **LIANG Chao** - see p.98

■ **LIANG Liwei** - see p.105

■ **LIANG Wang**, a 24-year-old worker formerly employed at the Changsha Woolen Mill, Hunan

Province, was administratively sentenced by the Changsha City Public Security Bureau to "only two years' re-education through labor" because of lack of evidence. He presumably was released upon completion of his term. Arrested after the 1989 pro-democracy movement, Liang allegedly instigated strikes and cooperated with students to "make disturbances."

■ **LIAO Zhengxiong**, a 24-year-old owner of a small private business in Changsha City, Hunan Province, was tried by the Changsha City South District Court in mid-June 1989 on a charge of robbery, and sentenced to three years' imprisonment. Arrested in connection with the April 22 "beating, smashing, looting incident" in Changsha, Liao served his sentence in Longxi Prison (Provincial No.6). He presumably was released after completing his term.

■ **LIU Chengwu[1]**, 25, a Shenyang, Liaoning Province resident, was arrested on October 30, 1989 for "openly propagating reactionary words and disrupting public order." According to an official Chinese response to inquiries by the U.S. government (November 1991), "legal responsibility was not pursued" in Liu's case, often a euphemism for re-education through labor. Since "re-education" sentences do not usually run longer than three years, it is presumed he has been released. The unemployed Liu, who allegedly served a prison sentence for theft in 1983-85, reportedly had set up a radio transmitter outside his mother's

restaurant on June 7, 1989 to relay *Voice of America* news about the Beijing massacre. "Many people stopped to listen to the radio. As a result traffic was seriously disrupted" (*Liaoning Fazhi Bao*, November 7, 1989).

■ **LIU Chengwu[2]**, a 24-year-old peasant from Huangtuhang Township, Suining County, Hunan Province, sentenced at the end of 1989 by the Changsha Eastern District Court to four years' imprisonment on a charge of "disrupting social order," presumably was released after completing his term. According to the authorities, "On May 18, 1989, [Liu] stirred up the blocking of vehicles in the square of the Changsha Railway Station. When public security cadres tried to get people to stop, he actually took pictures, trying to find some basis on which to stir up even more trouble. He was arrested on the spot" (*Hunan Ribao*, mid-June 1989). First held in Changsha No.1 Prison, Liu was later transferred to Yuanjiang Prison (Provincial No.1).

■ **LIU Congshu** (Chongxi on an International Labor Organization list), a leader of the Xi'an (Shaanxi Province) Workers Autonomous Federation and member of the "Xi'an Citizens Petition Group" and the "Workers' Pickets," has not been arrested nor has he come before judicial authorities, according to one Chinese response to ILO inquiries (November 1990); according to another response, he was "released after re-education through labor or absolved of criminal responsibility by the court" (ILO, November 1991). According to an official Chinese response to inquiries by the U.S. government (November 1991), "legal responsibility was not pursued" in Liu's case.

Liu was arrested on June 11, 1989 and accused of inciting citizens to "besiege" the Xi'an City Federation of Trade Unions, smash the union's signboard and go on strike. According to *Xi'an Radio* (June 12, 1989), "the reactionary declaration made by this group of people and their letter to all workers throughout the city viciously attacked the leaders of the party and state in an organized, planned and guided way." A total of 43 people, all publicly unidentified and all apparently members of seven banned student and worker federations, were arrested in Xi'an on June 11, 1989. It is not certain that Liu Congshu and Liu Chongxi are the same person.

■ **LIU Fengming**, a 40-year-old peasant from Changxu County, Liaoning Province, arrested in July 1990, was sentenced to three years in prison on charges of "counter-revolutionary propaganda and incitement." He was held in Lingyuan Prison and presumably was released upon completion of his term. So far as is known, Liu was not involved in any of the hunger strikes in the facility. (For details see Tang Yuanjuan p.105.) From 1976 until 1978, Liu was imprisoned for "counterrevolutionary crimes." Later, he was "rehabilitated."

■ **LIU Huanwen**[2], 28, a Standing Committee member of the Beijing Workers Autonomous Federation, had his sentence remitted or was released after "re-education through labor," according to a Chinese response to inquiries from the International Labor Organization (November 1990). He had been arrested at 10 P.M., June 13, 1989 by police of the Yongan Street Police Station of the Qiaoxi Sub-bureau of the Shijiazhuang Public Security Bureau; local citizens had reported his presence (*Hong Kong Standard*, June 17, 1989). A "most wanted" Beijing worker in charge of the Pickets Team, Liu fled Beijing on June 9. At the time of his arrest, he allegedly had in his possession passes signed by Wuerkaixi, one of the 21 "most wanted" students; a dagger; two rounds of ammunition; and a "picket certificate." Liu was accused of inciting sit-ins and demonstrations, "engaging in reactionary rebellious activities," erecting roadblocks in Tiananmen Square and burning military vehicles in Beijing districts where major confrontations occurred. Once a worker at the Special Steel Branch Company of the Capital Iron and Steel Company, Liu started receiving unemployment insurance at the end of 1987, according to a June 14 *Beijing Television* broadcast (FBIS, June 15, 1989).

■ **LIU Jianwei**, a 30-year-old worker in the Vehicle Section of the Passenger Transport Department of Changsha's Railway Bureau, Hunan Province, was sentenced in early 1990 by the Changsha Railway Public Security Bureau to three years' "re-education through labor." He presumably has been released after completing his term. During the 1989 pro-democracy movement, Liu allegedly participated in the Changsha Workers Autonomous Federation, and, in mid-June, secretly smuggled several leaders of the Hunan Students Autonomous Federation out of the city by train. Arrested in September 1989, Liu served his sentence at the Changsha City Xinkaipu Labor Re-education Center.

■ **LIU Ronglin** - see p.386

■ **LIU Wei**, a 25-year-old worker at a Changsha (Hunan Province) municipal factory arrested in July 1989, was administratively sentenced in November 1989 to two years' "re-education through labor." He presumably was released upon completion of his term. Liu joined the Changsha Workers Autonomous Federation during the 1989 pro-democracy movement and served on its picket squad. He allegedly participated in protest demonstrations and encouraged workers to strike.

■ **LIU Weihong²**, a 27-year-old worker at a Changsha (Hunan Province) factory, was tried by the Changsha Intermediate People's Court in mid-1990 on a charge of "counter-revolutionary propaganda and incitement" and sentenced to four years' imprisonment. During the 1989 pro-democracy movement, he allegedly organized workers in his factory to "go on strike and create disturbances" and "made impertinent remarks to the factory leaders." Arrested soon after

June 4, 1989, he was held in Lingling Prison (Provincial No.3) and presumably was released upon completion of his term.

■ **LIU Xiaolong, ZHU Lin, YU Yungang, LI Tao** (also known as **XU Tao), PANG Xiaobin, XIANG Yongbin** (also known as **WEI Yongbin**) and **WANG Jianjun**, all students and members of a "Dare-to-Die Corps" from Xi'an, had their sentences remitted or were released after "re-education through labor," according to a Chinese response to requests for information from the International Labor Organization (November 1991). A request for information by the U.S. government on Xiang's case elicited no response from Chinese authorities (November 1991).

All seven students were arrested at midnight on June 11, 1989 at a meeting in the Xingqinggong section of Xi'an City. According to a *Renmin Ribao* (June 13, 1989) report, led by Liu, they "set up barricades, intercepted traffic and disrupted transportation and social order." Although the Corps, one of seven illegal organizations in Xi'an, was banned before June 11, 1989, its members were accused of refusing to disband and carrying out "desperate resistance."

■ **LIU Xingqi** - see p.103

■ **LIU Yusheng** - see p.154

■ **LIU Yubin², CHE Hongnian, SHAO Liangchen, ZHANG Xinchao** and **HAO Jinguang**, all members of the Jinan (Shandong Province) City Workers Autonomous Federation and the Workers Democratic Federation, were arrested in Jinan on June 15, 1989. Liu and Zhang received three-year prison terms, the latter for disturbing the public peace; and Che was sentenced to two years' imprisonment, according to the International Labor Organization (November 1990, November 15, 1991). The same source reported Shao and Hao were "never brought to court," which could indicate they received administrative sentences of "re-education through labor." However, such an interpretation is not consistent with an official Chinese response to U.S. government inquiries (November 1991), which confirmed that Liu, Shao, Zhang and Hao had been tried and sentenced in court. It is presumed that Liu, Zhang and Che were released upon completion of their sentences. If Shao and Hao did receive "re-education through labor" sentences, usually no longer than three years, they too have presumably been released.

According to *Jinan Radio* (FBIS, June 16, 1989), an amalgam of the two organizations to which the men belonged planned to seize political power by armed force. Liu, a worker at the Qianqiaoju Textile Company of Jinan, and Che were named as the group's leaders.

■ **LU Zhaixing** - see p.103

■ **MA Heping**, an unemployed 29-year-old resident of Hengyang City, Hunan Province, was administratively sentenced in November 1989 by the Hengyang City Public Security Bureau to three years' "re-education through labor." Arrested in June 1989, he had allegedly "created disturbances" during the pro-democracy movement, "sneaked into" the ranks of the students to take part in demonstrations and "cursed" the public security authorities. It is presumed that Ma was released after completing his sentence.

■ **PANG Jiemin**, a worker in a space flight department factory, was sentenced to one-an-a-half years' "re-education through labor" for throwing rocks. There is no record of where his July 1989 arrest took place; and it is presumed he was released upon completion of his term.

■ **PENG Ditang**, a factory worker and member of the Xi'an (Shaanxi Province) Workers Autonomous Federation, was sentenced to three years' imprisonment for "counter-revolutionary propaganda and incitement" (*South China Morning Post*, March 19, 1991). Requests by the U.S. government for information about Peng's status elicited no response from Chinese officials (November 1991), but it is presumed he was released upon completion of his sentence.

■ **PENG Jing**, a member of the Beijing "Dare-to-Die Corps" and a worker at the Wuhan (Hubei Province) City Pharmaceutical Factory, had his sentence remitted or was released after "re-education through labor," according to the Chinese government's report to the International Labor Organization

(November 1990). Peng was arrested in Wuhan on June 16, 1989 and accused of fabricating rumors and blocking railroad traffic. He allegedly went to Beijing on May 20 and returned to Wuhan after June 4. Reporting his arrest on June 18, Chinese television showed Peng being escorted into a room, then being questioned by two uniformed men. On several previous occasions, Peng allegedly was detained and fined by public security organs for committing theft (*Beijing Television*, June 18, 1989, in FBIS, June 20).

■ **PENG Liangkun**, a 25-year-old worker in a large factory in Xiangxiang County, Hunan Province, was administratively sentenced in November 1989 by the Xiangxiang County Public Security Bureau to three years' re-education through labor. He presumably was released after completing his term. Peng was arrested after June 4 for allegedly going to many places to "stir up the wind and light a fire," wishing to "bring chaos" to society. He reportedly also disseminated news from "enemy stations" (i.e. *Voice of America* and BBC).

■ **QIAN Lizhu** (the surname may be incorrect), a 26-year-old peasant from Yueyang City, Hunan Province, was administratively sentenced in October 1989 by the Yueyang City Public Security Bureau to three years' "re-education through labor." He presumably was released upon completion of his term. Arrested after June 4, 1989, Qiang allegedly came to the city during the pro-democracy

movement to "create rumors;" he attacked the Party and the government, and took part in "making disturbances."

■ **QIN Huaiqing** - see p.87

■ **RUI Tonghu** - see p.582

■ **SHAN Guoguang**, a truck driver in Putuo District Truck Company and a member of the Shanghai Vehicle Flying Squad, was sentenced in Shanghai to a three-year term for disturbing the public peace, according to the Chinese government's response to repeated inquiries from the International Labor Organization (November 1990). He was presumably released upon completion of his sentence. Shan was arrested on June 9 or 10, 1989 in Shanghai (*June 4 China Support Group*, January 8, 1991). In response to requests for information by the U.S. government, Chinese authorities confirmed (November 1991) that one **SHAN Hongguang** (presumably the same person as Shan Guoguang) was sentenced.

■ **SHEN Jizhong**, a florist in his forties, and three other industrial workers reportedly were arrested in Shanghai on May 31, 1989 for making pro-democracy speeches. According to an official Chinese response to requests for information by the U.S. government (November 1991), he was "not found legally responsible," usually a euphemism for an administrative sentence of "re-education through labor." Since re-education sentences usually do not exceed three years, it is presumed he has been released. During the Cultural Revolution, Shen reportedly spent many years in jail for political reasons before he was released and rehabilitated in 1976.

■ *Ming Bao* (October 10, 1989) reported the arrests and sentencing to two and three years' "re-education through labor" of six unnamed persons, mostly workers, apparently in connection with the pro-democracy movement in Chongqing, Sichuan Province. It is presumed that all were released upon completion of their terms.

■ **SUN Chaohui** - see p.370

■ **TAN Minglu** - see p.124

■ **TANG Changye**, a 29-year-old resigned worker, was sentenced in 1990 by the Changsha (Hunan Province) Eastern District Court to three years' imprisonment on a charge of "disturbing social order." He presumably was released upon completion of his term. During the 1989 pro-democracy movement, Tang allegedly printed handbills and posted big-character posters. Arrested in October 1989, he suffered a great deal of abuse from fellow prisoners while detained in Changsha No.1 Prison, Cell 15. Later Tang was transferred to Yuanjiang Prison (Provincial No.1). Cadres and convicts alike considered him mentally ill.

■ **TIAN Suxin**, a worker at the Fushun Steel Plant, and two others were sentenced to two to three years' "re-education through labor." They

were arrested in Fushun, Liaoning Province, for allegedly shouting slogans and blocking traffic there on May 17-18, 1989. According to a June 15, 1989 *Liaoning Radio* report, all three also "brutally beat" those who refused to shout the slogans they provided. Requests by the U.S. government for information about Tian's whereabouts elicited no response from Chinese officials (November 1991), but he presumably was released upon completion of his term.

■ **WANG Changhuai** - see p.102

■ **WANG Guisheng**, a 40-year-old high school graduate from Dalian, was sentenced to three years in prison on charges of "counterrevolutionary propaganda and incitement." He was arrested either in June 1989 or on December 4 after being denounced by an informer for allegedly writing "counterrevolutionary tracts" and posting them in downtown Dalian, Liaoning Province. Wang reportedly "harbored resentment against the party" and "slandered" its leadership (Amnesty International, *ASA 17/24/90*). He presumably was released upon completion of his term which he served in Lingyuan Prison.

■ **WANG Hong[3]**, a leader of the Shanghai Workers Autonomous Federation, who was sentenced to one-and-a-half years in prison for "disturbing the peace" (International Labor Organization, November 1991), presumably was released upon completion of his term. That he was sentenced was confirmed by Chinese officials in a response to inquiries by the U.S. government (November 1991). Wang was arrested on June 9, 1989 and, along with nine others (see Wang Wang p.506), was accused of holding secret meetings, spreading rumors, distributing leaflets, advocating strikes, chanting reactionary slogans, advocating the overthrow of the government, setting up roadblocks and disrupting traffic. Allegedly, "they also vilified the Shanghai Council of Trade Unions as being totally paralyzed" (*Beijing Radio* in FBIS, June 12, 1989).

■ **WANG Lidong** - see p.93

■ **WANG Wei**[3] (Yang Wei[2] on an International Labor Organization list) was never arrested nor has he come before judicial authorities, according to the Chinese government's reply to the ILO (November 1990). He probably was sentenced administratively to "re-education through labor." Of three different people named "Wang Wei" listed in an official Chinese response to U.S. government inquiries (November 1991), one was "not found legally responsible" - often a euphemism for "labor re-education." If so, he presumably has been released since "re-education" terms usually run no longer than three years. Wang and another member (see Zhang Jun p.157) of a Beijing "Citizen's Dare-to-Die Corps" were detained on June 11, 1989 by the Martial Law Enforcement Command acting in coordination with the Public Security Bureau. According to a June 12, 1989 Beijing Television broadcast, Wang, allegedly a leader of the "No.9 Team" of the "Dare-to-Die Corps,"

was accused of assaulting soldiers with bottles on the night of June 3. According to the authorities: "On June 5, while corps members were escorting fleeing Beijing Students Autonomous Federation ringleaders, he unscrupulously spread [aboard the train] counterrevolutionary rumors about a bloodbath in Tiananmen Square" (FBIS, June 14, 1989).

■ **WANG Xia** - see p.374

■ **WANG Zhongxian** - see p.93

■ **WANG Zunning** - see p.370

■ **WEI Ren** - see p.93

■ **WENG Zhengming**, allegedly head of the *China Youth Democracy Party*, was sentenced to three years' imprisonment for "disturbing the peace," according to an official Chinese response to requests for information by the International Labor Organization (November 1991). He presumably was released upon completion of his term. Weng's name also appeared on a list of those sentenced which was presented by Chinese officials to the U.S. government in November 1991. A self-employed tailor, Weng was arrested on June 10, 1989 in Shanghai, according to *Beijing Radio*. After student demonstrations began in April 1989, Weng allegedly went to several universities around Shanghai to recruit members for the *China Youth Democracy Party* and to "instigate unrest" among students. He passed out membership registration forms and copies of the party's platform. During the demonstrations in Shanghai, a contingent from the *China Youth Democracy Party*, termed "counter-revolutionary" by the authorities, marched through the streets carrying a banner. Weng allegedly established the party as early as 1986, arguing that an opposition party must emerge in China.

■ **WU Changgui**, a 30-year-old worker, was administratively sentenced in early 1990 by the Xiangtan (Hunan Province) City Public Security Bureau to three years' "re-education through labor" and presumably was released upon completion of his term. Arrested in June 1989, for helping organize the Xiangtan Workers Autonomous Federation and serving as a member of its Standing Committee, Wu allegedly also organized demonstrations, sit-ins, and strikes by the workers.

■ **XIA Kuanqun**, a 34-year-old who worked at a government organ in Changde City, Hunan Province, was administratively sentenced in November 1989 by the Changde City Public Security Bureau to three years' "re-education through labor." He presumably was released upon completion of his term. During the pro-democracy movement, Xia allegedly donated several hundred *yuan* to the students and encouraged cadres in his unit to go out into the streets in their support.

■ **XIAO Sanfeng** - see p.370

■ **XIAO Shenhe**, a 32-year-old peasant from Ningxiang County, Hunan Province, was administratively

sentenced at the end of 1989 to three years' "re-education through labor" at the Changsha City Xinkaipu Labor Re-education Center. He presumably was released upon completion of his term. During the 1989 pro-democracy movement, Xiao allegedly participated in demonstrations and meetings and planned to set up an "Anti-Corruption Action Group." He was arrested after June 4 and initially held in the Changsha County Jail.

■ **XIONG Xiangwen**, a 28-year-old worker in a factory in Linli County, Hunan Province, was administratively sentenced in November 1989 by the Changde City Public Security Bureau to two-and-one-half years' "re-education through labor." He presumably was released upon completion of his term. During the 1989 pro-democracy movement, Xiong allegedly stirred up workers to strike, and disseminated all kinds of "rumors" and "reactionary speech," "trying to create chaos." He was arrested after June 4.

■ **XU Bingli**, 51, a worker at the Hongkou District Housing Management Company in Shanghai, had his sentence remitted or was released after "re-education through labor," according to the Chinese government's reply to International Labor Organization inquiries (November 1990). Xu was arrested in Shanghai on June 13, 1989 and accused of setting up an illegal organization, the *China Civil Rights Autonomous Federation*, on May 28 in Shanghai, and of making "numerous counterrevolutionary" speeches in People's Square in which he urged workers to join a general strike and "overthrow the corrupt government."

■ **XUE Wuyi**, a Beijing Capital Iron and Steel Factory worker, presumably has been released after serving a two-year "re-education through labor" sentence. According to an Asia Watch source, Xue was arrested in 1989 for "picking up" two bullets and a can of biscuits.

■ **YAN Xingan**, a 35-year-old worker in Fushun Municipality, Liaoning Province, arrested in June 1989, was sentenced to four years in prison on charges of "counter-revolutionary propaganda and incitement." He was held in Lingyuan Prison and presumably was released upon completion of his term. So far as is known, Yan was not involved in any of the hunger strikes in the facility. (For details see Tang Yuanjuan p.105.)

■ **YANG Fuqian**, 27, a worker at the Beijing No.4 Hydraulic Plant and a leader of the Beijing Workers Autonomous Federation, had his sentence remitted or was released after "re-education through labor," according to the reply to the International Labor Organization by Chinese authorities (November 1990). He was arrested on June 10, 1989. According to *Beijing Radio*, Yang, who became a member of the Federation on May 22 and was appointed leader of the Third Picket Detachment, made a "preliminary confession" that he had instigated people to storm the Beijing Public Security Bureau. That "confession" may, however, have been extracted by

force or intimidation. Yang appeared on state television in the presence of an interrogator on June 11, 1989. According to a UPI report, "The prisoner was groggy and his speech was slurred from an apparent beating that swelled his right cheek. Several of the other suspects also appeared to have suffered beatings."

■ **YANG Gechuang**, who was arrested in Wuhan, Hebei Province on June 7, 1989 for allegedly overturning trucks, blocking traffic and setting fire to a public vehicle, had his sentence remitted or was released after "re-education through labor," according to the Chinese government's report to the International Labor Organization (November 1990).

■ **YANG Hengwu** - see p.505

■ **YANG Liu**, a 20-year-old peasant from Yueyang Municipality, Xiangyin County, Hunan Province, was tried at the end of 1989 by the South District Court of Changsha on common criminal charges and sentenced to four years' imprisonment. While working in Changsha as a carpenter during the 1989 pro-democracy movement, he allegedly was involved in an incident in which "people burst into a government office." Arrested soon after June 4, he served his sentence at the Mijiang Tea Farm labor reform camp in Chaling County and presumably was released upon its completion.

■ **YANG Xiao**[1], a worker from Shanghai, may have been released, according to an official Chinese response to inquiries from the U.S. government (November 1991), but the reference probably was to a Beijing intellectual with the same name. An earlier report to the International Labor Organization (November 1990) that a Yang Xiao had never been arrested nor had he ever come before judicial authorities, implying a "re-education through labor" sentence probably refers to the Shanghai worker. First of all, Yang was charged with "smashing railway cars, setting fire to nine railway cars and six public security motor vehicles, turning over police boxes, beating up firemen to impede them from putting the fire out and fabricating rumors to mislead the people (*Zhong Xin She*, June 10, 1989, in FBIS, June 12). Secondly, others involved in the case received harsh sentences at their trial on June 18, 1989 (see Ai Qilong p.371 and Zhu Qin p.583). Since re-education sentences are usually no longer than three years, if Yang received such a sentence, he probably has been released.

■ **YANG Xiaogang**, a 35-year-old worker, was sentenced in September 1989 by the Changsha (Hunan Province) Eastern District Court to three years' imprisonment. In December, he was sent to Longxi Prison (Provincial No.6) for reform through labor; presumably he was released upon completion of his term. Son of the chairman of the Changsha Science [and Technology] Federation, where his family resides, Yang allegedly disseminated news from "enemy [broadcasting] stations" and spread "rumors" during the 1989

pro-democracy movement. He was arrested in May 1989 on a charge of "assembling the masses for beating, smashing, and looting."

■ **YANG Xiong**, a resident of Changsha in his late twenties, was sentenced to either three or four years' imprisonment after June 1989 for his involvement in the *Changsha Workers Autonomous Federation*. Responsible for the federation's picket squad, he organized members to go to local factories and urge the workers to go on strike. On June 8, 1989, Yang was in charge of the picket squad assigned to keep order at the mass public mourning ceremony held that day at the Changsha Railwat Station. He was arrested in mid-June and tried in early 1990 on charges of "disrupting social order." According to initial reports, he received a three-year sentence; but in January 1992, the Chinese authorities informed the International Labor Organization that Yang had been given a four-year sentence. He is presumed released after serving his term.

■ **YANG Yongming**, self-employed and **DU Wenge**, unemployed, two of the 29 "lawless elements" arrested in Xuzhou, Jiangsu Province before June 11, 1989, were both punished for their 1989 pro-democracy activities. According to an official Chinese response to U.S. government inquiries (November 1991), Du received a prison term and Yang was "not found legally responsible," a euphemism for "re-education through labor." According to another official Chinese response, this one to an International

Labor Organization inquiry (November 1991), Yang was "released following re-education or absolved of criminal responsibility by the courts." Du was handed a three-year sentence for "disturbing the public order." Presumably he was released upon its completion. Both men allegedly were ringleaders of the illegal Xuzhou Autonomous Federation of National Salvation and were accused of planning to "carry out a number of sabotage activities to create turmoil in Xuzhou." Du allegedly had already spent a year in prison for theft. Yang, according to an official report, had been punished by public security authorities for "hooliganism" in 1981 and again in 1988.

■ **YANG Zhizen** (Shizeng on the International Labor Organization list), a worker, had his sentence remitted or was released after "re-education through labor," according to the Chinese government's response to the ILO (November 1990). He was arrested for allegedly killing a soldier, Cui Guozheng, in Beijing on June 3-4, 1989.

■ **YAO Shanbai** (Shanbo), a peasant from Xinghua, Jiangsu Province, was sentenced to four years' imprisonment for joining demonstrations in Shanghai on June 5, 1989 and presumably was released upon completion of his term. He was alleged to have blocked traffic, deflated tires and shouted "counter-revolutionary slogans" (*Jiefang Ribao*, July 15, 1989). Yao's sentence was confirmed in an official Chinese

response to U.S. government inquiries (November 1991).

■ **YI Jingyao**, 20, a driver at the Beijing Civil Administration Bureau's Fourth Branch Construction Company (some sources list him as a waiter at the Beijing Duck Restaurant), and **TAN Minglu**, a driver at the Red Star Supply and Marketing Company, were tried and sentenced to four years and three-and-a-half years' imprisonment respectively. The two men allegedly tried to persuade workers at Beijing's Capital Iron and Steel Company to help set up blockades to prevent troops from moving into the city on May 20, 1989, the day martial law was declared. *Beijing Radio* (May 22 and 23, 1989) declared that Yi had "tried to incite workers to go on strike, shouted indiscreet slogans and disrupted social order." He was arrested on May 19, 1989 and reportedly tried at Shijingshan Court on June 1. After Yi's arrest, his family appealed for help to the *Joint Liaison Group for all Circles in the Capital,* a pro-democracy organization set up in the second half of May 1989 and led by, among others, Wang Juntao (see p.70). In Wang's February 1991 court verdict, Yi was named as being a "criminal" whom Wang had tried to "rescue" after his arrest. However, Chinese authorities confirmed only that Yi had been sentenced. Both Yi (who was acknowledged as sentenced by the Chinese authorities in a November 1991 reply to inquiries from the U.S. government) and Tan are presumed to have been released after serving their sentences. (See also **Wang Liqiang**, p.124).

- **YU Jiasong**, **GU Peijun**, **HUANG Ziqiang** and **ZHANG Kebin** received three to four-year prison terms for "inciting the masses" (*Shanghai Radio*, June 23, 1989, in FBIS, June 26). The sentences were announced by the Yangpu District People's Court at a public meeting on June 23, 1989 in the Shanghai Electric Plant. An official Chinese response to requests for information by the U.S. government (November 1991) confirmed that the men, all presumably workers, had been sentenced. It is assumed they were released upon completion of their terms.

- **YU Zhun(g)sheng**, identified only as a company employee, was sentenced to a three-year prison term. No additional information is available (China Coordination Group AI/USA), but it is presumed he was released upon completion of his sentence.

- **ZHANG Guohan**, an unemployed 32-year-old resident of Shuyuan Road in the Southern District of Changsha, Hunan Province, was administratively sentenced in December 1989 to two years' "re-education through labor." He presumably was released upon completion of his term. During the pro-democracy movement, Zhang actively supported the students and collected money on their behalf, from among others, the small private businessmen (*geti hu*). After June 4, Zhang continued to have contact with

student leaders; in August, he was arrested.

- **ZHANG Jianzhong** - see p.359

- **ZHANG Jun**[2] either had his sentence remitted or was released after "re-education through labor," as reported by the Chinese government to the International Labor Organization (November 1990) - or he may simply have disappeared. According to an official Chinese response to requests for information by the U.S. government, one person named Zhang Jun was released, but no reply was given in the case of another man of the same name. From the scant information available, it is impossible to determine which of the two is supposed to have been released.

Zhang and another member (see Wang Wei p.574) of a Beijing "Citizens Dare-to-Die Corps" were arrested on June 11, 1989 by the Martial Law Enforcement Command acting in coordination with the Public Security Bureau. According to a June 12, 1989 *Beijing Television* broadcast, Zhang, a native of Hebei, was in Tiananmen Square every night from May 20, 1989 until the army assault on June 3-4. He was accused of "shielding" the radio station there and spreading rumors against the party and government (FBIS, June 14, 1989).

- **ZHANG Meirong**, a worker and member of the Beijing Workers Autonomous Federation, was sentenced sometime before December 1990 to a three-year prison term for "counter-revolutionary crimes" (Amnesty

International *ASA 17/34/91*). Requests by the U.S. government for information about her have elicited no response from Chinese officials (November 1991), but it is presumed she was released upon completion of her term.

■ **ZHANG Qiang**, a worker, was sentenced to two years' "re-education through labor" for setting fire to two army uniforms in the woods in front of Beijing University's campus. He was arrested in June 1989; and it is presumed he was released upon completion of his term.

■ **ZHANG Qiwang**, sentenced to a prison term of three years for "disturbing the peace," according to an official Chinese response to requests for information by the International Labor Organization (November 1991), presumably was released upon completion of his term. His name also appeared on an official Chinese list of those sentenced which was handed over to the U.S. government in November 1991. Allegedly released from an earlier jail term in January 1988, Zhang, along with three other members of the Shanghai-based "Patriotic Volunteer Army" was arrested for taking part in a demonstration on the Shanghai Bund (*Shanghai Radio*, June 8, 1989). Demonstrators claimed that 200,000 troops were on their way to suppress the students. Zhang, a private entrepreneur and allegedly a "key" member of the Shanghai Workers Autonomous Federation, reportedly "incited" people to take the bodies of victims killed in the June 6 riot from

hospital mortuaries in order to create further turmoil.

■ **ZHANG Quancheng** - see p.375

■ **ZHANG Xudong** - see p.103

■ **ZHAO Jian** - see p.370

■ **ZHAO Weiguo**, 34, was tried by the Changde (Hunan Province) Intermediate People's Court on charges of "counterrevolutionary propaganda and incitement" and sentenced to four years' imprisonment. Arrested in October 1989 and initially held in Changde City Jail, Zhao was sent after trial to Yuanjiang Prison (Provincial No.1). Two others arrested at the same time were students from universities in Beijing who had been expelled for their 1989 pro-democracy activities. One was later released, but nothing is known of the fate of the second. Zhao, together with eight former students expelled from Beijing universities for participating in the 1986-87 student movement, had established a small private business in his home town, Changde, Hunan Province. During the 1989 movement, Zhao gave up his work with the company to help student activists, and later travelled to Changsha to join the Students Autonomous Federation there. He reportedly contributed almost 10,000 *yuan* to the cause.

■ **ZHAO Yuetang**, a peasant, arrested for allegedly killing a soldier, Cui Guozheng, in Beijing, on June 3-4, 1989, "had his sentence remitted or was released after re-education," according to a Chinese response to International Labor Organization inquiries (November 1990). Another ILO report (November 1991) listed **LI Weidong**, arrested for the same offense, as "released following re-education or absolved of criminal responsibility by the court." The report is consistent with an official Chinese response to U.S. government inquiries (November 1991), which also stated that Li had been released.

▪ **ZHONG Yinshan (ZONG Jingshan)**, a worker at Beijing's Capital Steel Factory, was sentenced in August 1990 to three years' imprisonment for "counterrevolutionary crimes." Court officials provided no additional information (*Reuters*, April 9, 1991), but it is presumed Zhong was released upon completion of his term.

▪ **ZHOU Endong**, alias **ZHOU Bo**, a 20-year-old worker at the Tianjin Cable Factory and a member of the Tianjin Workers Autonomous Federation, was arrested on June 9, 1989 by the Public Security Bureau in Yinchuan City, Ningxia Hui Autonomous Region. According to an official June 14 report, Zhou arrived in Yinchuan from Beijing on June 7 professing to be from the information department of the Tiananmen Square General Headquarters. In speeches made on June 7, 8 and 9 in front of the Statue of Heroes and Heroines in Yinchuan, Zhou further claimed he was an eyewitness to the Beijing massacre. However, he admitted upon interrogation that he had not been at the Square, but had spread rumors that

20,000 had died in order to incite workers and students to "intensify the counterrevolutionary rebellion." Requests for information by the U.S. government about Zhou's whereabouts elicited no response from the Chinese authorities (November 1991), but according to their report to the International Labor Organization (November 1991), he was "never brought to court," which may mean he was administratively sentenced to a term of "re-education through labor." If so, he presumably has been released since re-education terms usually do not run longer than three years.

▪ **ZHOU Shaowu**, a liaison representative between students and workers, was "released after re-education or absolved of criminal responsibility by the court," according to the Chinese response to the International Labor Organization's Freedom of Association Committee (November 11, 1991). According to previous accounts (*Beijing Television*, June 14, 1989; FBIS, June 15, 1989), he was arrested on June 10, 1989 in Shanghai in possession of "reactionary material" including a proposal to establish a *League of Democratic Parties*. A former worker at the Ningguo County Ferro-Alloy Plant in Anhui Province, Zhou reportedly became active in the Beijing Students Autonomous Federation, acting as a liaison between students and workers from his May 18, 1989 arrival in Beijing until he left on June 2. After reaching Shanghai on June 6, he allegedly made contact with "other illegal organizations." In June 1992,

Zhou was again arrested in connection with a crackdown on underground groups. He was held approximately forty days, then released.

■ **ZHOU Shuilong**, 39, a worker at the Changsha (Hunan Province) North Station of the Changsha Branch of the Railway Bureau, was sentenced by the Changsha Railway Public Security Bureau to two years' "re-education through labor" and presumably was released upon completion of his term. Arrested in mid-August 1989, he was sent to serve his sentence at the Changsha City Xinkaipu Labor Re-education Center. During the 1989 pro-democracy movement, Zhou served as deputy head of the picket squad for the Changsha Workers Autonomous Federation. He allegedly organized demonstrations and strikes and posted up numerous handbills.

■ **ZHOU Wenjie**, a worker in his twenties, formerly employed at a factory in Changsha, Hunan Province, was tried in mid-June 1989 by the Changsha City South District Court on a charge of robbery. Sentenced to four years' imprisonment, he presumably was released upon completion of his term. Zhou's arrest was in connection with the April 22 "beating, smashing, looting incident" in Changsha.

■ **ZHU Genhao** (Genbao on the ILO list), of the Shanghai Shipping Corporation was sentenced in Shanghai to a three-year term of imprisonment for destroying transport equipment, according to the Chinese government's reply to repeated International Labor Organization inquiries (November 1990). He presumably was released upon completion of his term. Requests by the U.S. government for information about him elicited no response from Chinese officials (November 1991). Zhu was arrested between June 6 and June 9, 1989 (See Cheng Qiyang p.497 and Liu Jian[2] p.125) and accused of setting up roadblocks in Shanghai, instigating others to do the same and attempting to "stop and overturn police cars." In all, 130 "lawless elements" were arrested in Shanghai for "disrupting traffic and obstructing official business" between June 6 and 9.

■ **ZHU Guanghua** had his sentence remitted or was released after "re-education through labor," according to the Chinese government's reply to International Labor Organization (November 1990) inquiries. Zhu and six "leading" members of the Hangzhou (Zhejiang Province) Workers' Autonomous Federation (see Gao Jin(g)tang p.562) were arrested on June 10, 1989 (*Beijing Ribao*, June 13, 1989). Several were subsequently sentenced.

■ **ZHU Huiming, LI Huling** and **RUI Tonghu** were arrested in Nanjing, Jiangsu Province, on June 10, 1989; they were sentenced along with seven others. According to an official Chinese response to U.S. government inquiries, Rui received a prison term while Zhu and Li were "not found legally responsible," a euphemism for an administrative sentence of "re-education through labor"

(November 1991). Another Chinese response, this one to the International Labor Organization (November 1991), stated that Zhu and Li were "released following re-education and absolved of criminal responsibility by the courts." Rui reportedly received a three-year sentence for disturbing the peace and presumably was released upon its completion. According to a *Xinhua* radio broadcast (June 10, 1989), all ten men were members of the Nanjing Workers Autonomous Federation and had established contacts with the Nanjing Students Autonomous Federation. The broadcast alleged the three named had previous convictions. Zhu, described as "a vagrant," was detained for "beating other people or acting indecently"; he was also accused of fabricating a story that his brother had been killed in Beijing. Li, a worker at the Nanjing Public Transportation Company's No.1 Farm, allegedly had served two years' "re-education through labor" for fighting. Rui, a workers' pickets leader, was a self-employed car repairman. In 1979, he allegedly served a year in prison for "injuring people." According to *Renmin Ribao* (June 11, 1989), Li and Zhu were accused of "repeatedly plotting to carry out counterrevolutionary acts, such as snatching guns..."

■ **ZHU Qin**, a Shanghai worker, may have been released "after education." Arrested on June 6, 1989, he was tried along with seven others on June 18 (see, for example, Ai Qilong p.371), but according to the deputy chief procurator, Zhu alone pleaded not guilty.

Occupation unknown

■ **QI Huaiqing**, arrested for involvement in the May-June 1989 protest movement, was reportedly sentenced to four years' imprisonment. He is presumed released upon completion of his term.

■ For participating in the 1989 pro-democracy movement, **SONG Jingwu** (Guowu) was sentenced to three years' "re-education through labor." No further details are available but it is presumed he was released upon completion of his term.

■ **ZHAN Haiyan** was "not found legally responsible" (a common euphemism for a term of "labor re-education"), according to an official Chinese response to inquiries about some 800 dissidents by the U.S. government (November 1991). However such a name did not appear on the submitted list and nothing further is known about Zhan. Since re-education terms usually do not run longer than three years, it is presumed he has been released.

■ **ZHAO Jun'an**, reportedly arrested after June 4, 1989, is said to have later been sentenced to four years' imprisonment for "disturbing social order" and is presumed to have been released after serving his sentence.

■ According to an Asia Watch source, **ZHENG Wenbin**, 23, from Zigong, Sichuan Province, was sentenced to three years in prison for his participation in the pro-democracy movement. It is presumed he was released upon completion of his term.

Ethnic Nationals

■ **AAJO**, a 24-year-old Chamdo monk, arrested in January 1989 and sentenced on February 5, 1991 by the Chamdo Court to three years in Chamdo Prison, presumably was released upon completion of his term.

■ **AGYAL TSERING** (also known as APHO AHGYA), a former Ganden monk, in his late thirties, tried and administratively sentenced in July 1990 to 18 months' imprisonment, presumably has been released from Jyekundo District Prison in Qinghai Province. He had been arrested on March 8, 1990 in Qinghai in connection with a late February wall-poster campaign in support of Tibetan independence (*International Campaign for Tibet*, April 1991).

■ **BAO BI** (Chinese name), a 20-year-old born in Lhasa Kyire, was arrested in 1989 and sentenced to four years in prison. He presumably was released from Drapchi Prison upon completion of his term.

■ **CHOEDRON**, a 28-year-old farmer from Lhokha Danak, arrested in 1989 and sentenced to a two-year term, presumably was released after its completion. He had been held in Drapchi Prison.

■ **DAWA**[7], a 23-year-old Shungsep nun from Lhokha, arrested between September and December 1990, was sentenced to a three-year prison term and was presumably released upon its completion. Reports from late 1991 indicated she had been moved from Gutsa Detention Center to Drapchi Prison. Despite the case similarities, it is believed that Dawa[7] and Samten Dawa (Dawa[17], see p.536) are not the same person.

■ **DAWA**[14], in his fifties, also known as SHOL DAWA, because he is a native of the Shol district of Lhasa, was arrested in late August 1985 (*Tibetan Review*, September-October 1985) and reportedly received a seven-year term which he served in Drapchi Prison. He allegedly had pro-independence posters in his home.

■ **DAWA**[15], 20, from Lhasa Sungchoe Ra, arrested in 1989 and sentenced to three years in prison, presumably was released after completing his term in Sangyip.

■ **DAWA**[16], a 14-year-old from Lhasa, Town-3, arrested in 1989 and sentenced to three years in prison, presumably was released from Drapchi upon completion of his term.

■ **DAWA CHUNGDAG**, a 17-year-old carpenter from Lhasa, arrested March 1989, and sentenced to a three-year prison term, appears to have been released from Drapchi Prison. An earlier report, that he received an eight-year sentence, was probably erroneous.

■ **DORJE**[5] - see p.353

■ **GOKYI**, a 22-year-old farmer from Gyaltse, detained in December 1990 and sentenced to a one-and-a-half year term, presumably was released upon its completion. He was in Drapchi Prison.

■ There is an unconfirmed report that **GYALPO**[2], a layman in his thirties, arrested in 1987 and held in Sangyip Prison, has been released. He reportedly was injured in prison and hospitalized in mid-1991. No other information is available.

■ Of eleven Garu nuns, arrested for demonstrating on the Barkhor in Lhasa on June 9, 1991, five are known to have received prison sentences, one reportedly has been released, and several presumably were released upon completion of their terms. Of the five identified as originally detained in Gutsa, four were transferred to Trisam. **GYALTSEN DROLMA**, 16, from Lhasa, who had been previously arrested - date unknown - received a two-year sentence and presumably has been released. An earlier source listed her as an Ani Tsangkhung nun. **NGAWANG LHAMO**, 20, from Lhokha, Nyethang, and **GYALTSEN PEMA**, 17, from Medro Gyama, also received two-year terms. The latter presumably has been released; there is a report that **Ngawang Lhamo** was released. **GYALTSEN LODROE**[1], 23, from Drigung, received a three-year sentence. There is some confusion about **NGAWANG NAMDROL**[2], 18, from Lhasa. She was first detained for her solo demonstration on April 30, 1991 on the Barkhor in Lhasa where

she allegedly put up posters and shouted Tibetan independence slogans. She also allegedly scattered leaflets around the streets and threw them at policemen. Arrested immediately, Ngawang Namdrol was taken to Kyire Police Station where she continued shouting slogans even as her arms were tied behind her back. Ngawang Namdrol may have been released in May and then re-arrested for her participation in the June 9 demonstration. Or there may be two Ngawang Namdrols from the same nunnery, one of whom reportedly was last released from Gutsa in September 1991. It is unclear if **GYALTSEN CHOEZANG**, a Garu nun in her twenties, from Chang Namtso, who was expelled from the nunnery, was arrested in connection with the demonstration. She had been arrested once before, on December 10, 1988 (see Gyaltsen Wangchuk p.521). Another Garu nun, **GYALTSEN LHAZOM** (whose name may be GYALTSEN LHAKSAM[2]), in her twenties, from Nyangrey, may also have been arrested on June 9. She, too, had been detained once before, on April 17, 1988, along with thirteen other nuns (see Gyaltsen Choetso, p.521).

■ **DAWA YANGZOM** - see p.536

■ **GYALTSEN OEZER**, (lay name DAWA[18]), 23, arrested March 13, 1989, and **GYALTSEN CHOEDRAG**, (lay name NANGKAR), 25, arrested April 26, both monks from Nyethang Ratoe Monastery and natives of Chushul County, were among eight

Tibetans sentenced on September 12, 1989. The two received respectively four and three-year prison terms and presumably were released from Drapchi Prison upon their completion. Gyaltsen Oezer also has had his political rights suspended for one year. According to a report in *Xinhua* (September 13, 1989), the monks "hung a Tibetan flag in the monastery, took part in disturbances and shouted reactionary slogans." Gyaltsen Oezer allegedly inscribed the banner with the "reactionary" phrases: "Tibet is independent," "This is its national flag," and "Do not remove." Gyaltsen Oezer was among the twenty-some Drapchi prisoners who, on April 27, 1991, were harshly disciplined for protesting the transfer and ill-treatment of five Drapchi prisoners, two of whom attempted to hand James Lilley a letter about prison conditions. (See Tenpa Wangdrag[2] p.177.)

- **HA RANGGON** - see p.192

- **JAMPA KELSANG**, a construction worker in Lhasa, arrested on September 26, 1986 and sentenced to a three-year prison term, presumably was released upon its completion. He reportedly was linked to printed materials advocating Tibetan independence that were distributed at Drepung Monastery. In addition, a police search of his home three days after his detention, allegedly turned up a copy in Tibetan of the Dalai Lama's autobiography.

- **JAMYANG[6]** - see p.195

- **KARMA[3]**, a 20-year-old native of Chushul County, arrested in 1989 and sentenced to three years in prison, presumably has been released from Sangyip Prison. No other information is available.

- **KARMA TRINLEY** - see p.181

- **KELSANG[3]**, 24, a carpenter from Lhasa Chagshing, arrested on March 14, 1989, was sentenced to a four-year prison term by the Lhasa Municipal Court on September 12, 1989, for "destruction of property" during the March 5, 1989 demonstration in Lhasa. He presumably has been released from Drapchi Prison.

- **KELSANG DROLKAR[1]** - see p.533

- **KHERGA**, a 20-year-old native of Kantse, arrested in 1989 and sentenced to three years in prison, presumably was released from Sangyip Prison upon completion of his term.

- **KHYENTSE LEGDRUB** (lay name PHURBU TSERING[5]), a 27-year-old Sungrabling monk, from Lhokha Gongkar, detained in March 1990 and sent to Drapchi, presumably was released upon completion of his three-year sentence.

- **KUNSEL**, a 26-year-old native of Yamdrog, arrested in 1989 and sentenced to three years in prison, presumably was released from Sangyip Prison upon completion of his term.

- **LHAKPA[5]**, a female from Lhasa Banakshol, in her late thirties, arrested in late May 1993, has probably been released.

- **LHAKPA TSERING[8]**, a 20-year-old native of Lhasa, arrested in 1989 and sentenced to a two-year term, presumably was released upon its completion. He had been held in Sangyip Prison.

- **LHAKPA TSERING[9]**, 20, from Lhasa Lugug, arrested in 1989, presumably was released from Sangyip Prison after three months. No additional information is available.

- **LHAKYET** - see p.195

- **LHUNDRUP SANGMO** - see p.181

- **LOBSANG[2]** - see p.539

- **LOBSANG DROLMA[3]** - see p.528

- **LOBSANG KHETSUN** (lay name KHETSUN), a 60-year-old, (there is a unexplained discrepancy in his age; another report gives it as 20), from Drongtse Monastery in Gyaltse, detained in September 1990, was sentenced to a three-year term and sent to Drapchi Prison. He presumably has been released.

- **LOBSANG NGAWANG[2]** - see p.203

- **LOBSANG NYIMA[2]**, a 26-year-old Chamdo monk from Chamdo, arrested on October 24, 1989 and sentenced on July 5, 1990 to a three-year term, presumably has been released. He had been held in Powo Tramo Prison.

- **LOBSANG SHERAB[2]**, a 30-year-old monk from Palkhor Choede Monastery, from Gyantse, arrested in July 1989 and sentenced to a three-year prison term, presumably was released upon its completion. He had been held in Drapchi Prison.

- **LOBSANG TOPCHU** - see p.188

- **LOBSANG WANGMO** - see p.521

- **LODROE[2]** - see p.196

- **MIGMAR SAMDRUP**, a 19-year-old native of Lhasa, arrested in 1989 and sentenced to three years in prison, presumably was released upon completion of his term. He had been held in Gutsa Detention Center.

- **NGAWANG KYIZOM**, a 20-year-old Ani Tsangkhung nun, from Medro Gongkar, arrested on September 13, 1990 (probably a Tibetan date) and sentenced to three years in prison, presumably was released upon completion of her term. First held in Gutsa Detention Center, she was transferred to Trisam sometime after February 1992.

- **NGAWANG RABSANG** - see p.183

■ **PAIGON** (whose name may also be PALGON or PELGON), sentenced to a two-and-a-half-year-term, probably in February 1990, presumably has been released. He had been arrested in March 1989 for distributing independence pamphlets and held in Ngaba District Prison.

■ **PEMA DROLKAR**[2] - see p.189

■ **PHURBU**[4], a 20-year-old from Lhasa, arrested in 1989, presumably was released after serving a two-year sentence in Sangyip Prison.

■ **PHURBU**[9] - see p.527

■ **SONAM GYALPO**[3], a 30-year-old native of Lhokha Gongkar County, was arrested on September 27, 1989 and reportedly sentenced to three years in prison. It is known that he was admitted to a hospital by prison authorities for an undiagnosed ailment. He is presumed to have been released upon the completion of his term.

■ **SONAM TSERING**[5], 30, from Kongpo, arrested in 1990 and sentenced to a one-and-a-half-year prison term, presumably was released upon its completion. As of late 1991, he was still held in Sangyip Prison. No other information is available.

■ **TAKRA PHUNTSOG**, a 58-year-old monk from Phenpo Lhundrup County, arrested in March 1989 and sentenced to a three-year term, presumably was released upon its completion. He had been held in Sangyip Prison.

■ **TAMDRIN**[1] - see p.351

■ **TASHI**[3], a 20-year-old monk from Lhokha, Samye Da, arrested sometime in 1990 and sentenced to three years in prison, presumably was released after completing his term. He had been held in the Fifth Division at Drapchi Prison.

■ **TASHI CHOEZOM** - see p.515

■ **TENZIN NGAWANG** - see p.181

■ **TENZIN NYIMA** - see p.172

■ **TENZIN TSULTRIM** - see p.177

■ **THUBTEN KELSANG THALUTSOGENTSANG**, a monk and horse cart driver, was about 40 years old when he was arrested on December 3, 1981 in Lhasa for shouting pro-independence slogans. He was taken to Sangyip prison. There were no reports of a trial, the official charges against him were ever known, and no further reports about him ever surfaced. It is assumed he has been released. Lobsang Kelsang Thalutsogentsang had also been arrested in 1959 and sent to the Nachen Hydroelectric labor reform brigade, according to Amnesty International.

■ **THUPTEN TSERING**[3] - see p.179

■ **TSERING NYIMA**, a 20-year-old businessman and native of Phenpo Lhundrup, whose date of arrest is unknown, was detained for some eleven months in Gutsa Detention Center, then presumably released.

■ **TSERING YANGZOM** - see p.536

■ **TSETEN YANGKYI**, 38, arrested on February 20, 1990, probably was not held for long, although her release has not been confirmed. She is the wife of Jampa Ngodrup (see p.15, 194) who received a thirteen-year prison sentence for copying lists of Tibetans who were arrested or injured in two demonstrations in 1988.

■ **TSICHOE** - see p.533

■ **UBUL EMIL** and **BALAT NIYAZ MOHAMMAT TOHTI** - see p.224

■ **YESHE TSERING** - see p.190

3. Miscellaneous

■ **GUO Chengdong**, a pro-democracy activist whose name appeared on a Chinese government "most wanted" list after June 1989; and **ZHANG Guozhong** and **WANG Jin**, described as husband and wife although they are not legally married, were all released from detention in Taiwan's Xinzhu Processing Center for Mainland People sometime in late 1993. The three had escaped to Taiwan in 1992 and been interned by the government pending a decision on their asylum claim. Zhang, a 31-year-old former technician in Tianjin Railway Signals Factory, and Wang, 25, a lab worker at the Tianjin Circulatory System Research Institute, claimed to have been the targets of a confidential "most wanted" list issued by the Tianjin authorities after June 1989. The couple first escaped to Taiwan later that same month, but nine months later, on March 7, 1990, they were forcibly repatriated to China. Wang managed to escape on the way back, but Zhang was administratively sentenced to one year's "re-education through labor," and four months were later added to his sentence for an attempted escape. In 1992, Zhang and Wang again escaped to Taiwan.

■ **HAN Jinming,** a pro-democracy activist who spent 19 months in Tianjin No.1 Prison after June 1989 on a charge of "counterrevolutionary propaganda and incitement," was re-arrested in mid-September 1992 following a meeting with U.S.-based dissident Shen Tong (see p.452), who had briefly returned to China that August. After several days questioning in a secret government guest house, Han was transferred to the Public Security Bureau's detention center at Tianjin No.1 Prison and interrogated almost continually for three days and two nights, during which time he was threatened with a 20-year sentence if he did not cooperate. During a visit under armed police escort to identify the building where he had met with Shen, however, he managed to evade his captors and eventually escaped from China. Han has now resettled in a Western country.

■ **SONAM DROLKAR**[2], a 25-year-old Tibetan nun, born in Lhasa, arrested on July 29, 1990 on suspicion of deep involvement in pro-independence activities, managed to escape from Tibet in August 1991. Held in Seitru Prison, she was tortured so badly that prison officials finally hospitalized her. In addition to the torture, she endured 300 days of solitary confinement without charge or trial, and with neither blanket nor mattress (*Tibet Information Network*, November 19, 1989). Starting on August 2, 1990, according to Sonam Drolkar's testimony, she was stripped naked and subjected to electric shocks every second day. Such torture continued for six months. In addition, she was sexually violated with an electric baton and beaten frequently. Not until February 1991, when a prison doctor warned that she was near death, did the torture sessions stop. At that point she was moved to a hospital and from the hospital made good her escape. Sonam Drolkar was arrested by twenty officers from the Public Security Bureau when another prisoner, **Gelek Yonten** (see p.193), was forced to give her name under interrogation. At that time, she was not living in a nunnery but at home, looking after her elderly parents and her child.

APPENDIX IV: ERRATA FROM
EARLIER ASIA WATCH REPORTS

■ **BAO Mi**, the pen name of a novelist who dropped out of sight in 1991 and who declines to disclose his real name or meet with journalists, was not, contrary to initial reports, arrested (*AP*, January 2, 1992). Bao's novel, *Huang Huo (Yellow Peril)*, published in Taiwan and circulating through photocopies and on computer disks in Beijing, predicts China's destruction in a nuclear war.

■ **CAO Jianhua**, whose name, address, photograph and I.D. number appeared on the Chinese government's August 19, 1989 compilation of "most wanted lists," appears to have escaped arrest. A 27-year old native of Yiyang, Hunan Province, he was a chemistry major, entering class of 1984, Tongji University. No additional information is currently available.

■ **CHEN Zhixiang**, sentenced by a Guangzhou court to 10 years' imprisonment in January 1990, is being held at a prison in Shaoguan, northern Guangdong Province, and has never been imprisoned in Hunan. In June 1992, Asia Watch reported that Chen might be held at Hunan's Yuanjiang Prison.

■ **DAO Zi** - see p.143

■ **HE Aoqiu**, a 55-year-old assistant professor in the Chinese Department at Yueyang Normal College, Hunan Province; **HUANG Yaru**, 47, a professor of political education at Yueyang Teachers College; **ZHANG Jizhong**, 30, a reporter for the official *Hunan Ribao*; **MEI Shi**, the 40-year-old editor-in-chief of the *Yueyang Evening News*; **CHENG Cun**, 30, a reporter at the Yueyang City bureau of the magazine *News Pictorial (Xinwen Tupian Bao)*; **YANG Shaoyue**, the 36-year-old head of the Yueyang Office of Criticism and Discussion; and **WU Weiguo**, 30, a cadre in the same office, were never in fact arrested. In June 1992, Asia Watch reported that the six men had received sentences of three to five years' imprisonment after June 1989 in connection with the "Yin Zhenggao Affair" of early 1989.

■ **HE Jiadong** (previously listed as He Jiandong), former deputy publisher at the Workers' Publishing House and later the publisher of *Jingjixue Zhoubao (Economics Weekly)*, was apparently not, contrary to previous reports, arrested in connection with the 1989 pro-democracy movement.

■   **HU Xuedong**, a 26-year-old student at the Central-South Industrial University, Hunan Province, was never arrested in connection with the pro-democracy movement. In June 1992, Asia Watch reported that Hu had been detained in March 1990 and held at Changsha No.1 Jail for nine months before being freed.

■   **HU Jiwei**, former *Renmin Ribao* editor, under whose leadership the paper was liberalized in 1989, is not in prison and has been permitted to travel abroad. He is not, however, permitted to work as a journalist. In late June 1989, Hu was included on a list of 17 "bourgeois-liberal intellectuals" whom the authorities regarded as having been deeply involved in the "counterrevolutionary rebellion." In March 1990, Hu was expelled from the Standing Committee of the National People's Congress; in September 1990, he was formally expelled from the Party (*Shijie Ribao*, September 10, 1989).

■   **LI Dan** was never arrested, according to an Asia Watch source, despite an official Chinese response to U.S. government inquiries stating that he had been "released" (November 1991). Li originally was thought to be the announcer on an unauthorized *Radio Beijing* program on June 4, 1989 which broadcast the news that thousands had been killed by the army in Beijing the previous night (see Wu Xiaoyong p.470).

■   **MIN Qi**, a 39-year-old former researcher at the Social and Economic Sciences Research Institute (SERI) and assistant to Wang Juntao (see p.70), was never imprisoned in connection with the 1989 pro-democracy movement, despite being listed as "released" in an official Chinese response to U.S. government inquiries (November 1991). In 1993, Min wrote to two Politburo members, Qiao Shi and Ren Jianxin, claiming he had been forced to live as a social outcast and denied the means to earn a living following the cancellation of his Beijing residency card and identity papers. "My status as a man without official identity means I cannot buy state grain, apply for a job, study, marry or even father a child. Officially, I no longer exist," he said (*Kyodo*, March 17, 1993, in FBIS, same day). Also in spring 1993, Min and a few friends issued a public appeal on behalf of Wang Juntao, demanding that he be transferred from prison to a hospital and given proper treatment for his hepatitis-B and other serious illnesses. Wang was moved to a hospital soon afterwards. Formerly secretary-general at SERI and editor of the magazine *Zhongguo Shehui Kexue (Chinese Social Sciences),* Min's pro-democracy activities extend back to the early 1970s when he was jailed for five years.

■   **SONG Song**, a surgeon at the Beijing Union Medical College Hospital, and **SHAN Gangzhi**, a urologist, both of whom were on volunteer medical duty in Tiananmen Square on the night of June 3-4, 1989, were never detained or arrested, contrary to previous reports. Both men had been quoted, along with students and intellectuals, in a *Xinhua* article, "Witnesses Report No Deaths at Tiananmen Square" (September 18, 1989). Although no locations were given for the interviews, the context had suggested that they might have taken place in prison or that quotations were taken directly from detainees' "confessions."

■ **SUN Changjiang**, former chief editor of Beijing's *Keji Ribao (Science and Technology News)*, was never arrested. According to an Asia Watch source, Sun lost his job as editor, but is teaching at the department of politics and law at Beijing Teachers Training College.

■ **TAO Sen**, a former student activist who led a hunger strike at Hunan Normal College in 1980, was not involved in the 1989 pro-democracy movement and was not arrested or sentenced thereafter. In June 1992, Asia Watch reported that Tao had been sentenced to four or five years' imprisonment in 1990.

■ **WANG Luxiang**, a co-author of the controversial 1988 television series "River Elegy" *(He Shang)*, was not rearrested in Hunan Province following his release from prison in 1990. In June 1992, Asia Watch reported that he had been rearrested and was being held in a prison in Lianyuan City, Hunan.

■ **WU Xinghua**, around 50 years old, a senior journalist at the Hunan Province branch office of *Xinhua*, was never arrested. In June 1992, Asia Watch reported that Wu had been detained in July 1989 and held for over a year before being released on medical bail.

■ **ZHANG Boli**, No.17 on the June 13, 1989 "21 most wanted students" list, escaped from China in June 1991 after two years on the run. Contrary to previous information, he was never arrested, except briefly by the Soviet authorities after a failed attempt to escape via the U.S.S.R. A 34-year-old native of Wangkui district, Heilongjiang Province, Zhang spent the greater part of his two years in hiding, first working as a migrant farm laborer in a remote village in Heilongjiang, hunting and fishing for his food; later working his own farm. During the April-May demonstrations in Beijing in 1989, Zhang was chief editor of Beijing University's *Xinwen Daobao (News Herald)*. Together with Chai Ling and Feng Congde, Zhang led the June 3-4 retreat from Tiananmen Square. He still suffers from severe kidney malfunction exacerbated by his experiences in Tiananmen Square and during his years in hiding.

■ **ZHANG Xianyang**, a 53-year-old research fellow at the Chinese Academy of Social Sciences, and one of 33 signers of the February 1989 petition calling for amnesty for political prisoners, was not arrested as previously reported. As of July 1991, he remained at the Institute of Marxism-Leninism-Mao Zedong Thought in Beijing and was a consultant to a research institute associated with the Capital Steel Company. It is not known whether he is still Director of the Institute and deputy editor of the magazine *Marxist Research*. Zhang earned a degree in European philosophy at People's University, and after graduation became a researcher at the Institute. An advocate of political reform, Zhang was accused by the authorities after June 1989 of promoting "counter-revolutionary" theories. With Su Shaozhi, now in exile in the U.S., he published

Marxism in China Since the Eleventh Session of the Third Party Plenum. This 1988 work is now officially banned in China (*Shijie Ribao*, February 4, 1991).

■   **ZHU Houze**, 58, former head of the All-China Federation of Trade Unions and the Communist Party's propaganda department, was not arrested after June 1989, contrary to initial reports, and retained his freedom throughout the subsequent crackdown. In his capacity as trade union chief, he urged China's workers to show caution during the pro-democracy movement and reportedly succeeded in preventing a threatened major strike.

■   The "No.48 Guangzhou-Beijing express train" incident, referred to on p.17 of *Anthems of Defeat: Crackdown in Hunan Province, 1989-92* (Asia Watch, June 1992), occurred not (as was stated) shortly before June 4, 1989, but on June 6, 1989. Also, on p.10 of the same report, reference was made to a "hunger strike of around 2000 students." There were in fact only several hundred student hunger strikers, although a mass sit-in by 1000 or more Changsha residents at the same location contributed to the impression that the hunger-strike group was considerably larger.

■   A number of arrest or trial reports concerning Tibetan pro-independence activists which appeared in Asia Watch's November 1993 report "China in 1993: One More Year of Political Repression" (Vol.5, No.20) were either superseded or rendered outdated by a large quantity of new information on the repression in Tibet that became available shortly after the report's publication. For all current information on arrests and trials carried out in Tibet as of January 1994, please refer to the present report only.

GEOGRAPHICAL INDEX
(Arrests and Detentions Only)

INDEX OF NAMES

600

601

606

LIANG Jianguo	100
LIANG Jianshe	147
LIANG Liwei	105, 567
LIANG Qiang	301, 379
LIANG Sanying	400
LIANG Wang	567
LIANG Weimin	32, 116
LIANG Xiang	549
LIANG Xiaozhong	96
LIANG Xihua	450
LIANG Xisheng	239
LIANG Yu	433
LIANG Zenguo	362
LIANG Zhenyun	148
LIAO * bin	306, 334
LIAO Baobin	159, 295, 548
LIAO Haiqing	234
LIAO Jia'an	5, 65, 294
LIAO Yiwu	88, 294, 458, 459, 555
LIAO Zhen'an	259, 297
LIAO Zheng	89, 294
LIAO Zhengxiong	568
LIAO Zhijun	367
LIN * qiu1	302
LIN * qiu2	304
LIN * shou	91, 295
LIN * yin	304
LIN Bingqi	307, 348
LIN Buxiang	433
LIN Guizhen	433
LIN Jiale	543
LIN Jianhua	47
LIN Lin	440
LIN Muchen	49
LIN Qiang	124
LIN Qiangguo	112, 284
LIN Shanming	394
LIN Shengli	434, 435
LIN Songlin	74, 294
LIN Tianlin	304
LIN Weiming	151
LIN Weisheng	304
LIN Wenming	394
LIN Xianggao	53, 400
LIN Yongkai	307, 348
LIN Zhaorong	311, 354
LIN Zilong	45
LIN Ziyong	97, 298

LIU * chen	308
LIU * cheng	306, 334
LIU * fang	279, 286, 295
LIU * feng	261
LIU * jie	306, 335
LIU * lin	251, 310
LIU * lu	308
LIU * ming	302
LIU * sheng	303
LIU * tang	306, 340
LIU * ting	260
LIU * xiang	311
LIU * xin	279, 299
LIU * yang	279, 286, 295
LIU * ying	259, 297
LIU *	311
LIU Anping	434
LIU Baiqiang	17, 96, 284, 294
LIU Baiyu	23, 116, 309
LIU Bangming	14, 120, 295
LIU Baode	311, 354
LIU Beihong	149
LIU Bihua	304, 389
LIU Bingjiang	131
LIU Changqing	361
LIU Chengwu1	568
LIU Chengwu2	568
LIU Chongyun	14, 120, 295
LIU Chunan	301, 377
LIU Congshu	568, 569
LIU Danhong	425, 434, 436, 472, 552
LIU De	275, 294, 549
LIU Di	26, 434, 487
LIU Difen	231
LIU Feng	435
LIU Fengming	569
LIU Fuan	135, 436, 549
LIU Fuyuan	152
LIU Gang1	65, 292
LIU Gang2	370
LIU Guandong	229, 394
LIU Guangpin	235, 396
LIU Gui	14, 120, 295
LIU Hanyi	434, 436, 472, 552
LIU Heping	11, 14, 284, 294
LIU Heping2	243
LIU Hongli	415
LIU Huanwen1	401

618

620

628

632